NTC's Dictionary of

LATIN AMERICAN SPANISH

Rafael A. Olivares, Ed.D.
School of Education, Queens College
City University of New York

NTC Publishing Group

Library of Congress Cataloging-in-Publication Data

Olivares, Rafael A.
    NTC's dictionary of Latin American Spanish / Rafael A. Olivares.
        p.   cm.
    Includes index.
    ISBN 0-8442-7963-3 (cloth)
    ISBN 0-8442-7964-1 (paper)
    1. Spanish language—Provincialisms—Latin America—Dictionaries.
    2. Spanish language—Dictionaries—English.   I. Title.   II. Title: Dictionary
of Latin American Spanish.
    PC4822.065   1997
    467'.98'03—dc21   97-22112
                                                    CIP

Interior design by Terry Stone

Published by NTC Publishing Group
A division of NTC/Contemporary Publishing Group, Inc.
4255 West Touhy Avenue, Lincolnwood (Chicago), Illinois 60646-1975 U.S.A.
Copyright © 1997 by NTC/Contemporary Publishing Group, Inc.
Printed in the United States of America
International Standard Book Number: 0-8442-7963-3 (cloth)
                                      0-8442-7964-1 (paper)
99 00 01 02 03 04 BC 19 18 17 16 15 14 13 12 11 10 9 8 7 6 5 4 3 2 1

Contents

Preface

Spanish is spoken in more American countries than any other language, and each national variety of Spanish has its own collection of unique words. These unique words differ from the standard Spanish usually taught in schools and, in many cases, the unique words spoken in one country are not recognized in other Spanish-speaking countries. Very few of these words, whether they are part of the local standard Spanish or the local slang, appear in the typical bilingual Spanish and English dictionary. Most of these are as unfamiliar to speakers of Spanish as they are to speakers of English.

NTC's Dictionary of Latin American Spanish is a collection of the Spanish variants used by Spanish-speaking people all over Latin America. It is an essential reference for both Spanish and English speakers who want to widen their language competence to include the many varieties of Spanish vocabulary spoken in the New World.

This dictionary does not define words that are part of standard Spanish or are easily found in other bilingual dictionaries. The vocabulary presented here is unique to only one or a few countries and not part of the common Spanish lexicon. In addition to this vocabulary, words borrowed from English that are commonly used in Spanish speech in the United States, sometimes referred to as "Spanglish," are included. Words borrowed from English that have been recognized in standard Spanish by the Real Academia de la Lengua Española are indicated in the text by the symbol "RAE."

NTC's Dictionary of Latin American Spanish was compiled over a period of several years from interviews with hundreds of Spanish-speaking people of different nationalities living in the United States. Many of the Spanish speakers interviewed were not even familiar with the standard Spanish equivalent for some words commonly spoken in their homeland and strongly believed that the word they used was the standard. For example, some Puerto Ricans believed that the word they use for garbage, *safacón*, is the standard Spanish term. This dictionary will prove fascinating for anyone interested in the differences in vocabulary among Spanish-speakers.

About This Dictionary

NTC's Dictionary of Latin American Spanish is divided into five sections. The main body of the dictionary lists words used by people from one or a few Latin American countries. Each entry identifies in italics where the word is used: *Argen.* (Argentina), *Bol.* (Bolivia), *Chile, Colo.* (Colombia), *Costa Rica, Cuba, Dom. Rep.* (Dominican Republic), *Ecua.* (Ecuador), *Salva.* (El Salvador), *from English, Guat.* (Guatemala), *Hond.* (Honduras), *Mex.* (Mexico), *Nic.* (Nicaragua), *Pan.* (Panama), *Para.* (Paraguay), *Peru, Puerto Rico, Uru.* (Uruguay), *Ven.* (Venezuela). Definitions of the word are given in English and in standard Spanish, and words that are considered vulgar are marked accordingly. The abbreviation "N.E." (no equivalent) appears in the definitions of words for which there is no direct equivalent either in standard Spanish or in English.

Three indexes follow the main body of the dictionary. The English Index is an alphabetical index of English words with their Latin American Spanish counterparts. The Spanish Index lists standard Spanish words and their variants from all over Latin America. Both are indexes of word forms, not meanings. Finally, lists of the words from each Latin American country are provided, along with a list of words used in Spanish that were borrowed from English.

Dictionary of Latin American Spanish

A

a capela (*Chile*) [to sing] without accompaniment = [cantar] sin acompañamiento de instrumentos musicales.

a concho (*Chile*) until the end = hasta el final.

¿a dónde la llevas?; ¿a dónde la tiras? (*Mex.*) Where are you going? = ¿a dónde vas?

¿a dónde la tiras? See **¿a dónde la llevas?**

a esta altura del partido (*Argen.*) it is too late = ya es muy tarde.

a gatas (*Argen.*) with great effort = apenas; con mucha dificultad.

a juro; a la machimberra (*Ven.*) by force = a la fuerza.

a la brava (*Dom. Rep., Mex., Puerto Rico*) by force = por la fuerza.

a la diabla (*Dom. Rep.*) to obtain something maliciously or illegitimately or through physical force = obtener algo por las malas, maliciosamente o con gran fuerza física.

¡a la gran puchica! See **¡joepuchita!**

a la hora del té (*Colo.*) at the moment of truth = a la hora de la verdad.

a la lata (*Colo.*) very much = mucho.

a la machimberra See **a juro.**

a la orden (*Colo.*) "you are welcome;" the response to "thanks" = "de nada;" la respuesta a "gracias."

a medio filo (*Chile*) almost drunk = casi borracho.

a pata; de mingo (*Ven.*) very close to something or someone = muy cerca de algo o alguien.

a rolete (*Argen.*) a waste; a lavish expenditure = derroche; gasto desmedido o a destajo.

a rolo (*Ven.*) with a blow = a golpes.

a secas (*Mex.*) singing or dancing without musical accompaniment = cantar o bailar sin acompañamiento musical.

a todo dar (*Mex.*) by all efforts; has all the qualities = con máximos esfuerzos; tiene todas las mejores cualidades.

a todo jender (*Puerto Rico*) at full power; as fast as possible = a toda fuerza; tan rápido como es posible.

abacorao (*Puerto Rico*) burdened with many tasks = muy atareado.

abacorar (*Ven.*) to harass = hostigar.

abalserar (*Hond.*) to pile up; to accumulate = amontonar; juntar acumular.

abandonado (*Peru*) a dissolute person; a reckless person = calavera; vicioso.

abanico 1. (*Cuba, Dom. Rep., Mex., Puerto Rico*) a fan = ventilador. **2.** (*Mex.*) an agreement that is easy to wiggle out of = asunto del cual es fácil desprenderse.

abarrotería (*Ecua., Guat., Hond., Mex., Salva.*) a grocery store = tienda de abarrotes; tienda de comestibles.

abasto (*Ven.*) a grocery store = tienda de comestibles.

abatatarse 1. (*Argen.*) to become confused = confundirse. **2.** (*Argen.*) to get scared = atemorizarse.

abatí; avatí 1. (*Argen., Para., Pan., Uru.*) corn; in Argentina, used only in the North = maíz; en Argentina se usa sólo en el norte del país. **2.** (*Argen., Para., Pan., Uru.*) a corncob; in Argentina, used only in the North = mazorca; en Argentina se usa sólo en el norte del país.

abiertazo (*Guat., Hond.*) generous = generoso.

abismar (*Hond.*) to surprise; to amaze = asombrar.

abolillar (*Mex.*) to become like a **gringo** = agringarse; comportarse como un anglo.

abollado (*Ven.*) an item that is not selling well = un artículo que no se vende fácilmente.

abombar (*Uru.*) to get drunk = embriagarse.

abombarse (*Puerto Rico, Ven.*) to rot; to give off a fetid smell = pudrirse; oliscar; empezar a oler mal.

abradera (*Ven.*) diarrhea (informal) = diarrea (informal).

¡ábrase! (*Colo.*) Stop being a nuisance!; Scram!; Get lost! = ¡déjese de molestar!; ¡váyase!; ¡piérdase!

abridor (*Dom. Rep.*) a can opener = un abrelatas.

abridura (*Hond.*) something thats gets opened continuously = abridero; lo que se abre continuamente.

abrigada (*Hond.*) a hiding place = escondite.

abrigadero (*Puerto Rico*) a hole; a den; a hideout = madriguera; guarida.

abrigo de lluvia (*Ecua., Peru*) a raincoat = impermeable.

abrirse 1. (*Argen.*) to run away; to shove off = dejar colgado; abandonar a alguien o a algo. **2.** (*Ven.*) to move to one side = apartarse para dar paso. **3.** (*Dom. Rep.*) to escape = huir; escaparse; rajarse. **4.** (*Dom. Rep.*) to crack = quebrarse. **5.** (*Dom. Rep.*) to be afraid = sentir miedo.

abrirse de piernas (*Argen.*) to pretend or feign ignorance of a problem = desentenderse de un problema.

abrocharse; acostar; acostarse (*Colo.*) to have sex = realizar el acto sexual.

abujazo (*Mex.*) to inject a drug = inyectar una droga.

aburrición 1. (*Bol.*) boredom = aburrimiento. **2.** (*Puerto Rico*) antipathy; hatred = antipatía; odio contra algo o alguien.

abusado(a) 1. (*Mex.*) to be clever; to be alert = ser astuto(a); estar alerta. **2.** (*Mex.*) to be a bully = ser pendenciero(a).

acabado (*Ecua.*) a sick person = una persona enfermiza.

acábala farolito (*Argen.*) stop talking nonsense = déjate de decir tonterías.

acabar 1. (*Argen., Chile, Para.*) to ejaculate; to have an orgasm (vulgar) = eyacular en la cópula; tener un orgasmo (vulgar). **2.** (*Ecua.*) a nasty remark about somebody = hablar mal de una persona; desollar a alguien.

acabose 1. (*Dom. Rep.*) a commotion = tumulto. **2.** (*Dom. Rep.*) very extraordinary = muy extraordinario.

acachao (*Chile*) a store manager or owner who has a large amount of an article that does not sell = comerciante que se queda con una gran cantidad de artículos sin poder venderlos.

acarajado; apendejado (*Colo.*) bewildered; confused; stupefied = abombado; alelado; atontado.

acarrear 1. (*Mex.*) to gossip = chismear; cotorrear. **2.** (*Mex.*) to gather a crowd for a political meeting = juntar gente para actos políticos.

acartonado (*Mex.*) a thin person = delgado.

acatar (*Hond., Guat., Mex., Salva., Ven.*) to realize; to notice = enterarse; caer en la cuenta; comprender.

acatarrar 1. (*Argen.*) to get tipsy = más o menos mareado o embriagado. **2.** (*Mex., Ven.*) to bother someone; to annoy someone = molestar; fastidiar a alguien. **3.** (*Mex., Ven.*) to realize = enterarse. **4.** (*Chile, Mex.*) to catch a cold = resfriar; contraer un catarro.

accidentado (*Ven.*) a broken-down vehicle; a vehicle that has stopped running = vehículo que sufre un desperfecto y deja de funcionar.

acepillado (*Puerto Rico*) a half-breed; a mixture of a Caucasian and an African (derogatory) = mulato; mestizo; la mezcla de blanco con negro (peyorativo).

acero (*Mex.*) a frying pan = sartén.

achanchado (*Argen.*) to be lazy; to like the easy life = dejarse ganar por la vida cómoda.

achantao (*Puerto Rico*) without ambition; half-heartedly; without interest or motivation = sin ambición; con desgana; sin motivación.

achantar (*Colo.*) to bring down an arrogant person = abatir la altivez de alguien.

achantarse (*Puerto Rico*) to be without enthusiasm = estar sin deseos de continuar; hacer algo con desgana.

achicar 1. (*Colo.*) to shorten; to shrink = acortar; reducir; empequeñecer. **2.** (*Colo.*) to humiliate = humillar. **3.** (*Colo.*) to kill = matar.

achicharrado (*Nic.*) burned = quemado.

achimería (*Guat., Hond., Salva.*) a junk shop; a flea market = buhonería; baratillo; lugar donde se venden baratijas.

achimero (*Guat., Hond., Salva.*) a peddler = buhonero; vendedor de baratijas; vendedor ambulante.

achimes (*Guat., Hond., Salva.*) trinkets; knick-knacks = baratijas.

achín (*Hond.*) a peddler = buhonero.

achinado (*Argen., Para.*) with physical features that show native origin = con rasgos físicos que indican ascendencia indígena.

achiote (*Cuba, Dom. Rep., Guat., Hond., Puerto Rico, Salva.*) annatto seed used to color food = colorante para las comidas preparado con la semilla de bija, un árbol tropical.

achispado (*Argen.*) tipsy and happy = estar ligeramente mareado y alegre por haber bebido alcohol.

acholado (*Chile, Peru*) embarrassed = avergonzado.

acholar (*Chile, Peru*) to put to shame = avergonzar.

acholarse (*Bol.*) to be frightened; to get frightened = acobardarse.

achucutar (*Hond., Guat.*) to wither; to shrivel = ajarse; marchitarse.

achucutarse (*Ven.*) to shrink back = acobardarse.

achumar (*Ecua.*) to make another feel ashamed = avergonzar.

achún (*Hond., Nic.*) a peddler = vendedor ambulante.

achuncharse (*Bol.*) to be ashamed = avergonzarse.

achurrascar (*Chile*) to squeeze; to compress = apretar; comprimir.

acial (*Ecua., Guat.*) a whip = látigo.

acidarse (*Colo.*) to turn sour = agriarse; avinagrarse.

ácido (*Puerto Rico*) annoying; impertinent = fastidioso; impertinente.

acogotar (*Para.*) to shout loudly at someone; to shout until one is hoarse = desgañitar.

acostar See **abrocharse**.

acostarse See **abrocharse**.

acreencia (*Colo., Peru*) a debt that is claimed by a creditor = deuda reclamada por el acreedor.

acriollarse (*Dom. Rep.*) to adopt the customs and uses of the natives = adoptar las costumbres y usos del nativo.

acuarium (*from English*) an aquarium = acuario.

acusete (*Argen., Bol., Chile, Ecua., Peru*) a tattletale; a blabbermouth = soplón(a).

¡adiós! (*Dom. Rep.*) an interjection that expresses incredulity = interjección que expresa incredulidad.

adiosito (*Dom. Rep.*) a farewell expressed with love and friendship = despedida cariñosa.

aeromoza (*Colo., Cuba*) a stewardess = azafata.

afanar (*Argen.*) to steal = robar.

afectar (*Puerto Rico*) to harm; to injure = lastimar; perjudicar.

afilador (*Argen., Para.*) flirtatious = galanteador.

afilar 1. (*Argen., Para.*) to sharpen = aguzar una herramienta. 2. (*Argen., Para.*) to court a woman gallantly = enamorar galantemente a una mujer. 3. (*Chile*) to have sex (vulgar) = tener relaciones sexuales (vulgar). 4. (*Uru.*) to get ready; to prepare oneself = prepararse; disponerse cuidadosamente para cualquier tarea.

aflojar (*Argen., Chile*) to let up = ceder; condescender.

afuerino (*Chile*) an outsider; a stranger = forastero; afuereño; un extraño.

agacharparse (*Dom. Rep.*) to take and keep something for oneself = embolsar; embolsillar.

agalla 1. (*Colo.*) greed; robbery; stinginess = avaricia; rapiña; cicatería. 2. (*Ecua.*) a fearless person = persona sin miedo.

agallado (*Argen., Chile, Puerto Rico*) valiant; courageous = valiente; con coraje.

agallarse (*Puerto Rico*) to become bold = envalentonarse.

agalludo 1. (*Ecua., Colo., Ven.*) ambitious; greedy = ambicioso; avaro. 2. (*Ecua., Colo., Ven.*) stingy = tacaño; mezquino.

agarrar (*Uru., Chile*) to take = tomar; coger.

agarrar chansa (*from English*) to take a chance = correr un riesgo.

agarrar clases (*Mex.*) to take courses in school = tomar cursos en la escuela.

agarrar de puro pedo (*Mex.*) to pursue someone continuously and insistently = perseguir a alguien de una manera continua e insistente.

agarrar la onda (*Chile, Mex.*) to tune in; to catch the drift of something; to be on the right track = comprender; captar lo que se dice o se hace.

agarrar la tetera (*Mex.*) to be a drunk = ser borracho.

agarrarse a cancos (*Mex.*) to get involved in a fist fight = pelear; irse a las manos.

agarrón 1. (*Chile*) to touch in a sexual manner (vulgar) = tocar en un sentido sexual (vulgar). 2. (*Ven.*) a fist fight = pelea a puñetazos.

agarroso 1. (*Guat., Hond., Salva.*) sharp = filudo; agudo. 2. (*Guat., Hond., Salva.*) bitter = amargo; agrio.

ágatas; agües; agüitas (*Mex.*) marbles = canicas.

agringado (*Mex.*) anglicized = latino que sigue los usos y costumbres anglosajonas.

agua de piringa; aguapiringa (*Puerto Rico*) a tasteless cold drink = refresco frío y sin sabor.

aguacate 1. (*Colo., Cuba, Mex., Puerto Rico, Salva.*) an avocado = fruto del aguacate o palta. 2. (*Colo., Cuba*) a policeman = agente de policía. 3. (*Hond., Guat., Salva.*) an idiot; a fool = idiota; tonto. 4. (*Ven.*) a tree that produces a nonedible fruit = árbol que produce un fruto no comestible. 5. (*Mex.*) downhearted; discouraged = desanimado.

aguachacha (*Guat., Hond., Salva.*) a drink that is not prepared properly and tastes bad = refresco mal preparado o de mala calidad.

aguachada (*Hond.*) a tasteless drink; a nasty-tasting drink = bebida sin gusto; bebida de sabor desagradable.

aguachar 1. (*Chile*) to use flattering language in order to obtain the goodwill of others = captar la voluntad de otro con palabras lisonjeras. 2. (*Chile*) to domesticate an animal = domesticar una bestia. 3. (*Chile*) to be fond of; to be attached to = querendar; encariñar.

aguachinarse (*Hond.*) to flood = inundarse; anegarse.

aguachoso (*Puerto Rico*) watery; insipid = aguachento; desabrido.

aguada(o) 1. (*Colo., Guat., Nic., Mex., Pan., Ven.*) soft; without consistency = cosa blanda y sin consistencia. 2. (*Guat., Mex., Nic., Pan.*) weak; faint = débil; desfallecido. **3.** (*Mex.*) a dull-witted person = persona sin viveza ni gracia. **4.** (*Pan., Ven.*) something loose; something untied = suelto; flojo. **5.** (*Pan., Costa Rica*) lazy = haragán. **6.** (*Ecua.*) a fruit juice and sugar drink = refresco de agua con azúcar y frutas.

aguadulce (*Costa Rica*) a drink of water and honey = refresco de agua con miel.

aguaje 1. (*Dom. Rep.*) a lie = una mentira. **2.** (*Dom. Rep.*) a fuss = aspaviento; gesticulación exagerada.

aguajero (*Puerto Rico, Ven.*) a loud-mouth; a braggart = fanfarrón; el que alardea de lo que no es o de lo que no tiene.

aguajirarse (*Cuba*) to become countrified = adoptar las costumbres del campo.

agualotal (*Hond.*) a swamp = pantano.

aguamiel (*Ven.*) sugar-cane firewater = guarapo; aguardiente de caña.

aguanoso (*Hond., Peru*) a tasteless fruit = fruto sin sabor.

aguantador (*Chile, Puerto Rico*) long-suffering = extremadamente paciente.

aguantar (*Cuba*) to put up with something = tener que tolerar algo.

aguántate (*Puerto Rico*) calm down = tranquilízate.

aguántele (*Chile*) wait = espere.

aguantón (*Cuba*) a person who accepts mistreatment without complaint = el que acepta abusos sin quejarse.

aguapanela (*Colo., Ven.*) a drink made of water, lemon, and **panela** = bebida de agua, limón y **panela**.

aguapiringa See **agua de piringa**.

aguarapado (*Colo., Ven.*) the color **guarapo**; a light brown color = del color del **guarapo**; color marrón o café claro.

aguares (*from English*) awards = premios.

aguasado (*Argen., Chile*) to behave shyly = comportarse tímidamente.

aguatero (*Argen., Chile*) a water carrier = aguador.

agüerista (*Colo.*) one who believes in omens; one who is superstitious = supersticioso; el que cree en agüeros.

agües See **ágatas**.

agüevado; ahuevado (*Colo.*) silly; a person of low intelligence = tonto; bobo; persona corta de entendederas.

agüitas See **ágatas**.

agujero (*Mex.*) the vagina (vulgar) = vagina (vulgar).

agujetas; cintas (*Mex.*) shoelaces = lazos o cordones de zapatos.

ahijuma (*Ecua., Peru*) son of a bitch (strong vulgar insult) = hijo de mala madre; hijo de perra (insulto fuerte y vulgar).

ahogado; ahogo; hogo (*Colo.*) a seasoning sauce = salsa para sazonar.

ahogo See **ahogado**.

ahora 1. (*Argen., Bol., Chile, Cuba, Peru*) right now = de inmediato. **2.** (*Mex.*) in a moment = en un momento. **3.** (*Nic.*) soon = pronto.

ahorita 1. (*Mex.*) soon = pronto. **2.** (*Nic.*) right now = en este instante.

ahoritica (*Ven.*) right now = en este momento; de inmediato.

ahoritita (*Mex.*) right now = de inmediato.

ahorrar (*Ecua.*) to avoid any kind of work; to refuse to work = evitar cualquier tipo de trabajo; negarse a trabajar.

ahuevado See **agüevado**.

aindiado 1. (*Ecua.*) Indian-like (derogatory); looking like a native of Ecuador and not like a Caucasian European = se ve como indio (peyorativo); de facciones indígenas y no europeas. **2.** (*Chile, Ecua.*) to behave as an Indian (derogatory) = comportarse como indio (peyorativo).

aiscon (*from English*) an ice cream cone = helado de barquillo.

aiscrim (*from English*) ice cream = helado.

ají 1. (*Argen., Bol., Chile, Colo., Ecua., Peru, Uru.*) a hot pepper; a red pepper; a

chili pepper = picante; pica; pique; **chile. 2.** (*Colo.*) stimulating = estimulante. **3.** (*Colo.*) annoying; bothersome = fastidioso; molestoso. **4.** (*Cuba*) a green pepper = chile verde.

ají picante (*Cuba*) a hot pepper = picante; chile.

ají verde (*Argen., Chile*) a green hot pepper = picante verde; jalapeño; chile verde.

ajiaco 1. (*Chile, Colo., Peru*) a dish prepared with potatoes and other ingredients = plato de patatas y otros ingredientes. **2.** (*Cuba*) a chili stew = guiso picante. **3.** (*Cuba*) a brawl; a rumpus = escándalo; reyerta; gresca.

ajibararse (*Puerto Rico*) to be afraid of people = sentirse cohibido frente a los demás.

ajonjear (*Colo.*) to caress = acariciar.

ajorado 1. (*Puerto Rico*) hurried = apurado. **2.** (*Puerto Rico*) busy = ocupado.

ajumado (*Colo., Pan., Ven.*) drunk = borracho.

ajumao (*Puerto Rico*) almost drunk; half drunk = medio borracho; casi borracho.

ajustador (*Cuba*) a brassiere = sostén; sostén de senos.

al bote y al miado (*Nic.*) everything is or has been wrong = todo está saliendo o salió mal.

al carajo (*Dom. Rep.*) with all possible strength = con toda la fuerza posible.

al clima (*Colo.*) at room temperature = a la temperatura ambiental.

al cuete 1. (*Chile*) straight = directo; sin rodeos. **2.** (*Chile*) without order; without sequence = sin orden; sin secuencia.

al hilo (*Mex.*) an uninterrupted action = un acto hecho ininterrumpidamente.

al mejor mico se le cae el zapote (*Nic.*) even the wisest people make mistakes = aún los más sabios cometen errores.

al pedo (*Argen.*) to do or say nonsense = decir o hacer tonterías (informal).

al tilín (*Cuba*) having something in mind and ready to answer = tener algo en la punta de la lengua y estar listo para responder.

al tuntún 1. (*Argen., Chile, Cuba*) only as an estimation; inexact; inaccurate = sólo como estimación; inexacto; no preciso. **2.** (*Argen., Chile, Cuba*) careless behavior = conducta descuidada.

alabao (*Dom. Rep.*) arrogant; haughty = altanero.

alacamunería 1. (*Ven.*) a brawl = alboroto; escándalo. **2.** (*Ven.*) gossip = chisme.

alaco (*Hond., Salva.*) a useless person or object = persona u objeto inútil.

alacranar (*Argen.*) to slander = difamar.

alacraneo (*Argen.*) slander = difamación.

alagartarse (*Guat., Nic.*) to behave with avarice = actuar con avaricia.

alambrista (*Mex.*) an illegal Mexican alien in the United States = mexicano indocumentado en los Estados Unidos.

alambrito; angarillo (*Colo.*) a thin person (informal) = persona delgada (informal).

alaraco (*Chile*) exaggerated; overly demonstrative; theatrical = exagerado; que aumenta las cosas mucho más de lo que son.

alaste (*Nic.*) gooey; sticky = pegajoso; empalagoso; mucoso.

albardear (*Hond.*) to annoy; to bother = fastidiar; molestar.

albarillo (*Hond.*) camomile = manzanilla.

albazo (*Mex.*) an early morning serenade = serenata muy temprano por la mañana.

alberca (*Mex.*) a swimming pool = piscina.

albóndiga 1. (*Argen.*) a battered or damaged object = cosa u objeto muy maltrecho y casi destruido. **2.** (*Argen.*) a fat or slow person = persona gorda o lenta.

alboroto; crispetas; maíz piro (*Colo.*) popcorn = palomitas de maíz.

alborotos (*Hond., Guat., Salva.*) popcorn = palomitas de maíz.

alcahuete (*Uru.*) a fawner = adulón.

alcanforarse (*Hond., Ven.*) to evaporate; to disappear; to hide; to vanish = evaporarse; desaparecer; ocultarse; disiparse.

alcapurria (*Puerto Rico*) a fritter of plantain, **yautía** or **yucca** filled with meat or crab = fritura de plátano, **yautía o yuca** relleno de carne o cangrejo.

alegrona (*Colo., Ecua.*) a prostitute (vulgar) = prostituta (vulgar).

alentar (*Colo., Ecua., Hond.*) to recover from an illness = recuperarse; restablecerse de una enfermedad.

aleonar (*Chile*) to encourage; to foster = animar; incitar; alentar.

alepantado (*Ecua.*) to become lost in thought; a daydreamer = ensimismado; embelesado.

alepate (*Costa Rica*) a bedbug = chinche.

aletazo 1. (*Chile, Cuba*) a slap = bofetada; puñetazo. **2.** (*Hond.*) a robbery = robo. **3.** (*Hond.*) fraud = estafa.

alfeñique (*Ven.*) a delicacy prepared with **panela** = golosina preparada con **panela**.

alférez (*Hond., Guat.*) a person who can be trusted; an honest person = persona a quien se le tiene confianza; persona honesta.

alfiler (*Ven.*) a safety pin = imperdible.

alfiler de criandera (*Cuba*) a safety pin = imperdible.

alfiler de gancho (*Chile, Ecua., Peru*) a safety pin = imperdible.

algaraza (*Hond.*) noisy voices = bullicio de voces.

alianza (*Bol., Ecua., Peru*) a wedding ring = sortija de compromiso.

alicate 1. (*Chile, Colo., Puerto Rico*) pliers = tenazas. **2.** (*Puerto Rico*) a close friend = amigo íntimo.

alicates (*Peru, Guat.*) pliers = tenazas.

aliento (*Mex.*) an illegal alien living in the United States = persona indocumentada que vive en los Estados Unidos.

aliñada (*Colo.*) a fine and delicate person = persona fina y delicada.

aliñado (*Mex.*) a well-dressed person = bien vestido; bien presentado.

aliñar 1. (*Colo.*) to bribe = sobornar. **2.** (*Colo.*) to cause someone to come to terms with oneself = inducir a otro para que se reconcilie consigo mismo.

alipego (*Costa Rica*) extra merchandise given as a gift from the seller, in addition to items purchased = mercancía regalada que el vendedor le da al comprador.

almacén (*Argen., Chile, Ecua., Peru, Uru.*) a grocery store = tienda de abarrotes.

almádana (*Hond.*) a mallet = mazo de hierro.

almágana (*Hond.*) a lazy person = haragán; persona perezosa.

almareado; birote; embolado (*Nic.*) drunk = ebrio; borracho.

almidonado (*Argen.*) a very formal person (derogatory) = una persona muy formal (peyorativo).

aloja (*Bol.*) a drink made from fermented fruits or corn = chicha; bebida hecha con fruta o maíz fermentado.

alpaca (*Bol.*) a mammal of the camel family that lives only in the Andes mountains = mamífero camélido que vive sólo en los Andes.

alpargatón; alpargatudo; ruanetas (*Colo.*) a person of low socioeconomic status = persona de baja condición socioeconómica.

alpargatudo See **alpargatón.**

alquitrán (*Guat.*) asphalt on the road = asfalto de los caminos.

altiro (*Chile*) at once = de inmediato.

altos (*Argen., Chile*) the upper floor of a two-story building = el piso de arriba.

alturado (*Peru*) dignified; calm = digno; mesurado.

alumbrado 1. (*Ven.*) a simple-minded person = persona de escaso entendimiento. **2.** (*Ven.*) a person who is bewitched = hechizado. **3.** (*Ven.*) a person who bewitches others; a person with supernatural powers; a wizard = persona con poderes sobrenaturales; el que puede hacer hechicerías; hechicero.

alunarse (*Colo.*) to lose one's mind = perder el juicio.

alverja; arveja; arverja (*Argen., Bol., Colo., Chile, Cuba, Ecua., Guat., Hond., Peru, Ven.*) a pea = guisante.

alverjón (*Mex.*) peas = guisantes.

alzacola (*Puerto Rico*) a servile person = servil; arrastrado.

alzado 1. (*Argen., Chile, Mex., Puerto Rico*) rebel = rebelde. **2.** (*Argen., Chile, Mex., Puerto Rico*) to be in heat = estar en celo.

alzafuelles; lambón(a) (*Colo.*) a flatterer; a blabbermouth = soplón; servil; lameculos.

alzar (*Argen.*) to steal; to take without authorization = robar o llevarse algo a escondidas.

alzo (*Guat., Hond., Nic.*) a robbery = robo; hurto.

amachada; machera (*Dom. Rep.*) a mannish woman; a woman who behaves like a man = marimacho; mujer que actúa como hombre.

amacharse (*Mex.*) to be stubborn = estar o ponerse obstinado.

amachinar (*Ven.*) to live together without being married = amancebarse; vivir juntos sin casarse.

amachinarse (*Pan.*) to be disheartened; to be sad = estar desilusionado; encontrarse triste; no tener ánimos.

amacolao (*Puerto Rico*) melancholic = melancólico.

amallarse (*Chile*) to delay or stop the payment of a debt = evitar o eludir el pago de una deuda.

amangaluar (*Colo.*) to conspire; to plot = confabular; conchabar.

amanta (*Peru*) the village elder = el anciano de la aldea; al que se le respeta por su antigüedad.

amañarse (*Colo., Ecua.*) to be accustomed to someone or something; to find doing something to be pleasant = acostumbrarse a algo o a alguien; gustarle lo que hace.

amapuchar (*Puerto Rico*) to hide the truth = esconder la verdad.

amarchantarse (*Ven.*) to become a client = hacerse cliente.

amargo 1. (*Argen., Uru.*) **mate** without sugar = **mate** sin azúcar. **2.** (*Argen., Uru.*) any drink without sugar = cualquier bebida sin azúcar. **3.** (*Peru*) angry; upset = enojado; molesto.

amariconado (*Chile*) effeminate (vulgar) = afeminado (vulgar); amaricado.

amarillo (*Puerto Rico*) fried ripe plantain = plátano maduro frito.

amarradijo (*Guat., Hond.*) a bad knot = nudo mal hecho.

amarrarse 1. (*Colo., Cuba, Guat., Mex., Nic., Pan., Puerto Rico, Salva.*) to get married = casarse; contraer un vínculo matrimonial. **2.** (*Colo., Cuba, Guat., Mex., Nic., Pan., Puerto Rico, Salva.*) to become engaged = comprometerse; juntarse para convivir. **3.** (*Ven.*) to be ready for action = estar listo para emprender una acción. **4.** (*Costa Rica, Pan., Salva.*) to get drunk = emborracharse.

amarrarse los huevos (*Mex.*) to take a stand on an issue or topic = tomar una postura firme en un asunto o cuestión.

amarrete; apretado(a) 1. (*Chile*) always saving; always letting others pay for him or her = está siempre ahorrando; dejar que otros siempre paguen por él/ella. **2.** (*Argen.*) miserly; mean (informal) = avaro; egoísta (informal).

amarroso 1. (*Salva.*) an acidic fruit = fruta ácida. **2.** (*Salva.*) sharp = agudo.

amasadito(a) (*Dom. Rep.*) a fat person = gordo(a).

amasandería (*Chile*) a bakery where the bread is prepared by hand in small amounts = panadería donde se amasa el pan a mano en pequeñas cantidades.

amasar (*Puerto Rico*) to touch in a sexual manner = tocar en un sentido sexual.

amauta (*Bol.*) the village elder; the elder respected for his or her age = el anciano de la aldea; al que se le debe respetar por su antigüedad.

amayorado (*Bol.*) a precocious child = niño precoz.

ambiente (*Chile, Peru, Uru.*) a room = habitación; aposento.

ambo (*Argen., Chile, Uru.*) a two-piece man's suit, each piece having a different color and texture = traje de hombre de dos piezas de diferentes colores y texturas.

amelcocharse (*Cuba*) to fall in love; to become attached to someone = enamorarse; estar emocionalmente muy pegado a alguien.

amellarse 1. (*Chile*) to leave a game as a winner too early = abandonar el juego como ganador antes que éste termine. **2.** (*Chile*) to be stingy or tight-fisted = comportarse como tacaño.

americana; chamarra; manuela (*Mex.*) a jacket = chaqueta.

ameritar (*Cuba, Mex., Peru, Ven.*) to deserve = merecer.

amistarse (*Para.*) to become friends = hacerse amigos.

amohosado (*Chile*) rusty = oxidado; mohoso.

amolar 1. (*Argen.*) to annoy; to bother (informal) = fastidiar; molestar (informal). **2.** (*Ven.*) to steal; to cheat = robar; engañar.

amongado (*Dom. Rep.*) sad = triste.

amontonar (*Ecua.*) to insult = insultar.

amorochados (*Ven.*) very close companions; people who are always together = personas que andan siempre juntas.

amostazar (*Ecua., Hond.*) to put to shame = avergonzar.

ampalagoso (*Chile*) too sweet and sticky = muy dulce y pegajoso.

ampolleta (*Chile*) a light bulb = bujía eléctrica.

amuñuñar; apurruñar (*Ven.*) to squeeze = apretujar; apretar a varias personas o cosas.

amurrarse 1. (*Chile*) facial gestures that show you do not want to do something = mostrar con gestos faciales que no se quiere hacer algo. **2.** (*Hond.*) to become sad = entristecerse; acongojarse.

amurrugado (*Ven.*) sad = triste.

amusgarse; azarearse (*Hond., Guat.*) to be daunted; to be ashamed = amilanarse; avergonzarse.

anafre (*Puerto Rico*) a prostitute = prostituta.

anamú (*Puerto Rico*) an herb used by the **santero** = hierba usada por el **santero**.

ananá (*Argen., Uru.*) a pineapple = piña.

ancas (*Argen.*) the buttocks (vulgar) = nalgas (vulgar).

ancheta 1. (*Bol.*) nonsense; talk that does not make any sense = palabrería insulsa. **2.** (*Colo.*) a basket or bag full of groceries = canasta o bolsa llena de comestibles. **3.** (*Colo., Ecua., Peru*) good business; a bargain; a good buy = buen negocio; ganga; bicoca. **4.** (*Ven.*) a bonus; a gift = gratificación; dádiva. **5.** (*Mex., Ven.*) a joke = broma. **6.** (*Mex., Ven.*) a small business = negocio de poca monta.

anchoveta (*Chile, Peru*) a variety of anchovy, typical of the Pacific Ocean near South America = variedad de anchoa, muy común en las costas del Océano Pacífico de Sudamérica.

ancón (*Puerto Rico*) a flat-bottomed boat used for cargo = bote grande y de fondo plano usado para la carga.

¡ándale! (*Mex.*) Hurry up! = ¡apúrate!

andar bravo (*Mex.*) to be angry = estar enojado.

andar con el gorila (*Argen.*) to be drunk (informal) = estar borracho (informal).

andar de jacalera (*Mex.*) spreading gossip = chismeando.

andar en pelotas (*Mex.*) to be naked = estar desnudo.

andar ficha; andar quebrado (*Mex.*) to be broke = estar sin dinero.

andar juntos (*Mex.*) going steady in a love affair = una pareja que se cita sólo entre los dos.

andar lurias (*Mex.*) to be crazy = estar fuera de sí; estar o comportarse como un loco.

andar pato; estar pato (*Argen., Chile, Uru.*) to be penniless = no tener dinero; estar sin un centavo.

andar pedo; andar pisto (*Mex.*) to be drunk = estar ebrio.

andar pisto See **andar pedo**.

andar quebrado See **andar ficha**.

andén 1. (*Colo., Guat., Hond., Salva.*) a sidewalk = acera; calzada. **2.** (*Peru*) a platform made in the mountains for cultivating soil = plataforma hecha en la montaña para cultivar la tierra.

andón (*Colo., Ven.*) a person who walks a lot and/or fast = el que anda mucho y/o con velocidad.

angarillo See **alambrito**.

angarrio 1. (*Colo.*) a thin person = persona delgada. **2.** (*Colo.*) an old person or animal = persona o animal viejo.

angelar (*Hond.*) to sigh = suspirar.

angola (*Hond.*) sour milk = leche agria.

angolo(a) (*Puerto Rico*) a black person (derogatory) = negro(a) (peyorativo).

angurria (*Argen.*) **1.** hunger = hambre. **2.** greed = codicia.

anillo (*Argen., Chile, Colo., Cuba, Ecua., Peru, Uru.*) a ring = sortija.

animita (*Chile*) a folkloric religious landmark to signify where someone died or was killed on the road = marca de carácter folclórico y religioso que señala el lugar donde alguien murió en el camino.

anotarse un poroto 1. (*Chile, Para.*) to make a point in a game = apuntarse un tanto en el juego. **2.** (*Chile, Para.*) to guess correctly = tener un acierto.

ansia (*Puerto Rico, Ven.*) nausea = náusea.

anteojos largavista (*Argen., Chile, Ecua., Peru*) binoculars = binoculares.

anticuchos (*Bol., Chile, Peru*) small pieces of meat and vegetables barbecued on a metal rod; a shish kebob = trozos pequeños de carnes y vegetales que se ensartan en un fierro y se asan a fuego abierto.

antifris (*from English*) antifreeze = anticongelante.

antipespirante (*Colo.*) deodorant = desodorante.

anuncio (*Colo.*) a sign = cartel.

añiñado(a); añiñao (*Chile*) a bully = valentón(a); matón(a).

añiñao See **añiñado(a)**.

añoñar (*Dom. Rep.*) to caress = mimar.

apachurrado (*Dom. Rep.*) **1.** a short man = enano; un hombre bajo de estatura. **2.** to be stunted in physical growth = atrofiado.

apachurrar (*Ecua., Guat., Hond., Mex., Peru, Salva.*) to smash; to squash; to crush = despachurrar; destruir; aplastar.

apagador (*Mex.*) a switch; an electric switch = interruptor; interruptor eléctrico.

apajuatao (*Puerto Rico*) to have swollen eyelids from too much sleep = mostrar los párpados hinchados de mucho dormir.

apanar 1. (*Chile*) to wrap beef or pork in bread crumbs = rebozar carnes de cerdo o vacuno en migas de pan. **2.** (*Peru*) a group of people beating up on one person = varias personas dan de golpes a una sola.

apañar 1. (*Argen.*) to conceal a crime = proteger; encubrir al autor de una acción delictiva. **2.** (*Chile, Mex.*) to obtain; to get (informal) = conseguir; obtener (informal). **3.** (*Mex.*) to arrest = arrestar.

aparato (*Mex.*) the buttocks = nalgas; asentaderas.

aparragarse (*Hond.*) to crouch down; to squat = agazaparse.

apartado 1. (*Mex.*) the process by which and/or the building in which metals are classified = la operación y/o el edificio en que se clasifican los metales. **2.** (*Hond., Nic.*) shy; unsociable = huraño; insociable.

apartido (*Ecua.*) in equal parts = en partes iguales.

apaste (*Guat., Hond., Mex.*) a basin = palangana.

apatronado(a) (*Chile*) a worker who defends the interests of the boss or the company against the interests of himself or other workers = el/la que defiende los intereses de la compañía o del jefe más que los suyos propios o los de otros trabajadores.

apechugar 1. (*Chile, Colo.*) to assume full responsibility for something = hacerse completamente responsable por algo. **2.** (*Chile, Colo.*) to have drive or initiative = tener empuje.

apendejado See **acarajado**.

apendejao (*Puerto Rico*) dumb; an idiot = tonto; idiota.

apensionado (*Argen.*) grieved = apesadumbrado.

apereá (*Para.*) a guinea pig = conejillo de indias.

api (*Bol.*) a drink made from corn = bebida de maíz.

apilonados 1. (*Ven.*) in a pile = apilados; amontonados. **2.** (*Ven.*) in a crowd = gentes aglomeradas en un lugar.

apintonearse (*Para.*) tipsy = achisparse; ponerse alegre con la bebida.

apitiguarse (*Chile*) to dress up; to dress elegantly = vestirse elegante.

apitutarse (*Chile*) to gain special privileges at work; to get a good position = obtener privilegios especiales en el trabajo; tener un buen trabajo o ubicarse en una buena posición en el trabajo.

aplanchar; vaciar (*Colo.*) a severe reprimand = reprimenda severa.

aplanche (*Colo.*) decay; gloominess = decaimiento; melancolía.

aplastado (*Argen.*) lacking enthusiasm; discouraged = carente de entusiasmo; sin fuerzas; desalentado.

aplatanao (*Puerto Rico*) lazy = holgazán.

aplatarse (*Dom. Rep.*) to crouch down = ponerse en cuclillas.

aplicación (*from English*) an application = solicitud; petición.

aplicar (*from English*) to apply = postular; presentar una solicitud.

apoinmen (*from English*) an appointment = cita; compromiso para encontrarse.

apolillar (*Uru.*) to sleep = dormir.

apolizmado (*Colo.*) to grow less than expected = retrasado en el crecimiento.

aposar (*Chile*) to form a pool = líquido que forma un charco.

apozarse 1. (*Dom. Rep.*) to stop = detenerse. **2.** (*Colo.*) a puddle; a liquid that forms a pool = un líquido que forma un charco.

apretado(a) See **amarrete**.

apretar (*Argen.*) to kiss = besar.

apricot (*from English*) an apricot = albaricoque.

aprontao (*Puerto Rico*) a busybody; a meddler = entrometido; metiche.

apronte (*Argen., Chile, Para.*) preparation; preliminary activities = preparación; preparativos.

¡apucha! (*Mex.*) an expression of surprise or astonishment = expresión de sorpresa o incredibilidad.

apuchungar (*Ven.*) to hug = abrazar; estrechar con mucho cariño.

apuercado (*Mex.*) dressed very poorly = vestido muy pobremente.

apuñalearse (*Dom. Rep.*) to keep part of the money won during a game = guardarse parte del dinero que se va ganando en el juego.

apurar (*Chile*) to rush = apresurar.

apurruñado (*Ven.*) to be squeezed by a crowd = apretujado por la multitud.

apurruñar See **amuñuñar**.

aquerenciar (*Argen.*) to become attached to a place = acostumbrarse a un lugar.

arao (*Puerto Rico*) stupid; thick-headed = estúpido; cabeza dura.

araucano (*Argen., Chile*) a native pre-Colombian people from the South of Argentina and Chile = pueblo precolombino nativo del sur de Argentina y Chile.

arbolario (*Ven.*) **1.** a person who exaggerates = persona exagerada. **2.** a busybody = entrometido.

arca (*Mex.*) an armpit = axila.

arenque (*Dom. Rep.*) a thin person (informal); skinny = delgado (informal); flaco.

arepa **1.** (*Colo., Guat., Hond., Salva.*) a fried corn tortilla = tortilla de maíz frita. **2.** (*Ven.*) a corn flour bread in a circular shape = pan de harina de maíz con forma circular.

arepera (*Colo.*) a lesbian (vulgar) = lesbiana (vulgar).

arete (*Peru*) an earring = pendiente; zarcillo.

aretes (*Cuba, Mex.*) earrings = pendientes; zarcillos.

argel (*Para.*) a bad temper = mal humor.

argelado (*Para.*) bad-tempered = malhumorado.

argolla (*Chile, Colo.*) a wedding ring = sortija o anillo de bodas.

argollero (*Colo.*) a person who sees the advantages; an opportunist = aprovechador; ventajista.

argüenda (*Mex.*) gossip = chisme.

argüende (*Mex.*) **1.** a brawl; a rumpus = alboroto. **2.** a lie; an exaggeration = mentira; exageración.

argüendero(a) **1.** (*Mex.*) a liar; a scandalmonger = mentiroso(a); chismoso(a). **2.** (*Mex.*) a person who is always complaining about something = el que siempre se queja acerca de algo.

aribe (*Hond.*) an intelligent boy or girl = niño(a) inteligente.

aritos (*Hond., Salva.*) earrings = pendientes; zarcillos.

¡aro! (*Chile*) to rest and drink between the two sections of the **cueca**, the national dance of Chile = descanso y el momento para beber entre dos secciones del baile nacional chileno, la **cueca**.

aro **1.** (*Bol., Peru*) an earring = zarcillo. **2.** (*Ven.*) a wedding ring = anillo matrimonial. **3.** (*Puerto Rico*) a ring = sortija.

aros (*Argen., Chile*) earrings = pendientes; zarcillos.

arquero (*Argen., Chile, Uru.*) a jail keeper = guardavallas; guardametas.

arranao (*Chile*) to behave lazily; not interested in work or other activities = perezoso; sin interés por trabajar o por otras actividades.

arrancado; arrancao (*Dom. Rep.*) to be broke = estar sin dinero.

arrancao See **arrancado.**

arrancar (*Chile, Mex.*) to flee; to run away = escapar; huir.

arranchado (*Colo.*) stubborn = obstinado.

arranchar (*Peru*) to lodge; to stay = alojar; permanecer.

arrastrado (*Colo.*) despicable; poor = miserable; pobre; despreciable.

arreado(a) (*Hond.*) lazy; idle = haragán; perezoso; holgazán.

arrebatao (*Puerto Rico*) to be high on drugs = estar bajo los efectos de la droga.

arrebolarse (*Puerto Rico*) to become more lively = animarse.

arrebrujar; rebrujar; rebujar (*Colo.*) to make a mess; to create a disorder = revolver; desordenar.

arrechado(a) **1.** (*Colo., Ven.*) to be sexually excited = estar excitado sexualmente. **2.** (*Colo., Ven.*) to be very upset; to be in a bad mood = estar muy enojado; estar de mal genio.

arrecharse **1.** (*Colo., Ven.*) to get furious = enfurecerse; indignarse. **2.** (*Colo., Ven.*) to get sexually excited = excitarse sexualmente.

arrechera 1. (*Colo.*) sexual excitement = excitación sexual. **2.** (*Colo.*) anger; irritation; bad temper = enojo; mal genio.

arrecho 1. (*Nic., Salva.*) anger; annoyance = enojo; molestia. **2.** (*Salva.*) very good = muy bueno. **3.** (*Ven.*) a bad-tempered person = persona iracunda y de mal carácter. **4.** (*Ven.*) courage = valentía. **5.** (*Colo., Ven.*) sexual excitement = excitación sexual.

arreglar (*Chile*) to castrate an animal = cortar los órganos genitales a un animal; capar.

arrejarse 1. (*Ven.*) to pause for a long time = detenerse por un largo tiempo. **2.** (*Ven.*) to dress elegantly = vestirse elegantemente.

arrequintado (*Ven.*) tight-fitting = apretado.

arribeño (*Colo.*) foreign = forastero.

arrimado(a) 1. (*Hond.*) a person who lives in the home of others; a lodger in another's home = alojado; el que vive en casas ajenas; hospedado en la casa de otro(a). **2.** (*Hond.*) someone who is always asking for favors = el que siempre anda pidiendo favores.

arrimarse (*Argen.*) to live together without being married = convivir sin haberse casado.

arriquín (*Guat., Hond.*) a person who is very attached to somebody else = persona que no se separa de otra.

arriscarse (*Peru*) to dress carefully = vestirse con esmero.

arrocero (*Ven.*) a person who likes to party (informal); a party animal = el que es aficionado a las fiestas (informal).

arrodajarse (*Costa Rica*) to sit with the legs crossed = sentarse con las piernas cruzadas.

arrollado (*Argen., Chile*) beef or pork tied in a roll, seasoned and boiled = carne de vacuno o cerdo enrollada en un cilindro aderezada y hervida.

arrosquetado (*Ven.*) a dark-skinned person = persona de piel oscura.

arrotado 1. (*Chile*) without manners = sin modales. **2.** (*Chile*) from a low social class = de baja condición social.

arroz (*Ven.*) a small party = fiesta pequeña.

arroz con mango (*Cuba*) a complicated thing = cosa complicada.

arrufar (*Ven.*) to lose one's temper; to get angry = irritarse; enojarse.

arrugarse (*Argen.*) to get scared = acobardarse; atemorizarse.

arrume (*Ven.*) a pile of objects in disarray = conjunto o montón de objetos en desorden.

arveja See **alverja**.

arverja See **alverja**.

asalto (*Puerto Rico*) a Christmas carol that is sung outside a house until the door is opened = canciones navideñas que se cantan fuera de una casa hasta que se abren las puertas.

asegurador; broche; segurito; seguro (*Mex.*) a safety pin = imperdible.

asistencia 1. (*Colo.*) a boarding house = casa de huéspedes. **2.** (*Colo.*) a restaurant of inferior quality = restaurante de mala calidad.

asomar (*Chile, Ecua., Peru*) to draw near; to approach = aproximarse; acercarse.

asopao 1. (*Puerto Rico*) something easy = cosa fácil. **2.** (*Puerto Rico*) a Puerto Rican dish with rice and meat, midway between a soup and dry rice = plato a base de arroz y carne que no es ni sopa ni arroz seco. **3.** (*Chile*) a naive person; a silly person = ingenuo; persona tonta.

asunto (*Argen.*) menstruation = menstruación.

atacar (*Ven.*) to court = cortejar; enamorar.

atajarse (*Para.*) to hold oneself back = contenerse.

atajona (*Hond.*) a whip = látigo.

atao (*Chile*) a mess = enredo.

atapuzar (*Ven.*) to fill; to pack = atiborrar; llenar demasiado; llenar hasta el borde.

atarrillarse (*Ven.*) to get sunstroke = sufrir una insolación.

ático (*from English*) an attic = desván.

atingencia (*Peru*) responsibility; concern = incumbencia.

atiquizar 1. (*Hond.*) to chase = acosar. **2.** (*Hond.*) to poke = atizar.

atolada (*Hond.*) a party where **atole** is served = fiesta donde se sirve **atole**.

atole (*Guat., Hond., Mex., Ven.*) a creamy drink prepared with water, sugar, and rice, wheat or oat flour = bebida con una consistencia cremosa preparada con agua, azúcar y harina de arroz, de trigo o de avena.

atotumarse (*Colo.*) to be bewildered; to be stunned = atolondrarse; aturdirse.

atracar 1. (*Hond., Nic.*) to argue; to quarrel = discutir; reñir. **2.** (*Mex., Puerto Rico*) to hit = pegar; zurrar. **3.** (*Mex., Puerto Rico*) to push against someone or something = empujar contra algo; arrimar. **4.** (*Nic.*) to tie up tightly; to truss = sujetar; asegurar con cuerdas y lazos; atar. **5.** (*Nic.*) to impose strict rules or discipline = imponer reglas o disciplina muy estricta. **6.** (*Puerto Rico*) to eat excessively = comer excesivamente. **7.** (*Puerto Rico*) to assault = agredir. **8.** (*Chile*) to fondle = tocar; acariciar eróticamente.

atrecho (*Puerto Rico*) a shortcut; a path = atajo; sendero.

atributo (*Hond.*) a platform used to carry a religious icon during a procession = plataforma sobre la que se carga una imagen religiosa durante una procesión.

atrincado (*Ven.*) tough; daring = corajudo; arriesgado.

atrincar 1. (*Chile, Costa Rica, Cuba, Dom. Rep., Ecua., Peru, Ven.*) to tie up tightly; to truss up = amarrar; sujetar; asegurar con cuerdas y lazos. **2.** (*Chile, Cuba, Mex., Peru*) to impose very strict rules or discipline = imponer reglas o disciplina muy estricta.

atrojar (*Mex.*) bewildered; unable to find a solution to a problem = aturdirse; no hallar alguien salida en algún empeño o dificultad.

atucuñar (*Hond.*) to fill; to pack = atiborrar; llenar algo hasta el máximo.

atufar (*Ecua.*) to get confused; to become bewildered = atolondrarse; aturdirse.

atufarse (*Guat.*) to be proud; to be vain = enorgullecerse; ensoberbecerse.

aunche; hunche (*Colo.*) the residue of a liquid in a container = sobras o residuos de un líquido en la botella.

auquénido (*Bol.*) the name for the alpaca, guanaco, llama, and vicuña animals of the camel family that live only in the Andes = denominación para los camélidos que viven sólo en las montañas de los Andes: alpaca, guanaco, llama y vicuña.

aut (*from English*) out = fuera.

autocarril 1. (*Chile*) a railway motor coach = autovía; automotor; autorriel. **2.** (*Nic.*) a short train pulled by a diesel locomotive = tren corto tirado por un motor diesel.

autoestop (*from English*) to hitchhike = (N.E. solicitar transportación gratuita por la carretera).

automación (*from English*) automation = automatización.

automático (*Cuba*) something that is happening now or has to be done quickly = lo que sucede o tiene que hacerse muy rápido.

autsai (*from English*) outside = fuera.

auxiliar de vuelo (*Chile*) a stewardess = azafata.

avatí See **abatí**.

avenidas (*Cuba*) to have several possibilities; to have more than one way out of a problem = tener posibilidades abiertas; tener más de una salida al problema.

aventado (*Puerto Rico*) meat or vegetables starting to rot = carnes o vegetales que empiezan a pudrirse.

aventar 1. (*Colo.*) to throw oneself over something or someone = arrojarse; lanzarse sobre alguna cosa o persona. **2.**

(*Cuba*) to dry sugar by exposing it to the air and the sun = secar la azúcar exponiéndola al aire y al sol. **3.** (*Mex.*) to throw; to fling; to hurl = tirar; arrojar; lanzar.

aventar a alguien (*Colo.*) to blow the whistle on someone = delatar o acusar a alguien.

averach (*from English*) average = promedio.

average (*from English*) average = promedio.

avería (*Mex.*) mischief = travesura.

aviador; pájaro; pato (*Cuba*) an effeminate man; a homosexual = hombre afeminado; homosexual.

avión; bebe-leche (*Mex.*) hopscotch = la pata coja; juego infantil en que se salta en un pie sobre marcas en el suelo.

avirote (*Mex.*) naked = desnudo(a).

aviso (*Cuba, Ecua., Peru, Puerto Rico*) a sign = cartel; letrero; anuncio.

avispa (*Ven.*) a clever person = persona lista y vivaz.

avispado (*Ecua.*) a clever person = persona astuta; persona lista y rápida para reaccionar.

avíspese (*Colo.*) be more alert = esté más alerta.

¡ay bendito! (*Puerto Rico*) an interjection; Hah!; Please! = interjección; ¡caramba!; ¡por favor!

¡ay chihuahua! See **¡chihuahua!**

azadón (*Hond.*) selfish = egoísta.

azarearse 1. (*Guat., Hond.*) to be ashamed = avergonzarse. **2.** See **amusgarse.**

azarozo (*Colo.*) in a rush = meteprisa.

azocararse (*Hond.*) to get scared = asustarse.

azotea (*Argen., Dom. Rep., Ven.*) the head (informal) = cabeza (informal)

azúcar negra (*Peru*) unrefined sugar; a syrup cake = chancaca; trozos de azúcar sin refinar.

azumagarse (*Chile*) to get moldy; to get rusty = enmohecerse.

azurumbado (*Guat.*) scatterbrained = atolondrado.

azurumbarse (*Guat., Hond.*) to be confused; to be stunned = atolondrarse; aturdirse.

azurumbrado 1. (*Hond.*) scatterbrained; silly = atolondrado; tonto. **2.** (*Hond.*) disoriented; confused = desorientado; confundido.

B

babosear (*Nic.*) to act silly = hacer o decir tonterías.

baboso (*Salva.*) a silly person = tonto.

baboso(a) (*Mex.*) ignorant; stupid = ignorante; estúpido(a).

babuchas (*Colo.*) slippers = pantuflos; pantuflas.

bacalaito (*Puerto Rico*) a fritter of cod fish = fritura de bacalao.

bacán 1. (*Argen.*) a fortunate person; a man who has luck with women and/or money = hombre afortunado con las mujeres y/o con el dinero. **2.** (*Ecua., Dom. Rep.*) great; very beautiful = magnífico; muy bonito. **3.** (*Cuba*) a dish prepared with pork and tomatoes wrapped in banana leaves = plato preparado con puerco y tomates envueltos en hojas de plátano.

bacana (*Argen.*) a woman who has several rich lovers = mujer que tiene varios amantes adinerados.

bacano; legal; soda (*Colo.*) very good; excellent = muy bueno; excelente.

bacha 1. (*Mex.*) a cigarette butt = colilla de cigarrillo. **2.** (*Mex.*) a marijuana cigarette = cigarrillo de marihuana. **3.** (*Mex.*) a barge; a flat boat = lanchón; bote plano para transportar carga.

bachaca (*Ven.*) a person with curly, red hair = persona del pelo rojizo ensortijado.

bachajé (*Colo.*) a butcher; a slaughterman = carnicero; matarife.

bachata 1. (*Dom. Rep.*) revelry = juerga. **2.** (*Dom. Rep.*) a bad or an obscene word = una palabra obscena. **3.** (*Dom. Rep.*) garbage = basura. **4.** (*Dom. Rep.*) cabaret music = música de cabaret. **5.** (*Puerto Rico*) a binge = parranda; diversión bulliciosa; juerga.

bachatear (*Puerto Rico*) to joke = bromear.

bachicha 1. (*Argen., Chile, Peru*) a nickname for an Italian = apodo para un italiano. **2.** (*Uru.*) a fat person = gordo.

bacilarlo (*Chile*) to make fun of something = burlarse de él; hacerlo el centro de las bromas.

bacilón 1. (*Dom. Rep.*) to charm women = conquistar mujeres. **2.** (*Dom. Rep.*) to show off = lucirse.

bacín (*from English*) a basin = palangana.

badget (*from English*) a budget = presupuesto.

bafle (*from English*) baffle = (RAE) dispositivo que facilita la mejor difusión y calidad del sonido de un altavoz.

bagre 1. (*Bol.*) an ugly woman = mujer fea y desgarbada. **2.** (*Bol.*) an unpleasant person = antipático(a). **3.** (*Bol.*) overly precious; without class = cursi; charro. **4.** (*Hond., Salva.*) a very clever person = persona muy astuta. **5.** (*Argen., Para.*) an ugly person = persona fea.

bai (*from English*) good-bye = adiós; hasta luego.

baicicle (*from English*) a bicycle = bicicleta.

bailar la suiza (*Cuba*) to jump rope = saltar a la cuerda.

bajaca (*Ecua.*) a ribbon used by some Ecuadorian women as an ornament in their hair = cinta usada como ornamento para el pelo por algunas ecuatorianas.

bajaollas (*Colo.*) a rag or cloth used for holding hot pots = tomador de ollas calientes.

bajareque (*Hond.*) a hut made of sticks and mud = choza construida con palos y lodo.

bajo (*Nic.*) a dish of salted beef and vegetables that are covered with plantain leaves and steam cooked = carne salada y vegetales que se cubren con hojas de plátanos y que se cocinan al vapor.

bakgraun (*from English*) a background = ambiente previo; antecedentes; experiencias anteriores.

bakin (*from English*) baking powder = polvos para hornear.

bala (*Mex.*) a very clever or astute person = una persona muy lista o astuta.

balaquear (*Argen.*) to boast = fanfarronear.

balasto (*from English*) a ballast = (RAE) capa de grava o piedras machacadas que sujetan las traviesas o rieles del ferrocarril.

balerina (*from English*) a dancer; a ballerina = bailarina.

balita (*Para.*) marble = canica.

balone; baloni (*Mex.*) the penis (vulgar) = pene (vulgar).

baloni See **balone**.

balrum (*from English*) a ballroom = salón de baile.

balsa (*Dom. Rep.*) a pile = pila; montón.

baluma; boche (*Ecua.*) a brawl = barullo; alboroto.

balumba; bayú; bembé (*Puerto Rico*) a din; a row = batahola; barullo; alboroto.

balumoso (*Hond.*) voluminous; massive = voluminoso; lo que abulta mucho.

balún (*from English*) a balloon = globo.

balurdo 1. (*Argen.*) a package of fake money used to cheat someone = envoltorio que se hace pasar por dinero para engañar o estafar. **2.** (*Ven.*) unpleasant = desagradable. **3.** (*Ven.*) something that seems out of place = lo que desentona; lo que no corresponde.

bambalina (*Ven.*) the paper or plastic decorations for a party = adorno de papel o plástico que se usa para decorar el lugar de una fiesta.

bamper (*from English*) a bumper = parachoques.

banana (*Argen.*) an intelligent and clever person = persona inteligente y pícara.

banasta 1. (*Puerto Rico*) a big shoe = zapatón; zapato grande. **2.** (*Puerto Rico*) a canoe = canoa.

bancar (*Uru.*) to tolerate = tolerar.

banco (*Mex.*) a pile of grain = montón de granos.

banda 1. (*from English*) a bandage; a Band-Aid™ = venda de parche; curita; parche adhesivo para las heridas pequeñas. **2.** (*Para.*) an easy woman (vulgar) = mujer fácil (vulgar).

banda de caucho (*Colo.*) a rubber band = bandita de goma.

bandear (*Guat.*) to go after someone continuously = perseguir a alguien continuamente.

bandeja (*Mex.*) a bowl = tazón; palangana; bolo.

banderazo (*Ven.*) the starting rate in a taxi ride = tarifa inicial en un viaje por taxi.

banderola (*Para.*) a doorpost = jamba.

bandola (*Ven.*) a musical instrument with four pairs of strings = instrumento musical con cuatro pares de cuerdas.

bandolero (*Ven.*) a musician who plays the **bandola** = el músico que toca la **bandola**.

bángalo (*from English*) a bungalow = (RAE) bungaló; casa pequeña de una sola planta que se construye en lugares destinados al descanso.

banquear (*from English*) to deposit or withdraw money from the bank = depositar o retirar dinero del banco.

banqueta (*Mex.*) a sidewalk = acera.

bañadera (*Cuba, Para.*) a bathtub = tina; bañera.

bañado (*Para.*) wet soil; flooded soil = terreno muy húmedo; anegado.

bañar (*Ven.*) to surpass others in abilities and skills = superar a otros en habilidades y destrezas.

baño (*Mex.*) a bathtub = bañera.

baqueano; baquiano 1. (*Argen., Bol., Chile, Ecua., Peru*) a native guide; a person who knows a place well = guía nativo; el que conoce bien el lugar. **2.** (*Argen., Bol., Chile, Ecua., Peru*) to have an intuitive sense of direction = tener un sentido intuitivo del camino que se debe seguir.

baquear; vaquear (*from English*) to back up = respaldar; apoyar.

baqueo; vaqueo (*from English*) support; an endorsement = respaldo; apoyo.

baquiano See **baqueano**.

baracutey (*Cuba*) lazy; a person who avoids work = haragán; el que evade el trabajo.

barajar (*Argen., Chile*) to catch something in the air = tomar en el aire un objeto que se arroja.

barajustar (*Ven.*) to attack; to charge against = embestir; arremeter bruscamente.

barajuste (*Ven.*) disorder; disorganization = desorden; desorganización.

baranda (*Argen.*) a stink = mal olor.

barata 1. (*Chile*) a cockroach = cucaracha. **2.** (*Colo., Mex.*) a sale; a bargain sale = baratillo; venta especial a bajos precios. **3.** (*Ecua.*) confusion; disorder = confusión; desorden.

baratero 1. (*Chile*) a place full of cockroaches = lugar lleno de cucarachas. **2.** (*Colo., Mex.*) a shop that sells cheap merchandise = tienda donde se vende mercancía de bajos precios.

baratieri (*Argen., Chile*) cheap; without value = barato; de poco valor.

baratillo 1. (*Chile*) a small store that sells many different kinds of items = tienda pequeña donde se venden mercaderías variadas. **2.** (*Cuba, Ecua., Peru*) cheap goods = baratijas. **3.** (*Puerto Rico*) a sale = liquidación.

baratos (*Argen.*) cheap goods = baratijas.

bárbaro 1. (*Argen., Para., Uru.*) big; excessive = grande; excesivo. **2.** (*Argen., Para., Uru.*) fantastic; extraordinary = fantástico; extraordinario. **3.** (*Cuba*) very good = muy bien o muy bueno.

barbear 1. (*Costa Rica*) to scold = regañar. **2.** (*Para.*) to shave = afeitar.

barbekiu (*from English*) a barbecue = barbacoa; asado.

barbero (*Costa Rica*) a person who scolds continuously = el que regaña continuamente.

barman (*from English*) a bartender = camarero; mesonero; cantinero.

barquilla (*Puerto Rico*) an ice cream cone = barquillo.

barra; gavilla (*Colo.*) a gang of teens = pandilla; grupo de muchachos.

barreta (*Chile*) a lie (informal) = mentira (informal).

barrigón; cagón (*Colo.*) a baby (according to the context, could be derogatory or affectionate) = niño de poca edad, según el contexto puede ser despectivo o afectivo.

barrilete 1. (*Ven.*) a hexagonal-shaped kite = cometa de forma hexagonal. **2.** (*Guat.*) any kite = cualquier cometa.

barrilito (*Puerto Rico*) a fat and short person = persona muy gorda y baja de estatura.

barro (*Mex.*) acne = acné.

barsa (*Chile*) abusive = abusón.

bartender (*from English*) a bartender = cantinero.

bartolear (*Chile*) to be lazy; to be idle = holgazanear.

bartolina; chirola (*Puerto Rico*) a jail = cárcel.

bas (*from English*) a bus = bus; ómnibus.

basca 1. (*Mex.*) vomit = vómito. **2.** (*Mex.*) a mean person = persona ruin.

bascoso (*Ecua.*) rude; gross = indecente; grosero.

basilico (*from English*) basil = albahaca.

básquetbol (*from English*) a basketball = (RAE) básquetbol; baloncesto.

bastimento (*Ven.*) carry-out food; meals taken to eat away from home = alimento que se lleva para comer fuera de la casa.

bastonero (*Ven.*) an accomplice = cómplice en un acto deshonesto o ilegal.

basura (*Cuba*) something that has no value = no tiene ningún valor.

bata (*Chile, Cuba*) a housedress; a bathrobe = mono; albornoz o bata.

bata de dormir (*Cuba, Mex.*) a nightgown = camisón; camisa de dormir.

batacazo (*Puerto Rico*) a crush; a bang = golpe.

batanear (*Colo.*) to steal (informal) = robar (informal).

batata 1. (*Argen.*) a scare; confusion = susto; confusión. **2.** (*Argen.*) an old and battered car = automóvil viejo y golpeado. **3.** (*Argen.*) a chubby and sloppy person = persona gorda y descuidada. **4.** (*Dom. Rep., Puerto Rico*) a calf = pantorrilla. **5.** (*Dom. Rep., Puerto Rico*) an easy, soft job = un trabajo simple y fácil. **6.** (*Dom. Rep., Puerto Rico*) a lazy person = holgazán.

batatazo 1. (*Chile*) to hit the jackpot; a big gain in a game = golpe de suerte en el juego; grandes ganancias en el juego. **2.** (*Puerto Rico*) a crush; a bang = golpe.

bate 1. (*from English*) a baseball bat = (RAE) palo más grueso por el extremo libre que por la empuñadura, con que se golpea a la pelota en el **béisbol**. **2.** (*Cuba*) to be in charge = estar a cargo. **3.** (*Puerto Rico*) a piece of paper with notes used to cheat on an exam = trozo de papel con apuntes para copiar en un examen.

batea (*Peru*) a bathtub = bañera.

batear (*Cuba*) to eat too much = comer mucho.

bateya 1. (*Guat.*) a trough = artesa. **2.** (*Guat.*) a tray = bandeja.

batiboleo (*Cuba, Mex.*) a brawl = alboroto; bochinche.

batida (*Puerto Rico*) a beating; a spanking = zurra; tunda; azotaina.

batir 1. (*Argen., Uru.*) to denounce = denunciar. **2.** (*Mex.*) to get dirty = ensuciarse.

bató (*Hond.*) a canoe = canoa.

batrom (*from English*) a bathroom = baño.

baúl (*Argen., Colo., Pan., Puerto Rico*) a car trunk = maletero o portaequipaje en el automóvil.

bausa (*Peru*) laziness = holgazanería; ociosidad; pereza.

bausón(a) (*Peru*) lazy = perezoso(a); ocioso(a).

bayeta (*Cuba*) a mop; a cleaning cloth = trapero; trapo de limpieza.

bayú 1. (*Puerto Rico*) a big party = una gran fiesta. **2.** (*Puerto Rico*) a party of homosexuals = fiesta de homosexuales. **3.** See **balumba**.

bazuca (*from English*) a bazooka = (RAE) lanzagranadas portátil.

bazuco(a) (*Colo.*) a marijuana or other hallucinogenic cigarette = cigarrillo de marihuana u otros alucinógenos.

beata (*Colo.*) an old maid = solterona.

beatificar (*Hond.*) to give a travel allowance = dar el viático para un viaje.

bebe-leche See **avión**.

bebida (*Argen., Bol., Chile, Peru*) soda pop = gaseosa.

bebito (*Cuba*) a baby = bebé.

bedspred (*from English*) a bedspread = cubrecama.

beeper [pron. bi per] (*from English*) a beeper = (N.E. aparato electrónico portátil que anuncia una llamada telefónica.)

beguiansa (*Puerto Rico*) a problem = problema.

behaviorismo (*from English*) behavior = (RAE) conductismo.

beibi (*from English*) a baby = bebé.

beibisiter (*from English*) a babysitter = niñera; cuidadora de niños.

beiby (*from English*) a baby = bebé.

beich (*from English*) beige = (RAE) beige; color marrón o castaño claro.

beicon (*from English*) bacon = (RAE) panceta ahumada; tocino entreverado.

beiquinparer (*from English*) baking powder = polvos para hornear.

béisbol (*from English*) baseball = (RAE) juego en que los jugadores han de recorrer bases de un circuito, en combinación con el lanzamiento de una pelota golpeada con un **bate**.

beisman (*from English*) a basement = sótano.

bejuco (*Ven.*) an old man (informal) = hombre viejo (informal).

bejuquear (*Peru*) to beat with a stick = apalear.

bemba 1. (*Colo., Dom. Rep., Pan., Ven.*) thick lips; a big mouth = labios gruesos y abultados; boca grande. **2.** (*Peru, Puerto Rico*) a snout; a mug (derogatory) = hocico; jeta (peyorativo).

bembé 1. (*Dom. Rep., Puerto Rico*) the lips = labios. **2.** (*Puerto Rico*) a brawl = barullo; alboroto.

bembeteo 1. (*Ecua.*) too much talk = mucha conversación. **2.** (*Puerto Rico*) small talk; gossip = chismorreo; contar chismes.

bembón(a) (*Cuba, Puerto Rico*) a person who speaks too much; a person who says stupid things = persona que habla mucho; persona que dice tonterías.

bembudo(a) (*Dom. Rep.*) someone with thick lips = persona con labios gruesos.

bencina (*Chile*) gasoline = gasolina.

berenjena (*Ven.*) a term used to describe any matters or things which are not named separately = cuestión; término que se usa para describir algo que no se específica con nombres concretos.

bergantín; fundoso; piñazo (*Dom. Rep.*) a blow in the eye = golpe al ojo.

bernia (*Hond.*) lazy; idle; good-for-nothing = haragán; holgazán; inútil.

berracá (*Cuba*) silly = tonto.

berraquera; verraquera 1. (*Colo.*) eagerness; initiative; enthusiasm = ahínco; empuje; entusiasmo. **2.** (*Colo.*) a complicated issue that is difficult to solve = cuestión enredada difícil de solucionar. **3.** (*Colo.*) sexual attraction = atracción sexual.

berrear 1. (*Ecua.*) to anger; to annoy = enojar; enfadar. 2. (*Ecua.*) to cry = llorar. 3. (*Chile*) to shout = gritar.

berretín (*Uru.*) to hang up = colgar.

berrinche (*Ven.*) a brawl = alboroto.

besito de coco (*Puerto Rico*) a cookie prepared with flour, coconut and sugar = galletita preparada con harina, coco y azúcar.

beso (*Ven.*) a sweet pastry prepared with wheat flour, coconut, and sugar = golosina preparada con harina de trigo, coco y azúcar.

best-séller (*from English*) a best-seller = (RAE) obra literaria de gran éxito y de mucha venta.

betabel (*Mex.*) a beet = remolacha.

betibú (*Cuba*) a provocative woman = mujer provocativa.

beutichian (*from English*) a beautician = maquillador(a).

biberón; chupón; tete (*Cuba*) a pacifier = chupete; artefacto de goma o plástico para que el bebé chupe.

bibi (*Puerto Rico*) a feeding bottle = biberón.

bibicho (*Hond.*) a domestic cat = gato doméstico.

biblioteca (*Argen., Para.*) a bookshelf = armario para libros.

bica (*Mex.*) a little money = bicoca; poco dinero.

bicha(o) 1. (*Ven.*) stuff; things = cosa; asunto. 2. (*Ven.*) the genitals (vulgar); could be the male or female genitals = genital masculino o femenino (vulgar).

bichar 1. (*Ven.*) to make a mess; to disorganize = revolver; desorganizar. 2. (*Ven.*) to damage; to harm = dañar; menoscabar. 3. (*Ven.*) to fix = componer; arreglar. 4. (*Ven.*) any action or activity for which the name is unknown or is not recalled = cualquier acción o actividad a la cual no se le conoce o no se le recuerda el nombre.

bicharango (*Ven.*) the disrespectful treatment of any object, animal or person = cualquier objeto, persona o animal a lo que se le quiere tratar despectivamente.

bichazo (*Ven.*) hitting someone; a strong blow = golpe fuerte y contundente.

biche 1. (*Colo., Pan.*) immature = inmaduro. 2. (*Colo.*) a person with a weak character = persona débil de carácter. 3. (*Mex.*) empty = vacío. 4. (*Mex.*) soft; spongy = fofo. 5. (*Peru*) a large cooking pot = olla de gran tamaño.

bichero (*Nic.*) a person who is in charge of maintenance and supply at a ranch = el que mantiene y provee de todo en la hacienda.

bichicome (*Uru.*) a street bum; a vagrant = vago; vagabundo.

bicho 1. (*Puerto Rico*) the penis (vulgar) = pene (vulgar). 2. (*Cuba*) a clever person = persona lista. 3. (*Ven.*) an expression and hand gesture used to curse someone = expresión que acompañada de un gesto con la mano significa un conjuro o maleficio. 4. (*Argen.*) the tiger that lives in the Chaco region = nombre del tigre en la región del Chaco.

bicho chillón (*Salva.*) someone who cries too much (informal) = llorón (informal).

biela (*Ecua.*) beer = cerveza.

bien hecho(a) (*Puerto Rico*) a beautiful and attractive person = persona bonita y atractiva.

bien padre (*Mex.*) really good; top notch = extraordinariamente bueno; realmente bueno.

bienmesabe 1. (*Colo.*) a pastry made of milk, coconut, potatoes, and sugar = dulce de leche, coco, patatas y azúcar. 2. (*Ven.*) a cold jam prepared with eggs, sugar, and coconut milk = manjar frío preparado con huevos, azúcar y leche de coco. 3. (*Dom. Rep., Puerto Rico*) a thick syrup made with milk, coconut, cinnamon, egg, and sugar = jarabe espeso que contiene leche, coco, canela, huevos y azúcar. 4. (*Nic.*) a jam made of bananas and brown sugar = dulce hecho de plátano y azúcar sin refinar.

bife (*Puerto Rico*) a steak = bistec.

bikini (*from English*) a bikini = traje de baño de dos piezas.

bil (*from English*) a bill = aviso; cuenta; boleta de venta o aviso de consumo.

bilding (*from English*) a building = edificio.

bilí; bizcocho; paseo (*Puerto Rico*) something that is very easy = lo que es muy fácil.

billete (*Dom. Rep., Puerto Rico*) a patch; a clothing patch = remiendo.

bimba 1. (*Hond.*) a thick-lipped mouth = boca de labios gruesos. **2.** (*Hond.*) a tall person = persona de elevada estatura.

bimbazo; bombazo; burrunazo (*Puerto Rico*) a punch = puñetazo.

binbín; huevo; güevo (*Dom. Rep.*) the penis (vulgar) = pene (vulgar).

bingo (*Cuba*) to hit the jackpot = sacarse el premio major.

biologista (*from English*) a biologist = biólogo.

biombo (*Pan.*) a slingshot = honda.

bipear (*from English*) to beep = llamar a través del **beeper**.

birdcontrol (*from English*) birth control = control de la natalidad; anticonceptivos.

biromé (*Argen.*) a ballpoint pen = bolígrafo.

bironga; chela (*Mex.*) beer = cerveza.

birote See **almareado**.

birria 1. (*Colo.*) a caprice = capricho. **2.** (*Colo.*) hatred = odio. **3.** (*Colo.*) obstinacy = obstinación. **4.** (*Mex.*) beer = cerveza.

birriñaque (*Hond.*) something that is not well done = lo que está mal hecho.

biscera (*Ecua., Peru*) a cap = gorra.

biscornio; bizcorneo (*Puerto Rico*) squinty-eyed = bizco; turnio.

bisnes (*from English*) business = negocio; asunto; comercio.

bisnesman (*from English*) a businessman = hombre de negocios.

bisquete (*from English*) a biscuit = panecillo.

bisté; bistec (*from English*) a beefsteak = (RAE) lonja de carne asada o frita.

bistec See **bisté**.

bit (*from English*) a bit = (RAE) unidad de medida de información equivalente a la elección entre dos posibilidades igualmente probables.

bíter (*from English*) bitter = (RAE) licor amargo.

biutichap (*from English*) a beauty shop = salón de belleza.

biyuya; biyuyo (*Argen.*) money (vulgar) = dinero (vulgar).

biyuyo See **biyuya**.

bizcocho 1. (*Colo.*) a good-looking person = persona bien parecida. **2.** (*Colo.*) the vulva (vulgar) = vulva (vulgar). **3.** (*Dom. Rep., Puerto Rico*) a cake = torta; pastel. **4.** (*Puerto Rico*) something that is very easy = lo que es muy fácil.

bizcochuelo (*Argen.*) a cake = torta.

bizconeto (*Colo.*) cross-eyed = bizco.

bizcorneado (*Dom. Rep.*) squint-eyed = turnio.

bizcorneo See **biscornio**.

blackpawer (*from English*) black power = el poder negro.

blanco (*Chile, Colo., Peru*) a bull's eye = centro del blanco.

blanquear 1. (*Cuba*) to win = ganar. **2.** (*Cuba*) to clear = limpiar. **3.** (*Cuba*) to destroy = destruir.

blanquillo 1. (*Chile*) a kind of fish; a white-meat fish = un tipo de pez; pez de carne blanca. **2.** (*Chile, Ecua.*) a white peach = melocotón blanco. **3.** (*Guat., Hond., Mex., Peru, Salva.*) an egg = huevo. **4.** (*Mex.*) the testicles (vulgar) = testículos (vulgar). **5.** (*Uru.*) a variety of tree with white bark = una variedad de árbol que tiene la corteza blanca.

blich (*from English*) bleach = blanqueador.

bloaut (*from English*) a blowout of an automobile tire or other inflatable device =

reventón de una goma de automóvil u otro artefacto inflado.

bloque (*from English*) a block; houses from one street to the other = (RAE) manzana de casas.

blue jeans [pron. blugin] (*from English*) blue jeans = pantalón de mezclilla; pantalón vaquero.

blues (*from English*) the blues = (RAE) música folclórica de los negros de Estados Unidos.

bluf (*from English*) a bluff = fanfarronada.

blufear (*from English*) to bluff = fanfarronar.

bobo 1. (*Guat., Puerto Rico, Salva.*) pacifier = tetera; chupador para el bebé; plástico o goma que se les da a los niños para que se entretengan chupando. **2.** (*Guat., Mex.*) a river fish that is easy to catch = un pez de río que es fácil de pescar.

boca de agua; bomba de agua (*Cuba*) a hydrant = toma de agua.

boca de incendio (*Puerto Rico*) a hydrant = toma de agua.

bocacalle (*Argen., Chile, Colo., Cuba, Uru.*) an intersection = intersección.

bocadillo; bocadito (*Cuba*) a sandwich = emparedado; sándwich.

bocadito See **bocadillo**.

bocatero(a) (*Cuba, Hond., Ven.*) swaggering; boastful; talkative; a person who talks too much = fanfarrón; charlatán; el que habla mucho.

bochar (*Ven.*) to snub someone = desairar.

boche 1. (*Argen.*) a nickname for a German = apodo para un alemán. **2.** (*Bol., Chile, Ecua., Peru*) a brawl = barullo; alboroto; pendencia; disputa. **3.** (*Ven.*) a strike in the game of bowling = un pleno o una chuza. **4.** (*Dom. Rep., Puerto Rico, Ven.*) a reprimand = regaño; reprimenda. **5.** (*Mex., Ven.*) a rebuff; a rejection = rechazo; desaire.

bochinche 1. (*Cuba, Puerto Rico*) gossip; lies; stories = chismes; mentiras; cuentos. **2.** (*Bol., Chile, Peru, Uru.*) noise = ruido.

bochinchero (*Puerto Rico*) a gossipmonger = chismoso.

bocho(a) (*Para.*) a clever person = una persona inteligente.

bodega 1. (*Cuba, Dom. Rep., Puerto Rico*) a grocery store = tienda de abarrotes. **2.** (*Uru.*) a storage place = lugar para almacenar.

bodeguero (*Cuba*) a grocery store clerk = dependiente en la tienda de abarrotes.

bodrio (*Argen., Chile*) a person or object of inferior quality = cosa, asunto o persona de poca calidad.

bofa (*Mex.*) a prostitute (vulgar) = prostituta (vulgar).

bohio (*Cuba, Dom. Rep., Pan., Puerto Rico*) a hut = choza.

boicot (*from English*) a boycott = (RAE) privar a una persona o entidad de toda relación social o comercial.

boila (*from English*) a boiler = caldera.

bojote (*Ven.*) bulk; a package = bulto; paquete; envoltorio.

bol 1. (*from English*) a bowl = (RAE) tazón grande sin asa. **2.** (*from English*) a ball = pelota.

bola 1. (*Argen., Colo., Cuba, Guat., Ven.*) false news that is publicized for personal interest = noticia falsa difundida con motivos interesados. **2.** (*Colo.*) stupid; silly = tonto; bobo. **3.** (*Colo.*) a police vehicle for the transportation of prisoners = vehículo policial para el transporte de presos. **4.** (*Ven.*) corn dough in a spheric shape = masa de harina de maíz de una forma esférica. **5.** (*Mex.*) a brawl; a noisy party = reunión bulliciosa. **6.** (*Mex.*) a noisy crowd; a noisy fight; a revolt = tumulto bullicioso; riña; revuelta. **7.** (*Peru, Pan., Puerto Rico*) a ball = pelota; balón.

bolas (*Cuba, Pan.*) marbles = canicas.

bolas de cuero (*Chile*) extremely stupid = extremadamente tonto.

bolate; volate (*Colo.*) confusion; a mess; a spree = bochinche; jaleo.

bolb (*from English*) a light bulb = bombilla.

boleadoras (*Argen., Uru.*) a **gaucho** tool made from three thongs with balls at the end that is thrown at the legs of animals to stop them = herramienta del **gaucho** que consiste en tres tiras unidas entre sí y con bolas a los extremos, se usa para detener la carrera de un animal enredándoselas en las patas.

boleadores (*Mex.*) a shoeshine = lustre al calzado.

bolear 1. (*Dom. Rep.*) to hitchhike = pedir transporte gratuito. **2.** (*Uru.*) to catch with **boleadoras** = cazar con las **boleadoras**. **3.** (*Uru.*) to involve; to implicate = envolver; enredar.

bolero 1. (*Costa Rica*) a cup-and-ball toy = boliche; juguete formado por una bola con hoyo y una asta para ensartarla. **2.** (*Guat., Hond.*) a top hat = sombrero de copa. **3.** (*Mex.*) a bootblack = lustrabotas. **4.** (*Peru*) bowling = boliche; juego de las bolas.

boletín (*from English*) a bulletin board = tablero de anuncios; anunciador mural.

boliche 1. (*Argen., Chile, Para.*) a small store with inferior-quality items = tienda de poco rango que vende artículos de baja calidad. **2.** (*Uru.*) a cheap bar = cantina de baja calidad.

bolichero (*Argen., Chile, Para.*) an owner of or clerk in a poor, inferior-quality store = dueño o empleado de una tienda pobre y de inferior calidad.

bolillo 1. (*Colo.*) a nightstick; a billyclub = porra de madera o caucho usada por la policía. **2.** (*Mex.*) a Caucasian; a white person = caucásico; persona blanca.

bolillos (*Mex.*) bread rolls = bollos.

bolitas (*Argen., Chile, Cuba, Mex., Peru, Puerto Rico*) marbles = canicas.

bollitos (*Peru, Puerto Rico*) rolls; small breads = bollos; panecillos.

bollo 1. (*Cuba, Dom. Rep., Ven.*) the vagina (vulgar) = vagina (vulgar). **2.** (*Hond.*) a blow with the fist = puñetazo. **3.** (*Dom. Rep., Ven.*) corn dough filled with meat and boiled = maza de maíz rellena de carne y hervida. **4.** (*Dom. Rep.,*

Ven.) an offense; an insult = ofensa; insulto.

bolo (*Costa Rica, Guat., Salva.*) drunk = borracho; ebrio.

bolón 1. (*Argen., Chile*) a big, rounded stone used for building a foundation = piedra grande casi redonda que se usa en los cimientos de una construcción. **2.** (*Mex.*) a multitude = multitud. **3.** (*Mex.*) fast = rápido.

bolones (*Puerto Rico*) the testicles (vulgar) = testículos (vulgar).

bolsa 1. (*Colo.*) stupid; silly = poco inteligente; tonto. **2.** (*Ven.*) a dull person; a clumsy person = lerdo; persona torpe. **3.** (*Dom. Rep.*) a very dirty word; a forbidden word in the Dominican Republic = palabra muy sucia; palabra tabú en la República Dominicana. **4.** (*Dom. Rep., Peru*) the scrotum; the pouch of skin enclosing the testicles = escroto (vulgar); piel que cubre los testículos. **5.** (*Mex.*) a purse = cartera. **6.** (*Mex.*) a pocket = bolsillo en las prendas de vestir.

bolsear 1. (*Chile*) to eat, drink, and seek lodging at the expense of others = aprovecharse de otros para obtener comidas, bebida y/o alojamiento gratuito. **2.** (*Costa Rica, Hond.*) to pick someone's pocket = carterear; robar del bolsillo. **3.** (*Costa Rica, Hond.*) to steal furtively = robar furtivamente.

bolsero (*Chile*) someone who is always exploiting others = aprovechador; siempre aprovechándose de otros.

bolsiflay (*Chile*) silly; stupid (vulgar) = tonto; estúpido (vulgar).

bolso (*Cuba*) a purse = cartera.

bolsón; bolsudo (*Cuba*) stupid; silly = poco inteligente; tonto.

bolsudo See **bolsón.**

boludo 1. (*Argen., Uru.*) silly; stupid (vulgar) = tonto; estúpido; bobo (vulgar). **2.** (*Mex.*) bumpy = con hinchazones; lleno de protuberancias.

bomba 1. (*Colo., Guat., Peru*) false news; rumors = noticias falsas; rumores. **2.** (*Colo.*) an annoying person = molestoso;

pesado. **3.** (*Guat., Hond., Peru*) a drinking spree; drunkenness = embriaguez; borrachera. **4.** (*Colo., Dom. Rep., Hond.*) a soap bubble = pompa; burbuja. **5.** (*Colo., Mex., Puerto Rico*) a balloon = globo. **6.** (*Mex.*) a round kite = cometa redondo. **7.** (*Mex.*) a top hat = sombrero de copa; chistera. **8.** (*Mex.*) a satirical remark = comentario satírico. **9.** (*Puerto Rico*) a drum; a percussion instrument of African origin = tambor; instrumento de percusión de origen africano. **10.** (*Puerto Rico*) the music that is played with that instrument = la música que se interpreta con ese instrumento.

bomba de agua 1. (*Colo., Ecua.*) a hydrant = toma de agua. **2.** (*Ecua.*) a drinking spree; drunkenness = tomar de parranda; borrachera.

bomba de bencina (*Chile*) a gas station = estación o bomba de gasolina.

bombachas (*Argen.*) the typical loose-fitting pants of the **gaucho** = pantalones típicos del **gaucho**, sueltos y ajustados a la cintura y a la pantorrilla.

bombazo See **bimbazo**.

bombear (*Puerto Rico*) to bum; to beg = mendigar.

bombillo (*Cuba*) intelligence = inteligencia.

bombita (*Argen., Uru.*) a light bulb = bombilla; bujía eléctrica.

bombo 1. (*Mex.*) pomp; ostentation = pompa; ostentación. **2.** (*Mex.*) fat = gordo; panzón.

bompa; bomper (*from English*) a bumper = parachoques; defensas del automóvil.

bomper See **bompa**.

bonchar (*Ven.*) to party; to have fun = andar de fiestas; andar en diversiones.

bonche (*Colo., Ven.*) a brawl = bochinche.

bonchón (*Ven.*) a person who is partying = enfiestado; el que anda en fiestas.

bonete (*Puerto Rico*) a car hood = capota del automóvil.

boniato (*Cuba, Uru.*) yams; sweet potatoes = batata; patata dulce.

boom (*from English*) an economic boom; a population boom = auge; gran incremento inesperado; prosperidad súbita.

boquiduro (*Puerto Rico*) argumentative = respondón; discutidor.

boquinche; boquineto(a) (*Colo., Ven.*) a person with a harelip = persona con labio leporino.

boquineto(a) See **boquinche**.

boquique (*Peru*) talkative = parlanchín; persona muy habladora.

boquisucio (*Puerto Rico*) foul-mouthed = mal hablado.

bordera(o) (*from English*) an owner or operator of a boarding house = dueño o encargado de una casa de huéspedes.

boricua (*Puerto Rico*) a Puerto Rican person; an authentic Puerto Rican = Puertorriqueño; lo que es auténticamente de Puerto Rico.

borincano; borinqueño (*Puerto Rico*) of Puerto Rican origin = lo que es de Puerto Rico.

borinqueño See **borincano**.

borlo (*Mex.*) a party = una fiesta.

borlote (*from English*) a brawl = alboroto.

borrado (*Peru*) pockmarked = con cicatrices de viruelas.

borrador (*Cuba, Mex., Pan., Peru*) an eraser = goma de borrar; goma.

borrego (*Guat., Hond., Mex., Salva.*) rumors; gossip = rumores; chismes.

boruquear (*Mex.*) to confuse; to disorient = confundir; desorientar.

bos (*from English*) a boss = patrón(a); el o la que manda.

bosgo(a) (*Mex.*) a glutton = glotón(a).

boslain (*from English*) a bus line = línea o recorrido de omnibuses.

boso (*Dom. Rep.*) a mustache = bigotes.

bosta (*Argen., Chile*) manure = excremento del ganado caballar o vacuno.

botafango (*Cuba*) a fender = guardafangos; guardabarros.

botago (*Puerto Rico*) very ugly = muy feo.

botalodo (*Puerto Rico*) a fender = guardafangos; guardabarros.

botana 1. (*Mex.*) a snack; anything small and quick to eat = tentempié; cualquier cosa pequeña y rápida de comer. **2.** (*Mex.*) a free taco for regular customers = taco gratuito para los clientes habituales. **3.** (*Mex.*) something that is easy to do = lo que es fácil de hacer.

botánica 1. (*Dom. Rep., Puerto Rico*) a store that sells **santería** and paraphernalia used to perform spiritism or other pseudo-religious activities = tienda que vende artículos para **santería** y adminículos para practicar otras formas de espiritismo o actividades seudo-religiosas. **2.** (*Dom. Rep., Puerto Rico*) a store that sells medicinal herbs = tienda donde se venden hierbas medicinales.

botar (*Puerto Rico*) to fire someone from a job = despedir a alguien de un trabajo.

botarata (*Chile, Colo.*) a spendthrift = derrochador; botarate.

bote 1. (*Guat., Hond., Mex., Salva.*) a jail = cárcel. **2.** (*Mex.*) a can of food = tarro de comida en conservas. **3.** (*Mex.*) a bucket = cubo; balde.

bote de basura (*Mex.*) a garbage can = basurero.

botella 1. (*Cuba, Mex.*) a feeding bottle = biberón. **2.** (*Puerto Rico*) an easy job (informal) = trabajo fácil (informal). **3.** (*Puerto Rico*) memorized information = información aprendida de memoria.

botija 1. (*Hond.*) a hidden treasure = tesoro escondido. **2.** (*Mex.*) a large, fat person = persona grande y gorda. **3.** (*Uru.*) a boy = niño.

botillería (*Chile*) a liquor store = tienda de vinos y licores.

botiquín (*Ven.*) a cheap bar; an establishment of the lowest level selling alcoholic drinks = cantina pobre; establecimiento de ínfima categoría donde se expenden bebidas alcohólicas.

botiquinero (*Ven.*) a waitress or barman in the **botiquín** = el que sirve las bebidas en el **botiquín**.

botón (*Argen.*) a nickname for a policeman = apodo para un agente de policía.

bototo 1. (*Chile*) a very strong shoe; a boot = zapato fuerte y resistente. **2.** (*Colo.*) the root of a medicinal tree = raíz de un árbol con propiedades medicinales.

bouling (*from English*) bowling = bolos, boliche.

box; boxeo (*from English*) boxing = (RAE) pugilato; deporte que consiste en la lucha de dos púgiles que se golpean con las manos enguantadas de acuerdo a ciertas reglas.

boxear (*from English*) to box = (RAE) practicar el boxeo.

boxeo See **box**.

boxer (*from English*) a boxer = (N.E. una de las razas caninas.)

bracero (*Mex.*) a day-laborer working in the fields = jornalero; trabajador del campo que recibe su paga por día.

bragado (*Dom. Rep.*) a bully = bravucón.

brandy (*from English*) brandy = coñac; (RAE) nombre que se da, por razones legales, a los tipos de coñac elaborados fuera de Francia.

brasier (*from English*) a brassiere = sostén de senos.

braun (*from English*) brown = marrón o castaño.

bravito (*Dom. Rep.*) to be angry; to be upset = estar enojado; estar molesto.

bravo (*Bol., Chile, Ecua., Guat., Hond., Mex., Peru, Salva.*) angry = enojado.

brazo; palanca (*Colo.*) a connection; a useful contact in politics or business = enchufe; persona de influencia; contacto político o comercial.

brea (*Colo., Puerto Rico*) asphalt = asfalto.

breca; breik; breique; breque 1. (*from English*) brake(s) = freno(s). **2.** (*from English*) a break = interrupción; descanso.

brega (*Ven.*) a courtship; a sentimental relationship = relación amorosa.

bregador (*Ven.*) a person who dates a lot = el que busca constantemente relaciones amorosas.

bregar 1. (*Dom. Rep., Puerto Rico*) to struggle = luchar contra algo. **2.** (*Dom. Rep., Puerto Rico*) to work = trabajar.

breik See **breca**.

breique See **breca**.

brejetero 1. (*Ven.*) a busybody = entrometido. **2.** (*Ven.*) fussy = quisquilloso. **3.** (*Ven.*) vain; a show-off = presuntuoso; fanfarrón.

breque See **breca**.

brete 1. (*Mex.*) a job = empleo. **2.** (*Argen.*) a corral in which to brand animals = lugar cercado donde se marca a los animales. **3.** (*Puerto Rico*) a love affair = relación amorosa. **4.** (*Puerto Rico*) a difficulty; a jam; a fix = aprieto; problema; enredo. **5.** (*Puerto Rico*) shackles; stocks; fetters = cepo o prisión estrecha de hierro; grillos.

breva (*Puerto Rico*) a cigar butt = colilla de cigarro puro.

brin (*Chile*) a fabric of inferior quality generally used as a lining = tela ordinaria que se suele usar para forros.

brincar (*Ven.*) to joke; to poke fun = chacotear; comportarse de una manera poco seria.

brincar a la cuerda (*Cuba*) to keep an eye out; to be alert = estar alerta.

brincar a la reata (*Mex.*) to jump rope = saltar a la cuerda.

brincar el charco (*Mex.*) to cross the Rio Grande; to emigrate to the United States = cruzar el Río Grande; emigrar a los Estados Unidos.

brincar la cuerda (*Mex.*) to jump rope = saltar a la cuerda.

broche See **asegurador**.

broco (*Puerto Rico*) an amputee; someone without arms = amputado; sin brazos.

brodcastin 1. (*from English*) broadcasting = radiodifusión. **2.** (*from English*) a radio station = radioemisora.

broder (*from English*) a brother; a buddy; a friend = hermano; compañero; amigo.

broga (*Ven.*) overalls; one-piece work clothing = guardapolvo; mono; traje de una sola pieza que se usa para trabajar.

brollero (*Ven.*) a liar; a scandalmonger = embustero(a); chismoso; enredoso.

brollo 1. (*Dom. Rep., Ven.*) confusion; disorder; uproar = embrollo; confusión; bochinche. **2.** (*Dom. Rep., Ven.*) a problem = problema.

broma (*Ven.*) stuff; things = asunto; cosas.

bronca 1. (*Argen., Chile*) an aversion to a person, object or issue = aversión hacia una persona, cosa o asunto. **2.** (*Cuba, Mex., Puerto Rico*) a brawl; a fist fight; a quarrel = alboroto; pelea; trifulca; pendencia.

bruja (*Mex.*) broke; poor = arruinado; pobre.

brujear (*Dom. Rep.*) to practice **santería** = practicar la **santería**.

brujo(a) (*Colo.*) an intruder; a meddler = entrometido(a).

brujulear 1. (*Ven.*) to plot = tramar; confabular. **2.** (*Ven.*) to work in odd jobs = hacer trabajos pequeños de poca duración. **3.** (*Dom. Rep.*) to walk without direction = vagar sin dirección. **4.** (*Dom. Rep.*) to hang around = estar en un lugar esperando sin ninguna razón para hacerlo.

bruquena (*Puerto Rico*) a river crab = cangrejo de río.

buca (*Mex.*) a girl = niña.

buchaca 1. (*Colo., Mex.*) a billiard pocket = tronera; cada una de las bolsas de la mesa de billar. **2.** (*Ecua.*) a jail = cárcel. **3.** (*Mex.*) the mouth (vulgar) = boca (vulgar).

buchipluma 1. (*Puerto Rico*) timorous; shy = temeroso; tímido. **2.** (*Puerto Rico*) an untrustworthy person = persona no confiable. **3.** (*Ven.*) pompous; showy = aparatoso; lo que aparenta mucho pero tiene poco valor.

budín (*Argen.*) a beautiful woman = mujer hermosa.

buena esa (*Peru*) very good = muy bueno.

buena pieza (*Puerto Rico*) irresponsible and informal; a person who only talks about something and does not act = irresponsable e incumplidor; el que habla pero no hace.

buenote(a) (*Mex.*) a sexually attractive person = persona sexualmente atractiva.

buey (*Mex.*) ignorant; stupid = ignorante; tonto.

bufar (*Mex.*) to swell = hincharse.

bufeo (*Puerto Rico*) ugly = feo.

bufete (*Nic.*) a cupboard = armario para guardar los utensilios de cocina.

bugarón (*Puerto Rico*) bisexual = bisexual.

búho (*Colo., Pan.*) an owl = lechuza.

buinsuan; suinsuan 1. (*Pan.*) a seesaw = balancín. **2.** (*Pan.*) a rocking chair = mecedora.

búlava (*from English*) a boulevard = bulevar.

bulchitero (*from English*) a bullshitter (vulgar) = (N.E. expresión vulgar para lo que no tiene valor o lo que es un gran problema).

buldog (*from English*) a bulldog = dogo; una raza de perros.

buldoser (*from English*) a bulldozer = motoniveladora; excavadora de orugas.

bule (*from English*) a bully = matón(a); valentón(a); persona que intimida.

bullaranga; chambrana (*Ven.*) a scandal; a noise; a rumpus = escándalo; alboroto; algazara.

bulto 1. (*Colo., Guat., Hond.*) a pumpkin; a squash = calabaza. **2.** (*Colo., Guat., Hond., Puerto Rico, Ven.*) a briefcase; a book bag; a schoolbook bag = cartapacio; bolsa para los libros; bolsa, maletín para transportar los útiles escolares.

bululú (*Puerto Rico*) a brawl; a scandal = alboroto; escándalo.

buquear (*from English*) to book someone or something = poner; anotar o entrar en un libro; fichar a alguien en los archivos policiales.

burra 1. (*Chile*) an old car; a battered automobile = automóvil antiguo y golpeado; automóvil en mal estado. **2.** (*Colo.*) a bicycle (informal) = bicicleta (informal).

burrero (*Argen.*) a racehorse gambler = el que juega a las carreras de caballos.

burrión (*Hond.*) a hummingbird = colibrí.

burro 1. (*Argen., Mex.*) a stepladder = escala de tijeras. **2.** (*Argen., Chile*) a slow learner = el que aprende lento. **3.** (*Cuba*) a sawhorse = caballete para serrar. **4.** (*Cuba*) an ignorant person = persona ignorante. **5.** (*Mex.*) an iron table = mesa para planchar.

burrunazo See **bimbazo**.

burujón (*Cuba*) lots; a pile of something = un montón; un rimero de cosas.

burundanga (*Puerto Rico*) unimportant objects = objetos sin importancia.

buruquena; juey (*Puerto Rico*) a crab = cangrejo.

buruza (*Ven.*) a crumb; a small piece = migaja; porción muy pequeña.

buscamoscas (*Mex.*) a troublemaker = buscapleitos.

busconear 1. (*Puerto Rico*) to make a living with a very small business = ganarse la vida con negocios muy pequeños. **2.** (*Puerto Rico*) to look for something = buscar; buscando algo.

buscones (*Dom. Rep.*) a guide for illegal immigrants = guía para inmigrantes indocumentados.

buseta (*Ven.*) a small bus = ómnibus pequeño.

busito See **chivita**.

butifarra (*Peru*) a sandwich with ham and lettuce or another kind of mixture = **sándwich** o emparedado de jamón y ensalada.

butléger (*from English*) a bootlegger = contrabandista.

butuco 1. (*Guat., Hond.*) shabby; corpulent and short = grueso; rechoncho. **2.** (*Costa Rica, Hond.*) a type of banana from Costa Rica = un plátano originario de Costa Rica.

butute (*Hond.*) a trumpet = trompeta.

buzeta (*Colo.*) a small bus = bus pequeño.

by pass [pron. baipás] **1.** (*from English*) a bypass = carretera de circunvalación. **2.** (*from English*) a by-pass = (N.E. procedimiento quirúrgico para reparar arterias obstruidas.)

byte [pron. bait] (*from English*) a series of eight bits = técnicamente es el nombre de un paquete de ocho **bits**.

C

caballada (*Dom. Rep.*) a mistake; foolishness = disparate; desatino.

caballazo (*Chile, Mex., Peru*) a bump; the collision of one person against another = encontronazo contra una persona.

caballete; caballito del diablo (*Mex.*) a cricket = grillo.

caballito del diablo See **caballete**.

caballo 1. (*Ven.*) familiarity between friends = tratamiento de famialiaridad entre amigos. **2.** (*Dom. Rep.*) awkward; clumsy = torpe. **3.** (*Dom. Rep.*) rude; impolite = grosero; mal educado; el que se comporta brutamente. **4.** (*Nic.*) a dish that combines different regional foods from Nicaragua = plato en que se combinan diferentes comidas regionales de Nicaragua. **5.** (*Ven.*) a pal = compinche.

caballón(a) 1. (*Mex.*) a large or tall person = persona grande o muy alta. **2.** (*Mex.*) to be high on drugs = volarse con drogas.

cabanga 1. (*Costa Rica, Pan.*) a broken heart = pena amorosa. **2.** (*Costa Rica, Pan.*) nostalgia for a loved one = nostalgia por el ser amado.

cabañuelas (*Bol.*) the first rains of the summer = primeras lluvias del verano.

cabaretera (*Colo.*) a prostitute = prostituta.

cabecearse (*Chile*) to think = pensar.

cabeciduro (*Dom. Rep.*) obstinate; stubborn = obstinado; testarudo.

cabecita negra (*Argen.*) a half-breed (derogatory); any person with dark skin and black hair = despectivo para mestizos(as) o personas de la piel oscura y el pelo negro.

cabellera (*Mex.*) a toupee = tupé.

cabestro 1. (*Ven.*) rustic; uncouth = rústico; persona de modales toscos. **2.** (*Ven.*) inefficient = incapaz. **3.** (*Mex.*) a rope; a cord = cuerda; cordón.

cabete (*Puerto Rico*) a shoelace = cordón o lazo de zapato.

cabezón (*Colo.*) rapids; a whirlpool in a river = rápidos; remolinos en el río.

cabinera (*Colo.*) a stewardess = azafata.

cabinete (*from English*) a cabinet = gabinete; estante; armario.

cabo; mocho (*Dom. Rep.*) a cigar butt = colilla de puro; lo que queda de un cigarro puro ya fumado.

cabra 1. (*Bol.*) dirt on the knees = suciedad de las rodillas. **2.** (*Colo.*) a brush = brocha para pintar. **3.** (*Colo., Cuba, Ven.*) a trick; a swindle; loaded dice = trampa en el juego; dados arreglados para hacer trampas. **4.** (*Puerto Rico*) a woman who goes with many men = mujer que tiene muchos hombres. **5.** (*Chile*) a girl (informal) = niña (informal).

cabreado 1. (*Colo.*) suspicious = receloso. **2.** (*Colo.*) a scare = asustado.

cabrear (*Puerto Rico*) the behavior of a woman who has many men = conducta de una mujer que tiene varios hombres.

cabrearse (*Argen.*) to lose one's cool = perder los estribos.

cabriado (*Chile*) fed up (informal) = harto (informal).

cabrilla; timón (*Colo.*) a steering wheel = volante del automóvil.

cabro 1. (*Puerto Rico*) a womanizer; a man who chases after women = mujeriego; conquistador; hombre que anda constantemente tras las mujeres. **2.** (*Chile*) a kid; a boy (informal); a guy = niño (informal); tipo; amigo.

cabrón 1. (*Chile, Colo., Peru*) a pimp = chulo; explotador de prostitutas. **2.** (*Colo., Mex., Puerto Rico*) a strong insult (vulgar) = insulto grave (vulgar). **3.** (*Colo., Mex., Puerto Rico*) a cuckold = cornudo. **4.** (*Mex.*) a man who has many women = galán; hombre que tiene varias mujeres.

cabrona (*Chile*) a madam; a brothel keeper = la administradora de un prostíbulo.

cábula (*Para.*) an amulet; a lucky charm = amuleto.

cabulear (*Peru*) to deceive = embaucar; engañar.

cabulla; cabuya (*Colo., Puerto Rico, Ven.*) a string = cuerda delgada; cordel.

cabuya See **cabulla**.

cacahuate 1. (*Mex., Puerto Rico*) a peanut = maní. **2.** (*Mex.*) a pill; a barbiturate pill = píldora; píldora de barbitúrico.

cacalota (*Hond.*) a debt = deuda.

cacana (*Colo.*) excrement (informal) = excremento (informal).

cacaquear (*Colo.*) to speak with a peasant's accent = hablar con acento acampesinado.

cacarear (*Mex.*) to gossip = chismear.

cacarico 1. (*Hond.*) a crab = cangrejo. **2.** (*Hond.*) weak; old = débil; viejo.

cacatúa (*Puerto Rico*) inefficient; an unproductive or useless person = ineficiente; una persona inútil.

cach (*from English*) cash = pago al contado; dinero en efectivo.

cachá (*Chile*) a great amount = una gran cantidad.

cacha (*Colo.*) a nickname for a very good friend = apelativo afectuoso para un buen amigo.

cachacascán (*from English*) a wrestling match in which the blows are faked; it is more like a show than a real match. (From catch-as-catch-can.) = lucha libre donde los luchadores dan golpes y hacen movimientos falsos; es un espectáculo y no un encuentro deportivo.

cachaco 1. (*Colo., Ecua.*) countrylike behavior; a person who lives away from the capital city = acampesinado; el que vive al interior del país. **2.** (*Colo., Ven.*) well-dressed; elegant = bien vestido; elegante. **3.** (*Peru*) a police officer = agente de policía. **4.** (*Peru*) any person in the military (derogatory) = cualquier persona en las fuerzas armadas (despectivo). **5.** (*Colo.*) an inhabitant of Bogotá and the metropolitan area = los que viven en Bogotá y el área metropolitana.

cachado (*Ven.*) under surveillance = observado; vigilado.

cachafaz (*Para.*) mischievous; cheeky = pillo; desvergonzado; atrevido.

cachaflín (*Colo.*) a joint; a marijuana cigarette = cigarrillo de marihuana.

cachaña (*Chile*) to show a fake intention to do something = aparentar intención de hacer algo.

cachapera (*Puerto Rico, Ven.*) a lesbian (vulgar) = lesbiana (vulgar).

cachar 1. (*from English*) to catch = (RAE) coger; alcanzar. **2.** (*from English*) to cash = convertir en dinero efectivo. **3.** (*Argen., Chile, Mex., Ven.*) to catch in the act = sorprender, descubrir a alguien o algo. **4.** (*Argen., Chile, Mex., Ven.*) to understand (informal) = entender (informal). **5.** (*Guat., Hond., Salva.*) to get; to obtain = conseguir; obtener. **6.** (*Peru*) to have sex; to screw (vulgar) = realizar el acto sexual (vulgar). **7.** (*Uru.*) to pull someone's leg = tomar el pelo.

cacharpas (*Peru*) junk = baratijas; trastos de poco valor.

cacharpearse (*Chile*) to dress up in the best clothes = adornarse de las mejores galas.

cacharra (*Ven.*) an old, battered car = automóvil viejo y golpeado.

cacharrero (*Colo.*) a peddler = buhonero; vendedor callejero; vendedor de baratijas.

cacharro 1. (*Chile, Colo.*) a battered automobile; a car of inferior quality = automóvil en mal estado o de pésima calidad. **2.** (*Chile, Colo.*) an old car = automóvil viejo. **3.** (*Colo.*) a trinket; a knickknack = baratija; chuchería.

cacharro de greda (*Chile*) a clay vessel = jarrón de arcilla.

cacharros (*Colo.*) cheap goods = baratijas.

¿cachay? (*Chile*) Do you understand? Do you see? = ¿entiendes? ¿ves?

cachaza 1. (*Colo.*) an inferior-quality cane alcohol; firewater = aguardiente de caña de baja calidad. **2.** (*Colo.*) nerve = desfachatez; conducta desvergonzada. **3.** (*Dom. Rep.*) a vegetable peel = cáscara de un vegetal. **4.** (*Dom. Rep., Puerto Rico*) the cheap liquor that is left over from cane alcohol production = hez del **guarapo** de caña; sobrante de la producción de alcohol de caña.

cache (*Ven.*) rotten coffee; an inferior-quality coffee = café descompuesto o de mala calidad.

cachencho (*Chile*) a simpleton = persona bobalicona.

cachero 1. (*Costa Rica, Ven.*) a liar; an untrustworthy person = embustero; indigno de confianza. **2.** (*Salva.*) eager; longing; demanding; insistent = ansioso; pedigüeño. **3.** (*Chile*) one who practices sex continuously (very vulgar) = el que practica el sexo continuamente (muy vulgar). **4.** (*Costa Rica*) cuckolded = cornudo; marido engañado.

cachetada (*Argen., Chile, Dom. Rep., Uru.*) a slap; a blow to the face with a fist = cachete; bofetada; golpe dado en la mejilla con la mano abierta.

cachete (*Argen., Chile, Uru.*) a buttock = nalga.

cacheteo (*Argen., Chile, Uru.*) to have a good time; to have an easy life = pasarlo bien; vivir la buena vida.

cachetón 1. (*Chile*) big cheeks = de grandes carrillos. **2.** (*Chile*) presumptuous; pretentious = presuntuoso; pomposo.

cachicha (*Hond.*) a temper tantrum; anger = berrinche; enojo.

cachifa(o) (*Ven.*) a servant = sirviente.

cachiflín (*Hond.*) to flee; to escape quickly = salir; escapar rápido.

cachifo (*Colo.*) a boy = niño.

cachilapo (*Ven.*) any small and/or cheap animal used to prepare a meal = animal pequeño y/o de poco valor que se usa para preparar una comida.

cachimba (*Ven.*) the vagina (vulgar) = vagina (vulgar).

cachimbear (*Nic.*) to punch = dar trompadas.

cachimbero (*Ven.*) a person who bewitches another by smoking a pipe = el que hace brujerías fumando una pipa o cachimba.

cachimbo (*Nic.*) a blow with the fist = puñetazo; golpe con el puño.

cachipil (*Nic.*) a fortune = una fortuna.

cachiporra (*Chile*) false; fraud; smug = farsante; vanidoso; pagado de sí mismo.

cachipuco (*Hond.*) a person with an irregular face, where one cheek is bigger than the other = persona con un carrillo más abultado que el otro.

cachirulo 1. (*Chile*) a bun in the hair at the side of the head = moño al lado de la cabeza. **2.** (*Mex.*) a patch = parche; remedo. **3.** (*Mex.*) a trick = truco. **4.** (*Mex.*) a half-brother = medio hermano.

cachito (*Chile*) a piece of something = trozo o pedazo de algo.

cachivaches (*Argen., Bol., Chile*) cheap goods = baratijas; objetos sin valor.

cacho 1. (*Chile*) a dice game; the single cup used to play that game = juego de dados; vaso de cuero para tirar los dados en ese juego. **2.** (*Chile*) merchandise that does not sell = mercancía que no se vende. **3.** (*Chile*) good-for-nothing = inútil. **4.** (*Colo.*) a joint; a marijuana cigarette =

porro; cigarrillo de marihuana. **5.** (*Costa Rica*) a robbery; a theft; a burglary = robo. **6.** (*Costa Rica, Ecua., Ven.*) an anecdote; an obscene joke = anécdota o charrasquillo generalmente obsceno. **7.** (*Mex.*) a part of a lottery ticket = parte de un boleto de lotería. **8.** (*Para.*) a whole bunch of bananas = racimo entero de bananas o plátanos. **9.** (*Uru.*) a piece of something = trozo o pedazo de algo.

cachola; chola (*Puerto Rico*) the head = cabeza.

cacholón (*Puerto Rico*) a person with a big head (informal) = cabezón; el que tiene la cabeza grande (informal).

cachón (*Colo.*) a cuckold = cornudo; marido engañado por la esposa.

cachorro 1. (*Cuba*) a malicious person; a sneaky person = persona rencorosa y mal intencionada. **2.** (*Ven.*) a surly person = persona hosca. **3.** (*Puerto Rico, Ven.*) obstinate; stubborn = terco.

cachos 1. (*Bol., Chile, Ecua., Peru, Pan.*) an animal's horns = cuernos. **2.** (*Pan.*) a bunch of bananas = racimo de bananas.

cachube (*Ven.*) the navel; the physical depression on the abdomen = ombligo.

cachucha 1. (*Colo., Cuba, Mex., Ven.*) a cap = gorra con visera. **2.** (*Mex.*) a drug supply = abastecimiento de drogas. **3.** (*Mex.*) the police force (derogatory) = la policía (peyorativo). **4.** (*Para.*) the vagina (vulgar) = vagina (vulgar).

cachuchazo (*Chile*) a strong blow with the hand = golpe fuerte con la mano.

cachudo 1. (*Chile*) it has big horns = tiene grandes cuernos. **2.** (*Chile*) suspicious; suspecting something = el que es o está sospechoso.

cachumbambé (*Cuba*) a seesaw = balancín.

cacique (*Chile*) a person who has influence and/or controls many voters = el que influencia y/o controla a muchos votantes.

cacorro; cucarrón (*Colo.*) a man who plays the masculine role in a homosexual relationship (vulgar) = el que desempeña el papel masculino en una relación homosexual (vulgar).

cacreca (*Nic.*) a convalescent = convaleciente.

caculear 1. (*Puerto Rico*) to attend social events often = asistir a fiestas continuamente. **2.** (*Puerto Rico*) to flirt with a man = coquetear con un hombre.

cacurúo(a) (*Ven.*) disheveled = desgreñado(a).

cada lora a su guanascate (*Nic.*) every bird in its nest = cada quien en su casa.

cadete (*Argen., Para.*) an apprentice = aprendiz; mandadero.

cadi (*from English*) a caddy = recogepelotas.

Cadilaque 1. (*from English*) a Cadillac = el automóvil de marca Cadillac. **2.** (*from English*) any large automobile = cualquier automóvil grande.

caer el veinte (*Mex.*) to get a joke; to understand the hidden meaning of something = entender una broma o un chiste; entender el significado de algo que no se ha expresado abiertamente.

caer mala (*Puerto Rico*) to menstruate (informal) = menstruando (informal).

caerle polilla (*Colo.*) to fall into disgrace = traer la deshonra.

cafetera (*Argen.*) a battered vehicle = vehículo en muy mal estado.

cafiche; cafiolo (*Argen., Chile*) a pimp; any man that lives on the money of a woman (vulgar) = chulo; explotador de prostitutas; cualquier hombre que vive con el dinero de una mujer (vulgar).

cafiolo See **cafiche**.

cagacatre (*Puerto Rico*) a coward = cobarde.

cagadera (*Argen., Cuba, Dom. Rep., Mex.*) diarrhea (vulgar) = diarrea (vulgar).

cagalera (*Colo., Cuba*) diarrhea (vulgar) = diarrea (vulgar).

cagarreta; churra (*Puerto Rico*) diarrhea (vulgar) = diarrea (vulgar).

cagón See **barrigón**.

cagueta; churria (*Dom. Rep.*) diarrhea (vulgar) = diarrea (vulgar).

cahuin 1. (*Chile*) a thorny or complicated issue; an immoral affair; an illegal business = asunto o cuestión inmoral o escabrosa; negocio ilegal. **2.** (*Chile*) a mess = enredo.

cahuinero (*Chile*) a mischief-maker; someone who makes things more complicated than they are = enredador; el que arma líos.

caibo (*Colo.*) a knock on the head = coscorrón.

caído del catre (*Chile*) silly; naive = tonto; ingenuo.

caite 1. (*from English*) a kite = cometa. **2.** (*Nic.*) an Indian shoe = el calzado del indio.

caja blanca (*Puerto Rico*) the blank piece in dominos = la pieza blanca del dominó.

caja de dientes (*Colo.*) false teeth = dentadura postiza.

cajeta (*Nic.*) milk candy = dulce de leche.

cajetilla (*Argen.*) a dude; a man who is a show-off = petimetre; hombre presumido.

cajetón (*Puerto Rico*) good-looking = guapetón.

cajón 1. (*Argen., Chile, Colo., Guat., Para.*) a casket; a coffin = féretro; ataúd. **2.** (*Chile, Mex.*) a large box or box made from hard material = caja grande o caja de material sólido. **3.** (*Chile, Guat., Mex., Uru., Ven.*) a long and deep ravine; a narrow canyon = barranco largo y profundo; cañón estrecho; corte profundo en el terreno producto del aluvión.

cajonero (*Ven.*) that which is obvious = lo que es obvio e inevitable.

cajuela; castaña 1. (*Mex.*) a car trunk = maletero o portaequipaje del automóvil. **2.** (*Mex.*) a big trunk = baúl grande.

calabaza 1. (*Mex.*) a stupid person = persona estúpida. **2.** (*Mex.*) the air filter of an engine = el filtro de aire de un motor.

calaca (*Mex.*) a sign of death = señal de muerte.

calalú (*Dom. Rep.*) a vegetable stew = guisado con varios vegetales.

calamorro (*Chile*) a big and heavy shoe = zapato grande y pesado.

calanchún (*Colo.*) a front man = testaferro o hombre de paja; el que se presta para esconder la identidad del contratante.

calandraca (*Nic.*) sick; unhealthy = enfermizo.

calango(a) (*Mex.*) an ambitious person = persona ambiciosa.

calar 1. (*Argen., Chile*) to see through = adivinar la intención. **2.** (*Colo.*) to bewilder; to confuse = apabullar; anonadar; confundir. **3.** (*Ven.*) to tolerate; to put up with something annoying = aguantar; soportar algo molesto y/o desgradable.

calato(a) (*Peru*) naked = desnudo(a).

calavera (*Mex.*) a taillight = luces traseras de un vehículo.

calcetas (*Chile*) socks = calcetines.

calceto (*Colo.*) a person who comes off badly = el que queda mal.

calculador (*Puerto Rico*) self-interested = interesado; el que todo lo hace interesadamente.

caldera (*Uru.*) a kettle = tetera.

caldillo 1. (*Chile*) a fish or shellfish soup = sopa de mariscos o pescado. **2.** (*Mex.*) a soup made with diced meat = caldo de picadillo de carnes.

caldo de cabeza (*Chile*) to daydream without connection to reality = imaginar sin fundamento.

calducho (*Chile*) a party; a celebration = fiesta; celebración.

calentar (*Dom. Rep., Uru.*) to upset someone; to make someone angry = alterar a alguien; poner a alguien furioso.

calentarse 1. (*Chile, Mex.*) to get sexually excited = excitarse sexualmente. **2.** (*Guat., Hond., Mex., Salva., Ven.*) to get cross; to get angry = enfadarse; enojarse.

calentera (*Ven.*) indignation; displeasure = indignación; disgusto.

calentón(a) (*Para.*) a person who gets sexually excited very easily = el o la que se excita sexualmente con facilidad.

calentura 1. (*Colo.*) a fit of temper = preparado para enfrentarse a algo. **2.** (*Colo.*) to be angry = estar enojado(a). **3.** (*Para.*) sexual excitation = excitación sexual.

calenturiento (*Chile*) with high fever = con mucha fiebre.

calesita (*Argen., Para.*) a merry-go-round = caballitos; tíovivo.

caleta (*Colo.*) a secret place to hide something or someone (informal) = escondrijo; lugar secreto para esconder algo o alguien (informal).

caletudo(a) (*Colo.*) a wealthy person (informal) = persona adinerada (informal).

caliente 1. (*Colo.*) a bold, brave person = persona atrevida; valiente. **2.** (*Colo.*) courage = coraje.

calificar (*from English*) to qualify = tener antecedentes; tener credenciales.

calilla 1. (*Guat., Hond., Mex.*) a boring, tedious person = persona aburrida; tediosa. **2.** (*Mex.*) the last piece of the soap = lo último que queda del jabón usado.

calillas (*Chile*) debts = deudas.

calimete (*Dom. Rep.*) a drinking straw = pajita.

callahuaya (*Bol.*) a native medicine man = curandero nativo.

callampas 1. (*Chile*) mushrooms = hongos; setas. **2.** (*Chile*) shanties = chozas provisionales hechas de material ligero.

callana 1. (*Peru*) a container = tiesto. **2.** (*Peru*) a piece of a clay container = trozo de una vasija de barro.

caló 1. (*Mex.*) a five-cent coin; a nickel = moneda de cinco centavos. **2.** (*Mex.*) slang = argot; jerga.

calpul (*Guat.*) a meeting = reunión; asamblea.

calumnia (*Chile, Ecua., Peru*) a lie; a slander; a defamation = mentira; difamación; chisme.

calzoncillo de baño (*Mex.*) a bathing suit = traje de baño.

calzones (*Chile, Colo.*) women's underwear; panties = bragas.

calzoneta (*Guat., Hond., Salva.*) a bathing suit = traje de baño.

calzonudo (*Chile*) disrespect for a man who is dominated by a woman = desprecio por el hombre que se deja dominar por la mujer.

camambuses (*Uru.*) oversized shoes = zapatos que quedan grandes.

camamila (*from English*) camomile = (RAE) manzanilla.

camanchaca (*Chile*) the Atacama desert's fog = niebla del desierto de Atacama.

camandulear 1. (*Para.*) to be hypocritical = proceder con hipocresía. **2.** (*Para.*) to intrigue = intrigar.

camarera (*Puerto Rico*) a stewardess = azafata.

camarón 1. (*Costa Rica*) a tip; a gratuity; extra work with special pay = propina; gratificación; trabajo extra pagado de manera especial. **2.** (*Dom. Rep.*) a scandalmonger = chismoso. **3.** (*Peru*) a turncoat = camaleón; el que muda de parecer con facilidad o por conveniencia. **4.** (*Puerto Rico*) an undercover agent = agente encubierto.

cambiado(a) (*Mex.*) a gay man or woman; a homosexual = hombre o mujer homosexual.

cambucho 1. (*Chile, Peru*) a paper or cardboard cone = cucurucho de papel o cartón en forma cónica. **2.** (*Chile, Peru*) a paper bag = bolsa de papel.

cambur 1. (*Ven.*) a banana = banana. **2.** (*Ven.*) public employment = puesto público.

camburrear (*Para.*) to mix = mezclar.

cambute (*Costa Rica*) a big snail; a conch = caracol grande.

cambuto; catimbao; petacón(a) (*Peru*) chubby = rechoncho(a).

camellar (*Colo.*) to work with determination = trabajar con ahínco.

camello (*Mex.*) a job; employment = trabajo; empleo.

camellón (*Colo.*) a promenade; an avenue lined with trees = alameda; vía pública ancha y generalmente arborizada.

cameraman (*from English*) a cameraman = camarógrafo.

camín (*Ecua.*) a ragamuffin boy = golfillo; granuja; niño de la calle; pilluelo.

camión (*Guat., Hond., Mex., Nic.*) a bus = autobús.

camisilla (*Dom. Rep., Para.*) an undershirt = camiseta.

camisola (*Para.*) a young boy's nightshirt = camisa de dormir de niño.

camisón 1. (*Argen., Chile, Cuba, Pan., Peru*) a nightgown = camisa de dormir. 2. (*Ven.*) a lightweight woman's dress = vestido liviano de mujer. 3. (*Peru*) a woman's shirt = camisa de mujer.

camita (*Mex.*) a crib = cuna.

camizón (*Mex.*) a nightgown = camisa de dormir.

camochar (*Hond.*) to prune = podar; desmochar árboles o plantas.

camotazos (*Mex.*) blows from a fist = golpes de puño.

camote 1. (*Argen., Bol., Chile, Ecua., Peru*) a sweet potato = batata. 2. (*Chile*) a large stone = piedra de gran tamaño. 3. (*Chile*) a bothersome person; a tedious person = persona aburridora, tediosa, molestosa o majadera. 4. (*Ecua., Mex.*) a silly person; a fool = bobo; tonto. 5. (*Guat.*) a calf = pantorrilla. 6. (*Guat.*) a nuisance; a bother = molestia; fastidio. 7. (*Mex.*) a rascal = pícaro. 8. (*Peru*) a sweetheart = novio(a); la persona querida.

camotera (*Chile*) a light beating given by a group as a joke = golpiza liviana dada por un grupo como broma.

campana (*Argen.*) a look-out thief = cómplice que vigila durante un robo.

campanero (*Colo.*) a look-out person in a crime = el vigía durante una fechoría.

campechana 1. (*Chile, Cuba*) an approachable person; a happy-go-lucky person = persona de trato agradable; despreocupada. 2. (*Ven.*) a hammock = hamaca. 3. (*Ven.*) a whore = prostituta; ramera. 4. (*Mex.*) a drink prepared with rum, cola, and soda water = bebida preparada con ron, Coca-Cola y soda. 5. (*Mex.*) a cocktail = bebida preparada con mezcla de licores.

cámper (*from English*) a camper = vehículo recreacional para acampar y vivir en él.

campera (*Argen., Uru.*) a short sports jacket = chaqueta deportiva corta.

campero (*Colo.*) a four-wheel drive vehicle = vehículo para todo terreno.

campin (*from English*) camping = acampar; campamento.

campirano (*Costa Rica*) country-like; rude; behaving like a peasant = lo que es del campo; persona rústica; acampesinado.

camposantero (*Mex.*) a cemetery caretaker = cuidador del cementerio.

camuliano (*Hond.*) a fruit that is starting to ripen = fruto que está comenzando a madurar.

cana 1. (*Argen., Chile, Peru, Uru.*) a jail; a police station = cárcel; cuartel de la policía. 2. (*Para.*) a police officer = agente de policía.

canacanear (*Mex.*) to stutter; to have speech problems = tartamudear; hablar con dificultad.

canal (*Cuba*) a playground slide = tobogán.

canana 1. (*Colo.*) handcuffs = esposas o manillas de hierro. 2. (*Colo.*) a straitjacket = camisa de fuerza.

canario (*Uru.*) a peasant; a person from the countryside = campesino; el que es del campo.

canasta(o) (*Argen., Bol., Chile, Peru, Puerto Rico*) a basket = cesta(o).

cancanear 1. (*Colo., Costa Rica, Dom. Rep., Nic.*) to stutter; to express oneself with difficulty = tartamudear; hablar con dificultad. **2.** (*Colo., Costa Rica, Dom. Rep., Nic.*) to squander money = derrochar el dinero.

cancel (*Colo.*) a folding screen = biombo.

cáncer (*Colo.*) an infected wound; a sore that does not look well = herida infectada; llaga de mal aspecto.

cancha 1. (*Peru*) popcorn = palomitas de maíz. **2.** (*Peru*) roasted beans = habichuelas tostadas. **3.** (*Colo.*) scabies = sarna.

canchar 1. (*Ven.*) to get someone into an issue; to involve others in something = encajarle a alguien un asunto. **2.** (*Ven.*) to drink a few glasses = tomarse unas copas. **3.** (*Ven.*) to slip on one's clothes = ponerse las prendas de vestir. **4.** (*Ven.*) to hit; to give a blow = asestar un golpe.

canche; chele (*Guat.*) a white person, male or female = persona blanca, se usa para el femenino y el masculino.

canchero 1. (*Peru*) a priest who takes advantage of the churchgoers as much as he can = clérigo que trata de sacar lo que se puede de los fieles. **2.** (*Argen., Chile*) an experienced, smart person; a person who behaves with ease and confidence = persona lista y con experiencia; el que actúa con facilidad y soltura; alguien que sabe lo que hace.

canchitas 1. (*Peru*) popcorn = palomitas de maíz. **2.** (*Peru*) roasted beans = habichuelas tostadas.

canco 1. (*Mex.*) a fist fight = pelea de puños. **2.** (*Mex.*) a hit on the opponent's spinning top in a spinning top contest = golpe en el trompo o peonza de un adversario cuando se compite en el juego del trompo.

candado 1. (*Colo.*) a goatee = perilla. **2.** (*Colo.*) a lock = cerradura.

candeleja (*Peru*) a washer = arandela.

candi (*from English*) candy = dulce; caramelo.

candil (*Mex.*) **1.** a chandelier = candelabro. **2.** a person who lays around = el que vagabundea.

candinga (*Hond.*) a mess = enredo.

candonga (*Hond.*) a bandage over the navel of a newborn = ombliguero; faja para el ombligo de un bebé.

candongas (*Colo.*) earrings = pendientes; zarcillos.

candungo (*Puerto Rico*) any container = cualquier receptáculo.

caneca 1. (*Colo.*) a large can; a garbage can = bidón; cubo para la basura. **2.** (*Puerto Rico*) a pint of rum = una pinta de ron.

caneco (*Bol.*) drunk = borracho; ebrio.

canela (*Puerto Rico*) the sperm (vulgar) = espermio (vulgar).

caney (*Ven.*) a hut = choza.

canfín (*Costa Rica*) oil; petroleum = petróleo.

cangallero (*Peru*) a peddler = buhonero; vendedor ambulante.

cangrejo (*Ven.*) a difficult crime to solve = problema policial difícil de resolver.

cangrimán; cocoroco (*Puerto Rico*) a very important person = persona muy importante.

canguil 1. (*Ecua.*) popcorn = palomitas de maíz. **2.** (*Ecua.*) roasted beans = habichuelas tostadas.

canilla 1. (*Argen., Uru.*) a faucet = grifo. **2.** (*Argen., Chile, Para.*) the shinbone = espinilla; parte anterior de la pierna. **3.** (*Colo., Peru*) a calf = pantorrilla. **4.** (*Guat., Hond., Salva.*) a newspaper boy; a newspaper seller = niño que vende el periódico; vendedor de periódicos. **5.** (*Mex.*) the wrist = muñeca; articulación de la mano con el brazo. **6.** (*Peru*) a dice game = juego de dados. **7.** (*Puerto Rico*) cowardice = cobardía.

canillera (*Argen., Chile, Para.*) a pad used to protect the shinbone = almohadilla para proteger la **canilla**.

canillita (*Argen., Chile, Para., Peru, Uru.*) a newspaper boy = vendedor de periódicos.

canjura (*Hond.*) a strong poison = veneno muy potente.

cano (*Puerto Rico*) a blond-haired person = persona del pelo rubio.

canquiza (*Mex.*) beating; thrashing = paliza o golpiza.

cansón (*Puerto Rico*) boring = aburrido.

cantaleta 1. (*Colo., Costa Rica*) to repeat again and again; to reprimand over and over = estribillo; regaño que se repite muchas veces. **2.** (*Guat., Hond.*) the chorus of a song = estribillo; canción o parte de una canción que se repite varias veces.

cantaso; cantazo (*Dom. Rep., Puerto Rico*) a crash; a blow = choque o colisión; golpe.

cantazo See **cantaso.**

cantegril (*Uru.*) a shanty town; a neighborhood with houses for the poor = chabolas; vecindario pobre con casas de material de baja calidad.

cantimplora 1. (*Guat.*) the mumps = paperas. **2.** (*Guat.*) a goiter = bocio.

cantinflear; cantinfleo (*Chile, Mex.*) to speak a lot without any substance = hablar mucho sin decir nada específico; hablar sin sentido.

cantinfleo See **cantinflear.**

cantó el manicero (*Cuba*) someone "kicked the bucket" = se murió.

canturria (*Peru*) a monotonous song = canto monótono.

canuto 1. (*Chile*) a member of any Protestant church = miembro de cualquier iglesia protestante. **2.** (*Ven.*) the handle of a fountain pen or ballpoint pen = mango de una pluma fuente o un bolígrafo. **3.** (*Mex.*) sherbet or ice cream in a cone = sorbete o helado en la forma de un cilindro.

caña 1. (*Argen., Colo., Uru.*) sugar-cane brandy = licor de caña de azúcar. **2.** (*Chile*) a big glass; a big glass of wine = vaso grande; vaso grande de vino. **3.** (*Colo., Ven.*) false news = noticias falsas. **4.** (*Colo., Ven.*) a boast = fanfarronada. **5.** (*Ven.*) any alcoholic beverage = cualquier bebida alcohólica.

caña hueca (*Chile*) a person who talks nonsense = el que habla tonterías.

cáñamo 1. (*Chile, Costa Rica, Hond.*) a string = cordel delgado; bramante. **2.** (*Chile, Costa Rica, Hond.*) cannabis; the plant of marijuana; a textile plant = planta de la marihuana; planta textil.

cañar (*Colo.*) to lie = mentir.

cañero; fafarachero; fafaracho (*Colo.*) a person who bluffs = el que fanfarronea; el que aparenta lo que no es.

cañita 1. (*Ecua., Peru*) a drinking straw = paja o pajita para beber. **2.** (*Puerto Rico*) an illegal rum; an inferior-quality rum = ron ilegal; ron de baja calidad.

caño 1. (*Peru*) a faucet = grifo. **2.** (*Ven.*) a branch in the river delta = brazo del delta de un río.

cañonazo 1. (*Argen., Bol., Chile, Ecua., Para., Peru, Uru.*) a strong kick to a soccer ball = potente golpe de pie en el **fútbol. 2.** (*Chile*) a large swallow of an alcoholic beverage = trago grande de bebida alcohólica.

cañoneado; cocido (*Chile*) drunk = borracho.

cañonero (*Ven.*) a person who provides the music at a family party = el que provee la música en una fiesta familiar.

cañuelas; choclos (*Chile*) calves = pantorrillas.

capa (*Hond.*) a beating; a thrashing = paliza; golpiza.

capa de agua (*Cuba, Mex.*) a raincoat = impermeable.

capacha (*Bol., Chile*) a jail; a prison = cárcel; prisión.

capear (*Chile, Guat.*) to cut classes; to avoid work = hacer novillos; escaparse del trabajo.

capear escuela (*Colo.*) to cut school = hacer novillos; ausentarse o faltar a la escuela sin razones justificadas.

caperuzo (*Chile*) skillful; clever = apto; hábil; astuto.

capirotada 1. (*Mex.*) a dessert prepared with bread, raisins, and sugar or honey = postre preparado con pan, pasas y azúcar o miel. **2.** (*Mex.*) a pie prepared with bread crumbs, meat and spices = pastel de pan remojado, carne y especias.

capo (*Chile*) able; efficient; competent = capaz; eficiente; competente.

capón (*Mex.*) a sterile person; someone who cannot procreate = persona estéril; él o la que no puede procrear.

capote 1. (*Chile*) a rape (vulgar) = violación (vulgar). **2.** (*Colo.*) humus; leaf mold = mantillo; capa superior muy fértil del suelo. **3.** (*Pan.*) a raincoat = impermeable.

capotera (*Hond.*) a coat stand = percha para la ropa.

capul (*Colo., Pan.*) fringe; bangs = flequillo.

capulín (*Mex.*) a cherry = cereza.

capulina 1. (*Mex.*) a prostitute = prostituta. **2.** (*Mex.*) a black widow spider = la araña viuda negra.

caquis (*Mex.*) feces; generally applied to baby feces = materia fecal; aplicado generalmente al excremento de un niño pequeño.

carabina 1. (*Ven.*) a mixture of several liquors = mezcla de varios licores. **2.** (*Ven.*) a ball of corn flour filled with black beans = esfera de harina de maíz rellena de habichuelas negras.

carabinero (*Bol., Chile*) a policeman = agente de policía.

caracha (*Para.*) the scabies; mange = sarna.

caracho (*Chile*) to show a face of distaste or anger = cara de disgusto o molestia.

carachoso (*Peru*) with scabs from infections, cuts or wounds = sarnoso; lleno de llagas.

carajada (*Chile*) a bad action; a dirty trick = una mala jugada; jugada sucia.

carajito 1. (*Ven.*) a boy (informal) = niño (informal). **2.** (*Ven.*) a young, inexperienced person = persona joven y sin experiencia.

¡carajo! (*Colo., Mex., Puerto Rico*) Good gracious!; Gosh!; a mild or violent interjection according to the context and the emphasis in the pronunciation = ¡caramba!; ¡caray!; interjección suave o violenta de acuerdo al contexto y al énfasis en la pronunciación.

carajo 1. (*Chile*) a person who behaves impolitely = el que se comporta sin modales. **2.** (*Chile*) a person of low social status = persona de baja condición social. **3.** (*Cuba*) a bad name; a very vulgar insult = insulto de gran calibre; insulto muy vulgar. **4.** (*Ven.*) a person without social value; a person of little importance (derogatory) = persona a la cual no se le da valor social alguno (peyorativo).

caramelo (*Pan.*) a lollipop = chupachupa; chupetín; pirulí.

carancho (*Argen., Uru.*) a buzzard = buitre.

caranga (*Hond.*) a louse = piojo.

caraota (*Ven.*) a bean = habichuela.

carapacho (*Ven.*) a frame; the framework of something = armazón; esqueleto de algo.

carapulca (*Peru*) a dish prepared with dry potatoes and hot pepper = guisado picante preparado con patatas secas.

caravana (*Hond., Mex.*) to bow as a sign of courtesy or politeness = reverencia; inclinación del cuerpo en señal de cortesía.

caravanas (*Argen., Uru.*) earrings = zarcillos; pendientes.

carboncillo 1. (*Chile*) coal dust = carbonilla. **2.** (*Chile*) small pieces of charcoal = trozos pequeños de carbón vegetal. **3.** (*Chile*) drawing charcoal = carbón para dibujar. **4.** (*Chile*) a charcoal drawing = dibujo al carbón.

carbonear (*Mex.*) to deceive someone who thinks of himself or herself as a clever person = engañar a aquel que se considera astuto.

carbonero 1. (*Chile*) one who encourages others to fight; or fosters disagreement = el que incita a la pelea; el que fomenta la discordia. **2.** (*Mex.*) a person who deceives someone who thinks of himself or herself as a very clever person = el que engaña a aquel que se considera astuto.

carca (*Peru*) dirt; grime = roña.

carcamán (*Argen., Peru*) a person who pretends to be important or wise when he or she is not = persona de muchas pretensiones y poco mérito.

carcancha (*Peru*) a skeleton; a structure = esqueleto; armazón.

carcasa 1. (*from English*) a carcass; an inner tube of a tire = parte interna de un neumático. **2.** (*from English*) a carcass = armado estructural de un objeto.

care gallo (*Chile*) the sun = el sol.

cargadora (*Ven.*) a nanny = niñera; la que cuida los niños.

cargoso (*Ecua.*) a person who insists too much; a bothersome person = muy insistente; molestoso.

caribería (*Ven.*) a clever move; an aggressive move = acción astuta; acción agresiva.

cariduro 1. (*Puerto Rico*) shameless; fresh = desvergonzado. **2.** (*Puerto Rico*) obstinate = obstinado.

caripelao (*Puerto Rico*) fresh; impudent = desvergonzado; fresco; descarado.

carlanca (*Hond.*) a bothersome person; an annoying person = persona fastidiosa; molestosa.

carmelita (*Cuba*) brown = pardo; color café.

carnaval (*Mex.*) a merry-go-round = tíovivo; caballitos.

carne bif (*from English, Dom. Rep., Puerto Rico*) corned beef = carne de vacuno conservada en salmuera.

carnero (*Peru*) a blackleg; a strikebreaker = rompehuelgas; el que sigue al patrón; el que no participa igual que sus compañeros defendiendo los intereses del grupo contra la autoridad.

carpa (*Argen.*) a tent = tienda; toldo.

carpet (*from English*) a carpet; a rug = alfombra.

carpeta 1. (*from English*) a carpet; a rug = alfombra. **2.** (*Ecua., Peru*) an office desk

= escritorio. **3.** (*Peru*) a school desk = pupitre.

carpetear (*Argen.*) to observe = observar.

carraplana (*Ven.*) indigence; misery; poverty = indigencia; miseria; pobreza.

carreta 1. (*Colo.*) a wheelbarrow = carretilla de mano. **2.** (*Colo.*) a series of lies = sarta de mentiras.

carretilla 1. (*Colo.*) a person who speaks too quickly = el que habla muy de prisa. **2.** (*Colo.*) a lie = mentira. **3.** (*Argen., Chile, Uru.*) a wheelbarrow = carro pequeño de mano generalmente de una rueda. **4.** (*Argen., Chile, Uru.*) the jaw; the jawbone = carrillera; mandíbula; quijada.

carreto (*Colo.*) a person who speaks too much without any substance = el que habla mucho pero sin substancia en lo que dice.

carretón (*Hond.*) a bobbin = carrete de hilo.

carretonero (*Chile*) a person with no manners; rude; impolite = el que se comporta sin modales; tosco; grosero.

carricito (*Ven.*) a very young boy = niño de corta edad.

carril (*Chile*) a lie = mentira.

carrilero (*Chile*) a blusterer; a braggart = fanfarrón; el que pretende ser o tener algo que no es; el que inventa historias.

carrizo 1. (*Mex.*) a fishing rod = caña de pescar. **2.** (*Pan.*) a drinking straw = paja; pajita para beber.

carro (*Chile, Colo., Cuba, Dom. Rep., Mex., Pan., Puerto Rico*) a car; an automobile = automóvil.

carrusel (*Chile, Colo., Cuba, Ecua., Peru*) a merry-go-round = tíovivo.

cartabón (*Hond.*) a unit or pattern used as a reference for measurement = unidad o patrón de referencia para medir.

cartapacio (*Mex.*) a folder = carpeta.

cartera dactilar (*Cuba*) a driver's license = permiso para conducir.

cartnetizar; cedular (*Ven.*) to get or give an identification document = otorgar o solicitar un carné o una cédula de identificación.

cartón (*Ven.*) a measurement used in the egg trade that is equal to thirty eggs = medida para la venta y compra de huevos, igual a treinta huevos.

cartucho (*Cuba, Ecua., Pan.*) a paper bag = bolsa de papel.

casabe; casave (*Dom. Rep., Ven.*) a thin omelet prepared with yucca = tortilla muy delgada preparada con yuca.

casaca (*Chile, Ecua., Peru*) a jacket = chaqueta.

casar (*Colo.*) to reach an agreement; to come to terms = concertar; convenir.

casarse por detrás de la iglesia (*Puerto Rico*) to live together without being married = vivir juntos sin estar casados.

casave See **casabe**.

cascarazo (*Puerto Rico*) a strong hit = golpe fuerte.

cascarria (*Chile*) a product of rust = producto de la herrumbre.

casco 1. (*Colo., Mex., Peru*) a segment of a fruit = gajo; segmento de una fruta. **2.** (*Ecua.*) the main building of a farm or a ranch = edificios principales de una granja o una hacienda.

casero 1. (*Chile*) a regular customer; a preferred store attendant = cliente regular; el vendedor preferido de la tienda. **2.** (*Peru, Ven.*) a delivery boy = el que reparte a domicilio. **3.** (*Mex.*) a babysitter = niñera(o); cuidador(a) de niños. **4.** (*Chile, Mex.*) a person who likes to do household chores = persona que gusta de hacer los quehaceres de una casa.

cash-flow (*from English*) cash-flow = movimiento de dinero en efectivo.

casilla (*Chile*) a post-office box = apartado de correos.

casimiro (*Chile*) silly = tonto.

casorio (*Argen.*) a wedding = casamiento.

casqueta (*Mex.*) masturbation = masturbación.

casquillo (*Ven.*) a horseshoe = herradura.

castaña See **cajuela**.

castañazo (*Argen., Chile*) a strong punch = golpe fuerte de puños.

castaño (*Colo.*) a brown color = color café.

castao (*Puerto Rico*) brave = valiente.

castigarse (*Argen.*) to provide pleasures for oneself = proporcionarse placeres.

casualidades (*from English*) casualties = muertos y heridos.

catajana (*Ven.*) a crowd; a large amount of people, objects or issues = multitud; cantidad de personas, cosas o asuntos.

catete (*Chile*) bothersome = molestoso.

catimbao See **cambuto**.

catinga (*Argen., Bol., Para.*) a strong animal or human odor = mal olor humano o animal.

catire (*Colo., Peru, Ven.*) a white person with blond hair and blue eyes = persona blanca de cabellos rubios y ojos verdes.

catirruano (*Ven.*) a person who pretends to be white and blonde = el que aparenta ser blanco y rubio.

catrachos (*Hond.*) a nickname that the Hondurans use for themselves = apodo con que los hondureños se llaman a sí mismos.

catre 1. (*Guat., Hond.*) a camping stool; a folding stool = banqueta desarmable que se usa para acampar. **2.** (*Mex., Ven.*) a camp bed; a folding bed = cama de campaña; cama plegable. **3.** (*Bol., Chile, Peru*) a bedstead = armazón que sostiene la cama.

catrin 1. (*Mex.*) a dandy; a very elegant person = petimetre; persona muy elegante. **2.** (*Mex.*) a person who tries to look rich = persona que hace esfuerzos para aparecer adinerada.

catuche (*Ven.*) a guanabana, a tropical fruit = guanabana, la fruta tropical.

caucho (*Cuba, Peru*) a tire = neumático; goma del automóvil.

caula (*Hond.*) a scheme; a trick; a plot = ardid; engaño.

cauntri 1. (*from English*) a country; the nation state; the fatherland = país. **2.** (*from English*) the countryside; rural areas = el campo.

causeo (*Chile*) a cold snack between meals; a dish prepared with pickles, cheese, and ham = tentempié frío entre las comidas; plato preparado con cebollas escabechadas, quesos y jamón.

cavanga (*Nic.*) nostalgic; nostalgia = nostálgico; nostalgia.

cayanco (*Hond.*) a cataplasm or poultice prepared with hot herbs = cataplasma preparado con hierbas calientes.

cayapa 1. (*Ven.*) those who attack something = los que arremeten contra algo. **2.** (*Ven.*) voluntary work = trabajo voluntario.

cazcorvo; chapín; garetas; patasagrias (*Colo., Ven.*) knock-kneed = patizambo.

cazo (*Mex.*) a bowl = tazón.

cazuela (*Puerto Rico*) a sweet dish made of sweet potatoes, pumpkin, coconut milk, and spices = dulce preparado con batata, calabaza, leche de coco y especias.

cebar (*Argen., Para., Uru.*) **1.** to put boiled water in a **mate** = poner agua caliente en el **mate**. **2.** to serve a **mate** = servir el **mate**.

cebiche; ceviche (*Chile, Ecua., Peru*) a dish prepared with raw shellfish and/or fish marinated with lime or lemon, oil, salt, and black pepper = plato preparado con pescado y/o mariscos crudos, sazonados con lima o limón, aceite, sal y pimienta.

cedular See **cartnetizar**.

célebre 1. (*Colo.*) a pretty woman = mujer bonita. **2.** (*Colo.*) a person who stands out because of his or her intellect and knowledge = el o la que se destaca por su intelecto y conocimientos. **3.** (*Colo.*) a person for whom everything is a joke or is funny = aquel a quien todo se le hace cómico. **4.** (*Mex.*) cute = simpático.

celeque (*Nic.*) a fruit that is not ripe = fruta que no está madura.

cenca (*Peru*) the crest of a bird; a comb on a rooster = cresta de las aves.

centro (*Hond.*) the vest of a suit = chaleco de un traje.

cepa (*Hond.*) several plants that share the same root = conjunto de plantas que comparten una raíz.

cepillado (*Ven.*) sherbet = sorbete; hielo raspado o molido al que se le agregan sabores.

cepillo (*Nic.*) a bootlicker; a sycophant = lameculos; adulador.

cereta (*Puerto Rico*) with one's hair standing on end = con los pelos de punta.

cerilla (*Colo.*) a climbing plant = planta trepadora.

cero (*Mex.*) kindergarten = jardín infantil; kindergarten.

cerrazón (*Argen., Para.*) fog = niebla.

cerrero 1. (*Colo.*) uncouth; coarse = cerril; brusco; tosco. **2.** (*Ven.*) not sweet; bitter = lo que no está o no es dulce; lo que es o está amargo.

cerros (*Chile, Mex., Puerto Rico*) hills = colinas.

cesto (*Bol.*) a measure of coca leaves weighing twenty-five pounds = medida de peso que equivale a veinticinco libras de hojas de coca.

ceviche See **cebiche**.

chabacano (*Mex.*) a variety of apricot = una variedad de albaricoque.

chabelón (*Guat.*) a coward; an effeminate person = cobarde; afeminado.

chacalines (*Nic.*) shrimp = camarón.

chacana (*Ecua.*) a stretcher = camilla.

chacára (*Colo.*) a coin purse = monedero.

chacarita (*Argen.*) a cemetery = cementerio.

chachae; traje (*Pan.*) a dress = vestido.

chachalaquero (*Mex.*) a talkative person = persona parlanchina.

cháchara (*Chile*) an unimportant chat = conversación sin importancia.

chachivaches; chunches; chalchiuite (*Salva.*) knick-knacks; bric-a-brac; small objects of little value = baratijas; objetos pequeños de poco valor.

chachos(as) (*Hond.*) twins = gemelos(as); mellizos(as).

Chaco; El Chaco (*Argen., Bol., Para.*) the geographic area of Paraguay, north of Argentina and east of Bolivia = area geográfica que incluye Paraguay, el norte de Argentina y el este de Bolivia.

chaco (*Ven.*) a sweet potato = batata; patata dulce.

chacolí (*Chile*) a mild, sweet young wine = vino joven, suave y dulce.

chacolín (*Hond.*) shrimp = camarón.

chacón (*Peru*) an Indian chief; a chief = cacique; jefe.

chacota (*Argen., Chile*) fun; a noisy party = diversión; fiesta ruidosa.

chacra 1. (*Bol., Chile, Colo., Ecua., Peru*) a cultivated field; a small farm = campo cultivado; campo pequeño de cultivo. **2.** (*Bol.*) a person who does not have the skills to perform a task = persona sin la habilidad para desarrollar una tarea.

chacuaco (*Salva.*) a cigar butt = colilla de cigarro.

chafa (*Mex.*) cheap; of inferior quality; low-class = lo que es barato y de baja calidad; de mala calidad; de clase baja.

chafirrazo (*Costa Rica*) to cut with a knife or a machete = golpe con un cuchillo o un machete; golpe con un **chafirro**.

chafirro (*Costa Rica*) a big knife; a machete = cuchillo grande; machete.

chagra (*Ecua.*) a peasant = campesino.

chaguala (*Colo.*) an old shoe = zapato viejo.

chagüer (*from English*) a shower = ducha.

chainar (*from English*) to polish; to shine = pulir; dar brillo.

chaito (*Chile*) bye-bye = adiosito.

chajal (*Ecua.*) a household servant; domestic help = empleado(a) doméstico(a).

chala (*Bol.*) a fuel made from corn stalks and used for cooking = tallo del maíz que se usa como combustible para cocinar.

chalaco (*Peru*) a person from the Callao region = originario de la región del Callao.

chalán 1. (*Colo.*) a good horseman = buen jinete. **2.** (*Mex.*) a shoe = zapato.

chalas (*Chile*) sandals = sandalias.

chalcha (*Chile*) a double chin = papada.

chalchazo (*Argen.*) a slap = cachetada; bofetada.

chalchiuite (*Guat., Salva.*) trinkets; knick-knacks = chucherías; baratijas; objetos pequeños.

chalchudo 1. (*Chile*) with big cheeks = con las mejillas abultadas. **2.** (*Chile*) double-chinned = papudo.

¡chale! (*Mex.*) I can't believe it! = ¡No lo puedo creer!

chale (*Mex.*) the penis (vulgar) = pene (vulgar).

chaleca (*Chile*) a sweater = suéter; chaqueta o blusa tejida de lana.

chalequear 1. (*Ven.*) to interrupt a conversation; to stop a narrative = interrumpir o parar una narración. **2.** (*Ven.*) to hinder or ruin a business deal or any other kind of deal = entorpecer o estorbar un negocio u otro asunto.

chalina (*Puerto Rico*) a tie = corbata.

chalona 1. (*Bol.*) dry lamb meat = carne de cordero seca. **2.** (*Peru*) cured mutton = carne de carnero hecha cecina.

chalungo; gurundango; matungo; muchitanga; pendango (*Puerto Rico*) clumsy; feeble = torpe; enclenque; débil.

chalupa 1. (*Colo., Mex., Uru.*) a canoe = canoa. **2.** (*Chile*) a long boat having a bow and stern that are identical = bote largo con los dos extremos iguales. **3.** (*Chile*) an old shoe = zapato viejo. **4.** (*Mex.*) a Mexican **tortilla** with sauce = **tortilla** mexicana con salsa.

chamaca (*Hond., Mex.*) a girl = niña.

chamaco (*Guat., Hond., Mex., Salva.*) a boy = niño.

chamanto (*Chile*) a heavy wool **poncho** used by peasants = **poncho** de lana gruesa usado por los campesinos.

chamaquito(a) (*Guat., Hond., Salva.*) a little boy; a little girl = niño(a) pequeño(a).

chamarra 1. (*Guat., Mex.*) a jacket = chaqueta. **2.** (*Ven.*) a blanket = frazada.

chamarreta; chamerrata (*Ven.*) (N.E. poncho; a blanket with a hole in the center for the head that is used as a cape) = **poncho**.

chamarro (*Hond.*) an inferior-quality piece of clothing = prenda de vestir tosca y de baja categoría.

chamba 1. (*Colo.*) a ditch = zanja. **2.** (*Ven.*) piecework = trabajo a destajo. **3.** (*Mex., Puerto Rico*) a job (informal) = trabajo (informal).

chambe 1. (*Dom. Rep.*) a thick mouth; thick lips = boca o labios gruesos. **2.** See **bemba**.

chambelona; colombina (*Cuba*) a lollipop = pirulín; dulce para chupar adherido a un palo paqueño.

chamberí (*Peru*) an ostentatious person = persona ostentosa.

chamberinada (*Peru*) ostentation; luxury = ostentación; lujo.

chambiar (*Colo.*) to work = trabajar.

chambón (*Puerto Rico*) a big shoe = zapatón; zapato grande.

chamborote (*Guat.*) with a big nose = narigón(a); narigudo(a).

chambrana See **bullaranga**.

chamerrata See **chamarreta**.

chamo (*Ven.*) a young man; a teenager = muchacho; adolescente.

chamorro (*Mex.*) the calf of the leg = pantorrilla.

champiñones (*Chile, Cuba, Mex., Peru*) mushrooms = hongos; setas.

champion (*from English*) a champion = campeón(a).

championes (*Uru.*) sneakers = zapatos deportivos de goma.

champions (*from English, Puerto Rico*) sneakers = calzado deportivo.

champola (*Dom. Rep.*) a drink of **guanabana** = refresco de **guanabana**.

champurreado (*Mex.*) chocolate mixed with **atole** = chocolate mezclado con **atole**.

champurriado (*Chile*) a mixture of very different things = una mezcla de cosas muy diferentes.

champús (*Colo.*) a sweet drink made with corn, lemon leaf, sugar, and other ingredients = bebida de maíz, hojas de limonero, azúcar y otros ingredientes.

chamuchina 1. (*Argen.*) a mob = populacho. **2.** (*Chile*) a disorder; a brawl = desorden; algarabía; jaleo.

chamullar (*Argen., Chile*) a lot of talk to impose one's viewpoint = hablar mucho para imponer el propio punto de vista.

chanca (*Chile*) a beating = tunda; golpiza.

chancaca 1. (*Argen.*) brown sugar honey = miel de azúcar sin refinar. **2.** (*Argen., Bol., Chile*) a syrup cake = trozos de azúcar sin refinar. **3.** (*Chile*) an easy thing = cosa fácil.

chancacazo (*Chile*) a big crash; a big blow; a big hit = un gran choque; un gran golpe.

chancaco 1. (*Ecua.*) blond = rubio. **2.** (*Peru*) a blond, green-eyed person = persona rubia de ojos verdes.

chancao (*Argen., Chile*) ground corn = maíz machacado.

chancar 1. (*Chile*) to do something halfway = ejecutar algo a medias. **2.** (*Chile*) to grind = moler.

chanchada (*Argen., Chile*) a dirty or disgusting trick = cochinada; mala jugada.

chancharreta (*Peru*) an old shoe = zapato muy usado y viejo.

chanchira(o) (*Colo.*) rags = andrajos; harapos.

chancho 1. (*Argen., Bol., Chile, Cuba, Ecua., Peru, Uru.*) a pig = cerdo; puerco. **2.**

(*Argen., Bol., Chile, Cuba, Ecua., Peru, Uru.*) a dirty person; a person without manners = persona sucia; persona sin modales. **3.** (*Chile*) a belch = eructo. **4.** (*Chile*) a domino piece with the same value on both sides = pieza del dominó con el mismo valor en ambos lados.

chanchullo (*Argen., Chile*) a crooked or illegal deal = asunto poco claro; asunto ilegal.

chanclas 1. (*Mex.*) slippers = pantuflas. **2.** (*Colo.*) sandals = sandalias.

chancleo (*Mex.*) a party = fiesta.

chancleta 1. (*Chile*) an old and battered shoe = zapato viejo y muy usado. **2.** (*Ven.*) a vehicle's accelerator = acelerador de un vehículo. **3.** (*Chile, Dom. Rep.*) a newborn baby girl = niña recién nacida.

chancletas (*Argen., Cuba, Dom. Rep., Pan., Peru*) slippers = pantuflas.

chancletero (*Dom. Rep.*) a person of very low social status = persona de baja categoría social.

chancuco (*Colo.*) the smuggling of alcoholic drinks and/or tobacco = contrabando de bebidas alcohólicas y/o tabaco.

chancuquear (*Colo.*) to smuggle = contrabandear.

chane (*Hond.*) an old hand; a person who knows a place well = baqueano; el que conoce bien el lugar.

chaneque 1. (*Guat.*) jovial; good humored = hombre jovial. **2.** (*Salva.*) an experienced guide; an old hand = guía que tiene experiencia del lugar.

chanfaina 1. (*Colo.*) a job with a good salary and little work that is obtained through political or social influences = empleo con buen sueldo y poco trabajo conseguido por medio de influencias. **2.** (*Argen., Chile*) a dish prepared with animal lungs = plato preparado con los pulmones de animal.

chanfle (*Argen., Chile, Dom. Rep., Uru.*) a hit or blow in a diagonal direction = golpe oblicuo; golpe torcido.

changa (*Mex.*) a little girl who amuses people = niña pequeña que entretiene a la gente.

changa(o); chuga; cuervo (*Mex.*) person of African origin; a black person (derogatory) = persona de origen africano de la raza negra (peyorativo).

changador (*Argen.*) a man who does odd jobs = el que realiza trabajos pequeños de breve duración.

changar (*Argen., Bol., Para.*) to make a living from odd jobs = ganarse la vida haciendo trabajos de poca monta.

changarro (*Mex.*) a grocery store = tienda de comestibles.

changle (*Mex.*) useless = inútil.

chango 1. (*Argen.*) a nickname for a young man = apodo para un adolescente. **2.** (*Puerto Rico*) a joker = bromista.

changuear 1. (*Colo.*) to joke = chancear; bromear. **2.** (*Mex.*) to imitate = imitar.

changuería (*Dom. Rep.*) a joke = broma.

chanse (*from English*) a chance = oportunidad.

chanta; chantún (*Argen., Uru.*) a person with pretentions of false attributes, power or abilities = el que presume gozar de cualidades, capacidades o poder fingidos.

chantada (*Argen.*) foolishness; nonsense = conjunto de tonterías.

chantar 1. (*Argen.*) to put = poner. **2.** (*Argen.*) to blow = golpear. **3.** (*Chile*) to stop suddenly = parar o detenerse bruscamente. **4.** (*Chile*) to put or leave someone in a place against his or her will = poner a alguien en un sitio contra su voluntad. **5.** (*Chile*) to miss a date = faltar a una cita. **6.** (*Colo.*) to jilt a boyfriend or girlfriend = plantar; abandonar al novio(a).

chante (*Mex.*) a house; a home = la casa; el hogar.

chantún See **chanta**.

chao (*Chile*) good-bye = adiós.

chapa 1. (*Bol., Chile, Guat., Hond., Peru, Salva.*) a lock = cerradura. **2.** (*Ecua.*) the police = policía. **3.** (*Ven.*) a joke = broma.

4. (*Mex.*) a pork chop = chuleta de cerdo. **5.** (*Puerto Rico*) the metallic cap from a bottle = tapa metálica de una botella.

chapacaca (*Ecua.*) a person who abuses his or her official status to get personal benefits = el que abusa de su autoridad para beneficio propio.

chapapote (*Cuba, Mex.*) asphalt = asfalto.

chapar 1. (*Argen.*) to get; to seize (vulgar) = apoderarse de algo; tomar; agarrar. **2.** (*Argen.*) to fondle (vulgar) = manosear sexualmente (vulgar). **3.** (*Ecua.*) to look; to watch; to lie in wait for = mirar; acechar.

chaparro 1. (*Ven.*) a thin and flexible stick used as a whip = rama delgada y flexible que se usa para azotar. **2.** (*Ven.*) a hit with that stick = golpe dado con esa rama. **3.** (*Mex.*) a short person = persona de baja estatura. **4.** (*Mex.*) a short tree that grows in the desert = árbol en el desierto.

chapear (*Salva.*) to cut with a machete = cortar con el machete.

chapeta 1. (*Mex.*) earrings = pendientes; zarcillos. **2.** (*Mex.*) diapers = pañales.

chapetear 1. (*Mex.*) to color the cheeks = colorear las mejillas. **2.** (*Mex.*) to have sex (vulgar) = realizar el acto sexual (vulgar).

chapetón (*Colo.*) a nickname for a Spaniard = apodo para un español.

chapín 1. (*Guat.*) a native of Guatemala City = el que es originario de Ciudad de Guatemala. **2.** (*Colo.*) knock-kneed = patizambo.

chapote (*Mex.*) an oak tree = roble.

chapucero (*Mex.*) a person who cheats = el que hace trampas.

chapul (*Mex.*) a child = niño o niña.

chapulín (*Guat., Hond., Mex., Salva.*) a grasshopper = saltamontes.

chapuzar (*Mex.*) to trick; to fake = engañar; estafar.

chaquetear 1. (*Mex.*) to betray = traicionar. **2.** (*Mex.*) to masturbate = masturbarse.

chaquiñán (*Ecua.*) a short cut = atajo; sendero más corto.

chaquira (*Hond.*) a sore = llaga.

charada 1. (*Guat.*) stuff; any object whose name is unknown or is not recalled = cuestión; cosa de la cual no se sabe o no se le recuerda el nombre. **2.** (*Guat.*) stupidity = tontería.

charanga; charranga (*Colo.*) a family party; a family dance = baile familiar.

charango (*Argen., Bol., Chile, Ecua., Peru*) a small, stringed instrument made from an armadillo shell = instrumento musical de cuerdas hecho con la caparazón de un armadillo.

charbasca (*Nic.*) garbage = basura.

charcheta (*Chile*) the hanging skin on a fat person; a roll of fat = piel que cuelga en un gordo; rollo de gordura.

charchiar (*from English*) to charge = cargar a la cuenta.

charchina (*Mex.*) an old car = automóvil viejo.

charcón (*Argen.*) thin; skinny = delgado; flaco.

charlón (*Ecua.*) a chatterbox; a talkative person = charlatán; parlanchín.

charola 1. (*Mex.*) a tray = azafate; bandeja. **2.** (*Mex.*) a badge = insignia; chapa de identificación.

charonga (*Puerto Rico*) a family dance or party = baile o fiesta familiar.

charquear (*Chile*) to stab; to knife several times = dar muchas cuchilladas.

charqui (*Argen., Bol., Chile, Peru, Uru.*) jerked meat; dried meat = carne seca.

charquicán (*Argen., Chile*) a traditional dish made with dry meat, pumpkin, potatoes, and other vegetables = plato tradicional a base de carne seca, calabaza, patatas y otras verduras.

charra (*Hond.*) a wide hat = sombrero de alas anchas.

charranga 1. (*Guat.*) a guitar = guitarra. **2.** (*Cuba*) a family party; a family dance = fiesta o baile familiar.

charrasquear 1. (*Ecua., Pan., Ven.*) to strum any stringed instrument = rasguear cualquier instrumento de cuerdas. **2.** (*Mex.*) to knife; to stab = herir con arma blanca; apuñalar.

charretada; charreteada; churretada (*Chile*) diarrhea (vulgar) = diarrea (vulgar).

charreteada See **charretada**.

charro 1. (*Mex.*) a Mexican cowboy = vaquero mexicano. **2.** (*Colo.*) funny = gracioso.

charrúa (*Uru.*) a native of Uruguay = nativo del Uruguay.

chárter (*from English*) charter = (RAE) viajes alquilados; viaje especial fuera del itinerario; viajes o vuelos no sujetos a horarios ni a programas regulares.

chasca (*Chile*) matted hair = cabello enmarañado.

chasco 1. (*Chile*) a disappointment; a failure = desengaño; fracaso. **2.** (*Chile*) an embarrassment = vergüenza.

chascón (*Chile*) disheveled hair = enmarañado; con el pelo enredado.

chasqui (*Uru.*) a courier = mensajero.

chasquilla (*Chile*) bangs; fringe = flequillo.

chata (*Puerto Rico*) an endearing term for a woman = forma cariñosa para llamar a una mujer.

chatino; chicharritas; mariquitas (*Cuba*) fried green plantain = plátano verde frito.

chau (*Peru*) bye-bye = hasta luego; adiosito.

chauchas (*Argen.*) green beans; string beans = habichuelas verdes.

chauchera (*Chile, Ecua., Peru*) a purse; a pocketbook = portamonedas; bolsa pequeña donde las mujeres transportan el dinero.

chauchón (*Argen.*) silly = tonto.

chaval 1. (*Nic.*) a boy = niño. **2.** See **chavala**.

chavala; chaval (*Mex.*) a sweetheart; a girlfriend; a boyfriend = novia; novio.

chavalo (*Nic.*) a baby = niño pequeño.

chavar; fuñir; jeringar (*Puerto Rico*) to bother; to annoy = molestar; fastidiar.

chavarse (*Puerto Rico*) to get hurt = sufrir daño.

chavo 1. (*Mex.*) a boy = niño. **2.** (*Puerto Rico*) a penny = un centavo.

chavón; jorobón 1. (*Puerto Rico*) troublesome = majadero; fastidioso; molestoso. **2.** (*Argen.*) a man = hombre.

chavona (*Argen.*) a woman = mujer.

chavos (*Puerto Rico*) money = dinero.

chayotada (*Guat.*) a foolish remark; nonsense = desatino; tontería.

chayote 1. (*Hond.*) a coward = cobarde. **2.** (*Hond.*) a type of pumpkin = un tipo de calabaza. **3.** (*Guat.*) foolish; silly = necio; tonto.

che 1. (*Argen.*) you (pronoun) = tú (pronombre). **2.** (*Bol., Chile, Ecua., Peru*) a nickname for Argentines = apodo para los argentinos.

cheche; chenche (*Puerto Rico*) a wiseguy = sabihondo; el que se las sabe todas.

chécheres; chunches (*Colo., Nic.*) knick-knacks = baratijas; cachivaches.

cheje (*Hond., Salva.*) a link in a chain = eslabón de una cadena.

chela See **bironga**.

chele 1. (*Guat., Hond., Salva.*) a white or blond person = una persona blanca o rubia. **2.** (*Dom. Rep.*) the smallest unit of money; a penny = centavo; la unidad más pequeña de moneda.

chelv (*from English*) a shelf; a bookcase = anaquel; estantería.

chenche See **cheche**.

chepa (*Colo.*) good luck = buena suerte.

chepe (*Mex.*) a hypocrite = hipócrita.

chepudo (*Colo.*) with good luck = con buena suerte.

chequear 1. (*from English*) to check = (RAE) revisar; examinar; cotejar; puntear; verificar. **2.** (*from English*) to shake = batir.

chequeo (*from English*) to check up; to examine = revision; cotejo; verificación; (RAE) reconocimiento médico general al que se somete una persona.

cherbet (*from English*) sherbet = sorbete.

chercha 1. (*Hond.*) joking; a hullabaloo = chacota; algarabía; barullo. **2.** (*Ven.*) jeering = burla. **3.** (*Ven.*) a noisy conversation = conversación bulliciosa.

cherche (*Hond.*) pale = pálido.

chereques; chunches (*Nic.*) things; objects; stuff = cosas; objetos; cuestiones.

cherife (*from English*) a sheriff = alguacil.

cherry (*from English*) a cherry = cereza.

cheto (*Argen.*) dressed in fine-quality clothes with a specific style = el que viste de ropa de gran calidad en un estilo específico.

cheuto (*Chile*) a person with a twisted or deformed lip; anything that is twisted, deformed or out of place = persona con el labio partido o deformado; cualquier cosa que está deformada, torcida o desviada de su lugar.

chévere (*Colo., Peru, Puerto Rico, Ven.*) good; very good; beautiful; nice; excellent; elegant; correct; appropriate = bueno; muy bueno; bonito; muy bonito; agradable; lo que luce muy bien; elegante; correcto; apropiado.

chi (*Mex.*) urine = urina.

chiba 1. (*Colo.*) a backpack = mochila. **2.** (*Colo.*) the news = noticias.

chicaneo (*Mex.*) typical **chicano** behavior = conducta típica del **chicano**.

chicanglo 1. (*Mex.*) a **chicano** who behaves as a gringo (derogatory) = un **chicano** que se comporta como un anglo. **2.** (*Mex.*) an Anglo who shows solidarity with **chicano** interests = anglo que simpatiza con la causa **chicana**.

chicanismo (*Mex.*) the ideology of the **chicano** culture = ideología de la cultura **chicana**.

chicano(a) 1. (*Mex.*) a United States citizen of Mexican origin who can be traced to several generations in the United States = ciudadano(a) estadounidense de origen mexicano que se remonta a varias generaciones de residencia en los Estados Unidos. **2.** (*Mex.*) the culture of the ethnic minority group of American citizens of Mexican origin = cultura del grupo étnico minoritario constituido por los ciudadanos estadounidenses de origen mexicano.

chicato 1. (*Argen.*) a short-sighted person = miope. **2.** (*Argen.*) unable to understand what is going on = el que no se da cuenta de lo que sucede a su alrededor.

chicha 1. (*Argen., Bol., Colo., Ecua., Hond., Ven.*) an alcoholic beverage made from the fermentation of diverse fruits or vegetables = bebida alcohólica que resulta de la fermentación de diversas frutas o vegetales. **2.** (*Chile*) an alcoholic beverage made from fermented grape juice = bebida alcohólica hecha de jugo de uva fermentada. **3.** (*Bol., Guat., Hond., Nic., Peru, Salva., Ven.*) an alcoholic drink made from fermented corn = bebida alcohólica hecha de maíz fermentado. **4.** (*Puerto Rico*) the vagina (vulgar) = vagina (vulgar).

chichar 1. (*Colo.*) to protest; to grumble; to complain = protestar; refunfuñar; quejarse. **2.** (*Dom. Rep., Puerto Rico*) to have sex (vulgar) = tener sexo (vulgar).

chícharo (*Dom. Rep., Mex., Puerto Rico*) peas = guisantes.

chicharra 1. (*Guat., Hond., Mex., Salva.*) a piece of fried pork or chicken = trozo de cerdo o pollo frito. **2.** (*Chile, Cuba*) a grasshopper = saltamontes. **3.** (*Chile*) a harsh-sounding musical instrument = instrumento musical que suena discordante. **4.** (*Colo.*) a portable radio = radio portátil.

chicharritas See **chatino**.

chicharrón (*Cuba, Guat., Hond., Mex., Salva.*) a piece of fried pork skin = trozo de la piel de cerdo frita.

chicharrones See **guita**.

chicharrones; chirola; guita; mosca (*Uru.*) money (informal) = dinero (informal).

chiche 1. (*Chile, Peru, Uru.*) a precious or delicate object = objeto delicado o fino. **2.** (*Chile, Peru, Uru.*) a well-dressed, elegant or nice-looking person = persona elegante, bien vestida o de aspecto agradable. **3.** (*Chile, Peru, Uru.*) delightful = cosa agradable o deliciosa. **4.** (*Cuba, Guat., Hond., Salva.*) a woman's breast (vulgar); a teat = pechos femeninos (vulgar); teta. **5.** (*Salva.*) something that is very easy = lo que es muy fácil.

chichí 1. (*Colo.*) piss = orina. **2.** (*Colo.*) a child's penis (informal) = pene de niño (informal). **3.** (*Dom. Rep., Pan., Salva.*) a baby = bebé.

chichi 1. (*Mex.*) a woman's breast (vulgar); a teat = pecho de mujer (vulgar); teta. **2.** (*Mex.*) a nanny; a nursemaid = nodriza.

chichigua (*Dom. Rep.*) a kite = cometa.

chichimeco 1. (*Mex.*) a bad man = hombre ruin. **2.** (*Mex.*) a man with an ugly body = hombre de mala figura. **3.** (*Mex.*) a small man = hombre pequeño.

chicho (*Colo.*) the very end of a marijuana cigarette = lo último que queda en un cigarrillo de marihuana.

chichos; mangoso (*Ecua.*) body fat = gorduras del cuerpo.

chicle 1. (*Ven.*) an annoying person = persona fastidiosa. **2.** (*Mex.*) asphalt = asfalto. **3.** (*Mex.*) an uninvited person = persona no invitada.

chico (*Peru*) a boy; a young person = niño; muchacho.

chicoco(a) (*Chile*) a short person (informal) = persona de poca estatura (informal).

chicote 1. (*Argen.*) a belt = correa o cinturón. **2.** (*Colo.*) a cigar butt = restos de un cigarro puro fumado. **3.** (*Colo.*) a short cigar or cigarette of inferior quality = cigarro o cigarrillo corto, barato y de baja calidad.

chicotear 1. (*Argen., Bol., Chile, Ecua., Peru*) to lash; to whip = dar de latigazos; dar cintarazos. **2.** (*Colo.*) to exhale smoke when smoking = exhalar el humo cuando se fuma.

chifles 1. (*Ecua., Peru*) fried green plantain chips = medallones de plátano verde frito. **2.** (*Puerto Rico*) horns = cuernos.

chifleta (*Hond.*) a gibe; a jeer; a satiric joke = pulla; burla; broma satírica; mofa.

chiflis (*Colo.*) daft = chiflado; medio loco.

chiforobe (*Puerto Rico*) a wardrobe (informal) = armario para guardar ropa (informal).

chifurnia (*Salva.*) an isolated place; a hidden place = lugar aislado; lugar escondido.

chigüin (*Hond., Nic.*) a small boy = muchacho pequeño.

¡chihuahua!; ¡ay chihuahua! (*Mex.*) an interjection whose meaning ranges from very good to very bad according to the emphasis in the pronunciation = interjección cuyo significado puede ir desde muy bueno hasta muy malo de acuerdo a la entonación que se use al pronunciarla.

chilango (*Mex.*) a native of Mexico City = nativo u originario de Ciudad de México.

chilaquila (*Costa Rica, Guat.*) a corn **tortilla** filled with cheese, herbs, and hot peppers = **tortilla** de maíz con relleno de queso, hierbas y pimientos picantes.

chile 1. (*Guat., Hond., Mex., Salva.*) a hot pepper; a chili = pimiento picante; ají. **2.** (*Guat.*) a lie; a story = mentira; cuento. **3.** (*Mex.*) the penis = pene.

chile verde (*Guat., Hond., Mex., Salva.*) a green hot pepper = picante verde; ají verde; pimiento verde picante.

chilillo (*Guat., Nic.*) a whip = látigo.

chilingo (*Colo.*) a small piece of something = pedazo pequeño de algo.

chilito (*Ecua.*) a kite = cometa.

chillar (*Argen.*) to complain = quejar.

chillarse (*Mex.*) to be offended = ofenderse; sentirse ofendido.

chillería (*Puerto Rico*) a group of people who misbehave = grupo de gente que muestra mala conducta.

chillo 1. (*Puerto Rico*) Be quiet! = quédate en silencio; cállate. **2.** (*Puerto Rico*) a love affair outside of marriage or engagement

= relación amorosa fuera del matrimonio o a espaldas del noviazgo.

chilote 1. (*Nic.*) baby corn = maíz tierno. **2.** (*Chile*) an inhabitant of the Chiloé island in the South region of Chile = habitante de la isla de Chiloé en la región sur de Chile.

chiltoma (*Nic.*) a green hot pepper = picante; ají verde.

chimba 1. (*Colo., Ecua.*) a small braid = trenza pequeña de pelo. **2.** (*Colo.*) the vagina (vulgar) = vagina (vulgar). **3.** (*Peru*) the ford of a river = vado; parte baja de un río.

chimbear (*Colo.*) to adulterate; to forge = adulterar; falsificar.

chimbero 1. (*Colo.*) a lecherous man (vulgar) = hombre lujurioso (vulgar). **2.** (*Colo.*) a womanizer (vulgar) = mujeriego (vulgar).

chimbo 1. (*Colo.*) fake; fraudulent = falso; fraudulento. **2.** (*Colo.*) the penis (vulgar) = pene (vulgar). **3.** (*Ven.*) a small business; an unimportant issue = negocio o asunto de poco valor. **4.** (*Ven.*) an inferior-quality object = objeto de mala calidad.

chimentar (*Argen.*) to gossip = llevar chismes.

chimentos (*Argen.*) gossip = chismes.

china 1. (*Argen.*) a peasant woman = mujer del campo. **2.** (*Colo.*) an elegant young lady = mujer joven elegante. **3.** (*Colo.*) a spinning top = juguete infantil; trompo o peonza. **4.** (*Chile, Ecua., Peru*) a maid (derogatory) = sirvienta doméstica (peyorativo). **5.** (*Nic.*) a nanny = niñera; la que cuida a un niño. **6.** (*Puerto Rico*) an orange = naranja. **7.** (*Uru.*) a mistress; a concubine = amante; concubina.

chinazo (*Colo.*) a very good-looking person = persona muy bien parecida.

chincharro (*Colo.*) dice = dado.

chinche 1. (*Argen.*) a venereal disease = enfermedad venérea. **2.** (*Colo.*) a bothersome boy or baby = niño molestoso.

chinchería; chinchero (*Mex.*) a filthy and/or messy place = lugar sucio y/o desordenado.

chinchero See **chinchería**.

chinchín 1. (*Ven.*) drizzle = llovizna; lluvia persistente y de gotas muy pequeñas. **2.** (*Ven.*) annoying repetition = situación repetitiva que se convierte en molestia. **3.** (*Ven.*) a small amount of money = pequeña cantidad de dinero. **4.** (*Dom. Rep., Puerto Rico*) a small piece = un pedacito. **5.** (*Dom. Rep., Puerto Rico*) a little bit = un poquito.

chinchinear (*Hond.*) to caress; to fondle = acariciar; mimar.

chinchorro 1. (*Ven.*) a type of hammock = un tipo de hamaca. **2.** (*Dom. Rep., Puerto Rico*) a small shop or store in a poor community = taller o tienda pequeña en una comunidad pobre.

chinchudo (*Argen.*) an irritable person = persona irritable.

chinchulines (*Argen.*) beef tripe served in the Argentine **parrillada** = intestinos delgados del vacuno que son parte de la **parrillada** argentina.

chinelas 1. (*Cuba, Puerto Rico*) slippers = pantuflas; chancletas. **2.** See **chancletas**.

chinga 1. (*Costa Rica*) a cigarette butt = colilla de cigarrillo. **2.** (*Costa Rica*) a worn-out **machete** = **machete** muy gastado. **3.** (*Hond.*) a gibe; a joke; a cutting remark = burla; chunga; pulla.

chingadazo See **chingazo**.

chingadera 1. (*Mex.*) an annoyance = molestia. **2.** (*Mex.*) an evil act = acción maliciosa; acto que produce daño. **3.** (*Mex.*) a trifle; a thing of no importance = insignificante; cosa sin importancia.

chingana (*Argen.*) a dance party with people of low social status = fiesta bailable de gente de baja condición social.

chingar 1. (*Argen., Chile, Uru.*) to fail or miss in assembling or hitting something; to fall through = fallar en armar o alcanzar algo; fracasar. **2.** (*Ecua., Mex., Salva.*) to bother; to annoy = molestar. **3.** (*Hond.*) to joke = bromear. **4.** (*Mex.*) to have sex (vulgar) = realizar el acto sexual (vulgar). **5.** (*Mex.*) to cheat = trampear; estafar; engañar. **6.** (*Mex.*) to avenge = vengarse;

tomar venganza. **7.** (*Mex.*) to defeat = derrotar.

chingazo; chingadazo (*Mex.*) a blow with the fist or a heavy object = golpe de puño o con un objeto pesado.

chingo 1. (*Ven.*) a small- or flat-nosed person = chato; de la nariz pequeña o aplastada. **2.** (*Nic.*) short = corto.

chingón 1. (*Mex.*) good = bueno. **2.** (*Mex.*) manly; a macho man = hombre muy viril; hombre muy macho. **3.** (*Puerto Rico*) a sexually active man with several partners (vulgar) = el que tiene sexo con varias mujeres (vulgar).

chingona (*Puerto Rico*) a sexually active woman with several partners (vulgar) = la que tiene sexo con varios (vulgar).

chingue (*Nic.*) a drink made with rice and cacao = refresco hecho con masa de arroz y cacao.

chinguear (*Costa Rica*) to bother; to annoy = molestar; fastidiar.

chinguero (*Costa Rica*) a gambling den manager = el que administra un garito.

chinguito 1. (*Dom. Rep.*) a small piece = pedacito. **2.** (*Dom. Rep.*) a crumb = migaja.

chinita (*Ven.*) a sarcastic reference to someone or something = alusión sarcástica a algo o a alguien.

chino(a) 1. (*Colo.*) a son; a daughter; a girl; a boy = hijo(a); muchacha(o) **2.** (*Dom. Rep.*) a nickname for anyone who looks like an Asian = apodo para cualquiera que tenga rasgos asiáticos. **3.** (*Mex.*) a person with curly hair = persona de pelo ensortijado. **4.** (*Colo.*) a poor or homeless child = niño(a) pobre o desamparado(a). **5.** (*Colo.*) a servant = sirviente(a).

chinola (*Ecua.*) (N.E. tropical fruit) = parcha; granadilla; fruta tropical.

chinzado(a) (*Mex.*) ruined; to produce, to give or to receive something bad or that doesn't work = fallido; producir, dar o recibir algo malo o que no funciona.

chip (*from English*) a computer chip = (RAE) pequeño circuito integrado que realiza numerosas funciones electrónicas.

chipe (*Guat.*) very attached to someone else = muy apegado(a) a otra persona.

chipe libre (*Chile*) you are free to choose = no hay restricciones.

chipiar 1. (*Chile*) to pay; to put up the money = pagar; poner dinero. **2.** (*Guat.*) to be fed up; to pester = molestar hasta cansar; importunar.

chipines (*Guat.*) a nickname that the Guatemalans use for themselves = apodo que los guatemaltecos se dan a sí mismos.

chipola (*Ven.*) a variety of Venezuelan folk music = un tipo de música folclórica venezolana.

chipón(a) (*Mex.*) a spoiled child = niño(a) malcriado(a).

chipote (*Nic.*) intelligence = inteligencia.

chiquear (*Hond.*) to swing one's hips = contonear; contonearse al andar.

chiquije (*Nic.*) the stinking odor of rotten meat = mal olor de la carne descompuesta.

chiquilín (*Uru.*) a boy = niño.

chira 1. (*Guat., Salva.*) a sore; a festering wound on the surface of the skin = llaga; úlcera; herida en la piel. **2.** (*Mex.*) a cheater = tramposo; engañoso.

chirajos; chiros (*Colo.*) shreds; rags = hilachas; jirones de vestimenta.

chirapa 1. (*Bol.*) old and worn clothes = ropa vieja y muy usada. **2.** (*Peru*) rain when it is sunny = lluvia con sol.

chiras 1. (*Hond., Salva.*) a balloon = globo. **2.** (*Colo.*) shreds; rags = hilachas; jirones de vestimenta.

chirigua (*Ven.*) a water container = vasija para cargar agua.

chirimbolo (*Dom. Rep.*) a vessel; a bowl = vasija; utensilio para líquidos.

chirimoya 1. (*Colo.*) the head (informal) = cabeza (informal). **2.** (*Chile, Colo., Ecua., Peru, Ven.*) a custard apple, the fruit = fruta aromática que tiene la cáscara verde, la pulpa blanca y semillas negras.

chiringa (*Mex., Puerto Rico*) a kite = cometa.

chiringo (*Hond.*) rags; tatters = harapos; andrajos.

chirinola 1. (*Colo.*) a brawl; a fight = alboroto; pendencia; reyerta. **2.** (*Mex.*) a gossiper = chismoso.

chiripa 1. (*Ven.*) a small cockroach = cucaracha pequeña. **2.** (*Chile, Nic.*) by chance = por casualidad. **3.** (*Puerto Rico*) a small job; an unimportant job = trabajo pequeño; trabajo de poca importancia.

chiririco (*Dom. Rep.*) restless = inquieto; el que no se está tranquilo.

chirla (*Ecua.*) a hit with the finger; a soft blow with the finger tip = golpe con la punta de los dedos; palmada suave con la palma de los dedos.

chirlito (*Chile*) a blow with the tips of two fingers = golpe con la palma de dos dedos.

chirlo (*Colo.*) a slap = bofetada.

chirmol (*Guat.*) a dish of onions, tomatoes, and meat = plato preparado con cebollas, tomates y carne.

chirola 1. (*Argen., Mex., Puerto Rico, Uru.*) a jail = cárcel. **2.** (*Argen., Uru.*) money (informal) = dinero (informal). **3.** (*Argen., Uru.*) change (money) = cambio (dinero).

chirona 1. (*Argen., Mex., Uru.*) a jail = cárcel. **2.** (*Argen., Uru.*) money (informal) = dinero (informal). **3.** (*Argen., Uru.*) change (money) = cambio (dinero).

chiros See **chirajos**.

chirotada (*Ecua.*) stupidity; foolishness = necedad; tontería.

chirote 1. (*Costa Rica*) big; beautiful = grande; hermoso. **2.** (*Costa Rica*) a rascal = niño travieso. **3.** (*Peru*) dumb; silly = torpe; tonto; bobo.

chirre (*Nic.*) watered down = aguado.

chirringo; chirriquitico; chirriquitín (*Colo.*) a very small boy = niño muy pequeño.

chirriquitico See **chirringo**.

chirriquitín See **chirringo**.

ichis! (*Guat.*) ugh! (interjection) = ipuf! (interjección)

chischí; chispito (*Puerto Rico*) a little bit = un poquito.

chispito See **chischí**.

chistes (*Ecua., Peru*) comics = historietas.

chitrulo (*Argen.*) silly; stupid = tonto.

chiva 1. (*Chile*) a lie; a deceit = mentira; embuste. **2.** (*Colo.*) interesting news = noticias novedosas. **3.** (*Ven.*) a beard = barba. **4.** (*Ven.*) a piece of clothing lent or given to someone = prenda de vestir que se regala o se presta. **5.** (*Ven.*) any used object = cualquier prenda u objeto usado. **6.** (*Ven.*) a trick = trampa; engaño. **7.** (*Dom. Rep.*) a coquettish woman = mujer coqueta. **8.** (*Dom. Rep.*) a prostitute = prostituta. **9.** (*Colo., Pan.*) a bus = autobús. **10.** (*Dom. Rep., Puerto Rico*) a goatee = perilla; barba que cubre sólo el mentón. **11.** (*Puerto Rico*) a completed domino game with a zero score for the loser = juego de dominó que termina con un puntaje de cero para el perdedor. **12.** (*Mex.*) handsome; beautiful = bien parecida; bella. **13.** (*Mex.*) anything for which the name is unknown = cualquier cosa o asunto al que se le desconoce el nombre. **14.** (*Mex.*) a ten-dollar bill = billete de diez dólares.

chivar See **chivatear**.

chivarse (*Argen.*) to get upset; to get angry = molestarse; enojarse.

chivas (*Mex.*) stuff; objects of little value = cosas; objetos de poco valor.

chivatear; chivar; sapear (*Colo.*) to denounce; to betray; to report to the authorities = denunciar; delatar; traicionar; informar a las autoridades.

chivato(a) (*Colo., Cuba*) a gossipmonger; a whistleblower; an informer; a squealer = chismoso(a); soplón(a).

chivear (*Dom. Rep.*) to cheat on an exam = copiar en un examen.

chivera (*Colo.*) a goatee = perilla; pera de la barba.

chivería (*Puerto Rico*) the practice of prostitution = práctica de la prostitución.

chivero (*Ven.*) a dealer of second-hand items = el que vende objetos usados.

¡chivísima! (*Nic.*) Look out! = ¡cuidado!.

chivita; busito (*Pan.*) a small bus = autobús pequeño.

chivo **1.** (*Colo.*) a rage; a tantrum = berrinche; rabieta. **2.** (*Colo.*) a man who is easily infatuated with women = hombre enamoradizo. **3.** (*Dom. Rep.*) a crib note; a small note used to cheat on an exam = chuleta; papelito para copiar en un examen. **4.** (*Mex.*) handsome; beautiful = buenmozo; bello. **5.** (*Mex.*) anything for which the name is unknown = cualquier cosa o asunto al que se le desconoce el nombre. **6.** (*Mex.*) a ten-dollar bill = billete de diez dólares.

¡icho! (*Nic.*) Shut up! = ¡cállate!

choapino (*Chile*) a handmade rug = alfombra tejida a mano.

choc **1.** (*from English*) chalk = tiza. **2.** (*from English*) an automobile choke = ahogador, obturador en el carburador del automóvil. **3.** (*from English*) a shock = choque; sacudida; golpe; sobresalto.

choca **1.** (*Guat.*) a cookie = galleta. **2.** (*Guat.*) a blind female = ciega. **3.** (*Chile*) milk (informal) = leche (informal).

chocante (*Argen., Bol., Chile, Colo., Peru, Ven.*) impertinent; annoying; unpleasant = impertinente; molesto; desagradable.

chocha (*Colo., Dom. Rep., Puerto Rico*) the vagina (vulgar) = vagina (vulgar).

chochas (*Guat., Salva.*) coins of little value = monedas de poco valor.

chocholear (*Colo.*) to pamper = mimar; tratar con especial cariño.

chocleros (*Chile*) teeth (incisors) = dientes (incisivos).

choclo **1.** (*Argen., Bol., Chile, Colo., Ecua., Peru, Uru.*) corn for human consumption = maíz para el consumo humano. **2.** (*Argen., Bol., Chile, Colo., Ecua., Peru, Uru.*) a corncob = mazorca.

choclón **1.** (*Chile*) a disorganized meeting = grupo de gentes agrupadas sin ningún orden. **2.** (*Chile*) a meeting of confeder-ates to plan a political action = reunión de partidarios de una idea para confabular el triunfo de la misma.

choclos See **cañuelas**.

choco(a) **1.** (*Chile*) short-tailed; having no tail = rabón. **2.** (*Guat., Hond., Salva.*) cross-eyed; one-eyed = bizco; tuerto. **3.** (*Guat., Hond., Nic., Salva.*) sour; fermented = agrio; fermentado. **4.** (*Bol.*) a white, blond person = persona blanca y rubia.

chocolate **1.** (*Guat., Hond., Salva.*) a black person = persona de la raza negra. **2.** (*Pan.*) a brown color = color café.

chocolo; choglo (*Colo.*) a corncob = mazorca del maíz.

chocolón (*Costa Rica, Salva.*) a game of marbles = juego de canicas.

chocoyo (*Nic.*) a green parrot = loro; perico verde.

chocozuela (*Colo.*) the knee (informal) = rodilla (informal).

chofero (*Mex.*) a chauffeur; a driver = chofer; conductor.

choglo See **chocolo**.

chola See **cachola**.

cholco **1.** (*Guat.*) without a tooth = persona a quién le falta un diente. **2.** (*Salva.*) an amputee; someone who is without a limb; without teeth = amputado; persona a la que le falta algún miembro del cuerpo; sin dientes.

choleta (*Chile*) a fabric of low quality used to provide body to a jacket = tela ordinaria que se usa como forro para dar consistencia a una prenda.

cholga (*Chile*) a big mussel = mejillón grande.

cholito(a) (*Chile*) a black person = persona de origen africano; negro(a).

cholla (*Colo.*) laziness = pereza.

cholo(a) **1.** (*Argen., Bol., Ecua., Peru, Uru.*) a half-breed = mestizo(a). **2.** (*Chile*) a derogatory nickname for a Peruvian = apodo peyorativo para un/una peruano(a). **3.** (*Costa Rica*) a strong, black person =

persona negra robusta. **4.** (*Peru*) any dark-skinned person = cualquier persona de la piel oscura.

chomba (*Chile*) a sweater = suéter.

chombo; jamaiquino; prieto (*Pan.*) a black person (derogatory) = negro; persona de origen africano (peyorativo).

chompa 1. (*Ecua., Peru*) a sweater = suéter. **2.** (*Mex.*) the head = cabeza.

chompipe (*Salva.*) a turkey = pavo.

choncaco (*Argen.*) a leech = sanguijuela.

chonchón 1. (*Chile*) a homemade kerosene lamp = lámpara rústica de parafina. **2.** (*Chile*) a kite made only from newspaper = cometa hecho sólo con papel de periódico.

chonco (*Costa Rica*) a stump = muñón de un miembro; lo que queda de una extremidad cuando se la ha cortado.

chongo 1. (*Argen.*) an uneducated person; one without manners = persona ordinaria; el que no sabe comportarse. **2.** (*Guat.*) a curl = rizo de pelo. **3.** (*Mex.*) a bun = moño. **4.** (*Puerto Rico*) an old, sickly or feeble horse = caballo viejo, enclenque o en muy mal estado.

chop; chopa; chope (*from English*) a shop = tienda.

chopa See **chop.**

chope See **chop.**

chopear (*from English*) to shop = ir de tiendas; ir de compras.

chopo (*Mex.*) the nose = nariz.

chopos; chanclas; chancletas (*Mex.*) slippers = pantuflas.

chorcha 1. (*Guat., Hond., Salva.*) the crest on a bird = cresta de ave. **2.** (*Guat., Hond., Salva.*) a goiter = bocio. **3.** (*Guat., Nic.*) a swelling; a lump = roncha; marca en la piel. **4.** (*Mex.*) a band; a gang = banda; pandilla. **5.** (*Mex.*) a rowdy party = fiesta vulgar o de mal gusto. **6.** (*Nic.*) a big mark on the skin; a scar = marca grande en la piel; cicatriz.

choreado (*Chile*) tired; fed up; cannot take it anymore (informal) = cansado; hastiado; no puede soportarlo más (informal).

chorear 1. (*Chile*) to steal (vulgar) = robar (vulgar). **2.** (*Chile*) to challenge (informal) = desafiar (informal).

choretear (*Ven.*) to harm = dañar.

choretó (*Puerto Rico*) in a large amount = en gran cantidad.

choreto (*Ven.*) a person with a physical deformity = el que tiene alguna deformidad en el cuerpo.

choripán (*Argen.*) an Argentine sausage sandwich = emparedado de chorizo argentino.

chorito (*Chile*) a small mussel = mejillón pequeño.

chorizo 1. (*Chile*) a person with an interesting or strong personality; a person who behaves in unconventional ways = persona con una personalidad interesante o fuerte; el que se comporta de manera no convencional. **2.** (*Chile*) things that are placed one after the other = cosas ordenadas, una tras la otra. **3.** (*Colo.*) a stupid and silly person = persona boba y mentecata. **4.** (*Mex.*) a roll of coins = rollo de monedas. **5.** (*Mex.*) bewitched; wicked = hechizado; malévolo. **6.** (*Uru.*) a beef cut; a sirloin = carne del lomo del vacuno.

chorlo (*Colo.*) the son of one's grandson = hijo del tataranieto.

choro 1. (*Chile, Peru*) a mussel = mejillón. **2.** (*Chile*) interesting; uncommon (informal) = interesante; fuera de lo común (informal). **3.** (*Chile*) a person with a peculiar or a strong personality (informal) = persona con una personalidad muy peculiar o muy fuerte (informal). **4.** (*Chile*) the vagina (very vulgar) = vagina (muy vulgar). **5.** (*Ecua.*) a thief = ladrón.

chorota 1. (*Dom. Rep.*) any sauce = cualquier salsa. **2.** (*Dom. Rep.*) a thick substance = substancia espesa.

chorote (*Puerto Rico*) a drink prepared with roasted corn and milk = refresco preparado con maíz tostado y leche.

chorreoso (*Dom. Rep.*) dirty = sucio.

chorrera 1. (*Puerto Rico*) a playground slide = tobogán. **2.** (*Puerto Rico*) a gutter = gotera; canal de desagüe.

chorro 1. (*Argen.*, *Chile*) a street thief who escapes by running at high speed = ladrón callejero que escapa corriendo a gran velocidad. **2.** (*Colo.*) a river rapids = rápidos de un río. **3.** (*Salva.*, *Ven.*) a faucet = grifo. **4.** (*Mex.*) diarrhea (vulgar) = diarrea (vulgar). **5.** (*Mex.*) a lot = mucho de algo.

chota 1. (*Colo.*) a police car = vehículo policial. **2.** (*Puerto Rico*) an informer = delator.

chotear 1. (*Cuba*) to make fun of something or someone = hacer risa de algo o alguien. **2.** (*Guat.*, *Hond.*, *Mex.*, *Salva.*) to idle = holgazanear. **3.** (*Guat.*, *Hond.*, *Mex.*, *Salva.*) to take a walk = pasear. **4.** (*Guat.*) to overwear; to overuse = usarlo demasiado; abusar de su uso. **5.** (*Mex.*) to give away; to inform on = acusar; delatar.

chotón (*Argen.*) silly = tonto.

choya (*Guat.*) laziness = pereza; flojera.

chucán (*Guat.*) a buffoon; a jester = bufón; el que continuamente hace bromas y chistes.

chucanear (*Guat.*) to joke = bromear.

chucear (*Argen.*) to urge; to provoke; to bother = aguijonear; provocar; molestar.

ichucha! (*Chile*) an interjection of amazement or surprise (vulgar) = interjección vulgar de asombro o sorpresa.

chucha 1. (*Colo.*) an opossum = zarigüeya; animal mamífero parecido a la zorra. **2.** (*Colo.*) an armpit = axila. **3.** (*Colo.*) an odor from the armpit = mal olor de las axilas. **4.** (*Chile*, *Ecua.*) the vagina (very vulgar) = vagina (muy vulgar). **5.** (*Puerto Rico*) the blank piece in dominos = la pieza blanca del dominó.

chuchazo; cuerazo (*Ven.*) a lash = latigazo.

chuchear (*Ven.*) to scratch = escarbar.

chuchin (*Puerto Rico*) good; nice = bueno; agradable.

chuchipluma 1. (*Puerto Rico*) timorous; shy = temeroso; tímido. **2.** (*Puerto Rico*) an untrustworthy person = persona no confiable. **3.** See **buchipluma**.

chucho 1. (*Cuba*) an electric switch = interruptor. **2.** (*Guat.*, *Hond.*) miserly; stingy = tacaño. **3.** (*Ven.*) a whip made of leather or braided fiber = látigo trenzado de cuero o fibra vegetal. **4.** (*Para.*) a shiver = escalofrío. **5.** (*Para.*) malaria = paludismo. **6.** (*Para.*) a fear; a fright = miedo; susto. **7.** (*Mex.*) astute = astuto.

chuchoca (*Argen.*, *Chile*) corn flour = harina de maíz.

chucumber (*from English*) a cucumber = pepino.

chucuto 1. (*Ven.*) bobtailed = rabón. **2.** (*Ven.*) a demon = demonio; diablo.

chueco 1. (*Nic.*) one-eyed = tuerto. **2.** (*Argen.*, *Bol.*, *Chile*, *Colo.*, *Ecua.*, *Peru*, *Uru.*) crooked = tramposo. **3.** (*Salva.*) a useless thing = inservible; cosa que no sirve. **4.** (*Argen.*, *Bol.*, *Chile*, *Colo.*, *Ecua.*, *Peru*, *Uru.*) bent; twisted = doblado; torcido.

chuequear (*Ven.*) to limp = cojear.

chuga See **changa(o)**.

chuingom (*from English*) chewing gum = chicle.

chulear (*Colo.*) to check; to make correction marks in a written piece = chequear; poner señales de revisión en un escrito.

chuleta (*Chile*) a kick in the buttocks = puntapié en el trasero.

chulo 1. (*Colo.*) a check mark = marca de revisión en un escrito. **2.** (*Colo.*) a buzzard = buitre. **3.** (*Argen.*, *Chile*, *Guat.*, *Mex.*) beautiful; pretty = bonito; hermoso. **4.** (*Mex.*) a particular kind of brush = un tipo específico de brocha.

chumado (*Ecua.*) drunk = borracho; ebrio.

chumar (*Argen.*) to get drunk = emborrachar.

chumpipe; jolote (*Guat.*, *Hond.*) a turkey = pavo.

chunche See **chécheres**.

chunches See **chereques**.

chuncho (*Chile*) an owl = búho.

chunchules (*Chile*) animal tripe prepared as a dish = tripas de animal preparadas para comer.

chunchullos; chunchurria 1. (*Colo.*) beef or lamb tripe = tripas de vacuno o cordero para comer. **2.** (*Colo.*) money or goods stolen by government functionaries or bureaucrats = dinero o bienes robados por funcionarios o burócratas gubernamentales.

chunchurria See **chunchullos**.

chuño (*Bol., Argen., Chile, Peru*) potato starch = almidón de patatas.

chupa 1. (*Colo.*) a traffic police woman = mujer que dirige o controla el tráfico vehicular. **2.** See **chupahueso**.

chupaflor (*Colo.*) a hummingbird = colibrí.

chupahueso; chupa (*Colo.*) a bootlicker; a brown-noser; a sycophant = lameculos; servilón; adulador.

chupaleta (*Mex.*) a lollipop = chupetín; pirulí.

chupalla (*Chile*) a straw hat = sombrero de paja.

chupamedia (*Argen.*) submissive = dócil; sumiso.

chupamedias (*Chile*) a bootlicker; a brown-noser = lameculos; zalamero.

chupa-mirto; chupa-rosa (*Mex.*) a hummingbird = colibrí.

chupar 1. (*Argen., Chile, Uru.*) to drink alcoholic beverages (vulgar) = consumir bebidas alcohólicas (vulgar). **2.** (*Hond.*) to smoke = fumar. **3.** (*Dom. Rep.*) to drink hard liquor = beber licores de alto grado alcohólico. **4.** to confront the consequences = afrontar las consecuencias.

chupa-rosa See **chupa-mirto**.

chupe 1. (*Argen., Peru*) a dish prepared with corn, meat, and potatoes = plato a base de maíz, carne y patatas. **2.** (*Chile*) a creamy dish prepared with animal tripe or shellfish = guiso con la consistencia de una crema preparado con estómago de vacuno o con mariscos.

chupeta (*Colo.*) a lollipop = pirulí.

chupete (*Argen., Chile, Ecua., Peru*) a lollipop = pirulí.

chupetín (*Argen.*) a lollipop = loly; pirulí.

chupo(a) (*Colo.*) **1.** a baby's bottle = biberón. **2.** the nipple on a bottle = tetilla del biberón.

chupo(a) de entretención (*Colo.*) a pacifier = tetera; chupete de entretención.

chupón 1. (*Ecua., Peru, Puerto Rico, Ven.*) a pacifier = tetera. **2.** (*Colo.*) a baby's bottle = biberón. **3.** (*Colo., Mex.*) the nipple on a feeding bottle = tetilla del biberón. **4.** (*Mex.*) a homosexual (vulgar) = homosexual (vulgar). **5.** (*Puerto Rico*) a passionate kiss = beso apasionado.

chuquiasa (*Peru*) a prostitute = prostituta.

churo 1. (*Ecua.*) a curl = rizo de pelo. **2.** (*Ecua.*) a snail = caracol.

churra See **cagarreta**.

churrasco 1. (*Argen.*) a steak = carne asada. **2.** (*Chile*) a steak sandwich = **sándwich** preparado con un **bistec**. **3.** (*Para., Uru.*) a piece of barbecued meat = carne asada a las brasas.

churretada See **charretada**.

churrete (*Argen., Chile*) with diarrhea (vulgar) = con diarrea (vulgar).

churria See **cagueta**.

churro (*Argen., Chile, Colo.*) an elegant and attractive person = persona elegante y atractiva.

churrusco 1. (*Colo.*) a butterfly larva = larva de la mariposa. **2.** (*Colo.*) a spiral brush used to clean bottles = cepillo espiral para limpiar botellas. **3.** (*Colo.*) the curly hair of black people = pelo crespo de personas negras. **4.** (*Colo.*) a contraceptive device = dispositivo anticonceptivo.

chusco (*Colo.*) a nice-looking person = persona agradable de buena presencia.

chusear (*from English*) to choose = elegir.

chuspira (*Colo.*) the vagina (vulgar) = vagina (vulgar).

chutar (*from English*) to shoot = (RAE) lanzar el balón fuertemente con el pié.

chute 1. (*from English*) to shoot; to kick; to hit the ball = golpe de pie en el **fútbol**. **2.** (*Chile*) elegant = elegante. **3.** (*Guat., Salva.*) a sting; a prick = aguijón; púa.

chuto(a) (*Bol.*) an amputee; a person who has lost a body part = amputado; persona que ha perdido cualquier parte de su cuerpo.

chuzar (*Colo.*) to prick = pinchar; punzar.

chuzo 1. (*Chile*) a pick axe = barra de hierro puntiaguda que se usa como herramienta para abrir los suelos. **2.** (*Chile*) a slow learner = el que aprende lento. **3.** (*Ven.*) a blade; the steel used as a weapon by prisoners in jail = la hoja o el acero de un arma que usan los prisioneros en las cárceles. **4.** (*Nic.*) a person with straight hair = persona de pelo liso.

cicla (*Colo.*) a bicycle = bicicleta.

ciclo (*Argen., Para.*) each level of the school system = períodos en que se dividen los niveles de escolaridad, ciclo primario, ciclo secundario, ciclo universitario.

cicote; sicote (*Dom. Rep.*) a bad odor from the feet = mal olor de los pies.

cicotudo; sicotudo (*Dom. Rep.*) someone with bad foot odor = el que tiene mal olor de pies.

cidi (*from English*) a CD; a compact disc = DC; disco compacto.

cierre (*Para.*) a zipper = cierre de cremallera.

cierre relámpago (*Argen.*) a zipper = cierre de cremallera.

cignato 1. (*Ven.*) rotten food = alimento podrido o en vías de descomposición. **2.** (*Ven.*) a sickly-looking person = persona pálida y de aspecto enfermizo.

cilampa (*Costa Rica, Salva.*) drizzle = llovizna.

cilindro (*Mex.*) a hand organ = organillo.

cilón (*Chile*) the special police forces = policía de las fuerzas especiales.

cimarra (*Chile*) to cut school = hacer novillos; faltar a la escuela.

cimbronazo (*Colo.*) a violent shake = sacudida; estremecimiento muy violento.

cinchazo (*Costa Rica*) to hit with a belt = cintarazo; golpe con un cinto.

cintas See **agujetas**.

ciodi (*from English*) "COD;" cash on delivery = pago contra entrega.

cipe 1. (*Costa Rica, Hond.*) a weak or unhealthy baby = niño lactante débil o enfermizo. **2.** (*Nic.*) a baby or young boy who cries too much = bebé o niño pequeño que llora mucho. **3.** (*Salva.*) a baby = bebé; niño lactante. **4.** (*Salva.*) the resin of a tree = resina de árbol.

cipote 1. (*Hond., Salva., Ven.*) a young man = muchacho; chiquillo. **2.** (*Ven.*) stupid; silly = bobo; tonto; zonzo. **3.** (*Nic.*) a boy between six and ten years of age (derogatory) = niño entre los seis y los diez años de edad (despectivo). **4.** (*Guat.*) shabby; corpulent and short = corpulento; rechoncho.

circunstanfláutico (*Colo.*) outlandish (informal) = estrafalario (informal).

cisca 1. (*Mex.*) shame = vergüenza. **2.** (*Mex.*) a fright; a scare = susto; miedo.

cismático (*Colo.*) a finicky person = melindroso; el que se asusta fácilmente; el que no se atreve.

cisnero(a) (*Mex.*) a liar = mentiroso(a).

cizote 1. (*Mex.*) a sore = inflamado; enconado. **2.** (*Mex.*) a wound = herida.

clam 1. (*from English*) a clam (shellfish) = almeja. **2.** (*from English*) a mechanical clamp; a device used to tighten a hose to a pipe in a machine = abrasadera; mordaza mecánica.

clapiar (*from English*) to clap = aplaudir.

claridoso (*Mex.*) outspoken; plain-spoken = francote; el que habla directo y simple.

claro (*Chile*) an affirmative expression; "yes" = expresion afirmativa; "sí."

clavar (*Colo.*) to involve someone in a difficult situation = comprometer a alguien en una situación difícil.

clavo 1. (*Colo.*) a surprise = sorpresa. **2.** (*Chile*) an unpaid debt = una deuda que no se paga.

clawn (*from English*) a clown = payaso.

cleimiar (*from English*) to claim = reclamar.

cliar (*from English*) clear = despejado; libre; diáfano; transparente.

clientelismo (*Colo.*) to give or receive political favors = dar o recibir favores políticos.

clin (*from English*) clean = limpio; limpieza.

clineja; crineja (*Ven.*) a woman's hairstyle with two braids on both sides of the head = peinado femenino en que el cabello se teje en dos trenzas a los lados de la cabeza.

cliner 1. (*from English*) the cleaners = tintorería. **2.** (*from English*) the dry cleaners = tienda de limpiado al seco.

clip (*from English*) a clip = (RAE) sujetapapeles.

clipa (*from English*) clippers = tijeras.

cloche (*from English*) an automobile clutch = (RAE) embreague del automóvil.

clorex; clorina (*from English*) chlorine = cloro.

clorina See **clorex**.

club 1. (*from English*) a club = (RAE) junta de individuos asociados para conseguir un interés común; asociación. **2.** (*from English*) a club = (RAE) centro; el lugar donde se reúnen los miembros de una asociación.

club nocturno (*from English*) a nightclub = (RAE) lugar de esparcimiento con espectáculos donde se bebe y se baila hasta altas horas de la noche.

clueco (*Dom. Rep.*) to think highly of oneself = el que tiene opinión grandiosa acerca de sí mismo.

coa 1. (*Chile*) slang = jerga de la gente del hampa; lenguaje del delincuente. **2.** (*Pan.*) a tool used to make holes in the ground = herramienta para hacer hoyos en el suelo.

coba (*Ven.*) a lie; a trick = mentira; engaño.

cobacha (*Puerto Rico*) a small room for storage; a shack = cuarto pequeño que se usa como bodega.

cobija (*Colo., Guat., Mex., Pan.*) a blanket = frazada.

cobo (*Costa Rica*) a bedspread = cubrecama.

cocaví (*Chile*) the food for a trip = víveres; comida para el viaje.

cocedor (*Mex.*) an oven = horno.

coch (*from English*) a coach = entrenador.

cocha 1. (*Ecua.*) a lagoon; a pond = laguna; charco. **2.** (*Peru*) a savanna = sabana, gran extensión de terreno plano y sin árboles.

cochambriento (*Peru*) greasy and smelly = grasiento y de mal olor.

cochayuyo (*Bol., Chile, Peru*) a type of edible seaweed = un tipo de planta marina comestible.

coche (*Argen., Uru.*) a car = automóvil.

cochera (*Colo.*) a pigsty = pocilga; chiquero.

cochino 1. (*Chile, Ven.*) dirty = sucio. **2.** (*Colo., Mex., Puerto Rico*) a pig; pork = cerdo; puerco. **3.** (*Ven.*) a coward = cobarde. **4.** (*Ven.*) vulgar = vulgar.

cochote (*Mex.*) a sweet daddy or mommy = querido papito o mamita.

cocido 1. (*Mex., Pan.*) a stew = estofado; guiso. **2.** (*Chile*) drunk (informal) = borracho (informal).

cocina (*Colo.*) a cocaine laboratory = laboratorio de cocaína.

cocinería (*Chile*) a place to eat inexpensive, popular dishes = lugar donde se sirven comidas preparadas al estilo popular y a bajos precios.

cocinero (*Colo.*) a cocaine laboratory technician = el técnico en el laboratorio de cocaína.

cocineta (*Colo.*) a small kitchen in a corner of a room = pequeña cocina en un rincón.

cocinol (*Colo.*) kerosene = queroseno.

coco 1. (*Cuba, Mex., Nic., Pan.*) the head (informal) = cabeza (informal). **2.** (*Ven.*) intelligence; judgment = inteligencia; juicio. **3.** (*Ven.*) obsession; insistence = obsesión; insistencia. **4.** (*Nic.*) the brain = cerebro.

cocoles (*Mex.*) beans = habichuelas.

cocolía 1. (*Puerto Rico*) a variety of small crab = variedad de cangrejo pequeño. **2.** (*Puerto Rico*) masturbation (vulgar) = masturbación (vulgar).

cocolmeca (*Mex.*) an herbal tea used medicinally for the kidneys = té de hierbas usado como medicina para los riñones.

cocopelao; coquipela; pelón (*Puerto Rico*) bald = calvo; sin cabellos.

cocora (*Peru*) dislike; animosity = ojeriza; rencor; disgusto.

cocoroco See **cangrimán**.

cocotazo; marranazo 1. (*Dom. Rep., Puerto Rico*) a blow on the head = coscorrón; golpe en la cabeza. **2.** (*Dom. Rep., Puerto Rico*) a bump = chichón.

cocote (*Dom. Rep.*) the neck = cuello; pescuezo.

cofiro (*Mex.*) coffee = café.

cógelo suave (*Puerto Rico*) take it easy = tómalo con calma; hazlo despacio.

coger 1. (*Argen., Mex., Ven., Uru.*) to have sex; coitus = practicar el acto sexual; coito. **2.** (*Ven.*) to go in a specific direction = dirigirse hacia un sitio.

coger pela (*Puerto Rico*) to get beaten up = ser golpeado; recibir una zurra.

cogotear (*Chile*) to get mugged in the street = asaltar por la calle.

coima (*Argen., Bol., Chile, Colo., Ecua., Peru, Uru.*) a bribe = soborno.

coime (*Colo.*) a waiter = camarero.

cojín 1. (*Mex.*) an adulteress = adúltera. **2.** (*Mex.*) a woman who practices the sexual act frequently = mujer que practica el acto sexual frecuentemente.

cola 1. (*Argen., Chile*) a line of people = fila de personas que esperan. **2.** (*Colo., Mex.*) the buttocks = nalgas; trasero. **3.** (*Ven.*) to hitchhike = pedir o dar transporte gratuito.

colada (*Colo.*) a nutritional paste prepared with flour, milk, sugar, and banana or yucca = pasta alimenticia preparada con leche, azúcar y harina de plátano o yuca.

colca (*Peru*) a barn; a granary; an attic used for food storage = granero; bodega; desván donde se guarda comida.

colcha 1. (*Chile, Colo., Mex., Peru, Puerto Rico*) a bedspread = cubrecama. **2.** (*Cuba, Salva.*) a blanket = frazada.

colear (*Ven.*) to cut in line = meterse indebidamente en la fila de personas que esperan.

colectar (*Puerto Rico*) to collect = recoger; recaudar; cobrar; sacar dinero de una agencia gubernamental.

colectivero (*Argen.*) a bus driver = conductor de ómnibus.

colectivo (*Argen.*) a bus = ómnibus.

colegiante (*from English*) a college student = estudiante universitario.

colero 1. (*Ven.*) a stowaway; a person who travels without paying for a ticket = polizonte; el que viaja sin pagar pasaje. **2.** (*Ven.*) a hitchhiker = el que pide transporte gratuito.

coleto (*Ven.*) a mop = trapero.

colgada 1. (*Colo.*) the task has not been completed on time = la tarea está incompleta; incumplimiento de una actividad. **2.** (*Colo.*) behind in the payments = retraso en los pagos.

colgado(a) (*Chile*) he or she doesn't understand anything at all = no entiende nada de nada.

colgarse 1. (*Dom. Rep., Puerto Rico*) to fail an exam; to fail a subject in school = reprobar un examen; reprobar una materia.

2. (*Colo.*) to fall behind = atrasarse; quedarse atrás.

colgarse en la escuela (*Cuba*) to fail an exam = fallar un examen.

colgarse en un examen (*Puerto Rico*) to fail an exam = fallar o reprobar un examen.

coliche (*Mex.*) a young person who consistently follows others = joven que sigue a los otros continuamente.

colino 1. (*Colo.*) a drug addict = persona adicta a las drogas. **2.** (*Colo.*) an adolescent = adolescente.

collera 1. (*Puerto Rico*) dumb; stupid = tonto. **2.** (*Chile, Colo.*) cufflink = gemelo de la camisa.

colmado (*Puerto Rico*) a grocery store = tienda de abarrotes.

colmena (*Mex.*) a bee = abeja.

colmilludo (*Puerto Rico*) a person who is involved in politics for personal gain only = el que está en la política para conseguir ganancias personales.

colocho 1. (*Costa Rica*) a hair curl = rizo del cabello. **2.** (*Costa Rica, Guat., Salva.*) a woodshaving = viruta de madera. **3.** (*Guat., Hond., Nic., Salva.*) curly hair = cabello ensortijado. **4.** (*Salva.*) a favor or a service = un favor o un servicio.

colombina 1. (*Colo., Cuba*) a lollipop = pirulí. **2.** (*Cuba*) a swing = columpio.

color (*Chile, Colo.*) a colored seasoning = condimento que da color a las comidas.

comal (*Nic.*) a clay artifact used to prepare **tortillas** = tiesto de barro o arcilla para hacer **tortillas**.

combiar (*from English*) to comb = peinar.

combo 1. (*Chile*) a punch = puñetazo. **2.** (*Puerto Rico*) a group of people associated to do or act on something = un grupo de personas asociadas para hacer algo. **3.** (*Puerto Rico*) a musical band = conjunto musical.

come mierda (*Puerto Rico*) a snob = esnob; el que aparenta o que trata de aparentar lo que no es.

comebola (*Dom. Rep.*) silly; stupid (vulgar) = tonto; estúpido (vulgar).

comedirse (*Ecua.*) to meddle = entrometerse o entremeterse.

comeivete (*Puerto Rico*) a fast-food place; a small eating stand = come y vete; lugar donde se come rápido.

comején 1. (*Colo.*) a glutton = glotón; el que come mucho o muy apurado. **2.** (*Ecua., Peru*) worry; anxiety = preocupación; ansiedad. **3.** (*Colo., Peru, Ven.*) termites = termitas.

comer 1. (*Ven.*) to surpass someone else = superar; sobrepasar a alguien en alguna actividad. **2.** (*Ven.*) to skip someone or something = omitir; pasar por alto.

comer bola (*Cuba*) to talk or speak nonsense = hablar o decir tonterías.

comer machica (*Ecua.*) to be quiet = callarse la boca.

comer pavo (*Puerto Rico*) to be tricked = ser engañado.

cómicas; comiquillas (*Pan., Puerto Rico*) cartoons = caricaturas; dibujos animados.

comiquillas See **cómicas**.

comiquitas (*Ven.*) comics = historietas.

como coco (*Puerto Rico*) great; fantastic = fabuloso; muy bueno.

como cuba; como huasca; como huevo; como pickle; como piojo; como poto'e guagua (*Chile*) drunk = borracho.

como cuete (*Chile*) very fast = muy rápido.

como el forro; como las huevas (*Chile*) very bad (vulgar) = muy mal (vulgar).

como huasca See **como cuba**.

como huevo See **como cuba**.

como la mona (*Argen., Chile*) bad; very bad = malo; muy malo.

como las huevas See **como el forro**.

como pickle See **como cuba**.

como piojo See **como cuba**.

como poto'e guagua See **como cuba**.

¿Cómo tú te llamas? (*from English*) What is your name? = ¿Cómo te llamas? o ¿Cuál es tu nombre?

como tuna (*Chile*) very good (informal) = muy bueno (informal).

compiuter (*from English*) a computer = computador.

complain 1. (*from English*) to complain = queja; quejarse. **2.** (*from English*) a complaint = querella; demanda.

componer 1. (*Chile, Colo.*) to set bones = volver un hueso a su lugar después de una dislocación. **2.** (*Chile, Colo.*) to castrate = castrar.

comprimido (*Colo.*) a prompt; a small note used to cheat on an exam = nota; apuntes para copiar en un examen.

computador (*from English*) a computer = (RAE) computador; máquina que computa y calcula.

con el cuerpo cortado; con el ropero a cuestas; con el hachazo; con la caña mala; con la mona viva (*Chile*) to have a hangover (informal) = estar con la resaca después de una borrachera (informal).

con el hachazo See **con el cuerpo cortado.**

con el ropero a cuestas See **con el cuerpo cortado.**

con la caña mala See **con el cuerpo cortado.**

con la mona viva See **con el cuerpo cortado.**

con mucho gusto (*Costa Rica*) "you are welcome;" the response to "thanks" = "de nada;" la respuesta a "gracias."

concha 1. (*Argen., Chile, Para., Peru, Uru.*) the vagina (vulgar) = vagina (vulgar). **2.** (*Colo.*) a nerve = descaro; desvergüenza. **3.** (*Ecua.*) a shellfish = marisco.

conchabar 1. (*Ven.*) to hire someone for a specific job = contratar para un trabajo específico. **2.** (*Mex.*) to live together without being married = vivir juntos sin casarse.

conchavar (*Argen.*) to hire someone for a specific job = emplear a alguien para la realización de un trabajo específico.

concheto (*Argen.*) a snobby person = el que es o se cree de la alta sociedad.

conchú (*Puerto Rico*) hardheaded; stubborn = cabeza dura; terco.

conchudo 1. (*Ven.*) shameless = el que no tiene vergüenza. **2.** (*Dom. Rep.*) to act or think slowly = cachazudo; ser lento para pensar o actuar. **3.** (*Puerto Rico*) with courage = el que se atreve; temerario.

conchupancia (*Ven.*) a political conspiracy = contubernio político.

condenar (*Ven.*) to anger; to irritate = enfadar; irritar.

conejear 1. (*Colo.*) to leave a place without paying the bill = abandonar un establecimiento sin pagar la cuenta. **2.** (*Colo.*) to swindle = estafar.

conejero (*Colo.*) a swindler = estafador.

conejo 1. (*Colo.*) the vulva (vulgar) = vulva (vulgar). **2.** (*Mex.*) the biceps = bíceps.

conejo de las indias (*Bol.*) a guinea pig = conejillo de indias.

confiscado (*Colo., Hond., Ven.*) mischievous; roguish = pícaro; travieso; bribón.

conformar (*Ven.*) to clear payment for a check = confirmar; verificar la información para pagar un cheque.

congri (*Dom. Rep.*) black beans and rice cooked together = arroz con habichuelas negras cocinados conjuntamente.

congrio 1. (*Chile*) conger eel = anguila o serpiente marina. **2.** (*Chile*) the lower grade in the army (informal) = el rango más bajo del ejército (informal).

cono (*Cuba, Mex.*) ice cream on a cone = helado de barquillo.

conserva (*Colo.*) a food can = tarro.

conservativo (*Mex.*) tight-fisted = tacaño.

constipado (*Chile*) to have a cold = estar resfriado.

consumir (*Colo.*) to sink; to dive = sumergir; zambullir.

container (*from English*) a container = contenedor; embalaje metálico grande y recuperable.

contra 1. (*Ven.*) an anti-poison; an antidote = antiveneno; antídoto. **2.** (*Ven.*) that which is used to fight a spell = lo que se usa para combatir los hechizos.

contre (*Argen., Chile*) a gizzard = molleja.

contrecho (*Mex.*) contradictory = contradictorio.

contreras (*Argen.*) one who is always against something; one who opposes everything = el que lleva siempre la contraria; el que siempre se opone.

controler (*from English*) a controller = inspector; interventor.

conventilleo (*Chile*) to spread gossip; to slander = acarrear chismes.

conventilleo; pelambre (*Chile*) gossip = chisme.

conventillera(o) (*Chile*) a scandalmonger = la/el que lleva chismes.

conventillo (*Argen., Bol., Chile, Peru*) many people living together in one or a few rooms = mucha gente que vive junta en un cuarto o en pocos cuartos.

coñazo (*Ven.*) to hit with a strong blow = golpazo; golpe fuerte.

¡coño! (*Puerto Rico*) Damn it all! Good heavens! = ¡demonios! ¡Dios santo!

coño (*Chile*) a nickname for a Spaniard = apodo para un español.

copera (*Colo.*) a waitress = camarera.

copetón; encopetonarse (*Colo.*) to be almost drunk = casi ebrio.

copia (*from English*) a copy; an issue of a printed item, magazine, newspaper, or book = ejemplar de algún impreso, una revista, un periódico o un libro.

copiarse (*Puerto Rico*) to cheat on an exam = hacer trampas durante un examen.

copietas (*Colo.*) a person who cheats on an exam = el que copia en un examen.

copiete (*Puerto Rico*) many students in the act of cheating on an exam = muchos estudiantes que hacen trampas durante un examen.

copirrait (*from English*) a copyright = derechos de autor.

copo de nieve (*Costa Rica*) sherbet = hielo raspado al que se le pueden agregar diferentes sabores.

copuchar (*Chile*) to gossip = chismear.

coquero (*Dom. Rep.*) a coconut seller = el que vende cocos.

coquí (*Puerto Rico*) a small frog, native to Puerto Rico = rana pequeña nativa de Puerto Rico.

coquipela See **cocopelao.**

coraje 1. (*Dom. Rep.*) anger = enojo. **2.** (*Mex.*) pathologically angry = enojado a un grado patológico.

corbata (*Colo.*) a job with a good salary and little work obtained through political or social influence = empleo con buen sueldo y poco trabajo conseguido por medio de influencias.

corbata de gato (*Mex.*) a bow tie = corbata de lazo.

corbata de humita (*Chile*) a bow tie = corbata de lazo.

corbejo (*Puerto Rico*) an easy woman = mujer fácil.

corchar (*Colo.*) to fail in something; to fail an exam = fracasar en algo; reprobar un examen.

corcholata (*Mex.*) a bottle cap = tapa de botella.

corcorear (*Puerto Rico*) to gargle = gargarizar; hacer gárgaras.

cordón (*Mex.*) a curb = cuneta.

corillo (*Puerto Rico*) a teenage gang = pandilla de adolescentes.

córner (*from English*) to kick the ball from the corner of the field in a soccer game = (RAE) tiro de esquina en el juego de **fútbol.**

corneta 1. (*Ven.*) a car horn = bocina del automóvil. **2.** (*Ven.*) a speaker; an amplifier = bocina; aparato amplificador de sonidos. **3.** (*Puerto Rico*) a moron = imbécil.

coronta (*Chile*) a corncob = mazorca.

coroto 1. (*Ven.*) stuff; any object or issue = cosa; asunto; cuestión; cualquier objeto. **2.** (*Ven.*) a high position in public administration = puesto público de alto nivel. **3.** (*Ven.*) a secret; private information = secreto; información privada. **4.** (*Ven.*) the male or female genitalia = genitales femeninos o masculinos. **5.** (*Dom. Rep.*) useless objects = trastos. **6.** (*Dom. Rep.*) words that do not make any sense = disparates; una palabra tonta que no hace sentido.

correa 1. (*Mex.*) an immigration officer on the United States side = agente de inmigración en el lado de los Estados Unidos. **2.** (*Mex.*) a shoelace = cordón de zapatos; lazo del calzado.

corredera 1. (*Colo., Dom. Rep., Mex.*) diarrhea (vulgar) = diarrea (vulgar). **2.** (*Ven.*) comings and goings; too many things to do = trajín; ajetreo por tener muchas cosas que hacer.

correrse (*Colo.*) to give up = desistir.

corretaje (*Hond.*) the payment of the rent for a piece of land with the product of the same land = pago del arrendamiento de un terreno con parte del producto del mismo.

corrincho (*Ven.*) a noisy conversation = conversación bulliciosa.

corroncha (*Hond.*) a shell = concha.

corroncho (*Ven.*) slow = lento; tardo.

corrotoco (*Puerto Rico*) a dwarf = enano.

cortahierro (*Argen., Para.*) the chisel used to cut cold iron or other metals = cortafrío.

cortar (*Chile*) to go in a specific direction = coger un camino; partir en una dirección específica.

cortar pantrucas (*Chile*) to take admission tickets = cortar la taquilla; recibir los boletos de entrada.

cortarla a cincel (*Chile*) to get great profits = sacar grandes ganancias.

cosa (*Ven.*) any genitals; human or animal genitals = cualquier genital; genitales de personas o animales.

coscacho (*Chile*) a rap on the head = coscorrón; golpe en la cabeza con los nudillos de los dedos.

coscorrones (*Chile*) white beans = habichuelas blancas.

coso 1. (*Puerto Rico*) stuff; objects = cosas; cuestiones; objetos o temas que no se saben como nombrar. **2.** (*Colo.*) joints; marijuana cigarettes = cigarrillos de marihuana.

costal 1. (*Ecua.*) a sack = bolsa fuerte y resistente para acarrear mercancía. **2.** (*Ecua.*) a rug made of agave or pita = alfombra de pita.

costear (*Peru*) to make fun of someone = burlarse; mofarse.

costeo (*Peru*) a gibe; a jest = burla; mofa.

costiante (*Peru*) funny = cómico.

costilla 1. (*Mex.*) a girlfriend = novia. **2.** (*Mex.*) a wife = esposa.

costura (*Colo.*) a school subject that is easy to pass = asignatura escolar fácil de aprobar.

cota 1. (*Ven.*) a blouse = blusa. **2.** (*Dom. Rep.*) the filth on the neck or ears = mugre en el cuello o las orejas.

cotaco (*from English*) female sanitary napkins; Kotex™ = toallas higiénicas femeninas; Kotex^MR.

cotita (*Puerto Rico*) a shirt for a small child = camisita para niños pequeños.

coto (*Chile, Ven.*) a goiter = bocio.

cotonear (*Hond., Nic.*) to please someone only for personal gain = complacer a una persona sólo por el interés de conseguir otra cosa.

cotorra 1. (*Chile, Puerto Rico*) a person who is too talkative = persona parlanchina. **2.** (*Cuba, Puerto Rico*) a parrot = loro. **3.** (*Ven.*) a long and tedious conversation = conversación larga y tediosa. **4.** (*Ven.*) an old maid; a woman who is not married = solterona.

cototo (*Chile*) a bump on the head; a bruise on any part of the body = chichón; hinchazón pequeña en cualquier parte del cuerpo.

cotufa; crispeto (*Ven.*) popcorn = palomitas de maíz.

couch (*from English*) a couch = sillón.

cowboy [pron. cauboi] (*from English*) a cowboy = vaquero.

coyote 1. (*Mex.*) a younger member of the family = el más joven de la familia. **2.** (*Mex.*) a person who helps others cross the United States border illegally for a fee = el que cobra por ayudar a otros a pasar la frontera de los Estados Unidos ilegalmente. **3.** (*Mex.*) a politician without scruples = político sin escrúpulos. **4.** (*Mex.*) a half-breed = mestizo. **5.** (*Mex.*) someone who works for a commission = el que trabaja por una comisión.

coyunda (*Nic.*) a whip = látigo.

cozco (*Mex.*) the devil = el diablo.

crab (*from English*) a crab = cangrejo; jaiba; juey.

crack (*from English*) a crack = quebradura; fisura.

craqueado (*from English*) cracked = quebrajado; partido.

craqueao (*Puerto Rico*) cracked = chalado; chiflado; loco.

creerse (*Puerto Rico*) showing-off behavior = estimarse a sí mismo como muy importante.

crestón 1. (*Chile*) silly; stupid; dumb (vulgar) = tonto; estúpido: bobo (vulgar). **2.** (*Colo.*) a gigolo = gigolo; hombre enamoradizo.

crica (*Dom. Rep.*) the vagina (vulgar) = vagina (vulgar).

crimen (*Ecua.*) a crime; any unlawful act = un delito; cualquier acto ilegal.

crineja See **clineja**.

crismas (*from English*) Christmas = navidad.

crispetas See **alboroto**.

crispeto See **cotufa**.

cross (*from English*) any kind of cross-country competition = (RAE) carrera de larga distancia a campo traviesa.

croto (*Argen.*) idle; lazy = haragán; flojo.

cruce (*Chile, Peru, Puerto Rico*) a street intersection = intersección de dos calles.

crucero (*Mex.*) an intersection = intersección.

cruda (*Mex.*) a hangover = resaca después de la borrachera.

crudo (*Colo.*) a badly-prepared school topic = tema o asignatura de estudios mal preparada.

crus (*from English*) a cruise = crucero.

cuache (*Guat.*) twins = gemelos(as); mellizos(as).

cuaco (*Mex.*) the horns of an animal = cuernos de un animal.

cuadrar (*Ven.*) to please; to come out of a situation with flying colors = agradar; quedar airoso.

cuadros (*Chile*) women's underwear = bragas; pantaloncillos íntimos de la mujer.

cuajada (*Nic.*) a soft and milky cheese = un queso blando y lechoso.

cuajado (*Colo.*) a big, physically well-developed person = persona grande y muy desarrollada físicamente.

¿Cual es su gracia? (*Nic.*) What is your name? = ¿Cómo se llama Ud.?

cuapes (*Nic.*) identical twins = gemelos.

cúaquer (*Peru*) oats = avena.

cuartada; cuartiza; cuartazo (*Mex.*) slashes on the buttocks from a belt = azotes en las nalgas con un cinturón.

cuartazo See **cuartada**.

cuartear (*Mex.*) to surrender; to back down; to go back on one's word = rendirse; ceder; no responder a la palabra empeñada.

cuarteo (*Chile*) to look at a nude person (vulgar) = mirar a una persona desnuda (vulgar).

cuarterón (*Mex.*) a person of Hispanic and African origin = persona de origin hispano y africano mezclado.

cuartilla (*Mex.*) a quarter = moneda de veinticinco centavos de dólar.

cuartiza See **cuartada**.

cuarto; habitación (*Cuba, Mex.*) a bedroom = dormitorio; alcoba.

cuate (*Mex.*) a pal; a buddy = compadre; compañero; amigo.

cuatezón(a) (*Mex.*) a very close friend = amigo(a) muy cercano(a).

cuatrero (*Peru*) sly = bribón; pícaro.

cuatriborleado (*Ven.*) an expert in several arts and/or sciences = experto en varias artes y/o ciencias.

cubeta (*Mex.*) a bucket = balde.

cúbilo (*Colo.*) a top hat = sombrero de copa.

cubo (*Cuba, Dom. Rep., Puerto Rico*) a bucket = balde.

cucamba; mantilla (*Hond.*) a coward = cobarde.

cucaracha 1. (*Colo.*) the vagina (vulgar) = vagina (vulgar). **2.** (*Mex.*) an old car = automóvil viejo.

cucarachero (*Puerto Rico*) a dirty and messy place = lugar sucio y desordenado.

cucarrón See **cacorro**.

cucarronear (*Colo.*) a display of effeminate gestures to show homosexuality = demostrar con gestos afeminados que se es homosexual.

cucha 1. (*Colo.*) mother, in an endearing sense = mamá, en un sentido cariñoso. **2.** (*Colo.*) a female teacher or professor = profesora.

¡cúchale!; ¡cúchele! (*Mex.*) an interjection to encourage the contenders in a fight = interjección para azuzar una pelea.

cuchara (*Colo.*) a job = empleo; trabajo.

¡cúchele! See **¡cúchale!**

cuchí (*Peru*) a pig = cerdo.

cuchifrito; cuchufrito 1. (*Puerto Rico*) fries made from the insides of a pig = interiores del cerdo fritos. **2.** (*Puerto Rico*) any fried meal = fritos en general.

cuchillero (*Mex.*) a troublemaker = pendenciero.

cuchito (*Chile*) to call for the cat = voz para llamar al gato.

cucho 1. (*Guat., Hond.*) a hunchback = jorobado. **2.** (*Chile*) a cat = gato. **3.** (*Colo.*) dad, in an endearing sense = papá, en un sentido cariñoso. **4.** (*Colo.*) a male teacher or professor = profesor. **5.** (*Colo., Ecua., Peru*) a hole = hoyo. **6.** (*Colo., Ecua., Peru*) the corner of a room = rincón. **7.** (*Colo., Ecua., Peru*) a hovel; a pigsty; a den = madriguera; pocilga; guarida.

cuchuco (*Colo.*) a soup with barley and meat = sopa de cebada con carne.

cuchufrito See **cuchifrito**.

cuco (*Chile*) a character used to scare children = personaje para asustar a los niños.

cucos (*Colo.*) women's underwear; panties = bragas.

cucufato 1. (*Chile*) half drunk; dizziness = medio ebrio; mareado. **2.** (*Peru*) sanctimonious = beato; mojigato.

cucurucho 1. (*Cuba*) ice cream on a cone = helado de barquillo. **2.** (*Cuba*) the cone of an ice cream cone = el barquillo para el helado.

cueca 1. (*Bol., Peru*) a Bolivian and Peruvian folk dance = baile folclórico boliviano y peruano. **2.** (*Chile*) a national Chilean dance = baile nacional de Chile.

cuechos (*Nic.*) pieces = pedazos; retazos.

cueco (*Pan.*) effeminate = amaricado; afeminado.

cuello (*Chile*) an unfulfilled desire; an unaccomplished personal project (informal) = quedarse con las ganas de hacer u obtener algo personal (informal).

cuellón (*Colo.*) beyond a person's capabilities = lo que excede las capacidades de una persona.

cuentamusa (*Uru.*) a liar; a tricky person = embustero; el que engaña con mentiras.

cuentazo (*Mex.*) a big lie or great gossip = una gran mentira o un chisme muy grande o muy largo.

cuentero (*Chile, Para.*) a trickster = estafador.

cuentista (*Para.*) a confident trickster; a con man = estafador; el que engaña contando cuentos.

cuentos (*Mex.*) comics = historietas.

cuerazo (*Ecua., Hond., Ven.*) a lash = azote; latigazo.

cuerda (*Ven.*) a teenage gang = pandilla de adolescentes.

cueriza (*Mex.*) a spanking = nalgadas.

cuero 1. (*Chile*) a good-looking person (vulgar) = persona bien parecida (vulgar). **2.** (*Ven.*) a whip = látigo. **3.** (*Dom. Rep., Puerto Rico, Ven.*) a woman with a bad reputation; a prostitute (vulgar) = mujer de mala reputación; prostituta (vulgar). **4.** (*Puerto Rico*) pig skin cooked and roasted = piel del cerdo cocida y tostada.

cuervo See **changa(o)**.

cuestión (*from English*) a question = pregunta.

cuete 1. (*Chile, Colo.*) a rocket; fireworks = fuego de artificio; cohete. **2.** (*Mex.*) drunk = borracho.

cuetear (*Colo.*) to jump as a **cuete** or rocket = saltar como un **cuete** o cohete.

cueva 1. (*Chile*) the bottom; a bum (vulgar) = trasero (vulgar). **2.** (*Chile*) luck (vulgar) = suerte (vulgar). **3.** (*Mex.*) the vagina (vulgar) = vagina (vulgar).

cufifo (*Chile*) drunk (informal) = ebrio (informal).

cuí (*Pan.*) a guinea pig = conejillo de indias.

cuica (*Puerto Rico*) a jump rope = cuerda para saltar.

cuico 1. (*Argen.*) a short and chubby person = persona chica rechoncha y gordiflona. **2.** (*Ecua.*) a thin person = persona delgada.

3. (*Chile*) overly affected = cursi. **4.** (*Chile*) meddlesome; a meddler = metiche; metido. **5.** (*Mex.*) a policeman (informal); a cop = policía (informal).

cuidar la cuchara (*Colo.*) to work hard and well to keep a job = trabajar bien y mucho para cuidar el empleo.

cuija (*Mex.*) a personal defect that attracts sympathy = defecto personal que atrae las simpatías de los demás.

cuilca (*Mex.*) a blanket = frazada.

cuita (*Chile*) a hidden or secret issue = asunto secreto; cuestión escondida.

cuki (*from English*) a cookie = galleta.

culear 1. (*from English*) to cool = enfriar. **2.** (*Chile, Colo.*) to have sex (very vulgar, taboo) = tener un coito; realizar el acto sexual (muy vulgar, tabú).

culebrear (*Dom. Rep.*) to elude a responsibility = eludir una responsabilidad.

culebrero (*Dom. Rep.*) clever; smart = astuto; listo.

cúler (*from English*) a cooler = heladera; caja o vasija para enfriar los alimentos.

culero 1. (*Salva.*) a homosexual (vulgar) = homosexual (vulgar). **2.** (*Cuba, Puerto Rico*) diapers = pañales.

culi (*from English*) a coolie = (RAE) trabajador o criado nativo de la China u otros países asiáticos.

culiche (*Salva.*) faint-hearted; insecure = miedoso; inseguro.

culilludo 1. (*Ven.*) a coward = cobarde. **2.** (*Ven.*) faint-hearted = miedoso.

culipando; culiseco (*Colo.*) a person with small buttocks = persona con pocas nalgas.

culipendearse (*Colo.*) to become frightened = acobardarse; amilanarse.

culirroto (*Colo.*) ragged; in tatters = andrajoso; desarrapado.

culisada; enrizado (*Pan.*) curly hair = crespo.

culiseco See **culipando**.

culo (*Argen., Bol., Chile*) a vulgar word for buttocks = forma vulgar para asentaderas.

cumbamba (*Colo.*) a chin = mentón.

cumbanchear (*Dom. Rep.*) to party = andar de fiestas.

cumbearse (*Hond.*) to praise mutually = elogiarse mutuamente.

cumbo (*Hond.*) a water container = recipiente para agua.

cuminar (*Hond.*) to take somebody else's things = apropiarse de una cosa ajena.

cuncuna (*Chile*) a caterpillar = oruga.

cuncuno (*Colo.*) bobtailed = rabón; sin cola o de la cola corta.

cuneco; cunene (*Ven.*) the youngest son = el benjamín; el menor de la familia.

cunene See **cuneco**.

cuña 1. (*Argen., Chile, Uru.*) a wedge; a splinter = soporte o apoyo. **2.** (*Argen., Chile, Uru.*) help from an influential person = ayuda de una persona de influencia.

cuño (*Cuba*) a stamp = estampilla; sello de correos.

cuora; peseta (*from English*) a quarter; a twenty-five cent coin = un cuarto de dólar; veinticinco centavos.

cupón (*Ven.*) a bill of one-hundred monetary units = billete de cien unidades monetarias.

cuquear 1. (*Dom. Rep.*) to provoke = provocar. **2.** (*Dom. Rep.*) to bother = molestar.

cuquera (*Colo.*) a delicate and beautiful thing = cosa bonita y delicada.

cuquiar (*from English*) to cook = cocinar.

cuquísima (*Colo.*) very beautiful = muy bonita.

curaca (*Colo.*) an Indian chief = cacique.

curado (*Argen., Chile, Peru, Uru.*) drunk = borracho; ebrio.

curanto (*Chile*) seafood, meat, and cheese cooked in a big pot or over hot stones in a hole in the ground = mariscos, pescados, carnes y quesos cocinados en una gran cacerola o sobre piedras calientes dentro de un hoyo.

curar 1. (*Argen., Chile*) to get drunk = emborrachar. **2.** (*Argen., Chile*) to heal = sanar. **3.** (*Chile*) to glue powdered glass to the thread used for a kite in order to cut the thread of other kites = pegar vidrio molido en el hilo que se usa para elevar cometas con el objeto de cortar el hilo de otros cometas.

curco (*Colo., Ecua.*) hunchbacked = jorobado.

curcuncho (*Bol., Chile, Ecua., Peru*) hunchbacked = jorobado; gibado; corcovado.

curda 1. (*Argen., Chile*) drunkenness = borrachera; embriaguez. **2.** (*Ven.*) an alcoholic beverage = bebida alcohólica.

curdeao; curdo (*Colo., Ven.*) drunk = borracho.

curdo See **curdeao**.

curepa; curepí (*Para.*) a nickname that the Paraguayans use for Argentineans = apodo que los paraguayos dan a los argentinos.

curepí See **curepa**.

curí (*Colo.*) a guinea pig = conejillo de indias.

curiche 1. (*Bol.*) a marsh; a swamp = poza fangosa; pantano. **2.** (*Chile*) a dark-skinned person = persona de la piel oscura.

curiel (*Cuba*) a guinea pig = conejillo de indias.

curiositas (*Mex.*) cartoons = dibujos animados; caricaturas.

curricán (*Puerto Rico*) a string; a cord = cordel; cordón.

currutaca (*Nic.*) diarrhea = diarrea.

cursera (*Colo.*) diarrhea (vulgar) = diarrea (vulgar).

cursor (*from English*) a cursor = (RAE) marca movible luminosa que sirve como indicador en la pantalla de un computador.

curtido 1. (*Chile*) a person with experience = persona con experiencia. **2.** (*Colo.*)

ingrained with dirt = percudido. **3.** (*Colo.*) discolored = desteñido. **4.** (*Colo.*) stained = manchado.

curtío (*Dom. Rep.*) dirty = sucio.

curtir (*Colo.*) to become ingrained with dirt = percudir.

curucutear 1. (*Colo.*) to win the heart of = enamorar. **2.** (*Ven.*) to move things around = cambiar las cosas de su sitio.

cururo (*Chile*) a black-skinned person = persona de la piel negra.

cusca (*Colo.*) a butt; a cigarette end = colilla; lo que queda del cigarrillo después de fumarlo.

cusuco (*Nic., Salva.*) an armadillo = armadillo.

cutacha (*Hond.*) a small machete = machete pequeño.

¡icutí!; icutú! (*Colo.*) a call to the chickens = llamada a los pollos.

cuto(a) 1. (*Salva.*) an amputee; a person without a limb = amputado; persona a quien le falta un miembro del cuerpo. **2.** (*Salva.*) a short person = persona muy baja de estatura.

icutú! See **icutí!**.

cutuco (*Salva.*) a pumpkin = calabaza.

cuy (*Argen., Bol., Chile, Ecua., Peru*) a guinea pig = conejillo de indias.

D

dailear; dalear; dialear (*from English*) to dial the telephone = discar el teléfono.

daim (*from English*) a dime = moneda de diez centavos de un dólar.

dala para atrás (*from English*) give it back = devuélvela.

dale un pico (*Colo.*) give him/her a kiss = dale un beso.

dalear See **dailear**.

dama gris (*Colo.*) a police car = patrullero policial.

damasco (*Argen., Bol., Chile, Ecua., Peru*) an apricot = albaricoque.

dame quebrada (*Mex.*) give me a break = dame un respiro; dame un descanso; déjame por un momento.

dámela para atrás (*Puerto Rico*) return it to me = devuélvemela.

dancing hall [pron. dancinjol] (*from English*) a dancing hall = salón de baile.

dandi (*from English*) a dandy = (RAE) hombre que se distingue por su extrema elegancia y buen tono; petimetre.

danza (*Puerto Rico*) one of the folk dances of Puerto Rico = baile criollo de Puerto Rico.

dañero (*Ven.*) a person who harms by means of a spell = el que causa daño a travez de brujerías.

daño 1. (*Colo.*) the damage to a vehicle that puts it out of order = desperfecto de un vehículo por el cual queda inservible. **2.** (*Ven.*) a curse; a spell = maleficio; hechizo.

dar birote (*Salva.*) to make it confusing = hacerlo confuso; tratar de confundir.

dar botella (*Cuba*) to hitchhike = dar o pedir transporte gratuito.

dar candela 1. (*Dom. Rep.*) to hit someone = golpear a alguien. **2.** (*Puerto Rico*) to bother; to annoy = molestar; fastidiar.

dar capote (*Ven.*) to deceive; to get ahead by using tricks = engañar; tomar la delantera con trucos.

dar carpeta 1. (*Dom. Rep.*) to bother constantly = molestar constantemente. **2.** (*Dom. Rep.*) to fondle; to touch sexually = manosear; tocar en un sentido sexual.

dar examen (*Chile*) to take an exam = tomar examen.

dar galleta (*Puerto Rico*) to slap = dar de bofetadas.

dar mateo; echar mateo 1. (*Ven.*) to perform an incomplete task = dejar algo incompleto. **2.** (*Ven.*) to do something in the wrong way = hacer algo imperfectamente.

dar picón (*Ven.*) to provoke sexually by exposing parts of the body = provocar sexualmente exponiendo ciertas partes desnudas del cuerpo.

dar un boniato (*Cuba*) to trip; to misstep = tropezar; dar un traspié.

dar un jalón (*Salva.*) to give a ride = dar transporte gratuito.

dar un pico (*Colo.*) to kiss = besar.

dar un pon (*Puerto Rico*) to give a ride = dar transporte gratuito.

dar una pela 1. (*Puerto Rico*) to beat up = pegarle. **2.** (*Puerto Rico*) to win big = vencer por mucho; ganar con gran ventaja.

dar una tanda (*Chile*) to beat; to punish physically = dar una paliza o golpiza.

darse un panzazo (*Para.*) to eat too much = comer demasiado.

darse un paseo (*Colo.*) to take drugs = endrogarse.

darse una jartera (*Puerto Rico*) to eat too much = comer demasiado.

darse zoca (*Salva.*) to fight = pelear.

ide a cachimba! (*Nic.*) This is very good! = iestá buenísimo!

de agua (*Mex.*) effeminate = afeminado; amaricado.

de cachete; ir de cachete (*Colo.*) to get a free ride on a project, activity or vehicle = participar en una actividad sin poner nada de su parte; viajar como polizón.

de cajón (*Chile, Puerto Rico*) obvious; for sure = obvio; de seguro.

de chiripa; por chiripa (*Argen.*) by chance = de casualidad.

de forro; ganancia (*Guat.*) in addition to; a gift from the seller to the buyer; a bonus; a tip; a commission = agregado a; lo que el vendedor le da al comprador como gratificación; propina; comisión.

de golilla (*Ven.*) free = gratis.

de la madona (*Colo.*) very good = muy bien o muy bueno.

de llapa; de ñapa; de yapa 1. (*Chile, Colo., Peru*) an extra amount of merchandise given by the vendor to the purchaser = cantidad extra de mercancía que el vendedor le da al comprador de más como regalo. **2.** (*Chile, Colo., Peru*) added to = agregado a.

de mingo See **a pata**.

de ñapa See **de llapa**.

de raspa (*Ven.*) in a rush = apresuradamente.

de rulo (*Chile*) unirrigated land; farms irrigated only with rain = tierra de secano; granjas regadas sólo por las lluvias.

de vicio 1. (*Argen., Chile, Para.*) in excess = en exceso. **2.** (*Argen., Chile, Para.*) just for the fun of it = por el puro gusto.

de yapa See **de llapa**.

ideacá! (*Nic.*) This is very good! = iestá buenísimo!.

dean (*from English*) an academic dean = decano (en el mundo académico).

debocar (*Bol., Peru*) to vomit = vomitar.

decolaje (*Colo.*) an airplane departure = despegue de un avión.

deit (*from English*) a date; an appointment = cita; compromiso.

dejen de relinchar (*Nic.*) Be quiet! = quédense tranquilos.

dejón (*Mex.*) a person who allows others to manipulate himself or herself = persona que se deja manipular por otros.

del año del caldo (*Mex.*) very, very old = sumamente viejo.

del carajo (*Colo.*) very good = sumamente bueno.

del coño de su madre (*Colo.*) very good (vulgar, indecent) = algo que está muy bien o es muy bueno (vulgar, indecente).

deletear (*from English*) to delete = suprimir; borrar.

den (*from English*) a room in the house that is used for rest = cuarto de la casa que se usa para descansar.

dengue 1. (*Colo.*) swinging hips = contoneo al caminar. **2.** (*Colo.*) any illness = cualquier enfermedad.

denso (*Argen.*) a person who cannot be tolerated anymore = alguien a quien no se le puede soportar.

deodoran (*from English*) a deodorant = desodorante.

dependiente (*Para.*) a store clerk = empleado que despacha en una casa de comercio.

deponer (*Guat., Hond., Mex.*) to vomit = vomitar.

derraparse (*Ven.*) social misbehavior = actuar incorrectamente; mal comportamiento social.

desabrochador (*Mex.*) a fastener; a clip = broche; presilla.

desaguar (*Colo., Mex.*) to urinate (informal) = orinar (informal).

desahijar (*Mex.*) to prune = podar; recortar las plantas.

desarmador (*Mex.*) a screwdriver = destornillador; atornillador.

desbarrigarse (*Puerto Rico*) a big belly during pregnancy = tener el vientre grande durante la preñez.

desbole; despelote; despiole 1. (*Argen.*) disorder = desorden. 2. (*Argen.*) confusión = confusión. 3. (*Argen.*) vagueness = imprecisión.

desborrador (*Mex.*) an eraser = goma de borrar; borrador.

descachalandrado 1. (*Ven.*) a person who dresses carelessly = persona descuidada en el vestir. 2. (*Ven.*) a dismantled or deteriorated object = objeto desarmado o deteriorado.

descache 1. (*Colo.*) impertinence = cometer una impertinencia. 2. (*Colo.*) the detachment of an axle from a vehicle = desprendimiento de un eje en un vehículo.

descamburador (*Ven.*) a person who takes away someone's job = el que destituye a otro de su empleo.

descarachar (*Colo.*) to peel = descascarar.

descascaranar (*Dom. Rep.*) to peel paint; to strip paint from a wall = descascarar; desprender la pintura de un muro.

descocorotarse (*Colo.*) to give oneself a bang on the head = descalabrarse; destutumarse.

descocotar (*Dom. Rep.*) to murder; to kill by cutting the head = dar muerte; matar cortando la cabeza.

descolar (*Guat.*) to dismiss someone from a job = destituir a alguien del trabajo.

descolgar (*Dom. Rep.*) to crash a party; to show up without invitation = irrumpir en una fiesta; presentarse en un lugar sin invitación.

descompasar (*Mex.*) to misbehave = descomportarse.

descompletar (*Colo.*) to make incomplete = descabalar; quitar una parte y dejarlo incompleto.

desconchabar (*Dom. Rep.*) to dislocate = dislocar.

desconchar (*Ven.*) to peel = pelar frutas o semillas; sacar la cáscara.

desconchiflado (*Mex.*) in disarray; dismantled; in poor working condition = en desorden; desmantelado; en muy malas condiciones.

desconchinflar (*Dom. Rep.*) to dissemble = desarmar; descomponer.

descorche; destape 1. (*Colo.*) the payment for the right to see a show in a restaurant = pago por presenciar el espectáculo en un restaurante. 2. (*Colo.*) the payment for the right to take one's own alcoholic beverages into a restaurant = pago por el derecho de llevar sus propias bebidas alcohólicas al restaurante.

descorotar (*Ven.*) to break a seed or an eggshell = quebrar la cáscara de una semilla o un huevo.

descrestada (*Colo.*) a fraud; a trick = fraude; engaño.

descrestarse (*Chile*) to work extra hard; to kill oneself in a job (vulgar) = trabajar con un ahinco extraordinario; matarse trabajando (vulgar).

descualificar (*from English*) to disqualify = descalificar.

descueve (*Chile*) very good (vulgar) = muy bueno (vulgar).

desembarañador (*Mex.*) a comb = peine; peineta.

desembuchar (*Argen.*) to tell; to reveal everything = confesar; decir todo lo que se sabe.

desespero (*Colo.*) a loss of hope = pérdida de esperanza.

desfrozar (*from English*) to defrost = descongelar.

desgonzarse (*Colo.*) to be left without strength = quedarse sin fuerzas.

desgraciarse (*Para.*) to injure fatally; to kill = provocar una herida mortal; matar a otra persona.

desgualetado (*Colo.*) sloven = desaliñado.

desguañangado (*Puerto Rico*) tired; without strength = cansado; sin fuerzas; desganado.

desharrapado (*Hond.*) shameless; daring = descarado; osado.

deshechar (*Colo.*) to take a short cut = tomar un atajo.

deshecho (*Colo.*) a short cut = atajo.

deslizadero (*Colo.*) a playground slide = tobogán.

desmoronamiento (*Colo.*) to crumble bread = desmigamiento; desmenuzar el pan en migas.

deso (*Puerto Rico*) stuff; things = cosas; cuestiones; objetos o temas que no se saben nombrar.

desobligado (*Mex.*) irresponsible = irresponsable.

desocupar (*Mex.*) to fire someone else or to get fired from a job = despedir a otro o ser despedido de un trabajo.

desorejado (*Peru*) an off-key person; one without musical ability = desafinado; el que canta mal porque no tiene oído musical.

despachante (*Para.*) a customs clerk or agent = agente de aduanas que despacha la mercadería.

despagar (*Mex.*) to cut the weeds = cortar las malezas.

despapucho (*Peru*) nonsense = disparate; tontería.

desparpajar (*Hond.*) to smarten up; to wake up = despabilar; espantar el sueño.

desparramar (*Mex.*) to spread gossip = repartir chismes.

desparringarse (*Ven.*) to waste; to spend without limits = despilfarrar; gastar sin medida.

despatarro (*Argen.*) to neglect oneself; to let oneself go = dejarse estar; estado de abandono.

despecho (*Puerto Rico*) weaning = destete; quitar o suspender la alimentación de pecho a un niño.

despelote See **desbole**.

despercudido (*Chile*) wise; with self-confidence; without shame = sabio; avisado; desparpajado.

desperfeccionar (*Ecua.*) to damage = dañar; estropear.

desperrindingarse (*Colo.*) to waste; to squander; to spend without limits = despilfarrar; gastar sin medida.

despichar (*Colo.*) to squash; to crush; to squeeze = despachurrar; aplastar; estrujar.

despintar (*Chile, Puerto Rico*) out of one's sight; to look the other way = perder de vista; apartar la mirada.

despiole See **desbole**.

desplomar (*Ven.*) to tear apart; to detach = desgarrar; desprender.

desplomo (*Ven.*) a reprimand = regañina; reprimenda.

despuesito (*Mex.*) immediately after = inmediatamente después.

despunte (*Chile*) what is left after a cut; a small remnant after a cut; chips = trozos pequeños que sobran después de un corte.

destaparse (*Dom. Rep.*) to run for escape = echarse a correr para escapar.

destape See **descorche**.

destemplar (*Guat.*) to have a toothache = tener un dolor de dientes.

destornillarse de risa (*Dom. Rep.*) to laugh a lot = desternillarse de risa.

69

destorrentarse 1. (*Guat., Hond.*) to get lost; to get disoriented = extraviarse; desorientarse. **2.** (*Guat., Hond.*) to act foolishly = actuar tontamente; perder el tino.

desván (*Mex.*) an attic = buhardilla.

desvaradar (*Colo.*) to repair a vehicle provisionally = reparar provisionalmente un vehículo.

desvarado (*Colo.*) he or she has a job = ha conseguido un empleo.

desvirolado (*Colo.*) crazy; nuts = chiflado; chalado.

detalle 1. (*Costa Rica*) one kind of municipal tax = un tipo de impuesto municipal. **2.** (*Costa Rica*) a person who takes care of all the details = el que es detallista.

determinar (*Colo.*) to pay special attention to one specific person = brindar atención manifiesta a una persona.

detur (*from English*) a detour = desvío.

diablito (*Chile*) a cross bar; a metal bar; a tool used as a lever = palanqueta; barra de acero que se usa como herramienta para palanquear.

diablo (*Hond.*) the delirium tremens = delirium tremens.

dialear See **dailear**.

diaper (*from English*) diapers = pañales.

diche (*from English*) a ditch = canal.

dinero-oro (*Mex.*) the currency of the United States = dinero circulante en los Estados Unidos.

dinero-plata (*Mex.*) the currency of Mexico = dinero circulante en México.

dinga (*Puerto Rico*) a defect = defecto.

discante (*Peru*) extravagant = extravagante.

discjokey (*from English*) a disc jockey = (N.E. presentador de discos; disquero; pinchadiscos).

disfuerzo (*Peru*) prudery; an affectation = melindre; remilgo.

disticoso (*Peru*) to be picky with food = selectivo; el que distingue mucho lo que comerá o dejará.

dita (*Guat.*) a debt = deuda.

divierta (*Guat.*) a cheap dance; a dance party of poor people = baile de baja categoría; baile en que participa gente de baja condición social.

divisa (*Colo.*) a panoramic view = panorama.

doblechequear (*from English*) to double-check = volver a revisar; verificar por segunda vez.

dobletroque (*Colo.*) a trailer = camión con remolque.

dock (*from English*) a dock = dársena; muelle rodeado de almacenes; depósito comercial de mercancías.

doctor (*Colo., Ven.*) respectful treatment, independent of an academic degree = trato respetuoso independiente del grado académico.

doméstico (*from English*) domestic = lo que es local; nacional; lo que no ha sido importado.

dompear (*from English*) to dump; to dispose of = botar o desprenderse de algo.

don de gentes (*Colo.*) good manners = modales decentes y refinados.

dona; donat (*from English*) a doughnut = buñuelo; rosca.

donat See **dona**.

donde el diablo perdió el poncho (*Argen., Chile, Peru*) in some godforsaken spot = en un lugar muy lejos.

donde la viste (*Chile*) I don't believe you; you are lying. = no te creo; estás mintiendo.

donkey (*from English*) a donkey engine; a small crane used in ships to lift cargo = grúa pequeña.

donquero (*from English*) a donkeyman; a small crane operator = operador de una grúa pequeña.

doña (*Puerto Rico*) a wife = esposa.

doña Rosa (*Puerto Rico*) menstruation = menstruación.

dopar (*from English*) to dope; to drug; to give dope to = (RAE) administrar substancias estimulantes; drogar.

doping (*from English*) doping; drugging; with the effects of dope = drogado.

dormida (*Costa Rica*) a place to sleep overnight = lugar para pasar la noche.

dormilona (*Ven.*) a nightgown = camisón para dormir usado por las mujeres.

dormir la mona (*Cuba*) to sleep off a hangover = dormir la borrachera.

dormitorio (*from English*) a college dormitory = residencia estudiantil en la universidad.

dostiar (*from English*) to dust = desempolvar; limpiar el polvo.

dragstor (*from English*) a drugstore = farmacia; droguería.

draicliner (*from English*) a dry cleaner = limpiado al seco; limpiador profesional de ropa.

draivear (*from English*) to drive = conducir el automóvil u otro vehículo motorizado.

draiver (*from English*) a driver, a kind of computer program = un tipo de programa del computador.

dres (*from English*) a dress = vestido; traje.

driblar (*from English*) to dribble = (RAE) esquivar al contrario en el juego de **fútbol**; regatear.

drive (*from English*) a drive, a place in which to insert a disk in a computer = disquetera; dispositivo controlador de disquetes.

droga (*Puerto Rico*) a crib note; a piece of paper with notes used to cheat on an exam = trozo de papel con apuntes para copiar en un examen.

dropeado (*from English*) expelled from school = expulsado de la escuela.

dropear (*from English*) to drop = dejar; abandonar.

dropearse (*from English*) to drop out = abandonar la escuela.

dulceabrigo (*Colo.*) a fabric used for underwear = tela para la confección de ropa interior.

dumper (*from English*) a dump truck = volquete.

dumping 1. (*from English*) a dump = botadero; basurero; vaciadero. **2.** (*from English*) dumping; selling at a price below the cost of production to beat the competition = (N.E. venta de existencias a un precio menor al costo de producción para derrotar a la competencia).

dundo (*Nic.*) silly = tonto; simplón.

durazno 1. (*Argen., Chile, Colo., Ecua., Guat., Mex., Pan., Peru*) a peach = melocotón. **2.** (*Argen.*) a slow-thinking person = persona de entendimiento lento.

duro (*Dom. Rep., Ecua., Peru, Puerto Rico*) hard; difficult = difícil.

E

echado (*Costa Rica*) lazy = holgazán; perezoso.

echar jareta 1. (*Ven.*) to annoy; to bother = fastidiar; molestar. **2.** (*Ven.*) to harm; to damage = perjudicar; dañar.

echar mateo See **dar mateo**.

echar pupila (*Colo.*) to look attentively = mirar con mucha atención.

echar tallas (*Chile*) to tell jokes = decir bromas.

echar un polvo (*Chile, Puerto Rico*) to have sex (vulgar) = tener sexo (vulgar).

echar una bomba (*Cuba*) flatulence (vulgar) = flatulencia (vulgar).

echar una pestaña (*Chile*) to take a short nap = tomar una pequeña siesta.

echarle al pelo (*Chile*) to have fun = entretenerse.

echarle las cacas (*Puerto Rico*) to blame someone = echarle las culpas a alguien.

echarse el pollo (*Chile*) to flee = irse; abandonar el lugar.

échele chicha al cumbo (*Nic.*) you are making one mistake after another; you keep goofing up = está cometiendo error tras error.

echón (*Ven.*) ostentatious = ostentoso.

echonería (*Ven.*) ostentation = ostentación.

edible (*from English*) edible = comestible.

edredón (*Colo., Peru*) a bedspread = cubrecama.

egresar (*Dom. Rep.*) to graduate = graduarse.

ejote (*Guat., Mex.*) a string bean = habichuela verde.

el bron (*from English*) the Bronx; a borough of New York City = El Bronx; una de las cinco áreas administrativas de la ciudad de Nueva York.

El Chaco See **Chaco**.

el chancho (*Argen.*) a train conductor; a public transportation supervisor = inspector de trenes u otros vehículos de transporte colectivo.

el chino (*Peru*) a grocery store = tienda de abarrotes.

el colochón; papachú (*Nic.*) God = Dios.

el fliper See **flipiadora**.

el look (*from English*) the look = el aspecto; la fisonomía.

el luche (*Chile*) hopscotch = juego infantil; rayuela; la pata coja.

el mono (*Mex.*) the movies = las películas; el cine.

el que con niños se acuesta, cagado amanece (*Colo.*) a person who gets involved emotionally with someone younger will pay for it later = el que se envuelve emocionalmente con alguien más joven lo pagará después.

el que no tiene dinga tiene mandinga 1. (*Puerto Rico*) if you don't have one defect then you surely have others = si no se tiene un defecto seguramente se tiene otro. **2.** (*Puerto Rico*) if you don't have a specific defect, then maybe you have African blood, but you must have something wrong (derogatory) = si no se tiene un defecto específico se tiene sangre negra (peyorativo).

el queque (*Chile*) the buttocks = nalgas.

el super (*from English*) the custodian; the building superintendent = el conserje; el guardia.

el tejo (*Cuba*) hopscotch = la pata coja; la rayuela; juego infantil en que se tira una ficha y se la sigue saltando en un pié sobre un trazado en el suelo.

el último domingo (*from English*) the last Sunday = el domingo pasado.

el uñudo (*Nic.*) the devil = lucifer; el diablo.

elástico (*Chile, Ecua., Peru*) a rubber band = bandita de goma.

electar (*from English*) to elect a candidate to office = elegir un candidato.

electroshock (*from English*) an electroshock = electrochoque.

elevador (*from English*) an elevator = ascensor.

elote 1. (*Guat.*) a tender corncob = mazorca del maíz tierno. **2.** (*Mex.*) corn = maíz. **3.** (*Mex.*) the person whom you are talking about, but whose name you don't want to mention = persona de quien se habla pero a quien no se desea nombrar.

embachichar (*Mex.*) to dupe; to besmirch = embaucar; engañar.

embalado (*Chile*) at full speed = a toda velocidad.

embalao 1. (*Chile, Puerto Rico*) fast = rápido. **2.** (*Puerto Rico*) the high from the effect of drugs = bajo los efectos de la droga.

embalar (*Puerto Rico*) to escape = escapar.

embancarse (*Argen., Chile, Cuba, Ecua., Puerto Rico, Uru.*) to become blocked by silt = quedar atrancado o obstruido un río como consecuencia de los materiales de aluvión.

embarado (*Mex.*) with a lot of indigestion = embotado; con indigestión.

embarazado(a) (*from English*) embarrassed = avergonzado(a).

embarbascar (*Ven.*) to mess up an issue = enredar un asunto o una situación.

embarcado (*Colo.*) in jail (informal) = preso; en la cárcel (informal).

embarcar (*Puerto Rico*) to be taken for a sucker (informal) = ser tratado como un estúpido (informal).

embarque 1. (*Ven.*) a long wait = plantón. **2.** (*Ven.*) a trick = engaño.

embarrada (*Chile, Peru, Puerto Rico*) a mistake = error.

embarrándola (*Chile, Colo.*) making a mistake = cometiendo un error; equivocándose.

embarrar 1. (*Chile, Colo.*) to make a mistake = cometer un error; equivocarse. **2.** (*Chile, Mex., Peru, Puerto Rico*) to damage; to create a problem = causar daño; crear un problema. **3.** (*Mex.*) to spread = esparcir.

embeleco (*Chile*) junk food = comida sin valor nutritivo.

emberrenchinarse (*Ven.*) to be penetrated or filled with a nasty smell = quedar impregnado de una substancia maloliente.

embijar 1. (*Mex.*) to paint; to smear = manchar con pintura; pintarrajear. **2.** (*Mex.*) to grease = engrasar; ensuciar con grasa.

embocar 1. (*Argen.*) to be successful; to hit the target = tener éxito; acertar. **2.** (*Colo.*) to go to a specific place = irse a determinado sitio.

embochinchar (*Dom. Rep.*) to provoke a fight = provocar una pelea.

embojotar (*Ven.*) to wrap; to pack = envolver; empaquetar.

embolado (*Guat., Hond., Nic., Salva.*) drunk = borracho; ebrio.

embolar (*Colo.*) to give a shoeshine = lustrar; dar lustre al calzado.

embolatar; envolatar 1. (*Colo.*) to deceive with false promises = engañar con falsas promesas. **2.** (*Colo.*) to get lost; to lose one's way = abstraerse; despistarse; desviarse.

embolsicar (*Dom. Rep.*) to take and keep for oneself = embolsar.

embonar 1. (*Ecua.*) to adjust; to fit = ajustar; acomodar. **2.** (*Ecua.*) to join; to assemble = empalmar; ensamblar.

emboque (*Chile*) a cup-and-ball toy = boliche; juguete de madera en que se procura encajar otro trozo de madera perforado cuando los dos se encuentran atados a una cuerda.

emborucar (*Mex.*) to confuse somebody else or to get confused = confundir a otro o estar confundido.

emborujar (*Puerto Rico*) to make things confused = hacer las cosas confusas.

emborujo (*Puerto Rico*) a pile of mixed-up things; a confused situation; a mess = conjunto de cosas mezcladas sin ningún sentido; confusión; enredo.

emboticarse (*Chile*) to become full of medicines = llenarse de medicinas.

embraguetarse (*Ven.*) to have courage = envalentonarse.

embrollao (*Puerto Rico*) to have many debts = estar cargado de deudas.

embrollón (*Puerto Rico*) a person who doesn't pay his debts = persona que no paga sus deudas.

embromado (*Colo.*) to be in a difficult situation = estar en una situación difícil.

embromar (*Mex.*) to get delayed = atrasarse.

embuchado (*Dom. Rep., Puerto Rico*) with a stomach ache = con indisposición de vientre.

empacar (*Mex.*) to eat until satiated = comer hasta quedar saciado.

empacarse (*Argen., Uru.*) to get angry = enojarse.

empacho (*Chile*) a child's upset stomach that is caused by an evil eye = niño enfermo del estómago por un mal de ojo.

empalarse (*Chile*) to be extremely cold = tener mucho frío.

empalmado (*Mex.*) to wear many clothes = estar vestido con mucha ropa.

empanada 1. (*Argen., Bol., Chile, Colo., Ecua., Peru, Uru.*) a small fried pie filled with meat, cheese or vegetables = frito de masa de harina de trigo que se rellena de carnes, queso o vegetales. **2.** (*Puerto Rico*) yucca dough with crab or meat wrapped in plantain leaves and cooked = masa de yuca con cangrejo u otras carnes envuelta en hojas de plátano y cocinada.

empancinao (*Puerto Rico*) to be full of food = estar lleno de comida; el que ha comido más de la cuenta.

empanizado (*Bol.*) a syrup cake; a solid piece of unrefined sugar = chancaca.

empanzar See **empanzurrar**.

empanzurrar; empanzar (*Mex.*) to eat in excess = comer en exceso.

empañetado (*Colo.*) the plaster of a wall = enlucido de un muro.

empaque 1. (*Colo.*) a gasket = junta mecánica. **2.** (*Ecua., Peru*) impudence = impudicia; descaro.

empaquetado (*Colo.*) well-dressed = acicalado.

emparamado (*Colo.*) numb = entumecido.

empatar 1. (*Colo., Ven.*) to join; to connect; to tie firmly together = empalmar; ajustar; juntar una cosa con otra. **2.** (*Ven.*) to bother = molestar.

empatucado (*Ven.*) to be under the influence of something or someone = estar bajo la influencia de algo o alguien.

empatucar 1. (*Ven.*) to dirty = ensuciar. **2.** (*Ven.*) to damage another's reputation = destruir la reputación de otro(s). **3.** (*Ven.*) to create confusion = provocar enredos.

empavar 1. (*Ecua.*) to anger; to irritate = enojar; irritar. **2.** (*Ven.*) to have or give bad luck = dar o tener mala suerte. **3.** (*Peru*) to shame; to make fun of someone = avergonzar; burlarse de alguien.

empedar; ponerse pedo (*Mex.*) to get drunk = emborracharse.

empelotado 1. (*Argen.*) confused; in a mess = confundido; desordenado. **2.** (*Mex.*) to be very much in love = estar muy enamorado. **3.** (*Mex.*) lazy = haragán.

empelotarse (*Argen., Chile, Colo., Cuba, Mex., Uru.*) to strip naked (vulgar) = desnudarse; quedarse uno en pelotas (vulgar).

empelotarse con (*Cuba*) to fall in love with = estar enamorado(a) de.

empepado (*Colo.*) to be high on drugs = estar bajo los efectos de narcóticos.

emperendengarse (*Hond.*) to adorn oneself with cheap objects = adornarse con objetos de poco valor.

empichar (*Hond.*) to dirty; to stain = ensuciar; manchar.

empicharse (*Ven.*) to get rotten = pudrirse.

empilcharse (*Argen.*) to dress elegantly = vestirse con buenas prendas o **pilchas**.

empleado(a) (*Mex.*) an immigration agent or policeman = agente de policía o de inmigración.

emplumar 1. (*Ecua.*) to send to prison = mandar a la prisión. **2.** (*Ven.*) to relegate = relegar; mandar a alguien a un lugar de castigo. **3.** (*Mex.*) to get older = envejecer; avanzar en edad.

emplumárselas (*Chile, Colo.*) to get off fast; to escape = largarse rápido; escaparse.

emponchado (*Peru*) suspicious = sospechoso.

emporrar (*Costa Rica*) to bother = molestar.

empuntar 1. (*Colo.*) to lead; to give directions = dirigir; orientar; encarrilar. **2.** (*Colo.*) to go; to leave = marcharse; irse. **3.** (*Ven.*) to be obsessed with a theme = obsesionarse con un tema.

empuntarlas (*Colo., Ecua.*) to disappear; to escape; to flee = desaparecer; huir.

empuñar (*Chile*) to clench = cerrar la mano haciendo un puño.

en cueros (*Chile*) nude (informal) = desnudo(a) (informal).

en especial (*Puerto Rico*) on sale = en liquidación.

en fuego; jumado (*Pan.*) drunk = ebrio; borracho.

en los quintos infiernos (*Para.*) very far = muy lejos.

en pelotas (*Chile*) naked (vulgar) = desnudo (vulgar).

en un improviso (*Colo., Mex.*) in a moment; very soon = en un momento; muy pronto.

en un tilín (*Colo.*) immediately = de inmediato.

enaguas; naguas (*Mex.*) a skirt = falda.

encabar (*Colo.*) to put the handle on a tool = poner cabo o mango a una herramienta.

encachado (*Chile*) beautiful; nice; good-looking (informal) = bonito; agradable; bien presentado (informal).

encachorrarse (*Colo.*) to get upset = enfadarse.

encaletado (*Colo.*) with a lot of money = con mucho dinero.

encaletar 1. (*Colo., Ven.*) to hide (informal) = esconder (informal). **2.** (*Ven.*) to steal (informal) = robar (informal).

encamarse (*Chile*) to go to bed with; to have sex (vulgar) = acostarse con alquien; tener relaciones sexuales (vulgar).

encamburarse (*Ven.*) to get public employment = lograr un cargo público.

encamisonado (*Ven.*) a transvestite = travestido; hombre que se viste de mujer.

encampanar 1. (*Ven.*) to rise on the social ladder = elevarse de rango social. **2.** (*Ven.*) to retire to a faraway place; to go to a place that is difficult to reach = retirarse a algún lugar lejano; dirigirse a un lugar difícil de alcanzar.

encandilado(a) 1. (*Puerto Rico*) very angry = muy enojado(a). **2.** (*Mex.*) to tire of an activity = estar cansado(a) de una actividad.

encarajinar (*Argen.*) to complicate things = hacer las cosas complicadas.

encarapichar (*Ven.*) to obtain more political and/or economic power = ascender política y/o económicamente.

encargo (*Chile, Puerto Rico*) a pregnancy = embarazo.

encartado (*Mex.*) to come from a mixed racial heritage = provenir de una mezcla racial.

encartuchar (*Ecua.*) to roll in the shape of a paper cone; to put in a paper bag = enrollar en forma de cucurucho; poner dentro de una bolsa de papel.

encatrado (*Chile*) a weak or poor design structure = estructura débil o de mal diseño.

enchafainarse (*Colo.*) to get a job or a position = conseguir un empleo o un cargo.

enchambrar (*Colo.*) to put in a ditch = meter en una zanja.

enchicarse (*Guat., Hond.*) to get annoyed; to be angry = enojarse; encolerizarse; irritarse; enfurecerse.

enchichar (*Nic.*) to ferment = fermentar.

enchilada 1. (*Guat., Hond., Mex.*) a Mexican **tortilla** filled with **chile**, bean sauce, hot pepper, and other ingredients = **tortilla** mexicana enrollada y rellena de chile, la salsa hecha de habichuelas con pimiento picante y otros ingredientes. **2.** (*Salva.*) a **tortilla** filled with hot pepper or **chile** and cabbage = **tortilla** en que se envuelve una porción de picante o **chile** y repollo.

enchilado 1. (*Guat., Mex.*) seasoned with **chile** = aderezado con **chile. 2.** (*Mex.*) to feel sick from eating too much **chile** = sentirse mal por haber comido mucho **chile**.

enchilar 1. (*Costa Rica*) to play or be the object of a trick = dar o recibir un chasco. **2.** (*Costa Rica*) to eat hot pepper; to put **chile** in food = comer chile picante; poner **chile** en la comida.

enchinado (*Mex.*) with curls = enrizado; con el cabello ensortijado.

enchinchado (*Argen.*) angry; bothered = enojado; molesto.

enchinchar (*Dom. Rep.*) to incite or provoke a fight = incitar o provocar una pelea.

enchipar (*Colo.*) to roll up; to wind up = arrollar; enrollar.

enchismar (*Puerto Rico*) to get mad at someone = enfadarse con alguien.

enchismarse (*Puerto Rico*) to be angry = enojarse; enfadarse.

enchivarse (*Colo., Ecua.*) to get furious; to get exasperated; to get upset = enfurecerse; encolerizarse; enfadarse; irritarse.

enchuecar (*Chile, Mex.*) to twist; to make crooked = torcer; encorvar.

enchumbar (*Ven.*) to soak = empapar.

enchute (*Hond.*) bowling = juego del boliche.

encielar 1. (*Chile*) to put a roof on = poner techo. 2. (*Guat.*) to cover = poner una cubierta sobre algo.

encimar 1. (*Colo.*) to add on; to give a gift to the customer = dar gratificación al cliente. 2. (*Colo.*) to allow an advantage = dar ventaja.

encintado de la acera (*Argen.*) a street curb = cuneta.

enclochar (*Colo.*) to press the clutch in a vehicle = embreagar un vehículo.

encochinar (*Colo.*) to involve someone in a crime = envolver a alguien en una fechoría.

encocorarse (*Argen.*) to show boldness with gestures = mostrar envalentonamiento con gestos y ademanes.

encohetarse (*Bol., Costa Rica*) to get angry; to get furious = encolerizarse; enfurecerse.

encomienda (*Argen., Chile, Colo., Costa Rica, Ecua., Guat., Para., Peru, Uru., Ven.*) parcel post = paquete postal.

enconchar (*Ven.*) to hide for political or judiciary reasons = esconderse por razones políticas o judiciales.

encopetonarse See **copetón.**

encuentro (*Guat.*) an armpit = axila; sobaco.

encuerar (*Dom. Rep.*) to strip; to leave a person naked = desnudar; desvestir hasta dejarlo(a) desnudo(a).

encuerarse (*Ven.*) to cohabit (vulgar) = amancebarse (vulgar).

encularse (*Colo.*) to fall in love (informal) = enamorarse (informal).

enculillarse (*Ven.*) to become frightened = acobardarse.

endiablado (*Argen., Chile, Mex., Uru.*) risky; dangerous = arriesgado; peligroso.

endilgar; endosar; enflautar (*Colo.*) to burden someone with something that is annoying = encasquetar; encargar; encajar a alguien en algún asunto, persona o cosa que causa molestia.

enditarse (*Guat.*) to have many debts = llenarse de deudas.

endosar See **endilgar.**

enfermo(a) 1. (*Argen.*) stupid = estúpido. 2. (*Argen.*) Are you out of your mind? = ¿estás trastornado?; ¿has perdido el juicio?

enfiestarse (*Hond.*) to party; to enjoy = estar en estado de jolgorio; pasar en fiestas.

enflautada (*Guat., Hond., Peru*) a foolish remark; a blunder = una disparatada; patochada.

enflautar See **endilgar.**

enfletar (*Colo.*) to run away fast; to slip away in a hurry = largarse rápido; escaparse de prisa.

enfogonarse 1. (*Dom. Rep.*) to become angry = enfurecerse. 2. (*Puerto Rico*) to get furious = enfurecerse.

enfuscarse (*Puerto Rico*) to fall in love suddenly = enamorarse repentinamente.

engalletar 1. (*Ven.*) to confuse = confundir. 2. (*Ven.*) the traffic becomes a mess = enredarse el tráfico de vehículos.

enganche (*Mex.*) a down payment = pago inicial en una cuenta a crédito.

engasado (*Guat.*) mentally unbalanced due to alcohol = trastornado por el alcohol.

engerirse (*Colo.*) to be depressed = ponerse alicaído.

englobado; envolatado (*Colo.*) absent-minded = distraído.

engorilado (*Argen.*, *Chile*) drunk (informal) = ebrio (informal).

engorrar (*Ven.*) to annoy; to bother = fastidiar; molestar; incomodar.

engrampar (*Colo.*) to staple = grapar; asegurar con grapas.

engrasar (*Chile*, *Ven.*) to bribe (informal) = sobornar (informal).

engreñao (*Dom. Rep.*) in a bad mood = de mal humor.

engrifado (*Colo.*) to be high on marijuana = estar bajo los efectos de la marihuana.

engrupir (*Argen.*, *Chile*) to use false arguments; to trick; to invent = usar argumentos falsos; engañar; fingir.

enguacar; enhuacar (*Pan.*) to hide = esconder.

enguainar (*from English*) to become drunk with wine = embriagarse con vino.

enguandocar (*Colo.*) to put in jail = encarcelar; meter a la cárcel.

enguayabado 1. (*Colo.*, *Ven.*) to have a hangover = estar con la resaca después de haber bebido mucho. **2.** (*Ven.*) sad; nostalgic = triste; nostálgico.

engurrioso (*Colo.*) envious; jealous = envidioso; celoso.

enhuacar See **enguacar**.

enhuevado (*Mex.*) to behave stubbornly = comportarse porfiadamente.

enjabonada (*Colo.*, *Ven.*) a reprimand = reprimenda.

enjaranado 1. (*Costa Rica*, *Guat.*) full of debts = endeudado. **2.** (*Guat.*) full of tricks = lleno de trampas o trucos.

enjaranarse (*Hond.*) to acquire debts = adquirir deudas.

enlagunado (*Colo.*) memory loss from alcohol consumption; a blackout = pérdida de la memoria por los efectos del alcohol.

enlatado(a) (*Peru*) canned food = comida de tarro.

enmarañado (*Dom. Rep.*) uncombed hair = cabellera sin peinar.

enmochilado (*Ven.*) hidden; in secret = lo que se tiene escondido o en secreto.

enmular (*Mex.*) to become stubborn as a mule = porfiar; comportarse porfiado como una mula.

enquesarse (*Ven.*) misappropriate = cometer desfalcos; apoderarse de dineros públicos o del dinero del cual se es responsable.

enredista (*Colo.*) a scandalmonger = chismoso.

enrizado See **culisada**.

ensabanado 1. (*Ven.*) to be free of any compromise = quedar librado de cualquier compromiso. **2.** (*Ven.*) satisfied; pleased = satisfecho; complacido.

ensalada (*Colo.*) mix = mezcla.

ensopar (*Argen.*, *Chile*, *Hond.*, *Ven.*) to soak = empapar; mojarse hasta quedar hecho una sopa.

entablar 1. (*Peru*) to boast = fanfarronear. **2.** (*Peru*) to impose a whim or personal criteria over others = imponer un capricho o criterio personal sobre los demás.

entablazón 1. (*Mex.*) a heavy obstruction = obstáculo muy fuerte. **2.** (*Mex.*) acute constipation = constipación aguda.

entablillar (*Mex.*) to cut chocolate into tablets or squares = cortar el chocolate en tiras cortas o en cuadrados.

entablonada (*Peru*) a brag; a boast = bravata; fanfarronada.

entambar (*Mex.*) to put in jail = poner en la cárcel.

enterar 1. (*Hond.*) to pay = pagar. **2.** (*Hond.*) a payment = pagar una cuota de una deuda.

enterciar (*Guat.*) to pack = empacar.

enterito (*Dom. Rep.*) the same = idéntico.

entero (*Guat.*) the same; very similar = idéntico; muy parecido.

enterrar (*Chile*, *Hond.*, *Puerto Rico*) to bury in = clavar; meter un objeto o instrumento punzante.

entilar (*Hond.*) to blacken = ennegrecer; tiznar.

entortar (*Costa Rica*) to involve somebody in debts or problems with the law = envolver a alguien en deudas o problemas judiciales.

entotorotar (*Costa Rica*) to fill with enthusiasm = entusiasmar.

entrabar (*Colo.*) to put up obstacles = poner trabas; estorbar.

entrada (*Mex.*) a beating = paliza; zurra.

entrador(a) 1. (*Chile, Colo.*) a busybody = entrometido(a). **2.** (*Chile, Colo.*) he/she gains familiarity very soon = el/la que logra familiaridad rápidamente.

¡iéntrale!; iéntrele! (*Mex.*) Come in!; Go ahead! = ¡adelante!; ¡pase!; ¡hágalo!

entre pisco y nazca (*Peru*) drunk = borracho; ebrio.

entrecerrar (*Chile*) half-closed = cerrar a medias; a medio cerrar.

¡iéntrele! See **¡iéntrale!**

entrepiernas (*Chile*) sport shorts = pantaloncillos para deportes.

entretecho (*Argen., Chile*) an attic = desván.

entripado (*Puerto Rico*) soaked = empapado; todo mojado.

entripar (*Ecua.*) to upset; to annoy = disgustar; molestar; incomodar.

entromparse (*Colo.*) to get angry; to get upset = enojarse; enfadarse.

entumirse (*Colo.*) to retreat; to get timid = retraerse; volverse tímido.

entunarse (*Colo.*) to get angry = enojarse.

envainar (*Ven.*) to harm = dañar.

envejigarse (*Colo.*) to blister = ampollarse.

envenenao (*Puerto Rico*) to be very angry = con mucha ira.

envolatado See **englobado**.

envolatar See **embolatar**.

envuelto 1. (*Colo.*) corn flour dough packed in corn leaves and steamed or baked = masa de harina de maíz envuelta en hojas del maíz cocinadas al vapor u horneadas. **2.** (*Mex.*) a Mexican **tortilla** rolled with **chile** inside; an **enchilada** = **tortilla** mexicana enrollada con **chile** en su interior.

enyerbar (*Mex.*) to bewitch someone or something = embrujar a alguien o algo.

enzanjonar (*Ven.*) to involve someone in a difficult or illegal situation = meter a una persona en un asunto grave o ilegal.

erjostes (*from English*) an air hostess; an airplane stewardess = azafata.

erogación 1. (*Chile, Peru, Ven.*) a contribution = dádiva; limosna; cuota voluntaria para fines de beneficencia. **2.** (*Colo.*) an expenditure; a payment = desembolso; gasto.

es óxido (*Nic.*) it is horrible; it is ugly = es horrible; es feo.

es papaya (*Chile, Ven.*) it is easy = es fácil.

es pintado (*Chile*) it is very similar; it is the same = es muy parecido; es igual.

es un clavo (*Argen., Chile, Uru.*) a person, a problematic situation or an object that is difficult to get rid of = persona, situación problemática u objeto del cual o de quien es difícil deshacerse.

escab (*from English*) a scab = esquirol; rompehuelgas.

escame (*Mex.*) terror; fear = terror; miedo.

escándalo (*Argen., Chile, Colo., Peru*) an uproar; a rumpus = alboroto; tumulto.

escáner; escanógrafo (*from English*) a scanner = (RAE) aparato para la exploración radiográfica.

escanógrafo See **escáner**.

escanograma (*from English*) an X-ray or picture taken by means of a scanning device = (RAE) radiografía obtenida con un **escáner**.

escaparate (*Colo., Ven.*) a wardrobe = ropero; mueble para guardar la ropa.

escarapelar (*Mex.*) to take chips = sacar pequeños trozos o astillas.

escarcha (*Mex.*) the cold season = la estación fría del año.

escarchar (*from English*) to scratch = raspar; rascar; rayar.

escarpines; medias (*Cuba, Mex.*) socks = calcetines.

eschoretar (*Ven.*) to deform; to ruin something that was right = deformar; descuadrar algo que estaba bien.

esclava (*Ecua., Peru*) a bracelet = brazalete; pulsera.

escoba (*Chile*) an informal expression meaning "the same to you" = expresión informal que significa "lo mismo para ti."

escocotarse (*Puerto Rico*) to fall = caerse.

escogencia (*Colo.*) a choice; a selection = elección; selección.

escor (*from English*) a score = puntaje; puntuación; puntos o resultado del puntaje obtenido.

escotch (*from English*) **1.** (Scotch) whisky = whisky escosés. **2.** Scotch Tape™ = cinta adhesiva.

escrachao 1. (*Puerto Rico*) in bad condition = en malas condiciones. **2.** (*Puerto Rico*) sloppily dressed = vestido de una forma desordenada.

escrachar (*Puerto Rico*) to break; to damage = quebrar; dañar.

escrin (*from English*) a screen = pantalla.

escrip (*from English*) a script = guión; libreto.

escuadra 1. (*Colo.*) a small handgun = pistola pequeña. **2.** (*Mex.*) any pistol = cualquier pistola.

escuela superior (*from English*) high school = escuela secundaria.

escuelante (*Colo.*) a school boy or girl = escolar.

escuelero(a) (*Para.*) a school boy; a school girl = escolar, colegial.

escuelita (*Colo.*) kindergarten = jardín infantil.

esferográfico (*Colo.*) a ballpoint pen = bolígrafo.

esgunfiar (*Argen.*) to bother; to incite; to provoke = molestar; incitar; provocar.

eslacks (*from English*) slacks = pantalones amplios y livianos.

eslilla (*Argen.*) the clavicle; the collar bone = clavícula.

eslip; slip (*from English*) a slip; however, in Spanish it does not mean an underskirt, but underwear for a male = calzoncillos, sin embargo cuando se refiere a prendas de vestir, el significado de esta palabra en inglés es enaguas o funda.

eslipincar (*from English*) a railway sleeping car = coche cama del tren.

eslogan (*from English*) a slogan = (RAE) lema breve y original utilizado para la publicidad, la propaganda política, etc.

esmachetarse (*Ven.*) to precipitate = precipitarse a algo.

esmandao (*Puerto Rico*) fast = rápido.

esmandarse (*Puerto Rico*) to do something quickly = hacer algo rápido; hacerlo rápidamente.

esmayao (*Puerto Rico*) selfish; self-centered = egoísta; el que piensa sólo en sí mismo.

esmeralda 1. (*Colo., Cuba*) a hummingbird = colibrí. **2.** (*Mex.*) a variety of pineapple = variedad de piña.

esmoquin (*from English*) smoking jacket; tuxedo = (RAE) prenda masculina de etiqueta.

esnikers (*from English*) sneakers = calzado deportivo de goma; zapatos de lona.

esnob (*from English*) a snob = (RAE) persona que imita con afectación las maneras, opiniones, etc. de aquellos que considera distinguidos.

espabilar (*Ven.*) to blink = pestañar; parpadear.

espaciador (*Ecua., Peru*) a bulletin board = tablero para anuncios; anunciador mural.

espalda mojada (*Mex.*) a wetback; an illegal Mexican immigrant who goes to the United States to work in the fields = el inmigrante indocumentado de México que va a los Estados Unidos para trabajar en los campos de cultivo.

espaldero (*Ven.*) a bodyguard = guardaespaldas.

espaldón (*Colo.*) with wide shoulders = de espaldas anchas.

espantar el lomo (*Cuba*) I am out of here = yo me largo de aquí.

espatear (*from English*) to spot; to locate = distinguir; avistar; localizar.

especial (*Dom. Rep.*) a sale = liquidación.

espejuelos (*Cuba, Puerto Rico*) eyeglasses = anteojos.

espejuelos de sol; lentes ahumados; lentes oscuros (*Cuba, Mex.*) sunglasses = gafas; anteojos de sol.

espelear; espeliar (*from English*) to spell = deletrear.

espeliar See **espelear**.

espepitar (*Puerto Rico*) to confess = confesar.

esperanza (*Cuba, Guat., Puerto Rico*) a grasshopper = saltamontes.

espichar (*Ven.*) to let the air out of a tire = sacar el aire de un neumático.

espiche (*from English*) a speech = discurso.

espiquer (*from English*) a loudspeaker = bocina; altavoz; altoparlante.

espiritero (*Puerto Rico*) someone who uses spiritualism = espiritista; el que practica el espiritismo.

esplayao (*Puerto Rico*) a person who makes things on his or her own = el que hace las cosas a su propio gusto.

espléndido (*Cuba*) generous = generoso.

esplín (*from English*) melancholy; low spirits = (RAE) melancolía; tedio de la vida.

esponcear (*from English*) to sponsor = patrocinar.

esponsor (*from English*) a sponsor = patrocinador.

esponsorizar (*from English*) a sponsorship = patrocinar.

esport (*from English*) a sport = deportivo.

esprín (*from English*) spring = primavera.

esquech (*from English*) a sketch = apunte; esbozo; boceto; bosquejo.

esquechar (*from English*) to sketch = trazar; esbozar; bosquejar.

esqueleto (*Colo.*) a printed form to fill out = formulario con renglones en blanco para llenar.

esquimal (*Colo.*) a romper = pelele; mameluco de niño.

esquinazo (*Argen., Chile*) a serenade = serenata.

esquinera (*Chile*) corner furniture = rinconera; mueble para un rincón.

esquite (*Mex.*) **1.** popcorn = palomitas de maíz. **2.** corn cooked in **chile** = maíz cocinado en **chile**.

está cabezón (*Chile*) **1.** with too much alcohol = tiene mucho alcohol. **2.** it is difficult = está difícil.

está cabrón (*Puerto Rico*) it is very good or it is very bad, according to the context = está o es muy bueno o muy malo de acuerdo al contexto en que se usa.

está chapetón (*Colo.*) he/she is almost drunk = está casi ebrio.

está chingado 1. (*Mex.*) it does not work; it is broken = no funciona; está descompuesto. **2.** (*Mex.*) it has no solution = no tiene solución.

está de cajón (*Chile*) it is obvious = es obvio.

está de maleta (*Chile*) it is upset; it is angry = está enojado; está molesto.

está del carajo (*Puerto Rico*) it is very difficult = es o está muy difícil.

está en la piyama de madera (*Nic.*) it is in the coffin = está en el ataúd.

está hasta el birote (*Nic.*) he/she is very drunk = está muy borracho.

está hecho un cabro (*Puerto Rico*) he/she is in love = está enamorado.

está jodido 1. (*Nic.*) it is ruined; it is full of problems = está arruinado; está lleno de problemas. **2.** (*Nic.*) it is upset = está molesto.

está papa (*Argen.*) he/she is beautiful = es hermoso; es bello.

está por la maceta (*Puerto Rico*) he/she is beautiful; is good = es bonito; está o es bueno.

establichment (*from English*) an establishment = sistema social; aparato de gobierno; sector o grupo social dominante.

estacar 1. (*from English*) to stack = apilar. **2.** (*Hond.*) to hold to the floor with stakes = sujetar al suelo con estacas. **3.** (*Hond.*) to wound; to prick = clavarse; punzarse.

estación de servicio (*Argen.*) a gas station = gasolinera; bomba de gasolina.

estadero (*Colo.*) a motel next to the road = motel a la orilla del camino.

estadista (*Puerto Rico*) someone in favor of making Puerto Rico another state = el que está a favor de la condición de estado de Puerto Rico.

estadolibrista (*Puerto Rico*) someone in favor of the Commonwealth of Puerto Rico = el que está a favor del Estado Libre Asociado de Puerto Rico.

estaf 1. (*from English*) stuff = cuestión; asunto; cosa. **2.** (*from English*) a staff = equipo; el personal; conjunto de empleados de una organización.

estampa; timbre (*from English*) a stamp = estampilla; sello de correos.

estancia (*Argen., Bol., Para.*) a ranch = hacienda.

estanciero (*Argen., Bol., Para.*) an employee at a ranch or **estancia** = empleado de la hacienda o **estancia**.

estanco; estanquillo (*Ecua.*) a liquor store = licorería; tienda de licores.

estand (*from English*) a stand = puesto; caseta; pabellón.

estandardizar See **estandarizar**.

estandarización (*from English*) standardization = (**RAE**) acción y efecto de **estandarizar**.

estandarizar; estandardizar (*from English*) to standardize = (**RAE**) uniformar; normalizar.

estanquillo See **estanco**.

estante (*Argen., Chile*) a cabinet (furniture) = armario; gabinete.

estar ahorcado (*Argen.*) to be broke = tener serios apuros económicos.

estar bomba (*Guat., Hond.*) to be drunk = estar borracho.

estar caliente 1. (*Colo.*) to be very upset and angry = estar muy enojado y de mal genio. **2.** (*Mex.*) to be sexually excited = estar excitado(a) sexualmente.

estar churrete (*Argen., Chile*) to have diarrhea (vulgar) = tener diarrea (vulgar).

estar como la chingada (*Mex.*) to be as ugly, mean, shy, insensitive, etc., as one can possibly be = estar tan feo, insensible o ser tan malo, tímido etc. como se pueda ser.

estar con el gorila (*Chile*) to be drunk (vulgar) = estar ebrio (vulgar).

estar con la caña (*Chile*) to be drunk = estar borracho.

estar con la mona 1. (*Argen., Chile*) to be drunk (informal) = estar borracho (informal). **2.** (*Cuba*) to have a hangover = tener una resaca después de haber bebido mucho.

estar cotizada(o) (*Colo.*) to be very well considered by the opposite sex = estar muy bien considerado(a) y ser pretendido(a) por el sexo opuesto.

estar en banda (*Argen.*) to be unemployed = no tener empleo.

estar en fuego; jumado (*Pan.*) to be drunk = borracho.

estar en la pitadora (*Colo.*) to have money problems = tener apuros económicos.

estar engomado (*Pan.*) to have a hangover = resaca; tener malestar después de beber.

estar gas (*Guat.*) to be in love = estar enamorado.

estar jai (*from English*) to be high on drugs or other stimulants = estar volado; estar bajo la influencia de drogas u otro estimulante.

estar montado en la vaca (*Colo.*) to face or confront a difficult situation = estar enfrentado a una situación difícil.

estar pato See **andar pato**.

estar pilas (*Colo.*) to be alert = estar alerta.

estar podrido (*Argen.*) to be bored; to be tired of something = estar muy aburrido o cansado de algo.

estar prendido (*Chile*) to be constipated = tener estreñimiento.

estar quemado 1. (*Colo.*) to be burned out = estar cansado de una actividad. **2.** (*Colo.*) to be ruined = estar arruinado.

estar rebotado (*Colo.*) to have a stomach ache = tener una indisposición estomacal.

estar salado (*Cuba, Ecua., Mex., Peru*) to be unlucky = ser de mala suerte; tener mala suerte.

estar satisfecho (*Chile*) to be full of food = estar harto de comida; no poder comer más.

estar sonado (*Argen.*) to have failed; to be finished = haber fracasado; estar acabado.

estariar (*from English*) to start an engine = arrancar un motor.

¿estás enfermo? (*Chile*) Are you stupid?; Are you out of your mind? = ¿eres estúpido?; ¿estás trastornado?; ¿has perdido el juicio?

estencil (*from English*) a stencil = patrón picado para reproducir un escrito.

estero 1. (*Chile*) a brook = riachuelo; arroyo. **2.** (*Para.*) a flooded and grassy land = terreno inundado o inundable cubierto de pasto.

estillar (*Dom. Rep.*) to chip = astillar.

estilozo(a) (*Guat.*) a vain person = persona vanidosa.

estirar la jeta (*Argen.*) to kick the bucket; to die = estirar la pata; morir.

estiró los caites; peló el ajo (*Nic.*) kicked the bucket; dead = estiró la pata; se murió.

estítico (*Chile, Colo.*) constipated = estreñido.

estoc (*from English*) stock = depósito; reserva; mercancía que se encuentra almacenada.

estofarse (*Puerto Rico*) to study or work hard = estudiar o trabajar con ahínco.

estofón (*Puerto Rico*) someone who studies or works hard = el que estudia o trabaja mucho.

estola; mantón (*Cuba*) a shawl = chal.

estop (*Colo.*) a stoplight = luz de freno en cualquier vehículo.

estor (*from English*) a store = tienda.

estoy cachimbeado See **estoy hecho pistola**.

estoy embalado(a) (*Colo.*) I am high on drugs = estoy drogado(a).

estoy hecho pistola; estoy jodido; estoy cachimbeado (*Nic.*) I am ruined = estoy arruinado.

estoy jodido See **estoy hecho pistola**.

estoy puto(a) (*Colo.*) I am very angry; I am furious = estoy muy enojado(a); estoy furioso(a).

estraberry (*from English*) a strawberry = fresa.

estrellón (*Chile, Colo., Hond.*) a crash; a collision = choque; colisión.

estrepitarse (*Dom. Rep.*) exhilarate = alborozarse.

estrés (*from English*) stress = (RAE) situación de un individuo o alguno de sus órganos o aparatos, que por exigir de ellos un rendimiento superior a lo normal, los pone en riesgo de enfermar.

estresante (*from English*) a stressful situation = (RAE) lo que produce estrés.

estroc (*from English*) a stroke = hemorragia cerebral.

estufa (*Colo., Cuba, Mex., Puerto Rico*) a stove = cocina; hornillo; artefacto para cocinar.

etiqueta (*Colo.*) a small portion of food left on the plate as a sign of good manners = pequeño resto de comida dejado en el plato como señal de buenos modales.

excusado 1. (*Colo., Mex., Pan., Peru*) a bathroom = lavabo; baño. **2.** (*Colo., Mex., Pan., Peru*) a toilet = inodoro.

excusar (*from English*) to excuse; to pardon = perdonar; disculpar.

exhibir (*Mex.*) to pay by installments = pagar en cuotas.

éxito (*from English*) an exit = salida.

expendio de gasolina (*Mex.*) a gas station = bomba de gasolina; estación de gasolina.

expres (*from English*) express = expreso.

exprimión (*Dom. Rep.*) pressing hard = estrujón.

F

faca (*Argen.*) a knife = cuchillo.

fachoso (*Chile*) presumptuous; swanky; ostentatious = presuntuoso; fachendoso; ostentoso.

facistol(a) See **facistor(a)**.

facistor(a); facistol(a) (*Ven.*) pedantic; stuck-up = pedante; engreído.

facón (*Argen., Uru.*) a dagger; a large knife = daga; cuchillo grande.

factoría (*from English*) a factory = fábrica.

facultoso(a) (*Mex.*) taking the authority or a right to which one is not entitled = tomarse la autoridad o el derecho que no le corresponde.

faena (*Guat.*) an extra job; overtime = trabajo especial; trabajo que se hace fuera de las horas reglamentarias.

faenar (*Argen., Chile*) to slaughter = matar animales para el consumo.

fafarachero See **cañero**.

fafaracho See **cañero**.

fain (*from English*) fine = estoy de acuerdo; está bien; de acuerdo.

fairplay (*from English*) fair play = juego limpio; conducta caballerosa.

faitoso(a) (*from English*) one who likes to fight; a fighter = persona a quien le gusta pelear; peleador(a).

fajar 1. (*Argen.*) to punish physically = castigar físicamente; golpear. **2.** (*Colo.*) an outstanding performance = realizar algo brillante o sobresalientemente. **3.** (*Dom. Rep., Ven.*) to attack = acometer. **4.** (*Mex.*) to beat up with a belt = dar de correazos. **5.** (*Puerto Rico*) to trade; to get something from someone = tratar de obtener algo de alguien.

fajarse 1. (*Ven.*) to work hard = dedicarse con ahínco. **2.** (*Ven.*) to start an activity with enthusiasm = iniciar una actividad con entusiasmo; acometer. **3.** (*Dom. Rep., Ven.*) to attack = agredir. **4.** (*Mex.*) to make a great effort; to sacrifice oneself = sacrificarse; hacer un gran esfuerzo.

fajazón (*Cuba*) a brawl; an uproar = alboroto; tumulto.

fajina 1. (*Ven.*) a group of persons working together in one activity = grupo de personas que realizan una actividad. **2.** (*Ven.*) the activity itself = la actividad misma. **3.** (*Ven.*) a fight; a disorder = pelea; desorden.

faldellín (*Ven.*) the special clothing for a baby's baptism = traje especial que usa el bebé el día de su bautizo.

faldero (*Dom. Rep.*) a womanizer = mujeriego.

faldón (*Mex.*) an automobile fender = cubrelodo o tapabarros del autómovil.

falencia (*Colo.*) an irregular performance = rendimiento irregular.

falfallota (*Puerto Rico*) the mumps = paperas o parotiditis.

falfullero; farfullero (*Puerto Rico*) blustering = fanfarrón.

fallo (*Cuba*) silly; foolish = tonto; bobo.

falopa 1. (*Argen.*) a poor, inferior-quality thing = cosa o asunto muy pobre; de poca calidad. **2.** (*Argen.*) an illegal drug = droga ilegal.

faltar 1. (*Guat., Hond., Mex., Salva.*) to insult; to offend; to be disrespectful = insultar; ofender; ser irrespetuoso. **2.** (*Guat.*) to miss = añorar; echar de menos.

falucho (*Puerto Rico*) a small kite = cometa pequeño.

fama (*Argen., Bol., Chile, Cuba, Ecua., Peru*) the bull's eye; the center of the target = centro del blanco.

fan 1. (*from English*) a fan = ventilador. **2.** (*from English*) a fan = admirador; devoto; aficionado.

fanfullero; fullero (*Dom. Rep.*) a person who leaves a restaurant without paying the check = el que se va del restaurante sin pagar la cuenta.

fanfultear; fullería (*Dom. Rep.*) to leave a place without paying the bill = irse del lugar sin pagar la cuenta.

fañoso (*Ven.*) nasal; twanging = gangoso; el que habla con una voz nasal.

farfullero 1. (*Ecua.*) someone who offers many things but doesn't deliver accordingly = el que ofrece mucho y no cumple. **2.** (*Puerto Rico*) blustering = fanfarrón.

farmaleta (*Colo.*) a structure; a mold used in construction = armazón; molde usado en construcción.

farmero (*from English*) a farmer = granjero; el que posee o trabaja una granja.

farolero (*Argen.*) exaggerated; ostentatious = el que hace ostentación; exagerado.

faso (*Argen.*) a cigarette = cigarrillo.

fastidiar (*Puerto Rico*) to hurt; to harm = herir; hacer daño.

fasulo (*Argen.*) a bill (money) = billete.

fatiga (*Ven.*) hunger = hambre.

faul (*from English*) a foul in a ball game = falta en un juego de pelota.

fax (*from English*) a fax = facsímil o facsímile.

fayuto 1. (*Argen.*) untrustworthy; disloyal = desleal. **2.** (*Argen.*) a humbug; a hypocrite = farsante; hipócrita.

feca (*Puerto Rico*) a fake; a lie = falsedad; mentira.

féferes 1. (*Dom. Rep.*) useless objects = cachivaches. **2.** (*Ecua.*) things; stuff = bártulos; trastos.

feilear (*from English*) to fail = fracasar; errar; reprobar un examen.

felony (*from English*) a felony = delito.

felpa (*Ecua.*) a beating; a thrashing = zurra; tunda.

felpudo (*Chile*) a doormat = limpiapiés.

feminil (*from English*) feminine = femenino.

fenda; fender (*from English*) an automobile fender = cubrelodo, guardafangos o tapabarros del automóvil.

fender See **fenda**.

feo (*Colo.*) bad; unpleasant = malo desagradable.

feria 1. (*Costa Rica*) a tip = propina. **2.** (*Mex.*) change (money) = cambio; sencillo; suelto (dinero). **3.** (*Salva.*) a celebration = celebración.

ferrocarrilero (*Ecua.*) a railroad man = ferroviario.

ferry (*from English*) a ferry = transbordador.

festinado (*Ven.*) busy = atareado; ocupado.

feto (*Argen.*) an ugly person = persona muy fea.

feúra (*Colo., Dom. Rep.*) ugliness = fealdad.

fiaca 1. (*Argen.*) laziness = flojera. **2.** (*Uru.*) hunger = hambre.

fiambrera (*Puerto Rico*) several food containers carried one over the other to keep the food warm = varios tiestos de comida que se transportan uno sobre el otro para mantener la comida caliente.

fiambrería (*Argen., Chile, Para., Uru.*) a delicatessen; a store that specializes in **fiambres** = tienda donde se venden **fiambres**.

fiambres (*Argen., Chile, Para., Uru.*) prepared meats such as ham, sausage, and others = carnes elaboradas como jamón, salchichas y otras.

ficha 1. (*Colo.*) a trustful or distrustful person, according to context = persona digna de confianza o desconfinaza de acuerdo al contexto en que se usa. **2.** (*Ven.*) a person who has a bad reputation (informal) = persona de mala reputación (informal). **3.** (*Mex.*) a bottle cap = tapa de latón de una botella.

fichera (*Mex.*) a woman who gets paid to dance = mujer a quien se le paga para bailar.

ficho (*Colo.*) a trustful or distrustful person, according to context = persona digna de confianza o desconfinaza de acuerdo al contexto en que se usa.

fider (*from English*) a feeder = alimentador; artefacto para alimentar.

fifí (*Argen.*) a person with delicate clothes and manners = persona de prendas y modales finos.

fifiriche (*Costa Rica*) weak; thin = enclenque; flaco.

fil (*from English*) a sports field or an agricultural field = campo deportivo o campo de cultivo.

file (*from English*) a file = archivo.

filear (*Mex.*) to eat = comer.

filera (*Mex.*) a knife = cuchillo.

filerear (*Mex.*) to cut with a knife = cortar con cuchillo.

film; filme (*from English*) film = (RAE) película.

filme See **film**.

finca 1. (*Cuba, Pan., Puerto Rico*) a ranch = hacienda. **2.** (*Mex.*) a building = edificio.

fiñe (*Cuba*) a boy = niño; muchacho.

firme como un peral (*Chile*) very strong; secure = fuerte; de mucha firmeza.

firulístico 1. (*Dom. Rep.*) silly = tonto. **2.** (*Puerto Rico*) pedantic = pedante.

fisca (*Ven.*) a little bit = pizca.

fiscal (*Ven.*) the traffic police = el que controla y dirige el tránsito de vehículos.

fiul (*from English*) fuel = combustible; carburante.

flacuchento (*Chile, Ecua., Peru, Ven.*) skinny = flacucho.

flagship (*from English*) a flagship = buque insignia.

flamenco (*Hond., Puerto Rico*) a very thin person; skinny (informal) = una persona muy delgada; flaco (informal).

flash 1. (*from English*) flash = (N.E. destello luminoso de luz muy intensa que se usa en la fotografía). **2.** (*from English*) a flashlight = linterna eléctrica.

flat (*from English*) a flat tire = una goma o neumático desinflado.

flato 1. (*Cuba, Guat.*) apprehension; fear = aprehensión; miedo. **2.** (*Mex., Ven.*) melancholy; sadness = melancolía; tristeza.

fletación (*Dom. Rep.*) a massage; rubbing = masaje; fricción; frotamiento.

fletar 1. (*Chile*) to beat up = dar una zurra. **2.** (*Chile, Peru*) to chuck out; to remove by force = echar; sacar por la fuerza. **3.** (*Chile, Cuba, Dom. Rep., Mex.*) to run away; to slip away = arrancarse; escaparse. **4.** (*Cuba*) to flirt = coquetear.

fletear (*from English*) to let the air out of a tire; to get a flat tire = desinflar una goma o neumático; el acto de recibir el desinflamiento de un neumático.

fletera (*Cuba*) a prostitute = prostituta.

fliche (*Puerto Rico*) skinny = delgado(a).

flipear (*from English*) to flip over = lanzar al aire; dar vueltas en el aire.

flipiadora; el fliper (*Puerto Rico*) a pinball machine; a flipper machine = (N.E. máquina electrónica de juego en la cual se marcan puntos).

flirtear (*from English*) to flirt = coquetear.

flochar 1. (*from English*) to flush = vaciar un líquido con fuerza. **2.** (*from English*) to blush = sonrojarse.

flonkear (*from English*) to flunk = reprobar una materia en la escuela.

flor (*Chile*) good; high quality (informal) = bueno; de buena calidad (informal).

florear (*Ven.*) to flower = florecer.

florecido (*Cuba, Peru, Puerto Rico*) flowery; with flowers = floreado; que tiene flores.

floretear (*Dom. Rep.*) a flirtation = coquetear; enamorar como pasatiempo.

flout (*from English*) to float = flotar.

flowshart (*from English*) a flow chart = diagrama de flujo; organigrama.

flu (*from English*) the flu = gripe; influenza.

flux (*Ven.*) a two- or three-piece men's suit of the same color and material = traje de hombre de dos o tres piezas del mismo color y de la misma tela.

¡fo! (*Dom. Rep.*) an interjection that shows repugnance = interjección que expresa repugnancia.

fo (*Ecua.*) stinks = que apesta.

focet (*from English*) a faucet = grifo; llave.

fochi (*Ecua.*) get out of here, you bother me = fuera de aquí, me estás dando lata.

foco 1. (*Bol., Colo., Cuba, Ecua., Mex., Peru*) a lightbulb = bombillo(a); bujía eléctrica. **2.** (*Cuba*) a street light = farol de la calle. **3.** (*Mex.*) eyeglasses = anteojos.

fodongo 1. (*Mex.*) an old car in bad shape = automóvil viejo y en mal estado. **2.** (*Mex.*) a lazy person = persona haragana. **3.** (*Mex.*) fat = gordo.

foete (*Puerto Rico*) a whip = látigo.

fogón 1. (*Costa Rica*) a stove that requires firewood = cocina de leña. **2.** (*Colo., Cuba, Mex., Pan., Puerto Rico*) a stove = cocina; artefacto para cocinar.

folder (*from English*) a folder = (RAE) carpeta liviana donde se guardan o se archivan documentos.

follisca (*Ven.*) a row; a fight = gresca; pendencia.

follón 1. (*Ecua.*) a skirt = falda. **2.** (*Puerto Rico*) a mania; an obsession for something = manía u obsesión por algo.

fome (*Chile*) dull = sin gracia; insípido.

fonazo (*from English*) to have great fun = pasarlo muy bien.

fonchar (*Mex.*) to cheat in a marble game = trampear en el juego de canicas.

fonda (*Chile*) a refreshment stall at a party during the national independence days = puesto donde se bebe y se baila durante los días de las fiestas nacionales.

fondeado (*Ven.*) wealthy = adinerado.

fondear (*Chile*) to hide = esconder.

fondo (*Cuba, Mex.*) a slip = enaguas.

fonis (*from English*) comics = historietas.

for sale [pron. for seil] (*from English*) for sale = en venta; para la venta.

forado (*Chile, Peru*) a hole that extends from one side to the other in a wall = horadado; que está horadado; hoyo que cruza una muralla de lado a lado.

forma (*from English*) a form = formulario.

forman (*from English*) a foreman = capataz; encargado de dar órdenes a los que trabajan.

formar (*Argen.*) each pays his or her share in the group's expenses = pagar la parte que corresponde a cada uno en un gasto hecho por un grupo.

formatear See **formateo de disco**.

formateo de disco; formatear (*from English*) to format a floppy disk = crear los campos de memoria en un disco de computación.

fórmula (*Colo.*) a medical prescription = receta médica.

formular (*Colo.*) to issue a prescription = recetar medicinas.

fornitura (*from English*) furniture = mueble(s).

forrar 1. (*Guat., Hond.*) to eat well = comer bien. **2.** (*Guat., Mex.*) to supply oneself with food = aprovisionarse de comida. **3.** (*Mex., Uru.*) to save money = ahorrar dinero.

forro 1. (*Chile*) a problematic situation (informal) = situación difícil o problemática. **2.** (*Cuba*) a swindle; a fraud = engaño; fraude. **3.** (*Cuba*) a cover-up = encubrimiento. **4.** (*Uru.*) dumb (vulgar) = tonto; de poca inteligencia (vulgar). **5.** (*Uru.*) a condom (vulgar) = condón (vulgar).

fortunoso (*Guat.*) fortunate = afortunado.

forwardear (*from English*) to go forward = avanzar; ir hacia adelante.

fósforos (*Chile, Cuba, Ecua., Pan., Peru, Puerto Rico, Uru.*) matches = cerillos.

frajo (*Mex.*) a cigarette = cigarrillo.

franela 1. (*Colo., Cuba, Dom. Rep., Puerto Rico, Ven.*) an undershirt = camiseta de hombre. **2.** (*Ven.*) a T-shirt = polo; camisa deportiva sin abertura en frente.

frangollo 1. (*Peru*) a badly-prepared meal = comida mal preparada. **2.** (*Peru*) a mixture; a muddle; a mess = mezcolanza; revoltijo.

franque (*from English, Mex.*) frank; honest = franco; honesto.

fregada (*Ven.*) a person or situation that is difficult and complicated = situación o persona difícil y complicada.

fregadera 1. (*Mex.*) a dishwasher = máquina lavadora de platos. **2.** (*Mex.*) harassment; annoyances = acoso; hostigamiento; acción de molestar o producir una situación desagradable.

fregado 1. (*Chile, Colo., Ecua., Peru*) bothersome; annoying = molestoso; fastidioso; inoportuno. **2.** (*Colo.*) stubborn = porfiado. **3.** (*Colo.*) strict = estricto; riguroso. **4.** (*Guat., Hond., Mex., Nic.*) brazen; a bad person = desvergonzado; inescrupuloso; persona mala. **5.** (*Puerto Rico*) fresh; indecent = fresco; indecente. **6.** (*Ven.*) difficult; complicated = difícil; complicado.

fregador (*Pan.*) a sink = fregadero.

fregar 1. (*Chile, Colo.*) to bother; to annoy = molestar; fastidiar. **2.** (*Ven.*) to harm = dañar. **3.** (*Ven.*) to annoy = molestar. **4.** (*Ven.*) to kill = matar.

fregón 1. (*Puerto Rico*) shameless = descarado; desvergonzado. **2.** (*Mex.*) a person who annoys others continuously; a bothersome person = molestoso(a); una persona que molesta continuamente.

frejoles; frijoles (*Mex.*) beans = habichuelas.

frenillo (*Dom. Rep.*) a kite string; the threads that control a kite = hilos que permiten controlar la cometa.

fresco 1. (*Colo., Guat., Hond., Salva.*) a cool drink = refresco. **2.** (*Puerto Rico*) a freshman = estudiante de primer año en la universidad.

fresquesito (*Puerto Rico*) clean = limpio.

fría (*Ven.*) a cold beer = cerveza helada.

friar (*from English*) to fry = freír.

frigider; nevera (*Cuba*) a refrigerator = refrigerador.

frijoles; frisoles; frísoles (*Colo., Pan.*) beans = habichuelas.

friquear 1. (*Puerto Rico*) to freak out = descontrolarse; no saber que hacer en una situación específica. **2.** (*Puerto Rico*) to lose mental control; to be high on drugs = perder el control mental; alucinarse; volarse con drogas.

friquitín (*Puerto Rico*) a small food stand = pequeño puesto de comida.

frisa 1. (*from English*) a blanket = cobija; manta para la cama. **2.** (*from English*) a freezer = caja congeladora; sección congeladora de una heladera o refrigerador. **3.** (*Para.*) the hair of some fabrics such as velvet = pelo de algunas telas así como la del terciopelo.

frisado (*from English*) frozen = congelado.

frisar (*from English*) to freeze = congelar.

frísoles See **frijoles.**

frisoles See **frijoles.**

fritera (*Colo.*) **1.** a difficult thing = asunto engorroso. **2.** bothersome; dull = asunto pesado o aburrido.

frivolité (*Chile*) tatting = encaje tejido a mano.

friza (*Puerto Rico*) a blanket = frazada.

fruncirse 1. (*Argen.*) to get scared = asustarse. **2.** (*Argen.*) to shrink back = acobardarse. **3.** (*Argen.*) to be repentant = arrepentirse.

fruta bomba (*Cuba*) a papaya = papaya.

frutillas (*Chile*) strawberries = fresas.

fuente (*Cuba, Puerto Rico*) a tray = bandeja; azafate.

fuereño (*Ecua., Mex., Peru*) an outsider = afuerano; el que no pertenece al lugar.

fuerte 1. (*Argen.*) a nice-looking young male = hombre joven de buena presencia. **2.** (*Mex.*) any strong liquor = cualquier licor de alto grado alcohólico. **3.** (*Mex.*) a very influential person = persona muy influyente. **4.** (*Mex.*) a very attractive or strong man = hombre muy atractivo o de mucha fuerza física.

fuete (*Dom. Rep.*) a whip = látigo.

fuetera; garrotera; muenda; trilla (*Colo.*) a beating; a thrashing; a spanking = azotaina; zurra; tunda.

fuetiza (*Dom. Rep.*) a severe chastisement = zurra; tunda; castigo severo.

fufú 1. (*Colo.*) mashed plantain with fried pork and other ingredients = puré de plátano con puerco frito y otros ingredientes. **2.** (*Puerto Rico*) witchcraft = brujería; hechizo.

fula(o) (*Pan.*) blonde = rubio(a).

fulear (*from English*) to fool = engañar.

fulera(o); julero(a) (*Chile*) fake (informal) = falsa(o) (informal).

full (*from English*) full = lleno; completo; copado.

fullería See **fanfultear**.

fullero 1. (*Colo.*) nice; graceful = agradable; gracioso. **2.** (*Ven.*) presumptuous = presumido; presuntuoso. **3.** (*Dom. Rep.*) a person who leaves a restaurant without paying the bill = persona que se va de un restaurante sin pagar la cuenta.

fultaim (*from English*) full-time = trabajo de horario completo.

fumar (*Argen.*) to cheat; to deceive = engañar; estafar.

fumón (*Ven.*) a marijuana smoker (informal) = marihuanero (informal).

funá (*Argen.*) take it easy = tómalo con calma.

funcar (*Argen.*) to function = funcionar.

funche (*Ven.*) corn flour = harina de maíz.

funda 1. (*Colo.*) a skirt = falda. **2.** (*Dom. Rep.*) a bag = bolsa.

fundifá; fundillo (*Ecua.*) the buttocks = nalgas.

fundillo See **fundifá**.

fundoso See **bergantín**.

fungir (*Hond.*) to substitute in a job = reemplazar en un empleo.

fuñir (*Puerto Rico, Ven.*) to damage; to bother = perjudicar; molestar.

furnitura (*Dom. Rep.*) furniture = muebles.

furruco (*Ven.*) a Venezuelan folkloric musical instrument = instrumento musical folclórico venezolano.

furrusca (*Colo.*) a disturbance; an uproar = alboroto; pelotera.

fútbol (*from English*) a soccer game = balompié, (RAE) juego entre dos equipos de once jugadores cada uno, cuya finalidad es hacer entrar un balón por una portería, golpéandole con los pies.

fute (*Colo.*) a whip = látigo.

futin (*from English*) footing = marcha; caminata.

futre (*Chile*) a dude = lechuguino; el que no acepta trabajos difíciles o pesados.

G

gabachero(a) (*Mex.*) to be fond of the Anglo-Saxons; to like Americans = persona a la que le gustan los anglosajones; entusiasta por lo que es estadounidense.

gabacho (*Mex.*) an Anglo-Saxon in the United States (derogatory); a **gringo** = anglosajón de los Estados Unidos (peyorativo); **gringo**.

gabán 1. (*Ven.*) a variation of the **joropo** = una de las variaciones del **joropo**. **2.** (*Puerto Rico*) a suit jacket = saco o chaqueta de hombre.

gabardina 1. (*Argen., Colo., Mex.*) a raincoat = impermeable. **2.** (*Mex.*) a variation of **gabacho**, an Anglo-Saxon in the United States (derogatory); a gringo = variación de **gabacho**, anglosajón de los Estados Unidos (peyorativo); **gringo**.

gabardinos (*Mex.*) those who live in the United States = norteamericanos; habitantes de los Estados Unidos.

gabela 1. (*Chile*) an issue; a matter = asunto; cuestión. **2.** (*Colo.*) an advantage; a profit = ventaja; provecho. **3.** (*Colo.*) a duty; a burden = impuesto; tributo; gravamen.

gabriela (*Chile*) a bill worth five-thousand pesos (informal) = billete de cinco mil pesos (informal).

gaceta (*Puerto Rico*) the thread used to control a kite = hilos usados para controlar una cometa.

gacho 1. (*Mex.*) bad; ugly; stinky = malo; feo; maloliente. **2.** (*Puerto Rico*) one-eared = con una sola oreja.

gachupín (*Mex.*) a Spaniard = de origen español.

gadejo (*Colo.*) a person who has the intention of annoying others = persona con las ganas de molestar a otros.

gafas 1. (*Cuba*) prescription glasses = anteojos para corregir la visión; lentes. **2.** (*Puerto Rico*) sunglasses = anteojos de sol; lentes oscuros.

gafo 1. (*Ven.*) a dim person = el de poca inteligencia. **2.** (*Ven.*) clumsiness = torpeza.

gafufa (*Colo.*) "four-eyes" (derogatory); a person who wears glasses = "cuatro ojos" (peyorativo); la persona que usa anteojos.

gagear (*Dom. Rep.*) to stutter = tartamudear.

gago (*Dom. Rep., Peru, Ven.*) a stutterer = tartamudo.

gagüear (*Puerto Rico*) to stutter = tartamudear.

gaguear (*Colo., Peru*) to stutter = tartamudear.

gaita (*Ven.*) a Venezuelan Christmas carol = canto folclórico navideño venezolano.

gajo 1. (*Chile*) one grape; one piece of a fruit that can be divided naturally into different sections = una uva; parte de una fruta que se puede dividir naturalmente en diferentes secciones. **2.** (*Hond.*) a lock of hair = mechón de pelo. **3.** (*Ven.*) a mistake; a failure = equivocación; fallo. **4.** (*Ven.*) penury and privation = penurias y privaciones.

galafardo (*Colo.*) a thief who steals cheap, unimportant objects = el que roba objetos baratos de poca importancia.

galgo (*Colo.*) always hungry; fond of sweets = siempre hambriento; bueno para los dulces.

galla (*Chile*) a gal; so-and-so = tipeja; fulana.

gallada (*Colo.*) an audacious or astute action = acción audaz o astuta.

gallego (*Argen., Uru.*) a nickname for any Spaniard = apodo para cualquier español.

gallera (*Colo., Dom. Rep., Guat., Hond., Pan., Puerto Rico, Salva.*) a cockfight ring = ruedo de gallos; lugar donde se efectúan peleas de gallos.

galleta 1. (*Ven.*) confusion; disorder; congestion = confusión; desorden; congestionamiento. **2.** (*Dom. Rep., Puerto Rico*) a slap = bofetada.

galletazo (*Cuba*) a slap = bofetada; cachetada.

galletica (*Colo., Cuba*) a cookie = galleta.

galletita (*Puerto Rico*) a cookie = galleta.

galletoso (*Ven.*) messy; confused = enredado; confuso.

gallinacea (*Colo.*) a man who flirts with a woman = hombre que coquetea para seducir a una mujer.

gallinazo 1. (*Colo., Ecua., Peru*) a buzzard = buitre. **2.** (*Colo.*) a ladies' man; he is always after women = hombre galante; el que anda siempre tras las mujeres.

gallinero (*Ven.*) the worst seat in the theater = la localidad más barata del teatro.

gallito (*Puerto Rico*) a child's game = juego infantil.

gallo 1. (*Argen., Mex.*) a serenade = serenata. **2.** (*Colo.*) each piece of chrome plating on a car = cada uno de los cromados que adornan un automóvil. **3.** (*Puerto Rico*) a good-looking man = hombre bien parecido. **4.** (*Chile*) a pal; a guy; so-and-so (informal) = informal para compinche; camarado; compañero; tipo; fulano.

galpón (*Argen., Bol., Chile, Colo., Ecua., Peru, Uru.*) a large, open shed; a roof without walls = cobertizo grande y abierto; techo sin murallas.

gamba 1. (*Argen.*) a bill of one-hundred pesos = billete de cien pesos. **2.** (*Chile*) a big foot = un pie grande. **3.** (*Chile*) a big shrimp = camarón grande.

gambetear (*Colo.*) to dribble = (N.E. **driblar**; movimiento rápido en los deportes para evitar un golpe del contrario).

gamín (*Colo.*) a street urchin = niño vagabundo.

gamonal 1. (*Bol.*) a landlord (derogatory) = despectivo para nombrar al dueño de las tierras o la propiedad. **2.** (*Colo.*) a political boss; a person who controls a number of voters = cacique político; el que controla votantes.

ganadero (*Para.*) the owner of a ranch = dueño de una hacienda.

ganancia See **de forro**.

ganbout (*from English*) a gunboat = cañonera.

ganchito; presilla (*Cuba, Pan.*) a hair pin = horquilla para el cabello.

gancho 1. (*Argen., Colo., Cuba, Guat., Hond., Mex., Nic., Peru, Uru.*) a hair pin = horquilla. **2.** (*Peru*) a connection; a social, political or professional contact = enlace o contacto social, político o profesional. **3.** (*Pan.*) a safety pin = imperdible.

gancho de nodriza (*Colo.*) a safety pin = imperdible.

ganchudo (*Colo.*) with thorns or spines = que tiene púas o espinas.

gandinga (*Puerto Rico*) a typical dish prepared with pork tripe, kidneys, and heart = plato típico preparado con tripas, riñones y corazón de puerco.

gandul (*Puerto Rico*) a vegetable shaped like a pea prepared with rice; it is a typical Puerto Rican dish = vegetal en la forma de un guisante que se prepara con arroz y constituye un plato típico de Puerto Rico.

ganga (*from English*) a gang = pandilla.

gangoche (*Costa Rica*) an inferior-quality fabric; a jute sack = tela de baja calidad; saco o bolsa de yute.

gangster (*from English*) a gangster = (RAE) miembro de una banda organizada de malhechores que actúa en las grandes ciudades.

ganguero (*from English*) a member of a gang = pandillero.

ganman (*from English*) a gunman = pistolero.

ganso (*Chile*) clumsy; ungainly = torpe; desgarbado.

gap (*from English*) a gap = espacio; vacío; intervalo.

garabato 1. (*Colo.*) a pitchfork (the farm tool) = horqueta. **2.** (*Colo.*) charm; grace = gracejo; gracia femenina. **3.** (*Puerto Rico*) an ugly woman = mujer fea.

gararey (*Dom. Rep.*) jealous = celoso.

garata (*Puerto Rico*) a brawl; an uproar = alboroto; tumulto.

garbinche; garvinche; bolitas (*Colo.*) marbles = canicas.

gardelito (*Argen.*) a good singer of popular songs = el que canta muy bien canciones populares.

garden party (*from English*) a garden party = (N.E. fiesta que se celebra en el jardín).

garetas See **cazcorvo**.

gargarear (*Chile, Guat., Peru*) to gargle = gargarizar.

garifo (*Costa Rica*) hungry; greedy = hambriento; codicioso; avaro.

garífuna 1. (*Hond.*) related to the African culture = relativo a la cultura africana. **2.** (*Hond.*) a person of African origin = persona de origen africano.

garita (*Mex.*) a customs house = oficina de aduana.

garnacha 1. (*Hond., Nic.*) strength; violence = fuerza; violencia. **2.** (*Hond.*) an old car = automóvil viejo.

gárnica (*Bol.*) a kind of green, very hot pepper = ají verde muy picante.

garoso (*Colo.*) hungry; fond of eating = comilón; hambriento.

garra 1. (*Chile, Uru.*) strength = fuerza. **2.** (*Colo.*) a remnant of clothing = ropa o zapatos viejos; vestimentas sobrantes. **3.** (*Colo.*) pork skin for cooking = piel de cerdo para cocinar. **4.** (*Mex.*) old clothes; inferior-quality, cheap clothes = ropa de bajo precio; ropa vieja o de mala calidad.

garrero (*Mex.*) a dealer of cheap clothing; a used-clothing dealer = vendedor de ropas usadas o de bajo precio por su mala calidad.

garrobo (*Nic.*) an iguana = iguana.

garrote (*Mex., Puerto Rico*) a stick = palo.

garrotear 1. (*Mex.*) to beat severely = golpear severamente; dar con el garrote; dar una paliza. **2.** (*Mex.*) to defeat by an ample margin in a sporting match = derrotar por un amplio margen en algún juego o encuentro deportivo. **3.** (*Chile*) to overcharge = cobrar un precio excesivo.

garrotera (*Colo.*) a fight; a violent discussion = pelea; discusión violenta.

garrotero 1. (*Chile*) a person who is always borrowing money from others = el que pide dinero prestado constantemente. **2.** (*Cuba*) stingy = cicatero; mezquino. **3.**

(*Ecua.*) a moneylender = prestamista. **4.** (*Peru*) a bully; a tough = guapetón; valentón.

garrotiza 1. (*Mex.*) a severe beating = golpes severos; una tunda que se da con el garrote; paliza. **2.** (*Mex.*) a defeat by an ample margin in a sporting match = derrota por un amplio margen en algún juego o encuentro deportivo.

garúa (*Argen., Bol., Ecua., Guat., Hond., Peru, Salva., Uru.*) drizzle = llovizna muy liviana.

garufa (*Argen.*) a party animal = el que gusta de las fiestas.

garuga (*Chile*) drizzle = llovizna liviana.

garvinche See **garbinche**.

gas 1. (*Colo., Puerto Rico*) gasoline = gasolina. **2.** (*Puerto Rico*) an alcoholic beverage = bebida alcóholica.

gas warfare [pron. gas worfear] (*from English*) gas warfare = guerra química.

gásfiter (*Chile, Peru*) a plumber = fontanero.

gasfitería (*Chile, Peru*) plumbing = fontanería.

gasolin (*from English*) gasoline = gasolina.

gasolinera (*Cuba, Dom. Rep., Mex., Pan., Puerto Rico*) a gas station = estación de gasolina; bomba de gasolina.

gata 1. (*Chile*) a car jack = gato del automóvil. **2.** (*Mex.*) a maid; a young and good-looking female maid = camarera; sirvienta; criada joven y bonita. **3.** (*Puerto Rico*) a variety of red fish = una variedad de pez de color rojo.

gatear (*Bol.*) to flirt = andar en aventuras amorosas.

gato 1. (*Argen.*) an urban folk dance = baile criollo de la ciudad. **2.** (*Cuba*) a pickpocket = carterista; ladrón de bolsillos. **3.** (*Dom. Rep.*) tongs = tenazas. **4.** (*Dom. Rep.*) a thief = ladrón. **5.** (*Guat.*) the biceps = bíceps.

gauchada (*Argen., Chile*) to provide a service; to do a big favor = hacer un favor desinteresadamente; prestar un servicio de gran valor.

gaucho 1. (*Argen., Uru.*) an Argentine or Uruguayan cowboy = vaquero de las pampas argentinas o uruguayas. **2.** (*Para.*) a flirtatious man = conquistador de mujeres.

gavilán (*Colo., Cuba, Mex., Pan., Puerto Rico*) a hawk = halcón.

gavilla See **barra**.

gay (*Argen.*) a homosexual = homosexual.

gaznate 1. (*Chile*) the gullet = garganta; pescuezo. **2.** (*Ecua., Peru*) a sweet meat prepared with pineapple or coconut = carne dulce cocinada con piña o coco.

gaznatón (*Colo.*) a slap = cachetada.

gazpacho (*Hond.*) the sediment; the dregs = heces; residuos.

gelati (*Argen.*) ice cream = helado.

gemelos 1. (*Colo.*) twin brothers = mellizos. **2.** (*Cuba, Mex.*) field glasses = binoculares.

gendarme 1. (*Argen.*) a policeman in the provinces = agente de policía de las provincias. **2.** (*Guat., Hond., Mex., Salva., Uru.*) a policeman = agente de policía.

gente copetuda (*Argen.*) important people = gente importante.

gentleman (*from English*) a gentleman = caballero.

gentleman agreement (*from English*) a gentleman's agreement = acuerdo entre caballeros.

gigabyte [pron. guigabait] (*from English*) a gigabyte; a unit of 1,073,741,824 bytes = unidad de 1.073.741.824 **bits**; se abrevia Giga o Gb.

gil; menso; menzo (*Argen., Chile, Colo., Ecua.*) silly; a person who is easy to cheat; naive; a sucker = jilipollas; tonto(a); papanatas; incauto(a); simplón; el/la que es fácil de engañar.

gira (*Puerto Rico*) to get high on drugs = volarse con drogas.

giro (*Dom. Rep.*) a yellow rooster = gallo de color matizado con amarillo.

gis (*Colo.*) blackboard chalk = tiza para el pizarrón.

glamur (*from English*) glamour = atractivo; encanto.

glándulas (*Colo.*) the tonsils = amígdalas.

globo 1. (*Argen.*) a lie; exaggerated gossip = mentira; noticia o chisme exagerado. **2.** (*Dom. Rep.*) a lamp = lámpara.

gloriado (*Chile*) an alcoholic beverage for a wake = bebida alcohólica para un velatorio.

glu 1. (*from English*) glue = goma de pegar. **2.** (*from English*) any adhesive = cualquier pegamento.

gobelinos (*Argen.*) the testicles (vulgar) = testículos (vulgar).

gocho 1. (*Ven.*) clumsy; a brute = torpe; bruto. **2.** (*Ven.*) hunchbacked = jorobado.

godo (*Colo.*) conservative = conservador.

godos (*Colo.*) long underpants = calzoncillos largos de hombre.

gofia (*Colo.*) a detective (informal) = detective (informal).

gofio 1. (*Ven.*) roasted corn flour = harina tostada de maíz. **2.** (*Ven.*) a pastry prepared with that flour = dulce hecho con esa harina. **3.** (*Nic.*) a pastry made with **pinol** = alfajores de **pinol**.

gogo-girl (*from English*) a gogo girl = (N.E. animadora de un bar que baila y charla con los clientes).

golilla 1. (*Chile*) a washer = arandela. **2.** (*Ven.*) easy to do or to get = lo que se hace o logra con facilidad.

golillero (*Ven.*) a person who wants things for free = el que desea obtener cosas gratuitamente.

golkiper (*from English*) a goal keeper = guardametas; arquero; portero.

golosa; peregrina; pata sola (*Colo.*) hopscotch = infernáculo; truque; rayuela.

goma (*Argen.*) a woman's chest (vulgar) = pechos de mujer (vulgar).

goma 1. (*Chile*) a gofer; a person who works hard and with loyalty for somebody else = el que trabaja para otro con lealtad y ahínco. **2.** (*Colo.*) a penchant; a desire to do something = afición; deseo por hacer alguna cosa. **3.** (*Puerto Rico*) a condom = condón.

goma elástica; liga (*Cuba*) a rubber band = bandita de goma.

gomita (*Argen.*, *Puerto Rico*) a rubber band = bandita de goma.

gorda 1. (*Chile*) a short and thick sausage = salchicha corta y gruesa. **2.** (*Mex.*) a very thick Mexican **tortilla** made from corn meal = una **tortilla** Mexicana muy gruesa hecha de harina de maíz.

gorila (*Argen.*) an officer of the army participating in a coup d'état = militar golpista.

gorozo 1. (*Ven.*) a big eater = comilón. **2.** (*Ven.*) hungry = hambriento.

gotario (*Chile*) a dropper = cuentagotas.

goterero (*Colo.*) someone who drinks and eats at another's expense = el que bebe y come a costas de otro.

gotero (*Argen.*, *Chile*, *Colo.*, *Cuba*, *Mex.*, *Peru*, *Puerto Rico*) a dropper = cuentagotas.

gozón (*Colo.*) a good dancer; a party animal = persona a quien le gusta bailar y andar de fiestas.

grabol (*from English*) gravel = piedrecillas; guijarros.

gracejo (*Guat.*) **1.** a buffoon; a clown = bufón; payaso. **2.** silly = tonto.

graficmode (*from English*) the graphic mode in a computer = modo gráfico en la computadora.

grajo (*Dom. Rep.*, *Ecua.*) armpit odor = olor de las axilas.

grama (*Cuba*, *Dom. Rep.*, *Puerto Rico*, *Salva.*) a lawn = césped.

gramilla (*Colo.*) a soccer field = cancha de fútbol.

grampa (*Colo.*) a staple = grapa.

grampadora (*Colo.*) a stapler = grapadora.

grandulón (*Argen.*) overgrown; a big boy who behaves as a child = grandullón; muchacho que se comporta como un niño.

granizado; raspado; rasco-rasco (*Cuba*) sherbet = sorbete.

gras (*from English*) grass; a lawn = yerba; césped; pasto.

grasa (*Mex.*) shoe polish = betún para el calzado.

greda (*Chile*) clay = arcilla.

greifrut (*from English*) a grapefruit = pomelo; toronja.

greifú (*Para.*) a grapefruit = pomelo; toronja.

greive (*from English*) gravy = jugo cremoso de la carne asada.

grifo 1. (*Bol.*, *Ecua.*, *Peru*) a cheap tavern that sells **chicha** = taberna pobre donde se compra **chicha**. **2.** (*Bol.*, *Ecua.*, *Peru*) a gas station = estación de gasolina. **3.** (*Colo.*) a drug addict = drogadicto. **4.** (*Puerto Rico*) a half-breed, between Caucasian and African = mestizo; hijo de una persona blanca y una negra. **5.** (*Puerto Rico*) a white person with curly hair = persona blanca con el pelo muy crespo.

gril (*from English*) a grill = parrilla.

grilla (*from English*) a grill = parrilla.

grillero (*Argen.*) the side pocket in a pair of pants = bolsillo lateral del pantalón.

grillo (*Ven.*) **1.** an obsession = obsesión. **2.** a mania = manía.

grima (*Colo.*) grief; sadness = pena; tristeza.

grin (*from English*) green = verde.

gringo 1. (*Argen.*, *Bol.*, *Chile*, *Ecua.*, *Para.*, *Peru*, *Uru.*) any white blond alien who speaks Spanish with a foreign accent = cualquier extranjero rubio que habla el español con acento. **2.** (*Mex.*) a Caucasian; a white person from the United States = estadounidense.

gripa (*from English*) the flu = gripe.

griseta (*Argen.*) a poor girl (vulgar) = muchacha pobre (vulgar).

grisma (*Guat., Hond.*) a bit; a pinch = brizna; pizca.

grocer; groceri; grocería (*from English*) 1. groceries = abarrotes. 2. a grocery store = tienda de abarrotes.

groceri See **grocer**.

grocería See **grocer**.

grogui (*from English*) groggy = tambaleante aturdido; sin conocimiento.

groso (*Chile*) good = bueno.

gross margin (*from English*) a gross margin = margen de ganancias brutas.

grupo (*Argen., Chile*) a lie; a falsehood; a fake argument = mentira; falsedad; argumento falso.

guabinear (*Ven.*) to avoid a definition; to stay away from a decision = evadir definiciones; evitar tomar partido.

guacal (*Colo., Ven.*) a box used as a measure to trade farm products = caja que se usa como medida para comerciar productos agrícolas.

guacamole 1. (*Cuba*) an avocado and tomato salad = ensalada de aguacate y tomate. 2. (*Mex.*) a salad whose main ingredient is avocado = ensalada a base de aguacates.

guacara (*Mex.*) vomit = vómito.

guacha (*from English*) a watch = reloj.

guachada (*Colo.*) a dirty word; a vulgarity = grocería; vulgaridad.

guachafita 1. (*Ven.*) a disturbance; a noisy crowd = alboroto; multitud bulliciosa. 2. (*Ven.*) inefficiency; disorganization = ineficacia; desorganización.

guachapear; guachapiar (*Chile*) to steal (informal) = hurtar; robar (informal).

guachapiar See **guachapear**.

guachar (*from English*) to watch = mirar.

guachatería (*from English*) a laundromat; a place with automatic washing machines = el lugar donde se lava; el lavadero automático.

guache (*Colo.*) a villain; a vulgar and rude person = villano; grocero; persona vulgar.

guachiman 1. (*from English*) a watchman = vigilante; guardia; el que cuida. 2. (*Nic.*) a servant = criado; sirviente.

guacho 1. (*Argen., Bol., Colo., Ecua., Peru, Uru.*) an orphan (derogatory) = peyorativo para referirse a un huérfano. 2. (*Argen., Chile*) a strong insult (vulgar) = insulto fuerte y vulgar.

guacuco (*Ven.*) a shellfish = molusco comestible.

guaflera (*from English*) a waffle machine = máquina para preparar **guafles**.

guafles (*from English*) a waffle = pan muy delgado y esponjoso que se cuece entre dos planchas calientes.

guagua 1. (*Bol., Chile, Ecua., Peru*) a baby = bebé. 2. (*Cuba, Dom. Rep., Puerto Rico*) a bus = bus; autobús. 3. (*Dom. Rep., Puerto Rico*) any large vehicle for transporting people = cualquier vehículo grande para pasajeros. 4. (*Dom. Rep., Puerto Rico*) a station wagon = (N.E. camioneta cerrada para transportar pasajeros).

guagualón (*Chile*) a young man who behaves as a child = joven que se comporta como un niño pequeño.

guaguero (*Dom. Rep.*) a bus driver = conductor de ómnibus.

guaife (*from English*) a wife = esposa.

guaina (*Chile*) a farmer; to behave as a farmer = el del campo; el que se comporta como campesino.

guaipe (*Chile, Ecua.*) burlap = estopa; hilachas de algodón que se usan para limpiar.

guaiper (*from English*) a windshield wiper = limpiaparabrisas.

guajiro 1. (*Cuba*) rustic; peasant-like = rústico; acampesinado. 2. (*Cuba*) a typical character from the Cuban countryside = personaje típico de los campos cubanos.

guajolote (*Mex.*) a turkey; a fool = pavo; tonto.

gualeta (*Chile*) a fin = aleta.

gualmo (*Colo.*) a wooden shovel = pala de madera.

gualuche (*Puerto Rico*) a swelling = hinchazón.

guamazo 1. (*Ven.*) a strong blow with a blunt object = golpe fuerte dado con un objeto contundente. 2. (*Ven.*) a wound from a shot = herida de bala. 3. (*Ven.*) a misfortune; a mishap = desgracia; contratiempo. 4. (*Ven.*) a swig of strong liquor = trago de licor fuerte. 5. (*Costa Rica*) a violent blow = golpe violento.

guame (*Puerto Rico*) an easy thing; a good deal = algo fácil; buen negocio; trato favorable.

guanaco 1. (*Chile*) a water cannon truck = carro policial que lanza agua. 2. (*Bol., Ecua., Peru*) an animal from the camel family that lives only in the Andes = mamífero camélido que vive sólo en los Andes. 3. (*Guat., Hond.*) a nickname for Salvadoreans = apodo para los salvadoreños. 4. (*Nic.*) an insult meaning silly or stupid = insulto con el significado de bobo o tonto.

guanacos (*Salva.*) a nickname that the Salvadoreans use for themselves = apodo con que los salvadoreños se llaman a sí mismos.

guandolo (*Colo.*) smuggled firewater = aguardiente de contrabando.

guangoche 1. (*Hond.*) a sack; a big bag = costal; bolsa grande. 2. (*Guat.*) a sack used in the coffee harvest = costal usado en la cosecha del café.

guanguero (*Colo.*) a noisy, bustling person = bullicioso; bullangero.

guano 1. (*Bol., Chile, Ecua., Peru, Uru.*) manure; any animal feces = cualquier tipo de heces de animal; excremento animal. 2. (*Cuba*) money (informal) = dinero (informal). 3. (*Cuba*) a person who is or acts crazy (informal) = loco; chiflado (informal). 4. (*Dom. Rep.*) a palm tree; palm leaves = palmera; hojas de palmera. 5. (*Peru*) bird dung used as fertilizer = excremento de las aves usado como fertilizante.

guantes (*Colo., Cuba, Puerto Rico*) mittens = mitones.

guapear (*Chile*) to boast; to bluster = echar bravatas.

guapo(a) 1. (*Colo., Cuba*) fearless; brave = temerario(a); valiente. 2. (*Ecua., Peru*) harsh; severe = riguroso(a); severo(a). 3. (*Dom. Rep.*) angry = enojado. 4. (*Dom. Rep.*) quarrelsome; a bully = pendenciero. 5. (*Dom. Rep.*) boastful = fanfarrón.

guaquear (*Colo.*) to look for hidden treasures = buscar tesoros escondidos.

guaquero (*Colo.*) a person who looks for hidden treasures = el que busca tesoros escondidos.

guaraca (*Ecua., Peru*) a sling = honda.

guaracazo (*Colo.*) a violent, unexpected blow = golpe violento, imprevisto y repentino.

guaracha (*Colo.*) a popular dance = baile popular.

guarachar; rumbear (*Puerto Rico*) to dance = bailar.

guarache; huarachas (*Mex.*) sandals = sandalias.

guaraches (*Guat.*) old shoes = chancletas; zapatos viejos.

guaracho (*Hond.*) an old, worn hat = sombrero viejo en mal estado.

guaragua; levante (*Hond.*) a lie = mentira.

guaraguao (*Puerto Rico*) a hawk = halcón.

guaral (*Ven.*) a fishing line = sedal; hilo de pescar.

guaramo (*Ven.*) courage; drive = valor; pujanza.

guarán (*Puerto Rico*) a very big banana = banana muy grande.

guarango (*Uru.*) a foolish or silly person (pejorative) = persona chistosa que hace tonterías (despectivo).

guaraní 1. (*Argen., Bol., Chile, Para., Uru.*) a native American of Paraguay, the northeast of Bolivia or the north of Argentina = nativo original del noreste de Bolivia, Paraguay y el norte de Argentina. 2.

(*Argen., Bol., Para.*) the language of those natives = la lengua de esos indígenas.

guarape; guarapeado; guarapero (*Ecua.*) drunk = borracho; ebrio.

guarapeado See **guarape**.

guarapear (*Dom. Rep.*) to get drunk = emborracharse.

guarapero See **guarape**.

guarapillo (*Puerto Rico*) a medicinal tea = infusión medicinal.

guarapo 1. (*Bol., Colo., Ecua., Guat., Hond., Peru, Ven.*) the juice of sugar cane fermented; liquor from sugar cane = jugo fermentado de la caña de azúcar; licor de caña. **2.** (*Bol., Colo., Ecua., Guat., Hond., Ven.*) any cheap brandy = cualquier aguardiente de baja calidad. **3.** (*Puerto Rico*) a medicinal tea = infusión medicinal. **4.** (*Dom. Rep., Guat., Hond.*) the juice of the cane = jugo de caña.

guardería (*Pan.*) kindergarten = jardín infantil.

guardó el carro (*Cuba*) it is dead = se murió.

guarén (*Chile*) a big rat that lives in the countryside = rata de gran tamaño que vive en los campos.

guareto (*Puerto Rico*) similar; equal = semejante; igual; muy parecido.

guargüero (*Colo.*) the gullet = gaznate.

guaricha; vagamunda (*Colo.*) a prostitute (vulgar) = prostituta (vulgar).

guarimba (*Ven.*) a hideout (informal) = guarida (informal); lugar para ponerse a salvo.

guaripola 1. (*Argen., Chile*) a baton = bastón del tambor mayor en una banda musical que marcha. **2.** (*Para.*) cheap brandy = aguardiente de mala calidad.

guaro 1. (*Colo.*) someone who gets drunk from cane firewater = el que se emborracha con aguardiente de caña. **2.** (*Guat., Hond., Salva.*) rum = ron. **3.** (*Salva.*) any cheap liquor = cualquier licor barato.

guasa (*Colo.*) a water-valve washer = arandela del grifo.

guasamaco (*Chile*) uneducated; impolite; without manners = el que no sabe comportarse en público; de modales toscos; no educado.

guasapa (*Guat.*) a spinning top = peonza; perinola.

guasca 1. (*Para.*) the penis (vulgar) = pene (vulgar). **2.** (*Argen., Bol., Chile, Ecua., Peru*) a leather or cord thong; a whip = correa de cuero o de cuerdas; látigo. **3.** (*Colo.*) farmer-like behavior; to be shy and timid in the city = comportamiento acampesinado; ser tímido en la ciudad.

guascazo (*Colo.*) a blow with the fist = golpe de puño.

guaso 1. (*Argen.*) a person who behaves like a peasant = una persona que se comporta como un campesino. **2.** (*Argen., Chile, Cuba*) an uneducated or ill-mannered person = persona sin educación y sin modales. **3.** (*Chile*) a proud title for the Chilean cowboy = título de orgullo para el personaje típico del campo chileno.

guasupyta (*Para.*) the red deer that live in the Rio de la Plata basin = venado rojo que habita la cuenca del Río de la Plata.

guata 1. (*Argen.*) animal tripe = callos; estómago del animal. **2.** (*Chile, Ecua., Peru*) a belly; a stomach; a paunch = barriga; estómago. **3.** (*Colo.*) a poisonous snake = una serpiente venenosa. **4.** (*Ven.*) a fib = paparruchada; decir o contar mentiras.

guatapique (*Chile*) a small firecracker that explodes when crushed against the floor = petardo que explota al arrojarlo al suelo con violencia.

guato 1. (*Bol.*) a string = cordel. **2.** (*Mex.*) a brawl; an uproar = alboroto; tumulto.

guatoco (*Bol.*) small = pequeño.

guatoso (*Mex.*) noisy = bullicioso.

guayaba 1. (*Nic.*) a big mouth = bocota. **2.** (*Colo., Ven.*) a lie = mentira. **3.** (*Colo., Cuba, Dom. Rep., Puerto Rico, Ven.*) a guava = fruta tropical; fruto del guayabo.

guayabear (*Puerto Rico*) to lie = mentir.

guayabera (*Cuba, Dom. Rep., Puerto Rico*) a typical shirt worn in the Caribbean = camisa típica del Caribe.

guayabo (*Colo.*) a hangover = resaca; después de la borrachera.

guayacán (*Puerto Rico*) a person of strong character = persona fuerte de carácter.

guayao (*Puerto Rico*) drunk = borracho.

guayaquí 1. (*Para.*) the natives that live in Southwest Paraguay = tribus de indios que habitan el suroeste del Paraguay. **2.** (*Para.*) the language of those natives = lengua que hablan esos indios.

guazapa (*Hond.*) teetotum; a small spinning top = perinola; peonza pequeña.

gueldear (*from English*) to weld = soldar.

güera(o) (*Mex.*) a blond person = persona rubia.

güero 1. (*Ven.*) cassava liquor = licor de yuca. **2.** (*Chile, Ven.*) a rotten egg = huevo podrido; huevo que tiene mal olor. **3.** (*Chile, Ven.*) empty; without substance = vacío; sin sustancia.

güevada; huevada 1. (*Argen., Chile*) something stupid; a foolish remark (very vulgar) = algo estúpido; observación tonta (muy vulgar). **2.** (*Argen., Chile*) anything with an unknown name; stuff (very vulgar) = cualquier cosa cuyo nombre se desconoce; cuestión; asunto (muy vulgar).

güevas; huevas (*Argen., Chile*) scrotum and/or testicles (very vulgar) = forma muy vulgar para los testículos y/o el escroto.

güevear; huevear 1. (*Chile*) to bother; to pester (vulgar) = molestar; importunar (vulgar). **2.** (*Chile*) to behave clumsily (vulgar) = actuar torpemente (vulgar).

güevo (*Dom. Rep.*) the penis (vulgar) = pene (vulgar).

güevón; huevón 1. (*Argen., Chile, Uru.*) stupid; silly; lazy; slow; dim-witted (vulgar) = estúpido; tonto; torpe; flojo; lento (vulgar). **2.** (*Colo.*) stupid (vulgar) = estúpido (vulgar).

güevonada; huevonada (*Argen., Chile, Colo., Ven.*) stupidity; a silly thing; an unimportant issue (vulgar) = estupidez; tontería; asunto sin importancia (vulgar).

gufeao (*Puerto Rico*) good = bueno.

gufear (*Puerto Rico*) to joke = bromear.

guía (*Mex., Puerto Rico*) a steering wheel = volante del automóvil.

güila 1. (*Chile*) rags; tatters = trapos; harapos. **2.** (*Costa Rica*) a small spinning top = pequeño trompo. **3.** a prostitute = prostituta. **4.** (*Mex.*) a small kite = cometa pequeño.

güilas; huilas (*Chile*) rags; tatters = andrajos.

guillado (*Puerto Rico*) sly; deceitful = solapado.

guillar (*Ven.*) to watch = vigilar.

güimo (*Puerto Rico*) a guinea pig = conejillo de indias.

güincha; huincha 1. (*Chile*) a metallic band = cinta metálica. **2.** (*Chile*) a tape measure = cinta de medir. **3.** (*Chile*) any tape = cualquier cinta.

güinchil (*from English*) a car windshield = parabrisas del automóvil.

guinda (*Argen., Chile*) a cherry = cereza.

guindar 1. (*Ven.*) to hang; to suspend = colgar; suspender. **2.** (*Ven.*) to fight = pelear. **3.** (*Ven.*) to sleep = dormir.

guindo (*Mex.*) a dark, red color = color rojo oscuro.

guindó los tenis (*Dom. Rep.*) died; kicked the bucket = se murió; estiró la pata.

guineo (*Guat., Pan., Puerto Rico*) a sweet banana = plátano dulce; banana.

guineo cuadrado (*Nic.*) a special kind of banana = tipo especial de banana.

guineo niño (*Puerto Rico*) a very sweet, small banana = banana pequeña muy dulce.

güiña (*Chile*) always demanding help = pedigüeño.

guiro(a) (*Dom. Rep.*) a musical instrument = instrumento musical.

guiso (*Ecua., Peru*) a stew = guisado; estofado.

güisquil (*Guat., Salva.*) (N.E. chayote; a tropical fruit with the shape of a pear) =

chayote; fruta tropical con la forma de una pera.

guita (*Argen.*, *Uru.*) money (informal) = dinero (informal).

guita loca (*Argen.*) a large amount of money (informal) = informal para mucho dinero.

gumarra 1. (*Colo.*) a hen (informal) = gallina. **2.** (*Colo.*) a nice person = persona agradable.

gurbia (*Colo.*) hunger; fatigue = hambre; fatiga.

gurgucia (*Dom. Rep.*) a poor and ugly woman = una mujer pobre y fea.

gurí (*Uru.*) a country boy = niño del campo.

gurrumina (*Guat.*) a triviality = pequeñez; cosa baladí.

gurundango See **chalungo.**

gurupie (*Dom. Rep.*) a croupier = el que da las cartas en el casino de juego.

gusano (*Argen.*, *Chile*) a person with low or no morality; without ethical values = persona de baja moral o sin moral; sin ética.

gutara (*Ven.*) a slipper; a sandal = chancleta; chinela; sandalia.

H

habiloso (*Chile*) skillful = habilidoso.

habitación See **cuarto.**

hacer bulto (*Hond.*) to obstruct the way = obtaculizar el camino; ocupar demasiado espacio.

hacer chi (*Mex.*) to urinate = urinar.

hacer cuchara (*Chile, Costa Rica, Hond., Puerto Rico*) to pout = hacer pucheros; gesto que precede al llanto.

hacer dedo (*Chile*) to hitchhike = solicitar transporte gratuito en la carretera.

hacer el dos (*Ecua.*, *Peru*) to defecate (informal) = defecar (informal).

hacer fiero (*Colo.*) to show off = alardear; llamar la atención.

hacer gancho (*Argen.*, *Chile*) to help a couple get acquainted = ayudar a que una pareja se conozca.

hacer garra (*Guat., Hond., Mex., Nic., Peru, Ven.*) to destroy; to tear = hacer pedazos; desgarrar; hacer tiras.

hacer la caca (*Colo.*) to defecate (informal) = defecar (informal); cagar.

hacer la cama (*Argen.*) to pave the way for another to fail or make mistakes = preparar las condiciones para que otro falle o cometa errores.

hacer la chancha See **hacer la cimarra.**

hacer la cimarra; hacer la chancha (*Chile*) to play hooky = hacer novillos.

hacer la pata (*Chile*) to flatter = adular.

hacer la roña (*Colo.*) to work reluctantly = trabajar con desgana.

hacer perro muerto (*Bol., Chile, Peru*) to leave a place without paying the bill = irse del lugar sin pagar la cuenta.

hacer pinta (*Mex.*) to cut school; to play hooky = hacer novillos; salir hacia la escuela para irse a otro lado.

hacer pucheros (*Argen.*) to pout = mostrar las expresiones faciales del que llora en silencio.

hacer pupu (*Pan.*) to defecate (informal) = defecar (informal).

hacer sonar 1. (*Chile*) to punish = castigar duramente. **2.** (*Chile*) to disgrace somebody else = poner a otro en desgracia.

hacer tapa 1. (*Chile*) hand gestures that show no interest whatsoever (vulgar) = gesto con las manos que muestra total desinterés (vulgar). **2.** (*Chile*) to ignore; to reject (informal) = ignorar; rechazar (informal).

hacer tira (*Chile*) to break in pieces = hacer pedazos.

hacer tuto (*Chile*) to sleep = dormir.

hacerse el cucho (*Chile*) to behave shyly = comportarse furtivamente.

hacerse el/la pituco(a) (*Chile*) a derogatory term for a person who wants to show sophisticated and refined manners = despectivo para la persona que pretende ser de modales finos y sofisticados.

hacerse la paja (*Chile, Para.*) to masturbate (vulgar) = masturbarse (vulgar).

hall [pron. jol] (*from English*) a hall = vestíbulo; salón.

hallulla (*Chile*) a round bread = pan con forma redonda.

hamaquearse (*Colo.*) to swing = columpiarse.

hambriento (*Colo.*) avaricious; a miser = avaro; tacaño.

hambrío(a) (*Guat.*) starving = hambriento(a).

handboll [pron. janbol] (*from English*) handball = balón-mano.

handicap (*from English*) a handicap = desventaja; obstáculo; dificultad.

hangear (*from English*) to hang out with friends = holgazanear; estar en un lugar o salir a pasear con los amigos sin un objetivo determinado.

hangueando (*from English*) hanging out = holgazaneando; rondando en un sitio sin hacer nada; estar sin hacer nada.

haraca (*Peru*) a sling = honda.

hardwear [pron. jargüear] (*from English*) computer hardware = equipo; soporte físico del sistema informativo; maquinaria; lógica cableada de la computadora.

harinear (*Ven.*) to drizzle = lloviznar.

harnear (*Colo.*) to sift = cerner o cernir; pasar por el harnero.

harto (*Chile, Colo., Ecua., Peru*) a lot; plenty = mucho; una gran cantidad.

hasta la tusa (*Chile*) to be utterly fed up = hasta la coronilla.

hato (*Ven.*) a ranch = hacienda; finca; gran extensión de terreno donde se crían animales.

hay a patadas (*Argen.*) there is a great amount = hay una gran cantidad.

hay ropa tendida (*Argen., Chile*) there are unwanted witnesses to what is being said or is going on = hay testigos no deseados de lo que se dice o se hace.

hebrudo (*Guat.*) full of fibers = fibroso; con muchas hebras.

hechizo (*Chile*) handmade or made as a craft = lo que se ha hecho a mano o artesanalmente.

hecho torta (*Argen.*) it is very deteriorated = está muy deteriorado.

hediondo (*Argen.*) a skunk = zorrino.

heladera (*Argen., Para., Uru.*) a refrigerator = refrigerador.

helado 1. (*Chile*) without money = sin dinero. **2.** (*Ven.*) a glacé = confitado; cubierto de azúcar.

helado de agua (*Argen.*) sherbet = sorbete.

helaje (*Colo.*) extremely cold = frío intenso; frío penetrante.

hereje (*Ven.*) plenty; a lot = mucho; gran cantidad de algo.

herido (*Chile*) the foundations of a wall = zanja donde se construyen los cimientos de una pared.

hielera (*Mex.*) a refrigerator = refrigerador.

hierbatero (*Chile*) a person who prescribes and sells medicinal plants = el que vende y receta hierbas medicinales.

higadoso (*Costa Rica*) not nice; unfriendly; unpleasant = antipático.

high school [pron. jai eskul] (*from English*) high school = escuela secundaria.

hijoemadre; hijoepucha (*Colo.*) a strong insult; "son of your mother" (vulgar) = insulto de gran calibre; "hijo de tu madre" (vulgar).

hijoepucha See **hijoemadre**.

¡híjole! (*Mex.*) an interjection of surprise that varies in meaning according to the volume and pitch; can go from a simple "Damn!" to something much stronger = interjección de sorpresa que varía en su significado de acuerdo al volumen de la voz y a la intensidad de la entonación; puede ir de un simple "¡Demonios!" hasta algo mucho más fuerte que eso.

hijuela (*Chile*) a small farm = finca pequeña.

hilachento(a) (*Colo.*) ragged; tattered = andrajoso; deshilachado; hecho tiras.

hincada (*Ven.*) a wound made with a sharp object = herida producto de un objeto punzante.

hincarle el diente (*Chile*) to start doing something = comenzar a hacer algo.

hinchar (*Argen., Chile, Para.*) to bother; to upset = molestar; enfadar.

hisopo (*Chile*) a shaving brush = brocha de afeitar.

hobby [pron. jobi] (*from English*) a hobby = afición; pasatiempo; trabajo que se ejecuta por gusto.

hogo See **ahogado**.

hoja de gilet (*Bol., Chile, Peru*) a razor blade = cuchilla de afeitar; hoja de afeitar.

hojillas (*Ven.*) razor blades = cuchillas de afeitar.

hol (*Puerto Rico*) a hall = corredor; antesalón.

horita; horitita (*Mex.*) right now = ahorita.

horitita See **horita**.

hormadoras (*Colo.*) underskirts = enaguas.

horro; jorro (*Colo.*) a sterile animal = animal estéril.

hostigar (*Chile*) to surfeit; to be cloying = estar harto, especialmente de una comida o bebida.

hostigoso (*Chile*) too sweet = muy dulce; ampalagoso.

hot dog [pron. jotdo] (*from English*) a hot dog = (N.E. emparedado de salchicha).

hoya (*Colo.*) the river basin = cuenca de un río.

huaca (*Peru*) a sacred place = lugar sagrado.

huacal 1. (*Guat.*) a bag = bolsa. **2.** (*Guat., Hond., Salva.*) a water container made from a plant; a container made from the **jícaro** = recipiente para el agua fabricado de una planta; recipiente hecho del **jícaro**. **3.** (*Colo.*) a frame or basket used to carry delicate objects = armazón o cesta para transportar objetos delicados.

huachafería (*Peru*) affected behavior = cursilería; comportamiento cursi.

huacho(a) (*Chile*) an orphan (derogatory) = huérfano (peyorativo).

huarachas See **guarache**.

huáscar (*Chile*) a water cannon truck = carro policial que lanza agua.

huaso (*Chile*) a proud title for the Chilean cowboy = título de orgullo para el personaje típico del campo chileno.

hueco 1. (*Colo.*) a bump; a hole in the road = hoyo; bache en el camino. **2.** (*Guat.*) a homosexual = homosexual.

huelefrito (*Ven.*) a busybody = entrometido.

huella (*Argen., Bol., Chile, Ecua., Peru*) a path = sendero; vereda.

huero 1. (*Chile, Dom. Rep., Ven.*) a rotten egg = huevo podrido. **2.** (*Mex.*) blond = rubio. **3.** (*Ven.*) cassava liquor = licor de yuca.

huesillo (*Chile*) a sun-dried peach = melocotón o durazno deshidratado.

hueso (*Colo.*) an article that does not sell; inferior-quality merchandise = mercancía invendible; artículo de mala calidad.

huesudo (*Colo.*) a thin person = persona delgada.

huevá 1. (*Chile*) a mistake (vulgar) = error (vulgar). **2.** (*Chile*) stupidity; an absurdity (vulgar) = estupidez; lo que es absurdo (vulgar).

hueva 1. (*Colo.*) a person with low intelligence (vulgar) = poco inteligente (vulgar). **2.** (*Colo.*) a testicle (vulgar) = testículo (vulgar). **3.** (*Colo.*) naive = ingenuo.

huevada See **güevada**.

huevas (*Argen., Chile, Uru.*) the scrotum (vulgar) = escroto (vulgar).

huevear See **güevear**.

hueviar (*Hond.*) to steal = hurtar; robar.

huevo 1. (*Dom. Rep.*) the penis (vulgar) = pene (vulgar). **2.** (*Argen.*) the lowest school grade; zero grade = la nota más baja de la escuela; nota cero.

huevochimbo (*Nic.*) a pastry with a spherical shape = dulce o pastel con forma de bola.

huevón; güevón 1. (*Argen., Chile, Para., Peru, Uru., Ven.*) an insult (vulgar); stupid = insulto (vulgar); estúpido. **2.** (*Mex.*) lazy (vulgar) = haragán (vulgar). **3.** (*Mex.*) good-for-nothing = bueno para nada.

huevonada See **güevonada**.

huevonear (*Colo.*) to do stupid things = hacer tonterías.

huevos 1. (*Cuba, Pan.*) the testicles (vulgar) = testículos (vulgar). **2.** (*Pan.*) the scrotum (vulgar) = escroto (vulgar).

huevos pericos (*Colo.*) scrambled eggs = huevos revueltos.

huila (*Nic.*) a kite = cometa.

huilas See **güilas**.

huilón (*Ecua.*) elusive = huidizo.

huinca (*Argen.*) any white man in **araucano** language = cualquier hombre blanco en lenguaje **araucano**.

huincha See **güincha**.

huipil (*Nic.*) a typical dress that Nicaraguan Indians wear during folkloric festivities = traje típico que usan los indios e indias nicaragüences para las fiestas folclóricas.

huiro (*Chile*) any non-edible seaweed = cualquier planta marina no comestible.

huisache (*Guat.*) a pettifogger = picapleitos; tinterillo; leguleyo.

huistora (*Hond.*) a turtle = tortuga.

hulado (*Hond.*) waxed; plastic-coated = encerado; forrado en hule o plástico.

hule (*Colo.*) a rubber tree = gomero.

hulte (*Chile*) the edible part of the **cochayuyo** stem = parte comestible en el tallo del **cochayuyo**.

humista (*Bol.*) ground fresh corn seasoned and boiled, wrapped in corncob leaves = maíz fresco molido y aderezado que se cuece envuelto en las hojas de la mazorca; tamales.

humita (*Chile*) ground fresh corn seasoned and boiled, wrapped in corncob leaves = maíz fresco molido y aderezado que se cuece envuelto en las hojas de la mazorca; tamales.

hunche See **aunche**.

hunco (*Bol.*) a **poncho** or cape without tassels = **poncho** de lana sin flecos.

húngaro (*Mex.*) a gypsy = gitano.

hureque (*Colo.*) a hole = agujero.

hurgandilla (*Hond.*) a person who shakes or tosses something = persona que sacude o menea algo.

hurgüetear (*Chile*) to poke; to jab; to stir = hurgar; huronear.

¡huy que avión! (*Colo.*) How greedy! = ¡qué persona más avara!

I

ichu (*from English*) an issue = asunto; cuestión.

ideático (*Hond.*) ingenious = ingenioso.

¿ideay? (*Nic.*) What is happening? = ¿qué hay?

ideoso (*Guat.*) ingenious = ingenioso.

iglú (*from English*) an igloo = (RAE) vivienda construida con bloques de hielo.

imilla (*Bol.*) a young woman = mujer joven.

impase (*from English*) an impasse = atasco; atolladero; estancamiento; punto muerto; crisis.

impavidez (*Argen., Chile, Para., Uru.*) cheekiness = descaro; frescura.

implementar (*Ven.*) to make it possible; to do something = habilitar; realizar; ejecutar.

impruviar (*from English*) to improve = mejorar.

incaible (*Mex.*) a hair pin = horquilla.

incentivar (*from English*) to incite; to stimulate = estimular; incitar.

income tax (*from English*) an income tax = impuestos sobre la renta o sobre los salarios.

incomtax (*from English*) an income tax = impuesto sobre la renta o sobre los salarios.

indentar (*from English*) to indent = dejar sangría; comenzar un renglón más adentro que los otros.

indio comido puesto al camino (*Nic.*) to leave a party immediately after eating = retirarse de una fiesta inmediatamente después de la comida.

indio viejo (*Nic.*) a native Nicaraguan dish prepared with corn = comida indígena nicaragüense preparada con maíz.

infiernillo (*Colo.*) below the stairs or other small space in the house = bajo la escalera u otro espacio pequeño de la casa.

infraccionar (*from English*) to summon; to impose a fine for a violation of the law = citar; multar.

íngrimo 1. (*Ven.*) an isolated or empty place; an abandoned place = lugar solitario o vacío; lugar desamparado. **2.** (*Ven.*) a lonely person = persona sin compañía.

inocente (*Mex.*) a child in any of the different degrees of mental retardation = niño(a) en cualquier de los diferentes grados del retraso mental.

inodoro (*Cuba*) a toilet = lavabo; **retrete**.

inoficioso (*Colo.*) unnecessary = innecesario.

input (*from English*) input = (N.E. entrada; información recibida; puerto de entrada).

inquieto (*Hond.*) fond of; enthusiastic for = aficionado; entusiasmado por algo.

inquilino (*Chile*) a peasant who receives a small piece of land and a house as part of his salary = campesino que recibe como parte del salario un pequeño terreno y una casa.

inquirriado (*Hond.*) happy = alegre.

insoria (*Ven.*) a trifle = pequeñez.

inspectar (*from English*) to inspect = revisar; inspeccionar.

instructar (*from English*) to instruct = instruir.

insulto (*Mex.*) a stomach ache = dolor estomacal.

intermediaria (*Ven.*) an evening show = función vespertina; función que se realiza entre la de la tarde y la de la noche.

internalizar (*from English*) to internalize = convertir una idea o un conocimiento en algo propio; interiorizar.

interviú (*from English*) an interview = entrevista; conversación.

intratar (*Hond.*) to insult; to mistreat = insultar; tratar mal.

introducir (*from English*) to introduce a person = presentar a una persona.

invierno 1. (*Colo., Costa Rica, Ven.*) the rainy season = la temporada de las lluvias. **2.** (*Ven.*) a downpour = aguacero.

ipegue (*Nic.*) in addition to; an extra amount given free in a transaction = agregado a; lo que se da como pago de gratificación o bonificación en un trámite.

ir a fiesta (*Colo.*) a sure thing = cosa segura; ir sobre seguro.

ir de cachete See **de cachete**.

irrigar (*from English*) to irrigate = regar.

irse al chancho (*Chile*) to exaggerate = exagerar.

irse al tacho (*Argen.*) to fail; to lose = fallar; perder.

irse de levante (*Hond.*) young men looking for young women = jóvenes buscando muchachas.

itemizar (*from English*) to itemize = desglosar; detallar; pormenorizar.

izquierdista (*Mex.*) a left-handed person = zurdo.

J

jaba (*Cuba*) a shopping bag = bolsa para las compras.

jabear (*Guat.*) to steal; to rob = hurtar; robar.

jabón (*Argen.*) a fright = susto; miedo.

jabonarse (*Argen.*) to be scared = asustarse.

jacal (*Mex., Ven.*) a hut = choza.

jacalear (*Mex.*) to go from one house to the next spreading gossip = ir de casa en casa difundiendo chismes.

jachado(a) (*Hond.*) marked with a scar = marcado(a) con una cicatriz.

jachi (*Bol.*) bran = afrecho o salvado de trigo.

jaconta (*Bol.*) a dish prepared with meats, vegetables and fruits; especially one prepared for the carnival celebration = plato que se prepara con carnes, vegetales y frutas especialmente para las fiestas del carnaval.

jacú (*Bol.*) a **yucca**, banana or bread served with other meals = yuca, plátano o pan servidos como acompañantes de otras comidas.

jai (*Colo.*) the jet set; high society = la élite social; la alta sociedad.

jaiba 1. (*Argen., Chile, Colo., Ecua.*) a crab = cangrejo. **2.** (*Dom. Rep., Puerto Rico*) smart; cunning = listo; astuto(a); mañoso(a).

jaibería (*Puerto Rico*) cunningness = astucia.

jaibón (*Chile*) a wealthy person = persona adinerada.

jaic (*from English*) a hike = caminata.

jaiguey (*from English*) a highway = autopista.

jaiyakin (*from English*) to hitchhike; to ask for free rides on the road = (N.E. pedir transporte gratuito por la carretera).

jalabola; jalador; jalamecate (*Ven.*) a flatterer (vulgar) = adulador (vulgar).

jalada (*Ven.*) a servile compliment = halago servil.

jaladera (*Ven.*) continuous flattering = adulación continuada.

jalado (*Ven.*) drunk (informal) = borracho (informal).

jalador See **jalabola**.

jalamecate See **jalabola**.

jalapeño (*Guat., Hond., Mex.*) a specific variety of green hot pepper = una variedad específica de pimiento verde picante; ají verde; **chile verde**.

jalar 1. (*Chile, Ven.*) to pull = halar. **2.** (*Ven.*) to drink alcohol = beber bebidas alcohólicas. **3.** (*Ven.*) to drag = resistencia al avance. **4.** (*Ven.*) to go to someplace = dirigirse a un sitio. **5.** (*Ven.*) to get drunk = emborracharse. **6.** (*Ven.*) to have sex = tener relaciones sexuales. **7.** (*Mex.*) to steal = robar. **8.** (*Mex.*) to work = trabajar.

jalar el examen (*Peru*) to fail an exam = fallar un examen.

jalar para (*Ven.*) to have a preference for something = tener afición por algo; tener preferencia por algo.

jalársela (*Mex.*) to masturbate (vulgar) = masturbarse (vulgar).

jale (*Mex.*) a job = empleo.

jaleo 1. (*Puerto Rico*) a stomach ache = malestar o dolor de estómago. **2.** (*Puerto Rico*) a problematic situation; a disorder = situación problemática; desorden.

jalf (*from English*) half-time in a ball game = medio tiempo en el juego.

jalón 1. (*Bol., Guat., Hond., Puerto Rico, Salva.*) it is relatively far = trecho; está a cierta distancia. **2.** (*Guat., Hond., Mex., Salva.*) a swallow of liquor = trago de licor. **3.** (*Guat.*) hitchhiking; a free ride = transporte gratuito en un vehículo. **4.** (*Chile, Ven.*) a great distance between two places = distancia grande entre dos lugares.

jama (*Hond.*) a small iguana = iguana pequeña.

jamaiquino See **chombo**.

jamaquear (*Ven.*) to move something fast and with energy = mover algo rápido y con energía.

jamaqueo (*Ven.*) a violent shake = sacudida brusca.

jambar (*Hond.*) to eat too much = comer mucho.

jamburguer (*from English*) a hamburger = (RAE) hamburguesa; **sándwich** hecho de un disco de carne molida asada o frita.

jamón 1. (*Ven.*) a bargain = ganga. **2.** (*Ven.*) a person with exceptional qualities = persona con cualidades excepcionales. **3.** (*Ven.*) the erotic games of a couple in love (informal) = juego erótico de una pareja enamorada (informal).

jamonear 1. (*Ven.*) to touch sexually (vulgar) = acariciar eróticamente (vulgar). **2.** (*Ven.*) to eat lavishly (informal) = comer opíparamente (informal).

janano(a) (*Guat., Salva.*) a person with a mouth deformity = persona con deformidades en la boca.

jando; lana; pachocha; pisto (*Mex.*) money (informal) = dinero (informal).

jangiar (*Dom. Rep.*) to hang around = matar el tiempo.

janiche (*Salva.*) a person with a mouth deformity = persona con deformidades en la boca.

jara 1. (*Bol.*) to rest during a walk = descanso durante una caminata. **2.** (*Puerto Rico, Ven.*) the police (informal) = la policía (informal).

jarabe de lengua (*Ven.*) a long and insipid conversation = conversación prolongada e insulsa.

jaracotal 1. (*Guat.*) an abundance = abundancia; hay una gran cantidad. **2.** (*Guat.*) a crowd; a multitude = multitud; gran número de gentes en un lugar.

jarana 1. (*Colo.*) a fib = mentirilla; bola. **2.** (*Colo., Ecua., Puerto Rico*) an informal dance = fiesta; baile informal. **3.** (*Cuba*) a joke; a practical joke = burla; chanza. **4.** (*Guat., Hond.*) a trick = engaño; ardid; truco. **5.** (*Hond.*) a debt = deuda. **6.** (*Mex.*) a small guitar = guitarra pequeña. **7.** (*Peru*) a regional dance = un baile regional. **8.** (*Peru*) a festival of folk dances = festival regional de bailes folclóricos.

jardín de infancia; jardín de niños; la creche (*Cuba*) kindergarten = jardín infantil.

jardín de niños See **jardín de infancia**.

jardinera prescolar (*Colo.*) a kindergarten teacher = maestra de párvulos.

jarrete (*Colo., Dom. Rep.*) a heel = talón; tacón del zapato.

jarretera (*Colo.*) an ulceration of the heel = ulceración en el talón.

jarta (*Colo.*) a boring school topic = tema escolar aburrido.

jartar 1. (*Ven.*) to eat everything that is served = comer íntegramente. **2.** (*Ven.*) to devour = devorar.

jarto (*Colo.*) boredom = aburrimiento.

jauja (*Chile*) easy = fácil.

jaula 1. (*Colo.*) a heavy-duty truck = camión para carga pesada. **2.** (*Ven.*) a police vehicle used to transport prisoners = vehículo policial para el transporte de presos.

jazz (*from English*) jazz = (N.E. música folclórica y popular de los Estados Unidos).

jeans [pron. gins] (*from English*) jeans = pantalones vaqueros, tejanos o de mezclilla.

jebo 1. (*Ecua.*) a husband = esposo. **2.** (*Ecua.*) a lover = amante.

jecho 1. (*Colo.*) ripe fruit = fruto maduro. **2.** (*Colo.*) a middle-aged person = persona de edad madura.

jeep [pron. gip] (*from English*) any passenger all-terrain vehicle; a Jeep™ = (N.E. cualquier vehículo de pasajeros diseñado para todo terreno; tomado de la marca Jeep^MR).

jefaturear (*Ven.*) to lead; to command = dirigir; mandar.

jeme (*Argen., Bol., Chile, Colo., Mex., Peru*) (N.E. the distance from the end of the extended thumb to the end of the extended forefinger) = la distancia comprendida entre la punta del dedo pulgar y la punta del dedo índice cuando estos están extendidos.

jerga 1. (*Mex.*) a rug = alfombra. **2.** (*Mex.*) a cloth = paño.

jericoplear (*Guat.*) to annoy; to bother = fastidiar; molestar.

jerigonzo (*Ven.*) bothersome = molestoso.

jeringar (*Dom. Rep., Puerto Rico*) to bother = importunar; molestar.

jeringón; jodón (*Puerto Rico*) bothersome = molestoso; fastidioso.

jeringuear (*Colo.*) to bother; to annoy = molestar; fastidiar.

jersey (*from English*) a jersey = (RAE) prenda de vestir de punto que cubre de los hombros a la cintura.

jeruza; joyolina (*Guat., Hond., Salva.*) a jail = cárcel.

jesusear (*Guat.*) to commit perjury = declarar falsamente; hacer una declaración falsa.

jet (*from English*) a jet = avión a chorro.

jeta 1. (*Chile, Nic.*) the lips (vulgar) = labios (vulgar). **2.** (*Chile, Nic.*) the mouth (vulgar) = boca (vulgar).

jetón 1. (*Chile*) silly; stupid (vulgar) = tonto; estúpido (vulgar). **2.** (*Colo.*) a person with a big mouth and big lips = persona con la boca y los labios grandes.

jetset (*from English*) the jet set = élite de la alta sociedad; los que están constantemente en las noticias sociales.

jeva 1. (*Puerto Rico*) a woman = mujer. **2.** (*Puerto Rico*) a girlfriend = novia.

jevo (*Puerto Rico*) a man = hombre.

jíbaro (*Puerto Rico*) a Puerto Rican peasant = campesino puertorriqueño.

jicaque (*Guat.*) rude; ignorant = cerril; necio; inculto.

jícara 1. (*Guat.*) a gourd with a thick and hard peel used to make containers = calabaza de cáscara dura que se usa para hacer tiestos o recipientes. **2.** (*Nic.*) a container made from the **jícaro** = recipiente hecho del **jícaro**.

jícaro (*Nic.*) a tropical fruit with a hard peel which, when dry, can be used to make containers = fruta tropical de cáscara dura que cuando se seca se usa para fabricar tiestos.

jicate 1. (*Hond.*) foolish = necio. **2.** (*Hond.*) impolite = mal educado; sin urbanidad.

jil (*Chile*) silly; naive (informal) = tonto; ingenuo (informal).

jimaguas (*Cuba*) twins = mellizos(as).

jincho (*Nic.*) a person of low social class (derogatory); also used as an insult = persona de la clase baja (peyorativo); también se usa como insulto.

ijipa! (*Ven.*) an interjection of happiness = interjección de alegría.

jipa (*Colo.*) a very fine straw hat made from **jipijapa** = sombrero fino de **jipijapa**.

jipar (*from English*) to hiccup = hipar.

jipato (*Ven.*) paleness; an unhealthy appearance = palidez; aspecto enfermizo.

jipijapa (*Bol.*) grass used to make hats = pasto o hierba que se usa para tejer sombreros.

jira; jiter (*from English*) a heater = calentador.

jiriola (*Mex.*) to cut classes = faltar a la escuela; hacer novillos.

jirón (*Peru*) an avenue; a boulevard = avenida; bulevar.

jit (*from English*) a hit in the field of music = un suceso en el campo de la música.

jiter See **jira**.

ijito! (*Mex.*) Gosh! = icáspita!

jobo (*Guat.*) a cheap brandy = aguardiente barato.

jocha (*Ecua.*) a gift for the person who is giving a party = regalo que se lleva al que hace una fiesta.

jochear (*Bol.*) to urge; to incite = azuzar; incitar; torear.

joco (*Guat.*) sour; fermented = agrio; fermentado.

jocoque (*Mex.*) yogurt = yugurt.

jocote (*Nic.*) a kind of tropical fruit = (N.E. fruta tropical).

joda (*Ven.*) a grotesque joke = broma grotesca.

joder 1. (*Argen., Chile, Ecua., Para., Salva.*) to bother = molestar. 2. (*Colo., Mex., Ven.*) to hurt; to harm (vulgar) = herir; hacer daño (vulgar).

jodido 1. (*Argen., Chile, Para.*) a mean person = maligno; perverso. 2. (*Argen., Chile, Para., Salva.*) a person who is difficult to deal with = persona de trato difícil. 3. (*Mex.*) it is in bad shape; it is not working; it is out of order = está en malas condiciones; está fuera del estado normal; no funciona. 4. (*Salva.*) a dangerous person = persona peligrosa.

jodienda (*Argen., Chile*) a bother; a nuisance = molestia.

jodión (*Salva.*) bothersome = molestoso.

jodón 1. (*Colo., Dom. Rep., Puerto Rico*) bothersome; annoying = molestoso; fastidioso. 2. (*Mex.*) a bad person; a person who does not care about others = persona mala; el o la que no se preocupa por los demás.

¡joepuchita!; ¡puchita!; ¡a la gran puchica! (*Nic.*) a very vulgar expression; "son of a b...!;" an interjection whose meaning changes with different intonations: surprise, fury, happiness, and others = expresión muy vulgar; ¡hijo de p...!; interjección que cambia su significado de acuerdo a la entonación usada: sorpresa, ira, felicidad y otros.

jojoto 1. (*Dom. Rep.*) rotten fruit = fruto podrido. 2. (*Dom. Rep.*) a person who does not get involved with others = el que no se relaciona con otros. 3. (*Dom. Rep.*) a vegetable that is not completely cooked = vegetal a medio cocinar. 4. (*Ven.*) a tender and fresh cob; a fresh spike = mazorca de maíz tierno.

jol (*from English*) a hall = corredor; salón; vestíbulo.

joldin (*from English*) holding = reteniendo; refrenando.

jolopear (*Dom. Rep.*) to steal; to mug = robar; asaltar.

jolote (*Guat., Hond.*) a turkey = pavo.

joni 1. (*from English*) honey = miel. 2. (*from English*) honey; dear; a term of endearment = querido(a); palabra cariñosa para dirigirse a otra persona.

jonrón (*Puerto Rico*) a home run in baseball = (N.E. carrera completa en el juego de béisbol).

jornal (*Argen., Bol., Chile, Peru, Uru.*) a day's pay or a day's wages = el pago de una jornada de trabajo diaria; salario diario.

jorobado 1. (*Argen.*) to be ill = estar enfermo. 2. (*Argen.*) to be broke = estar en la bancarrota.

jorobón 1. (*Puerto Rico*) bothersome; annoying = molestoso; fastidioso. 2. (*Puerto Rico*) See **chavón**.

jorongo (*Mex.*) a Mexican **poncho**; a cape = **poncho** mexicano.

joropo (*Ven.*) a Venezuelan folk dance = baile folclórico venezolano.

jorro See **horro**.

jote (*Chile*) a buzzard = buitre.

joto (*Colo.*) bound; a package bound for transporting = atado; paquete para transportar cosas en un viaje.

joyolina See **jeruza**.

juanetes (*Hond.*) the hips = caderas.

jubilado(a) (*Ven.*) a person who plays hooky at work or at school = el/la que se ausenta de la escuela o el trabajo sin justificación.

jubilarse 1. (*Colo.*) to deteriorate; to go downhill = deteriorarse; abandonarse; descuidarse. 2. (*Cuba, Mex.*) to acquire skills; to gain experience; to learn about something = adquirir práctica; ganar experiencia; instruirse en un asunto. 3. (*Ven.*) to play hooky; to play truant at school or at work = hacer novillos; ausentarse del trabajo o de la escuela sin justificación. 4. (*Mex.*) to learn about something = instruirse en un asunto.

juco (*Hond.*) sour; fermented = agrio; fermentado.

judío; machete (*Uru.*) a cheap person (derogatory); stingy = tacaño (despectivo).

juey (*Puerto Rico*) a crab = cangrejo.

jueyero (*Puerto Rico*) a crab fisherman = (N.E. el que pesca cangrejos).

jugar (*Argen., Bol., Chile, Para.*) to move a loose object within another object = moverse una cosa dentro de otra por no estar ajustada.

jugar vicio (*Colo.*) to play a game without betting money = hacer juego sin apostar con dinero.

juguetón(a) (*Mex.*) an adulteress; an adulterer = adúltera; adúltero.

juicio (*Hond.*) deaf = sordo.

juila (*Mex.*) a bicycle = bicicleta.

julepe (*Puerto Rico*) a plot = enredo creado intencionalmente.

julero(a) See **fulera(o)**.

julia (*Mex.*) a police vehicle; a paddy wagon = vehículo policial para transportar detenidos.

juma (*Bol., Colo., Cuba, Ecua., Mex., Puerto Rico*) drunkenness = borrachera.

jumado 1. (*Bol., Colo., Cuba, Ecua., Mex., Pan., Puerto Rico*) drunkenness = borrachera. **2.** See **estar en fuego**.

jumarse (*Colo.*) to get drunk = emborracharse; embriagarse.

jumeta; petardo; picao; rajao (*Puerto Rico*) drunk = borracho.

jumo (*Dom. Rep., Puerto Rico, Ven.*) drunk = borracho.

jumpear (*from English*) to jump = saltar; crear un puente eléctrico entre dos vehículos.

junípero(a) (*Colo.*) silly; dumb = necio(a); tonto(a).

jupa (*Hond., Nic.*) the head (informal) = cabeza (informal).

juque (*Salva.*) a musical instrument used to play Salvadoran folk music = instrumento musical para interpretar música folclórica salvadoreña.

juqui (*from English*) to play hooky = hacer novillos; ausentarse de la escuela sin permiso.

jura (*Mex.*) the cops = policías.

jurel (*Chile*) a mackerel = caballa.

jurungar (*Ven.*) to poke; to search for something = hurgar; revolver buscando algo.

justiniano (*Argen.*) fear = justo.

K

kantuta (*Bol.*) Bolivia's national flower = la flor nacional de Bolivia.

kerosene (*from English*) kerosene = queroseno.

kibord (*from English*) a keyboard = teclado.

kilo (*Cuba*) a penny = centavo.

kilobite [pron. kilobait] (*from English*) a kilobyte; a unit of 1024 bytes = (N.E. unidad equivalente a 1024 **bits**).

kimono (*Argen., Para.*) a long robe used by some women as a house dress = bata larga usada por algunas mujeres como vestido de casa.

kindergarterina (*Ven.*) a kindergarten teacher = maestra de kindergarten.

krumiro (*Chile*) a strikebreaker; a blackleg; a scab = esquirol; rompehuelgas; el que no se adhiere a la huelga.

kupia-kume 1. (*Nic.*) to make a deal = hacer un pacto o un trato. **2.** (*Nic.*) to agree = estar de acuerdo.

L

la cana (*Para.*) the police = la policía.

la chota (*Nic.*) the police (informal) = la policía (informal).

la creche See **jardín de infancia**.

la fulera; la pelada (*Argen.*) dead = la muerte.

la gallá (*Chile*) a multitude (derogatory); a mob = multitud (peyorativo); la pandilla.

la migra (*from English*) the United States immigration system; immigration officers = el sistema de inmigración en los Estados Unidos; los agentes de inmigración.

la mosca (*Argen.*) money (vulgar) = dinero (vulgar).

la pelada See **la fulera**.

la raza See **latinos**.

la refrigeradora; nevera (*Pan.*) a refrigerator = refrigerador.

la sabiola (*Argen.*) the head = la cabeza.

la última chupá (*Chile*) the most modern; the best; the most up-to-date (informal) = lo más moderno; lo mejor; lo último conocido, alcanzado o producido (informal).

la vieja; viejita (*Para.*) the endearing treatment of a mother or grandmother = forma cariñosa y afectiva para referirse a la madre o la abuela.

la yapa; de yapa (*Bol.*) an extra amount of merchandise given by the seller to the buyer; in addition to (colloquial) = cantidad adicional de mercancía que el vendedor le da al comprador como regalo; agregado a (coloquial).

la yegua (*Argen., Chile*) very big (informal) = muy grande (informal).

laberinto 1. (*Mex.*) a scandal = escándalo. **2.** (*Mex.*) a noise = ruido. **3.** (*Mex.*) an intrigue = intriga.

labia (*Puerto Rico*) a smooth tongue = tener facilidad de palabra.

labioso(a) (*Mex.*) a flatterer = adulador.

labor (*from English*) labor; a farming field = (N.E. se usa para significar un campo de cultivo).

laburanta (*Argen.*) a female factory worker = operaria; obrera.

laburar (*Argen., Uru.*) to work (informal) = trabajar (informal).

laburo (*Argen., Uru.*) work = trabajo.

lachar (*Chile*) what a womanizer does; to date many women = lo que hace el mujeriego; perseguir a las mujeres.

lacho (*Chile*) extremely fond of women = mujeriego.

lacra (*Argen., Chile, Peru, Puerto Rico*) a sore wound = costra que se forma en las llagas o en las heridas.

ladilla 1. (*Chile, Ven.*) a bothersome person (vulgar) = persona molestosa (vulgar). **2.** (*Ven.*) a boring person (vulgar) = persona aburrida (vulgar).

ladino(a) 1. (*Mex., Ven.*) a talkative person = persona conversadora. **2.** (*Guat., Mex.*) a Spaniard; of Spanish origin = cualquier español; de origen español. **3.** (*Chile*) a clever person = persona astuta.

lágach (*from English*) luggage = valijas.

lagartija (*Colo.*) the biceps = bíceps.

lagarto 1. (*Chile, Colo.*) the biceps = bíceps. **2.** (*Ven.*) a type of beef cut = un corte de carne de res.

laidi (*from English*) a lady = señora; mujer educada y fina.

laira (*from English*) a cigarette lighter = encendedor.

laja (*Chile*) sandstone; slab; flagstone = piedra plana y delgada que se usa en la construcción.

lambeache; lambiache; lambehuevos (*Mex.*) a brown-noser (vulgar); a bootlicker = lameculos (vulgar).

lambebotas (*Peru*) a bootlicker = servilón; zalamero.

lambeculo; lambiscón (*Colo., Salva.*) a bootlicker = lameculos.

lambehuevos See **lambeache**.

lambeojo (*Dom. Rep., Puerto Rico*) a bootlicker; a brown-noser = lameculos; servil; adulador.

lamber 1. (*Dom. Rep., Ven.*) to lick = lengüetear. **2.** (*Dom. Rep.*) to eat at another's home = comer en la casa de otro.

lambetazo (*Dom. Rep.*) the act of licking = lengüetazo.

lambiache See **lambeache**.

lambío 1. (*Puerto Rico*) a glutton = glotón. **2.** (*Puerto Rico*) selfish = egoísta.

lambiscón See **lambeculo**.

lambizque (*Mex.*) a person who avoids paying = el que evita tener que pagar.

lambón(a); sacamicas (*Colo.*) a flatterer = adulador; lameculos.

lambucear (*Ven.*) to lick = lamer.

lampa (*Peru*) a hoe = azada.

lamparazo 1. (*Colo.*) a one-swallow drink = se bebe de un solo trago. **2.** (*Colo.*) a direct hit; a direct blow = un golpe directo.

lamparita (*Argen.*) a lightbulb = bombilla; bujía eléctrica.

lámparo (*Colo.*) broke; without money = sin dinero.

lamprear; lampriar (*Mex.*) to cover a piece of roasted meat with scrambled eggs = cubrir un trozo de carne asada con un huevo revuelto.

lampriar See **lamprear**.

lana 1. (*Colo., Ecua., Mex.*) money (informal) = dinero (informal). **2.** (*Guat., Hond.*) a person of low social status = persona de baja condición social. **3.** (*Guat., Hond.*) a trickster; a swindler = tramposo; estafador. **4.** (*Guat., Hond.*) a scoundrel = sinvergüenza. **5.** (*Mex.*) a lie = mentira.

lanceta (*Chile*) goad = aguijón.

lancha 1. (*Ecua.*) hoarfrost; frost = escarcha; helada. **2.** (*Ecua.*) a fog = niebla.

landromat (*from English*) a laundromat = (N.E. lugar público para lavar ropa en las máquinas automáticas).

lángara 1. (*Mex.*) sly = disimulada(o). **2.** (*Mex.*) an astute person = persona astuta.

langaruto (*Colo.*) a thin person = persona delgada.

langosta (*Chile*) a grasshopper = saltamontes.

lanudo (*Ven.*) gross; impolite; rustic; rude = tosco; malcriado; rústico; grosero.

lanza 1. (*Argen., Chile*) a thief (informal) = ladrón (informal). **2.** (*Ven.*) a clever person; a tricky person = persona astuta y mañosa.

lapicera (*Uru.*) a pen = bolígrafo.

lapicero (*Guat., Hond., Mex., Peru, Salva.*) a ballpoint pen = bolígrafo.

lápiz de pasta (*Chile*) a ballpoint pen = bolígrafo.

laquear (*from English*) to lock = encerrar; asegurar con cerradura o candado.

largar 1. (*Argen., Chile, Para.*) to throw = arrojar; lanzar. **2.** (*Argen.*) to give = dar. **3.** (*Argen.*) a hangover = resaca después de una borrachera. **4.** (*Colo.*) to lend = prestar. **5.** (*Mex.*) to abandon a spouse = abandonar a la esposa o al marido.

largona (*Chile*) authorization without restrictions = permiso sin restricciones.

lata (*Chile, Cuba, Mex., Pan., Peru, Puerto Rico*) a can; canned food = tarro; comida de conservas.

latear (*Argen., Chile, Ecua., Peru, Puerto Rico*) to talk too much; to talk so much that it is boring = hablar mucho; hablar tanto que aburre.

latería (*Argen., Para.*) tinware; tinwork = hojalatería.

latifundio (*Peru*) a muddle; a confusion = embrollo; enredo.

latiguear (*Hond.*) to slash = azotar; zurrar.

latinos; la raza (*Mex.*) the Latin-Americans known as an ethnic group in the United States = los latinoamericanos que viven en los Estados Unidos, identificándose a sí mismos como un grupo étnico.

latir (*Ven.*) to disturb; to bother = inquietar; molestar.

latón de basura (*Cuba*) a garbage can = basurero.

laucha 1. (*Chile*) a small mouse = ratón pequeño. **2.** (*Chile*) the steel wire used to penetrate pipes = alambre de acero que se usa para penetrar cañerías.

lava (*Ven.*) anything that bothers = cualquier cosa que cause molestia.

lavabo (*Puerto Rico*) a wash basin = fregadero.

lavacara; lavatorio (*Ecua.*) a basin = palangana.

lavadero (*Ecua., Peru*) a sink = fregadero.

lavado 1. (*Cuba, Mex.*) a washing basin = palangana. **2.** (*Ven.*) a person with fair skin = persona con la piel clara.

lavamanos (*Chile, Pan.*) a lavatory; a sink = lavabo.

lavaplatos (*Chile, Colo., Mex., Peru*) a kitchen sink = fregadero.

lavativoso (*Ven.*) bothersome; annoying = el o lo que causa molestia.

lavatorio 1. (*Argen., Chile, Cuba, Para., Peru*) a lavatory; a washbasin = lavabo; lavamanos. **2.** (*Chile, Peru*) a sink = palangana. **3.** See **lavacara**.

lavatory (*from English*) a lavatory = lavabo; lavamanos.

lazo (*Colo., Hond.*) a string = cordel; cuerda.

le dieron el paseo (*Colo.*) they killed him or her = le mataron.

le dió la quiebra (*Nic.*) breaking an engagement = terminar un noviazgo.

le falta la persiana (*Colo.*) missing front teeth = sin los dientes del frente de la boca.

le fue de la patada (*Guat.*) he or she did bad = le fue mal.

le pegaron el tarro (*Cuba*) cuckolded = cornudo; esposo engañado.

le pegó el gordo (*Guat.*) he or she hits the jackpot = ganó la lotería.

le pica 1. (*Chile*) impatient = está impaciente. **2.** (*Chile*) annoying = está molesto.

le ronca el clarinete; le zumba el mango (*Cuba*) amazing; fantastic = es asombroso; es increíble.

le zumba el mango See **le ronca el clarinete**.

lease (*Puerto Rico*) to lease = contrato de arrendamiento o contrato de renta.

leche 1. (*Bol., Colo., Ecua., Guat., Hond., Peru, Salva.*) luck = suerte. **2.** (*Mex.*) semen (vulgar) = semen (vulgar).

leche nevada; nieve (*Mex.*) ice cream = helado.

lecherear (*Ven.*) to be mean; to be stingy = escatimar; proceder con mezquindad.

lechero 1. (*Colo.*) slow public transportation = transporte público muy lento. **2.** (*Colo.*) a vehicle that stops continuously = vehículo que se detiene continuamente. **3.** (*Ven.*) mean; stingy = mezquino; tacaño.

lechina (*Ven.*) chickenpox = varicela.

lechón (*Puerto Rico*) roasted pork = cerdo asado.

lechonera (*Puerto Rico*) a restaurant that specializes in pork = negocio de comidas especializado en cerdo.

lechoza (*Dom. Rep.*) papaya = papaya.

lechugas (*Chile*) dollar bills (informal) = billetes de dólares (informal).

lechuguita (*Argen.*) a young and interesting woman = mujer joven y agraciada.

lechuza (*Mex.*) a bat = murciélago.

leco (*Ven.*) a noisy moan = lamento muy sonoro.

legal 1. (*Bol., Cuba, Ecua., Peru*) excellent = excelente. **2.** (*Peru*) correct = correcto.

legalismo (*from English*) to legalize only as a formality; legalism = (N.E. lo que impone la legalidad sólo como un formalismo).

leído (*Mex.*) an informed person; an educated person = instruido; informado; persona educada.

lejecito (*Mex.*) an ironic expression conveying the idea of keeping others away = forma irónica para expresar la idea de estar o mantener a otros lejos.

lenco (*Hond.*) stutterer = tartamudo.

lenguachuta; tartancho(a) (*Bol.*) stutterer = tartamudo(a).

lenguón(a) (*Mex.*) a scandalmonger = chismoso(a).

lenteja (*Chile*) too slow = muy lento.

lentes ahumados See **espejuelos de sol**.

lentes oscuros See **espejuelos de sol**.

leñazo (*Dom. Rep.*) to stroke with a heavy stick = garrotazo.

leño (*Cuba*) a stick = palo.

lepe 1. (*Mex.*) a rascal = pícaro. **2.** (*Mex.*) to squirt; to spray = en chorritos; en chorros cortos. **3.** (*Mex.*) a short person = persona de baja estatura. **4.** (*Mex.*) a baby = niño pequeño.

lesear (*Chile*) to behave in a silly way; to say silly things = tontear; decir o hacer una **lesera**.

lesera; lesura 1. (*Chile*) nonsense = necedad; tontería. **2.** (*Chile*) something with little or no value = lo que tiene poco o ningún valor.

leso(a) (*Argen., Bol., Chile*) silly; a fool = tonto(a); necio(a).

lesura See **lesera**.

leva (*Mex.*) a suit jacket = chaqueta de un traje.

levantadera (*Colo.*) a nightgown = bata de dormir.

levantador(a) (*Ven.*) a sexually and socially attractive person = persona atractiva sexual y socialmente.

levantar (*Colo.*) to get what you want = conseguir lo que se desea.

levante See **guaragua**.

liberación de aduanas (*Chile*) duty free = exención de impuesto de aduana.

liberación (*Colo.*) to give birth = parir; el acto de parir.

librera (*Guat., Pan.*) a bookcase = estantería para libros.

licencia; placa (*Cuba, Mex.*) a car license plate = matrícula de un vehículo.

licenciado 1. (*Argen., Guat., Hond., Salva.*) a lawyer = abogado. **2.** (*Mex.*) anyone with a university diploma = cualquiera que tenga estudios universitarios completos.

líder (*from English*) a leader = (RAE) director, jefe o conductor de un grupo.

liderato; liderazgo (*from English*) leadership = (RAE) condición de **líder**; el o lo que se encuentra al frente de una actividad.

liderazgo See **liderato**.

liendra (*Dom. Rep., Ven.*) a nit; the larva of the louse = liendre; la larva del piojo.

lienza (*Chile*) a twisted string made of cotton = cordón torcido de hilo de algodón.

life belt [pron. laifbelt] (*from English*) a life belt = cinturón de salvavidas.

life boat [pron. laifbout] (*from English*) a lifeboat = bote salvavidas.

liga 1. (*Argen., Para.*) good luck = buena suerte. **2.** (*Colo., Mex., Pan., Peru*) a rubber band = bandita de goma. **3.** (*Hond.*) a link; a joint = vínculo; lo que junta o une dos cosas.

limosnero (*Chile, Ven.*) a beggar = mendigo.

limpiamanos (*Hond.*) a napkin = servilleta; toalla de manos.

linda (*Mex.*) the vagina (vulgar) = vagina (vulgar).

lindero (*Hond.*) a landmark; a milestone = mojón; señal en el camino hecha con material durable y sólido.

link (*from English*) a link = enlace; conexión; vínculo.

linterna (*Mex.*) a small business or store = tienda o negocio pequeño.

linyera (*Argen.*) a bum; a homeless person = vagabundo; desamparado.

lipa (*Ven.*) a big belly = barriga abultada.

lipestic (*from English*) a lipstick = lápiz labial.

lipón(a) (*Ven.*) a person with a big belly (informal) = barrigudo(a) (informal).

liquea 1. (*from English*) it leaks; if it is liquid, it drips = si es líquido gotea. **2.** (*from English*) it leaks; if it is a gas, it filters = si es un gas, se filtra, tiene una fuga o un escape.

liquear 1. (*from English*) to lick = lamer; lengüetear. **2.** (*from English*) to leak = gotear (líquido); filtrar (gas.)

lírico 1. (*Mex.*) a person who plays musical instruments without reading music; to play by ear = persona que puede interpretar con instrumentos musicales sin saber leer música; el que toca por oído. **2.** (*Mex.*) anyone with a special gift for the performing arts = cualquiera que tenga habilidades interpretativas en el arte de la representación.

lis (*from English*) to lease = (N.E. contrato de arrendamiento o contrato de renta).

liso 1. (*Colo.*) slippery = resbaladizo; resbaloso. **2.** (*Bol., Colo., Ecua., Guat., Hond., Peru, Salva., Ven.*) fresh; impudent; a person who takes liberties with others = fresco; sin vergüenza; confianzudo; imprudente. **3.** (*Colo.*) someone who avoids a commitment = el que evita comprometerse.

listerina; listerine (*from English*) any type of mouthwash antiseptic; Listerine™ = cualquier antiséptico para la boca; (tomado de la marca Listerine^MR).

listerine See **listerina**.

listing (*from English*) a listing = cuadro de calificación.

listones (*Mex.*) a child's game played by two teams that compete against each other = juego infantil que se juega entre dos grupos que compiten entre ellos.

lisura (*Bol., Ecua., Guat., Peru, Ven.*) a strong insult; an indecent expression; a rude word; insolence = una expresión insultante o indecente; grosería; insolencia; falta de respeto.

litro (*Puerto Rico*) a quarter of a gallon = un cuarto de galón.

living (*from English*) a living room = sala de estar; cuarto de estar.

llama (*Bol., Chile, Peru*) (N.E. llama; a mammal of the camel family that lives only in the Andes) = llama (el animal).

llamar (*Mex.*) to take back a promise or one's word = retractarse de una promesa o de la palabra empeñada.

llambaroso (*Ecua.*) pompous; to be conceited; to give importance to oneself = pomposo; aparecer engreído; hacerse el importante.

llanero 1. (*Colo.*) a Colombian cowboy = vaquero colombiano. **2.** (*Colo.*) any person from the Colombian flatlands = cualquiera que viva en los llanos colombianos.

llanta 1. (*Chile*) a rim = aro; sección metálica en la rueda del automóvil. **2.** (*Colo., Guat., Mex., Pan., Uru.*) a tire = neumático; goma del automóvil. **3.** (*Ecua., Peru*) a large sunshade used in street markets = sombrilla de gran tamaño que se usa en los mercados.

llantería (*Colo.*) a tire repair shop = lugar donde se reparan los neumáticos.

llantón (*Mex.*) a person of African origin; a black person from the United States (derogatory) = estadounidense de origen africano (peyorativo).

llapa 1. (*Bol., Chile, Colo., Ecua., Peru*) in addition to = añadidura; agregado a. **2.** (*Bol., Chile, Colo., Ecua., Peru*) an extra amount of merchandise given by the vendor to the purchaser = cantidad adicional de mercancía que el vendedor le regala al comprador.

llave 1. (*Chile, Cuba, Mex.*) a faucet = grifo; canilla del agua. **2.** (*Colo.*) a pal; the affectionate treatment shown for a friend = compadre; trato afectuoso para el amigo.

llave de luz (*Argen.*) an electric switch = interruptor eléctrico.

llenador 1. (*Chile*) heavy food = alimento pesado; lo que sacia pronto. **2.** (*Colo.*) an annoying person = molestoso.

lleva y trae (*Pan.*) a scandalmonger = chismoso.

llevacuentos (*Ecua., Peru*) a scandalmonger = chismoso.

llévalo para atrás (*from English*) bring it back = devuélvelo.

llevar el bulto (*Colo.*) to suffer the consequences = sufrir las consecuencias.

llokalla (*Bol.*) a young woman = mujer joven.

lluqui (*Ecua.*) left-handed = zurdo.

lluvia (*Nic.*) a shower = ducha.

lo peor es un indio repartiendo chicha (*Nic.*) a person who is socially out of place and does not know how to behave = una persona desorientada socialmente que no sabe comportarse.

lobi (*from English*) a lobby = vestíbulo; antecámara.

lobo 1. (*Chile*) an elusive person; a difficult person = huraño; persona difícil. **2.** (*Mex.*) an astute and clever person = persona lista y astuta.

loca 1. (*Argen., Para.*) scatterbrained woman = mujer liviana, casquivana. **2.** (*Chile*) a homosexual (vulgar) = homosexual (vulgar).

locero (*Colo.*) a potter = alfarero.

locha (*Colo.*) laziness = flojera.

locho(a); mono(a) (*Colo.*) a blond person = persona rubia.

lock out [pron. lokaut] (*from English*) lock-out = (N.E. paro forzoso de una faena o una fábrica).

iloco! (*Argen.*) a friendly greeting to a very close friend = manera amigable y cariñosa de referirse a un amigo cercano.

loco (*Chile*) an abalone = molusco comestible.

locote (*Para.*) any hot pepper = cualquier tipo de ají o **chile**.

locoto; rocoto (*Bol., Peru*) a type of very hot pepper = un tipo de ají o **chile** muy picante.

locro (*Argen.*) a traditional Argentine dish made with corn, pumpkin, and meats = plato tradicional argentino preparado con maíz, calabaza y carnes.

lolei (*Chile*) an adult who behaves in an infantile way = adulto que se comporta como joven.

lolo(a) (*Chile*) a young person = joven.

lomo (*Chile*) loins = corte de carne de la espalda del animal.

lon (*from English*) a lawn = césped.

lona (*Argen., Para.*) cheap, inferior-quality fabric = tela barata de baja calidad.

lonch; lonche; lunche (*from English*) lunch = almuerzo.

lonchar; lonchear; lunchiar (*from English*) to have lunch = almorzar.

lonche 1. (*from English*) lunch = almuerzo. **2.** (*Colo.*) a child's party held in the afternoon = fiesta infantil por la tarde. **3.** (*Colo.*) a snack = merienda fría y ligera.

lonchear See **lonchar**.

lonchera (*from English*) a lunch box; a container used to take lunch to work, school or any other place = (N.E. caja para transportar el almuerzo al trabajo, a la escuela o a otro lugar).

lonchería (*Colo., Ven.*) a place to eat a snack; a place that serves fast food = lugar para meriendas ligeras; lugar donde se sirven platos de preparación rápida.

lonchero (*Ven.*) a clerk in a fast-food restaurant = el dependiente que despacha en un lugar de comidas rápidas.

lonchrum (*from English*) a lunch room = comedor.

longo (*Ecua.*) a young Ecuadorian Indian = indio ecuatoriano joven.

lorea (*Chile*) look (informal) = mira (informal).

loro 1. (*Chile*) a look-out for a crime = el vigía cuando se comete una fechoría. **2.** (*Mex.*) a friend = amigo.

los altos (*Chile, Para.*) the upper floor = el piso de arriba.

loundri 1. (*from English*) a laundry (the place) = lavadero; lavandería. **2.** (*from English*) the laundry (clothing) = ropa sucia; ropa para lavar.

luca (*Argen., Chile, Colo.*) a bill of one-thousand pesos (informal) = billete de mil pesos (informal).

luche 1. (*Chile*) a specific kind of edible seaweed = un tipo específico de alga marina comestible. **2.** (*Chile*) hopscotch = juego infantil; la pata coja.

lúcuma (*Chile*) an edible fruit which is the size and shape of a plum; its peel is dark-green and its meat, yellow = fruta comestible del tamaño y la forma de una ciruela; su cáscara es verde oscura y su pulpa, amarilla.

lueguito (*Colo.*) later = más tarde; después.

luis(a) morales (*Mex.*) the Spanish version of the English expression "loose morals;" a person without principles or moral values = calco en español de la expresión en inglés "loose morals," la cual significa una persona sin principios ni valores morales.

lujar (*Dom. Rep., Hond.*) to shine; to polish shoes = lustrar; dar lustre al calzado.

lulo 1. (*Chile*) a cylindrical object = objeto cilíndrico. **2.** (*Chile*) a bundle; wrapping with a cylindrical shape = un atado; un envoltorio en la forma de un cilindro.

luma 1. (*Chile*) a police stick; a nightstick = bastón policíaco. **2.** (*Chile*) a severe reprimand = reprimenda severa.

lumbrero (*Mex.*) a firefighter = bombero; el que apaga incendios.

lumbriz (*Mex.*) a thin person = persona delgada.

luna (*Mex.*) menstruation; the menstrual period = menstruación; regla de la mujer.

lunche See **lonch**.

lunchiar See **lonchar**.

lunfardo (*Argen.*) slang; an Argentine underworld dialect = dialecto del bajo mundo argentino.

lunguero (*Colo.*) a day laborer = jornalero.

lup (*from English*) a loop = vuelta; circuito cerrado.

luquear (*Chile*) to look = mirar.

lustrabotas; lustrador (*Argen., Chile, Para.*) a bootblack; a shoeshine person = limpiabotas.

lustrador See **lustrabotas**.

lustrín (*Chile*) a shoeshine box = caja para apoyar el pie y dar brillo al calzado.

luz (*Para.*) the space between two objects = distancia entre dos objetos.

luz de la calle, oscuridad de la casa (*Colo.*) someone who neglects his or her family to help others = el que descuida la familia por ayudar a otros.

M

mabita 1. (*Ven.*) the evil eye = mal de ojo. **2.** (*Ven.*) a person who brings or has bad luck = persona que tiene o trae mala suerte.

macacoa (*Ven.*) sadness = tristeza.

macalililia (*Mex.*) a child's game where the word **macalililia** is used as a repeated refrain to link questions and answers = juego infantil en que la palabra **macalililia** se usa como estribillo para ligar preguntas y respuestas.

macán (*Ven.*) a bothersome issue; an annoying situation = cosa o situación molestosa o engorrosa.

macana 1. (*Argen., Bol., Chile, Pan., Para.*) an absurdity; a piece of nonsense; an unimportant issue = disparate; cosa o asunto que no hace sentido. **2.** (*Bol.*) a heavy piece of wood used as a blunt weapon = garrote; pieza de madera pesada usada como arma contundente. **3.** (*Chile, Pan.*) a doubtful thing = cosa dudosa. **4.** (*Chile, Pan.*) a falsehood = falsedad. **5.** (*Chile, Pan., Uru.*) a tale = cuento; historia fantástica; producto de la imaginación. **6.** (*Costa Rica*) a sharp tool used to make holes = herramienta aguzada para hacer hoyos. **7.** (*Puerto Rico*) a policeman's nightstick = bastón que usan los agentes de la policía.

macanear (*Para.*) to make irrational statements; to talk without making any sense = hacer afirmaciones sin fundamentos; charla sin sustancia.

macano(a) (*Mex.*) cheap; of inferior quality = barato; de baja calidad.

macanudo 1. (*Argen., Chile, Para., Uru.*) fine; very good = bien; muy bueno. **2.** (*Colo.*) a big and strong person = persona fuerte, robusta y resistente.

maceta 1. (*Chile*) corpulent = corpulento. **2.** (*Dom. Rep., Puerto Rico*) avaricious; tight; miserable = avaro; tacaño; miserable.

maceteado (*Chile, Peru*) big and strong; stoutly built; well-built = grande y fuerte; fornido.

macetero (*Chile*) a flowerpot = maceta.

mach (*from English*) a match = cerillo; fósforo.

macha 1. (*Chile*) an edible bivalve mollusk that has the shape of a triangle = molusco bivalvo comestible en la forma de un triángulo. 2. (*Ven.*) a responsible and courageous woman = mujer valiente y responsable. 3. (*Ven.*) a heavy and strong thing = cosa fuerte y resistente.

machacante (*Puerto Rico*) money (informal) = dinero (informal).

machala (*Nic.*) a snake = culebra.

machear 1. (*from English*) to match = igualar; emparejar. 2. (*from English*) to match = parear; combinar.

machera 1. (*Colo.*) a good thing; an excellent thing = cosa buena; objeto excelente. 2. See **amachada**.

machete 1. (*Ven.*) an efficient and able person = persona capaz y eficaz. 2. (*Ven.*) a physically strong person = persona con mucha fuerza física. 3. (*Uru.*) a cheap person; a stingy person (derogatory) = tacaño mezquino (despectivo).

machetear 1. (*Chile*) to ask for money = pedir dinero. 2. (*Colo.*) to sell cheap = vender barato. 3. (*Colo.*) to insist; to be stubborn = insistir; porfiar; ser persistente. 4. (*Colo.*) to do something in a disorganized way; to leave work unfinished = hacer algo de una forma desorganizada; dejar un trabajo a medias o sin terminar.

machetero(a) 1. (*Ven.*) ignorant = ignorante. 2. (*Ven.*) a violent person = violento(a).

machetiar 1. (*Argen.*) to crush; to flatten = apabullar. 2. (*Argen.*) to surpass = superar. 3. (*Argen.*) to strike = golpear.

machetón(a) 1. (*Mex.*) a lazy person = haragán(a). 2. (*Mex.*) a clumsy person = torpe para ejecutar o hacer cosas.

machi (*Argen., Chile*) a native medicine man or woman = curandero(a) nativo; curandero(a) indígena.

machín 1. (*Colo.*) a monkey = mono; mico. 2. (*Mex.*) strong = fuerte. 3. (*Mex.*) good = bueno(a).

machina 1. (*Guat., Hond., Puerto Rico, Salva.*) a merry-go-round = caballitos; tíovivo. 2. (*Mex.*) strong = fuerte. 3. (*Mex.*) good = bueno(a).

machito (*Mex.*) a dish prepared with pork and other ingredients = plato preparado con puerco y otros ingredientes.

machitún (*Chile*) a badly organized meeting = reunión desorganizada.

macho 1. (*Chile*) stubborn = porfiado. 2. (*Colo.*) very big = muy grande; de grandes proporciones. 3. (*Cuba*) a pig = cerdo. 4. (*Costa Rica*) blond = rubio.

machona (*Argen., Colo., Ecua., Para.*) a tomboy; a mannish woman; a woman who looks and behaves like a man = marimacho; mujer ahombrada; mujer que se ve y se comporta como hombre.

machonear (*Argen., Para.*) to behave as a **machona** = comportarse como una marimacho.

machorra (*Puerto Rico*) a sterile woman (vulgar) = mujer estéril (vulgar).

machota (*Puerto Rico*) a sexy woman; an attractive woman = mujer sexy; mujer atractiva.

machote 1. (*Hond.*) a model; a pattern = modelo; ejemplo. 2. (*Puerto Rico*) handsome; an attractive man = guapo; bien parecido; hombre atractivo.

machrum (*from English*) a mushroom = hongo.

machucón (*Chile*) a bruise = moretón; parte afectada por un golpe.

machún; maco 1. (*Ven.*) unique = único. 2. (*Ven.*) one unit = una sola unidad.

macita (*Mex.*) a beautiful woman (informal) = mujer guapa o hermosa (informal).

macizar (*Mex.*) to secure = asegurar o poner en un lugar seguro.

maco See **machún**.

macuache (*Mex.*) a good-for-nothing person = inútil.

macuco 1. (*Chile, Peru*) clever; crafty = cuco; astuto; sagaz. 2. (*Peru*) an oversized young man = muchacho grande; grandullón.

macueco (*Mex.*) left-handed = zurdo.

macumba (*Colo.*) a speaker of lies = el que dice mentiras.

mádam (*from English*) a madam = señora.

madama (*Argen., Bol., Chile, Para.*) a brothel keeper = regenta de un prostíbulo.

madera (*Mex.*) flattery = adulación.

madrazo (*Colo.*) any insult involving one's mother = cualquier insulto que menciona a la madre.

madubí (*Bol.*) a peanut = maní.

maduro (*Colo., Puerto Rico*) a sweet ripe banana, the fruit = plátano dulce y maduro; banano, la fruta que se come cruda.

maestro (*Ven.*) cordial treatment given to someone who is respected = tratamiento de cordialidad a quien se le respeta.

magancear; mangancear (*Colo.*) to work a little or not at all = holgazanear; trabajar poco o nada.

maganza; manganza (*Colo.*) laziness; idleness = holgazanería; ociosidad.

maganzón; manganzón (*Colo., Costa Rica*) lazy = holgazán.

magna (*Ven.*) a disappointment = chasco; decepción.

magnarse (*Ven.*) to be disappointed = llevarse un chasco.

magüey (*Mex.*) (N.E. a plant originally from Mexico that has thick, long leaves, the juice of which is fermented to make) **pulque** = planta de origen mexicano, sus hojas son gruesas y carnosas y producen un jugo que fermentado da origen al **pulque**.

maicillo (*Chile*) a yellow, heavy sand used to cover the ground in yards = arena amarilla gruesa que se usa para pavimentos de patios.

mailing list [pron. mailinlist] (*from English*) a mailing list = lista para preparar envíos.

maíz (*Argen., Chile*) the corn used to feed animals or corn seed = se usa sólo para denominar el maíz destinado a alimentar animales o para sembrar.

maíz caqueado (*Dom. Rep.*) a dessert made with corn, milk, sugar, and raisins = postre preparado con maíz, leche, azúcar y pasas.

maíz piro See **alboroto**.

majarete (*Puerto Rico*) a dessert prepared with coconut milk, rice, sugar, and cinnamon = postre preparado con leche de coco, arroz, azúcar y canela.

majunche 1. (*Ven.*) without any good qualities = sin cualidades. **2.** (*Ven.*) someone or something that is unattractive = lo que no es atractivo. **3.** (*Ven.*) mediocre = mediocre.

mala leche (*Argen.*) bad luck = mala suerte.

malacaroso (*Colo.*) an angry or infuriated look on one's face = cara de enfado; cara de enojado.

malaley (*Colo.*) easy to upset or irritate = fácil de enojarse o irritarse.

malamé (*Mex.*) corn used to feed poultry = maíz para alimentar aves de corral.

malanco(a) 1. (*Mex.*) in bad shape = lo que está en mal estado. **2.** (*Mex.*) rotten fruit = fruta podrida. **3.** (*Mex.*) a sick person = persona enferma.

malancón (*Mex.*) having **malanco** = que tiene **malanco**.

malanocharse (*Ecua.*) to stay up very late = trasnochar.

malaya 1. (*Chile*) a rag used to clean tables in a restaurant = trapero para limpiar mesas del restaurante. **2.** (*Chile*) a beef cut = un corte de carne de vacuno.

maldingo(a) (*Colo.*) damned = maldito(a).

maldito(a) (*Mex.*) superior; super = superior; tremendo; fantástico.

maleta 1. (*Colo., Guat., Hond., Salva.*) a bundle of clothes on the back; a long bag = atado de ropa que se carga en la espalda. **2.** (*Colo.*) a hump = joroba; jiba. **3.** (*Guat.,*

Hond., Salva.) a rogue; a rascal = pícaro; pillo; bribón. **4.** (*Mex.*) the excrement of a baby in diapers = excremento del bebé en los pañales.

malevo (*Argen., Bol., Chile, Para.*) malicious; a criminal; a bad person = malévolo; malhechor; persona mala.

malgansón (*Puerto Rico*) a big, young man who behaves as a child = grandulón; muchacho grande que actúa como niño.

malhora (*Guat., Hond., Salva.*) trouble; misfortune = lío; situación desafortunada.

malicia (*Chile*) a little bit of alcohol added to a nonalcoholic drink = un poco de alcohol que se le agrega a una bebida sin alcóhol.

malinche (*Mex.*) bad; evil; a traitor = malo; malvado; traicionero.

malla (*Argen.*) a bathing suit = traje de baño.

malón 1. (*Chile*) a meeting of the Indian tribes = reunión de las tribus indias. **2.** (*Chile*) a party in which everybody brings drinks and food = fiesta en la que los participantes llevan comida y bebida.

maloso(a) (*Ven.*) something or someone who is not absolutely or totally bad = lo que no es totalmente o absolutamente malo(a).

malpractis (*from English*) malpractice = (N.E. procedimientos o conductas ilegales en una profesión.)

malta (*Chile*) any dark beer = cualquier cerveza oscura.

maluco (*Ven.*) perverse = malvado; perverso.

maluquera 1. (*Colo.*) an illness; an indisposition = enfermedad; indisposición. **2.** (*Colo.*) ugliness = fealdad.

malva (*Mex.*) astute; clever = astuto; listo.

mamá (*Colo.*) a term used before the first name of a grandmother as a sign of affection = término que se usa antes del nombre de pila de la abuela como señal de cariño.

mama grande (*Mex.*) a grandmother = abuela.

mamada (*Mex.*) a sinecure = trabajo fácil y bien pagado.

mamadera (*Argen., Chile, Ecua., Peru*) a feeding bottle = biberón.

mamado 1. (*Argen., Uru.*) drunk = borracho; ebrio. **2.** (*Colo.*) without strength = se ha quedado sin fuerzas.

mamador(a) (*Mex.*) a person who lives at the expense of others = persona que vive a expensas de otros.

mamalón (*Dom. Rep.*) lazy = haragán; perezoso.

mamalón(a) (*Mex.*) a gay person = homosexual; lesbiana.

mamao (*Puerto Rico*) clumsy; dim; easily seduced = torpe; idiota; el que se deja seducir.

mamar 1. (*Colo.*) to fail to live up to a commitment = no cumplir con un compromiso. **2.** (*Chile, Uru.*) to drink heavily = beber copiosamente. **3.** (*Chile*) to take something without complaint; to take it by force = aceptarlo sin reclamo; aceptarlo por la fuerza. **4.** (*Guat., Hond., Nic.*) to kill = matar.

mamar gallo (*Colo.*) to pull someone's leg; to bother = tomarle el pelo a alguien; molestar.

mamarse 1. (*Ven.*) to do something unwillingly = hacer algo a disgusto. **2.** (*Colo.*) to fail to live up to a commitment = no cumplir con un compromiso.

mamazota; mazota (*Colo.*) a very attractive woman = mujer muy atractiva.

mameluco 1. (*Chile*) overalls = mono. **2.** (*Hond.*) shorts; baggy trousers = calzón; bombachos.

mamerto; menso 1. (*Chile, Ecua.*) silly = tonto; bobo. **2.** (*Chile, Ecua.*) slow-witted = torpe.

mamila (*Dom. Rep., Mex.*) a feeding bottle = biberón.

mamito (*Puerto Rico*) a well-dressed man = hombre muy bien vestido.

mamón 1. (*Chile*) a baby that sucks a lot = bebé que mama mucho. **2.** (*Guat., Hond., Nic.*) a public employee (derogatory) = empleado público (peyorativo). **3.** (*Hond.*) a club; a heavy stick = un palo; garrote. **4.** (*Colo., Hond.*) (N.E. tropical fruit) = (N.E. fruta tropical). **5.** (*Dom. Rep.*) a big, young man who behaves like a child = grandullón; muchacho muy crecido que se comporta puerilmente. **6.** (*Mex.*) a special kind of cake = un tipo especial de pastel. **7.** (*Mex.*) a pompous person = persona pomposa. **8.** (*Mex.*) a pacifier = chupete; trozo de goma o plástico que se le da al bebé para que chupe y se entretenga.

mamonazo 1. (*Ven.*) a strong blow = golpe fuerte. **2.** (*Ven.*) a disgrace or obstacle = desgracia o contratiempo.

mamonsillo (*Colo.*) (N.E. tropical fruit) = (N.E. fruta tropical.)

mamotreto 1. (*Chile, Puerto Rico*) a shapeless object = objeto sin forma. **2.** (*Chile, Puerto Rico*) a very big book = libro voluminoso.

mampara (*Chile, Peru*) a glass door = puerta vidriada; puerta de bastidores y vidrio.

man (*from English*) a man = hombre.

manayer; manejador(a) (*from English*) a manager = administrador; gerente de un negocio; director; empresario.

mancha (*Guat.*) a circle on the ground used to play spinning top = círculo en el suelo para jugar al trompo.

mancha negra (*Mex.*) the black sheep in the family = oveja negra de la familia.

mancheta (*Ven.*) a short editorial comment in the newspaper = comentario editorial corto en el periódico.

mancorna (*Colo.*) cufflinks = gemelos de la camisa.

mancornar (*Chile*) to fight violently hand-to-hand = pelear cuerpo a cuerpo violentamente.

mandar (*Chile*) to lead in cards, dominos, or a dice game = dirigir el juego de dominó, barajas, o dados por llevar la mano ganadora.

mandar un golpe (*Ven.*) to hit = propinar un golpe.

mandarse mudar (*Argen., Chile, Cuba, Uru.*) to go away = irse de un lugar.

¡mándese mudar! (*Chile*) Get out of here! = ¡váyase de aquí!

mandinga (*Dom. Rep., Ven.*) the devil = el diablo.

mandioca (*Bol.*) a yucca = yuca.

maneado (*Chile*) caught in a mess; involved in a mess = enredado; ineficiente porque todo se le hace un lío.

manear (*Mex.*) to brake a vehicle = frenar un vehículo.

manearse (*Chile, Colo.*) to ramble; to get entangled = trabarse; enredarse.

manejador(a) See **manayer**.

manejar (*Ven.*) to drive a vehicle = conducir un vehículo.

manejera (*Mex.*) the handlebars of a bicycle; the steering wheel of a car = manubrio de la bicicleta; volante del automóvil.

maneto (*Guat., Ven.*) knock-kneed = patizambo; el que camina torcido.

manflor (*Mex.*) a gay person = homosexual o lesbiana.

manflora (*Para.*) effeminate = afeminado; marica.

manga 1. (*Argen.*) a loan of money = préstamo de dinero. **2.** (*Colo.*) a lawn = césped. **3.** (*Mex.*) a well-dressed person = persona bien vestida.

mangancear See **magancear**.

manganear (*Ecua.*) to bother; to annoy = fastidiar; molestar; importunar.

manganza See **maganza**.

manganzón See **maganzón**.

mangar (*Puerto Rico*) to understand something = entender; comprender de lo que se trata algo.

mangazo (*Colo.*) a blow with a fist = puñetazo.

mangó (*Puerto Rico*) (N.E. mango, the tropical fruit) = mango, la fruta tropical.

mango (*Ven.*) an attractive person = persona atractiva.

mangonear (*Puerto Rico*) to waste time = perder el tiempo.

mangos (*Argen.*) money (informal) = dinero (informal).

mangoso See **chichos**.

mangú See **mofongo**.

manguala 1. (*Colo.*) a fraud = fraude. **2.** a conspiracy = confabulación.

manguarear; manguerear (*Ven.*) to be lazy = holgazanear.

manguareo (*Ven.*) idleness; laziness = vagancia; holgazanería.

manguerear See **manguarear**.

manigordo (*Guat.*) (N.E. an ocelot; a Central American tiger) = ocelote; tigre de Centro América.

manigua (*Ven.*) a swamp covered with weeds = pantano cubierto de malezas.

manilarga 1. (*Chile*) a thief = ladrón. **2.** (*Chile*) a willingness to enjoy fondling = gusto de tocar sexualmente.

manilargo (*Dom. Rep.*) a thief = ladrón.

manillas (*Mex.*) mittens = mitones.

manirroto (*Colo.*) generous = generoso.

manito (*Mex.*) a very close friend; a real buddy = un amigo muy cercano; un verdadero amigo.

mano (*Mex.*) a buddy; a typical Mexican expression used when talking to a friend = compadre; compañero; expression típica mexicana para referirse a un amigo.

manoabierta (*Cuba, Peru*) generous = generoso.

manopla 1. (*Argen., Chile, Peru*) a knuckleduster; brass knuckles = puño de hierro; nudilleras de metal. **2.** (*Argen., Mex.*) mittens = mitones.

manoseada (*Mex.*) a woman who has had sex with many men = la que ha tenido sexo con muchos hombres.

manotada (*Colo.*) a handful = puñado.

manseque (*Chile*) a child's game and song = juego y baile infantil.

manso(a) (*Chile*) very big; extraordinary; a lot = muy grande; muy extraordinario; mucho.

manta (*Bol., Chile, Ecua., Peru*) a blanket = frazada.

mantadril (*Hond.*) a fabric of cheap quality = tipo de tela ordinaria.

manteca (*Para., Uru., Ven.*) butter (informal) = mantequilla (informal).

mantecado (*Cuba, Puerto Rico*) ice cream = helado.

manteco 1. (*Colo.*) a dirty person = persona sucia; desaseado(a). **2.** (*Colo.*) one who has sexual relations with the servants = el que tiene relaciones sexuales con la servidumbre.

mantelito (*Mex.*) a napkin = servilleta.

mantequilla 1. (*Ven.*) an easy and highly profitable business = negocio fácil y ventajoso. **2.** (*Ven.*) a person who complies or consents easily = persona condescendiente.

mantilla 1. (*Colo.*) a shawl = chal. **2.** (*Hond.*) a coward = cobarde.

mantillas (*Mex.*) diapers = pañales.

mantón See **estola**.

manuela 1. (*Mex.*) a jacket = chaqueta. **2.** (*Chile*) masturbation (informal) = masturbación (informal).

manyar (*Argen.*) to eat (informal) = comer (informal).

manzanear (*Mex.*) to seek favors through gifts = buscar favores a través de regalos.

mañanitas (*Mex.*) a typical Mexican song that is sung to celebrate a birthday or a saint's day = canción típica mexicana que se canta para celebrar un cumpleaños o el día del santo.

mapear (*from English*) to mop up = fregar el suelo; limpiar el suelo con un trapo húmedo o fregasuelos.

mapo (*from English*) a mop = fregasuelos; trapo o tiras de cordones para limpiar el piso.

mapuche (*Chile*) a native Chilean Indian = indio nativo de Chile.

maqueta (*Colo.*) lazy = haragán; holgazán.

maquetear (*Colo.*) to idle = haraganear.

maquetería (*Colo.*) laziness; idleness = holgazanería; haraganería.

máquina 1. (*Argen.*) a beautiful girl = muchacha bonita. **2.** (*Mex.*) a car = automóvil.

maraca 1. (*Chile*) a prostitute (vulgar) = prostituta (vulgar). **2.** (*Colo.*) a useless person = persona inútil. **3.** (*Ven.*) the youngest daughter = la menor de las hijas. **4.** (*Ven.*) a useless person = persona inútil. **5.** (*Colo., Costa Rica, Cuba, Dom. Rep., Guat., Hond., Puerto Rico, Salva., Ven.*) (N.E. musical instrument used to carry the rhythm of tropical music) = instrumento musical para marcar el ritmo de la música tropical.

maraco 1. (*Chile*) a homosexual (vulgar) = homosexual (vulgar). **2.** (*Ven.*) the youngest son = el menor de los hijos.

margayate (*Mex.*) a brawl; an uproar; a disorder = tumulto; lío; confusión; desorden.

maría (*Ven.*) marijuana (informal) = marihuana (informal).

marías; marujas (*Colo.*) a woman's breast (informal) = pechos femeninos (informal).

marico (*Colo., Ven.*) homosexual; effeminate = homosexual; afeminado.

mariela; marimba (*Colo.*) marijuana (informal) = marihuana (informal).

marifinga 1. (*Dom. Rep.*) ladyfingers, the dessert = postre de leche, huevos y otros ingredientes. **2.** (*Puerto Rico*) ladyfingers; a dessert prepared with creamed corn and white beans = postre preparado con crema de maíz y habichuelas blancas.

mariguanza 1. (*Chile*) hand gestures = gestos o movimientos de las manos. **2.** (*Chile*) magic gestures = gestos con sentido mágico.

marimba See **mariela**.

marimbero (*Colo.*) a marijuana dealer = traficante de marihuana.

marinera (*Bol., Ecua., Peru*) a popular dance of the Andean region = baile popular de la región andina.

marinovios (*Ecua.*) an unwed couple = pareja amancebada sin casarse.

mariposón (*Dom. Rep.*) a man who courts many women = hombre galanteador que corteja a muchas mujeres.

mariquear 1. (*Colo.*) a man with effeminate gestures = mariconear; hombre con gestos afeminados. **2.** (*Ven.*) to diminish the virility in a man = disminuir la virilidad en un hombre.

mariquitas (*Argen., Colo.*) fried plantain chips = medallones de plátano frito.

marisoñado (*Dom. Rep.*) oats with orange juice, milk, and sugar = avena con jugo de naranja, leche y azúcar.

maritata (*Mex.*) a peddler; a street vendor = vendedor callejero.

marketing (*from English*) marketing = (RAE) mercadotecnia; estudio del mercado.

marmolín (*Argen.*) a person of slow intelligence = persona de entendimiento lento.

marocha (*Hond.*) a thoughtless young woman = muchacha alocada.

marota (*Mex.*) a girl who behaves like a boy; a woman who behaves like a man = marimacho; mujer o jovencita que se comporta como varón.

marquesa (*Chile*) a wooden cot = catre de madera.

marqueta (*from English*) the market = mercado.

marquetero (*from English*) a person who works in the market = el que trabaja en la **marqueta** o mercado.

marrana (*Mex.*) an insult equivalent to "bitch" = insulto muy fuerte dirigido a una mujer.

marranazo See **cocotazo**.

marranear (*Colo.*) to cheat = engañar.

marrano 1. (*Colo.*) naive = ingenuo. **2.** (*Mex.*) a pig = cerdo.

marraqueta (*Chile*) a soft bread with a cut that facilitates splitting it in half = pan suave con un corte que permite partirlo fácilmente en dos.

marrón 1. (*Argen., Uru.*) brown = color café; pardo. **2.** (*Colo.*) a curl = rizo. **3.** (*Ven.*) coffee with a little milk = café con poca leche.

marrueco (*Chile*) the zipper in trousers or pants = bragueta.

marrunga See **mandinga.**

martillero (*Argen., Chile, Peru*) an auctioneer = subastador; el que dirige una subasta pública.

maruga (*Cuba*) a baby's rattle = cascabel; sonajero.

marujas See **marías.**

más cansón(a) que un mico al hombro (*Colo.*) someone who is a pain in the neck = persona que es insoportable.

más enamorado que un cabro (*Puerto Rico*) someone who is totally smitten = está muy enamorado.

más loco(a) que una cabra (*Colo.*) crazier than a loon = el o la que está muy desquiciado.

más perdido(a) que el hijo de Limber (*Colo.*) not to know which end is up = muy perdido; no entiende nada.

más perdido(a) que el teniente Bello (*Chile*) not to know which end is up; not to understand anything = muy perdido; no entiende nada.

masacota; masacote (*Mex.*) a mixed-up and unorganized object = objeto mezclado y desorganizado.

masacote See **masacota.**

masatudo (*Colo.*) lumpy; sticky; shapeless = amazacotado; pegajoso y sin forma definida.

mascada 1. (*Argen., Chile, Colo., Cuba*) a piece of food that fits in the mouth = cantidad de comida que cabe de una vez en la boca. **2.** (*Mex.*) a scarf = bufanda; mantilla; pañuelo.

mascadura (*Hond.*) a bread roll eaten when drinking chocolate = bollo que acompaña al chocolate.

mascota (*Ven.*) a baseball glove = guante de **béisbol.**

masilla (*Cuba*) clay = arcilla.

mastique 1. (*Chile*) food = comida. **2.** (*Ven.*) a substance used in construction to fill surfaces = substancia usada en la construcción para rellenar superficies.

mataburros (*Dom. Rep.*) a dictionary = diccionario.

mataculín (*Colo.*) a swing = balancín.

matada 1. (*Hond.*) a fall = caída. **2.** (*Ven.*) a fall that produces serious injuries = caída que provoca heridas serias.

matagusano (*Guat.*) a sweet dessert of orange peels and honey = dulce de cáscaras de naranjas y miel.

matamama (*Nic.*) a traitor to a country = vendepatrias.

matambre (*Argen., Para.*) a roll of meat seasoned and boiled, which is served in slices as an appetizer before a meal = carne aderezada y enrollada que se cuece en agua y se sirve en rodajas como tentempié mientras llega la comida principal.

matapiojo (*Chile*) a dragonfly = libélula.

matatudo (*Bol.*) with a big snout = hocicudo.

match (*from English*) a match = lucha; combate; asalto; encuentro; partido; juego.

mate 1. (*Argen., Chile, Para., Uru.*) a drinking vessel made from a gourd = vasija hecha de una calabaza seca. **2.** (*Argen., Chile, Uru.*) the head = cabeza. **3.** (*Argen., Chile, Uru.*) intellectual ability; intelligence = capacidad intelectual; inteligencia. **4.** (*Argen., Bol., Para., Uru.*) an herbal tea; a typical drink of the Argentines and Uruguayans = té de hierbas; bebida típica de los argentinos y los uruguayos. **5.** (*Colo., Ecua., Peru*) any small pot = cualquier tiesto pequeño.

matearse (*Chile*) to study hard = estudiar con ahinco.

mateo (*Chile*) a person who studies a lot = el que estudia mucho.

materia; postema (*Colo.*) pus; the liquid matter in an infected wound = pus; materia líquida en una herida infectada.

matraca 1. (*Ven.*) a bribe = soborno. **2.** (*Ven.*) a battered vehicle that make noises = vehículo muy usado que produce ruidos.

matracaso 1. (*Ven.*) a strong hit = golpe fuerte. **2.** (*Ven.*) a negative and painful influence = influencia negativa y dolorosa. **3.** (*Ven.*) a swallow of an alcoholic beverage = trago de bebida alcohólica.

matraquear; matraqueo (*Ven.*) to receive or to give a bribe = cobrar o dar soborno.

matraqueo See **matraquear**.

matrear (*Bol.*) to wander; to idle; to bum = andar errante; vagabundear.

matrero (*Argen., Uru.*) a bandit = bandido.

matrimonio (*Puerto Rico*) a plate of rice and beans (informal) = plato de arroz con habichuelas (informal).

matropa (*Hond.*) hysteria = histeria.

matungo See **chalungo**.

maula (*Argen.*) a coward; lazy = cobarde; flojo.

maus (*from English*) a mouse = ratón.

mayordomo (*Peru*) any servant = criado; cualquier sirviente.

mazacotudo 1. (*Ven.*) thick = espeso. **2.** (*Chile, Colo.*) sticky, lumpy, and shapeless = amazacotado pegajoso y sin forma definida.

mazamorra 1. (*Argen., Chile*) a mixture; a mess; confusion = mescolanza; confusión. **2.** (*Bol.*) the mud from an avalanche = lodo de un alud. **3.** (*Colo., Ven.*) a thick drink = bebida espesa. **4.** (*Dom. Rep.*) an irritation in the toes = irritación en los dedos de los pies. **5.** (*Peru*) soft and sweet mush = papilla suave y dulce.

mazorca de maíz (*Cuba*) a corncob = corazón del fruto del maíz.

mazota See **mamazota**.

mbarigüí (*Para.*) any small mosquito = cualquier mosquito pequeño.

me colgué en el examen (*Hond.*) I failed the exam. = fracasé en el examen.

me esta arañando el tigre (*Nic.*) I am hungry. = tengo hambre.

me hace tilín (*Cuba*) something appeals to me; it rings a bell = creo recordarlo; entiendo de que se trata.

me importa tres pitos (*Cuba*) I don't give a damn. = no me importa nada.

ime lleva la chingada! (*Mex.*) I will be God-damned! (vulgar) = ¡estoy maldito! (vulgar).

me rajaron en el examen (*Chile*) I failed the exam (informal). = reprobé el examen.

me tinca (*Chile, Peru*) I have a hunch. = tengo una corazonada.

me vale un cacao; me vale un pepino (*Nic.*) I don't care! = a mí no me importa.

me vale un pepino See **me vale un cacao**.

meca (*Chile*) excrement = excremento.

mecate 1. (*Colo., Mex., Ven.*) a rope = cuerda gruesa de hilos retorcidos. **2.** (*Ven.*) flattery = adulación.

mecatear (*Ven.*) to flatter = adular.

mecato (*Colo.*) a sweet treat = golosina.

mecha 1. (*Argen., Chile, Peru*) a bit = taladro. **2.** (*Argen., Chile, Peru*) a hair (informal) = un pelo (informal). **3.** (*Colo.*) a worthless thing = una cosa sin valor. **4.** (*Colo.*) old clothes = ropa vieja. **5.** (*Colo.*) to get what has been desired = conseguir lo que se desea. **6.** (*Hond.*) a setback; adversity = contrariedad; adversidad. **7.** (*Ven.*) a nuisance = molestia. **8.** (*Ven.*) a joke = broma.

mechicolorado (*Colo.*) red hair = pelirrojo.

mechón (*Chile*) a college freshman = estudiante universitario del primer año.

media (*Chile*) very big = muy grande.

mediagua (*Chile*) a small building with only one pitch in the roof = construcción pequeña con el techo en declive en una sola dirección.

medias (*Cuba, Pan., Puerto Rico*) socks = calcetines.

medicaid [pron. mediqueid] (*from English*) Medicaid = asistencia médica; asistencia de salud; servicio de salud gratuita.

mediero (*Chile*) a farmer who pays the rent on a field with its product = el que paga la renta de un terreno con lo que produce el mismo terreno.

medio pelo 1. (*Argen.*) of inferior quality = de calidad inferior. **2.** (*Argen., Chile*) the middle class = la clase media.

megabytes [pron. megabaites] (*from English*) megabytes; Mb or Mega unit equal to 1,048,576 bytes = (N.E. unidad de memoria de la computadora igual a 1.048.576 **bits**, se abrevia Mb o Mega).

meidin (*from English*) made in = fabricado en; hecho en.

meinfreim (*from English*) a mainframe computer = (N.E. unidad centro de la computadora; computador central).

meinjole (*from English*) the main hole in a sewer = tapa del alcantarillado.

mellos (*Pan.*) identical twins = gemelos.

melón de agua (*Cuba*) a watermelon = sandía.

memela (*Hond.*) a corn **tortilla** packed in banana leaves = **tortilla** de maíz envuelta en hojas de plátano.

memoria de gallina (*Colo.*) a bad memory = mala memoria.

memory (*from English*) a computer's memory = memoria de la computadora.

mene (*Ven.*) a natural spring of petroleum = manantial natural de petróleo.

meneada (*Mex.*) to stir; to whip a liquid = colar; batir un líquido.

mengalo (*Nic.*) without class (derogatory); without style = el que no tiene clase (despectivo); el que no tiene estilo.

menso; menzo 1. (*Chile, Ecua., Mex.*) ignorant; foolish = ignorante; tonto. **2.** See **gil**.

mentar (*Argen.*) to name someone = nombrar.

menudo 1. (*Cuba, Puerto Rico*) change (money) = cambio (dinero); unidades pequeñas de dinero. **2.** (*Mex.*) a tripe soup = callos; sopa de tripas o interiores del animal. **3.** (*Peru*) a brunette = persona de la tez blanca y del pelo negro.

menudo chichero (*Ven.*) several coins of low value = cantidad de monedas de poco valor.

menzo See **menso**.

mercería (*Chile*) a hardware store = ferretería.

merequetén (*Ven.*) a noisy disorder = desorden bullicioso.

mero 1. (*Mex.*) the special . . . ; the one and only . . . = el especial . . . ; el único . . . **2.** (*Mex.*) the great . . . ; the super . . . = el gran . . . ; el super. . . .

mesanín (*Colo.*) the mezzanine = entrepiso; entresuelos.

imétele! (*Mex.*) Do it!; Hit'em'!; Hurry up! = ¡hazlo!; ¡dale!; ¡apúrate!

métele chala (*Chile*) to accelerate a vehicle = acelera el vehículo.

meter el choclo (*Argen.*) to mislead into a difficult task = engañar para involucrar a alguien en un trabajo difícil.

meter la cuchara (*Chile, Dom. Rep.*) to intrude in someone else's conversation = intervenir en conversación ajena.

meter La Habana en Guanabacoa (*Cuba*) to try to squeeze something into a small space = tratar de meter algo grande en un espacio pequeño.

meter la pata (*Peru, Chile*) to make a mistake; to talk at the wrong moment or place = cometer un error; decir algo en el momento incorrecto o a la persona equivocada.

meter las extremidades (*Nic.*) to make a mistake = cometer una imprudencia.

metete (*Chile, Guat.*) a busybody; a meddler = entrometido(a).

metiche (*Chile*) meddlesome = intruso; entrometido.

metido 1. (*Chile*) an upstart = entrometido. **2.** (*Chile*) a social climber = arribista social.

metra (*Ven.*) marble = canica.

metro (*Chile*) a subway; a metropolitan train = tren subterráneo.

mezcal (*Mex.*) an alcoholic drink made from fermented **magüey** = bebida alcohólica del **magüey** fermentado.

mezclote (*Ven.*) a heavy and thick mixture of materials used in construction = mezcla gruesa de materiales usados en construcción.

mezquino (*Mex.*) a wart on the finger = berruga en un dedo.

mi cielo (*Mex.*) "darling" = querido(a).

mica 1. (*Colo.*) a chamberpot = orinal; recipiente para orinar. **2.** (*Guat.*) a coquette = mujer coqueta.

micada (*Guat., Hond.*) a ridiculous way of acting; a monkey-face; a monkeyish way = monada; acción ridícula; actividad graciosa.

miche (*Ven.*) cane alcohol mixed with spices and aromatic herbs = aguardiente de caña mezclado con hierbas aromáticas y especias.

mico 1. (*Guat., Hond., Salva.*) a monkey = mono. **2.** (*Guat., Hond., Salva.*) a car jack = gato; aparato para levantar el automóvil. **3.** (*Salva.*) a show-off person = persona presumida.

micro (*Chile*) a bus = ómnibus.

microbus (*Colo.*) a small bus = vehículo pequeño para el transporte público.

microfilm (*from English*) microfilm = microfilme.

mieditis (*Dom. Rep.*) a nickname for fear = apodo para designar el miedo.

migra; la migra 1. (*from English*) the Immigration and Naturalization Service of the United States = el Servicio de inmigración de los Estados Unidos. **2.** (*from English*) the United States immigration officers = agentes de Inmigración de los Estados Unidos.

migueleño (*Hond.*) discourteous; rude = descortés; descomedido.

mijito(a) (*Dom. Rep.*) "my very dearest," in a protective tone = contracción para "mi hijo," expresión que se usa para dirigirse a otro con cariño y en un sentido protector.

mijo(a) (*Dom. Rep.*) "my dear" = contracción para "mi hijo," la cual se usa para dirigirse a otro con cariño.

milico (*Argen., Bol., Chile, Para., Uru.*) any member of the military forces = nombre para cualquier miembro de las fuerzas armadas.

milpa (*Guat., Hond., Mex., Salva.*) a corn field = campo sembrado de maíz.

milque (*from English*) milk = leche.

mimeógrafo (*from English*) a mimeograph = (RAE) multicopista que reproduce el texto o las figuras grabadas en una lámina de papel que permite pasar la tinta por las incisiones hechas en ella.

mimosear (*Argen., Para.*) asking to be pampered = pedir mimos.

minga 1. (*Colo.*) a group working for the benefit of one of its members = trabajo de grupo para beneficiar a uno de los miembros del mismo. **2.** (*Puerto Rico*) an active person = persona muy activa.

mingonear (*Ven.*) to behave as a spoiled person = hacerse el consentido y mimado.

minguero (*Colo.*) a person who participates in a **minga** = el que participa en una **minga**.

mingui (*Hond.*) an alcoholic drink made from fermented fruit juice = bebida alcohólica que es producto de la fermentación de jugo de fruta.

miñoco (*Colo.*) a wry face; a grimace = gesto irónico; gestos graciosos; monerías.

miquear (*Colo.*) to play around = travesear.

mirringo; pirringa (*Colo.*) a small person = persona pequeña.

misia (*Colo.*) a lady = señora.

missy (*Puerto Rico*) the respectful treatment for a female teacher or any authoritative female figure = tratamiento de respeto a la profesora, a la maestra o a cualquier mujer que representa la autoridad.

mistear (*from English*) to miss or to fail = faltar; no asistir a un acto o cita.

mister 1. (*Colo.*) any male, blond foreigner = cualquier extranjero rubio. 2. (*Puerto Rico*) the respectful treatment for a male teacher or any authoritative male figure = tratamiento de respeto a un profesor, a un maestro o a cualquier hombre que representa autoridad.

místico (*Colo.*) with fine and delicate manners = con modales finos y delicados.

misturar (*Argen.*) to prepare a mixture; to mix = mezclar.

miti miti (*Colo.*) fifty-fifty = a partes iguales.

mitiar (*from English*) to meet = juntarse; reunirse; encontrarse.

mitié (*from English*) I met. = me junté; me reuní; me encontré.

mitin (*from English*) a meeting = (RAE) reunión donde se discuten públicamente asuntos políticos o sociales.

mixtiar (*from English*) to mix = mezclar.

moca (*Mex.*) a mug = vaso con asa; pequeña jarra para beber.

mocha (*Chile*) a fight (informal) = pelea (informal).

mochar 1. (*Colo.*) to be laid off from a job = ser despedido(a) de un trabajo. 2. (*Colo.*) to cut = cortar.

mochila (*Colo.*) a knapsack = morral; bolsa para colgar del hombro o terciada.

mochilas (*Colo.*) the scrotum (vulgar) = escroto (vulgar).

mochilón (*Colo.*) a type of basket = un tipo de canasto.

mocho 1. (*Cuba*) a cigar butt = lo que queda de un cigarro puro ya fumado. 2. (*Ven.*) a nag = caballo que luce muy mal. 3.

(*Mex.*) a conservative; a reactionary = conservador; reaccionario. 4. (*Mex.*) extremely religious; very Catholic = extremadamente religioso; muy católico.

mochuelo (*Colo.*) an owl = lechuza.

mofler (*from English*) an automobile muffler = silenciador del automóvil.

mofongo; mangú (*Dom. Rep., Puerto Rico*) a dish with plantain, fried pork, and other ingredients = plato preparado con plátano, chicharrón de cerdo y otros ingredientes.

mogallar (*Bol.*) to cheat = trampear.

mogolla (*Colo.*) a small whole wheat bread = panecillo de trigo integral.

mogollo (*Colo.*) easy; simple = fácil; muy sencillo de hacer.

mohair (*from English*) mohair = moaré.

mojado(a) (*Mex.*) a wetback; a nickname for an illegal immigrant to the United States (derogatory) = espaldas mojadas; apodo para los inmigrantes ilegales en los Estados Unidos (peyorativo).

mojiganga (*Ven.*) a grotesque person; a person who dresses oddly = persona que provoca risas y burlas especialmente por su atuendo extraño.

mojito (*Ven.*) a dish prepared with fish, coconut milk, and spices = plato preparado con pescado, leche de coco y especias.

mojojó (*Colo.*) an edible insect larva = larva comestible de insecto.

mojón (*Chile*) a stool; solid excrement (vulgar) = excremento sólido (vulgar).

mojonear (*Ven.*) to lie (vulgar) = mentir (vulgar).

mojonero (*Ven.*) a liar (vulgar) = mentiroso (vulgar).

molacha(o) (*Ecua.*) a girl; a boy = niña(o).

mole (*Mex.*) a dish prepared with turkey and hot peppers = plato preparado con pavo y pimientos picantes.

molenillo (*Nic.*) a mixer = mezcladora de bebidas o jugos.

molleja (*Mex.*) a pocket watch = reloj de bolsillo.

molleja de pollo (*Cuba*) a gizzard = molleja.

mollera (*Pan.*) biceps = bíceps.

mollero (*Puerto Rico*) biceps = bíceps.

molleros (*Cuba, Peru*) biceps = bíceps.

mollete (*Mex.*) a cake in the shape of a loaf = pastel o bizcocho con la forma de una hogaza de pan.

molleto (*Colo.*) a black person = negro.

molo 1. (*Chile*) a breakwater; a seawall = malecón. **2.** (*Ecua.*) mashed potatoes = puré de patatas.

mololoa (*Hond.*) a loud conversation = conversación en voz muy alta.

molote (*Mex.*) hair in a bun = moño; pelo atado.

molotera (*Guat., Hond.*) a brawl; an uproar; public outrage = alboroto; tumulto; gresca; escándalo.

mompes (*from English*) the mumps = amígdalas.

mona 1. (*Argen.*) a hangover = resaca. **2.** (*Hond.*) a bad section of a whole; the bad part of a complete set = lo que está o es malo dentro de un conjunto.

monate (*Dom. Rep.*) armpit odor = mal olor de los sobacos.

mondíngalo (*Dom. Rep.*) a dish prepared with the stomach and the intestines of an animal = plato preparado con el estómago y los intestinos del animal.

mondongo 1. (*Cuba, Guat., Hond.*) tripe soup = callos; sopa de callos o estómago de animal. **2.** (*Dom. Rep., Puerto Rico*) a soup prepared with pigs' feet, stomach of a cow, yucca, banana, and other ingredients = sopa preparada con patas de cerdo, estómago de vacuno, yuca y otros ingredientes. **3.** (*Guat.*) a freakish or outlandish person; an eyesore = adefesio; vestimenta ridícula.

monear 1. (*Hond.*) to work hard; to work with determination = trabajar con tesón.

2. (*Hond.*) to punish oneself = darse de golpes.

monga (*Puerto Rico*) the flu; influenza = gripe; influenza.

monguera 1. (*Puerto Rico*) laziness = flojera. **2.** (*Puerto Rico*) numbness = entumecimiento.

moni (*from English*) money = dinero.

monicongo 1. (*Colo.*) an ugly doll; a doll of inferior quality = muñeca fea de mala calidad. **2.** a doll used for witchcraft = muñeco para brujería.

monifato (*Ven.*) presumptuous; fatuous = presuntuoso; fatuo.

monitos (*Colo.*) comics = tiras cómicas.

mono 1. (*Ven.*) a specific kind of baby's attire = un traje específico que usan los niños pequeños. **2.** (*Colo.*) a blond person = persona rubia.

monos 1. (*Chile*) a derogatory term for a bunch of personal and/or household objects = forma peyorativa para referirse a un conjunto de objetos personales o del hogar. **2.** (*Colo.*) a cartoon = dibujos animados; caricaturas.

monquiar (*from English*) to monkey around = (N.E. darse vueltas o caminar sin destino fijo con el objeto de desperdiciar el tiempo).

monrero (*Peru*) a thief who uses force to break into a place = ladrón que entra en el lugar del robo por la fuerza.

montante (*Hond.*) a disturbance; a riot = alboroto; motín.

montañero (*Colo.*) a peasant = campesino.

montar 1. (*Uru.*) to have sex (vulgar) = forma vulgar para el acto sexual. **2.** (*Ven.*) to put a meal on the fire to cook = poner la comida al fuego para cocinarla.

montera 1. (*Bol., Peru*) a multicolored cone-shaped hat used by people living in the Andes high plateau = gorro multicolor con forma de cono usado por gentes que viven en el altiplano andino. **2.** (*Hond.*) drunkenness = borrachera.

moña (*Colo.*) a bun = moño.

mopear (*from English*) to mop = trapear.

moquetazo (*Mex.*) a punch in the nose = golpe de puño en la nariz.

moquete (*Uru.*) a slap = bofetada; cachetada.

mora (*Hond.*) a raspberry = frambuesa.

moray (*Hond.*) an oak = roble.

morder (*Ven.*) to cheat = estafar.

mordida (*Bol., Mex.*) a bribe = soborno.

moreno (*Uru.*) a black person = persona de la raza negra.

morete (*Hond.*) a bruise = moretón.

morir soñando (*Colo.*) an orange milkshake = batido de leche y jugo de naranja.

¡morite! (*Argen.*) an interjection of surprise or displeasure = interjección que puede significar sorpresa o desagrado.

morlacos (*Chile*) money (informal) = dinero (informal).

moro (*Bol., Chile, Colo., Ecua., Peru*) an unbaptized person = una persona sin bautizar.

morocho 1. (*Uru.*) a dark-skinned person = persona de tez oscura. 2. (*Colo.*) strong; tough = fuerte. 3. (*Colo.*) well-preserved = bien conservado. 4. (*Ecua.*) a dish made with corn = comida de maíz. 5. (*Hond.*) a person with a harelip = persona con el labio leporino. 6. (*Ven.*) a twin; an identical twin = mellizo; gemelo.

morochos (*Ven.*) twins; identical twins = mellizos; gemelos.

morolo (*Hond.*) silly; with limited intelligence = tonto; de inteligencia limitada.

moronga (*Guat., Hond.*) a blood-pudding sausage; a sausage = morcilla; salchicha.

moros y cristianos (*Cuba*) a dish of black beans and white rice mixed together = plato en que se mezclan el arroz blanco con habichuelas negras.

morral 1. (*Colo.*) a backpack = mochila. 2. (*Nic.*) a game bag; a book bag; a bag = bolsa; cartera de mano; maletín.

morrocotudo 1. (*Argen., Chile*) big; strong; of large size and weight = fornido; corpulento; de gran tamaño; de gran peso o importancia. 2. (*Colo.*) rich = adinerado; rico.

morroño 1. (*Hond.*) rough = áspero. 2. (*Peru*) weak; sickly; someone with rickets = débil; enfermizo; raquítico.

morrudo (*Uru.*) big = grande; fornido; corpulento.

mortual (*Hond.*) an inheritance = herencia.

mosca 1. (*Mex.*) the bull's eye; the center of a target = centro del blanco. 2. (*Argen.*) money (informal) = dinero (informal).

moscarrofio (*Hond.*) an ugly person = persona fea.

mosquear 1. (*Chile*) to bother; to annoy = molestar; importunar. 2. (*Uru.*) to snoop = curiosear; husmear.

mosquero 1. (*Dom. Rep.*) many flies = mosquerío; hervidero de moscas. 2. (*Dom. Rep.*) a person who goes from house to house = el que anda de casa en casa.

mota (*Mex.*) marijuana = marihuana.

mote 1. (*Argen., Chile, Peru*) a grammatical mistake = error gramatical. 2. (*Argen., Chile, Peru*) boiled wheat = trigo hervido. 3. (*Argen., Chile, Peru*) a very small fish = pez muy pequeño. 4. (*Bol., Ecua., Peru*) a nickname = apodo. 5. (*Bol., Ecua., Peru*) stewed whole grain of corn = grano entero del maíz cocido. 6. (*Peru*) an accent in the speech of the people living in the Peruvian Andes = acento distinto en el hablar de los que viven en los andes peruanos.

motete (*Guat., Hond., Nic., Salva.*) a backpack = mochila.

motilado (*Colo.*) a haircut = corte de pelo.

moto 1. (*Puerto Rico*) a marijuana joint = cigarrillo de marihuana. 2. (*Puerto Rico*) a junkie = drogadicto.

motocross (*from English*) a motorcross = (N.E. carrera de motocicletas a campo traviesa).

motoso (*Peru*) a peasant; a rustic = campesino; rústico.

movida 1. (*Argen., Chile*) a smart business; an interesting affair = buen negocio; asunto interesante. **2.** (*Ven.*) a party = fiesta. **3.** (*Mex.*) a love affair = aventura amorosa.

moyo (*Puerto Rico*) a black person from the continental United States = negro del territorio continental de los Estados Unidos.

mozón (*Peru*) a joker; a sarcastic person = persona bromista y burlona.

mucama (*Bol., Ecua., Peru*) a chambermaid; a servant = camarera; sirviente.

múcaro (*Puerto Rico*) an owl = lechuza.

mucepo (*Hond.*) sadness; grief = tristeza; pena.

¡muchacho! (*Puerto Rico*) an interjection that could mean several things according to the stress and the intonation; I am telling you!; Don't you see! How awful! = interjección que puede significar varias cosas según la entonación; ¡te lo digo!; ¡acaso no lo ves!; ¡que terrible!

muchacho (*Colo., Ven.*) the meat cut from the leg of an animal = corte de carne de la pierna del animal.

muchitanga 1. (*Peru*) a rude mob = muchedumbre soez y grosera. **2.** (*Puerto Rico*) clumsy = torpe. **3.** (*Puerto Rico*) feeble = enclenque; débil.

muco (*Hond.*) an animal without its horns = animal sin cuernos.

mudenco (*Hond.*) stuttering = tartamudo.

mueco (*Colo.*) without teeth = sin dientes.

muela; pena (*Hond.*) an embarrassment = vergüenza.

muenda See **fuetera**.

muérgano 1. (*Colo.*) an old object; knick-knacks; merchandise that does not sell = trasto viejo; chucherías; objeto que no se vende. **2.** (*Ven.*) a vile and despicable person = persona vil y despreciable.

mufa (*Argen.*) bad luck = mala suerte; sucesión de hechos nefastos.

mugre; mugroso (*Colo.*) a bad person = persona de baja calaña.

mugroso See **mugre**.

mula; paquete (*Uru.*) a lie = mentira.

mulato(a) (*Cuba*) a light-skinned black person = negro(a) de la piel clara.

mulero 1. (*Argen.*) a crook = tramposo. **2.** (*Uru.*) a liar = mentiroso.

muñequear (*Argen., Chile*) to negotiate with great political ability = gestionar con mucha habilidad política.

muñequitos (*Cuba, Puerto Rico*) comics; cartoons = historietas; caricaturas.

murruco (*Nic.*) a curly-haired person = de pelo muy rizado.

music hall [pron. miusic jol] (*from English*) a music hall = teatro de variedades.

musuco (*Hond.*) a curly-haired person = el que tiene el pelo rizado.

N

na' que ver (*Chile*) it doesn't belong here; it is not relevant = no corresponde aquí; no está relacionado.

nabo; vejiga (*Uru.*) silly = tonto.

nacatamal (*Nic.*) a corn dish with pork that is very spicy and has the consistency of dough = masa de maíz con carne de cerdo bien condimentada.

nacido (*Para.*) a boil; a big bump in the skin filled with pus = furúnculo; bola llena de pus en la piel.

nada que ver (*Argen., Chile*) it doesn't bear any relation (to the subject at hand) = lo que no está relacionado en absoluto con el tema.

nadita (*Dom. Rep.*) very little of something = muy poco de algo.

nafta (*Argen., Uru.*) gasoline = gasolina.

naftazo (*Argen.*) a hike in the price of gasoline = una subida en el precio de la gasolina.

nagual (*Hond.*) the skirt used by indigenous Honduran women = falda usada por las indígenas hondureñas.

naguas 1. (*Mex.*) a skirt = falda. **2.** (*Colo.*) an underskirt = enaguas.

naiboa (*Ven.*) a **casabe**, the tropical fruit, filled with sugar cane juice, cheese, and spices = la fruta tropical **casabe**, rellena de jugo de la caña de azúcar, queso y algunas especias.

nalgón(a) (*Hond.*) having big buttocks = nalgudo(a).

nambira (*Hond., Nic.*) a vessel made from half of a squash that is used by peasants to transport water = vasija hecha con la mitad de la calabaza y usada por los campesinos para transportar agua.

nancear (*Hond.*) to reach; to take = alcanzar; coger.

naranja (*Puerto Rico*) a bitter orange = naranja amarga.

nariz (*Mex.*) a busybody = entrometido.

natilla (*Colo.*) a Christmas dessert made of corn starch, milk, and sugar = postre navideño hecho de maicena, leche y azúcar.

naturaleza 1. (*Colo.*) semen (informal) = semen (informal). **2.** (*Colo.*) sexual desire = apetito sexual.

navajas de rasurar (*Mex.*) razor blades = cuchillas de afeitar.

navajas (*Puerto Rico*) razor blades = hojas para afeitar.

nave (*Ven.*) a big luxury automobile (informal) = automóvil grande y lujoso (informal).

navo (*Argen.*) clumsy = torpe.

necio (*Colo.*) touchy = quisquilloso.

negocio (*Chile*) a store = tienda; lugar donde se vende o se compra.

negrear 1. (*Colo.*) to humiliate = humillar. **2.** (*Colo.*) to isolate; to segregate = marginar.

negritas (*Ven.*) black beans = habichuelas negras.

negro; tinto (*Ven.*) black coffee = café solo.

neme (*Colo.*) tar = brea.

nena (*Argen., Colo., Uru.*) a girl = niña.

nene (*Argen., Colo., Uru.*) a boy = niño.

neneque (*Hond.*) to be weak = el que es o está muy débil.

nenito (*Argen., Guat., Uru.*) a baby = bebé.

neta (*from English*) a net = red.

network (*from English*) a network = red; cadena.

neumático (*Argen., Bol., Chile, Ecua.*) a tire = goma del automóvil.

nevera (*Colo., Puerto Rico*) a refrigerator = refrigerador.

ni cacho (*Guat.*) I did not get anything. = no saqué nada; no gané nada.

ni fu ni fa (*Argen.*) not this or the other; noncommittal = ni esto ni lo otro; ambiguo.

ni muy muy ni tan tan (*Argen.*) to not be so exaggerated and exigent = no hay que ser ni tan exagerado ni tan exigente.

niche (*Ven.*) a person with features that show African origin from black ancestors (derogatory) = persona con rasgos negroides (despectivo).

nicos (*Nic.*) a nickname that the Nicaraguans use for themselves = apodo que los nicaragüenses usan para llamarse a sí mismos.

nieve 1. (*Argen., Ecua., Peru, Uru.*) sherbet = sorbete. **2.** (*Mex.*) ice cream = helado.

nievero (*Mex.*) an ice cream vendor = el que vende helados.

night club [pron. naigtclab] (*from English*) a nightclub = cabaret; club nocturno.

niple (*from English*) a mechanic nipple = manguito de unión; tubo corto que se usa para unir otros dos tubos.

nítido (*Puerto Rico*) good; beautiful = bien; buena(o); bonita(o).

nixte 1. (*Hond.*) pale = pálido. **2.** (*Hond.*) ashen; ash-colored = ceniciento; de color ceniza.

no chillar (*Guat., Hond.*) to not say a word = no decir ni una palabra.

no estar el palo para cuchara (*Colo.*) it is not the time or the place for jokes = no es el momento para bromas.

no estar en nada (*Colo.*) to be a loser = ser un fracasado.

no estay ni ahí (*Chile*) you do not understand; you don't know = no entiendes; no sabes.

ino fuña! See **inojuña!**

no raja ni presta el hacha (*Colo.*) does not do and doesn't allow others to do something = no hace ni deja hacer nada.

no vuelvo ni a buscar billetes (*Puerto Rico*) there is nothing that will make me come back = no volveré por ninguna razón.

nochera (*Argen.*) a prostitute = prostituta.

nocomen (*from English*) no comment = sin comentario.

inojuña!; ino fuña! (*Ven.*) an interjection; Do not mess up! = interjección; ino lo estropees!

nombre de familia (*from English*) the family name = apellido.

nominar (*from English*) to nominate = presentar, designar, proponer la candidatura.

noqueado (*from English*) to be knocked out = (N.E. estar sin sentido; perder el conocimiento).

noquear (*from English*) to knock out = (N.E. dejar sin sentido; hacer perder el conocimiento).

norsa (*from English*) a nurse = enfermera; niñera; aya.

norseri (*from English*) a nursery = sala cuna.

norte 1. (*Ven.*) rain that is out of season = lluvia que cae fuera de estación. **2.** (*Guat., Hond., Salva.*) any wind; a wind that blows from any direction = viento que sopla desde cualquier dirección. **3.** (*Mex.*) to drive someone crazy or to go crazy = poner a otro o ponerse loco uno mismo.

nublazón (*Dom. Rep.*) very cloudy = muy nublado.

nulificar (*from English*) to nullify = anular; cancelar.

número (*Colo.*) the opportunity to have sex with a prostitute without paying = la oportunidad de tener sexo con una prostituta sin pagar.

Ñ

ñachi (*Chile*) a dish prepared with raw animal blood seasoned with salt, hot pepper, and other spices = plato preparado con sangre cruda condimentada con sal, **ají** y otras especias.

ñame 1. (*Ven.*) a big foot = pie grande. **2.** (*Ven.*) a swollen foot = pie hinchado.

ñandutí (*Para.*) handmade lace = encaje hecho a mano.

ñangue (*Puerto Rico*) an idiot; stupid = idiota; estúpido.

ñaña (*Peru*) a girl = niña.

ñañara (*Dom. Rep.*) a little scar = cicatriz pequeña.

ñaño 1. (*Ecua.*) a brother = hermano. **2.** (*Peru*) a boy = niño. **3.** (*Colo.*) the most spoiled child in the family = el/la más consentido(a) de los hermanos.

ñapa (*Ven.*) a gift = regalo.

ñapango (*Colo.*) a half-breed = mestizo; mulato.

ñatas (*Dom. Rep.*) a nose = narices.

ñau (*Dom. Rep.*) meow; the sound of a cat = miau; el sonido que hace el gato.

ñecla 1. (*Chile*) a small kite = cometa muy pequeña. **2.** (*Chile*) a weak person or animal = persona o animal enclenque.

ñeco (*Ecua.*) a blow with the fist = puñetazo; golpe con el puño.

ñeñeñe (*Puerto Rico*) foolish behavior = conducta necia.

ñoco (*Colo.*) a stump = muñón.

ñoña (*Puerto Rico*) feces = heces.

ñoñerías (*Dom. Rep.*) a fondness; an indulgence = mimos; halagos.

ñoño 1. (*Puerto Rico*) immature; a crybaby = inmaduro; niño que llora. **2.** (*Puerto Rico*) vain; a person who likes to be flattered = vano; persona a quien le gusta ser adulada.

ñuto (*Ecua.*) ground; powdered = molido; convertido en polvo.

O

obradera (*Argen., Cuba, Dom. Rep., Mex., Pan.*) diarrhea (vulgar) = diarrea (vulgar).

of 1. (*from English*) off (to turn off an appliance) = apagado. **2.** (*from English*) off (to disconnect) = desconectado. **3.** (*from English*) off = fuera.

of de record (*from English*) off the record = confidencialmente; no oficialmente; extraoficialmente; sin que conste en las actas.

ofendor(a) (*from English*) an offender = ofensor(a); transgresor(a); delincuente.

oferta (*Ecua., Peru*) a sale = liquidación; barata.

oficial de policía (*from English*) a police officer = agente de policía.

ofside (*from English*) offside = fuera del juego.

ojal (*Colo.*) the anus (vulgar) = ano (vulgar).

ojete (*Mex.*) **1.** the anus (vulgar) = ano (vulgar). **2.** a selfish person = persona egoísta.

ojo (*Argen.*) to be attentive; to watch out = ponga atención; tenga cuidado.

ojotas (*Bol., Chile, Ecua., Peru, Uru.*) the sandals used by Indians and poor peasants = sandalias usadas por los indios y campesinos pobres.

okei (*from English*) O.K.; good = está bien; de acuerdo; bien.

olor fuerte (*Argen., Chile, Para.*) an acidic odor; a rotten odor = olor ácido; olor a podrido.

olote 1. (*Guat., Hond., Mex.*) a corncob = mazorca. **2.** (*Guat., Hond., Mex.*) a corncob; the remainder of the cob when the grains have been removed = zuro; lo que queda de la mazorca después de que ha sido desgranada.

omelet (*from English*) an omelet = tortilla; fritura de huevos con otros ingredientes.

omnibus (*Ecua., Peru, Uru.*) a bus = bus; autobús.

on 1. (*from English*) on = encendido. **2.** (*from English*) on = conectado.

onces (*Chile*) an afternoon snack of tea, sandwiches and/or cookies = té o café acompañado por un bocadillo y/o galletas que se sirven en la media tarde.

operático 1. (*from English*) operatic = operístico o relativo a la ópera. **2.** (*from English*) operational = operacional; que puede funcionar bien.

iórale! (*Mex.*) Hurry up!; Over here!; It is O.K.; Stop it!; Sure!; Throw it!; and other meanings = iapúrate!; iapúrese!; iaquí!; está bien; idéjese!; idéjalo!; iseguro!; ibótalo!; itíralo! y otros significados.

oranch (*from English*) an orange = naranja.

orchata (*Nic.*) a cool drink made from rice and **jícaro** seed = refresco hecho de arroz con semilla de **jícaro**.

oreja (*Argen.*) a scandalmonger = chismoso.

orejear (*Argen.*) to spy = espiar.

orejero (*Puerto Rico*) distrustful = receloso.

organillo (*Para.*) a harmonica = armónica.

orilla (*Dom. Rep.*) a gutter along a paved street = cuneta de la calle.

ormy (*from English*) the army = el ejército; los militares.

oso (*Argen.*) a rejected greeting = saludo rechazado.

otate (*Guat., Hond., Mex., Salva.*) the native bamboo of Central America and

Mexico = bambú nativo de Centro América y México.

output [pron. autput] (*from English*) output = (N.E. salida; información que sale; puerto de salida).

over booking [pron. overbukin] (*from English*) over-booking = (N.E. exceso de contratación).

overol 1. (*from English*) overalls = mono; guardapolvo; traje de trabajo de una pieza que cubre todo el cuerpo. **2.** (*Ven.*) pants with straps and a front that covers the chest = pantalón con pechera y tirantes.

P

pabellón; raspado (*Mex.*) sherbet = sorbete.

paca (*Ven.*) a package for sale in bulk = bulto grande para vender ciertas mercaderías al por mayor.

pacaya (*Guat.*) a difficulty = dificultad.

pacha 1. (*Nic., Salva.*) a feeding bottle = biberón. **2.** (*Nic.*) a bottle used to carry liquids = botella para transportar líquidos.

pachamama (*Bol.*) the Incan spirit of Mother Earth = madre tierra en la cultura inca.

pachanga 1. (*Colo.*) a Caribbean dance = baile caribeño. **2.** (*Mex., Ven.*) a party; a festivity = fiesta; celebración.

pachango (*Nic.*) chubby = regordete; rechoncho.

pachanguear (*Ven.*) to party = parrandear.

pacheco (*Ecua., Ven.*) very cold = frío muy intenso.

pachigua (*Hond.*) full; fed up = lleno; harto.

pachó (*Puerto Rico*) an embarrassment = sentirse avergonzado(a); ponerse en una situación indeseada.

pacho (*Nic.*) flat; thin = aplanado; delgado.

pachocha See **jando.**

pachón (*Hond.*) hairy = lanudo; peludo.

pachorrada (*Dom. Rep.*) sluggishness = pachotada.

pachuco (*Mex.*) another N.E. name for **chicano** = otro nombre para un **chicano.**

pachulí (*Ven.*) a perfume of inferior quality = perfume de baja calidad.

pachuquismo (*Mex.*) that which is typical or exclusive of the **chicano** culture = lo que es típico o propio de la cultura **chicana.**

pacifair (*from English*) a pacifier = chupador del bebé; chupete de entretención.

paco (*Chile*) a cop; a policeman (informal) = agente de la policía (informal).

pacón (*from English*) popcorn = palomitas de maíz.

pacotilla (*Ven.*) a cheap thing; an item of inferior quality = cosa barata de baja calidad.

pacueca (*Colo.*) a bad odor from the feet = mal olor de los pies.

padastro (*Chile*) a hangnail = padrastro.

padoc (*from English*) a paddock = (N.E. localidad cerca de la pista en las carreras de caballos).

padre; padrísimo (*Mex.*) something great; very good; something cool = algo tremendo; muy bueno; fabuloso.

padrísimo See **padre.**

padrón 1. (*Chile*) a registration; a vehicle's license = registro; número de matrícula; documento que identifica al propietario de un vehículo. **2.** (*Colo.*) a stud = semental.

padrotear (*Ven.*) to intimidate = intimidar.

pafarilla (*Colo.*) an animal's pancreas = páncreas del animal.

paganini (*Chile, Colo.*) the one who always pays for everybody = el que siempre paga por todos.

pai (*from English*) a pie = tarta o tartaleta rellena de fruta confitada o cremas.

paico (*Puerto Rico*) ice cream = helado.

paila (*Nic.*) a machete used to cut sugar cane = machete para cortar la caña de azúcar.

pailón (*Chile*) an adult who behaves like a child; an overgrown person = grandulón; grandote; persona que se comporta puerilmente.

paipa 1. (*from English*) a pipe = cañería. 2. (*from English*) a smoking pipe = pipa para fumar.

paja (*Argen., Chile, Colo., Dom. Rep., Para.*) masturbation (vulgar) = masturbación (vulgar).

pajarear 1. (*Chile*) to miss what is going on = perder lo que sucede alrededor. 2. (*Chile*) to hang out = estar en un lugar sin hacer nada.

pajarito (*Puerto Rico*) a bug = bicho; insecto o cualquier animal de tamaño pequeño.

pájaro 1. (*Cuba, Pan.*) effeminate = amaricado; afeminado. 2. (*Cuba, Dom. Rep.*) a homosexual = homosexual. 3. (*Colo.*) the penis (vulgar) = pene (vulgar).

pajarón 1. (*Argen., Chile*) a person with slow reactions = lento para entender. 2. (*Chile*) a clumsy person; a person who does not realize what is going on = persona torpe; el que no entiende lo que sucede a sus alrededores.

pajear (*Ven.*) to denounce; to inform on or against (informal) = denunciar; delatar (informal).

pajearse (*Argen., Chile, Colo., Dom. Rep., Para.*) to masturbate = masturbarse.

pajero(a) (*Argen., Chile, Colo., Dom. Rep., Para.*) someone who practices masturbation frequently = el o la que practica la masturbación frecuentemente.

pajonal (*Argen., Para.*) a field of grass = yerbazal.

pajudear (*Colo.*) to talk a lot without substance = hablar mucho sin sustancia en lo que se dice.

pajudo; pajuo (*Ven.*) 1. a gossiper = chismoso. 2. a liar = mentiroso.

pajuela (*Mex.*) a prostitute = prostituta.

pajuelazo (*Mex.*) a strike; a blow with the fist or an object = puñetazo; golpe propinado con el puño o con un objeto.

pajuo See **pajudo**.

pala (*Puerto Rico*) connections with people of influence = contactos con personas de influencia.

palabrota (*Mex.*) a big word; an erudite word = palabra grandielocuente; una palabra erudita.

palanca (*Argen.*) a person with connections in the system = persona de influencia política y/o social.

palangana (*Argen., Chile, Peru*) a person who talks too much; a blusterer = el que habla mucho; fanfarrón.

palangre (*Ven.*) an illegal business = negocio ilícito.

palanquear (*Argen., Colo.*) to use influence; to use political connections to get something = usar influencias; acto de influenciar en una institución para conseguir algo.

palchó (*from English*) to patch = poner un parche.

paleada (*Cuba*) a beating = golpiza; paliza.

palenque (*Mex.*) a cockfight ring = gallera; ruedo de gallos; el lugar donde se realizan peleas de gallos.

palero (*Mex.*) a person who covers the mistakes of others = persona que cubre los errores de otros.

paleta (*Puerto Rico*) a lollipop = pirulí.

paletó (*Chile*) a suit jacket = chaqueta de un traje masculino; saco.

paliacate (*Mex.*) a handkerchief = pañuelo.

palillo (*Colo.*) a thin person = persona delgada.

palitroqui (*Pan.*) a thin person (informal); skinny = persona delgada (informal); flaco.

pallasá (*Chile*) nonsense; an issue; stuff; any object for which the name is unknown = tontera; cuestión; cosa; cualquier objeto al que no se le sabe el nombre.

pallasa (*Chile*) a straw mattress = colchón de paja.

palo 1. (*Argen., Uru.*) a reprimand = reprimenda. **2.** (*Argen.*) one millon money units (informal) = un millón de unidades monetarias (informal). **3.** (*Puerto Rico, Ven.*) a swig = trago. **4.** (*Puerto Rico, Ven.*) a small cup of rum or any alcoholic drink (informal) = copita de ron o trago de cualquier bebida alcohólica (informal).

palo verde (*Argen.*) one million dollars (informal) = un millón de dólares (informal).

paloma 1. (*Colo.*) the penis (vulgar) = pene (vulgar). **2.** (*Colo.*) a short ride in a vehicle on loan = paseo corto en un vehículo prestado. **3.** (*Mex.*) a butterfly = mariposa.

palomilla 1. (*Chile, Peru*) a ragamuffin; a rascal = muchacho vagabundo; pillín; golfillo; pilluelo. **2.** (*Colo.*) an insect that attacks a cane plantation = insecto que ataca la plantación de caña. **3.** (*Cuba, Puerto Rico*) a cut of beef; the meat from the leg = corte de carne de vacuno; carne de la pierna del vacuno. **4.** (*Hond., Mex., Pan.*) a mob of kids; a gang = pandilla de amigos; pandilla de vagabundos o matones.

palomita (*Mex.*) a moth = polilla; palomilla.

palomo 1. (*Colo.*) a white horse = caballo blanco. **2.** (*Dom. Rep.*) a delinquent (informal) = delincuente (informal).

palotazo (*Mex.*) a blow with a heavy stick = golpe con un palo grande.

palote 1. (*Argen., Cuba, Mex.*) a rolling pin = rodillo de pastelero. **2.** (*Chile*) a praying mantis = mantis religiosa. **3.** (*Chile*) a very rich person = persona muy adinerada.

palta 1. (*Argen., Chile, Ecua., Peru, Uru.*) an avocado = aguacate. **2.** (*Chile*) all dressed up = vestido formalmente; vestido elegantemente.

pamita (*Mex.*) the herb used to prepare a medicinal tea = hierbas que se usan para preparar un té medicinal.

pampa (*Argen., Bol., Chile, Colo., Ecua., Peru, Ven.*) a savannah; the Quechua word for a plain or flat, treeless area = llanura sin árboles.

pampalinas (*Colo.*) women's breasts = pechos femeninos.

pampear (*Chile*) to win big = ganar con gran ventaja.

pamplona (*Puerto Rico*) a fat person = gorda(o).

pampón (*Peru*) a big corral = corral grande.

pana 1. (*Mex.*) fluff; lint = esponjoso; mullido. **2.** (*Chile*) an animal's liver = hígado de animal. **3.** (*Chile*) a machine failure = avería de una maquinaria. **4.** (*Chile*) courage = valentía. **5.** (*Ecua., Puerto Rico*) a close friend; a buddy = amigo íntimo; compañero.

panatela (*Dom. Rep.*) a cake = bizcocho.

pancearse (*Para.*) any object that rests on its belly; a plane that lands without its landing gears = cualquier objeto que se deposita en el suelo en su parte inferior; avión que aterriza sin ruedas.

pancho 1. (*Argen.*) a hot dog = (N.E. se puede entender como un emparedado de salchicha). **2.** (*Ecua.*) the vagina (vulgar) = vagina (vulgar).

pancista; panzú (*Puerto Rico*) a political opportunist; a person who uses politics for personal gain = oportunista político; el que usa la política para obtener beneficios personales.

pancitos (*Pan.*) a bread roll = bollo.

pancutras; pantrucas (*Chile*) a strip of wheat flour dough boiled in soup = tira de masa de trigo sobada que se cuece y sirve en una sopa.

pandebono (*Colo.*) a corn flour and cheese bread = pan de harina de maíz y queso.

pando (*Colo.*) wide and flat = ancho y aplastado.

pandorga 1. (*Colo.*) a joke = broma; chanza; diablura. **2.** (*Para.*) a kite = cometa.

panecillos; panecitos (*Cuba*) rolls; bread = bollos.

panecitos See **panecillos**.

panel (*Colo.*) a small delivery truck = camión pequeño de reparto.

panela (*Colo., Ecua., Guat., Hond., Pan., Salva., Ven.*) a syrup cake; unrefined sugar in a solid block = chancaca; azúcar sin refinar en una melaza sólida.

panetela; raspadura (*Cuba*) a cake made of hard unrefined sugar = melaza sólida de azúcar sin refinar.

pánfilo(a) 1. (*Colo.*) pale; a person without color = pálido; descolorido; macilento. 2. (*Chile*) silly = tonto(a). 3. (*Chile*) he or she does not understand what is going on = el/la que no entiende lo que pasa a sus alrededores.

panga 1. (*Nic.*) a boat; a canoe = bote; canoa. 2. (*Nic.*) a raft = balsa.

pango (*Argen.*) a brawl; a mess; confusion = desorden; enredo; bochinche; confusión.

paniqueado (*from English*) to be in a panic = asustado; tener pánico; estar con pánico.

panita; pana (*Mex.*) fluff; lint = esponjoso; mullido.

panocha 1. (*Colo.*) a corn patty = pastel de maíz. 2. (*Colo., Mex.*) the vagina (vulgar) = vagina (vulgar). 3. (*Mex.*) a sugar syrup cake; an unrefined sugar cake = chancaca; trozos de azúcar sin refinar.

panqueque (*Chile*) a crepe; a soft and thin fried tortilla = filloa; crepé; tortilla frita suave y muy delgada.

pantaleta (*Ven.*) women's underwear = pantaloncillos interiores de la mujer.

pantalla 1. (*Costa Rica*) a person who always has a reason to argue = persona que siempre tiene un pretexto o una razón para argumentar. 2. (*Puerto Rico*) earrings = zarcillos; pendientes. 3. (*Ven.*) a false appearance = apariencia falsa.

pantallear (*Ven.*) to show off; to presume = fanfarronear; presumir.

pantallero (*Colo., Ven.*) swanky; boastful = fanfarrón.

pantaloncillo (*Puerto Rico*) men's underwear = calzoncillos.

pantaloneta 1. (*Colo.*) shorts = shorts; pantalones cortos de deportes. 2. (*Colo.*) a bathing suit = traje de baño.

pantis (*from English*) panties = braga; calzones.

pantrucas See **pancutras**.

panty (*from English*) pantyhose = (N.E. medias femeninas que cubren hasta la cintura.)

panucha (*Colo.*) a pastry made of milk, coconut, and sugar = golosina de leche, coco y azúcar.

panudo(a) (*Chile*) with courage; brave = valiente; atrevido(a).

panuela (*Hond.*) unrefined sugar = chancaca; azúcar sin refinar.

panzazo (*Para.*) to give or receive a blow in the belly = golpe que se da o se recibe en la panza.

pañar (*Colo.*) to pick up; to catch = recoger; agarrar.

paño 1. (*Mex.*) a shawl = chal. 2. (*Mex.*) a handkerchief = pañuelo.

pañoleta (*Pan.*) a shawl = chal.

pañoso (*Colo.*) a person with stains on the skin = persona con manchas en la piel.

panzú See **pancista**.

papa 1. (*Argen.*) a hole in the socks = agujero en las medias. 2. (*Chile*) it is easy to do (informal) = lo que es fácil de hacer (informal).

papa caliente (*Puerto Rico*) a difficult matter = asunto muy complicado o peligroso.

papa grande (*Bol., Ecua., Mex.*) grandfather = abuelo.

Papa Noel (*Colo., Peru*) Santa Claus = (N.E. personaje que tipifica la navidad).

papachú See **el colochón**.

papagallo; papagayo (*Cuba, Ven.*) a small kite = cometa pequeño.

papagayo See **papagallo**.

papalina (*Nic.*) to be drunk = borrachera.

papalote (*Cuba, Mex.*) a kite = cometa.

papango (*Bol.*) marble = canica.

papapúa 1. (*Ven.*) a very important person = persona muy importante. **2.** (*Ven.*) an above-average person = persona muy destacada.

paparrotear (*Peru*) to repeat by memory without understanding = repetir de memoria sin entender el contenido.

papasote (*Ecua.*) an elegant and good-looking man = hombre elegante y bien parecido.

papaya (*Cuba*) the vagina; the female genitals (vulgar) = vagina; genitales femeninos (vulgar).

papayudo (*Colo.*) silly; naive = tonto; ingenuo.

papazote (*Colo.*) a good-looking man = hombre bien parecido.

papel 1. (*from English*) a newspaper = el diario o periódico. **2.** (*Colo.*) a one-peso bill = billete de un peso.

papel de toile (*Puerto Rico*) toilet paper = papel higiénico.

papelada (*Colo.*) a farce; a simulation = farsa; simulación.

papelera (*Colo.*) a suitcase = portadocumentos.

papelero 1. (*Colo.*) deceitful = farsante; simulador. **2.** (*from English*) a newspaper seller = vendedor de periódicos.

papelón (*Chile*) to put oneself in a ridiculous situation = hacer el ridículo.

papi (*Puerto Rico*) a term of endearment that a woman uses for a man or a boy whom she loves = término cariñoso usado por una mujer para referirse a un hombre o un niño querido.

paponia (*Argen.*) a wonderful or excellent thing = cosa excelente o magnífica.

paquete 1. (*Argen., Uru.*) an insincere person; a liar = una persona insincera; el que miente. **2.** (*Argen., Puerto Rico, Uru.*) a lie (informal) = una mentira (informal).

3. (*Colo.*) easily infatuated with another person = enamoradizo. **4.** (*Colo.*) a little serious = poco serio. **5.** (*Mex.*) the best; the first prize = el mejor; el primer premio.

paquetería 1. (*Argen., Para.*) a set of jewelry and other body ornaments used to look well-dressed = conjunto de adornos y lujos que una persona usa para verse bien vestida. **2.** (*Chile*) a store that sells articles for sewing and knitting = tienda que vende artículos de costura y tejido.

paquetero (*Argen., Puerto Rico, Uru.*) a liar (informal) = mentiroso (informal).

paquínes (*Guat., Hond., Mex., Pan., Puerto Rico, Salva.*) comics = historietas.

para acabarla de chingar (*Mex.*) to make matters worse = para hacer o dejar que las cosas se empeoren.

¿Para donde tú vas? (*from English*) Where are you going? = ¿A dónde vas?

paracaidista (*Argen., Chile, Colo.*) an uninvited guest at a party = persona que llega a la fiesta sin haber sido invitada.

parachutista (*from English*) a parachutist = paracaidista.

parada (*Colo.*) an audacious and resolute action = acción audaz y resuelta.

paragolpes (*Para.*) a bumper = parachoques.

paragüe (*Mex.*) an umbrella = paraguas.

paragüita de sapo (*Pan.*) a mushroom = hongo.

parála (*Argen.*) stop it now; stop it here = deja de hacerlo ahora; déjalo aquí.

parar la olla (*Argen., Chile*) to provide money for food = proveer dinero para comida.

paratatú (*Dom. Rep.*) what happens suddenly = lo que sucede de improviso.

parcela (*Bol.*) a plot of land = área de terreno de unas pocas hectáreas.

parche (*Mex.*) **1.** a person who takes advantage of others = ventajista; persona que se aprovecha de los demás. **2.** a disagreeable person = persona desagradable.

parcho (*Ven.*) a medicinal patch used on the skin = parche medicinal que se usa sobre la piel.

pardo (*Argen.*, *Uru.*) a brown-skinned person = persona morena; persona de piel oscura.

parece un silbido de culebra (*Colo.*) it is very thin = está o es muy delgado.

parejero 1. (*Chile*) a secret motel for illegal sexual relations = hotel o motel done las parejas ilegales tienen relaciones sexuales. **2.** (*Cuba*) fresh; a wise-guy = confianzudo; el que cree que las sabe todas. **3.** (*Ven.*) a person who tries to be seen with people of high social prestige; a person who tries to imitate important people = quien procura andar acompañado por personas de prestigio social; el que trata de imitar a aquellos que son importantes. **4.** (*Puerto Rico*, *Ven.*) presumptuous; brazen = presumido; vanidoso.

parián (*Mex.*) a big market = un mercado muy grande.

parientes (*from English*) parents = padres.

pariguayo; periguallo 1. (*Dom. Rep.*) clumsy = torpe. **2.** (*Dom. Rep.*) easily seduced = el/la que es fácil de seducir. **3.** (*Dom. Rep.*) without taste = el/la que no tiene gusto. **4.** (*Dom. Rep.*) he or she doesn't know how to dress or behave = el/la que no sabe vestirse o comportarse.

parkear (*from English*) to park the car = estacionar el automóvil.

parkin; parking (*from English*) a parking lot = aparqueadero; estacionamiento.

parking See **parkin**.

parlante (*Chile*) a speaker = bocina; altavoz.

parna; parner (*from English*) a partner = socio(a); compañero(a); pareja.

parner See **parna**.

parranda (*Colo.*) a great number of people or things = un gran número de personas o cosas.

parraneto (*Puerto Rico*) a chubby person = rechoncho; gordo y bajo.

parrilla; parrillada (*Argen.*, *Chile*, *Peru*, *Uru.*) a barbecue = barbacoa; asado a las brasas.

parrillada See **parrilla**.

parrillero (*Ven.*) a motorcycle passenger = pasajero en la motocicleta.

partir (*Colo.*, *Ecua.*) to fail a student on an exam = reprobar a un estudiante en un examen.

partuza (*Chile*) an orgy (informal) = orgía (informal).

pary (*from English*) a party = fiesta; reunión social.

pasa (*Cuba*) a curly-haired person = crespo(a); de pelo ensortijado.

pasabocas (*Colo.*) a snack = tentempié.

pasabordo (*Colo.*) a boarding card = tarjeta de embarque.

pasacalle (*Colo.*) a sign that hangs from one side to the other in the street = aviso que cuelga de un lado al otro de la calle.

pasacintas (*Colo.*) a tape recorder = tocacintas; grabadora; magnetófono.

pasaderas (*Ecua.*) shoelaces = lazos de zapatos.

pasado (*Mex.*) dried fruit = fruta seca.

pasador 1. (*Colo.*) what someone drinks or eats after drinking hard liquor = lo que se come o bebe después de un licor fuerte. **2.** (*Mex.*) a hair pin = horquilla.

pasaje (*Colo.*) an anecdote = anécdota.

pasante (*Colo.*) what someone drinks or eats after drinking hard liquor = lo que se come o bebe después de un licor fuerte.

pasao (*Puerto Rico*) it is old; it is worn out = está viejo; está muy usado.

pasarse la nota (*Ven.*) to exaggerate = exagerar.

pase 1. (*Colo.*) a driver's identification or license = permiso o licencia de conducir. **2.** (*Colo.*) a portion of cocaine that has been snorted = porción de cocaína que se aspira. **3.** (*Puerto Rico*) a rub; a special movement practiced in spiritualism = un frote; movimiento que se hace en la práctica del espiritismo. **4.** (*Puerto Rico*) the use of any illegal drug = uso de cualquier droga ilegal.

paseo See **bilí.**

pasmarse (*Colo.*) to be suddenly overcome with drunkenness = quedar aturdido de repente por la embriaguez.

pasme (*Puerto Rico*) to feel embarrassed = sentir vergüenza.

paspadura (*Para.*) to get chapped skin or lips from the cold = erosión de la piel producida por el frío.

pasparse (*Para.*) skin that is eroded by the cold = agrietarse la piel por efectos del frío.

pastel 1. (*Cuba, Mex.*) a cake = torta. **2.** (*Puerto Rico*) a typical Puerto Rican dish prepared with a dough of corn, banana, **yautía** and pork wrapped in banana leaves and boiled = plato típico de Puerto Rico preparado con una masa de maíz, plátano, **yautía** y cerdo que se envuelve en hojas de plátano y se hierve.

pastelear (*Colo.*) to cheat on an exam = copiar en un examen.

pastelero (*Colo.*) someone who cheats on an exam = el que copia en un examen.

pastelillo (*Puerto Rico*) a beef patty made with different kinds of meat = empanadilla rellena de diferentes carnes.

pasto (*Colo.*) inferior-quality marijuana = marihuana de mala calidad.

pastorejo (*Colo.*) a flick = capirotazo.

pasudo 1. (*Colo.*) curly hair = pelo ensortijado. **2.** (*Colo.*) a person with that kind of hair = la persona que tiene ese tipo de pelo.

pata (*Puerto Rico*) a lesbian = lesbiana.

pata de gallina (*Nic.*) a stool = butaca.

pata de rolo; paterrolo 1. (*Ven.*) indifferent = indiferente. **2.** (*Ven.*) lazy = holgazán.

pata sola See **golosa.**

patacón (*Colo., Pan.*) fried plantain chips = medallones de plátano frito.

patacones (*Pan.*) a small card pinned on guests for a child's baptism = tarjeta que se le prende a los invitados a un bautizo.

patalear; pitear (*Chile*) to complain = reclamar.

patalegre (*Colo.*) a party animal = aficionado a las fiestas.

patanear (*Colo.*) to behave in a rude and clumsy manner = comportarse en forma grosera y torpe, como un patán.

patasagrias See **cazcorvo.**

patasca 1. (*Bol.*) a stew of corn with pork meat = guisado de maíz con carne de cerdo. **2.** (*Peru*) a fight; a quarrel = pendencia; reyerta; disputa.

pataste (*Hond.*) N.E. chayote; a tropical fruit with the shape of a pear = chayote; fruta tropical con la forma de una pera.

pategallina (*Colo.*) a short signature = forma recortada de la firma de identificación personal.

patente (*Argen., Chile*) a car's plate = matrícula de un vehículo.

patero(a) (*Chile*) a flatterer = adulador(a).

paterrolismo 1. (*Ven.*) indifference = indiferencia. **2.** (*Ven.*) laziness = holgazanería.

paterrolo See **pata de rolo.**

pateteada (*Guat.*) dead = defunción; muerte.

patilla 1. (*Chile*) a silly thing = tontería. **2.** (*Chile*) a cutting from a plant = esqueje o gajo que se usa para reproducir una planta. **3.** (*Colo., Dom. Rep., Puerto Rico, Ven.*) a watermelon = sandía; melón.

patín (*Chile*) a prostitute (vulgar) = prostituta (vulgar).

patineta (*Ven.*) a rolling board = tabla pastelera.

patiquín (*Ven.*) a young man from the city who doesn't like to work and is presumptuous = joven de la ciudad que es presumido y a quién no le gusta trabajar.

pato 1. (*Cuba, Dom. Rep., Ecua., Pan., Puerto Rico, Ven.*) a homosexual = homosexual. **2.** (*Argen.*) a thief = ladrón. **3.** (*Colo.*) a stowaway = polizón.

pato malo (*Chile*) a delinquent; a criminal (informal) = delincuente (informal).

patojito (*Guat., Hond., Mex., Salva.*) a little boy = niño pequeño.

patojo 1. (*Colo., Guat., Hond., Mex., Salva.*) a boy = muchacho; niño. **2.** (*Colo.*) a lame person = persona coja.

patona (*Puerto Rico*) a whorehouse madam = regenta de un prostíbulo.

patota (*Argen., Chile, Uru., Ven.*) a gang = pandilla.

patotero (*Argen., Chile*) a member of a gang = pandillero.

patricia (*Ven.*) a big foot = pie grande.

patuleco 1. (*Chile*) weak; dizzy = débil; mareado. **2.** (*Argen., Bol., Chile, Ecua., Peru*) bowlegged = patituerto; el que camina de forma irregular por tener un defecto en las piernas.

patuletas; patojo (*Colo.*) a lame person = persona coja.

paturro (*Colo.*) a short, fat person = rechoncho; persona gorda de baja estatura.

pava 1. (*Argen.*) a kettle = tetera. **2.** (*Argen.*) a teapot = tetera para preparar el té.

pavada (*Argen., Para.*) nonsense; stupidity; an unimportant issue = tontería; cosa de poca o sin importancia.

pavear 1. (*Chile*) to not pay attention; to look and not see = estar desatento; mirar sin ver. **2.** (*Colo.*) to spy on with the intent to kill = acechar con la intención de matar. **3.** (*Chile, Dom. Rep.*) to look or walk without a specific objective = mirar o caminar sin hacer nada.

paviarse (*Pan.*) to cut school = hacer novillos.

pavito(a) 1. (*Ven.*) a teenager = adolescente. **2.** (*Ven.*) ill-bred = gamberro; libertino; el que comete actos de grosería o incivilidad.

pavo 1. (*Chile*) a stowaway = polizón; el que viaja escondido para no pagar. **2.** (*Argen., Chile, Dom. Rep.*) a person who behaves disgracefully = persona que se comporta torpemente.

pavuncio(a) 1. (*Chile*) naive = ingenuo. **2.** (*Chile*) a person who does silly things = necio(a); persona que hace tonterías.

payada (*Argen., Chile*) a song of the **payador** = canto del **payador**.

payador (*Argen., Chile*) a folk singer who improvises verses on a theme spontaneously = cantor popular que crea versos improvisados sobre un tema que se presenta al momento.

payamas (*Cuba, Puerto Rico*) pajamas = pijamas.

PC [pron. picí] (*from English*) a personal computer (PC) = computadora personal.

pechar 1. (*Argen., Chile*) to take advantage; to take advantage of hospitality received = aprovecharse de una situación o de otros; aprovecharse de la hospitalidad brindada. **2.** (*Argen., Chile*) to get something without the right to it = conseguir las cosas aunque no se tenga derecho a ellas. **3.** (*Chile*) to make efforts to get something = hacer esfuerzos para conseguir algo.

pechazo (*Argen.*) to ask for a loan = pedir dinero prestado.

pechoño(a) (*Bol., Chile*) a fanatic Catholic = católico(a) fanático(a).

pechuga 1. (*Bol., Chile, Ecua.*) audacity; courage = audacia; coraje. **2.** (*Chile, Colo., Ecua., Pan., Peru, Ven.*) a person who takes liberties without the right to them; a person who abuses the trust of others = el/la que se toma libertades que no le corresponden; persona que abusa de la confianza de otros.

pechugas (*Chile*) a woman's breasts (informal) = pechos femeninos (informal).

pecueca; pesuña (*Ecua.*) foot odor = olor de los pies.

peculado (*Colo.*) a misappropriation = malversación.

pedigrí (*from English*) a pedigree = (RAE) genealogía de un animal.

pedir bola (*Cuba*) to hitchhike = (N.E. pedir transporte gratuito en el camino o la carretera.)

pedir limosna con escopeta (*Colo.*) to ask for a favor aggressively = pedir un favor con tono agresivo.

pedir un aventón (*Mex., Pan.*) to hitchhike = (N.E. pedir transporte gratuito en el camino o la carretera.)

pedir un pon (*Puerto Rico*) to hitchhike = (N.E. pedir transporte gratuito en el camino o la carretera.)

pedir una paloma (*Colo.*) to hitchhike = (N.E. pedir transporte gratuito en el camino o la carretera.)

pedo (*Colo.*) a problem; trouble = problema; lío.

pedrero (*Colo.*) rude; vulgar; without manners = tosco; basto; pedestre; de modales vulgares.

pees [pron. piis] (*from English*) peas = guisantes; arvejas.

pega 1. (*Chile, Cuba, Ecua.*) a job (informal) = trabajo; empleo (informal). **2.** (*from English*) adhesive = pegamento.

pegado (*Puerto Rico*) the rice that sticks to the inside of the pot after cooking = residuo que queda adherido a la olla después de cocer el arroz.

pegadura (*Mex.*) glue = goma; pegamento; goma de pegar.

pegante (*Colo.*) glue = pegamento; goma; goma de pegar.

pegostre (*Colo.*) filth = mugre.

pegotudo (*Colo.*) sticky = pegajoso.

peinar (*Argen., Uru.*) to flatter = adular.

peineta (*Argen., Chile, Para., Peru, Uru.*) a comb = peine.

peinilla (*Colo., Ecua., Puerto Rico*) a comb = peine.

peiperbac (*from English*) a paperback = encuadernación en rústica; libro en rústica.

peismeker (*from English*) a peace-maker = conciliador.

pela 1. (*Puerto Rico, Ven.*) a physical punishment; a beating = castigo corporal; golpiza. **2.** (*Ven.*) a defeat = derrota.

pelada (*Colo.*) a mistake; an error; a bad choice = equivocación; desacierto.

pelado 1. (*Colo.*) a boy = niño. **2.** (*Colo., Dom. Rep.*) to be broke = estar sin dinero. **3.** (*Mex.*) a haircut = corte de pelo. **4.** (*Mex.*) a very poor person = persona muy pobre.

pelaíto (*Colo., Pan.*) a toddler = niño pequeño; el que recién comienza a caminar.

pelambre See **conventilleo**.

pelao (*Colo., Pan.*) a boy; a young man = niño; muchacho.

pelar 1. (*Chile*) to gossip; to talk badly about someone else = chismear; hablar mal de alguien. **2.** (*Colo.*) to kill = matar. **3.** (*Ven.*) to be confused = estar confundido. **4.** (*Ven.*) to be careless = ser descuidado. **5.** (*Ven.*) to slip away; to die = irse; morir.

pelarse (*Colo.*) to make a mistake, an error or a bad choice = equivocarse; cometer un error; tener un desacierto.

pelegrina See **peregrina**.

peleros (*Nic.*) rags; tatters = trapos.

peletería (*Cuba*) a shoe store = zapatería.

pellejo (*Dom. Rep.*) a prostitute (derogatory) = prostituta (despectivo).

pelliscada (*Mex.*) a **tortilla** with Mexican salsa = **tortilla** con salsa mexicana.

peló el ajo See **estiró los caites**.

pelo enrulado (*Argen.*) curly hair = crespo; ensortijado.

pelo malo (*Dom. Rep.*) curly, thick, black hair = pelo rizado, negro y grueso.

pelo rizo (*Salva.*) curly hair = crespo(a); de pelo ensortijado.

pelón See **cocopelao**.

pelota 1. (*Bol.*) a canoe = piragua. **2.** (*Argen., Chile, Uru.*) a stupid or silly person (vulgar) = estúpido; tonto (vulgar).

pelotudo 1. (*Argen., Chile, Colo., Para., Uru.*) a sucker; stupid (vulgar) = papanatas; estúpido (vulgar). **2.** (*Argen.,*

Chile, Colo., Para., Uru.) sloppy; negligent; naive (vulgar) = descuidado; negligente; ingenuo (vulgar).

pelpa (*Colo.*) a small envelope of marijuana = pequeño sobre de marihuana.

peludo (*Colo.*) difficult = peliagudo.

peluqueada; peluqueado (*Colo., Para., Ven.*) a haircut = corte de pelo.

peluqueado See **peluqueada**.

peluquear (*Colo., Para., Ven.*) to cut and comb hair = cortar y peinar el cabello.

peluquearse (*Colo., Para., Ven.*) to get a haircut = cortarse el pelo.

pena (*Colo., Cuba, Guat., Mex., Salva., Ven.*) an embarrassment = vergüenza.

penal (*from English*) a penalty = castigo máximo en el juego.

penca 1. (*Chile*) of bad quality; in bad taste = de mala calidad; de mal gusto. 2. (*Chile*) the penis (vulgar) = pene (vulgar). 3. (*Chile*) cardone; an edible stem from the wild prickly pear plant = tallo comestible de una planta silvestre. 4. (*Chile*) a thick and short leather whip used by the Chilean cowboy = látigo de cuero corto y grueso usado por el **huaso** chileno. 5. (*Chile*) a reprimand = reprimenda.

pendango 1. (*Puerto Rico*) a coward = cobarde. 2. (*Puerto Rico*) clumsy; feeble = torpe; enclenque; débil.

pendejada 1. (*Chile, Colo., Dom. Rep.*) stupidity; a silly thing = estupidez; tontería. 2. (*Dom. Rep.*) cowardice = cobardía.

pendejo(a) 1. (*Colo., Dom. Rep.*) silly; stupid; a jerk = tonto(a); estúpido(a). 2. (*Dom. Rep.*) a coward = cobarde. 3. (*Dom. Rep., Puerto Rico*) a strong insult (vulgar) = insulto grave y vulgar. 4. (*Chile, Puerto Rico*) a worthless person = el/la que no vale nada.

pendenciero (*Cuba*) a scandalmonger = chismoso.

peni (*from English*) a penny = centavo.

penoso (*Colo., Cuba, Guat., Hond., Mex., Salva., Ven.*) timid; shy = tímido; vergonzoso.

pensión (*Colo.*) apprehension = preocupación; ansiedad.

peñascazo (*Chile*) the throw of a stone = pedrada.

peñasquear (*Chile*) to throw stones = apedrear.

peñazco (*Chile*) a rock; a big stone = roca; piedra de gran tamaño.

peo (*Chile*) flatulence; a fart (informal) = pedo; flatulencia que se expele por el ano (informal).

pepa y palmo (*Ven.*) a marbles game = un juego de canicas.

pepa 1. (*Colo., Ecua., Puerto Rico, Ven.*) a pit; the seed from a fruit = cuesco; hueso de la fruta. 2. (*Chile*) a marijuana cigarette = cigarrillo de marihuana. 4. (*Colo.*) a pill; a tablet = píldora; tableta. 4. (*Colo.*) the human head (informal) = cabeza (informal).

pepazo (*Ven.*) a blow with any spherical object = un golpe con cualquier objeto de forma cilíndrica.

pepe 1. (*Bol., Ven.*) a dandy; a fop; a dude; a vain person = petimetre; presumido; lechuguino. 2. (*Guat.*) a pacifier = tetera; chupador para el bebé.

pepeado 1. (*Ven.*) beautiful; nice = hermoso; agradable. 2. (*Ven.*) excellent = excelente.

pepermin (*from English*) a peppermint = menta.

pepián (*Peru*) a dish prepared with corn, hot pepper, meat, and fresh cheese = guisado preparado con maíz, picante, carne y queso fresco.

pepino de fruta (*Chile*) (N.E. fruit cucumber; a short, thick, sweet pink cucumber) = (N.E. pepino de fruta; pepino grueso y corto de la pulpa rosada y dulce).

pepino (*Argen.*) a goal in a soccer game = gol en el **fútbol**.

pepita (*Ecua., Puerto Rico, Ven.*) a pit = cuesco; hueso de la fruta.

pepo (*Colo.*) a person who is high from drug consumption = el que está bajo los efectos de un alucinógeno.

perchudo See **titino**.

percocho (*Hond.*) dirty clothes = tela o traje muy sucio.

perecoso; perecudo (*Colo.*) annoying; a bothersome person = molestoso; pesado.

perecudo See **perecoso**.

peregrina; pelegrina; golosa (*Puerto Rico*) hopscotch = rayuela; juego de niños en que se tiran fichas en una cancha y se salta en un pié tras ella.

perencejo (*Colo.*) so-and-so = perengano; fulano.

pereque (*Nic.*) a party = fiesta.

perezosa (*Argen., Colo., Peru, Ven.*) a deck chair = silla de descanso.

performans 1. (*from English*) a performance = desempeño; cumplimiento; ejecución. **2.** (*from English*) a performance = representación; actuación.

perico 1. (*Colo.*) a small coffee = café pequeño. **2.** (*Colo., Mex.*) cocaine = cocaína. **3.** (*Cuba, Mex.*) a parrot = loro. **4.** (*Ecua.*) the penis (vulgar) = pene (vulgar). **5.** (*Chile*) a so-and-so person = fulano; perengano.

pericote (*Chile, Peru*) a big rat that lives in the countryside = rata grande que vive en el campo.

periguallo See **pariguayo**.

perinola (*Mex.*) a kid; a child = muchacho; niño.

pernicioso 1. (*Colo.*) lazy; someone who works a little in order to party = haragán; parrandero; el que no trabaja lo suficiente por andar de fiesta. **2.** (*Colo.*) a drunk; an alcoholic = borracho; alcohólico.

perol 1. (*Ven.*) an issue; stuff = asunto; cosa. **2.** (*Ven.*) a tinware container = envase de hojalata.

perola (*Ven.*) a tinware container = envase de hojalata.

perra (*Peru*) a prostitute (vulgar) = prostituta (vulgar).

perrería (*Colo.*) a dirty trick = travesura que hace daño.

perrerreque (*Nic.*) a corn cake = torta de maíz.

perro (*Dom. Rep.*) a bad person = persona mala.

perro caliente (*Cuba, Mex., Pan., Ven.*) a hot dog = (N.E. emparedado de salchicha).

perulero (*Peru*) slang for Peruvian = vulgarismo con que los peruanos se nombran a sí mismos.

pesa (*Ven.*) a butcher shop = carnicería.

pesador (*Ven.*) a butcher shop attendant = carnicero.

pesar (*Ven.*) to sell meat = vender carne.

peseta See **cuora**.

pesetear (*Uru.*) to be nasty = tratar mal.

pestañina (*Colo.*) eyeshadow = rimel.

pestillo 1. (*Puerto Rico*) two people in love = dos personas enamoradas. **2.** (*Puerto Rico*) a boyfriend; a girlfriend = novio; novia.

pesuña 1. (*Pan.*) in addition to = agregado a. **2.** (*Pan.*) a gift from the seller to the buyer = regalo o gratificación que el vendedor le da al comprador. **3.** (*Ecua.*) foot odor = olor de los pies.

petaca 1. (*Bol., Mex.*) a leather box or trunk = baúl o caja de cuero. **2.** (*Mex.*) a trunk = maletero; baúl.

petacón(a) See **cambuto**.

petardo See **jumeta**.

petejota (*Ven.*) a detective from the Judiciary Technical Police (PTJ) = detective de la Policía Técnica Judicial (PTJ).

peteteada (*Nic.*) death = defunción; muerte.

peticionar (*from English*) to present a petition = pedir; solicitar.

peticote (*Pan.*) a petticoat; an underskirt = enaguas.

petipóas (*Pan.*) peas = guisantes.

petipúa 1. (*Cuba, Puerto Rico*) peas = guisantes. **2.** (*Ven.*) canned peas = guisantes enlatados o en conserva.

petiso; petizo (*Argen., Bol., Chile, Para., Uru.*) a short person = de baja estatura.

petizo See **petiso**.

petota (*Ven.*) a big rat = rata común de gran tamaño.

piacha (*Ven.*) a native medicine woman = curandera.

piantadura (*Argen.*) madness = locura.

piba (*Argen.*) a young, beautiful woman = mujer joven y bonita.

pibe (*Argen., Para.*) a boy; a young man = niño; muchacho.

pica 1. (*Chile, Colo., Peru*) resentment = despecho; resentimiento. **2.** (*Peru, Colo., Ecua.*) the tapping of the rubber tree = perforación hecha en el árbol que produce caucho. **3.** (*Colo., Ecua., Guat., Ven.*) a forest trail; a narrow path = sendero en el bosque; camino o sendero estrecho. **4.** (*Puerto Rico*) roulette = ruleta.

picada 1. (*Chile*) a very special place to eat or shop = lugar muy especial para comer o comprar. **2.** (*Cuba*) a path; a trail through a forest = sendero o vereda que cruza la vegetación tupida. **3.** (*Ven., Mex.*) a peck = pico; picotada. **4.** (*Uru.*) a snack while drinking = tentempié que se come mientras se bebe.

picadito (*Colo.*) a snack; a bite while drinking = tentempié; lo que se come entretanto se bebe.

picado(a) de la araña (*Chile*) amorously pursuing someone of the opposite sex = entusiasta por establecer relaciones con el sexo opuesto.

picana 1. (*Argen.*) to spur; to goad = caña para picar al buey. **2.** (*Argen.*) a cut of beef = corte de carne de vacuno.

picante 1. (*Chile*) bad-looking = de mala facha. **2.** (*Chile*) in bad taste; ordinary; without class = de mal gusto; ordinario; sin clase.

picao See **jumeta**.

picar 1. (*Ven.*) to rebound an object = rebotar un objeto. **2.** (*Ven.*) to leave = irse; marcharse.

picarón (*Chile*) a donut prepared with pumpkin = buñuelo frito que tiene la forma de aro, preparado con harina de trigo, calabaza y levadura.

picarones pasados (*Chile*) **picarones** boiled in molasses with pieces of oranges and spices = **picarones** hervidos en una sopa de chancaca con especias y trozos de naranjas.

picárselas (*Argen.*) to go away = alejarse; irse.

pich (*from English*) a peach = melocotón; durazno.

picha (*Mex., Pan.*) the penis (vulgar) = pene (vulgar).

pichanga 1. (*Chile*) an informal soccer match = juego informal de fútbol. **2.** (*Chile*) an antipasto salad; a snack with a mixture of pickled ham, sausages, and cheese = bocadillo o tentempié preparado con jamón, quesos y vegetales escabechados. **3.** (*Chile*) an informal game of soccer in the street = juego informal de **fútbol** en la calle. **4.** (*Colo.*) a broom = escoba.

pichar (*Colo.*) to have sex (vulgar); to fuck = tener sexo (vulgar).

picharse (*Para.*) to be ashamed = avergonzarse.

pichete (*Hond.*) a small lizard = lagartija.

pichí (*Chile*) piss; urine (informal) = orina (informal).

pichicata (*Argen., Chile*) a hallucinogenic drug; an illegal drug = droga alucinógena; droga ilegal.

pichicatero (*Argen., Chile*) a drug addict = adicto a las drogas.

pichicho (*Chile*) a small and tame dog = perro chico y manso.

pichiflina (*Argen.*) cheap goods = cosa de poca monta; baratija.

pichincha (*Argen., Para.*) a bargain = ganga; lo que se adquiere por menos de su valor real.

pichinchero(a) (*Para.*) a person who buys something only if it is a bargain; a cheap person = persona que sólo compra gangas o cosas de baja calidad.

pichirre (*Ven.*) mean; stingy = malo; tacaño; roñoso.

pichirrear (*Ven.*) stinginess = tacañería.

pichiruche (*Chile*) insignificant; very small; very little = insignificante; muy poquito; muy pequeño.

pichón (*Argen., Chile, Cuba, Peru, Puerto Rico*) the chick of any bird except the hen = pollo de cualquier ave excepto el de gallina.

pichula (*Chile*) the penis (vulgar) = pene (vulgar).

pichulear 1. (*Argen.*) to work in a small job = realización de un trabajo de poca monta o de poco valor. **2.** (*Argen.*) a job that is not completely honest = trabajo poco honesto. **3.** (*Chile*) to deceive; to trick; to cheat = engañar; burlarse.

pichulín (*Chile, Para.*) a child's penis = pene de los niños.

pick up [pron. picap] (*from English*) a pickup truck = (N.E. camión pequeño con la sección de carga abierta y separada de la cabina del conductor).

pickle (*from English*) a pickle = encurtido; escabechado.

picnic (*from English*) a picnic = merienda en el parque, en el campo, en la playa u otro lugar abierto.

pico 1. (*Chile*) the penis (vulgar) = pene (vulgar). **2.** (*Colo.*) a kiss = beso. **3.** (*Ecua.*) many; a large amount of something = mucha; una gran cantidad de algo. **4.** (*Ven.*) a toucan = tucán.

picotón (*Chile*) peck = picotazo.

piduye (*Chile*) the worms that live in the human intestine = lombrices parásitas del intestino humano.

pié (*Chile*) a down payment = pago inicial.

pierna (*Argen.*) a smart and quick person = persona sagaz y despierta, rápida de pensamiento y de acción.

pieza (*Argen., Chile, Mex.*) a room; a bedroom = cuarto; dormitorio.

pifia (*Argen., Chile, Peru*) booing = abucheo.

pifiar (*Argen., Chile, Peru*) to whistle at; to boo = rechiflar; abuchear.

pigmeo (*Colo.*) of little intelligence = poco inteligente.

pija; verga (*Argen., Uru.*) the penis (vulgar) = pene (vulgar).

pije 1. (*Chile*) pseudo-refined; affected = cursi. **2.** (*Chile*) stuck-up; fop = encopetado; pituco.

pijotear (*Argen.*) to avoid a compromise = eludir un compromiso.

pila (*Cuba*) a faucet = grifo.

pilchas (*Argen., Chile, Uru.*) cheap clothing (derogatory) = ropa barata; prendas baratas (peyorativo).

pileta 1. (*Argen.*) a sink = fregadero. **2.** (*Argen.*) a swimming pool = piscina.

pililo (*Chile*) dirty and ragged; in tatters = andrajoso y sucio.

pilinqui (*Pan.*) a person of poor taste = chabacano; el que no tiene calidad.

pillar (*Argen., Uru.*) to urinate (vulgar) = orinar (vulgar).

pilón 1. (*Puerto Rico*) mortar = mortero; trozo de madera, metal o piedra que se usa para machacar alimentos o especias. **2.** (*Puerto Rico*) a lollipop = pirulí; dulce de paleta.

piloto (*Argen.*) a raincoat = impermeable.

piltrafas; piltrajas 1. (*Chile*) rags = harapos. **2.** (*Chile*) clothing of inferior quality = vestimentas de mala calidad.

piltrajas See **piltrafas**.

pilucho (*Chile*) naked = desnudo.

pimpo (*Puerto Rico*) full of food = harto; lleno de comida.

pin 1. (*from English*) a hair pin = horquilla para el cabello. **2.** (*from English*) a pin = broche; prendedor; alfiler.

pin printer (*from English*) a dot matrix printer = impresora de agujas; impresora matricial.

pinche 1. (*Argen.*) a worker at the lowest level of specialization in a work place = el más bajo nivel de especialización en una obra o actividad. **2.** (*Mex.*) a mean person = persona mala; de malas intenciones. **3.** (*Mex.*) a nobody = un don nadie; persona sin importancia social. **4.** (*Nic.*) stingy = tacaño. **5.** (*Chile, Puerto Rico*) a hair pin = horquilla para el pelo. **6.** (*Puerto Rico*) an informer = delator.

pinga (*Cuba*) the penis (vulgar) = pene (vulgar).

pinganilla 1. (*Chile*) a person of low social status = persona de baja categoría social. **2.** (*Chile*) someone who is not serious = persona poco seria o frívola.

pingo 1. (*Argen., Bol., Chile, Ecua., Peru, Uru.*) a saddle horse = caballo de sillín. **2.** (*Mex.*) the devil; a bad person = el diablo; persona mala.

pinol (*Nic.*) corn roasted and ground to prepare a cool drink = maíz tostado y molido bien fino para hacer una bebida fría.

pinole; piñol (*Hond.*) a cool drink made of roasted corn and honey = bebida refrescante de maíz tostado y miel.

pinolillo 1. (*Nic.*) a cool drink made with **pinol** and cacao = refresco preparado con **pinol** y cacao. **2.** (*Hond.*) a cool drink made of roasted corn and honey = bebida refrescante de maíz tostado y miel.

pinta (*Chile*) the appearance of a person = el aspecto; cómo se ve una persona.

pintado (*Chile, Mex., Peru, Puerto Rico*) equal; similar = igual; semejante.

pintón (*Argen.*) a good-looking man = hombre de buena presencia.

pintonear (*Ven.*) to look young; to feel young = conservarse bien; sentirse joven; verse joven.

pintor (*Argen.*) a conceited and boastful person = persona presumida y jactanciosa.

pintoso (*Colo.*) elegant; well-dressed = elegante; bien vestido.

pinuca (*Chile*) a mollusk that is shaped like a short worm = molusco en la forma de un gusano corto.

pínut (*from English*) a peanut = maní; cacahuate.

pinzas (*Argen., Colo., Cuba, Dom. Rep., Mex., Uru.*) pliers = tenazas.

piña (*Argen., Uru.*) a blow with the fist; a punch = puñetazo.

piñazo (*Colo., Dom. Rep., Uru.*) a strong punch; a heavy blow with the fist = puñetazo muy violento.

piñiscar (*Chile*) to pinch; to nip = pellizcar.

piñisco 1. (*Chile*) a nip = pellizco. **2.** (*Chile*) a little bit = un poquito.

piñol See **pinole.**

piocha (*Mex.*) Great!; Excellent! = imagnífico!; ¡excelente!

piojosa (*Argen.*) the head (vulgar) = cabeza (vulgar).

piola (*Argen.*) a fast-thinking, roguish person = persona pícara y rápida de pensamiento.

pioscota (*Hond.*) a big, heavy girl = muchacha de gran tamaño.

pipa 1. (*Colo., Dom. Rep., Puerto Rico*) a belly = barriga. **2.** (*Colo.*) a green coconut = coco verde.

pipeline [pron. paiplain] (*from English*) a pipeline = acueducto o gaseoducto.

pipi (*Pan.*) the penis (vulgar) = pene (vulgar).

pipián (*Dom. Rep.*) a stew prepared with the insides of an animal = guisado preparado con con los interiores de un animal.

pipilacha 1. (*Nic.*) a dragonfly = libélula. **2.** (*Nic.*) a small airplane = avión pequeño.

pipiolo (*Puerto Rico*) a person who is for Puerto Rican independence = independentista; el que está por la independencia de Puerto Rico.

pipo 1. (*Colo.*) a censure; a criticism = censura; crítica. **2.** (*Colo.*) a complaint = queja. **3.** (*Colo.*) an indirect insult = insulto indirecto.

pipocho; piponcho; popocho (*Colo.*) full of food = lleno de comida.

pipón; pipudo (*Colo., Dom. Rep.*) big-bellied = barrigón; barrigudo.

piponcho See **pipocho**.

pipote (*Ven.*) a big container = recipiente grande.

pipudo See **pipón**.

pique 1. (*Colo., Peru*) resentment = despecho; resentimiento. **2.** (*Peru, Colo., Ecua.*) the tapping of a rubber tree = perforación hecha en el árbol que produce caucho. **3.** (*Colo., Ecua.*) a forest trail; a narrow path = sendero en el bosque; camino o sendero estrecho.

piqueteadero (*Colo.*) a place next to the road to drink and eat; a place to get a **picadito** = establecimiento a la orilla de la carretera donde se come y se bebe; el lugar donde se come un **picadito**.

piragua 1. (*Colo., Cuba, Mex.*) a canoe = canoa. **2.** (*Puerto Rico*) sherbet = hielo raspado al que se le agrega un sabor.

pirco (*Chile*) a popular dish with corn, pumpkin and fresh beans = guiso de maíz, calabaza y habichuelas tiernas.

pirinola (*Chile, Ven.*) a teetotum = perinola; peonza pequeña.

piririta (*Para.*) a small bird = ave pequeña.

pirquinero (*Chile*) an independent miner who works a small mine, paying the owner according to production = minero independiente que trabaja una pequeña mina y paga al dueño de acuerdo a la producción.

pirringa See **mirringo**.

pirujo (*Guat.*) a heretic; incredulous = hereje; incrédulo.

pirulí (*Puerto Rico*) a lollipop = loly; dulce de paleta.

pirulo 1. (*Chile*) the penis, in child's language = pene, en el lenguaje infantil. **2.** (*Chile*) beautiful; nice = bonito; agradable.

pisco 1. (*Colo.*) a rum-based alcoholic beverage = bebida alcohólica a base de ron. **2.** (*Colo.*) a turkey = pavo. **3.** (*Bol., Chile, Ecua., Peru*) firewater made from grapes = un tipo de aguardiente de uvas.

piscucha (*Salva.*) a kite = cometa.

pisón (*Ven.*) stamping of the foot = pisotón.

pispar; pispiar 1. (*Argen., Para.*) to hear = oír; indigar. **2.** (*Argen., Para.*) to snoop; to pry = fisgonear; mirar escondido; husmear.

pispiar See **pispar**.

pispireta 1. (*Nic.*) flirtatious = coqueta. **2.** (*Chile, Nic.*) a very talkative person = persona muy habladora.

pistero (*Colo.*) a black eye = ojo amoratado.

pisto (*Guat., Mex.*) money (informal) = dinero (informal).

pistola 1. (*Colo.*) to show the middle finger; an insulting hand gesture = gesto insultante con los dedos de la mano. **2.** (*Ven.*) silly = tonto.

pistolada (*Ven.*) a silly thing = tontera.

pistolita (*Puerto Rico*) an easy woman = mujer fácil.

pistolo (*Ven.*) silly = tonto.

pita (*Chile, Colo., Cuba, Mex.*) a string = cordel; cuerda.

pitanza (*Chile*) a gibe; a taunt = burla.

pitar 1. (*Chile, Peru, Uru.*) to smoke = fumar. **2.** (*Chile*) to pull someone's leg = tomar el pelo. **3.** (*Colo., Nic., Salva., Ven.*) to escape fast; to fly = salir o abandonar el lugar rápido. **4.** (*Colo.*) to give a present = dar un regalo. **5.** (*Colo.*) to sell = vender. **6.** (*Cuba, Mex.*) to steal = robar.

pite (*Colo.*) a small amount = pizca; un poquito.

pitear See **patalear**.

pitillo 1. (*Colo., Ven.*) a drinking straw = pajita o pajilla para beber. **2.** (*Argen., Chile, Uru.*) a cigarette = cigarrillo.

pitipuas (*Salva.*) a pea = guisante.

pitiyanqui (*Puerto Rico*) a Puerto Rican who is more American than the Americans (derogatory) = el puertorriqueño que es más norteamericano que los mismos norteamericanos (peyorativo).

pito (*Chile, Puerto Rico*) a marijuana joint = cigarrillo de marihuana.

pitón (*Hond.*) a nozzle; a hose gun = boquete de manga o manguera.

pituco 1. (*Argen., Chile, Para., Uru.*) elegant and fine = cosas o ambiente elegante y fino. **2.** (*Argen.*) a dude; derogatory for people who pose as being rich when they are not = lechuguino(a); despectivo para las personas que posan de adineradas cuando no lo son; de actuación cursi para simular elegancia.

pituto 1. (*Chile*) an odd job; a short or small job = trabajo temporal; trabajo pequeño o breve. **2.** (*Chile*) a special job done in addition to a regular job = trabajo especial que se hace fuera del trabajo regular o como agregado a él.

piure (*Chile*) an edible shellfish rich in iodine = marisco comestible rico en yodo.

piyamas (*Argen., Chile, Colo., Cuba, Mex., Pan., Peru*) pajamas = pijamas.

pizca (*Mex.*) a harvest = cosecha.

placa 1. (*Colo., Pan.*) a car's license plate = matrícula del automóvil. **2.** (*Mex.*) a police officer = agente de la policía.

plagiar (*Ven.*) to kidnap = secuestrar.

plagio (*Ven.*) a kidnapping = secuestro.

plaguear 1. (*Para.*) to talk about one's misfortune constantly = hablar siempre de los propios infortunios. **2.** (*Para.*) to scold constantly = regañar constantemente. **3.** (*Para.*) to grumble; to moan = rezongar; gemir.

pláier (*from English*) pliers = tenazas.

plancha (*Chile*) to put oneself in a ridiculous situation = hacer el ridículo.

planchar 1. (*Argen.*) to be embarrassed = pasar una vergüenza. **2.** (*Puerto Rico*) to have everything under control = tener todo bajo control.

planin (*from English*) planning = planeamiento; planificación.

plante (*Colo.*) the starting money in a business = capital con que se inicia un negocio.

plantilla (*Ecua.*) swanky; boastful = fanfarrón.

plasticola (*Argen.*) glue = adhesivo; pegamento.

platanutre (*Dom. Rep., Puerto Rico*) fried plantain chips = medallones de plátano frito.

platón (*Colo.*) a basin for washing = palangana.

playa (*Argen., Chile, Para.*) a wide and clear space in a town that is used as a parking lot or as a storage yard = espacio amplio, despejado y de mucha superficie dentro de un poblado destinado al estacionamiento de vehículos o al movimiento de mercaderías.

playa de estacionamiento (*Argen., Chile, Pan., Peru, Ven.*) a parking lot = terreno cercado destinado al estacionamiento de vehículos.

playo (*Ecua.*) small pliers = tenazas pequeñas.

playoff (*from English*) a play-off game = partido de desempate.

plegoste (*Puerto Rico*) any sticky substance = cualquier substancia pegajosa.

pleibac (*from English*) playback = sonido previo; sonido pregrabado.

pleigraun (*from English*) a playground = campo de juego; patio de recreo.

pleit (*from English*) a car's license plate = matrícula del automóvil.

pleno (*Ecua.*) good = bueno.

plomazo (*Colo., Dom. Rep.*) a gun shot = balazo.

plomera (*Colo., Dom. Rep.*) shooting = tiroteo.

ploming (*from English*) plumbing = plomería; fontanería.

plomo (*Chile, Mex.*) a gray color = color gris.

pluma 1. (*Colo., Dom. Rep.*) a fountain pen = lapicera; pluma fuente. **2.** (*Cuba, Mex., Puerto Rico*) a ballpoint pen = bolígrafo. **3.** (*Cuba, Dom. Rep., Puerto Rico*) a faucet = grifo. **4.** (*Cuba*) a shower = ducha.

plumígrafo (*Colo.*) a marker = marcador.

pluto (*Ecua.*) absolutely drunk = completamente borracho.

po (*Chile*) a suffix that some Chileans add to the end of many words which does not have any meaning; for example sí'po, no'po, ya'po = sufijo que algunos chilenos agregan al final de varias palabras; no tiene significado específico; algunos ejemplos son sí'po, no'po, ya'po.

población callampa (*Chile*) a shanty town = chozas; caseríos muy pobres; viviendas de material ligero.

poceta (*Ven.*) a toilet = taza del retrete.

pochos (*Mex.*) the Mexicans that live on the United States side of the border = Mexicanos que viven en el lado estadounidense de la frontera.

poconón; pocotón (*Colo.*) a great amount (informal) = una gran cantidad (informal).

pocotón See **poconón**.

podrido (*Argen.*) a mean, dishonest person = persona que actúa de manera deshonrada o malintencionada.

pola (*Colo.*) beer (informal) = cerveza (informal).

polarización (*Ven.*) two political parties taking turns in power = alternancia de dos partidos políticos en el poder.

polenta 1. (*Argen.*) strength = fuerzas. **2.** (*Argen.*) very good; out of this world = lo que es extremadamente bueno; fuera de categoría. **3.** (*Argen., Chile, Para., Uru.*) a type of corn flour = un tipo de harina de maíz. **4.** (*Argen., Chile, Para., Uru.*) a dish prepared with that flour = comida que se prepara con esa harina.

polera (*Chile*) a T-shirt = polo; camisa deportiva sin abertura al frente.

policamburismo (*Ven.*) to hold several political offices at the same time = desempeño de varios cargos políticos a la vez.

poliéster (*from English*) polyester = (RAE) resina termoplástica que se usa en la fabricación de fibras.

polígrafo (*Costa Rica*) a stencil machine = máquina que reproduce lo que se ha cortado según un patrón; máquina copiadora de troquel.

polín (*Colo.*) a railroad sleeper car = durmiente en la vía del tren.

polisman (*from English*) a policeman = agente de la policía.

pollera 1. (*Argen., Bol., Chile, Colo., Ecua., Para., Peru, Uru.*) a skirt = falda. **2.** (*Ecua.*) a woman who likes younger men = una mujer a quien le gustan los hombres mas jóvenes que ella. **3.** (*Ven.*) a restaurant that sells charcoal-roasted chicken = restaurante donde se venden pollos a la brasa.

pollerudo 1. (*Argen., Chile*) a man who hides himself behind women for protection = hombre que se refugia detrás de las mujeres. **2.** (*Argen., Chile*) a boy or young man who likes to play with girls only = muchacho que prefiere jugar sólo con niñas.

pollina (*Puerto Rico, Ven.*) bangs; fringe = flequillo.

pollo (*Chile*) phlegm (vulgar) = flema; gargajo (vulgar).

pololear (*Chile*) to court; to flirt with = estar de novios sin un compromiso formal; galantear.

pololo(a) 1. (*Chile*) a steady boyfriend or girlfriend = novio(a) sin formalizar un compromiso. **2.** (*Chile*) an odd job = trabajo esporádico o irregular.

polución (*from English*) pollution = contaminación.

polucionar (*from English*) to pollute = contaminar.

polvo (*Argen., Chile, Uru.*) coitus (vulgar) = coito (vulgar).

polvorón (*Nic.*) a cookie made from corn and roasted honey = galleta hecha de maíz y miel tostada.

pomo (*Ecua.*) a carafe = garrafa.

pomo de leche (*Cuba*) a feeding bottle = biberón.

pompa (*from English*) a pump = bomba.

pompo (*Colo.*) blunt = romo; que no tiene filo.

pompón (*Nic.*) **1.** a toilet = letrina; excusado. **2.** it is over; it is finished = se acabó.

pon (*Puerto Rico*) to hitchhike = (N.E. pedir transporte gratuito en la carretera.)

ponchar 1. (*Ven.*) to put the pitcher out of the game in baseball = poner al lanzador fuera de juego en el béisbol. **2.** (*Ven.*) to turn on the TV or the radio = encender la televisón o el radio. **3.** (*Ven.*) to cut something more than what is needed = cortar algo más de lo necesario. **4.** (*Ven.*) to defeat an adversary in a quarrel = ganar una discusión. **5.** (*Ven.*) to fail = fallar; fracasar. **6.** (*Ven.*) to lose something very dear or important = perder algo muy querido o muy importante. **7.** (*Ven.*) to fail an exam or a course = fallar o reprobar un examen o un curso. **8.** (*from English*) to punch a card at the workplace = marcar la tarjeta en el lugar de trabajo.

ponchar el examen (*Cuba*) to fail an exam = suspender un examen.

ponche (*Colo.*) a punch = mezcla de varios tipos de bebidas.

poncho (*Argen., Bol., Chile, Colo., Ecua., Para., Peru, Uru.*) (N.E. poncho; a square, heavy blanket with a hole in the center that is used as a cape) = manta gruesa con un agujero en el centro, se usa como capa que cuelga de los hombros.

poncho de sesenta listas (*Para.*) a multicolored **poncho** typical of Paraguay = **poncho** multicolor típico del Paraguay.

pondo (*Ecua.*) a large earthenware jar = tinaja.

poner el gorro (*Chile*) to betray someone in a love affair = traicionar a otra persona en una relación amorosa.

poner sebo (*Colo.*) to bother; to annoy = molestar; fastidiar.

ponerle empeño; ponerle pino (*Chile*) to make a real effort; to put oneself into it = hacer un gran efuerzo; hacerlo con ahínco.

ponerle la tapa al pomo (*Cuba*) to reach the highest achievement = lograr lo máximo.

ponerle mucha tiza (*Colo.*) to work very hard; to make a big effort to succeed = trabajar con mucho esmero.

ponerle pino See **ponerle empeño.**

ponerse (*Argen.*) to agree to pay a high price to get something done = aceptar condiciones onerosas para conseguir algo.

ponerse pedo See **empedar.**

ponerse tere (*Colo.*) to become whimsical = ponerse caprichoso.

póney; poni (*from English*) a pony = (RAE) caballo de raza de poca alzada.

póngase las pilas (*Colo.*) to be alert; to be prepared to do something very soon = esté alerta; esté preparado para hacer algo muy pronto.

poni See **póney.**

pool [pron. pul] **1.** (*from English*) a consortium; an association; a group; a pool = consorcio; asociación; grupo; mancomunidad. **2.** (*from English*) a swimming pool = piscina.

popcón (*from English*) popcorn = palomitas de maíz.

popi; popín; popó (*Chile*) the buttocks and/or genitals in children's language = trasero y/o genitales en lenguaje infantil.

popín See **popi.**

popó See **popi.**

popocho(a) (*Colo.*) full = harto; repleto.

poporopos (*Guat.*) popcorn = palomitas de maíz.

poposeador (*Colo.*) a baby that defecates a lot = bebé cagón; niño que defeca frecuentemente en sus ropas.

popote (*Mex.*) a drinking straw = paja; pajita; pajilla para beber.

por chiripa See **de chiripa.**

por el libro (*Puerto Rico*) a beautiful and attractive person = persona bonita y atractiva.

por la maceta (*Puerto Rico*) it is very good; it is very beautiful = es muy bueno(a); es muy bonito(a).

porongo (*Peru*) a clay container used to hold liquids = vasija de barro para guardar líquidos.

poronguito (*Argen.*) a small gourd used to prepare **mate** = calabaza pequeña en la que generalmente se ceba el **mate**.

pororó (*Para.*) popcorn = rosetas de maíz.

porotal (*Para.*) a bean field = sembrado de porotos.

porotos (*Bol., Chile, Ecua., Para., Peru, Uru.*) beans = habichuelas.

porra (*Colo.*) an intelligent person = persona inteligente.

porro (*Colo.*) one of the dances of the black people in Colombia = uno de los bailes de los negros colombianos.

portable (*from English*) portable = portátil.

posta (*Argen.*) a sure thing = cosa segura; lo que está o es seguro.

postema See **materia**.

poster (*from English*) a poster = (RAE) cartel que se cuelga en la pared como elemento decorativo; afiche.

postrera (*Colo.*) the last portion of milk when milking a cow = la última porción de leche en la ordeña.

pote (*Puerto Rico*) canned food = lata.

poto (*Chile, Peru*) the ass; the buttocks and/or the anus (vulgar) = culo; trasero y/o ano (vulgar).

potoco (*Chile*) short; shabby = bajo; rechoncho.

potrero (*Argen., Bol., Chile*) a big field; a neglected piece of land = terreno abandonado.

potrillo (*Chile*) a big drinking glass = vaso grande para beber.

potro(a) 1. (*Argen.*) a nice-looking person = persona bonita. **2.** (*Argen.*) something that looks well = lo que se ve bien.

pozo (*Para.*) a hole = hoyo.

pozol (*Nic.*) a beverage made from purple corn = bebida hecha de maíz purpúreo.

pozole 1. (*Guat.*) the corn used to feed poultry = maíz para alimentar a las aves de corral. **2.** (*Guat.*) one kind of **atole** = un tipo de **atole**. **3.** (*Mex.*) a dish prepared with pig's head and hominy = plato preparado con cabeza de cerdo y maíz machacado.

prado (*Colo.*) a lawn = césped.

prefaciar (*from English*) to preface = prologar.

preferencial (*from English*) preferential = preferente.

preguntadera (*Ven.*) asking many questions = el acto de preguntar mucho.

prelación (*Colo.*) the right to pass on the road = derecho de paso en las vías públicas.

premiación (*from English*) to give or receive a prize; to reward = premiar; dar o recibir un premio.

premier (*from English*) a prime minister = primer ministro.

prenda (*Ven.*) jewelry = joyas.

prender (*Chile, Puerto Rico, Ven.*) to turn on an electric device = conectar; encender; hacer funcionar un aparato eléctrico.

prenderse (*Puerto Rico*) to become angry = enojarse.

prendido (*Dom. Rep.*) drunk = ebrio; borracho.

prepucio (*Colo.*) a military cap = gorro militar.

preseki (*from English*) to press a key = pulsar una tecla.

presilla (*Pan.*) a hair pin = horquilla para el cabello.

presin (*from English*) pressing = poner presión.

prieta 1. (*Chile*) blood sausage = morcilla. **2.** (*Puerto Rico*) black woman = mujer negra.

prieto 1. (*Cuba, Dom. Rep., Guat., Pan., Puerto Rico*) black; a black person (derogatory) = negro; persona de rasgos negroides (despectivo). **2.** (*Cuba*) dark = oscuro.

printer (*from English*) a printer = impresora.

prójima (*Para.*) a woman who looks poor = mujer de aspecto pobre.

propela (*from English*) a propeller = hélice.

prosa (*Bol., Chile, Ecua., Guat., Peru*) to take on an attitude of being extremely important = tomar una actitud para demostrar que se considera a si mismo(a) tremendamente importante.

prospecto (*Colo.*) he or she is promising in sports = persona prometedora en los deportes.

prosudo (*Bol., Chile, Ecua., Guat., Peru*) affected; solemn; pompous; a person who takes on an attitude of being extremely important; a person who shows **prosa** = pomposo; el que se da excesiva importancia; el que tiene **prosa**; engreído.

provisorio (*Chile, Guat., Hond., Mex., Nic.*) provisional = provisional.

provista (*Para.*) the food and other items prepared for a trip = alimentos y otros elementos que se preparan para hacer un viaje.

provocación (*Colo.*) a desire to eat or drink = deseos de comer o beber.

pub (*from English*) a pub = taberna.

ipucha! (*Argen., Chile*) an interjection of surprise, admiration or other emotion depending on the context and use = interjección que expresa sorpresa, admiración u otros estados según el contexto en que se usa.

puchecas (*Colo.*) a woman's breasts = pechos femeninos.

pucherear (*Argen.*) to make only enough money to buy inexpensive food or **puchero** = ganar sólo lo indispensable para el **puchero**.

puchero (*Argen., Chile, Para.*) a traditional inexpensive meal prepared with meats and vegetables = comida tradicional de bajo costo preparada con carnes y vegetales.

ipuchica! (*Salva.*) Crumbs! = ¡recórcholis!

ipuchita! See **ijoepuchita!**

pucho 1. (*Argen.*) a cigar or cigarette butt = colilla de cigarro o cigarrillo. **2.** (*Colo.*) a handful = puñado. **3.** (*Colo.*) a small amount left = el poco que queda. **4.** (*Ecua.*) the younger son = hijo menor de la familia.

pudin (*from English*) a pudding = budín.

pujagua (*Nic.*) purple corn = maíz purpúreo.

pujar para adentro (*Puerto Rico*) to take something without complaint = aguantar sin quejarse.

pulento (*Chile*) very good; of high quality or value (informal) = muy bueno; de gran calidad o valor (informal).

pullman (*from English*) a pullman car = (N.E. clase de lujo en transportes públicos).

pulover 1. (*Argen.*) a sweater = suéter. **2.** (*from English*) a pullover = jersey; chaqueta de punto.

pulpear (*Chile*) to defraud or swindle someone in the price = estafar o timar en el precio.

pulque (*Mex.*) an alcoholic beverage; the fermented juice of the **magüey** = bebida alcohólica hecha de jugo de **magüey** fermentado.

pulsera (*Pan.*) a bracelet = brazalete.

pulso (*Colo., Cuba*) a bracelet = pulsera; brazalete.

puna 1. (*Bol., Chile, Ecua., Peru*) the tableland of the Andes = meseta de los Andes. **2.** (*Bol., Chile, Ecua., Peru*) high-altitude sickness = soroche; mareos y malestares producidos por las grandes altitudes del altiplano.

punch 1. (*from English*) a punch (a blow) = golpe. **2.** (*from English*) a punch (force) = empuje.

punga (*Argen., Chile*) a thief; a criminal (informal) = ladrón; delincuente (informal).

puntada (*Chile, Ecua., Peru*) a shooting pain; a spasm; a sharp pain in a specific part of the body = punzada; dolor agudo en un lugar específico del cuerpo.

puntal (*Colo.*) snacks between meals = tentempié entre las comidas.

punto jersey (*Chile*) flexible knitting = tejido de punto flexible.

punto rojo (*Colo.*) the best quality marijuana = marihuana de la máxima calidad.

puntudo 1. (*Argen., Bol., Chile, Ecua., Peru*) a sharp person = rápido para actuar. **2.** (*Chile*) a person who acts with familiarity too soon = el que se toma mucha confianza demasiado pronto.

punzada (*Bol.*) a sharp pain in a specific part of the body = dolor agudo que se siente en un lugar específico del cuerpo.

puñeta (*Puerto Rico*) masturbation (vulgar) = masturbación (vulgar).

puño (*Puerto Rico*) a punch = puñetazo.

pupú (*Ven.*) a piece of excrement expelled in one section (informal) = porción de excremento expelido de una vez (informal).

pupurrí (*Argen., Bol., Chile, Colo., Cuba, Peru, Uru.*) mixture; several things mixed into a whole = mezcla; varias cosas mezcladas en un todo.

pupusa 1. (*Nic.*) a sweet bread with a triangular shape = pan dulce con forma triangular. **2.** (*Salva.*) a corn **tortilla** filled with meat and cheese = **tortilla** de maíz rellena de carne y queso.

pura paja (*Nic.*) entirely a lie = una mentira por completo.

purrete (*Argen.*) a young boy = muchachito; niño pequeño.

puscafé (*Colo.*) a hard-liquor drink served with coffee after meals = trago fuerte que acompaña al café después de la comida.

puteada (*Para.*) a reprimand (vulgar) = reprimenda (vulgar).

putear 1. (*Ven.*) to degenerate (vulgar) = degenerar (vulgar). **2.** (*Ven.*) to degrade something or someone (vulgar) = degradar algo o a alguien (vulgar).

puya (*Dom. Rep.*) a provocation = provocación.

puyar 1. (*Chile, Colo.*) to urge someone to do something = incitar con ahínco a hacer algo. **2.** (*Ven.*) to make great effort at work = esforzarse grandemente en el trabajo. **3.** (*Nic.*) to prick = pinchar; punzar. **4.** (*Puerto Rico*) to accelerate a car = acelerar el automóvil.

puzzle (*from English*) a puzzle = (RAE) rompecabezas; crucigrama; acertijo.

Q

¡Qué brete! (*Cuba*) a mess; a problem = aprieto; lío; problema.

¡¿Qué chingados quieres?! (*Mex.*) What the hell do you want? (vulgar) = ¡¿Qué diablos quieres?! (vulgar).

¡Qué clase de bomba! (*Cuba*) How unpleasant! = ¡Qué desagradable!

que la felicidad te atropelle (*Colo.*) I hope you will bump into happiness = espero que tengas una gran felicidad.

ique plato! 1. (*Argen., Chile*) How funny! = ¡qué chistoso(a)! **2.** (*Argen., Chile*) How ridiculous he or she is! = ¡qué ridículo!

¡qué vaina! 1. (*Hond.*) What bad luck! = ¡qué mala suerte! **2.** (*Hond.*) What a complicated problem! = ¡qué problema más complicado!

quebrar (*Colo.*) to kill = matar.

quedado(a) (*Chile*) a slow thinker; someone of low intelligence = lento(a) para pensar; de inteligencia lenta.

quedarse mocho (*Cuba*) to have one's hair cut very short = hacerse un corte de pelo muy corto.

quedarse piola (*Argen.*) to perform below expectations = no actuar a la altura de los acontecimientos.

quedarse tieso (*Guat.*) to die = morirse.

¡quedetallaso! (*Colo.*) a big detail = un tremendo o un gran detalle.

quedó la escoba (*Chile*) it is a mess; there is much damage (informal) = quedó un desorden; es un desbarajuste; está muy dañado (informal).

queik (*from English*) a cake = torta; pastel; bizcocho.

quemada (*Dom. Rep.*) a burn = quemadura.

quemado 1. (*Chile*) to have bad luck = el que tiene mala suerte. **2.** (*Cuba, Mex.*) ruined = arruinado. **3.** (*Cuba, Mex.*) to be burned out; to be fed up = estar cansado de una actividad; estar harto.

quemarse (*Dom. Rep., Puerto Rico*) to fail an exam; to fail a subject in school = reprobar un examen; reprobar una materia.

quemón 1. (*Mex.*) a big burn = una quemadura grande. **2.** (*Mex.*) an insult = insulto. **3.** (*Mex.*) an embarrassment; ridiculous = vergüenza; ridículo.

quena (*Bol., Chile, Ecua., Peru*) a flute made with several bamboos; a typical instrument of the Andes tableland = flauta hecha con varios bambúes; instrumento típico del altiplano andino.

quenepa; quenepe (*Puerto Rico*) (N.E. tropical fruit) = (N.E. una fruta tropical).

quenepe See **quenepa**.

queque (*Mex., Nic.*) a cake = torta; bizcocho.

quequisque (*Nic.*) (N.E. **yautía**) = (N.E. **yautía**).

querencia (*Argen.*) a favorite spot; home ground or familiar territory = lugar querido donde se ha nacido, se vive o se ha vivido.

querendón 1. (*Dom. Rep.*) to cherish others = cariñoso. **2.** (*Puerto Rico*) the pampered child = el regalón; el más mimado de los hijos.

quesillo (*Ven.*) a sweet jelly prepared with milk, sugar, and eggs = dulce gelatinoso preparado con leche, azúcar y huevos.

quillarse 1. (*Puerto Rico*) to conceal; to pretend = disimular; pretender. **2.** (*Puerto Rico*) to give oneself airs of being important = presumir; engreírse.

quilombero(a) (*Para.*) a person who provokes disasters = persona que provoca desastres.

quilombo 1. (*Argen., Para., Uru.*) a big mess; a brawl = un gran desorden o tumulto. **2.** (*Argen., Para., Uru.*) a whorehouse = casa de prostitutas. **3.** (*Ven.*) a hut = choza. **4.** (*Para.*) a disaster = desastre.

quilto (*from English*) a quilt = edredón; acolchado.

quiltro (*Chile*) a stray dog; a dog without pedigree = perro vago; perrucho; perro sin raza conocida.

quincalla (*Ven.*) a store that sells small, cheap objects = tienda que vende objetos pequeños y baratos.

quinde (*Ecua.*) a hummingbird = colibrí.

quiñar 1. (*Colo.*) to hit = golpear. **2.** (*Colo.*) to kill = matar.

quiñazo (*Chile*) a wreck; a collision = encontrón; empujón.

quipe (*Peru*) bulk carried on the back = bulto o fardo que se carga sobre las espaldas.

quiquirigüiqui 1. (*Ven.*) a turbid, muddy and/or secret activity = actividad turbia y/o secreta. **2.** (*Ven.*) a secret love affair = amorío secreto.

quirquincho (*Bol., Chile*) an armadillo = armadillo.

quisco (*Chile*) a cactus = cacto.

quisio (*Dom. Rep.*) lazy = haragán.

R

rabo (*Colo., Ven.*) the buttocks (informal) = nalgas, trasero (informal).

rabúa; refistolera (*Puerto Rico*) a woman with a bad reputation = mujer cualquiera.

rachar (*from English*) to rush = apurarse; darse prisa.

radiotelefonía (*Para.*) the telephone conversations on a radio talk show = conversaciones telefónicas durante un programa de radio.

raglan (*from English*) a tailored style for the sleeves of a jacket in which the sleeves begin at the collar of the jacket = (RAE) estilo de manga que nace del cuello de la chaqueta.

ragú (*Argen.*) a hunger = hambre.

raid (*from English*) a trip = viaje.

raja (*Dom. Rep.*) the vagina (vulgar) = vagina (vulgar).

rajado (*Ven.*) legitimate; authentic = legítimo; auténtico.

rajao See **jumeta**.

rajar 1. (*Chile, Colo., Cuba*) to fail a student = reprobar a un estudiante. **2.** (*Colo., Ecua., Mex., Peru*) to insult = insultar. **3.** (*Cuba*) to change one's mind = cambiar de opinión; arrepentirse de hacer algo. **4.** (*Mex.*) to back down = retirarse o arrepentirse de hacer una actividad; hacerse atrás.

rajarse 1. (*Puerto Rico*) to get drunk = embriagarse; emborracharse. **2.** (*Puerto Rico*) to give up = abandonar; darse por vencido.

rajarse en el examen (*Colo.*) to fail an exam = suspender o reprobar un examen.

rajatablas (*Colo.*) a reprimand = reprimenda.

rally [pron. rali] (*from English*) a rally = manifestación; concentración de gentes para hacer una manifestación pública.

RAM (*from English*) Random Access Memory (RAM) = (N.E. memoria de acceso aleatorio).

ranada 1. (*Argen.*) craftiness = picardía. **2.** (*Argen.*) a smart move = acción astuta.

ranchería (*Para.*) a shanty town = poblaciones de viviendas pobres.

rancho 1. (*Colo., Cuba, Mex.*) a ranch = hacienda. **2.** (*Uru., Ven.*) a shanty = casa construida de cartones y de otros materiales de baja calidad.

ranquear (*from English*) to rank = ordenar en rangos; categorizar.

ranquin (*from English*) a ranking = categoría; posición.

rapista (*from English*) a rapist = violador.

raport (*from English*) to have a good rapport or affinity = buena relación; afinidad.

rasca 1. (*Chile*) anything that is poor and neglected = cualquier cosa descuidada y pobre. **2.** (*Chile*) something of inferior quality = lo que es de baja calidad; sin clase. **3.** (*Ven.*) drunkenness = borrachera.

rascado (*Colo.*) drunk = embriagado.

rascar (*Ven.*) to get drunk = causar embriaguez.

rascazón (*Ven.*) collective drunkenness = embriaguez colectiva.

rasco-rasco See **granizado**.

rasgado (*Colo.*) generous = generoso.

raspa; trancada (*Colo.*) a severe reprimand = reprimenda severa.

raspadilla (*Peru*) sherbet = sorbete.

raspado 1. (*Colo., Cuba, Dom. Rep., Mex.*) sherbet = sorbete. **2.** (*Ven.*) daring; shameless = atrevido; desvergonzado.

raspadura See **panetela**.

raspar 1. (*Ven.*) to escape; to go out quickly = salir apresuradamente. **2.** (*Ven.*) to fail an exam, a course or a subject = suspender o reprobar un examen, un curso o una asignatura.

rasquera (*Mex.*) an itching sensation = picazón.

rastrero (*Colo.*) a firework that trails on the ground = cohete; fuego de artificio que se arrastra por el suelo.

rastrojo 1. (*Chile*) what is left in the field after the crops = lo que queda en el terreno después de la cosecha. **2.** (*Ven.*) neglected farming land = terreno de cultivo abandonado.

ratearse de la escuela (*Argen.*) to cut school = hacer novillos; faltar a la escuela cuando se aparenta asistir a ella.

ratero (*Chile, Cuba, Peru*) a thief = ladrón.

ratio (*from English*) a quotient; a proportion; a ratio = cociente; proporción; tasa.

ratón 1. (*Chile*) a coward; pusillanimous = cobarde; pusilánime. **2.** (*Costa Rica*) the biceps = bíceps; músculo del brazo. **3.** (*Ven.*) to annoy = molestar. **4.** (*Ven.*) a hangover = resaca después de beber.

ratonera 1. (*Chile, Peru*) a hovel; a slum = vivienda pobre y sucia; lugar maloliente y desordenado. **2.** (*Chile*) a small sling = honda pequeña. **3.** (*Puerto Rico, Ven.*) a little, cramped shop = tienducha; tienda muy estrecha y pequeña.

raund (*from English*) round = asalto en un combate de boxeo.

raya 1. (*Colo.*) a detective (informal) = detective (informal). **2.** (*Mex.*) a payday = día de paga.

rayado (*Mex.*) a person who has a large sum of money = estar en posesión de una gran cantidad de dinero.

re (*Argen., Chile*) very; a prefix used as a superlative, for example, "rebuena" very good, "remala" very bad (informal) = muy; prefijo usado como superlativo, por ejemplo "rebuena" significando "muy buena," "remala" significando "muy mala" (informal).

realengo 1. (*Ven.*) an idler = ocioso. **2.** (*Ven.*) he or she does not obey or listen to anyone = el/la que no obedece o le hace caso a nadie. **3.** (*Ven.*) things that do not belong to anyone = cosas que no le pertenecen a nadie.

realero (*Ven.*) a large amount of money = cantidad grande de dinero.

realización (*Chile, Colo.*) a sale = liquidación.

realizar (*from English*) to realize = darse cuenta de.

reatazo 1. (*Mex.*) a blow with the fist = puñetazo. **2.** (*Mex.*) a slash with a rope = azote con una cuerda.

reatiza (*Mex.*) a severe beating = paliza.

rebaja (*Colo.*) a sale = liquidación.

rebaje (*Mex.*) a discount = descuento en el precio de algo.

rebanar (*Colo.*) to reduce the size of something to make it fit into another thing = disminuir el tamaño de una cosa para que encaje en otra.

reblujo; rebujo (*Colo.*) a mess; a disorder = revoltijo; desorden.

rebolotú (*Colo.*) a brawl = alboroto.

reborujo (*Mex.*) a brawl; noise; confusion = alboroto; tumulto; barahúnda.

rebotado (*Colo.*) a violent temperament = temperamento violento.

rebote (*Colo.*) a bile attack = ataque de bilis.

rebrujar See **arrebrujar.**

rebujar See **arrebrujar.**

rebujo See **reblujo.**

rebullir (*Colo.*) to mix liquids = revolver líquidos.

rebuscador (*Colo.*) a person who handles things with skill to reach his or her objective = el que se maneja bien para conseguir su objetivo.

rebusque 1. (*Colo.*) to work day by day, earning only enough money for the meals of the day = buscar el sustento diario; trabajar día a día alcanzando a hacer el dinero sólo para las comidas del día. **2.** (*Para.*) an illegal business = negocio ilícito. **3.** (*Ven.*) an extra job; a second job = el trabajo extra; el segundo trabajo que se tiene además del trabajo regular. **4.** (*Ven.*) an odd job = trabajo esporádico. **5.** (*Ven.*) a dishonest activity; an illegal job = actividad deshonesta; trabajo ilegal. **6.** (*Ven.*) a sporadic love affair = relación amorosa esporádica.

reca 1. (*from English*) a tow truck = camión grúa. **2.** (*from English*) a wreck = vehículo totalmente descompuesto.

recado (*Dom. Rep.*) spices = especias para aderezar la comida.

recalcadura (*Para.*) the dislocation of a bone = dislocación de un hueso.

recámara (*Mex., Pan.*) a bedroom = dormitorio.

recao (*Puerto Rico*) a condiment; a seasoning prepared with several ingredients = condimento; sazón preparado con varios ingredientes.

recargado (*Mex.*) arrogant; presumptuous = arrogante; presumido.

recaudo (*Mex.*) spices; seasoning = especias; hierbas y otros elementos para sazonar comidas.

rechinarse (*Colo.*) a meal that gets burned = alimento que se ha quemado.

reciencito (*Chile, Para.*) just a few minutes ago = hace muy poco.

recocho(a) (*Colo.*) he or she does not like to do anything = persona a quien no le gusta hacer nada.

recolectar (*from English*) to recollect = recordar.

recomendado (*Colo.*) certified mail = correo certificado.

reconociencia (*from English*) a recognition; an acknowledgment of another's behavior or status = reconocimiento de la conducta, el lugar o la condición que le corresponde a otro.

record (*from English*) a record = marca; (RAE) el mejor resultado en competencias deportivas.

recorderis (*Colo.*) the remainder = hacer recordar.

recordman (*from English*) one who holds a record; a record holder = plusmarquista; el último que ha quebrado el record.

recorrido(a) (*Colo.*) a person of great experience = hombre o mujer de mundo.

recorte (*Mex.*) a slander; a defamation = chisme; difamación.

recorte de pelo (*Puerto Rico*) a haircut = corte de pelo.

recuerdo (*Ven.*) awake = despierto.

recursivo(a) (*Colo.*) he or she has many means to be effective = tiene muchos recursos para ser efectivo(a).

recurso (*Para.*) a clever person = persona astuta.

redoblón (*Colo.*) a group rape = violación por un grupo.

redondo 1. (*Ecua., Peru*) stupid = estúpido. **2.** (*Mex.*) honest = honesto.

refajo 1. (*Cuba, Puerto Rico*) a slip = enaguas. **2.** (*Colo.*) a mixture of beer and soda = mezcla de cerveza con gaseosa.

refalar 1. (*Argen.*) to take off; to take away = sacar; quitar. **2.** (*Argen.*) to steal = hurtar.

réferi (*from English*) a referee = árbitro.

refistolero(a); refitolero(a) 1. (*Ven.*) a person who appears elegant and rich = el/la que presume de elegante y rico. **2.** (*Ven.*) a busybody = entrometido. **3.** (*Puerto Rico*) a person who has a bad reputation = persona de mala reputación.

refitolero(a) See **refistolero(a)**.

¡reflauta! (*Chile*) an interjection of surprise = interjección de sorpresa.

refresco (*Cuba, Ven.*) a soda = gaseosa.

regadera (*Colo., Cuba, Mex., Ven.*) a shower = ducha.

regarse (*Colo.*) to speak vehemently with the passion of fury = hablar con vehemencia por estar enfurecido.

registro (*Colo.*) a holy card = estampa religiosa.

reguerete (*Dom. Rep., Puerto Rico*) a mess of objects = desorden; regadero de objetos.

regueretear (*Puerto Rico*) to make a mess = desordenar; dejar las cosas en desorden.

reja (*Chile*) a fence = cerca; valla.

rejazo (*Colo.*) a blow with the **rejo** = golpe dado con el **rejo**.

rejo (*Colo.*) a whip made of twisted leather or other materials = látigo de cuero u otro material retorcido.

relacionista (*Colo.*) a public-relations person = publicista; persona encargada de las relaciones públicas.

relajante (*Chile*) extremely sweet = extremadamente dulce.

relajo 1. (*Dom. Rep.*) to make fun of someone = hacer burla de una persona. **2.** (*Mex.*) a disorder = desorden. **3.** (*Mex., Puerto Rico*) unconventional behavior; misbehavior = una conducta no convencional; conducta desordenada.

relativo (*from English*) a relative = pariente.

relís (*from English*) to release; to liberate = soltar; librar; dejar ir.

remar (*Argen.*) to work hard physically or intellectually in order to succeed = esforzarse física o intelectualmente para triunfar.

remascar (*Colo.*) to ruminate; to ponder = rumiar; meditar.

rematador (*Bol., Para.*) an auctioneer = subastador.

rematar (*Argen., Bol., Chile, Para.*) to buy or sell something in an auction = subastar; comprar o vender en subasta pública.

remate (*Argen., Bol., Chile, Para.*) an auction = subasta.

remodelar (*from English*) to remodel = modificar; mejorar; restructurar; reformar.

remoler (*Guat.*) to bother; to annoy = fastidiar; incomodar.

remolienda (*Peru*) a binge = juerga; jarana.

remontar (*Colo.*) a change of a shoe's sole = cambio de suela en el calzado.

rendir examen (*Argen., Chile, Para.*) to take an exam = tomar examen.

rentar (*Guat., Hond., Mex., Puerto Rico, Salva.*) to rent = alquilar; arrendar.

reparar 1. (*Para.*) to imitate; to mock = remedar. **2.** (*Ven.*) to take an exam or a subject a second time = tomar un examen o una asignatura por segunda vez.

repasador (*Colo.*) a dishcloth = paño o trapo de cocina.

repelar (*Chile*) to regret = lamentar.

repiocha (*Mex.*) extremely beautiful = extremadamente bonito(a).

repocheta (*Nic.*) a fried corn tortilla with cheese = tortilla frita de maíz con queso.

reposero (*Ven.*) an employee who abuses the right to be absent from work = el que abusa del permiso que se otorga en el trabajo para ausentarse.

repuñoso(a) (*Mex.*) selfish = egoísta.

requesón (*Nic.*) a sweet dessert prepared with sour milk = postre dulce preparado con leche cortada.

resabiado (*Colo.*) squeamish; easily frightened = melindroso; asustadizo.

resaca (*Mex.*) a reservoir; an artificial lake = represa; lago artificial.

resbaladera 1. (*Ven.*) a drink prepared with rice, sugar, water, and cinnamon = bebida preparada con arroz, azúcar, agua y canela. **2.** (*Colo., Mex.*) a slide in a playground = tobogán.

resbaladero; resbaladilla (*Mex.*) a slide in a playground = tobogán.

resbaladilla See **resbaladero**.

resfalar (*Argen., Chile*) to slip = resbalar.

resfriado 1. (*Argen.*) unable to keep a secret = el que no sabe guardar un secreto. **2.** (*Uru.*) indiscreet = indiscreto.

resistol (*Mex.*) glue = adhesivo; pegamento.

resorte (*Colo.*) a rubber band = bandita de goma.

respirator (*from English*) a respirator = respirador.

resquicio (*Chile, Mex.*) a crack; an opening = quebradura; abertura.

retacón (*Para.*) short and shabby = rechoncho; retaco.

retaliación (*from English*) a retaliation = desquite; represalia; revancha; venganza.

retallón (*Ven.*) leftover food = sobras de comida.

retamblar (*Peru*) to be enthusiastic; to energize others = energizar; comunicar más energía.

retar 1. (*Argen., Chile, Para.*) to scold; to reprimand = regañar; reprender. **2.** (*Argen., Bol., Chile*) to insult = denostar.

reto (*Bol.*) an insult; an offense = insulto; injuria.

retobo (*Colo.*) a waste = desperdicio; cosa inservible.

retranca (*Colo.*) a vehicle's brake = freno de un vehículo.

retratería (*Guat., Uru.*) a photo studio = taller del fotógrafo; lugar para sacarse un retrato fotográfico.

reverbero (*Colo.*) a small stove = cocinilla; pequeño artefacto para calentar comidas y cocinar.

reversa (*Chile, Colo.*) reverse = marcha atrás en los vehículos.

revirado (*Argen.*) a person who displays incoherent or irrational behavior = persona de actuar incoherente; el que no actúa cuerdamente.

revirar (*Para.*) to have seconds when eating = repetirse uno de los platos durante una comida.

revival (*from English*) revival; re-emergence; rebirth = resucitación; reanimación; restablecimiento; resurgimiento; renacimiento.

revolica (*Hond.*) a row; confusion; a mess = barullo; confusión; enredo.

revolú (*Dom. Rep., Puerto Rico*) a disorder; a brawl; a scandal; trouble = desorden; alboroto; escándalo; lío.

revuelto(a) (*Ven.*) a dish prepared with chicken, eggs, and spices = guisado preparado con pollo, huevos y especias.

revulú (*Pan.*) a brawl = alboroto.

rezandero(a) (*Ven.*) a paid mourner = el/la que cobra por rezar en el funeral.

rezar (*Colo.*) to take a spell off someone by praying = quitar un encantamiento con rezos.

rezondrar (*Peru*) to insult = insultar; injuriar.

ricoto (*Peru*) a Peruvian variety of hot pepper = una variedad peruana de pimiento picante.

rin 1. (*from English*) a ring = anillo. **2.** (*from English*) a rim = llanta en la rueda de un vehículo; aro metálico de la rueda del automóvil.

ring (*from English*) an enclosed space for boxing matches; a boxing ring = cuadrilátero para los encuentros pugilísticos.

ringlete (*Colo.*) a windmill = juguete infantil; molinete; molinillo.

ringuear (*from English*) to ring = hacer sonar un timbre; repicar la campanilla; sonar el timbre del teléfono; resonar.

riña (*Puerto Rico*) hatred; dislike; a grudge = odio; tirria.

ripio (*Colo.*) inferior-quality marijuana = marihuana de mala calidad.

ripostar 1. (*Colo.*) to hit back = devolver los golpes. **2.** (*Ven.*) to reply; to answer back = responder; contestar.

risés 1. (*from English*) a recess = interrupción de una actividad. **2.** (*from English*) a recess break at school = descanso entre dos períodos de enseñanza en la escuela.

rispar (*Hond.*) to flee; to escape quickly = marcharse de manera apresurada.

rizado (*Cuba, Ecua., Peru*) curly hair = cabello ensortijado o crespo.

robón(a) (*Mex.*) a thief = ladrón(a).

rochar (*Chile*) to catch in the act (informal) = sorprender u observar una acción impropia o ilícita (informal).

roche (*from English*) a cockroach = cucaracha.

rochela (*Colo.*) a noise = bulla; ruido.

rochelar (*Colo.*) to make noise = hacer ruido.

rock (*from English*) rock and roll = (N.E. tipo de música bailable derivada del **jazz**).

rocoroco (*Bol.*) a small mosquito = mosquito muy pequeño.

rocoto See **locoto**.

rodado (*Argen., Chile*) any vehicle with wheels = cualquier vehículo con ruedas.

rodillo (*Para.*) a rolling pin = uslero; rollo de amasar.

rodillón (*Colo.*) a very old person = persona muy anciana.

rodón (*Chile*) a moulding with a right angle and a curve in the opposite side to the angle = moldura con un ángulo recto y una curva del lado opuesto al ángulo.

rol (*from English*) a role = desempeño de un papel.

rolazo (*Ven.*) a hit with a police night-stick; a hit with a **rolo** = golpe con el bastón que usa la policía; golpe con el **rolo**.

rollo (*Dom. Rep.*) a speech without meaning = discurso poco sustancioso.

rolo 1. (*Ven.*) a police nightstick = bastón policíaco. **2.** (*Ven.*) any stick = cualquier palo. **3.** (*Ven.*) a piece; a part of a whole = trozo; parte de un todo.

rolos; rols (*from English*) rolls = bollos.

rols See **rolos**.

rompepecho (*Colo.*) an inferior-quality cigarette = cigarrillo de mala calidad.

romper (*Argen.*) to bother insistently = molestar con insistencia.

roncar (*Argen.*) to impose personal power on others; to behave in a bossy way = imponer el poder personal sobre otros; ser mandón.

roncear (*Chile*) to move a heavy object by swinging it on its corners = mover un objeto pesado balanceándolo por las esquinas.

roncha (*Ven.*) a nuisance = molestia; disgusto.

ronda 1. (*Argen., Chile*) a ring-around-the-rosy game = juego del corro. **2.** (*Ven.*) a guard = guardián.

rondana (*Dom. Rep.*) a pulley-wheel = roldana.

rondín (*Bol., Chile*) a night watchman = vigilante nocturno que hace la ronda alrededor de una propiedad.

rondpoint (*Colo.*) a traffic circle = cruce de círculo; redondel; plazoleta redonda que permite el cruce de varias vías en diferentes direcciones.

ron-ron (*Nic.*) a beetle = escarabajo.

ronrón (*Hond.*) a baby's rattle = cascabel; sonajero.

roña (*Colo.*) a trick used to avoid work = astucia que se usa para evitar el trabajo.

roñoso(a) (*Ecua.*) rough = áspero; tosco.

ropa de baño (*Ecua., Peru*) a bathing suit = traje de baño.

ropa vieja 1. (*Argen.*) a meal prepared with leftovers = comida preparada con los restos de otra. **2.** (*Cuba*) a meal prepared with shredded beef and cooked in tomato sauce = comida preparada con carne de res cortada en tiras y cocinada en salsa de tomates.

ropero (*Argen.*) a big person with a strong body = persona de gran tamaño y desarrollo físico.

ropo (*Hond.*) a rope; a string = cuerda; cordel.

roquero (*from English*) a rock and roll fanatic = fanático de la música **rock**.

roquet (*from English*) a rocket = cohete.

rosbif (*from English*) roast beef = asado de vacuno.

rosca 1. (*Colo.*) a caucus of influence = camarilla de influencia. **2.** (*Ecua., Peru*) a homosexual = homosexual. **3.** (*Chile*) a fight; a row; a rumpus = pelea; disputa; trifulca. **4.** (*Mex., Ven.*) a ring used to carry a load on the head = anillo para cargar un peso en la cabeza.

rosco (*Colo.*) a caucus of influence = camarilla de influencia.

roscón 1. (*Colo.*) a sweet bread = pan dulce. **2.** (*Colo.*) a good-looking man = hombre de buena presencia.

rosetas de maíz (*Cuba, Mex.*) popcorn = palomitas de maíz.

rositas de maíz (*Cuba*) popcorn = palomitas de maíz.

rosquete (*Peru*) a homosexual = homosexual.

rost (*from English*) roast = asado.

rosticería (*Guat.*) a deli = fiambrería; charcutería; rotisería.

roto 1. (*Argen., Peru*) a nickname for a Chilean = apodo para un chileno. **2.** (*Chile*) a poor person; a stereotypical Chilean type; depending on the context, it could be either a derogatory term or a term of self-pride = de la clase baja; personaje representativo del tipo chileno, el cual, según el contexto puede ser un tratamiento peyorativo o de orgullo. **3.** (*Ecua.*) a half-breed = mestizo.

rotos (*Peru*) a nickname for Chileans = apodo para referirse a los chilenos.

rotoso (*Argen., Chile*) ragged = andrajoso; mal vestido; pobremente vestido.

rótulo (*Mex., Puerto Rico*) a sign = cartel; letrero.

ruana 1. (*Colo.*) a wool **poncho** = **poncho** de lana. **2.** (*Ven.*) (N.E. any **poncho**) = cualquier tipo de **poncho**.

ruanetas See **alpargatón**.

rubro (*Argen., Chile, Para.*) an entry = asiento contable; partida de artículos en el comercio.

ruca (*Chile*) a typical hut of the **araucanos** = choza típica de los **araucanos**.

rucio(a) (*Chile*) blond = rubio(a).

rufo (*from English*) a roof = techo.

rula (*from English*) a ruler = regla.

ruleteo (*Ven.*) to impose or ask for unnecessary paperwork = pedir trámites innecesarios.

ruma (*Ecua., Peru, Ven.*) a pile = pila; montón; rimero.

rumbeador (*Argen.*) familiar with the route; **baqueano** = conocedor del camino o el derrotero; **baqueano**.

rumbear See **guarachar**.

rumbero 1. (*Colo.*) a person who likes to dance = al que le gusta mucho bailar. **2.** (*Puerto Rico*) a reveller = juerguista.

rumbo (*Guat.*) a spree = parranda; juerga.

rungo (*Hond.*) shabby; short = rechoncho; pequeño.

runrún 1. (*Argen.*) the sound of voices = hablar en voz baja. **2.** (*Argen.*) a murmur = murmuración. **3.** (*Chile*) a toy made with a big baton and a piece of string = bramadera; juguete hecho de un bastón grande y un bramante o cordel.

rustir 1. (*Ven.*) to work patiently = trabajar con paciencia. **2.** (*Ven.*) to endure pain patiently = soportar las penas con paciencia.

ruter (*from English*) a rooter; a machine that cuts roots = desarraigadora; máquina para cortar raíces.

rutero (*Mex.*) a newspaper deliverer = repartidor del periódico.

S

sabido (*Colo.*) an expert = experto.

sabora (*Ven.*) a light fog = niebla poco densa.

sabrosón (*Dom. Rep.*) a delightful person = persona muy simpática.

sabrosura (*Dom. Rep.*) a delight = dulzura; deleite.

sacamicas See **lambón**.

sacar chocoliya (*Salva.*) to hurry up; to speed up = apresurar.

sacar la leche (*Colo.*) to take advantage = aprovecharse.

sacarle la ñoña (*Chile*) to beat someone up = darle una gran golpiza.

sacarle ñachi (*Chile*) to give someone a punch in the nose that produces blood (informal) = dar un golpe en la nariz que saca sangre (informal).

sacarse el clavo (*Colo.*) to retaliate; to take revenge = desquitarse; vengarse.

sacarse el ratón (*Ven.*) to drink a little bit of alcohol to get rid of a hangover = beber un poco de licor para liberarse de la resaca.

sacarse el sombrero (*Chile*) to show respect and/or admiration = mostrar respeto y/o admiración.

sacarse la cresta 1. (*Chile*) to make sacrifices (vulgar) = sacrificarse (vulgar). **2.** (*Chile*) to suffer a hard blow (vulgar) = sufrir un golpe duro; golpearse fuertemente (vulgar).

sacatear (*Mex.*) to avoid = evitar.

saco 1. (*Colo., Cuba, Dom. Rep., Mex., Pan.*) a suit jacket = chaqueta; chaqueta del traje. **2.** (*Chile, Puerto Rico*) a sack; a big and strong bag = costal; bolsa grande y fuerte.

saco de viaje (*Colo.*) a suitcase = valija; maleta.

sacoleva; sacolevita (*Colo.*) a tuxedo; a tailored dress coat = traje de etiqueta; esmoquín.

sacolevita See **sacoleva.**

sacotín (*Colo.*) an illegal distillery = destilería ilegal.

safacón; zafacón (*Puerto Rico*) a garbage can = basurero; tacho de la basura.

safornado; sollamado (*Nic.*) with a rash = con la piel irritada.

sail (*from English*) a sale = liquidación; oferta especial; venta especial.

sain (*from English*) a sign = cartel.

sainear (*from English*) to sign = firmar; estampar la firma.

salado 1. (*Argen., Chile*) difficult; expensive = difícil; caro. **2.** (*Bol.*) to be unlucky = tener mala suerte. **3.** (*Colo.*) bad luck = mala suerte. **4.** (*Costa Rica, Puerto Rico*) a misfortune; a mishap = desgracia; infortunio; fatalidad.

salame (*Argen.*) silly; slow; naive = tonto; poco listo; ingenuo.

salar (*Colo., Cuba, Mex., Puerto Rico*) to bring or give bad luck = traer o dar mala suerte.

salarete (*Mex.*) baking powder; bicarbonate of soda = polvos para hornear; bicarbonato de sosa.

salazón (*Guat.*) bad luck = mala suerte; desgracia.

salchicha (*Colo., Ecua., Peru*) a hot dog = (N.E. emparedado de salchicha).

salcochar (*Dom. Rep.*) to boil = sancochar.

salcocho; sancocho 1. (*Colo., Puerto Rico, Ven.*) a stew prepared with varieties of meats and vegetables = estofado; guisado preparado con carnes y vegetales variados. **2.** (*Cuba*) leftovers; food scraps used to feed pigs = sobras de comida; sobrantes para alimentar a los cerdos. **3.** (*Dom. Rep.*) a dish prepared with yucca, meat, plan-tains, and cocoa = plato compuesto por yuca, carne, banana y cacao.

sale (*from English*) a sale = liquidación.

salitre (*Chile*) saltpeter; nitrate = nitrato natural que se produce en el desierto del norte chileno.

salón (*Colo., Dom. Rep., Puerto Rico*) a classroom = aula de enseñanza.

salpicón 1. (*Colo., Ecua.*) a drink made with pieces of different fruits = bebida con trozos de diferentes frutas. **2.** (*Chile*) a mixed salad with vegetables and meats = ensalada mixta de verduras y carnes.

salquipanqui (*Dom. Rep.*) a male or female prostitute = hombre o mujer que ejerce el comercio sexual.

salsa (*Colo.*) (N.E. a specific kind of popular Caribbean dance music) = (N.E. salsa; un tipo específico de música caribeña popular bailable).

salsamentaria (*Colo.*) a retail store for meats and sausages = expendio de carnes y embutidos.

salsómano (*Colo.*) a **salsa** music fanatic = fanático de la música **salsa.**

salta pa'l lado 1. (*Chile*) Do not interfere (informal). = no interfieras (informal). **2.** (*Chile*) What you are saying is a lie; I don't believe you (informal). = lo que dices es una mentira; no te creo (informal).

saltagatos (*Colo.*) a grasshopper = saltamontes; langosta de campo.

saltar el lazo (*Colo.*) to jump rope = saltar a la cuerda.

saltar la cuica (*Puerto Rico*) to jump rope = saltar a la cuerda.

saltar la soga (*Cuba, Ecua., Peru*) to jump rope = saltar a la cuerda.

saltar matojo (*Colo.*) to have money problems = estar en dificultades económicas.

salteñas (*Bol.*) a small pie of vegetables and/or meats and spices; a typical Bolivian patty = empanada pequeña de vegetales y/o carnes y especias; empanadas típicas bolivianas.

saltón (*Chile, Colo.*) half-cooked = a medio cocinar.

salvar (*from English*) to save = ahorrar; guardar; poner a recaudo.

sambumbia (*Puerto Rico*) badly-prepared food or drink = comida o bebida mal preparada.

samuro; zamuro (*Colo., Ven.*) a buzzard = buitre; zopilote.

sanandresito (*Colo.*) a contraband merchandise market = mercado de artículos de contrabando.

sanata (*Argen.*) an argument; a reproach = argumento; reprobación.

sancochao (*Puerto Rico*) heated = acalorado; sudado.

sancochar (*Colo.*) to cook in water with salt = cocer un alimento en agua con sal.

sancocho See **salcocho**.

sanduche (*Colo.*) a sandwich = emparedado; sándwich.

sandunga (*Chile, Mex., Peru, Puerto Rico*) a spree = jarana; algarabía; jolgorio.

sándwich; sánguche (*from English*) a sandwich = (RAE) emparedado hecho con dos rebanadas de pan entre las que se coloca jamón, queso u otros alimentos.

sángano 1. (*Puerto Rico*) an insult = insulto. **2.** (*Puerto Rico*) stupid = estúpido.

sangaraña (*Ecua.*) an indirect way to say something = lo que se dice de una manera indirecta.

sango (*Peru*) stilts = zancos.

sangre (*Ven.*) blood pudding; blood sausage = morcilla.

sangriento (*Dom. Rep.*) an unfriendly person = hostil; poco amistoso.

sanguaraña (*Peru*) to say something indirectly = decir algo de una manera indirecta.

sánguche See **sándwich**.

sanjuanear (*Colo.*) to be uneasy = estar inquieto.

sanjuanito (*Colo.*) a dance = baile; aire musical.

santa clos (*from English*) Santa Claus = (N.E. el que trae regalos para navidad; San Nicolás)

santería (*Puerto Rico*) a mixture of ancestral African beliefs and Catholic traditions; the practice of commingling magic and religion = mezcla de creencias africanas ancestrales y tradiciones católicas; práctica de una mezcla de magia y religión.

santero (*Puerto Rico*) a person who practices **santería** = el que practica la **santería**.

santulario(a) (*Para.*) sanctimonious = santurrón(na).

sapear See **chivatear**.

sapo 1. (*Chile*) a spy = espía. **2.** (*Chile*) the lookout person during a crime = el vigía durante una fechoría. **3.** (*Chile*) You are looking too much; You are looking for something that you shouldn't (informal). = estás mirando mucho; estás mirando algo que no debes mirar (informal).

saquito (*Colo.*) a boy's suit jacket = chaqueta de traje de niño.

sarapa (*Colo.*) leftovers = sobrados; sobras de comida.

sarape (*Guat.*) a cape = **poncho**; capote de monte.

sarazo; zarazo (*Colo., Ven.*) half-ripe fruit; fruit that is not ripe and gets hard = fruto a medio madurar; fruto inmaduro que se endurece.

sardina(o) 1. (*Mex.*) a person without any social value; socially insignificant = persona sin valor social; sin significado social. **2.** (*Colo.*) a teenager; an adolescent = adolescente.

sardinel 1. (*Colo.*) a sidewalk = acera. **2.** (*Ven.*) a curb = cuneta.

sarmiento (*Chile*) a slip; a cutting = esqueje; tallo o cogollo que se introduce en la tierra para reproducir la planta.

saya (*Cuba*) a skirt = falda.

saya interior; sayuela (*Cuba*) an underskirt; a slip = enaguas.

sayuela See **saya interior**.

se choteó (*Guat.*) it has been used too much = se ha usado mucho; es muy trillado.

se formó el tilingo (*Cuba*) something that causes an uproar; a problem has arisen; there is a problem = algo ha causado un alboroto; se produjo un lío; hay un problema.

se fue al pihuelo (*Chile*) it failed = falló; fracasó.

se le encendió el bombillo (*Cuba*) he or she got it = lo entendió.

se le pegaron las cobijas (*Mex.*) to oversleep = dormir más de la cuenta.

se le pegó el vellón (*Puerto Rico*) he or she did not like the joke = no le gustó la broma.

se puso hasta los queques (*Nic.*) he or she got drunk as a fish = se emborrachó del todo.

seboro (*Bol.*) a freshwater crab = cangrejo de agua dulce.

secador (*Mex.*) napkins = servilleta.

secante (*Argen.*) bothersome; annoying = molesto; pesado.

secarse (*Colo.*) to become rigid from laughing, crying or the effects of anger = ponerse rígido por efectos de la risa, el llanto o la ira.

seco 1. (*Chile*) parsimonious; serious = grave; serio; mezquino. **2.** (*Chile*) without money = sin dinero. **3.** (*Colo.*) a main course at lunch or dinner = plato principal del almuerzo o de la cena.

seguranza 1. (*from English*) insurance = seguro del automóvil o la casa. **2.** (*from English*) an insurance company = compañía de seguros.

segurito See **asegurador**.

seguro 1. (*Argen., Bol., Ecua., Mex., Peru, Uru.*) honest = honesto; honrado. **2.** See **asegurador**.

seibó (*Puerto Rico*) the furniture in which silverware and other articles for the dinner table are kept = mueble donde se guarda la vajilla y otros artículos para la mesa.

seibo (*Dom. Rep.*) a sideboard = mueble donde se guardan la vajilla y otros artículos para el cubierto de la mesa.

self control (*from English*) self-control = autocontrol.

selfservice [pron. selfservis] (*from English*) self-service = autoservicio.

sello (*Cuba, Peru, Puerto Rico*) a stamp = estampilla; sello de correos.

sencillero (*Ecua., Peru*) a peddler = buhonero; vendedor callejero que vende a plazos.

sencillo (*Chile*) money; change = menudo; cambio.

sendo (*Ven.*) the superlative for big, magnificent = superlativo para descomunal, magnífico.

sentador(a) (*from English*) a babysitter = cuidador(a) de niños.

sentarse en la palabra (*Colo.*) to monopolize the conversation = monopolizar toda la conversación.

sentencia (*from English*) a grammatical sentence = oración gramatical.

señorita (*Ven.*) a small crane = grúa pequeña.

sepe (*Bol.*) termites = termitas.

ser aguasado (*Peru*) to be shy; to behave shyly = ser tímido; comportarse tímidamente.

ser arrecho (*Salva.*) to be good = ser bueno.

ser calzón (*Dom. Rep.*) to be stupid = comportarse estúpidamente.

ser la sal (*Colo.*) to have bad luck = tener mala suerte.

ser pavo (*Chile*) to be a turkey; to behave in a silly way = comportarse tontamente o estúpidamente.

serape (*Mex.*) a light blanket; a shawl = frazada o manta liviana; chal.

serenar (*Colo.*) a light rain; a drizzle = lluvia liviana; llovizna.

serruchar (*Dom. Rep.*) to saw = aserruchar.

serrucho (*Dom. Rep.*) a contribution in equal parts to buy something as a group = contribución en partes iguales para comprar algo en grupo.

servicial (*Bol.*) a servant; the domestic service personnel = criado; sirviente; personal de servicio doméstico.

sestear (*Dom. Rep.*) to take a nap = tomar una siesta.

sesudo (*Hond., Mex.*) stubborn; obstinate = terco; testarudo; tozudo.

set (*from English*) a set = serie; juego; conjunto.

setas (*Puerto Rico*) mushrooms = hongos.

setear (*from English*) to set = acomodar; arreglar; poner en orden.

sex appeal [pron. sexapil] (*from English*) sex appeal = gancho; atractivo sexual.

sexapiloso (*Colo.*) with sex appeal = que tiene atractivo sexual.

sexy 1. (*from English*) a sexy (person) = atractivo sexual o sensual. **2.** (*from English*) a sexy environment = ambiente sexual o sensual.

sherry [pron. cherri] (*from English*) sherry = licor de cerezas; jerez.

shock (*from English*) a shock = conmoción; choque psicológico.

shop (*Argen., Chile*) a draft beer = cerveza del barril.

shoquer (*from English*) a shock absorber = amortiguador de un vehículo.

short (*from English*) short = pantalón corto.

show 1. (*from English*) a show (performance) = función; espectáculo. **2.** (*from English*) a show (arts) = exposición; exhibición.

showman (*from English*) a showman = director del espectáculo; animador.

sicote; cicote (*Costa Rica, Cuba, Dom. Rep., Puerto Rico*) the smell of dirty feet = mal olor de los pies.

sicotudo See **cicotudo.**

siete (*Argen.*) the bottom (informal) = trasero (informal).

sifón (*Colo.*) a draft beer = cerveza del barril.

sifrino (*Ven.*) a snob = (N.E. **esnob**, el que trata de aparentar elegancia y sofisticación).

isiga! (*Colo.*) Go ahead! Come in! = ¡adelante!; ¡entre!

silbatina (*Argen., Chile, Para.*) booing by whistling or hissing for a long time = abucheo o rechifla prolongada.

silgado (*Ecua.*) thin = delgado; flaco.

simpa (*Peru*) a braid = trenza.

simpático (*Colo.*) good-looking = de buena presencia.

sinc (*from English*) a sink = fregadero.

sindicado (*Chile, Colo., Ecua., Ven.*) accused = acusado.

sindicar (*Chile, Colo., Ecua., Ven.*) to accuse = acusar.

single 1. (*from English*) single = sencillo; único. **2.** (*from English*) single (person) = soltero.

síper (*from English*) a zipper = cierre relámpago; cierre de cremallera.

sipo (*Ecua.*) pockmarked = picado de viruelas.

siripita 1. (*Bol.*) a cricket = grillo. **2.** (*Bol.*) a meddlesome child = niño(a) entrometido(a).

sirop (*from English*) syrup = jarabe acaramelado.

sisote (*Mex.*) a skin inflammation = inflamación de la piel.

siútico (*Chile*) pseudo-refined; affected = cursi.

skating [pron. eskeitin] (*from English*) skating = patinaje.

skeitinrom (*from English*) a skating rink = salón de patinaje.

slaid [pron. eslaid] (*from English*) a slide = diapositiva; filmina.

slip See **eslip.**

smog (*from English*) the smog = niebla tóxica.

snack (*from English*) a snack = tentempié; bocadillo.

sobada; sobijo (*Colo.*) to set bones = encajar; arreglar una fractura o una dislocación de hueso.

sobadera (*Colo.*) an annoying thing; a bothersome thing = fastidio; molestia.

sobado 1. (*Colo.*) a difficult, bothersome person = persona difícil; cargante; pesado. **2.** (*Colo.*) a dangerous thing = lo que acarrea riesgo peligroso.

sobador; sobandero (*Colo.*) a bonesetter = el que encaja huesos quebrado; el que arregla fracturas o huesos dislocados.

sobandero See **sobador**.

sobar (*Argen.*) to flatter = adular.

sobijo See **sobada**.

soborno (*Ecua.*) an extra load; a load that is over the limit = carga en exceso; más carga que la que se pueda soportar.

sobrado(a) (*Chile*) presumptuous; he or she acts superior to everybody else = impertinente; engreído; presumido; el/la que se cree mejor o superior a los demás.

sobrar (*Argen.*) to anticipate someone's intentions; to act quickly before others = anticiparse; adivinar las intenciones del otro; actuar con astucia anticipadamente.

sobrebarriga (*Colo.*) a cut of beef = corte de carne de res.

sobrecama (*Colo., Cuba, Mex., Pan., Peru*) a bedspread = cubrecama.

sobretodo (*Chile*) a woman's coat = abrigo femenino.

socapar a uno (*Bol., Ecua., Mex.*) to cover up for someone = reemplazar; cubrir la actividad de otro.

socate (*Ven.*) an electric socket or bulbholder = portalámparas.

socket (*from English*) an electric socket = portalámparas.

soco; zoco 1. (*Colo.*) one-armed = manco. **2.** (*Colo.*) a broom or mop that is completely worn out = escoba o trapero completamente gastados. **3.** (*Colo.*) a stump = muñón; parte que queda de un miembro recortado.

socola (*Colo.*) to clear of shrubs = desbrozar; desmalezar.

soda 1. (*Mex., Pan., Peru*) soda = gaseosa. **2.** (*Cuba*) excellent = excelente.

softwere [pron. sofgüear] (*from English*) software = (N.E. procedimiento; procesos; lógica programable computarizada).

soga (*Ven.*) a rope = cuerda.

soguear; triscar (*Colo.*) to mock someone; to make fun of someone = burlarse de alguien.

solera 1. (*Chile*) curb = cuneta; encintado de la acera. **2.** (*Chile*) a summer dress = vestido de verano. **3.** (*Mex.*) a floor tile; a paving stone = piso de baldosa; piso de piedra.

solfear (*Argen.*) to rob = hurtar; robar.

sólido (*Costa Rica*) a wealthy person = persona adinerada; persona solvente.

sollamado See **saforno**.

soltar prenda (*Argen.*) to reveal a secret = revelar un secreto.

solterón (*Colo.*) an individual's clothes rack that is placed next to the bed = perchero individual que se usa junto a la cama.

soltura (*Colo., Mex., Ven.*) diarrhea = diarrea.

somatar (*Hond.*) to slash; to beat = zurrar; dar de golpes.

sombrilla 1. (*Colo., Cuba, Dom. Rep., Peru, Puerto Rico*) an umbrella = paraguas. **2.** (*Puerto Rico*) a beach umbrella = quitasol.

somier (*Chile*) a spring mattress = colchón de muelles.

sonajear (*Mex.*) to spank a child = dar de palmadas a un niño.

sonar 1. (*Argen., Chile*) to fail = fracasar. **2.** (*Argen., Chile*) to have a big loss = sufrir una gran pérdida.

sonastes (*Argen., Chile*) you lose = perdiste; fracasaste.

sonsonete (*Colo.*) a scolding that lasts and lasts = regañina continuada.

soñar con pajaritos de oro (*Colo.*) to have illusions or fantasies about something = hacerse vanas ilusiones.

sopa de cuerda (*Nic.*) to gossip continuously = chismear continuamente.

sopaipilla (*Chile*) thin, fried round bread made of wheat flour and pumpkin = pan frito redondo y delgado preparado con harina de trigo y calabaza.

soplado 1. (*Colo.*) fast = muy rápido. **2.** (*Colo.*) angry = enfadado.

soplador (*Bol., Ecua., Guat.*) a prompter in the theater = apuntador; el que ayuda a los actores susurrándoles el libreto a medida que transcurre la obra.

soplar 1. (*Ven.*) to defeat others in a contest = vencer a los otros en un concurso. **2.** (*Ven.*) to kill = matar.

sopletón (*Mex.*) a severe beating = paliza muy severa.

sorbete 1. (*Cuba, Peru, Puerto Rico*) a drinking straw = pajita; paja para beber. **2.** (*Guat., Hond., Mex., Salva.*) an ice cream cone = barquillo.

sorbeto 1. (*Puerto Rico*) a drinking straw = paja para beber. **2.** (*Pan.*) sherbet = sorbete.

sorete 1. (*Argen., Uru.*) solid human feces (vulgar) = excremento humano sólido (vulgar). **2.** (*Uru.*) an insult; stupid = insulto; estúpido.

sorochi (*Bol.*) high-mountain sickness; **puna** = **puna**; enfermedad producida por la altura de la montaña.

sorullo (*Argen.*) villainous; a nasty person = persona vil; canalla.

sota (*Chile*) ten years off my age = diez años de mi edad.

spankear (*from English*) to spank = dar de nalgadas a un niño.

spich (*from English*) a speech = discurso.

spiker (*from English*) a speaker = locutor.

sportivo (*from English*) sporty = deportivo.

sportman (*from English*) a sportsman = deportista.

spot (*from English*) a spot = espacio publicitario en radio o televisión.

spreadsheet [pron. spridshit] (*from English*) a spreadsheet on the computer screen = hojas de cálculo; planilla.

sprint (*from English*) a sprint = esfuerzo final en una carrera deportiva.

sprintar (*from English*) to sprint = acelerar.

stand (*from English*) a stand = puesto; cada uno de los locales en una exposición.

star (*from English*) a star = estrella del espectáculo o del cine.

starter (*from English*) a starter = motor de arranque.

status 1. (*from English*) a position of status = posición; condición; rango; categoría. **2.** (*from English*) social status = prestigio; reputación; estado; situación.

stencil (*from English*) a stencil = (RAE) papel de troquel para multicopiar en un **mimeógrafo**.

stepiar 1. (*from English*) to step (on) = poner el pie encima; pisar. **2.** (*from English*) to step (walk) = dar un paso.

stering (*from English*) a steering wheel = volante del automóvil.

stocar (*from English*) to stock = almacenar; guardar existencias.

stock 1. (*from English*) stock (in the store) = surtido; existencias. **2.** (*from English*) stock (storage) = mercancías almacenadas; existencia; provisión. **3.** (*from English*) stocks (financial market) = valores; acciones; capital comercial.

stop 1. (*from English*) a (traffic) stop = alto; pare. **2.** (*from English*) to stop = parar; detener. **3.** (*from English*) a stop (telegraphic transmissions) = punto en las transmisiones inalámbricas.

straique (*from English*) to strike = herir; golpear; azotar.

string (*from English*) a string = cordel.

striptease [pron. striptis] (*from English*) a striptease = (N.E. espectáculo en que un artista se desprende lentamente de la ropa).

suamp (*from English*) a swamp = ciénaga; pantano.

suampo (*Hond.*) a swamp = pantano.

suapear (*Dom. Rep.*) to mop the floor; to swab = trapear; limpiar el piso con un trapo.

suave 1. (*Mex.*) soft; smooth = blando; muelle; tierno. **2.** (*Mex.*) very good; cool = fantástico; muy bueno.

sube y baja (*Argen., Mex., Peru, Puerto Rico*) a seesaw = balancín.

subterráneo (*Chile, Pan.*) a basement = sótano.

suche 1. (*Chile, Nic.*) the lower status in a job = empleado de última categoría. **2.** (*Chile, Nic.*) a subordinate = subalterno. **3.** (*Ecua., Peru*) a tree that produces lumber for construction = suchil; árbol que produce madera para construcción. **4.** (*Ven.*) bitter; not ripe enough = agrio; sin madurar.

sucucho (*Chile*) a small and neglected house = casa muy pequeña y arruinada.

sudor (*Colo., Para.*) a hot medicine that makes one sweat = medicina caliente para provocar sudor.

sueco; zueco (*Dom. Rep.*) an old shoe = zapato viejo.

suelazo (*Ecua.*) a heavy fall; a nasty bump = butacazo; golpe contra el suelo.

suera (*from English*) a sweater = chaqueta o blusa tejida; **suéter**.

suerte (*Peru*) a lottery ticket = boleto de la lotería.

suertero 1. (*Ecua.*) a lucky one; fortunate = afortunado. **2.** (*Peru*) a lottery ticket seller = el que vende boletos de la lotería.

suertudo(a) (*Argen., Chile, Para.*) a lucky person = el que tiene suerte; afortunado.

suéter (*from English*) a sweater = (RAE) **jersey**, chaqueta de lana con tejido de punto.

suich (*from English*) a switch = interruptor.

suiche (*Colo.*) a switch = interruptor eléctrico.

suing 1. (*from English*) a swing made with the fist, as to strike a blow = golpe lateral. **2.** (*from English*) a swing = balanceo. **3.** (*from English*) swing (music) = ritmo.

suinsuan See **buinsuan**.

suitqueis (*from English*) a suitcase = valija.

sulfúrico (*Ecua.*) irascible; irritable = irascible; irritable; el que se enoja fácilmente.

suncán (*Hond.*) a fool; silly = bobo; tonto.

suncho (*Chile*) a metallic tape used to package heavy loads = cinta metálica para empaquetar carga pesada.

suple 1. (*Chile*) a part of the wages paid in advance = lo que se adelanta a cuenta del jornal. **2.** (*Chile*) supplementary = suplemento; añadido a.

suplementero(a) (*Chile*) a newspaper boy = vendedor(a) de periódicos.

surf (*from English*) surfing = (N.E. deporte que se practica deslizándose sobre las olas).

surfear (*from English*) to surf = (N.E. practicar el **surf**).

surfista (*from English*) a surfer; a person who surfs = (N.E. el que practica el **surf**).

surrunguear (*Colo.*) to strum = rasguear; tocar un instrumento de cuerdas.

surumbo (*Guat., Hond.*) bewildered; a prize idiot; foolish; stupid = aturdido; tonto lelo; idiota.

sute (*Colo., Ven.*) a weak or puny person = enteco; canijo; persona débil.

suvenir (*from English*) a souvenir = recuerdo; objeto recordatorio.

symposium (*from English*) a symposium = simposio.

T

ta (*Uru.*) it is all right = está bien.

tabaco 1. (*Colo., Cuba, Ven.*) a cigar = cigarro puro; cigarro; puro. **2.** (*Colo.*) a blow with the fist = golpe con el puño cerrado.

tabanco (*Nic.*) the second floor = segundo piso.

tabas (*Argen.*) foot or hand bones = huesos de las piernas y/o de los pies.

tablero (*Colo., Dom. Rep., Mex., Pan.*) a blackboard = pizarrón; pizarra.

tablero de anuncios (*Colo.*) a bulletin board = tablero mural; anunciador mural.

tablilla (*Puerto Rico*) a car's plate = matrícula de identificación de un vehículo.

tablilla de anuncios (*Cuba*) a bulletin board = anunciador mural; tablero mural.

taca (*Chile*) a small clam = almeja pequeña.

tacazo (*Dom. Rep.*) a big drink of hard liquor = trago grande de licor fuerte.

tachero (*Argen.*) a taxi driver = taxista.

tacho de la basura (*Argen.*) a garbage can = basurero.

taco 1. (*Chile*) a traffic jam = atasco del tráfico. **2.** (*Chile*) a short person = persona de poca estatura. **3.** (*Ecua., Peru*) a short and fat person = persona gorda de baja estatura. **4.** (*Mex.*) (N.E. a Mexican **tortilla** made of corn flour folded and filled with different ingredients) = (N.E. **tortilla** mexicana de maíz doblada y rellena de diferentes ingredientes.) **5.** (*Ven.*) an expert = experto.

tacón (*Ven.*) pieces of bread soaked in eggs with sugar and fried = fritos preparados con rodajas de pan duro remojados en huevos y azúcar.

tacotillo (*Mex.*) a tumor; a skin irritation = tumor; irritación de la piel.

tacuache (*Mex.*) drunk = ebrio.

tacuara (*Para.*) the native bamboo of the Río de la Plata basin = bambú nativo de la cuenca del Río de la Plata.

tafia (*Ven.*) rum = ron.

taguara (*Ven.*) any small store that sells food and liquor = cualquier tienda pequeña que vende licor y comida.

tai (*from English*) a tie = corbata.

tailor (*from English*) a tailor = sastre.

taimado (*Chile*) obstinate; stubborn = tenaz; porfiado en no hacer algo.

taimin (*from English*) timing = tiempo empleado; duración.

taipear; tipear (*from English*) to type = teclear; escribir en un teclado.

tair (*from English*) a tire = goma o neumático del automóvil.

taita 1. (*Bol.*) "father" in the Quechua and Aimará languages = padre, en las lenguas aimará y quechua. **2.** (*Argen., Chile*) a term of respect for a father or any old man = tratamiento de respeto al padre o a un anciano. **3.** (*Ven.*) father or mother = padre o madre.

tajada (*Ven.*) a slice of fried ripe banana = rebanada de plátano maduro frito.

tajamar 1. (*Argen., Chile, Colo.*) a breakwater; a dike; a sea wall = dique; malecón; defensa en las orillas de un río. **2.** (*Para.*) a small pond = pequeña laguna. **3.** (*Para.*) a pond from which animals drink = pozo para que beba el ganado.

tajeadura (*Argen., Chile*) a big wound from a cut on the body = gran herida cortante en el cuerpo.

tala (*Puerto Rico*) a parcel = sembrado; hacienda pequeña; parcela.

talaje (*Chile*) animal food = alimento para los animales.

talamoco (*Ecua.*) an albino = albino.

talanquera (*Colo.*) a fence made with cane = cerca de cañas.

talego (*Colo.*) shoelaces = lazos de zapatos.

talla (*Chile*) a joke; a practical joke = chiste; broma que se hace a otra persona.

tallar (*Mex.*) to scrub; to wash clothes = resfregar; lavar la ropa.

tambembe (*Chile*) the buttocks (informal) = trasero (informal).

tambo (*Mex.*) a jail = cárcel.

tambor (*Mex.*) a spring mattress = colchón de muelles.

tamboreatear (*Mex.*) to beat up = golpear; dar una paliza.

tan rápido como entierro de pobre (*Cuba*) something happened very quickly = algo pasó muy rápido.

tanda 1. (*Colo., Cuba, Mex., Ven.*) a section of a theatrical performance = sección de una función teatral. 2. (*Peru*) a beating = golpiza. 3. (*Ven.*) a short, dramatic play = pieza dramática corta.

tandear (*Chile*) to make jokes and tease each other = hacerse bromas y reírse unos de otros.

tanela (*Costa Rica*) pastries = repostería.

tangalear (*Hond.*) to waste time = empatar; demorar intencionalmente; hacer tiempo.

tángana 1. (*Cuba, Mex.*) a brawl = alboroto. 2. (*Ven.*) a quarrel; a verbal fight = riña; discusión.

tangána; titingó (*Puerto Rico*) a brawl = alboroto.

tanganazo (*Ven.*) a strong blow = golpe muy fuerte.

tango (*Hond.*) a percussion instrument = instrumento de percusión.

tano (*Uru.*) a nickname for an Italian = apodo para un italiano.

tantear 1. (*Hond.*) to be on the watch for = estar al acecho. 2. (*Mex.*) to fool = engañar.

tapabarros (*Chile*) a fender = guardafangos.

tapado 1. (*Argen., Chile, Para., Salva.*) a light and fancy woman's coat = abrigo liviano y elegante de señora. 2. (*Colo., Guat., Hond.*) meat and plantain packed in leaves that are cooked in a hole in the ground = carnes y plátano envueltos en hojas y cocinados en un hoyo en el suelo. 3. (*Colo.*) clumsy; ignorant = torpe; ignorante. 4. (*Colo.*) a hypocrite; sly; sneaky = hipócrita; solapado. 5. (*Mex.*) constipated = estreñido. 6. (*Peru*) buried treasure = tesoro enterrado. 7. (*Salva.*) a sweet prepared with **panela** = dulce preparado con **panela**. 8. (*Ven.*) stupid = bruto.

tapalodo (*Puerto Rico*) an automobile fender = guardabarro; cubrelodo o tapabarro del automóvil.

tapanco (*Guat.*) an attic = buhardilla.

taparrabos (*Ecua., Peru*) diapers = pañales.

taparse (*Colo.*) to make a fortune = amasar una fortuna.

tapatío 1. (*Mex.*) a native of Guadalajara = originario de Guadalajara. 2. (*Mex.*) something that is very Mexican; it is pure Mexican = lo que es auténticamente mexicano; lo que es bien mexicano o puro mexicano.

tapeque (*Bol.*) travel gear = avíos de viaje.

tapesco (*Nic.*) a mat used over the fire to smoke food = estera que se usa sobre los fogones para ahumar comida.

tapilla (*Chile, Costa Rica, Ecua.*) a spike = estaquilla; suela del tacón.

tapiscar (*Hond.*) to rip the leaves off the corncob = desgarrar las hojas de la mazorca.

tapón 1. (*Colo.*) varnish = barniz. 2. (*Puerto Rico*) a traffic jam = atasco; embotellamiento del tráfico.

tapudo (*Nic.*) a tattletale = chismoso.

taqueada (*Colo.*) a reprimand = reprimenda.

taqueado(a) (*Colo.*) full of food = lleno(a) de comida.

taquear 1. (*Colo.*) to obstruct; to cover = obstruir; tapar. 2. (*Colo.*) to rebuke; to reprimand = amonestar; reprender. 3. (*Colo.*) to pack; to cram; to stuff with = atiborrar; atestar.

taquiara (*Colo.*) a body ornament of the Guajiro Indians = adorno corporal de los indios guajiros.

taquilla 1. (*Ecua., Peru*) a tack = tachuela. 2. (*Guat., Hond., Salva.*) a liquor store = tienda de licores. 3. (*Guat., Hond., Salva.*) a bar = taberna.

tarabita (*Colo.*) a cableway; a cable ferry = andarivel.

tarado (*Uru.*) dumb (vulgar) = tonto; torpe; (vulgar).

tarajallo (*Ven.*) a youngster who is physically overdeveloped = muchacho muy crecido y corpulento para su edad.

taramba (*Hond.*) a stringed instrument used to play Honduran folk music = instrumento de cuerda que se usa para tocar música folclórica hondureña.

taranta (*Hond.*) a faint = desvanecimiento.

tarantín (*Ven.*) a small and poor store = tienducha; tienda pequeña y pobre.

tarasca (*Chile, Colo., Costa Rica, Peru*) a big mouth = boca grande.

tarascón (*Argen., Bol., Chile, Ecua.*) a big bite = mordiscón.

tarea (*Para.*) a harvest performed by several people = cosecha ejecutada entre varios.

tareco (*Cuba, Ecua.*) odds and ends; junk = cachivaches; chatarra; desperdicios.

tarjar (*Chile*) to cross out = tachar.

tarro de la basura (*Chile, Ecua., Peru*) a garbage can = basurero.

tarro 1. (*Argen.*) luck = suerte. **2.** (*Colo., Ecua., Para., Peru*) a tin can = lata; envase de hojalata. **3.** (*Cuba*) the horns on animals = cuernos. **4.** (*Guat.*) the native bamboo of Central America = bambú nativo de Centro América.

tartana (*Puerto Rico*) an old car; a car that is in bad shape = automóvil viejo o en mal estado.

tartancho(a) See **lenguachuta**.

tarugo (*Colo.*) a concern = preocupación.

tasajudo (*Bol.*) thin and long = flaco y largo.

tasin (*Ecua.*) a nest = nido; nidal.

tatá See **tata**.

tata; tatá 1. (*Bol.*) "father" in the Quechua and Aimará languages = padre, en las lenguas aimará y quechua. **2.** (*Argen.,*

Chile) a term of respect for a father or any old man = tratamiento de respeto al padre o a un anciano. **3.** (*Chile*) a grandfather = abuelo.

tatú (*Para.*) the vagina (vulgar) = vagina (vulgar).

taun (*from English*) a town = ciudad; pueblo.

tax; taxa (*from English*) a tax = impuesto.

taxa See **tax**.

taxi girl [pron. taxiguer] (*from English*) a taxi girl = (N.E. mujer pagada para bailar con los clientes de un local; prostituta que visita al cliente después de ser solicitada por teléfono.)

taza del baño (*Peru*) a toilet = retrete; inodoro; excusado.

te la comiste (*Cuba*) You did a hell of a job. = has hecho un magnífico trabajo.

te llamo para atrás (*from English*) I will call you back. = te devuelvo la llamada.

te miteo (*from English*) I will meet with you. = me reuniré o me juntaré contigo.

te voy a chillar (*Salva.*) I will shut you up. = te voy a callar.

tecato (*Puerto Rico*) a drug addict = drogadicto.

tecla shift (*from English*) the shift key = tecla de bloqueo de mayúsculas.

tecolote (*Mex.*) an owl = lechuza; búho.

tegua (*Colo.*) a medicine man = curandero.

teip (*from English*) any tape = cinta; tela adhesiva.

teipear (*from English*) to tape = grabar electrónicamente.

tembleque (*Puerto Rico*) a dessert with jelly and coconut = postre de jalea y coco.

tembó (*Para.*) the penis (vulgar) = pene (vulgar).

temperar (*Ven.*) to change the environment temporarily in order to rest = cambiar de ambiente para descansar.

templado (*Bol., Ecua., Peru*) to be in love; to be in an amorous disposition = estar enamorado; enamoradizo; ser enamorado.

templar (*Bol., Ecua., Peru*) to fall in love = enamorarse.

templarse (*Guat., Ecua.*) to die = morirse.

tenche (*Puerto Rico*) a strong man = hombre fornido y fuerte.

tendajo (*Mex.*) a small store = tienda pequeña.

tendal 1. (*Para.*) several things spread on a surface = profusión de cosas diseminadas. **2.** (*Para.*) an abundance; a large amount = abundancia; gran cantidad.

tendalada 1. (*Chile*) a disorder = desorden; profusión de cosas desordenadas. **2.** (*Chile*) a disaster = desastre.

tener agallas (*Chile*) to have courage; to be brave = ser osado; ser audaz.

tener coraje (*Dom. Rep.*) to be angry = estar enojado(a).

tener dengue (*Colo.*) to be ill = estar enfermo.

tener guano (*Cuba*) to have money (informal) = tener dinero (informal).

tener leche (*Puerto Rico*) to be lucky = tener suerte.

tener muñeca 1. (*Chile*) to play well in the political field; to handle difficult social conflicts skillfully = ser hábil en la política; saber manejar bien situaciones sociales difíciles. **2.** (*Dom. Rep.*) to be cruel = ser cruel.

tener pana (*Chile*) to have courage = tener coraje.

tener pasas (*Cuba*) to have very curly hair (derogatory) = tener el cabello muy ensortijado (peyorativo).

tener polenta (*Argen.*) the ability and will to do something well = capacidad y voluntad de hacer algo bien.

tener un bajón (*Uru.*) to be depressed = estar deprimido.

tener una botella (*Cuba*) to be in a position of making large amounts of money without working for it = estar en una posición en que se hace mucho dinero sin trabajar.

tengo el hojo empillamado (*Colo.*) I am sleepy. = tengo sueño.

tenida (*Chile*) the best clothing for special events; party clothing = la mejor vestimenta para ocasiones especiales; ropa de fiesta.

tenis (*Colo., Cuba, Dom. Rep., Guat., Hond., Mex., Puerto Rico*) sneakers = (N.E. zapatos deportivos de goma; calzado deportivo).

tentenelaire (*Argen., Peru*) a hummingbird = colibrí; picaflor.

tepalcates (*Mex.*) goals or objects of little value = propósitos o cosas de muy poco valor.

tercena (*Colo., Ecua.*) a butcher shop = carnicería.

terciador (*Colo.*) a porter = cargador; el que lleva carga en su espalda.

terciar (*Colo.*) to carry on the back = cargar; llevar carga en la espalda.

terciazo (*Ven.*) an extraordinary person = persona con cualidades extraordinarias.

tercio (*Colo.*) a measure equal to five arrobas; five times 11.5 kilos = medida igual a cinco arrobas; cinco veces 11.5 kilos.

terco (*Ecua.*) insipid; without grace = desabrido; sin gracia.

tereque 1. (*Dom. Rep., Puerto Rico, Ven.*) a piece of junk = trasto viejo; cachivache; chatarra. **2.** (*Nic.*) any object or thing = cualquier objeto o cosa.

ternejo (*Ecua., Peru*) a brave person; a strong person = persona valiente, fuerte y vigorosa.

ternera (*Argen.*) a calf = pantorrilla.

terno (*Chile*) a two- or three-piece suit of the same color and fabric = traje de dos o tres piezas del mismo color y la misma tela.

terquedad (*Ecua.*) a harshness; a lack of feeling; an indifference = aspereza; falta de sentimientos; indiferencia.

terraza; testa; tusta (*Colo.*) the human head = cabeza humana.

terronera (*Colo.*) a scare; a fright = susto; miedo.

teruteru (*Para.*) the onomatopoeic name for the bird that makes that sound = voz onomatopéyica para el pájaro que emite ese sonido.

teso (*Colo.*) difficult; complicated = difícil; complicado.

test (*from English*) a test = (RAE) examen; prueba.

testa; tusta See **terraza**.

testiar (*from English*) to test = probar; tomar o dar un examen.

tete See **biberón**.

tetelque (*Nic.*) the taste of fruit when it is not ripe = sabor de la fruta que no está madura.

tetera (*Colo., Dom. Rep., Mex., Puerto Rico*) a feeding bottle = biberón.

tetero (*Colo.*) a feeding bottle = biberón.

text mode [pron. texmoud] (*from English*) the text mode in the computer = (N.E. en forma de texto.)

teyú (*Para.*) any kind of lizard = cualquier tipo de lagarto.

tía rica (*Chile*) a pawnshop = casa de empeño.

tiburón (*Argen.*) a popular man among women = hombre que tiene éxito con las mujeres.

ticher 1. (*from English*) a teacher = maestro(a); profesor(a). **2.** (*from English*) T-shirt = polo; camiseta.

ticos (*Costa Rica*) (N.E. nickname that Costa Ricans use for themselves) = apodo con que los costarricences se llaman a sí mismos.

tierno(a) (*Guat., Nic.*) the youngest in the family = el/la más joven de la familia.

tiestazo; totazo (*Colo.*) to bump into something = porrazo; mamporro.

tiesto (*Chile*) any pot or container; a vessel = cualquier vasija.

tilango(a) 1. (*Argen.*) a simpleton = persona simple. **2.** (*Argen.*) silly = tonto(a). **3.** (*Argen.*) irresponsible and without social values = irresponsable y sin valores sociales.

tiliches (*Mex.*) stuff; junk; old clothes = cuestiones; objetos sin valor; ropa muy usada y vieja.

tilico 1. (*Bol.*) diffident = apocado. **2.** (*Bol.*) weak; a coward = débil; cobarde. **3.** (*Bol.*) silly = tonto.

tilingo 1. (*Para.*) reckless; irresponsible = inquieto; irresponsable. **2.** (*Para., Peru*) scatterbrained; silly = atolondrado; bobo; tonto.

tilingo-tilango (*Cuba*) the end of the story = se acabó el cuento.

tilinguear 1. (*Argen.*) to speak nonsense = hablar tonterías. **2.** (*Para.*) to behave in a silly manner; to behave as a **tilingo** = atolondrarse; comportarse como un **tilingo**.

tilinte (*Nic.*) rigid = tieso.

timba (*Argen.*) an illegal casino = casino ilegal.

timbre (*Mex.*) a stamp = estampilla; sello de correos.

timbre See **estampa**.

timón See **cabrilla**.

tina (*Chile, Ecua., Peru*) a bathtub = bañadera; bañera.

tina de baño (*Guat., Pan.*) a bathtub = bañadera; bañera.

tinaco (*Ecua.*) a tall earthenware vessel = vasija grande.

tincada (*Chile*) the intuition; a presentiment = intuición; presentimiento.

tincazo (*Ecua.*) a flick = capirotazo; papirotazo; golpe dado en la cabeza.

tincute; zopilote (*Guat.*) a buzzard = buitre.

tinglar (*Chile*) each board is mounted over one section of the next one to cover a wall = montar una tabla sobre una sección de la siguiente para cubrir una pared.

tinoso (*Ven.*) skillful; clever = diestro; hábil.

tinto (*Colo., Pan., Ven.*) black coffee; strong coffee without sugar = café fuerte sin azúcar; café negro; café sin leche; café solo.

tiñoza (*Cuba*) a buzzard = buitre.

tipa (*Argen., Bol., Chile, Para., Ven.*) a bitch (derogatory) = tipeja; cualquier mujer a la que no se le tiene respeto o consideración (despectivo).

tipazo (*Ven.*) an attractive man = hombre atractivo.

tipear (*from English*) to type; to write with a keyboard = teclear; escribir en un teclado.

típical (*from English*) typical = típico.

tíquet 1. (*from English*) a ticket (theater; raffle) = boleto; billete; recibo; taquilla. **2.** (*from English*) a ticket (elections; ballot) = lista de los candidatos que se postulan para una elección.

tiquete (*Colo.*) a ticket = billete; boleto.

tiquetear (*Colo.*) to cut a ticket; to punch a ticket = picar o cortar el boleto.

tirá (*Puerto Rico*) run-down looking; ill-kept = en decadencia; descuidado.

tira (*Argen., Chile*) a detective (vulgar) = detective (vulgar).

tiradera (*Costa Rica*) a gibe; a jeer = burla; pulla.

tirador (*Cuba*) a slingshot = honda.

tiraje (*Chile*) a chimney flue = tiro de la chimenea.

tirao (*Puerto Rico*) sloppy = el que hace las cosas descuidadamente.

tirar el dedo 1. (*Ecua., Peru*) to hitchhike = pedir transporte gratuito en la carretera. **2.** (*Peru*) to report to the police = informar a la policía.

tirarse la fiesta (*Colo.*) to spoil the fun at a party by disruptive behavior = echar a perder una fiesta por una conducta indebida.

tirarse la plana (*Colo.*) to make a mistake that produces some damage = cometer un error que produce daño.

tiras cómicas (*Guat., Hond.*) comics = historietas.

tiras (*Chile*) rags = trapos.

tire (*from English*) a tire = neumático.

tiros (*Ecua., Peru*) marbles = canicas.

tirubaqué (*Ven.*) a teetotum = perinola.

tiste (*Nic.*) a drink prepared with a mixture of tortilla and cacao = masa de tortilla y cacao para preparar una bebida.

títere (*Puerto Rico*) a street urchin = pilluelo; golfillo.

titingó (*Cuba, Puerto Rico*) a brawl = alboroto.

titino; perchudo (*Colo.*) elegant = elegante.

tiví (*from English*) a TV; a television = la tele; televisión.

tizate 1. (*Hond., Nic.*) chalk = tiza. **2.** (*Hond., Nic.*) plaster of paris = yeso.

toast (*from English*) toast = tostada; pan tostado.

tocado 1. (*Argen.*) psychologically disturbed (informal); crazy = enfermo mental (vulgar); loco. **2.** (*Argen.*) not serious; someone who is irresponsible = poco serio; el que actúa irresponsablemente.

tocar el piano (*Para.*) to steal = robar; hurtar.

tocotal (*Hond.*) a muddy place; a mud hole = ciénaga; lodazal.

tocotoco (*Ven.*) a pelican = pelicano.

tocuyo (*Argen., Chile*) a strong and ordinary fabric = tela ordinaria y resistente.

todero (*Colo.*) one who does everything; a person without any specialty = el que hace de todo; el que no tiene especialidad.

tóilet (*from English*) a toilet = inodoro.

tolda (*Colo.*) an awning; a canopy = toldo.

toldillo (*Colo.*) a mosquito net = mosquitero.

toletazo (*Ven.*) a strong blow with a stick = golpe fuerte con un palo.

toletear (*Colo.*) to cut in pieces = trozar; cortar en trozos.

toletole (*Argen., Chile*) a scandal; a fight; a brawl = escándalo; gresca; desorden de gentes.

tolonguear (*Costa Rica*) to caress; to pamper = acariciar; mimar o dar mimos.

tomado 1. (*Colo.*) drunk = ebrio; borracho. **2.** (*Mex.*) tipsy; short of being drunk = mareado; casi borracho.

tomador (*Argen., Bol., Chile, Para.*) a drinker = bebedor.

tomar examen (*Chile*) to give an exam = dar examen.

tomar para el fideo (*Argen., Chile*) to pull someone's leg = burlarse de alguien.

tomatera (*Chile*) a heavy drinking occasion = ocasión en que se bebe mucho; borrachera.

tomaticán (*Chile*) a dish with onions, tomatoes, and corn = guiso de cebollas, tomates y maíz.

tombo 1. (*Colo.*) a police officer (derogatory) = agente de policía (despectivo). **2.** (*Ven.*) a police agent of the Federal District, in uniform = policía uniformado del Distrito Federal.

tongonear 1. (*Puerto Rico*) to spoil = regalonear. **2.** (*Ven.*) to swing one's hips = contonear.

toples (*from English*) topless = (N.E. pecho femenino al descubierto; con los pechos desnudos.)

topeadura (*Chile*) a rider who goads the bull with his horse in the Chilean rodeo = con su cabalgadura, un jinete empuja o aguijonea a un toro en el rodeo chileno.

toperol 1. (*Chile*) the small cylindric bumps used to mark lines in the street = protuberancias cilíndricas con que se marcan las calles. **2.** (*Chile*) a bump in the sole of soccer shoes or other sport shoes that helps prevent slipping = remache o protuberancia en la suela de los zapatos que se usan en los deportes para evitar que éstos se deslicen.

tópico (*from English*) a topic = tema.

topo (*Colo.*) a small, spherical earring = zarcillo pequeño de forma esférica.

toque (*Colo.*) inhaling marijuana = inhalación de marihuana.

toqui (*Chile*) a great Indian chief; the leader of the Caciques = gran jefe indio; líder de los caciques.

torcido 1. (*Hond.*) offended = agraviado. **2.** (*Hond.*) with bad luck = con mala suerte. **3.** (*Dom. Rep.*) unfortunate = desafortunado. **4.** (*Dom. Rep.*) miserable = desgraciado.

torcidos (*Colo.*) those who steal from drug dealers = los que roban a los traficantes de drogas.

tornillo (*Argen.*) extremely cold = frío intenso.

torolo (*Para.*) effeminate = afeminado.

toronja (*Cuba, Mex.*) a grapefruit = pomelo; fruta cítrica parecida a la naranja pero de mayor tamaño.

torpedo (*Chile*) a crib note; a small note used to cheat during an exam = chuleta; pequeña nota para copiar durante un examen.

torreja 1. (*Chile*) a slice of fruit or vegetables = rodaja de frutas o vegetales. **2.** (*Chile*) without value or of little value = con poco o sin ningún valor.

torta 1. (*Mex.*) a sandwich = emparedado; sándwich. **2.** (*Mex., Pan.*) an omelet = tortilla; fritada de huevo batido en figura redonda o alargada, se le pueden agregar diferentes ingredientes.

torteado (*Chile*) with a lot of money (informal) = con mucho dinero (informal).

tortilla 1. (*Guat., Hond., Mex., Salva.*) a N.E. thin bread made of corn or wheat flour = pan muy delgado hecho de harina de maíz o trigo. **2.** (*Argen., Peru*) a bread with a round shape baked in hot ashes and coal = pan en una forma redonda que se hornea dentro de cenizas calientes y brazas.

tortilla de rescoldo (*Chile*) a bread baked in hot coals = pan horneado en las brazas.

tortillera (*Argen., Chile, Cuba, Puerto Rico*) a lesbian (vulgar) = lesbiana (vulgar).

tórtolo (*Colo.*) stupid; silly = tonto; bobo.

tostao (*Puerto Rico*) crazy; mad = loco; desquiciado.

tostón 1. (*Dom. Rep., Puerto Rico*) fried plantain chips = rodajas pequeñas de plátano verde frito. **2.** (*Puerto Rico*) a difficult person or situation = situación o persona difícil.

totazo 1. (*Colo.*) bursting; an explosion = reventón; explosión. **2.** (*Colo.*) to bump into something = porrazo; mamporro. **3.** (*Hond.*) a blow with a cudgel = golpe con un barrote u otro artefacto pesado.

tote (*Colo.*) a firecracker = petardo.

totearse 1. (*Colo.*) to break = quebrarse; romperse. **2.** (*Colo.*) to die = morir.

totora (*Bol.*) the high grass that grows on lake shores = pasto alto que crece a la orilla de los lagos.

totuma (*Dom. Rep.*) a hump; a prominence in the back = joroba.

toya (*Colo.*) an inferior-quality potato = patata de mala calidad.

traba; tronada (*Colo.*) a personal disturbance that is produced by drugs = alteración producida por la droga.

trabado (*Colo.*) disturbed due to drug consumption = alterado por consumo de drogas.

trabajo a trato (*Chile*) piecework = trabajo a destajo.

trabajoso (*Colo.*) a person who is difficult to get along with = persona muy exigente y poco complaciente.

traboco (*Colo.*) vomit = vómito.

trabucarse (*Argen.*) to get all mixed up = atolondrarse.

tracalá (*Ecua.*) a crowd = multitud de gentes.

tractomula (*Colo.*) a trailer = camión pesado.

trademark (*from English*) a trademark = marca registrada.

traga (*Colo.*) a strong attraction to another person = gran atracción hacia otra persona.

tragada (*Argen.*) an illegal profit = ganancia ilícita.

tragado (*Colo.*) completely in love = completamente enamorado.

traguearse (*Colo.*) to get drunk = embriagarse; emborracharse.

trailer (*from English*) a trailer = acoplado.

traje (*Pan., Puerto Rico*) formal dress = vestido de mujer.

trajebaño (*Chile*) a bathing suit = traje de baño.

trama (*Mex.*) a wheat flour bread = pan de harina de trigo.

tranca 1. (*Argen.*) drunkenness (vulgar) = borrachera (vulgar). **2.** (*Ven.*) a traffic jam = atasco; congestionamiento de tráfico vehicular.

trancada See **raspa.**

trancado 1. (*Chile*) constipated (informal) = constreñido; con estreñimiento (informal). **2.** (*Colo.*) severe; exigent = severo; exigente.

trancar (*Colo.*) to reprimand severely = reprender severamente.

trancarse (*Argen., Chile, Para.*) to be constipated (informal) = estreñirse (informal).

trancas (*Nic.*) long legs = piernas largas.

trancón (*Colo.*) a traffic jam = embotellamiento del tráfico.

transformista (*Ven.*) a transvestite = travestido.

transpiración (*Chile*) sweat = sudor.

trapeador (*Cuba, Mex., Pan., Peru*) a mop = fregasuelos; trapo o estropajo para limpiar los suelos.

trapero (*Chile*) a mop = fregasuelos; trapo o estropajo para limpiar los suelos.

trapicar (*Chile*) to swallow the wrong way = atorarse.

trapichar (*Colo.*) to smuggle = contrabandear.

traqueado (*Colo.*) ailing; unwell; looking old = achacoso; enfermizo; envejecido.

trasbocar (*Colo.*) to vomit = vomitar.

traste 1. (*Chile, Para.*) the buttocks = nalgas; asentaderas. **2.** (*Colo.*) a piece of junk = trasto; cachivache.

trastear; trostear (*from English*) to trust = confiar.

trasteo (*Colo.*) moving of furniture = mudanza.

trasvasijar (*Chile*) to pour into another container = trasvasar.

travelchek (*from English*) a traveler's check = cheque de viajero.

trencha (*from English*) a trench = zanja.

trenza 1. (*Argen.*) people that stick together in search of power or money = agrupación de individuos para obtener poder o beneficios económicos. **2.** (*Ven.*) a shoelace = cordón o lazo para el calzado.

trenzarse (*Bol., Chile, Ecua., Peru*) to get involved in a fight = envolverse en una pelea.

trigueño(a) (*Argen., Bol., Ecua., Peru*) a brown-skinned person; a black-haired person = persona con la piel morena; de cabello moreno.

trilla See **fuetera**.

trillo (*Costa Rica, Cuba, Puerto Rico*) a path = senda; vereda.

trincar 1. (*Argen.*) to surprise = sorprender. **2.** (*Argen.*) to catch = agarrar. **3.** (*Argen.*) to beat = golpear.

trinco 1. (*Puerto Rico*) stiff = tieso. **2.** (*Mex.*) drunk = borracho.

tringo (*Puerto Rico*) stiff = tieso.

tripear (*from English*) to make trips = viajar; hacer viajes.

tripón 1. (*Mex.*) fat = gordo. **2.** (*Nic.*) with a big belly = barrigudo; panzón.

tripulina (*Argen.*) a brawl; a fight; a row = desorden; pelea; trífulca.

trique (*Mex.*) household utensils of poor quality = utensilios de la casa de mala calidad.

trisca (*Colo.*) a gibe; a jeer; a quip = burla; pulla.

triscar See **soguear**.

triscón (*Colo.*) a fault-finder = sacafaltas; criticón.

troc; troca; troces (*from English*) a truck = camión.

troca See **troc**.

troces See **troc**.

trolo (*Argen.*) an effeminate man (vulgar) = hombre afeminado (vulgar).

trompa (*Argen.*) a boss (informal) = patrón (informal).

trompada (*Argen., Peru*) a blow with the fist = puñetazo.

trompeta (*Bol., Ecua., Peru*) drunk = borracho; ebrio.

trompicón (*Puerto Rico*) a beating = paliza.

trompón (*Ecua., Peru*) a blow with the fist = puñetazo.

tronada See **traba**.

troncha 1. (*Colo.*) a dislocation = dislocación. **2.** (*Peru*) a slice; a piece = tajada; lonja.

tronco (*Argen.*) without the ability to perform intellectually or in sports = poco hábil en el deporte o en alguna actividad intelectual.

tronk (*from English*) a trunk = maletero.

trostear See **trastear**.

trozo (*Colo.*) a very attractive woman = mujer muy atractiva.

trucho (*Argen.*) a cheap imitation = imitación barata.

trusa (*Cuba, Mex.*) a bathing suit = traje de baño.

trust (*from English*) trust = confianza.

trustí (*from English*) a trustee = fideicomisario; persona que merece crédito y confianza; acreditado como representante de una autoridad u organización.

trutro; tutro (*Chile*) a poultry leg = muslo de las aves de corral.

trutruca (*Argen.*) a musical instrument of the **Araucanos** = instrumento musical de los **araucanos**.

tuanis (*Guat., Hond.*) good = bueno.

tuero (*Guat.*) a hide-and-seek game = el escondite, juego infantil.

tuerto (*Guat.*) blind = ciego.

tufo (*Argen., Chile*) bad breath = mal olor de la boca.

tufoso (*Guat.*) proud = orgulloso.

tugar-tugar (*Chile*) the child's game of hide-and-seek = juego infantil a las escondidas.

tuines (*from English*) twins = mellizos; gemelos.

tula 1. (*Chile*) the penis, in a child's language = pene, en el lenguaje infantil. 2. (*Colo.*) a travel bag with a cylindrical shape = bolsa de viaje con forma cilíndrica.

tumba (*Argen.*) inferior-quality food; jail meals = comida de baja calidad; comida de la cárcel.

tumbado (*Ecua.*) a ceiling = cielo raso de las habitaciones.

tumbe (*Puerto Rico*) to be robbed = ser robado.

tumbear (*Bol.*) to move or walk from one side to the other = andar de arriba a abajo.

tuna (*from English*) tuna fish = atún.

tunco 1. (*Hond.*) crippled = lisiado. 2. (*Hond.*) pork; a pig = cerdo; marrano; puerco. 3. (*Nic.*) with one limb shorter than the other = con una extremidad más corta que la otra.

tunda (*Colo., Pan.*) a beating = golpiza.

tungo (*Chile*) the nape of the neck = cerviz; testuz.

tunjo 1. (*Colo.*) a PreColombian divinity = divinidad preColombina. 2. (*Colo.*) an ornament in the form of such a divinity = adorno en la forma de esa divinidad.

tunta (*Bol.*) potato starch = almidón de patatas.

tun-tun (*Argen., Colo., Cuba, Ecua., Peru, Puerto Rico, Ven.*) "knock-knock;" the sound of someone knocking at the door = pum-pum; la voz que indica golpes de llamada en la puerta.

tupido 1. (*Chile, Cuba, Peru, Puerto Rico*) impeded = impedido. 2. (*Chile, Cuba, Dom. Rep., Peru, Puerto Rico*) obstructed = obstruido.

tupir (*Dom. Rep.*) to obstruct = obstruir.

tupirse (*Colo.*) to feel silly; to get embarrassed = ruborizarse; avergonzarse.

turcaso (*Nic.*) a blow = golpe.

turco 1. (*Chile, Colo., Dom. Rep., Ven.*) a nickname for any person from the Middle East, except Jews = apodo dado a cualquier persona del medio oriente, excepto los judíos. 2. (*Colo.*) unscrupulous in business = sin escrúpulos en los negocios.

turmas (*Colo.*) the scrotum (vulgar) = escroto; bolas (vulgar).

turno (*Costa Rica*) a fair; a market = feria; mercado de alimentos.

turo (*Bol.*) a snail = caracol.

turqueada (*Nic.*) a beating = golpiza.

turra 1. (*Argen.*) a prostitute = prostituta. 2. (*Colo.*) the effects of a narcotic = los efectos de un narcótico.

turro (*Ecua.*) no good; without value = malo; sin valor.

turulato (*Argen.*) dazed; stunned = mareado; atontado.

turuleta 1. (*Puerto Rico*) crazy = loco. 2. (*Puerto Rico*) bewildered = turbado.

turupe 1. (*Colo.*) a bump; a lump = tolondrón; chichón. 2. (*Colo.*) awkward; daft = torpe; zopenco.

tusa 1. (*Argen.*) a horse's mane = crines del caballo. 2. (*Colo., Puerto Rico, Ven.*) a corncob = zuro; carozo; corazón de la mazorca después de estar desgranada. 3. (*Colo.*) pockmarks = hoyos de viruela. 4. (*Colo., Puerto Rico*) a despicable person; a worthless person = persona despreciable; el/la que no vale nada. 5. (*Costa Rica*) a lively woman = mujer alegre y vivaracha. 6. (*Cuba*) a cigarette made with corn leaves = cigarrillo hecho de las hojas de maíz.

tusada (*Colo.*) a bad haircut = mal corte de pelo.

tusar 1. (*Colo.*) to cut the hair very close; to shave the head = rapar. **2.** (*Guat.*) to criticize = criticar.

tuso(a) (*Colo.*) a bald person = calvo(a); pelado(a); pelón(a).

tusta See **terraza**.

tutifruti (*Chile, Colo.*) a mixture of different fruits = mezcla de diferentes frutas.

tuto 1. (*Chile*) sleep = sueño. **2.** (*Chile*) a poultry leg = muslo de las aves de corral.

tutro See **trutro**.

tutuma 1. (*Bol.*) a canteen or bowl = cantimplora o tiesto para guardar o transportar líquidos. **2.** (*Dom. Rep.*) a bump = chichón.

U

ulpo 1. (*Argen.*) the cream of corn flour = alimento de consistencia cremosa que se prepara con harina de maíz. **2.** (*Chile, Peru*) a drink made of toasted wheat flour, water, and sugar = bebida de harina de trigo tostada, agua y azúcar.

ultraboludo (*Argen.*) absolutely stupid = absolutamente tonto; tonto de capirote.

umbrela (*from English*) an umbrella = paraguas.

un carajo (*Ven.*) very little or nothing = poco o nada.

un palo (*Argen.*) one million monetary units = un millón de unidades monetarias.

una barbaridad (*Argen., Para.*) a large amount = una gran cantidad de algo.

unión (*from English*) a union = sindicato; gremio.

untar la mano (*Argen.*) to bribe = sobornar.

uñita (*Ven.*) a special kind of marble game = un tipo especial de juego de canicas.

up to date [pron. ap tu deit] (*from English*) up-to-date = al día; a la moda.

¡upe! (*Costa Rica*) hello!; hey, there! = ¿hay alguien aquí?

urraca (*Mex.*) a person with a dark complexion (derogatory) = persona de tez morena (peyorativo).

uslero (*Chile*) a rolling pin; a cylinder used to spread dough = rodillo de pastelero; palo cilíndrico que se usa para extender la masa de harina.

V

vaca 1. (*Chile*) an insult; a bad or cruel person (vulgar) = insulto; persona mala o cruel (vulgar). **2.** (*Chile, Ven.*) money collected within a group for a specific purpose = dinero que se recolecta dentro de un grupo para un propósito específico. **3.** (*Ecua.*) coconut pulp = carne o pulpa del coco.

vaca blanca (*Cuba*) a cola with vanilla ice cream = Coca-Cola con helado de vainilla.

vaca lechera (*Puerto Rico*) candy prepared with sugar and milk = caramelo preparado con azúcar y leche.

vaca negra (*Cuba*) a cola with chocolate ice cream = Coca-Cola con helado de chocolate.

vacano (*Dom. Rep.*) a great character (informal); a cool person = el que tiene una gran personalidad; el que es fantástico (informal).

vaciar See **aplanchar**.

vacilada (*Colo.*) a joke that causes damage = broma que causa daño.

vacilar 1. (*Mex.*) to have fun; to have a good time = pasarlo(a) bien. **2.** (*Ven.*) to make jokes = hacer bromas. **3.** (*Ven.*) to mock; to laugh at = burlarse.

vacilón 1. (*Colo.*) a joke that causes damage = broma que causa daño. **2.** (*Mex.*) a joker = bromista. **3.** (*Puerto Rico*) drunkenness = borrachera. **4.** (*Puerto Rico*) a rude joke = relajo.

vacuna (*Colo.*) the payment or tax collected by the guerrillas = tributo cobrado por guerrilleros.

vade (*Colo.*) a desk cover = carpeta sobre el escritorio.

vagamunda See **guaricha**.

vagamundo 1. (*Colo.*) a party animal = juerguero. **2.** (*Colo.*) a womanizer = conquistador de mujeres.

vaina 1. (*Colo., Dom. Rep., Puerto Rico, Ven.*) anything; stuff; an issue or object with an unknown name = cualquier cosa; objeto o asunto del cual no se sabe el nombre **2.** (*Colo., Costa Rica*) a nuisance; a troublesome thing = contrariedad; molestia.

vainica (*Costa Rica*) a vegetable; a type of plant = vegetal; un tipo de planta.

valdiviano (*Chile*) a soup made of dried meat, onions, and potatoes = sopa de **charqui**, cebollas y patatas.

valija (*Argen., Para., Uru.*) a suitcase = maleta.

valla comercial (*Colo.*) a sign = cartel.

valle (*Para.*) any place or region = cualquier lugar o región.

vaquear See **baquear**.

vaqueo See **baqueo**.

vaquero (*Argen.*) blue jeans = pantalón de mezclilla.

vaquilla (*Argen., Chile, Para., Uru.*) a calf; a young cow = ternera.

varado (*Colo.*) a vehicle that doesn't work = vehículo averiado.

vararse (*Colo.*) a vehicle that fails or stops working = averiarse un vehículo.

vareto; varillo (*Colo.*) a joint; a marijuana cigarette = cigarrillo de marihuana.

varilla (*Colo.*) marijuana = marihuana.

varillero (*Mex.*) a peddler = vendedor ambulante.

varillo See **vareto**.

vaselino (*Colo.*) conceited; to put on airs = presumido; darse aires de importancia.

vaya pues (*Salva.*) so be it; it is O.K. = que así sea; está bien.

vega 1. (*Cuba*) a tobacco plantation = plantación de tabaco; terreno sembrado de tabaco. **2.** (*Ecua.*) a stretch of alluvial soil = terreno que se forma por las avenidas del río, generalmente en los recodos del mismo; terreno de aluvión.

vegetable (*from English*) a vegetable = verdura.

veintiúnico (*Colo.*) the only one (informal) = el único (informal).

vejentud (*Argen.*) a funny expression for old age = expresión para referirse de una manera picaresca a la edad madura.

vejiga 1. (*Guat., Mex., Salva.*) a balloon = globo. **2.** (*Uru.*) silly = tonto.

vejuco; vejucón (*Ven.*) an old man (derogatory) = viejo (despectivo).

vejucón See **vejuco**.

velar 1. (*Colo.*) to stare at someone with desire = mirar fijamente mostrando deseo. **2.** (*Dom. Rep.*) to eat at somebody else's home = comer en casa ajena.

velís (*from English*) a suitcase = valija.

vellón 1. (*Puerto Rico*) any coin = cualquier moneda. **2.** (*Puerto Rico*) a quarter; a twenty-five-cent coin = moneda de un cuarto de dólar. **3.** (*Puerto Rico*) to play a joke on a person = gastar una broma a una persona.

vellón de cinco (*Puerto Rico*) a nickel = cinco centavos.

vellón de diez (*Puerto Rico*) a dime = diez centavos.

vellonera (*Puerto Rico*) a jukebox = máquina de discos.

velón 1. (*Chile, Peru*) a thick tallow candle = cirio o vela de gran tamaño. **2.** (*Colo.*) a person who stares at someone else with desire = persona que mira a otra fijamente con deseo.

velorio (*Chile*) a wake = velatorio.

vendaje (*Colo., Ecua.*) a gratuity; a tip; a bonus = propina; gratificación; lo que se da como agregado por contrato.

vendido (*Argen., Chile*) a person who shows loyalty to someone or something but at the same time is doublecrossing him or her = el que aparenta fidelidad a algo o alguien pero que al mismo tiempo lo está traicionando.

vendita (*Colo., Mex.*) a Band-Aid™ = tafetán adhesivo; curita.

venta (*Cuba*) a sale = liquidación.

ventero (*Colo.*) a peddler = buhonero; vendedor ambulante.

ventorrillo 1. (*Colo.*) a small business on the street = puesto de venta callejero. **2.** (*Colo.*) a small shop = tienducha; negocio de poca monta.

ventoso (*Mex.*) a fart (vulgar) = pedo; flatulencia expelida por el ano (vulgar).

verde (*Colo.*) a police officer (derogatory) = agente de la policía (peyorativo).

vereda 1. (*Argen., Chile, Peru, Uru.*) a sidewalk = acera. **2.** (*Colo.*) a small village = aldea pequeña. **3.** (*Costa Rica*) a country road = camino rural. **4.** (*Guat., Nic., Salva.*) the bank of a stream = banco de una corriente de agua. **5.** (*Mex.*) a path = sendero.

verga 1. (*Ven.*) a whip made with the penis of a bull = látigo hecho con el pene de un toro. **2.** (*Ven.*) a punishment with that whip (vulgar) = castigo con ese látigo (vulgar). **3.** (*Ven.*) an adverse situation = situación adversa. **4.** (*Argen., Uru., Ven.*) the penis (vulgar) = pene (vulgar). (See also **piya**.) **5.** (*Argen., Uru., Ven.*) stuff; a thing (vulgar) = asunto; cosa; cuestión (vulgar).

vergajo (*Colo., Ven.*) a villain; a shameless person; a despicable person (vulgar) = villano; sinvergüenza; persona despreciable (vulgar).

verja (*Puerto Rico*) a fence = valla; cerca de la casa.

vermuth (*Argen., Chile, Uru.*) an evening performance = función vespertina.

verraquera See **berraquera**.

vertiente (*Chile*) a spring; a fountain = manantial.

vestido (*Colo.*) a two- or three-piece suit in which all the pieces are made of the same fabric = traje de dos o tres piezas de la misma tela.

vestido de baño (*Colo., Pan.*) a bathing suit = traje de baño.

vestido de sastre (*Colo.*) a woman's suit = traje sastre.

vestón (*Chile*) a suit jacket = chaqueta de un traje masculino; saco.

vetazo (*Ecua.*) each lash in a beating = cada uno de los golpes durante una zurra.

veterano(a) (*Argen., Chile*) an old person = viejo(a).

vianda (*Puerto Rico*) the vegetables served with the meats = los vegetales que se sirven como acompañamiento a las carnes.

viandas (*Chile*) food containers that are carried one over the other to keep them hot = tiestos de comidas que se transportan uno sobre otro para mantenerlos calientes.

vicarios (*Colo.*) old people = viejos; ancianos.

vichar (*Argen.*) to spy = espiar.

victimar (*Colo.*) to kill = matar.

vicuña (*Bol., Chile, Peru*) a wool-bearing quadruped that lives only in the Andes mountains = cuadrúpedo productor de lana que vive sólo en las montañas de los Andes.

vidriera (*Mex.*) a windshield = parabrisas.

vidurria (*Colo.*) a lousy life = vida llena de reveses y padecimientos.

vieja 1. (*Colo.*) a young woman (informal) = muchacha (informal). **2.** (*Mex.*) a woman of any age; a term commonly used for a wife = mujer de cualquier edad; comunmente se usa para nombrar a la esposa.

viejita See **la vieja**.

vienesa (*Chile*) a hot dog = (N.E. emparedado de salchicha).

vigo (*Hond.*) a poultice = emplasto; parche medicinal.

villa miseria (*Argen.*) a shanty town = viviendas precarias construidas de material ligero que se levantan alrededor de las grandes ciudades.

violín (*Ven.*) to make a fool of oneself = quedar en ridículo.

virado (*Argen., Bol., Chile, Peru, Puerto Rico*) twisted = torcido.

viringo (*Colo.*) naked = desnudo; sin ropa.

virivira (*Puerto Rico*) a succession of rapid events = sucesión muy rápida de eventos.

virola (*Argen.*) a silver ornament = adorno de plata.

viroteao (*Puerto Rico*) twisted; placed in the wrong direction = mal colocado; algo que no está derecho; algo que está en la dirección equivocada.

virusa (*Colo.*) shavings = virutas.

visage (*Colo.*) malice; cunning = malicia; astucia.

visita flor (*Pan.*) a hummingbird = colibrí.

visitadora (*Ven.*) an enema = lavativa; aparato para hacer lavados intestinales.

visorioco 1. (*Puerto Rico*) twisted = torcido. **2.** (*Puerto Rico*) out of its place = fuera de sitio.

vitrina (*Chile, Colo.*) a shop window = escaparate.

vivaceta; vivaracho (*Chile*) unscrupulous; grasping = aprovechador; inescrupuloso; el que se aprovecha de los demás.

vivanco (*Argen.*) unscrupulous; self-serving = aprovechador; ventajista; ventajero; el que actúa sólo en beneficio personal.

vivandero(a) (*Hond.*) a salesperson in the food market = vendedor(a) en el mercado de comestibles.

vivaracho See **vivaceta**.

víveres (*Dom. Rep.*) edible fruits or roots = frutos o raíces comestibles.

vividor (*Colo.*) one who lives at another's expense = el que vive a costas de otros.

vivir arrimado (*Argen.*) to live together without being married = pareja que vive amancebada sin haberse casado.

voceador (*Colo.*) a newspaper boy = vendedor ambulante de periódicos.

volada (*Mex.*) a love affair = aventura amorosa.

volado 1. (*Colo.*) a balcony = balcón. **2.** (*Colo.*) scatterbrained = atolondrado. **3.**

(*Colo.*) an irritable person = persona irritable; el que se irrita con facilidad.

voladora (*Colo.*) a motorcraft launch = lancha de velocidad.

volantín 1. (*Chile*) a kite = cometa. **2.** (*Mex.*) a merry-go-round = tiovivo; carrusel. **3.** (*Mex.*) a love affair = aventura amorosa.

volarse de la escuela (*Colo.*) to cut school = hacer novillos; no asistir a la escuela e irse a otro lado.

volate See **bolate**.

volatero (*Ecua.*) a fireworks rocket = cohete de fuegos de artificio; volador.

volcán (*Colo.*) an avalanche = alud.

voleo 1. (*Colo.*) a job; work = trabajo ocupación. **2.** (*Colo.*) a disorder = desorden.

volteado (*Colo.*) an effeminate man = hombre afeminado.

voltear 1. (*Colo.*) to turn a vehicle = girar un vehículo; cambiar la dirección en que se mueve un vehículo. **2.** (*Colo.*) to go around in business; to go on an errand = andar de un lado para otro en diligencias. **3.** (*Colo.*) to change ideology or political affiliation = cambiar de ideología o afiliación política. **4.** (*Colo.*) to knock down; to pull down = derribar con violencia; derramar.

vos (*Argen.*) you = tú.

votar (*Puerto Rico*) to defecate (vulgar); to shit = defecar (vulgar); cagar.

vuelto (*Peru*) a change of money = cambio; suelto; sencillo.

W

waquitoki (*from English*) a walkie-talkie = transmisor-receptor portátil.

water; waterclo 1. (*from English*) a bathroom = baño; excusado. **2.** (*from English*) a water closet; a toilet = inodoro; retrete.

waterclo See **water**.

waxear (*from English*) to wax = encerar el piso de una habitación o encerar el automóvil.

welfare [pron. guelfear] (*from English*) welfare = bienestar social.

western (*from English*) a western = película de vaqueros; película del oeste.

wiken (*from English*) a weekend = fin de semana.

window (*from English*) a computer window = ventana gráfica.

wordprosesor (*from English*) a word processor = procesadora de textos.

wuiza (*Ecua.*) a prostitute = prostituta.

Y

yacaré (*Para.*) a South American alligator = caimán sudamericano.

yacks; yaquis (*from English*) jacks; fireworks = estrellitas; fuego de artificio que se sostiene en la mano y produce chispas.

yaket (*from English*) a jacket = chaqueta.

yapa (*Para., Uru.*) an extra amount of merchandise that the seller gives to the buyer = lo que el vendedor le da al comprador como extra o como gratificación.

yaque (*from English*) a car's jack = gato o gata del automóvil.

yaquis See **yacks**.

yarda (*from English*) a yard = patio.

yatiri (*Bol.*) a native medicine man = curandero nativo.

yautía (*Costa Rica, Dom. Rep., Guat., Hond., Nic., Puerto Rico, Salva.*) (N.E. tuber used to prepare different dishes; a tropical vegetable used in Central American and Caribbean meals) = (N.E. tubérculo que se usa para preparar diferentes platos; vegetal tropical usado en las comidas centroamericanas y caribeñas.)

yeguo(a) 1. (*Argen.*) a nice-looking person = persona bonita. **2.** (*Argen.*) what looks very good = lo que se ve muy bien.

yely (*from English*) jelly = jalea.

yerba 1. (*Argen., Uru.*) a typical Argentinean tea; **mate** = té de la hierba **mate**. **2.** (*Cuba, Pan., Puerto Rico*) a lawn = césped. **3.** (*Puerto Rico*) marijuana = marihuana.

yerbatero 1. (*Argen., Chile, Uru.*) a medicine man that cures with herbs = curandero que receta yerbas medicinales. **2.** (*Para.*) a **mate** dealer = el que comercia en la yerba **mate**.

yersey (*from English*) a jersey; a sweater = chaqueta o blusa tejida.

yetatore (*Para.*) without luck = sin suerte.

yin (*Colo.*) blue jeans = (N.E. pantalones vaqueros; pantalones de mezclilla).

yo no me chupo el dedo (*Cuba*) I am not stupid; You cannot cheat me. = no soy bobo; a mí no se me puede engañar.

yoltamal (*Nic.*) corn dough wrapped in corn leaves and cooked; after that it is cooked again for a long time, wrapped in plantain leaves = masa de maíz que se cuece primero envuelta en hojas de maíz y se vuelve a cocer por largo tiempo envuelta en hojas de plátano.

yompear (*Puerto Rico*) to jump a car when the battery is dead = (N.E. extender un puente eléctrico entre dos automóviles cuando la batería de uno está sin electricidad.)

yoni (*Argen.*) any foreigner (vulgar) = cualquier extranjero (vulgar).

yonker (*from English*) a junkyard; a worthless car = depósito de chatarra; deshuesadero; automóvil casi inservible.

yonquear (*from English*) to junk = botar como desperdicio.

yóquey; yoqui (*from English*) a jockey = (RAE) jinete profesional de carreras de caballos.

yoqui See **yóquey**.

yuca (*Puerto Rico*) a yucca; tapioca; manioca; a cassava; a vegetable served with meat or seafood = mandioca; tapioca; manioca; vegetal que se usa como acompañamiento de carnes y pescado.

yuta (*Argen.*) the police (vulgar) = policía (vulgar).

Z

zabeca (*Argen.*) the head (informal) = cabeza (informal).

zácate 1. (*Mex.*) a lawn = césped; pasto. **2.** (*Mex.*) inferior-quality marijuana = marihuana de baja calidad.

zafacón (*Dom. Rep.*) a garbage can = tacho de la basura.

zafado 1. (*Argen., Bol., Chile, Para.*) brazen; shameless = atrevido; imprudente. **2.** (*Chile*) spirited; brave = enérgico; corajudo. **3.** (*Chile*) one who does not anticipate the consequences of one's actions = el/la que no mide las consecuencias de sus acciones.

zamarro (*Hond., Ven.*) clever; roguish; astute = sagaz; bribón.

zambo (*Ecua., Peru*) a dark-skinned person = persona de la piel muy morena.

zamuro See **samuro**.

zanahoria (*Ven.*) an honest and pure person = persona sana y honesta.

zanahorio (*Colo.*) naive = ingenuo.

zancudo (*Bol., Chile, Ecua., Mex.*) a mosquito = mosquito.

zanja (*Ecua.*) a fence; a wall = cerca; muro.

zanjón (*Chile*) a big ditch = canal.

zapallo (*Argen., Colo., Ecua., Pan., Para., Peru*) a pumpkin; a squash = calabaza.

zapatillas (*Argen., Bol., Chile, Ecua., Pan., Peru*) sneakers = zapatos deportivos de goma.

zapatillas de levantarse (*Bol., Chile*) slippers = pantuflos o pantuflas.

zapatones (*Colo.*) rubber shoes used to protect regular shoes from the rain = zapatos de goma para proteger de la lluvia los zapatos regulares.

zapeta (*Mex.*) a diaper = pañal.

zapoyol (*Costa Rica*) an orange-colored tropical fruit = (N.E. fruta tropical de color anaranjado.)

zaragate 1. (*Peru, Ven.*) despicable = despreciable. **2.** (*Peru*) undesirable = indeseable. **3.** (*Peru*) a meddler = entrometido. **4.** (*Ven.*) a rascal = pícaro.

zaramullo 1. (*Peru, Ven.*) a busybody = entrometido. **2.** (*Peru, Ven.*) a fool = tonto.

zaranda (*Ven.*) a spinning top = peonza; trompo.

zarandear (*Para.*) to spank; to beat = dar de azotes; castigar físicamente.

zaratán (*Hond.*) trichinosis = triquinosis.

zarate (*Hond.*) scabies = sarna.

zaraza (*Colo.*) an inferior-quality cotton fabric = tela de algodón ordinario.

zarazo See **sarazo**.

zarpear (*Hond.*) to splash = salpicar.

zoco See **soco**.

zoncura (*Peru*) nonsense = tontería.

zopilote 1. (*Guat., Hond., Mex., Nic., Salva.*) a buzzard = buitre. **2.** (*Mex.*) a policeman = agente de policía.

zoquete 1. (*Colo., Guat.*) wicked = bellaco; mentecato. **2.** (*Colo.*) a duffer = inútil. **3.** (*Chile*) short socks = calcetín corto. **4.** (*Cuba*) a punch = puñetazo; golpe de puño. **5.** (*Ecua., Peru*) dirty; filthy = sucio.

zorrongo (*Colo.*) clever = astuto.

zueco See **sueco**.

zumbado (*Guat.*) drunk = borracho.

zumbador 1. (*Colo.*) a child's toy that buzzes = bramadera; juguete de niño que hace un zumbido. **2.** (*Puerto Rico*) a hummingbird = colibrí.

zumbar (*Guat.*) to speak ill of someone = hablar mal de alguien.

zumbido (*Mex.*) a gossip = chismes.

zunzun (*Cuba*) a hummingbird = colibrí.

zuro (*Colo.*) a pigeon = paloma doméstica.

zurra (*Argen.*) a beating = golpiza; paliza.

zurra-zurra (*Pan.*) a playground slide = tobogán.

zurumbático (*Colo.*) groggy; stunned = atontado; aturdido.

English Index

abalone loco
abandon a spouse largar
abandoned place íngrimo
able capo
above-average person papapúa
absent-minded englobado;
envolatado
absurdity macana
abundance jaracotal; tendal
abusive barsa
accelerate a vehicle métele chala;
puyar
accelerator chancleta
accent, Peruvian Andes mote
accompaniment, without a capela; a
secas
accomplice bastonero
accumulate abalserar
accuse sindicar
accused sindicado
acne barro
act foolishly destorrentarse
act quickly before others sobrar
act slowly conchudo
active person minga
added to de llapa; de ñapa; de yapa;
ipegue; la yapa; llapa
adhesive glu; pega
adjust embonar
adolescent chamo; colino; pavito;
sardina(o)
adorn oneself with cheap objects
emperendengarse
adult who behaves like a child lolei;
pailón
adulterate chimbear
adulterer juguetón
adulteress cojín; jugetona
advantage gabela
adverse situation verga

adversity mecha
affectation disfuerzo
affected pije; prosudo; siútico
affected behavior huachafería
afraid, be abrirse; ajibararse
African culture, related to
garífuna
African origin, person of (derogatory)
changa(o); chuga; cuervo; garífuna;
llantón; niche
agree kupia-kume
agreement, reach an casar
ailing traqueado
air filter of an engine calabaza
airplane, small pipilacha
albino talamoco
alcohol added to a drink malicia
alcohol, with too much está cabezón
alcoholic pernicioso
alcoholic beverage for a wake
gloriado
alcoholic beverage, special kind of
campechana; caña; chica; curda; gas;
mezcal; pisco; pulque
alcoholic beverage, swallow of a
cañonazo; guamasco; jalón;
matracaso; palo; tacazo
alert, be abusado(a); avíspese; brincar
a la cuerda; estar pilas; póngase las
pilas
alien, illegal aliento
alligator, South American yacaré
allow an advantage encimar
alluvial soil vega
amaze abismar
amazing le ronca el clarinete; le
zumba el mango
ambitious person agalludo;
calango(a)
amplifier corneta; parlante; spiker

amputee broco; cholco; chuto(a); cuto(a)
amulet cábula
anecdote cacho; pasaje
anger arrechera; arrecho; berrear; cachicha; condenar; coraje; empavar
anglicized agringado
Anglo-Saxon in the U.S. (derogatory) gabacho; gabardina
angry, be amargo; andar bravo; bravito; bravo; coraje; encandilado(a); enchicarse; enchinchado; enchismarse; envenenao; guapo(a); soplado; tener calentura; tener coraje
angry, get arrufar; calentarse; chivarse; empacarse; encohetarse; enfogonarse; entromparse; entunarse; prenderse
angry look malacaroso
animal food talaje
animal, old angarrio
animal tripe prepared as a dish chunchules; guata; mondongo
animal without its horns muco
animosity cocora
annatto seed achiote
annoy acatarrar; albardear; amolar; berrear; chavar; echar jareta; engorrar; entripar; fregar; fuñir; jericoplear; jeringar; jeringuear; manganear; mosquear; poner sebo; remoler
annoyance arrecho; chingadera
annoyed, get enchicarse; macán
annoying ácido; chocante; fregado; jodón; jorobón; lavativoso; le pica; perecoso; secante; sobadera
annoying person bomba; chicle; fregón; gadejo; llenador
annoying repetition chinchín
anticipate someone's intentions sobrar
antidote contra
antifreeze antifris
antipasto salad pichanga

antipathy aburrición
anus (vulgar) ojal; ojete; poto
anyone with a university diploma licenciado
anything for which the name is unknown bicha(o); broma; chereques; chiva; chivo; chunches; coroto; coso; deso; estaf; perol; tereque; vaina
apartment, upstairs altos
appearance of a person pinta
application aplicación
apply aplicar
appointment apoinmen; deit
apprehension flato; pensión
appropriate chévere
apricot apricot; chabacano; damasco
aquarium acuarium
Argentineans (nickname) che
Argentineans, nickname Paraguayans use for curepa; curepí
argue atracar; pantalla
argument sanata
argumentative boquiduro
armadillo cusuco; quirquincho
armpit arca; chucha; encuentro
armpit odor grajo; monate
army ormy
arrest apañar
arrogant alabao; recargado
article that does not sell cacho; hueso
ashamed, be achuncharse; amusgarse; azarearse; picharse
ashen nixte
Asian, nickname for anyone who looks like an chino(a)
asking to be pampered mimosear
asphalt alquitrán; brea; chapapote; chicle
assemble embonar
astute person abusado(a); chucho; culebrero; jaiba; lángara; macuco; malva; zorrongo

at once altiro
attached to somebody else, person who is very arriquín; chipe
attached to someone, become amelcocharse
attack barajustar; fajar; fajarse
attend social events caculear
attentive, be ojo
attic ático; desván; entretecho; tapanco
attraction to another person, strong traga
attractive person bizcocho; churro; cuero; levantador(a); machote; mango; tipazo(a)
auction remate
auctioneer martillero; rematador
audacious action gallada; parada
audacity pechuga
authentic rajado
authorization without restrictions largona
automation automación
automobile, battered batata; burra; cacharra; cacharro; cafetera; charchina; cucaracha; fodongo; garnacha; tartana
automobile, large cadilaque; nave
avalanche volcán
avarice, behave with alagartarse; hambriento; maceta
avenge chingar
avenue jirón
avenue lined with trees camellón
average averach; average
aversion to a person, object or issue bronca
avocado aguacate; palta
avoid guabinear; pijotear; sacatear
awake recuerdo
awards aguares
awkward turupe
awning tolda

baby barrigón; bebito; beibi; beiby; cagón; chavalo; chichí; cipe; guagua; lepe; nenito
baby that cries too much chinche; cipe
baby that defecates a lot poposeador
baby that sucks a lot mamón
baby's attire, specific kind of mono
babysitter beibisiter; casero; sentador(a)
back down rajar
back up baquear; vaquear
background bakgraun
backpack chiba; morral; motete; quipe
bacon beicon
bad condition, in escrachao
bad luck, bring or give empavar; salar
bad luck, having mala leche; mufa; quemado; salado; salazón; torcido
bad luck, person who brings or has mabita; ser la sal
bad man chichimeco
bad mood, in a arrechado(a); engreñao
bad or cruel person (vulgar) fregado; jodón; malevo; mugre; mugroso; perro; pingo; vaca
bad quality, of penca
bad reputation, person who has a cuero; ficha; rabúa; refistolera; refistolero
bad section of a whole mona
bad shape, in malanco(a)
bad taste, in penca; picante
bad temper argel; arrechera
bad, very (vulgar) como el forro; como la mona; como las huevas; feo; gacho; malinche; pichirre; turro
bad word bachata
badge charola
bad-looking picante
bad-tempered person argelado; arrecho

baffle bafle
bag funda; huacal; morral
bag, paper cambucho; cartucho
bag, shopping jaba
baking powder bakin; beiquinparer; salarete
balcony volado
ball bol; bola
ballast balasto
ballerina balerina
balloon balún; bomba; chiras; vejiga
ballpoint pen biromé; esferográfico; lapicero; lápiz de pasta; pluma
ballroom balrum
bamboo of Central America and México otate; tarro
bamboo of the Río de la Plata basin tacuara
banana, slice of fried ripe tajada
banana, sweet butuco; cambur; guineo; maduro; plátano
banana, very big guarán
bananas, bunch of cacho; cachos
band chorcha; combo
Band-Aid™ banda; vendita
bandit matrero
bang batacazo; batatazo
bangs capul; chasquilla; pollina
bank banquear
bank of a stream vereda
bar taquilla
bar, cheap boliche; botiquín
barbecue barbekiu; parrilla; parrillada
barbecued meat, piece of churrasco
bargain ancheta; jamón; pichincha
barge bacha
barn colca
bartender barman
baseball béisbol
baseball bat bate
baseball glove mascota
basement beisman; subterráneo
basil basilico
basin apaste; bacín; platón

basket canasta(o); huacal; mochilón
basketball básquetbol
bat murciélago
bathing suit calzoncillo de baño; calzoneta; malla; pantaloneta; ropa de baño; trajebaño; trusa; vestido de baño
bathrobe bata
bathroom batrom; excusado; water; waterclo
bathtub bañadera; batea; baño; tina; tina de baño
baton guaripola
battered object albóndiga
bazooka bazuca
be on the watch for tantear
bean field porotal
beans caraotas; cocoles; frejoles; frijoles; frisoles; frísoles; porotos
beans, black negritas
beans, roasted cancha; canchitas; canguil
beans, white coscorrones
beard chiva
beat with a belt fajar
beat with a stick bejuquear
beaten up, get coger pela
beating batida; canquiza; capa; chanca; entrada; felpa; fuetera; garrotera; muenda; paleada; pela; tanda; trilla; trompicón; tunda; turqueada; zurra
beating, severe dar una tanda; garrotiza; reatiza; somatar; sopletón; trincar
beautician beutichian
beautiful chévere; chirote; chiva; chivo; chulo; encachado; nítido; pepeado; pirulo; polenta
beautiful person bacán; bien hecho(a); budín; cuquísima; está papa; polenta; por el libro; por la maceta; repiocha
beauty shop biutichap

bed, folding catre
bedbug alepate
bedroom cuarto; habitación; pieza;
recámara
bedspread bedspred; cobo; colcha;
edredón; sobrecama
bedstead catre
bee colmena
beef, cut of lagarto; malaya;
palomilla; picana; sobrebarriga
beef or lamb tripe chunchules;
chunchullos; chunchurria
beef, roast rosbif
beefsteak bisté; bistec
beep bipear
beeper beeper
beer biela; bironga; birria; chela; pola
beer and soda, mixture of refajo
beer, cold fría
beer, dark malta
beer, draft shop; sifón
beet betabel
beetle ron-ron
beg bombear
beggar limosnero
behave as a spoiled person
mingonear
behave in a bossy way roncar
behave in a rude and clumsy manner
patanear
behave in a silly way destorrentarse;
lesear; ser pavo; tilinguear
behave shyly aguasado; hacerse el
cucho
behavior behaviorismo
behavior, careless al tuntún
beige beich
belch chancho
belly guata; lipa; pipa
belly during pregnancy, big
desbarrigarse
belly, person with a big lipón(a);
pipón; pipudo; tripón
belt chicote

bent chueco
best, the la última chupá; paquete
best-seller best-séller
betray chaquetear; chivatear; chivar;
poner el gorro; sapear
bewildered acarajado; apendejado;
atrojar; surumbo; turuleta
bewildered, be atotumarse
bewildered, become atufar
bewitch someone or something
enyerbar
bewitched chorizo
beyond a person's capabilities
cuellón
bicarbonate of soda salarete
biceps conejo; gato; lagartija; lagarto;
mollera; mollero; molleros; ratón
bicycle baicicle; burra; cicla; juila
big and strong person cuajado;
macanudo; maceteado; ropero; sendo
big, very bárbaro; chirote; la yegua;
macho; manso(a); media;
morrocotudo; morrudo
bile attack rebote
bill (money) bil; fasulo
bill of one-hundred monetary units
cupón; gamba
bill of one-thousand pesos luca
bill worth five-thousand pesos
gabriela
billiard pocket buchaca
binge bachata; remolienda
binoculars anteojos largavista;
gemelos
biologist biologista
bird dung used as fertilizer guano
bird, small piririta
birth control birdcontrol
biscuit bisquete
bisexual bugarón
bit grisma; mecha
bitch (derogatory) tipa
bite, big tarascón
bitter agarroso; bíter; cerrero; suche

black (color) prieto
black eye pistero
blackout enlagunado
black person (derogatory) angolo(a); chocolate; cholito(a); cholo(a); chombo; cururo; jamaiquino; molleto; moreno; prieto(a)
black person from the U.S. (derogatory) llantón; moreno; moyo
black person, light-skinned mulato(a)
black power blackpawer
black sheep of the family mancha negra
black widow spider capulina
blackboard tablero
blacken entilar
black-haired person trigueño(a)
blade chuzo
blame echarle las cacas
blanket chamarra; cobija; colcha; cuilca; frisa; friza; manta; poncho
blanket, light serape
bleach blich
blind tuerto
blind female choca
blink espabilar
blister envejigarse
block bloque
blond person cano; chancaco; fula(o); güera(o); huero; locho(a); macho; mono(a); rucio(a)
blood sausage prieta; sangre
blouse cota
blow camotazos; cantaso; cantazo; guamazo; guaracazo; lamparazo; turcaso blow, to chantar
blow in the belly panzazo
blow in the eye bergantín; fundoso; piñazo
blow on the head cocotazo; marranazo
blow, strong bichazo; chancazo; mamonazo; tanganazo

blow the whistle on someone aventar a alguien
blow, with a a rolo
blow with a blunt object guamazo
blow with a cudgel totazo
blow with a heavy stick palotazo; toletazo
blow with any spherical object pepazo
blow with the fingers chirlito
blow with the fist bollo; cachimbo; chingadazo; chingazo; guascazo; mangazo; ñeco; pajuelazo; piña; piñazo; reatazo; tabaco; trompada; trompón
blow with the hand, strong cachuchazo
blowout bloaut
blue jeans vaquero; yin
blues, the blues
bluff bluf bluff, to blufear
bluffs, person who cañero; fafarachero; fafaracho
blunder enflautada
blunt pompo
blush flochar
blustering falfullero; farfullero
boarding card pasabordo
boarding house asistencia
boarding house, owner or operator of a bordera(o)
boast balaquear; caña; entablar; entablonada; guapear
boastful aguajero; bocatero(a); carrilero; chanta; chantún; clueco; falfullero; farfullero; guapo(a); pantallero; plantilla
boat panga
boat used for cargo ancón
bobbin carretón
bobtailed chucuto; cuncuno
bodyguard espaldero
Bogotá, inhabitant of cachaco
boil nacido; salcochar

boiler boila
bold cocopelao; coquipela; pelón
  bold, to become agallarse
bold person tuso(a)
bones, foot or hand tabas
bonesetter sobador; sobandero
bonus ancheta; de forro; ganancia;
  vendaje
boo pifiar
booing pifia; silbatina
book someone buquear
bookcase biblioteca; estantería;
  librera
boot bototo
bootblack bolero
bootlegger butléger
bootlicker chupamedias; lambeache;
  lambebotas; lambeculo;
  lambehuevos; lambeojo; lambiache;
  lambiscón
bored, be estar podrido
boredom aburrición; jarto
boring person calilla; cansón; ladilla
**borrowing money, person who is
  always** garrotero
boss bos; trompa
bother (vulgar) acatarrar; amolar;
  chavar; chingar; chinguear; cuquear;
  dar candela; dar carpeta; echar jareta;
  empatar; emporrar; engorrar;
  esgunifar; fregar; fuñir; güevear;
  huevear; hinchar; jericoplear; jeringar;
  jeringuear; joder; jodienda; latir;
  manganear; mosquear; poner sebo;
  remoler; romper
bothersome issue lava; macán;
  sobadera
bothersome person (vulgar) ají;
  camote; cargoso; carlanca; catete;
  fregado; fritera; jerigonzo; jeringón;
  jodión; jodón; jorobón; ladilla;
  lavativoso; perecoso; perecudo;
  secante; sobado
bottle cap chapa; corcholata; ficha

bottle, feeding bibi; botella;
  chupo(a); chupón; mamadera;
  mamila; pacha; pomo de leche;
  tetera; tetero
bottle used to carry liquids pacha
bottom (vulgar) cueva; siete
boulevard búlava; jirón
bound joto
bow caravana
bow tie corbata de gato; corbata de
  humita
bowl bandeja; bol; cazo; chirimbolo;
  tutuma
bowlegged patuleco
bowling bolero; bouling; enchute
box boxear
box, large cajón
boxer boxer
boxing box; boxeo
boxing ring ring
boy botija; cabro; cachifo; carajito;
  chamaco; chaval; chavo; chico; chino;
  chiquilín; cipote; fiñe; molacho; ñaño;
  nene; patojo; pelado; pelao; pibe
boy, bothersome chinche
boy, country gurí
boy, intelligent aribe
boy, young carricito; chamaquito;
  chigüin; chirringo; chirriquitico;
  chirriquitín; patojito; purrete
boycott boicot
boyfriend, steady chaval; pestillo;
  pololo
bracelet brazalete; esclava; pulsera;
  pulso
braggart aguajero; carrilero
braid chimpa; simpa
brain coco
brake manear
brake(s) breca; breik; breique; breque;
  retranca
brandy, cheap guarapo; guaripola;
  jobo
brash person zafado

brass knuckles manopla
brassiere ajustador; brasier
brave, be tener agallas
brave person caliente; castao;
  guapo(a); panudo(a); ternejo; zafado
brawl ajiaco; alacamunería; argüende;
  baluma; batiboleo; bembé; berrinche;
  boche; bola; bonche; borlote; bronca;
  bululú; chamuchina; chirinola;
  fajazón; garata; guato; margayate;
  molotera; pango; quilombo; rebolotú;
  reborujo; revolú; revulú; tángana;
  tangána; titingó; toletole; tripulina
brazen zafado
bread panecillos; panecitos
bread, a kind of hallulla; marraqueta;
  mogolla; pupusa; roscón; tacón;
  tortilla de rescoldo; trama
bread, corn flour arepa
bread, crumbled desmoronamiento
bread rolls bolillos; pancitos
break breca; breik; breique; breque
  break, to escrachar; totearse
break a seed or an eggshell
  descorotar
break in pieces hacer tira
breakwater molo; tajamar
breasts, woman's (vulgar) chiche;
  chichi; goma; marías; marujas;
  pampalinas; pechugas; puchecas
breath, bad tufo
bribe aliñar; coima; coimear; engrasar;
  matraca; matraquear; matraqueo;
  mordida; untar la mano
briefcase bulto
bring down an arrogant person
  achantar
broadcasting brodcastin
broke, be andar ficha; andar pato;
  andar quebrado; arrancado; arrancao;
  estar ahorcado; estar pato; helado;
  jorobado; lámparo; pelado
broken heart cabanga
brook estero

broom pichanga
broom, completely worn out soco;
  zoco
brothel keeper cabrona; madama
brother broder; ñaño
brown braun; carmelita; castaño;
  chocolate; marrón
brown, light aguarapado
brown sugar honey chancaca
brown-skinned person pardo;
  trigueño(a)
bruise cototo; machucón; morete
brunette menudo
brush cabra; chulo
brush, shaving hisopo
brush used to clean bottles
  churrusco
brute gocho
bubble bomba
bucket bote; cubeta; cubo
buddy manito; mano; pana
budget badget
buffoon chucán; gracejo
bug pajarito
building bilding; finca
bulldog buldog
bulldozer buldoser
bulletin board boletín; espaciador;
  tablero de anuncios; tablilla de
  anuncios
bull's eye blanco; fama; mosca
bullshitter (vulgar) bulchitero
bully abusado(a); añiñado(a); añiñao;
  bragado; bule; garrotero; guapo(a)
bum bichicome; linyera
bump cocotazo; marranazo; hueco;
  suelazo; turupe; tutuma
bump into something caballazo;
  tiestazo; totazo
bump on the head cototo
bumper bamper; bompa; bomper;
  paragolpes
bumps to mark a street toperoles
bumpy boludo

bun in the hair cachirulo; chongo; moña
bundle lulo; maleta
bungalow bángalo
burden gabela
burden someone with something that is annoying endilgar; endosar; enflautar
burdened abacorao
burglary cacho
burlap guaipe
burn quemada
burn, big quemón
burned achicharrado
burned out quemado
bury in enterrar
bus bas; camión; chiva; colectivo; guagua; microbus; omnibus
bus driver colectivero; guaguero
bus line boslain
bus, small buseto; busito; buzeta; chivita; microbus
business bisnes
business, easy and highly profitable mantequilla
business, go around in voltear
business, illegal palangre; rebusque
business, small ancheta; chimbo; linterna; ventorrillo
business, smart movida
businessman bisnesman
busy ajorado; festinado
busybody aprontao; arbolario; brejetero; entrador(a); huelefrito; metete; nariz; refistolero(a); refitolero(a); zaramullo
butcher bachajé; pesador
butcher shop pesa; tercena
butter manteca
butterfly paloma
butterfly larva churrusco
buttocks (vulgar) ancas; aparato; cachete; cola; culo; el queque;

fundifá; fundillo; poto; rabo; tambembe; traste
buttocks and/or genitals in children's language popi; popín; popó
buttocks, having big nalgón(a)
buttocks, person with small culipando; culiseco
buy or sell something in an auction rematar
buzzard carancho; chulo; gallinazo; jote; samuro; tincute; tiñoza; zamuro; zopilote
by chance a juro; a la brava; a la machimberra; chiripa; de chiripa; por chiripa
bye-bye chaito; chau
cabinet cabinete; estante
cable ferry tarabita
cactus quisco
caddy cadi
Cadillac cadilaque
cake bizcocho; bizcochuelo; panatela; pastel; queik; queque
cake in the shape of a loaf mollete
cake made of hard unrefined sugar azúcar negra; empanizado; panela; panetela; panocha; panuela; raspadura
cake, special kind of mamón
calf ternera; vaquilla
calf (of the leg) batata; camote; canilla; chamorro
call for the cat cuchito
calm down aguántate
calves cañuelas; choclos
cameraman cameraman
camomile albarillo; camamila
camper cámper
camping campin
can lata; pote; tarro
can opener apridor
candle, thick tallow velón
candy candi

candy prepared with sugar and milk vaca lechera

cane alcohol, inferior quality cachaza

cannabis cañamo

canned food bote; enlatado(a); lata; pote

canoe banasta; bató; chalupa; panga; pelota; piragua

canopy tolda

canteen tutuma

canyon, narrow cajón

cap biscera; cachucha

cape jorongo; sarape

caprice birria

car carro; coche; máquina

car hood bonete

car jack gata; mico; yaque

car, old and/or battered batata; burra; cacharra; cacharro; cafetera; charchina; cucaracha; fodongo; garnacha; matraca; tartana

car trunk baúl; cajuela; castaña; tronk

car, worthless yonker

carafe pomo

carcass carcasa

careless, be pelar

caress ajonjear; añoñar; chinchinear; tolonguear

carpet carpet

carry on the back terciar

carry-out food bastimento

car's plate licencia; patente; placa; tablilla

cartoons cómicas; comiquillas; curiositas; monos; muñequitos

cash cach **cash, to** cachar

cash-flow cash-flow

casino, illegal timba

casket cajón

castrate an animal arreglar; componer

casualties casualidades

cat bibicho; cucho

catch cachar; pañar; trincar

catch a cold acatarrar

catch in the act cachar; rochar

catch something in the air barajar

caterpillar cuncuna

Catholic, fanatic mocho; pechoño(a)

Caucasian bolillo; gringo

caucus of influence rosca; rosco

CD cidi

ceiling tumbado

celebration feria

cemetery chacarita

cemetery caretaker camposantero

censure pipo

certified mail recomendado

chalk choc; tizate

chalk, blackboard gis

challenge chorear

chambermaid mucama

chamberpot mica

champion champion

chance chanse

chandelier candil

change (money) chirola; chirona; feria; menudo; sencillo; vuelto

change ideology or political affiliation voltear

change one's mind rajar

charcoal drawing carboncillo

charge charchiar

charm garabato

charm women bacilón

charter chárter

chase atiquizar

chastisement, severe fuetiza

chat, unimportant cháchara

chatterbox charlón

chauffeur chofero

cheap baratieri; chafa; macano(a)

cheap goods cacharros; cachivaches; pichiflina

cheap imitation trucho

cheap person (derogatory) judío; machete; pichinchero(a)

cheap thing pacotilla

cheat amolar; chingar; fumar; marranear; mogallar; morder; pichulear
cheat in a marble game fonchar
cheat on an exam chivear; copiarse; pastelear
cheater chapucero; chira
cheats on an exam, person who copietas; pastelero
check chequear; chulear
check mark chulo
check up chequeo
cheekiness impavidez
cheeks, with big cachetón; chalchudo
cheese, soft and milky cuajada
cherish others querendón
cherry capulín; guinda
chewing gum chuingom
chick of any bird except the hen pichón
chickenpox lechina
chief chacón
child chapul; perinola
child, meddlesome siripita
child, most spoiled ñaño
child, pampered chipón(a); querendón
child, poor or homeless chino(a)
child, precocious amayorado
Chilean (nickname) roto
Chilean cowboy guaso; huaso
Chilean dance, national cueca
chili stew ajiaco
chimney flue tiraje
chin cumbamba
chip estillar
chlorine clorex; clorina
choice escogencia
choke (automobile) choc
choose chusear
chorus of a song cantaleta
Christmas crismas
Christmas carol asalto
chubby and sloppy person batata

chubby person cambuto; catimbao; pachango; parraneto; petacón(a)
cigar tabaco
cigar butt breva; cabo; chacuaco; chicote; mocho
cigarette faso; frajo; pitillo
cigarette butt bacha; chinga; cusca; pucho
cigarette, inferior-quality chicote; rompepecho
cigarette lighter laira
cigarette made with corn leaves tusa
claim cleimiar
clam clam; taca
clap clapiar
classroom salón
clavicle eslilla
clay greda; masilla
clay vessel cacharro de greda
clean clin; fresquesito
cleaners cliner
clear blanquear; cliar
clear payment for a check conformar
clench empuñar
clerk in a fast-food restaurant lonchero
clerk in a poor, inferior-quality store bolichero
clerk, store dependiente
clever, be abusado(a)
clever move caribería; gallada; parada; ranada
clever person avispa; avispado; bagre; bala; banana; bicho; bocho(a); caperuzo; chucho; culebrero; jaiba; ladino(a); lángara; lanza; lobo; macuco; malva; recurso; tinoso; zamarro; zorrongo
client, become a amarchantarse
clip clip
clippers clipa
close, very a pata; de mingo
cloth jerga
cloth, cleaning bayeta

clothes, dirty percocho
clothes, old chirapa; garra; mecha; tiliches
clothes, wear many empalmado
clothing, cheap (derogatory) garra; pilchas; piltrafas; piltrajas
clothing for a baby's baptism faldellín
clothing for special events tenida
clothing lent or given to someone chiva
cloudy, very nublazón
clown clawn; gracejo
cloying, be hostigar
club mamón
clumsily, behave (vulgar) güevear; huevear
clumsy person bolsa; caballo; chalungo; gafo; ganso; gocho; gurundango; machetón(a); mamao; matungo; muchitanga; navo; pajarón; pariguayo; pendango; periguallo; tapado
clutch, automobile cloche
clutch in a vehicle, press the enclochar
coach coch
coal dust carboncillo
coat stand capotera
coat, woman's sobretodo; tapado
cob, tender and fresh jojoto
cocaine perico
cocaine laboratory cocina
cocaine laboratory technician cocinero
cocaine, portion that has been snorted pase
cockfight ring gallera; palenque
cockroach barata; chiripa; roche
cockroaches, place full of baratero
cocktail campechana
coconut, green pipa
coconut pulp vaca
coconut seller coquero

COD; cash on delivery ciodi
cod fish fritter bacalaito
coffee cofiro
coffee, black negro; tinto
coffee, inferior-quality cache
coffee, rotten cache
coffee, small perico
coffee with a little milk marrón
cohabit (vulgar) encuerarse
coin, any vellón
coins of little value chochas; menudo chichero
coitus (vulgar) polvo
cola with chocolate ice cream vaca negra
cola with vanilla ice cream vaca blanca
cold, extremely helaje; pacheco; tornillo cold, to be extremely empalarse
cold, have a constipado
cold season escarcha
collect colectar
college freshman mechón
collision quiñazo
Colombian flatlands, person from the llanero
color the cheeks chapetear
colored seasoning color
comb desembarañador; peineta; peinilla comb, to combiar
comics chistes; comiquitas; cuentos; fonis; monitos; muñequitos; paquínes; tiras cómicas
comings and goings corredera
command jefaturear
commission, someone who works for a coyote
commotion acabose
compact disc cidi
companions, very close amorochados
competent capo
complain chichar; chillar; patalear; pitear

complaining, person who is always argüendero(a)
complaint complain; pipo
complicate things encarajinar
complicated teso
complicated issue arroz con mango; berraquera; cahuin; verraquera
complies or consents easily, person who mantequilla
compliment, servile jalada
computer compiuter; computador
computer chip chip
computer window window
conceal quillarse
conceal a crime apañar
conceited llambaroso; vaselino
conceited and boastful person pintor
concern atingencia; tarugo
conch cambute
condiment achiote; color; recao
condom (vulgar) forro; goma
cone of an ice cream cone cucurucho
cone, paper or cardboard cambucho
confess espepitar
confront a difficult situation estar montado en la vaca
confront the consequences chupar
confuse boruquear; calar; emborucar; engalletar
confused, be acarajado; apendejado; azurumbarse; azurumbrado; empelotado; galletoso; pelar
confused, become abatatarse; atufar; emborucar
confused situation emborujo
confusion barata; batata; bolate; brollo; desbole; despelote; despiole; galleta; latifundio; mazamorra; pango; reborujo; revolica
confusion, create emborujar; empatucar
conger eel congrio
congestion galleta
connect empatar

connections with people of influence brazo; gancho; pala; palanca
conservative godo; mocho
consortium pool
conspiracy manguala
conspire amangaluar
constipated estítico; tapado; trancado
constipated, be trancarse; estar prendido
constipation, acute entablazón
container callana; candungo; pipote; porongo; tiesto
contraband merchandise market sanandresito
contraceptive device churrusco
contradictory contrecho
contribution erogación
controller controler
convalescent cacreca
conversation, long and insipid cotorra; jarabe de lengua
conversation, noisy chercha; corrincho; mololoa
cook cuquiar
cook in water with salt sancochar
cookie choca; cuki; galletica; galletita
cool suave **cool, to** culear
cool person vacano
cooler cúler
coolie culi
cops jura
copy (magazine, newspaper) copia
copyright copirrait
coquettish woman chiva; mica
cord cabestro
corn abatí; avatí; choclo; elote
corn, baby chilote
corn cake perrerreque
corn, dish made with morocho
corn field milpa
corn flour chuchoca; funche; polenta
corn flour and cheese bread pandebono
corn flour, cream of ulpo

corn flour, dish prepared with polenta

corn flour, roasted gofio

corn, ground chancao

corn patty panocha

corn, purple pujagua

corn tortilla with cheese, fried repocheta

corn used to feed poultry maíz; malamé; pozole

corn, whole grain, stewed mote

corncob abatí; avatí; choclo; chocolo; choglo; coronta; mazorca de maíz; olote; tusa

corncob, tender elote

corned beef carne bif

corner of a room cucho

corpulent maceta

corral, big pampón

correct chévere; legal

Costa Ricans ticos

cot, wooden marquesa

couch couch

countrified, become aguajirarse

country cauntri

country-like cachaco; campirano

countryside cauntri

couple, unwed marinovios

courage arrecho; caliente; guaramo; pana; pechuga

courage, have embraguetarse; tener pana

courage, with conchudo

courier chasqui

court afilar; atacar; pololear

courtship brega

cover encielar; taquear

covers the mistakes of others palero

cover-up forro; socapar a uno

coward cagacatre; chabelón; chayote; cochino; cucamba; culilludo; mantilla; maula; pendango; pendejo(a); ratón; tilico

cowardice canilla; pendejada

cowboy, Argentine or Uruguayan gaucho

cowboy, Colombian or Venezuelan llanero

crab buruquena; cacarico; cocolía; jaiba; juey; seboro

crab fisherman jueyero

crack resquicio **crack, to** abrirse

cracked craqueado

craftiness ranada

crane, small donkey; señorita

crash cantaso; cantazo; chancacazo; estrellón

crash a party descolgar

crazy andar lurias; guano; más loco(a) que una cabra

crazy, go desvirolado; norte; tocado; tostao; turuleta

crepe panqueque

crest cenca; chorcha

crib camita

crib note bate; chivo; comprimido; droga; torpedo

cricket caballete; siripita

cries too much, someone who bicho chillón

crime crimen

criminal malevo; palomo; pato malo; punga

crippled tunco

criticize pipo; tusar

crook mulero

crooked chueco

crooked deal chanchullo

cross bar diablito

cross out tarjar

cross the Rio Grande brincar el charco

cross-country competition cross

cross-eyed bizconeto; choco(a)

crouch aparragarse; aplatarse

croupier gurupie

crowd bola; bolón; catajana; jaracotal; la gallá; tracalá

crowd, in a apilonados
cruel, be tener muñeca
cruise crus
crumb buruza; chinguito
Crumbs! ipuchica!
crush apachurrar; batacazo; batatazo; despichar; machetiar
cry berrear
cuckold (vulgar) cabrón; cachero; cachón; le pegaron el tarro
cucumber chucumber
cufflinks collera; mancorna
cunning jaiba; visage
cup-and-ball toy emboque
cupboard bufete
curb cordón; encintado de la acera; sardinel; solera
curly-haired person chongo; churo; churrusco; colocho; enchinado; marrón; murruco; musuco; pasa; pasudo
currency of Mexico dinero-plata
currency of the U.S. dinero-oro
curse daño
curse, expression and hand gesture to bicho
cursor cursor
custard apple chirimoya
custodian el super
customer, regular casero
customs clerk or agent despachante
customs house garita
cut and comb hair peluquear
cut hair very close tusar
cut in line colear
cut in pieces toletear
cut school capear; capear escuela; hacer la chancha; hacer la cimarra; hacer pinta; jiriola; paviarse; ratearse de la escuela; volarse de la escuela
cut weeds despagar
cut with a knife or a machete chafirrazo; chapear; filerear **cut** mochar

cute célebre
cutting from a plant patilla; sarmiento
cylindrical object lulo
dad, in an endearing sense cucho
daddy cochote
daft chiflis
dagger, a facón
damage bichar; desperfeccionar; embarrar; escrachar; fuñir
damaged object albóndinga
Damn it all! icoño!
damned maldingo(a)
dance guarachar; rumbear
dance, family charanga; charranga
dance music, popular Caribbean salsa
dance party of poor people chingana; divierta
dance, regional guaracha; jarana; marinera; pachanga; porro; sanjuanito
dancer, good gozón; rumbero
dancing hall dancing hall
dandy cajetilla; catrin; dandi; pepe
dangerous endiablado; jodido; sobado
daring atrincado; desharrapado; raspado
dark complexion, person with a (derogatory) arrosquetado; cholo(a); curiche; morocho; prieto; urraca; zambo
darling mi cielo
date deit
date many women bregador; lachar
daughter china
daughter, youngest maraca
daunted, be amusgarse; azarearse
daydream caldo de cabeza
daydreamer alepantado
day-laborer working in the fields bracero
day's pay jornal
dazed turulato
dead estiró los caites; peló el ajo

dead, the la fulera; la pelada; pateteada; peteteada
deaf juicio
deal, good guame
dealer of second-hand items chivero; garrero
death, sign of calaca
debt acreencia; cacalota; calillas; dita
debt, unpaid clavo
debts, acquire enjaranarse
debts, have many embrollao; enditarse; enjaranado
decay aplanche
deceitful guillado; papelero
deceive cabulear; dar capote; embolatar; envolatar; fumar; pichulear
deck chair perezosa
decorations, party bambalina
defamation recorte
defeat others in a contest chingar; garrotear; garrotiza; pela; soplar
defecate (vulgar) hacer el dos; hacer la caca; hacer pupu; votar
defect cuija; dinga
deform eschoretar
deformity, person with a physical choreto
defraud or swindle someone pulpear
defrost desfrozar
degrade something (vulgar) putear
delay payment of a debt amallarse
delayed, get embromar
delete deletear
deli fiambrería; rosticería
delicate and beautiful thing cuquera
delicate person aliñada; don de gentes; fifí; místico
delight chiche; sabrosura
delightful person sabrosón
delinquent malevo; palomo; pato malo; punga
delirium tremens diablo
delivery boy casero
demanding cachero

demon chucuto
den abrigadero
denounce aventar; batir; chivar; chivatear; chotear; pajear; sapear
deodorant antipespirante; deodoran
depressed, be engerirse; tener un bajón
deserve ameritar
desire goma
desire to eat or drink provocación
desire, unfulfilled cuello
desk carpeta
desk cover vade
despicable person (vulgar) arrastrado; tusa; vergajo; zaragate
dessert, special kind of capirotada; maíz caqueado; majarete; marifinga; matagusano; natilla; requesón; tembleque
destroy blanquear; hacer garra
detective (vulgar) gofia; petejota; raya; tira
deteriorate jubilarse
detour detur
devil cozco; el uñudo; mandinga; pingo
devour jartar
dial the telephone dailear; dalear; dialear
diapers chapeta; culero; diaper; mantillas; taparrabos; zapeta
diarrhea (vulgar) abradera; cagadera; cagalera; cagarreta; cagueta; charretada; charreteada; chorro; churra; churretada; churria; corredera; currutaca; cursera; obradera; soltura
dice chincharro
dice game cacho; canilla
dice, loaded cabra
dictionary mataburros
die estirar la jeta; guindó los tenis; pelar; quedarse tieso; templarse; totearse
difficult matter fritera; papa caliente

difficult person or situation duro; embromado; fregada; fregado; jodido; peludo; salado; teso; tostón; trabajoso

difficulty brete; pacaya

diffident tilico

dignified alturado

dike tajamar

dim person gafo

dim-witted (vulgar) güevón; huevón

dime daim; vellón de diez

diminish the virility in a man mariquear

din balumba; bayú; bembé

directions, give empuntar

dirt carca

dirt on the knees cabra

dirty chorreoso; cochino; curtío

dirty and messy place cucarachero

dirty, get batir; curtir; empichar; empatucar

dirty person chancho; chorreoso; cochino; curtido; curtío; manteco; pililo

dirty word guachada

disagreeable person parche

disappear alcanforarse; empuntarlas

disappointment chasco; magna

disaster quilombo; tendalada

disasters, person who provokes quilombero(a)

disc jockey discjokey

discolored curtido

discount rebaje

discouraged aguacate; aplastado

disgrace somebody else hacer sonar; mamonazo

dishcloth repasador

disheartened, be amachinarse

disheveled cacurúo(a)

dishwasher fregadera

dislike cocora; riña

dislocate desconchabar; recalcadura; troncha

dismantled descachalandrado; desconchiflado

dismiss someone from a job descolar

disorder barajuste; barata; brollo; desbole; despelote; despiole; jaleo; reblujo; rebujo; relajo; revolú; revulú; tendalada; voleo

disorganization guachafita

disorganize bichar

displeasure calentera

disqualify descualificar

dissemble desconchinflar

distance between two places, great jalón

distillery, illegal sacotín

distrustful orejero

disturb latir

disturbance furrusca; guachafita; montante

disturbed due to drug consumption trabado

ditch chamba; diche; zanjón

dive consumir

dizzy cucufato; patuleco

do something in a disorganized way chancar; machetear

do something quickly esmandarse

do something unwillingly mamarse

do stupid things (vulgar) huevonear

dock dock

dog, small and tame pichicho

dog without pedigree quiltro

doll, ugly monicongo

dollar bills lechugas

domestic doméstico

domesticate aguachar

dominos, blank piece in caja blanca; chucha

donkeyman donquero

doormat felpudo

doorpost banderola

dormitory, college dormitorio

dot matrix printer pin printer

double-check doblechequear

double chin chalcha
double-chinned chalchudo
doubtful thing macana
doughnut dona; donat; picarón
down payment enganche; pie
downpour invierno
drag jalar
dragonfly matapiojo; pipilacha
dress chachae; dres; traje
dress elegantly apitiguarse; arrejarse;
  arriscarse; cacharpearse; empilcharse
dress, summer solera
dressed up cheto; palta
dresses carelessly, person who
  apuercado; descachalandrado;
  mojiganga
dribble driblar; gambetear
drink a few glasses canchar
drink, a kind of alcoholic aloja;
  campechana; caña; chicha; curda;
  gas; mezcal; mingui; pisco; pulque
drink, a special kind of aguada(o);
  aguadulce; atole; campechana;
  chingue; chorote; pinole; pinolillo;
  piñol; puscafé; resbaladera; salpicón;
  tiste; ulpo
drink alcohol chupar; jalar; mamar
drink alcohol to get rid of a hangover
  sacarse el ratón
drink, cool fresco
drink, one-swallow cañonazo;
  guamazo; jalón; lamparazo;
  matracazo; palo; tacazo
drink, tasteless agua de piringa;
  aguachada; aguapiringa
drink, thick mazamorra
drink without sugar amargo
drinker tomador
drinking glass, big potrillo
drinking spree bomba; bomba de
  agua
drinking vessel made from a gourd
  mate
drive draivear; manejar

drive or initiative, have apechugar
driver (computer) draiver
driver's license cartera dactilar; pase
drizzle chinchín; cilampa; garúa;
  garuga; harinear; serenar
drop dropear
drop out dropearse
dropper gotario; gotero
drug dopar
drug addict colino; grifo; moto;
  pichicatero; tecato
drug, illegal falopa; pichicata
drug, inject a abujazo
drug supply cachucha
drug, use of any illegal pase
drugs, make darse un paseo
drugs, personal disturbance from
  traba; tronada
drugstore dragstor
drum bomba
drunk ajumado; almareado; birote;
  bolo; caneco; cañoneado;
  chumadococido; como cuba; como
  huasca; como huevo; como pickle;
  como piojo; como poto'e guagua;
  cuete; cufifo; curado; curdeao;
  embolado; en fuego; engorilado;
  entre pisco y nazca; guarape;
  guarapeado; guarapero; guaro;
  guayao; jalado; jumado; jumeta;
  jumo; mamado; papalina; pernicioso;
  petardo; picao; prendido; rajao;
  rascado; tacuache; tomado; trinco;
  trompeta; zumbado
drunk, absolutely pluto
drunk, almost a medio filo; ajumao;
  copetón; encopetonarse
drunk, be agarrar la tetera; andar con
  el gorila; andar pedo; andar pisto;
  estar bomba; estar con el gorilla;
  estar con la caña; estar con la mona;
  estar en fuego; jumado
drunk, get abombar; amarrarse;
  chumar; curar; empedar; guarapear;

jalar; jumarse; ponerse pedo; rajarse; rascar; traguearse

drunk with wine, become enguainar

drunkenness (vulgar) bomba; bomba de agua; curda; juma; jumado; montera; pasmarse; rasca; rascazón; tranca; vacilón

dry cleaners cliner; draicliner

dry lamb meat chalona

dry sugar aventar

dude futre; pituco

duffer zoquete

dull fome; fritera

dull-witted person aguada(o)

dumb (vulgar) apendejao; chirote; collera; crestón; forro; junípero(a); mamerto; menso; tarado

dump dompear; dumping

dump truck dumper

dupe embachichar

dust dostiar

duty gabela

duty-free liberación de aduanas

dwarf corrotoco

eager cachero

eagerness berraquera; verraquera

earrings aretes; aritos; aros; candongas; caravanas; chapeta; pantalla; topo

easily seduced pariguayo; periguallo

easy asopao; bilí; bizcocho; botana; chancaca; chiche; golilla; guame; jauja; mogollo; paseo

easy to upset or irritate malaley

easy woman (vulgar) banda

eat filear; manyar

eat and drink at the expense of others bolsear; pechar; sacar la leche

eat at another's home lamber; velar

eat everything that is served jartar

eat excessively atracar; batear; darse un panzazo; darse una jartera;

empanzar; empanzurrar; jambar; jamonear

eat until satiated empacar

eat well forrar

eater, big garoso; gorozo

Ecuadorian Indian, young longo

editorial, newspaper mancheta

educated person leído

effeminate (vulgar) amariconado; aviador; cueco; de agua; manflora; marico; pájaro; pato; torolo; trolo; volteado

efficient capo; machete

efforts, by all a gatas; a todo dar

egg blanquillo

egg, rotten güero; huero

eggs, scrambled huevos pericos

ejaculate (vulgar) acabar

elect a candidate to office electar

electric socket socate; socket

electric switch chucho; llave de luz

elegant cachaco; chévere; chiche; churro; chute; perchudo; pintoso; pituco; titino

elegant and rich, person who appears refistolero(a); refitolero(a)

elevator elevador

elude a responsibility culebrear

elusive huilón; lobo

embarrassed acholado; embarazado(a); pasme

embarrassed, be planchar

embarrassed, get tupirse

embarrassment chasco; muela; pachó; pena; quemón

emigrate to the U.S. brincar el charco

employment, public cambur

empty biche; güero

encourage others to fight aleonar; carbonero

end of the story tilingo-tilango

end, until the a concho

endorsement baqueo; vaqueo

endure pain patiently rustir

enema visitadora
engaged, become amarrarse
engagement, breaking an le dio la quiebra
enthusiasm berraquera; verraquera
enthusiasm, fill with entotorotar
enthusiasm, lacking achantarse; aplastado
enthusiastic, be retamblar
enthusiastic for inquieto
entry rubro
envious engurrioso
equal guareto; pintado
equal parts, in apartido
eraser borrador; desborrador
erotic games of a couple in love atracar; jamón
errand, go on a voltear
escape abrirse; embalar; emplumárselas; empuntarlas; pitar; raspar
establishment establichment
evening show intermediaria
evil act chingadera; malinche
evil eye mabita
exaggerated alaraco; arbolario; farolero
exaggeration argüende; irse al chancho; pasarse la nota
exam, give an dar examen
exam, take an tomar examen
exasperated, get enchivarse
excellent chévere; legal; machera; paponia; pepeado; piocha; soda
excess, in de vicio
excessive bárbaro
excrement cacana; meca
excrement of a baby in diapers maleta
excuse excusar
exhale smoke when smoking chicotear
exhilarated estrepitarse
exigent trancado

exit éxito
expelled from school dropeado
expenditure erogación
expensive salado
experience, gain jubilarse
experience, person of great canchero; curtido; recorrido(a)
expert cuatriborleado; sabido; taco
explosion totazo
express expres
extraordinary acabose; bárbaro; manso(a)
extraordinary person terciazo
extravagant discante
eyeglasses espejuelos; foco; gafas
eyeglasses, person who wears (derogatory) gafufa
eyeshadow pestañina
eyesore mondongo
fabric, inferior quality brin; choleta; gangoche; lona; mantadril; tocuyo
face, person with an irregular cachipuco
factory factoría
factory worker, female laburanta
fail chingar; corchar; feilear; irse al tacho; mistear; ponchar; sonar
fail a course colgarse; ponchar; quemarse; raspar
fail a student partir; rajar
fail an exam colgarse; colgarse en la escuela; colgarse en un examen; corchar; jalar el examen; ponchar el examen; quemarse; rajarse en el examen
fail to live up to a commitment mamar; mamarse
failure chasco; gajo
faint taranta
faint-hearted culilludo
fair turno
fair play fairplay
fake chimbo; fulera(o); julero(a)
fall escocotarse; matada; suelazo

fall behind colgarse
fall in love suddenly enfuscarse
fall in love (vulgar) empelotarse con; encularse; templar
fall into disgrace caerle polilla
false cachiporra; fayuto; papelero
false appearance pantalla
false news bola
false teeth caja de dientes
falsehood feca; macana
falsify chimbear
familiar territory querencia
familiar with the route rumbeador
familiarity between friends caballo
family party charonga; charranga
fan abanico; fan
fantastic bárbaro; como coco; le ronca el clarinete; le zumba el mango
far, very en los quintos infiernos
farce papelada
farewell adiosito
farm, small chacra; hijuela
farmer farmero; guaina; mediero
farming land, neglected rastrojo
fart (vulgar) hechar una bomba; peo; ventoso
fast bolón; como cuete; embalao; esmandao; soplado
fastener desabrochador
fast-food place comevete; lonchería
fast-thinking, roguish person piola
fat person albóndiga; amasadito(a); bachicha; barrilito; bombo; chichos, fodongo; mangoso; pamplona; tripón
father taita; tata; tatá
fatigue gurbia
faucet canilla; caño; chorro; focet; llave; pila; pluma
fault-finder triscón
favor colocho
favorite spot querencia
fawner alcahuete
fax fax

fear chucho; escame; justiniano; mieditis
fearless person agalla; guapo(a)
features that show native origin achinado
feces, solid human (vulgar) caquis; mojón; ñoña; pupú; sorete
fed up, be cabriado; chipiar; choreado; hasta la tusa; quemado
feeble muchitanga
feeder fider
felony felony
female, blind choca
female sanitary napkins cotaco
feminine feminil
fence reja; verja; talanquera; zanja
fender botafango; botalodo; faldón; fenda; fender; tapabarros; tapalodo
ferment enchichar
fermented choco(a)
ferry ferry
festival of folk dances jarana
fib guata; jarana
fibers, full of hebrudo
field, big potrero
field glasses anteojos largavista; gemelos
field of grass pajonal
field, sports or agricultural fil
fifty-fifty miti miti
fight fajina; follisca; garrotera; mocha; patasca; rosca; tángana; toletole; tripulina **fight, to** darse zoca; guindar; mancornar; trenzarse
fighter faitoso(a)
file file
fill atapuzar; atucuñar
film film; filme
filth cota; pegostre
filthy person zoquete
filthy place chinchería; chinchero
fin gualeta
fine fain; macanudo
finicky person cismático

finished, be estar sonado
fire someone botar; desocupar
firecracker cuete; guatapique; tote
firefighter lumbrero
firewater made from grapes
  pisco
firewater, smuggled guandolo
fireworks, a kind of cuete;
  guatapique; tote; volatero; yacks;
  yaquis
first prize paquete
fishing line guaral
fishing rod carrizo
fist fight agarrarse a cancos; agarrón;
  bronca; canco
fit of temper calentura
fix bichar
flash flash
flashlight flash
flat pacho
flatter aguachar; hacer la pata;
  mecatear; peinar; sobar
flattered, person who likes to be
  ñoño
flatterer (vulgar) alcahuete;
  alzafuelles; jalabola; jalador;
  jalamecate; labioso(a); lambón(a);
  patero(a); sacamicas
flattering, continuous jaladera
flattery madera; mecate
flat tire flat
flat tire, get a fletear
flatulence (vulgar) echar una bomba;
  peo; ventoso
flea market achimería
flee arrancar; cachiflín; echarse el
  pollo; rispar
flick pastorejo; tincazo
flies, many mosquero
fling aventar
flip over flipear
flirt caculear; fletar; flirtear; gatear;
  pololear
flirtation floretear

flirtatious afilador; gaucho; lacho;
  pispireta
float flout
flood aguachinarse
flow chart flowshart
flower florear
flowerpot macetero
flowery florecido
flu, the flu; gripa; monga
flunk flonkear
flush flochar
flute made with several bamboos
  quena
fog camanchaca; cerrazón; lancha;
  sabora
folder cartapacio
folding screen cancel
folk dance of Puerto Rico danza
folk singer who improvises verses
  payador
fond of inquieto
fond of, be aguachar
fond of women, extremely lacho
fondle (vulgar) atracar; chapar; dar
  carpeta; jamonear
fondness ñoñerías
food mastique
food can bote; conserva; enlatado(a);
  lata; pote; tarro
food containers fiambrera;
  viandas
food for a trip cocaví; provista
food, heavy llenador
food, inferior-quality tumba
food, leftover retallón
food or drink, badly-prepared
  frangollo; sambumbia
food, rotten cignato
food scraps salcocho; sancocho
food stand, small friquitín
food, supply oneself with forrar
food that fits in the mouth, piece of
  mascada
fool fulear; tantear

foolish or silly person (vulgar)
aguacate; agüevado; ahuevado;
apendejao; azurumbrado; baboso;
berraca; bola; bolsa; bolsiflay; bolsón;
bolsudo; boludo; buey; caido del
catre; camote; casimiro; chauchón;
chayote; chitrulo; chotón; cipote;
collera; comebola; crestón; dundo;
fallo; firulístico; forro; gil; gracejo;
guajolote; guanaco; guarango;
güevón; huevón; jetón; jicate; jil;
mamerto; menso; menzo; morolo;
nabo; pánfilo(a); papayudo; pendejo;
pigmeo; pistolo(a); salame; suncán;
surumbo; tarado; tilango(a); tilico;
tilingo; tórtolo; vejiga; zaramullo
foolish remark (very vulgar) güevada;
huevada
foolishness al pedo; caballada;
chantada; charada; chayotada;
chirotada; ñeñeñe; pallasa; patilla;
pavada; pistolada; zoncura
foot, big gamba; ñame; patricia
foot odor pecueca; pesuña
foot odor, someone with bad
cicotudo; sicotudo
foot, swollen ñame
footing futin
for sale for sale
ford of a river chimba
foreigner (vulgar) arribeño; yoni
foreman forman
forest trail pica; pique
form a pool aposar
form to fill out esqueleto; forma
formal dress traje
formal person (derogatory)
almidonado
format a floppy disk formatear;
formateo de disco
fortunate person bacán; fortunoso;
suertero
fortune cachipil
fortune, make a taparse

forward, go forwardear
foul in a ball game faul
foul-mouthed boquisucio
foundations of a wall herido
fountain vertiente
fountain pen pluma
frame carapacho
frank franque
fraud aletazo; descrestada; forro;
manguala
freak out friquear
freakish or outlandish person
mondongo
free de golilla
freeze frisar
freezer frisa
fresh fregado; liso
freshman fresco
fried meal cuchifrito; cuchufrito
friend, close alicate; broder; cabro;
cuatezón(a); iloco!; loro; manito;
pana
friends, become amistarse
fright cisca; jabón
frightened, become acholarse;
culipendearse; enculillarse
front man calanchún
frost lancha
frozen frisado
fruit, dried pasado
fruit, ripe jecho
fruit, rotten jojoto; malanco(a)
fruit, tasteless aguanoso
fruit that is not ripe camuliano;
celeque; sarazo; zarazo
fruits, mixture of different
tutifruti
fry friar
fuel chala; fiul
full full; pachigua; popocho(a)
full of food, be empancinao; estar
satisfecho; pimpo; pipocho; piponcho;
popocho; taqueado(a)
full-time fultaim

fun, have bonchar; echarle al pelo; vacilar
function funcar
funny charro; costiante
furious, get arrecharse; enchivarse; encohetarse; enfogonarse
furniture fornitura; furnitura
fuss aguaje
fussy brejetero
gain special privileges at work apitutarse
gal galla
gambler (horses) burrero
gambling den manager chinguero
game, a special kind of child's gallito; listones; macalililia; manseque
gang barra; chorcha; corillo; cuerda; ganga; gavilla; palomilla; patota
gang, member of a ganguero; patotero
garbage bachata; charbasca
garbage can bote de basura; caneca; latón de basura; safacón; tacho de la basura; tarro de la basura; zafacón
garden party garden party
gargle corcorear; gargarear
gas station bomba de bencina; estación de servicio; expendio de gasolina; gasolinera; grifo
gasoline bencina; gas; gasolin; nafta
gather a crowd acarrear
gay person (vulgar) aviador; cacorro; cambiado; chupón; cucarrón; culero; gay; hueco; loca; mamalón(a); manflor; maraco; marico; pájaro; pato; rosca; rosquete
generous abiertazo; espléndido; manirroto; manoabierta; rasgado
genitals (vulgar) bicha(o); coroto; cosa
genitals, female (vulgar) papaya
German (nickname) boche
get (vulgar) chapar
get all mixed up trabucarse

get great profits cortarla a cincel
get or give an identification document cartnetizar; cedular
get something without the right to it pechar
get what has been desired levantar; mecha
gibe chifleta; chinga; costeo; pitanza; tiradera; trisca
gift, for the person giving a party jocha
gigabyte gigabyte
gigolo crestón
girl buca; cabra; carajita; chamaca; changa; chapul; china; molacha; nena; ñaña
girl, beautiful máquina
girl, big heavy pioscota
girl, intelligent aribe
girl, little chamaquita
girl, newborn baby chancleta
girl, poor (vulgar) griseta
girl who amuses people changa
girl who behaves like a boy machona; marota
girlfriend chavala; costilla; jeva; pestillo; polola
give largar
give birth liberación
give up correrse; rajarse
gizzard contre; molleja de pollo
glacé helado
glamour glamur
glass, big caña; potrillo
glass door mampara
gloominess aplanche
glue glu; pega; pegadura; pegante; plasticola; resistol
glutton bosgo(a); comején; lambío
go after someone continuously bandear
go away mandarse mudar; picárselas
go in a specific direction cortar
go to a specific place embocar; jalar

goad lanceta; picana
goal in a soccer game pepino
goal keeper golkiper
goals or objects of little value
 tepalcates
goatee candado; chiva; chivera
God el colochón; papachú
gofer goma
gogo girl gogo-girl
goiter cantimplora; chorcha; coto
good chévere; chingón; chuchin; flor;
 groso; gufeao; machín; machina;
 nítido; pleno; tuanis
good, be ser arrecho
Good heavens! ¡coño!
good luck chepa; liga
good luck, with chepudo
good thing machera
good, very arrecho; bacano; bárbaro;
 bien padre; buena esa; chévere;
 como tuna; de la madona; del carajo;
 del coño de su madre; descueve;
 legal; macanudo; padre; padrísimo;
 polenta; pulento; soda; suave
good-bye bai; chao
good-for-nothing person bernia;
 cacho; macuache
good-looking bizcocho; cajetón;
 chinazo; cuero; gallo; mamito;
 papasote; papazote; pintón; roscón;
 simpático
goods, cheap baratillo; baratos;
 cacharros; cachivaches
Gosh! ¡jito!
gossip acarrear; alacamunería;
 argüenda; bembeteo; bochinche;
 borrego; chimentos; cacarear;
 chimentar; conventilleo; copuchar;
 pelambre; pelar; zumbido
gossip continuously andar de
 jacalera; bembeto; sopa de cuerda
gossip, great cuentazo
gossip, spread andar de jacalera;
 conventilleo; desparramar; jacalear

gossiper bochinchero; camarón;
 chirinola; conventillero(a); enredista;
 lleva y trae; oreja; pajudo; pajuo;
 pendenciero; tapudo
gourd used to make containers jícara
grace garabato
grace, without terco
graceful fullero
graduate egresar
grammatical sentence sentencia
grandfather papa grande; tata; tatá
grandmother la vieja; mama grande;
 viejita
grapefruit greifrut; greifú; toronja
graphic mode in a computer
 graficmode
grasping vivaceta; vivaracho
grass gras
grass used to make hats jipijapa
grasshopper chapulín; chicharra;
 esperanza; langosta; saltagatos
gratuity vendaje
gravel grabol
gravy greive
gray color plomo
grease embijar
greasy and smelly cochambriento
Great! piocha
great bacán; como coco; padre;
 padrísimo
great amount cachá; poconón;
 pocotón
great character vacano
great number of people or things
 parranda
greed agalla; angurria
greedy agalludo; garifo
green grin
green beans chauchas; ejotes
greeting, rejected oso
grief grima
grieved apensionado
grill gril; grilla
grimace miñoco

grind chancar
groceries grocer; groceri; grocería
grocery store abarrotería; abasto; almacén; bodega; changarro; colmado; el chino; grocer; groceri; grocería
grocery store clerk bodeguero
groggy grogui
gross lanudo
gross margin gross margin
grotesque person mojiganga
ground ñuto
group pool
grudge riña
grumble plaguear
Guadalajara, native of tapatío
guard ronda
Guatemala City, native of chapín
Guatemalans (nickname) chipines
guava guayaba
guess correctly anotarse un poroto
guide, experienced chaneque
guide for illegal immigrants buscones
guinea pig apereá; conejo de las indias; cuí; curí; curiel; cuy; güimo
guitar charranga; jarana
gullet gaznate; guargüero
gun shot plomazo
gunboat ganbout
gunman ganman
gutter chorrera
guy cabro; gallo
gypsy húngaro
Hah! ¡Ay bendito!
hair mecha
hair, curly colocho; culisada; enrizado; pasudo; pelo enrulado; pelo malo; pelo rizo; rizado
hair, disheveled chascón
hair in a bun cachirulo; chongo; molote; moña
hair, lock of gajo

hair, matted chasca
hair, person with curly chino(a); tener pasas
hair, person with curly red bachaca
hair, person with straight chuzo
hair pin ganchito; gancho; incaible; pasador; pin; pinche; presilla
hair, red mechicolorado
hair, uncombed enmarañado
haircut motilado; pelado; peluqueada; peluqueado; recorte de pelo
haircut, bad tusada
hairstyle, woman's clineja; crineja
hairy pachón
half-breed cabecita negra; cholo(a); coyote; grifo; roto; ñapango
half-brother cachirulo
half-closed entrecerrar
half-cooked saltón
half-heartedly achantao
half-time in a ball game jalf
hall hall; hol; jol
hamburger jamburguer
hammock campechana; chinchorro
hand gestures mariguanza
hand organ cilindro
handball handboll
handcuffs canana
handful manotada; pucho
handicap handicap
handkerchief paliacate; paño
handlebars of a bicycle manejera
handmade hechizo
handsome bien hecho; biscocho; chinazo; chiva; chivo; churro; cuero; fuerte; gallo; macanudo; machote; papasote; papazote; pintón; por el libro; potro; roscón; tipazo; yeguo
hang guindar
hang around brujulear; hangear; hangueando; jangiar; pajarear; pavear
hang up berretin
hanger ragú
hangnail padastro

hangover cruda; guayabo; largar; mona; ratón

hangover, have a con el cuerpo cortado; con el hachazo; con el ropero a cuestas; con la caña mala; con la mona viva; enguayabado; estar con la mona; estar engomado

happy inquirriado

happy-go-lucky person campechana

harass abacorar

harassment fregadera

hardware, computer hardwear

hardware store mercería

harelip, person with a boquinche; boquineto(a); morocho

harm afectar; choretear; echar jareta; envainar; fregar; joder

harmonica organillo

harsh guapo(a)

harshness terquedad

harvest pizca

hat, old guaracho

hat, straw chupalla; jipa

hat, wide charra

hatred aburrición; birria; riña

have a good time cacheteo

have everything under control planchar

hawk gavilán; guaraguao

head (vulgar) azotea; cachola; chirimoya; chola; chompa; coco; jupa; la sabiola; mate; pepa; piojosa; terraza; testa; tusta; zabeca

head, person with a big cacholón

heal curar

hear pispar; pispiar

heat, in alzado

heated sancochao

heater jira; jiter

heel jarrete

help a couple get acquainted hacer gancho

help, always demanding güiña

help from an influential person cuña; palanca

hen gumarra

hiccup jipar

hidden enmochilado

hidden issue cuita

hidden treasure botija

hide alcanforarse; encaletar; enguacar; enhuacar; fondear

hide for political or judiciary reasons enconchar

hide-and-seek game tuero; tugar-tugar

hideout abrigada; abrigadero; guarimba

high fever, with calenturiento

high on drugs, be arrebatao; caballón(a); empepado; estar jai; friquear

high on drugs, get gira; turra

high on marijuana engrifado

high position in public administration coroto

high quality flor; pulento

high school escuela superior

high society jai

high-mountain sickness sorochi

highway jaiguey

hike jaic

hills cerros

hips juanetes

hips, swinging dengue

hips, swing one's chiquear; tongonear

hire someone conchabar; conchavar

Hispanic and African origin, person of cuarterón

hit a ball chute

hit back ripostar

hit, diagonal chanfle

hit, direct lamparazo

hit (musical) jit

hit, strong atracar; canchar; cascarazo; chancacazo; coñazo; dar candela; mandar un golpe; matracaso; quiñar

hit the jackpot batatazo; bingo
hit with a belt cinchazo
hit with a police nightstick rolazo
hit with the finger chirlo
hitchhike autoestop; bolear; cola; dar
  botella; dar un jalón; dar un pon;
  hacer dedo; jaiyakin; jalón; pedir
  bola; pedir un aventón; pedir un pon;
  pedir una paloma; pon; tirar el dedo
hitchhiker colero
hoe lampa
hold oneself back atajarse
holding joldin
hole cucho; hureque; pozo
hole in the socks papa
holy card registro
home ground querencia
home run in baseball jonrón
homosexual (vulgar) aviador;
  cambiado(a); chupón; culero; gay;
  hueco; loca; maraco; marico; pájaro;
  pato; rosca; rosquete
Hondurans (nickname) catrachos
honest person alférez; franque;
  redondo; seguro; zanahoria
honey joni
hope, loss of desespero
hopscotch avión; bebe-leche; el luche;
  el tejo; golosa; luche; pata sola;
  pelegrina; peregrina
horn (car) corneta
horns of an animal cachos; chifles;
  cuaco; tarro
horse, old chongo
horse, sickly chongo
horse, white palomo
horseman, good chalán
horseshoe casquillo
hot dog pancho; perro caliente;
  salchicha; vienesa
house chante
house, neglected sucucho
housedress bata
hovel cucho

hug apuchungar
humiliate achicar; negrear
hummingbird burrión; chupaflor;
  chupa-mirto; chupa-rosa; chupaflor;
  esmeralda; quinde; tentenelaire; visita
  flor; zumbador; zunzun
hump maleta; totuma
humus capote
hunchbacked cucho; curco;
  curcuncho; gocho
hunger angurria; fatiga; fiaca; gurbia;
  ragú
hungry galgo; garifo; garoso; gorozo;
  hambrío(a)
hurl aventar
hurried ajorado
Hurry up! iándale! **hurry up, to**
  sacar chocoliya
hurt charrasquear; fastidiar; joder;
  straique
hurt, get chavarse
husband jebo
hut bajareque; bohio; callampa;
  caney; jacal; quilombo; rancho;
  ruca
hydrant boca de agua; boca de
  incendio; bomba de agua
hypocrite chepe; fayuto; tapado
hypocritical, be camandulear
hysteria matropa
ice cream aiscrim; gelati; leche
  nevada; mantecado; nieve; paico
ice cream cone aiscon; barquilla;
  canuto; cono; cucurucho; sorbete
ice cream vendor nievero
idiot aguacate; apendejao;
  ñangue
idle arreado(a) **idle, to** chotear;
  maquetear
idler realengo
igloo iglú
ignorant person baboso(a); buey;
  burro; jicaque; machetero(a); menso;
  menzo; tapado

ignore hacer tapa
iguana garrobo; jama
ill, be jorobado; tener dengue
ill-bred pavito
illegal alien alambrista; aliento
illegal business cahuin
illegal drug falopa
illness dengue; maluquera
imitate changuear; reparar
immature biche; ñoño
immediately en un tilín
immediately after despuesito
immigration agent empleado(a)
Immigration and Naturalization Service of the U.S. la migra; migra
immigration officers, U.S. correa; la migra; migra
impasse impase
impatient le pica
impeded tupido
impertinence descache
impertinent chocante; sobrado
implicate bolear
impolite person carajo; jicate; lanudo
important, give oneself airs of being quillarse
important people gente copetuda
important person, very cangrimán; cocoroco; papapúa
impose a fine infraccionar
impose strict rules or discipline atracar; atrincar
impose unnecessary paperwork ruleteo
improve impruviar
impudence empaque
impudent caripelao; liso
in addition to de forro; de llapa; de ñapa; de yapa; ganancia; ipegue; llapa; pesuña
in a moment ahora
in charge, be bate
in disarray desconchiflado
inaccurate al tuntún

Inca spirit of Mother Earth pachamama
incite esgunfar; incentivar; jochear
income tax incomtax
incomplete, make descompletar
incredulous pirujo
indecent fregado
indent indentar
Indian chief curaca
Indian-like aindiado
indifference paterrolismo; terquedad
indifferent pata de rolo; paterrolo
indigestion, with embarado
indirect way to say something sangaraña
indiscreet resfriado
indulgence ñoñerias
inefficiency guachafita
inefficient cabestro; cacatúa
inferior quality bodrio; chimbo; rasca
influential person cacique; fuerte
inform on chotear; pajear
informer chivato(a); chota; pinche
ingenious ideático; ideoso
inhaling marijuana toque
inheritance mortual
initiative berraquera; verraquera
inject a drug abujazo
injure afectar
inner tube carcasa
input input
insect larva, edible mojojó
insecure culiche
insignificant chingadera; pichiruche
insipid aguachoso; terco
insist machetear
insistence coco
inspect inspectar
instruct instructar
insult bollo; quemón; reto; sángano; sorete **insult, to** amontonar; faltar; intratar; rajar; retar; rezondrar
insult, strong (vulgar) cabrón; vaca
insulting hand gesture pistola

insurance seguranza
insurance company seguranza
intelligence bombillo; chipote; coco;
  mate
intelligence, of little pigmeo
intelligent person banana; bocho(a);
  pierna; porra
interesting choro
internalize internalizar
interrupt a conversation chalequear
intersection, street bocacalle; cruce;
  crucero
interview interviú
intimidate padrotear
intrigue laberinto intrigue, to
  camandulear
introduce a person introducir
intrude in someone else's
conversation meter la cuchara
intruder brujo(a)
intuition tincada
intuitive sense of direction, person
who has an baqueano, baquiano
involved in a mess maneado
involved with others, does not get
  jojoto
involve others canchar
involve someone in a crime
  encochinar
involve someone in a difficult
situation bolear; clavar; entortar;
  enzanjonar
irascible sulfúrico
iron table burro
irrational behavior, person who
displays revirado
irresponsible buena pieza;
  desobligado; tilango(a); tilingo;
  tocado
irrigate irrigar
irritable person chinchudo; sulfúrico;
  volado
irritate condenar; empavar
irritation arrechera

isolate negrear
isolated place chifurnia
issue broma; coso; gabela; ichu;
  pallasá; perol; vaina
it looks well potro(a)
it seems out of place balurdo
Italian, nickname for an bachicha;
  tano
itching sensation rasquera
item that is not selling well abollado
itemize itemizar
jack, car gata; mico; yaque
jacket americana; campera; casaca;
  chamarra; manuela; yaket
jacket, suit gabán
jacks yacks; yaquis
jail bartolina; bote; buchaca; cana;
  capacha; chirola; chirona; jeruza;
  joyolina; tambo
jail, in embarcado
jail keeper arquero
jail meals tumba
jam made of bananas and brown
  sugar bienmesabe
jar, large earthenware pondo
jaw carretilla
jazz jazz
jealous engurrioso; gararey
jeans jeans
Jeep™ jeep
jeer tiradera; trisca
jeering chercha
jelly yely
jelly prepared with milk, sugar, and
  eggs quesillo
jerk pendejo(a)
jersey yersey
jet set, the jai; jetset
jewelry paquetería; prenda
jilt chantar
job brete; camello; chamba; cuchara;
  jale; pega; voleo
job, easy batata; botella;
  mamada

job, get a enchafainarse
job, illegal pichulear; rebusque
job, lower status in a suche
job obtained through influence
chanfaina; corbata
job, person who takes away
someone's descamburador
job, second faena; pituto; pololo(a);
rebusque
job, small chiripa; pituto
jockey yóquey; yoqui
join empatar
joke ancheta; changuería; chapa;
chercha; jarana; mecha; pandorga;
talla; vellón **joke, to** bachatear;
brincar; changuear; chingar;
chucanear; echar tallas; gufear;
tandear; vacilar
joke that causes damage cacho; joda;
vacilada; vacilón
joker célebre; chango; mozón;
vacilón
jovial chaneque
judgment coco
juice of the cane guarapo
jukebox vellonera
jump jumpear
jump a car yompear
jump rope bailar la suiza; brincar a la
reata; brincar la cuerda; cuica; saltar
el lazo; saltar la cuica; saltar la soga
junk cacharpas; tareco; tereque;
traste; tuliches **junk, to** yonquear
junk food embeleco
junkie moto
junkyard yonker
kerosene cocinol
kettle caldera; pava
keyboard kibord
kick cañonazo; chute
kick in the buttocks chuleta
kid cabro
kidnap plagiar
kidnapping plagio

kill achicar; desgraciarse; fregar;
mamar; pelar; quebrar; quiñar; soplar;
victimar
kilobyte kilobite
kindergarten cero; escuelita;
guardería; jardín de infancia; jardín de
niños; la creche
kindergarten teacher jardinera
prescolar; kindergarterina
kiss chupón; pico **kiss, to** apretar;
dar un pico
kitchen, small cocineta
kite barrilete; bomba; caite; chichigua;
chilito; chiringa; chonchón; huila;
pandorga; papalote; piscucha;
volantín
kite, small falucho; güila; ñecla;
papagallo; papagayo
kite string frenillo; gaceta
knapsack mochila
knee chocozuela
knick-knacks achimes; baratillo;
cacharro; chachivaches; chalchiuite;
chécheres; chunches; muérgano
knife faca; filera
knitting, flexible punto jersey
knock down voltear
knock-kneed cazcorvo; chapín;
garetas; maneto; patasagrias
knock-knock tun-tun
knock on the head caibo
knock out noquear
knot, bad amarradijo
laborer, day lunguero
lace, handmade ñandutí
ladies' man gallinazo
lady laidi; misia
lady, elegant young china
ladyfinger marifinga
lagoon cocha
laid off from a job, be mochar
lake, artificial resaca
lame person patojo; patuletas
lamp globo

lamp, homemade kerosene chonchón
land, neglected piece of potrero
landlord (derogatory) gamonal
landmark lindero
large amount choretó; una barbaridad
large person botija; caballón(a)
lash chuchazo; cuerazo; vetazo
later lueguito
laugh at vacilar
laundromat guachatería; landromat
laundry loundri
lavatory lavatory
lawn grama; gras; lon; manga; prado; yerba; zácate
lawyer licenciado
lays around, person who candil
laziness bausa; cholla; choya; fiaca; locha; maganza; manganza; manguareo; maquetería; monguera; paterrolismo
lazy aguada(o); almágana; aplatanao; arreado(a); baracutey; batata; bausón(a); bernia; croto; echado; empelotado; fodongo; machetón(a); maganzón; mamalón; manganzón; maqueta; maula; pata de rolo; paterrolo; pernicioso; quisio
lazy (vulgar) güevón; huevón
lazy, be achanchado; arranao; bartolear; manguarear; manguerear
lead empuntar; jefaturear
lead in a game mandar
leader líder
leadership liderato; liderazgo
leaf mold capote
leak liquear
learn about something jubilarse
lease lis
leather box or trunk petaca
leave empuntar; picar
leave a place without paying the bill conejear; fanfultear; fullería; hacer perro muerto
lecherous man (vulgar) chimbero

leech choncaco
left-handed person izquierdista; lluqui; macueco
leftovers salcocho; sancocho; sarapa
legalism legalismo
legitimate rajado
legs, long trancas
lend largar
lesbian (vulgar) arepera; cachapera; pata; tortillera
let the air out of a tire espichar; fletar
let up aflojar
liar (vulgar) argüendero(a); brollero; cachero; cisnero(a); cuentamusa; mojonero; mulero; pajudo; pajuo; paquete; paquetero
license plate, car licencia; placa; pleit
lick lamber; lambucear; liquear
licking, act of lambetazo
lie aguaje; argüende; barreta; calumnia; carretilla; carril; chile; chiva; coba; cuentazo; feca; globo; grupo; guaragua; guayaba; lana; levante; mula; paquete; pura paja
lie (vulgar) cañar; guayabear; mojonear
lies bochinche; carreta
lies, speaker of macumba
life belt life belt
life, lousy vidurria
lifeboat life boat
light bulb ampolleta; bolb; bombita; foco; lamparita
likes Americans, he/she gabachero(a)
limp chuequear
line of people cola
link liga
link in a chain cheje
lint panita; pana
lip, person with a deformed cheuto
lips (vulgar) bemba; bembé; chambe; jeta

lips, someone with thick
bembudo(a)
lipstick lipestic
liquor, cassava güero; huero
liquor, cheap cachaza; guaro
liquor from sugar cane guarapo
liquor store botillería; estanco;
estanquillo; taquilla
liquor, strong fuerte
liquor, swig of strong cañonazo;
guamazo; jalón; matracaso; palo;
tacazo
little bit chinchín; chischí; chispito;
fisca; piñisco
little, very un carajo
live together without being married
amachinar; arrimarse; casarse por
detrás de la iglesia; conchabar; vivir
arrimado
lively, become more arrebolarse
liver, animal's pana
living room living
lizard, any kind of teyú
lizard, small pichete
load, extra soborno
loan, ask for a pechazo
loan of money manga
lobby lobi
lock candado; chapa **lock, to**
laquear
lock-out lock out
lodge arranchar
lodger in another's home
arrimado(a)
loins lomo
lollipop caramelo; chambelona;
chupaleta; chupeta; chupete;
chupetín; colombina; paleta; pilón;
pirulí
lonely person íngrimo
long-suffering aguantador
longing cachero
look lorea **look, to** busconear;
chapar; echar pupila; luquear

look at a nude person (vulgar)
cuarteo
look for hidden treasures guaquear
Look out! ¡chivísima!
look the other way despintar
lookout person for a crime
campanero; loro; sapo
loop lup
loose morals luis(a) morales
lose irse al tacho
lose one's cool cabrearse
lose one's mind alunarse; friquear
lose one's temper arrufar
lose something very dear ponchar
loser, be a no estar en nada
loss, have a big sonar
lost, get destorrentarse; embolatar;
envolatar
lot, a chorro
lottery ticket suerte
lottery ticket, part of cacho
lottery ticket seller suertero
loudmouth aguajero
loudspeaker espiquer
louse caranga
love affair brete; chillo; movida;
quiquirigüiqui; rebusque; volada;
volantín
love, be in empelotado; estar gas;
templado; tragado
love, fall in amelcocharse
love, two people in pestillo
lover jebo
luck (vulgar) cueva; leche; tarro
luck, without yetatore
lucky person suertero; suertudo(a);
tener leche
luggage lágach
lump turupe
lumpy masatudo
lunch lonch; lonche; lunche
lunch box lonchera
lunch, have lonchar; lonchear;
lunchiar

lunch room lonchrum
luxury chamberinada
machete chafirro; chinga; cutacha;
  paila
machine failure pana
mackerel jurel
mad at someone, get enchismar
madam cabrona; mádam; patona
made in meidin
madness piantadura
magic gestures mariguanza
maid (derogatory) china; gata
mailing list mailing list
main course at lunch or dinner
  seco
mainframe computer meinfreim
make a deal kupia-kume
make a fool of oneself violín
make a living from odd jobs
  busconear; changar
make a point in a game anotarse un
  poroto
make a real effort fajarse; pechar;
  ponerle empeño; ponerle pino; puyar
make fun of someone bacilarlo;
  chotear; costear; empavar; relajo;
  soguear; triscar
make it possible implementar
make matters worse para acabarla de
  chingar
make sacrifices (vulgar) sacarse la
  cresta
malaria chucho
male teacher cucho
malice visage
malicious person cachorro
mallet almádana
malpractice malpractis
man chavón; jevo; man
man, lecherous (vulgar) chimbero
man, old bejuco
man, sexually active with several
  partners (vulgar) chingón
man, short apachurrado

man, strong chingón; fuerte; tenche
man who behaves like a child
  mamón
man who courts many women
  bacán; cabrón; chivo; gallinacea;
  gaucho; lacho; mariposón; tiburón
man who does odd jobs changador
man who hides behind women
  calzonudo; pollerudo
man with an ugly body chichimeco
manager manayer; manejador(a)
mange caracha
mania follón; grillo
manners, good don de gentes;
  místico
manners, person with no arrotado;
  carretonero; chancho; chongo
manure bosta; guano
marbles ágatas; agúes; agüitas;
  balitas; bolas; bolitas; garbinche;
  garvinche; metras; papangos; tiros
marbles game chocolón; pepa y
  palmo; uñita
marijuana maría; mariela; marimba;
  mota; varilla; yerba
marijuana, best quality punto rojo
marijuana cigarette bacha;
  bazuco(a); cachaflín; cacho; coso;
  moto; pepa; pito; vareto; varillo
marijuana cigarette, end of a chicho
marijuana dealer marimbero
marijuana, inferior-quality pasto;
  ripio; zácate
marijuana, small envelope of pelpa
marijuana smoker fumón
marker plumígrafo
market marqueta; parián; turno
marketing marketing
married, get amarrarse
marsh curiche
massage fletación
massive balumoso
masturbate chaquetear; hacerse la
  paja; jalársela; pajearse

masturbation (vulgar) casqueta; cocolía; manuela; paja; puñeta
match mach **match, to** machear
matches fósforos
mattress, spring somier; tambor
mattress, straw pallasa
meal, badly-prepared frangollo
meal prepared with leftovers ropa vieja
meal that gets burned rechinarse
mean, be lecherear
mean person amarrete; basca; cachorro; jodido; jodón; lechero; muérgano; perro; pichirre; pinche; pingo; podrido; sorullo
meat, dried charqui
meat or vegetables starting to rot aventado
meat, sell pesar
mechanic nipple niple
mechanical clamp clam
meddle comedirse
meddler aprontao; arbolario; brejetero; brujo(a); cuico; entrador(a); huelefrito; metete; metiche; metido; nariz; refistólero; refitolero; zaragate; zaramullo
Medicaid medicaid
medicinal patch used on the skin parcho
medicine, hot sudor
medicine man callahuaya; hierbatero; machi; tegue; yatiri; yerbatero
medicine woman, native machi; piacha
medicines, become full of emboticarse
mediocre majunche
meet mitiar
meeting calpul; choclón; machitún; malón; mitin
megabytes megabytes
melancholic amacolao
melancholy esplín; flato

memorized information botella
memory, bad memoria de gallina
memory, computer memory
menstruate caer mala
menstruation asunto; doña Rosa; luna
mentally unbalanced due to alcohol engasado
meow ñau
merchandise, inferior-quality hueso
merchandise that does not sell cacho; muérgano
merry-go-round calesita; carnaval; carrusel; machina; volantín
mess atao; cahuin; candinga; emborujo; frangollo; julepe; mazamorra; pango; quilombo; reblujo; rebujo; reguerete; revolica
mess, make a arrebrujar; bichar; rebrujar; rebujar; regueretear
mess up an issue embarbascar
messy galletoso
metallic band güincha; huincha
Mexican cowboy charro
Mexican, very tapatío
Mexicans who live in the U.S. pochos
Mexico City, native of chilango
mezzanine mesanín
microfilm microfilm
middle class medio pelo
Middle East, nickname for person from the turco
middle-aged person jecho
milestone lindero
military cap prepucio
military, person in the (derogatory) cachaco; milico
milk choca; milque
milk candy cajeta
milk, sour angola
mimeograph mimeógrafo
misappropriate enquesarse
misappropriation peculado
misbehave descompasar

misbehavior relajo
mischief avería
mischief-maker cahuinero
mischievous cachafaz; confiscado
miser hambriento; torcido
miserly amarrete
misfortune guamazo; malhora; salado
mishap salado
mislead into a difficult task meter el
  choclo
miss faltar; mistear
miss a date chantar
miss what is going on pajarear
mistake, grammatical mote
mistake, make a caballada;
  embarrada; embarrar; gajo; meter la
  pata; meter las extremidades; pelada;
  pelarse; tirarse la plana
mistake, making a embarrándola
mistreat intratar
mistress china
mittens guantes; manillas;
  manopla
mix ensalada **mix, to** camburrear;
  misturar; mixtiar
mix liquids rebullir
mixer molenillo
mixture carabina; champurriado;
  frangollo; mazamorra; pupurrí
moan leco; plaguear
mob chamuchina; la gallá; palomilla
mob, rude muchitanga
mock bacilar; chotear; costear; relajo;
  reparar; soguear; tandear; tomar para
  el fideo; triscar; vacilar
model machote
mohair mohair
mold used in construction farmaleta
moldy, get azumagarse
moment, in a en un improviso
mommy cochote
money biyuya; biyuyo; chavos;
  chicharrones; chirola; chirona; guano;
  guita; jando; la mosca; lana;

machacante; mangos; moni;
  morlacos; mosca; pachocha; pisto;
  sencillo
money, ask for machetear
money, have encaletado; rayado;
  tener guano; torteado
money, large amount of guita loca;
  realero
money, small amount of bica;
  chinchín
money stolen by government
  functionaries chunchullos;
  chunchurria
money, without estar en la pitadora;
  helado; saltar matojo; seco
moneylender garrotero
monkey machín; mico
monkey around monquiar
monopolize the conversation
  sentarse en la palabra
mop bayeta; coleto; mapo; trapero
mop, completely worn out soco;
  zoco
mop the floor suapear
mop up mapear; mopear; trapeador
moron corneta
mortar pilón
mosquito mbarigüí; rocoroco; zancudo
mosquito net toldillo
motel for illegal sexual relations
  parejero
motel next to the road estadero
moth palomita
mother cucha; la vieja; viejita
mother or grandmother la vieja;
  viejita
motorcraft launch voladora
motorcross motocross
motorcycle passenger parrillero
moulding rodón
mourner, paid rezandero(a)
mouse laucha; maus
mouth, big bemba; buchaca; guayaba;
  jeta; tarasca

mouth deformity, person with a janano(a); janiche

mouth, thick-lipped bimba; chambe; jetón

mouthwash antiseptic, any type listerina; listerine

move or walk from one side to the other tumbear

move something fast jamaquear

move things around curucutear

move to one side abrirse

movies, the el mono

mud from an avalanche mazamorra

muddy place tocotal

muffler, automobile mofler

mug moca **mug, to** cogotear; jolopear

multitude bolón

mumps, the cantimplora; falfallota; mompes

municipal tax detalle

murder descocotar

murmur runrún

mush, soft and sweet mazamorra

mushrooms callampas; champiñones; machrum; paragüita de sapo; setas

music, cabaret bachata

music hall music hall

musical instrument, special kind of bandola; furruco; guiro(a); juque; taramba

mussel choro

mussel, big cholga

mussel, small chorito

mustache boso

mutton, cured chalona

my dear mijo(a)

nag mocho

naive (vulgar) asopao; caído del catre; gil; hueva; jil; marrano; papayudo; pavuncio(a); pelotudo; salame; zanahorio

naked (vulgar) avirote; calato(a); en cueros; en pelotas; pilucho; viringo

naked, be andar en pelotas

name, family nombre de familia

name someone mentar

nanny cargadora; chichi; china

nap echar una pestaña; sestear

nape of the neck tungo

napkin limpiamanos; mantelito; secador

nasal fañoso

nasty, be pesetear

nasty person sorullo

native guide baqueano; baquiano; chane

nausea ansia

navel cachube

neck cocote

negative and painful influence matracaso

neglect oneself despatarro

negligent (vulgar) pelotudo

negotiate with great political ability muñequear

nerve cachaza; concha

nest tasin

net neta

network network

news chiba

news, false caña

news, interesting chiva

newspaper papel

newspaper boy canilla; canillita; papelero; suplementero(a); voceador

newspaper deliverer rutero

Nicaraguans (nickname) nicos

nice chévere; chuchin; encachado; fullero; pepeado; pirulo

nice person gumarra

nice-looking person chiche; chusco; potro(a); yeguo(a)

nice-looking young male fuerte

nickel caló; vellón de cinco

nickname mote

nickname for a very good friend cacha

night watchman rondin
nightclub club nocturno
nightgown bata de dormir; camisón;
  camizón; dormilona; levantadera
nightshirt, young boy's camisola
nightstick bolillo; luma; macana; rolo
nip piñisco **nip, to** piñiscar
nipple on a bottle chupo(a);
  chupón
nit liendra
no comment nocomen
no good turro
nobody pinche
noise bochinche; bullaranga;
  chambrana; laberinto; merequetén;
  reborujo; rochela
noise, make rochelar
noisy person guanguero; guatoso
nominate nominar
nonsense al pedo; ancheta; chantada;
  charada; chayotada; despapucho;
  lesera; lesura; pallasá; patilla; pavada;
  pistolada; zoncura
nonsense, speak al pedo; caña
  hueca; comer bola
nose chopo; ñatas
nose, with a big chamborote
nostalgia cabanga; cavanga
nostalgic cavanga; enguayabado
not say a word no chillar
not well done birriñaque
nothing un carajo
notice acatar
nozzle pitón
nuisance camote; chingadera;
  jodienda; mecha; roncha; vaina
nullify nulificar
numb emparamado
numbness monguera
nurse norsa
nursery norseri
oak moray
oak tree chapote
oats cúaquer

object, battered or damaged
  albóndinga
object or thing burundanga;
  tereque
obscene word bachata
observe carpetear
obsessed with a theme, be
  empuntar
obsession coco; follón; grillo
obstacle mamonazo
obstacles, put up entrabar
obstinacy birria
obstinate arranchado; cabeciduro;
  cariduro
obstruct hacer bulto; taquear; tupir
obstructed tupido
obstruction, heavy entablazón
obtain apañar; cachar
obtain political and/or economic
  power encarapichar
obtain something maliciously a la
  diabla
obvious de cajón
odds and ends tareco
odor from the armpit chucha; grajo;
  monate
odor from the feet cicote; pacueca;
  pecueca; pesuña; sicote
odor of rotten meat chiquije
odor, strong catinga; olor fuerte
off of
off the record of de record
offend faltar
offended torcido
offended, be chillarse
offender ofendor(a)
offense bollo
offside ofside
oil canfín
O.K. okei
old age vejentud
old animal angarrio
old, looking traqueado
old maid beata; cotorra

old man (derogatory) angarrio; bejuco; rodillón; vejuco; vejucón; veterano(a)

old, very cacarico; del año del caldo; pasao

older, get emplumar

omelet casabe; casave; omelet; torta

on on

one million monetary units palo; palo verde; un palo

one piece of a fruit gajo

one who does everything todero

one who lives at another's expense bolsero; vividor

one-armed soco; zoco

one-eared gacho

one-eyed choco(a); chueco

one-peso bill papel

only one, the veintiúnico

open continuously abridura

opening resquicio

operatic operático

operational operático

opossum chucha

opportunist argollero

orange china; oranch

orange milkshake morir soñando

ordinary picante

orgy partuza

ornament, silver virola

orphan (derogatory) guacho; huacho(a)

ostentatious chamberí; echón; echonería; fachoso; farolero

out aut

out of its place visorioco

outlandish circunstanfláutico

output output

outside autsai

outsider fuereño

outspoken claridoso

oven cocedor

overalls broga; mameluco; overol

over-booking over booking

overcharge garrotear

overgrown grandulón

overly affected cuico

oversleep se le pegaron las cobijas

overtime faena

overuse chotear

owl búho; chuncho; mochuelo; múcaro; tecolote

pacifier biberón; bobo; chupo(a) de entretención; chupón; mamón; pacifair; pepe; tete

pack atapuzar; atucuñar; embojotar; enterciar; taquear

package bojote

package for sale in bulk paca

pad used to protect the shinbone canillera

paddock padoc

pain, sharp puntada; punzada

paint embijar

pajamas payamas; piyamas

pal gallo; caballo; cuate; llave

pale cherche; nixte; pánfilo(a)

paleness jipato

palm leaves guano

palm tree guano

pamper chocholear; tolonguear

pan, frying acero

pancreas, animal's pafarilla

panic, be in a paniqueado

panoramic view divisa

panties calzones; cuadros; cucos; pantaletas; pantis

pantyhose panty

papaya fruta bomba; lechoza

paperback peiperbac

paper bag cambucho; cartucho

parachutist parachutista

Paraguay, native of guaraní

parcel tala

parcel post encomienda

parents parientes

park a car parkear

parking lot parkin; parking; playa; playa de estacionamiento
parrot cotorra; perico
parrot, green chocoyo
partner parna; parner
party (n) borlo; calducho; chancleo; cumbanchear; movida; pachanga; pary; pereque
party (v) bonchar; enfiestarse; pachanguear
party animal arrocero; bonchón; garufa; gozón; patalegre; vagamundo
party, big bayú
party, family charanga; charranga
party, noisy bola; chacota; chorcha
party, small arroz
pastries tanela
pastry, a special kind of beso; bienmesabe; cazuela; gofio; huevochimbo; matagusano; panucha; quesillo; tapado
patch billete; cachirulo; palchó
path huella; pica; picada; pique; trillo; vereda
pause for a long time arrejarse
pave the way for another to fail hacer la cama
pawnshop tía rica
pay chipiar; enterar
pay attention, not pavear
pay by installments enterar; exhibir
pay his debts, person who doesn't embrollón
pay one's own share in the group's expenses formar
pay special attention to one person determinar
payday raya
paying, person who avoids lambizque
payment enterar
payment for the right to see a show in a restaurant descorche; destape

payment or tax collected by guerrillas vacuna
pays for everybody, one who always paganini
peas alverja; alverjón; arveja; arverja; chícharo; pees; petipóas; petipúa; pitipuas
peace-maker peismeker
peach durazno; pich
peach, sun-dried huesillo
peach, white blanquillo
peanut cacahuate; madubí; pínut
peasant canario; chagra; montañero; motoso
peasant, behaving like a campirano; guaso
peasant woman china
peck picada; picotón
pedantic facistol(a); facistor(a); firulístico
peddler achimero; achín; achún; cacharrero; cangallero; maritata; sencillero; varillero; ventero
pedigree pedigrí
peel descarachar; desconchar
pelican tocotoco
pen lapicera
pen, handle of canuto
penalty penal
penchant goma
penis (vulgar) balone; baloni; bicho; binbín; chale; chile; chimbo; guasca; güevo; huevo; pájaro; paloma; penca; perico; picha; pichula; pico; pija; pinga; pipi; tembó; verga
penis, child's chichí; pichulín; pirulo; tula
penniless, be andar ficha; andar pato; andar quebrado; arrancado; arrancao; estar ahorcado; estar pato; pelado
penny chavo; chele; kilo; peni
penury gajo
people who stick together amorochados; trenza

pepper, eat hot enchilar
pepper, green hot ají verde; chile verde; chiltoma; jalapeño
pepper, hot ají; ají picante; chile; gárnica; locote; locoto; ricoto; rocoto
peppermint pepermin
percussion instrument tango
perform an incomplete task dar mateo; echar mateo; falencia
perform below expectations quedarse piola
performance performans
performance, evening vermuth
performance, outstanding fajar
perfume of inferior quality pachulí
perjury, commit jesusear
person of low intelligence (vulgar) agüevado; ahuevado; hueva; marmolín
person who accepts mistreatment aguantón
person who allows others to manipulate himself dejón
person who behaves disgracefully pavo
person who behaves with ease and confidence canchero; puntudo
person who bewitches another cachimbero
person who cannot be tolerated anymore denso
person who comes off badly calceto
person who lives at the expense of others argollero; bolsero; mamador(a); parche; pechuga; vivaceta; vivanco; vivaracho
person who provides music at a party cañonero
person who uses his status to get benefits chapacaca
person who wants things for free golillero
person with exceptional qualities célebre; jamón

person without color pánfilo(a)
person without skills chacra
personal defect that attracts sympathy cuija
personality, person with a peculiar or strong chorizo; choro
Peruvian, nickname for a (derogatory) cholo(a); perulero
perverse maluco
pester chipiar
petroleum canfín
petroleum, natural spring of mene
petticoat peticote
pettifogger huisache
phlegm (vulgar) pollo
photo studio retratería
pick axe chuzo
pick someone's pocket bolsear
pick up pañar
pickle pickle
pickpocket gato
picky with food, be disticoso
picnic picnic
pie pai
piece of clothing, inferior-quality chamarro
piece, small cachito; cacho; chamarro; chilingo; chinchín; chinguito; rolo; troncha
pieces cuechos
piecework chamba; trabajo a trato
pig chancho; cochino; cuchí; macho; marrano; tunco
pig skin cooked and roasted cuero
pigeon zuro
pigsty cochera; cucho
pile arrume; balsa; burujón; ruma
pile, in a apilonados
pile of grain banco
pill cacahuate; pepa
pimp (vulgar) cabrón; cafiche; cafiolo
pin pin
pinball machine el fliper; flipiadora

pineapple ananá; esmeralda
pipe paipa
pipeline pipeline
piss chichí
pistol escuadra
pit pepa; pepita
pitchfork garabato
place or region, any valle
place to eat or shop, very special picada
place to sleep overnight dormida
plain-spoken claridoso
planning planin
plant, one type of cerilla; vainica
plantain chips, fried amarillo; chatino; chicharritas; chifles; mariquitas; patacón; platanutre; tostón
plants that share the same root cepa
plaster empañetado; tizate
plastic-coated hulado
plate, car's tablilla
play a joke on a person vellón
play around miquear
play hooky capear; hacer la chancha; hacer la cimarra; hacer pinta; jirola; jubilado(a); jubilarse; juqui; paviarse; ratearse de la escuela; volarse de la escuela
play, short dramatic tanda
play well in the political field tener muñeca
playback pleibac
playground pleigraun
play-off game playoff
please cuadrar
please someone only for personal gain cotonear
plenty harto; hereje
pliers alicate; alicates; pinzas; pláier; playo
plot julepe **plot, to** brujulear
plot of land parcela
plumber gásfiter

plumbing gasfitería; ploming
pocket bolsa
pockmarked borrado; sipo
pockmarks tusa
poison, strong canjura
poke atiquizar; hurgüetear; jurungar
police car bola; chota; dama gris; jaula; julia
police forces, special cilón
police station cana; chapa; jara; la cana; la chota
police, traffic chupa; fiscal
policeman aguacate; botón; cachaco; cachucha; cana; carabinero; cuico; gendarme; oficial de policía; paco; placa; polisman; tombo; verde; yuta; zopilote
polish chainar; lujar
political boss gamonal
political connections, use palanquear
political conspiracy conchupancia
political favors, give or receive clientelismo
political offices, hold several policamburismo
political opportunist colmilludo; coyote; pancista; panzú
political parties taking turns in power polarización
pollute polucionar
pollution polución
polyester poliéster
pomp bombo
pompous buchipluma; llambaroso; mamón; prosudo
pond cocha; tajamar
ponder remascar
pony póney; poni
pool pool
poor, inferior-quality thing falopa; pilinqui; rasca
poor person arrastrado; bruja; pelado; roto

popcorn alboroto; alborotos; cancha; canchitas; canguil; cotufa; crispetas; crispeto; esquite; maíz piro; pacón; popcón; poporopos; pororó; rosetas de maíz; rositas de maíz

pork chancho; cochino; cuchí; macho; marrano; tunco

pork chop chapa

pork, piece of fried chicharra; chicharrón

pork, roasted lechón

pork skin for cooking garra

portable portable

porter terciador

position of status status

poster poster

post-office box casilla

pot, any tiesto

pot, large biche

potato, inferior-quality toya

potato starch chuño; tunta

potatoes, mashed molo

potholder bajaollas

potter locero

poultice cayanco; vigo

poultry leg trutro; tuto; tutro

pour into another container trasvasijar

pout hacer cuchara; hacer pucheros

poverty carraplana

power, at full a todo jender

practice of commingling magic and religion santería

praise mutually cumbearse

praying mantis palote

precious object bagre; chiche

precipitate esmachetarse

preface prefaciar

preference jalar para

preferential preferencial

pregnancy encargo

prepare afilar; apronte; póngase las pilas

prescription, medical fórmula

present a petition peticionar

present, give a pitar

press a key preseki

pressing presin

pressing hard exprimión

presume pantallear

presumptuous brejetero; cachetón; fachoso(a); fullero(a); monifato; parejero; recargado; sobrado(a); vaselino

pretends to be important, person who carcamán; parejero; prosudo

pretentious cachetón; chanta; chantún; quillarse

pretty célebre; chulo(a)

prick chuzar; estacar; puyar

prime minister premier

printer printer

prison bartolina; bote; buchaca; cana; capacha; chirola; chirona; jeruza; joyolina; tambo

privation gajo

prize, give or receive a premiación

problem beguiansa; brete; brollo; cangrejo; forro; pedo

problem, create a embarrar

profit gabela; tragada

promise, take back a llamar

propeller propela

proportion ratio

prostitute (vulgar) alegrona; anafre; bofa; cabaretera; campechana; capulina; chiva; chuquiasa; cuero; fletera; guaricha; güila; maraca; nochera; pajuela; patín; pellejo; perra; salquipanqui; turra; vagamunda; wuiza

prostitute, male salquipanqui

prostitution chivería

protest chichar

Protestant church, member of canuto

proud tufoso

proud, be atufarse

provide a service gauchada

provide pleasures for oneself
castigarse
provisional provisorio
provocative woman betibú; chiva; dar
picón; mica
provoke chucear; cuquear; puyar
provoke a fight embochinchar;
enchinchar
prudery disfuerzo
prune camochar; desahijar
pry pispar; pispiar
psychologically disturbed tocado
pub pub
public employee (derogatory)
mamón
public employment, get
encamburarse
public transportation, slow lechero
public-relations person relacionista
pudding pudin
puddle apozarse
**Puerto Rican independence, person
who is for** pipiolo
Puerto Rican origin, of borincano;
borinqueño
Puerto Rican peasant jíbaro
Puerto Rican person boricua
**Puerto Rican who is more American
than the Americans** pitiyanqui
pull jalar; voltear
pull someone's leg cachar; mamar
gallo; pitar; tomar para el fideo
pulley-wheel rondana
pullman car pullman
pullover pulover
pump pompa
pumpkin bulto; chayote; cutuco;
zapallo
punch bimbazo; bombazo; burrunazo;
castañazo; combo; moquetazo; piña;
piñazo; ponche; puño; zoquete
punch, to cachimbear
punch a card at the workplace
ponchar

punish dar una tanda; fajar; hacer
sonar; monear
purse bolsa; bolso; chacára;
chauchera
pursuing the opposite sex picado(a)
de la araña
pus materia; postema
push atracar
put chantar
put in a ditch enchambrar
put in a paper bag encartuchar
put in jail enguandocar; entambar
put oneself in a ridiculous situation
papelón; plancha
put to shame acholar; achumar;
amostazar; empavar
put up with something aguantar
puzzle puzzle
qualify calificar
quarrel bronca; fajina; garrotera;
mocha; rosca; tángana **quarrel, to**
atracar
quarrelsome guapo(a)
quarter (coin) cuartilla; cuora;
vellón
quarter of a gallon litro
question cuestión
quiet!, Be chillo; dejen de relinchar
quiet, be comer machica
quilt quilto
quotient ratio
radio, portable chicharra
radio station brodcastin
raft panga
ragamuffin camin; palomilla
ragged chivo; culirroto; hilachento(a);
rotoso(a)
rags chanchira(o); chirajos; chiras;
chiringo; chiros; güila; güilas; huilas;
peleros; piltrafas; piltrajas; tiras
railroad man ferrocarrilero
railroad sleeper car eslipincar; polín
railway motor coach autocarril
rain when it is sunny chirapa

raincoat abrigo de lluvia; capa de agua; capote; gabardina; piloto
rains of the summer, first cabañuelas
rainy season invierno
rally rally
ramble manearse
ranch estancia; finca; hato; rancho
rank ranquear
ranking ranquin
rap on the head coscacho
rape (vulgar) capote; redoblón
rapids cabezón; chorro
rapist rapista
rapport raport
rascal camote; chirote; lepe; palomilla; zaragate
rash, with a safornado; sollamado
raspberry mora
rat guarén; pericote; petota
ratio ratio
rattle, baby's maruga; ronrón
ravine cajón
razor blades hoja de gilet; hojillas; navajas; navajas de rasurar
reach nancear; ponerle la tapa al pomo
ready, get afilar; amarrarse
ready to answer al tilín
realize acatar; acatarrar; realizar
rebel alzado
rebirth revival
rebound an object picar
rebuff boche
rebuke taquear
recess risés
reckless abandonado; tilingo
recognition reconociencia
recollect recolectar
record record
record holder recordman
recover from an illness alentar
red, dark guindo
referee réferi

refrigerator frigider; heladera; hielera; la refrigeradora; nevera
registration padrón
regret repelar
reject hacer tapa
relative relativo
release relís
relegate emplumar
religious, extremely mocho; pechoño(a)
remainder recorderis
remark, nasty acabar
remnant of clothing garra
remodel remodelar
remove by force fletar
rent rentar
repeat again and again cantaleta
repeat by memory paparrotear
repentant, be fruncirse
reply ripostar
report to the police tirar el dedo
reprimand aplanchar; boche; desplomo; enjabonada; luma; palo; penca; puteada; rajatablas; raspa; retar; taqueada; taquear; trancada; vaciar
reputation, damage another's empatucar
resentment pica; pique
reservoir resaca
residue of a liquid in a container aunche; hunche
resin of a tree cipe
respect and/or admiration, show sacarse el sombrero
respected, someone who is maestro
respirator respirator
responsibility atingencia
responsibility, assume apechugar
restaurant asistencia; descorche; destape
restaurant that specializes in pork lechonera
restless chiririco

retaliate sacarse el clavo
retaliation retaliación
retire to a faraway place encampanar
retreat entumirse
reveal a secret soltar prenda
reveller rumbero
revelry bachata
reverse reversa
revival revival
revolt bola
reward premiación
ribbon, hair bajaca
rice and beans, plate of matrimonio
rich person caletudo; catrin;
  fondeado; jaibón; morrocotudo;
  palote; sólido
rickets, someone with morroño
ride in a vehicle paloma
ridiculous way of acting micada
right now ahora; ahorita; ahoritica;
  ahoritita; horita; horitita
right to pass on the road prelación
rigid tilinte
rim llanta; rin
ring alianza; anillo; argolla; aro; rin
  ring, to ringuear
ring-around-the-rosy game ronda
riot montante
rip the leaves off a corncob tapiscar
ripe enough, not suche
rise on the social ladder encampanar
risky endiablado
river basin hoya
road, country vereda
roast rost
rob solfear
robbed tumbe
robbery aletazo; alzo; cacho
rock peñazco
rock and roll rock
rock and roll fanatic roquero
rocket cuete; roquet
rocking chair buinsuan
rogue maleta

role rol
roll of coins chorizo
roll up enchipar
rolling board patineta
rolling pin palote; rodillo; uslero
rolls bollitos; panecillos; panecitos;
  rolos; rols
romper esquimal
roof rufo
room ambiente; pieza
room temperature al clima
rooter ruter
rope cabestro; mecate; ropo; soga
rot abombarse; cignato; empicharse
rough morroño; roñoso(a)
roulette pica
round raund
row balumba; bayú; bembé
rub (spiritualism) pase
rubber band banda de caucho;
  elástico; goma elástica; gomita; liga;
  resorte
rubber tree hule
rude bascoso; caballo; campirano;
  jicaque; lanudo; migueleño; pedrero
rug choapino; costal; jerga
ruin something eschoretar
ruined chinzado(a); estar quemado;
  quemado
ruler rula
rum cañita; guaro; tafia
rum, pint of caneca
ruminate remascar
rumors bomba; borrego
rumpus ajiaco; bullaranga;
  chambrana; rosca
run away abrirse; arrancar;
  destaparse; enfletar; fletar
run-down looking tirá
rush apurar; azarozo; de raspa;
  rachar
rust, product of cascarria
rustic cabestro; campirano; guajiro;
  guaso

rusty, get amohosado; azumagarse
sack costal; guangoche; saco
sacred place huaca
sad amongado; amurrugado; enguayabado
sad, become amachinarse; amurrarse
saddle horse pingo
sadness grima; macacoa; mucepo
safety pin alfiler; alfiler de criandera; alfiler de gancho; asegurador; broche; gancho; gancho de nodriza; segurito; seguro
salad, a kind of guacamole; salpicón
sale barata; baratillo; especial; oferta; realización; rebaja; sail; venta
salesperson in the food market vivandero(a)
saltpeter salitre
Salvadoreans, nickname for guanacos
same enterito; entero; pintado
sanctimonious cucufato; santulario(a)
sandals chalas; chanclas; guarache; gutara; huarachas; ojotas
sandstone laja
sandwich bocadillo; bocadito; butifarra; sanduche; sándwich; sánguche; torta
Santa Claus Papa Noel; Santa Clos
sarcastic reference to someone or something chinita
satirical remark bomba
satisfied ensabanado
sauce chorota
sausage gorda; moronga
sausage sandwich, Argentine choripán
savanna cocha; pampa
save forrar; salvar
saw serruchar
sawhorse burro
say something indirectly sanguaraña
scab escab
scabies cancha; caracha; zarate
scabs, with carachoso

scandal bullaranga; bululú; chambrana; laberinto; revolú; toletole
scandalmonger camarón; conventillera(o); enredista; lenguón(a); lleva y trae; llevacuentos; oreja; pendenciero
scanner escáner; escanógrafo
scar chorcha; ñañara
scar, marked with a jachado(a)
scare batata; cabreado; cisca; terronera
scared, get abatatarse; arrugarse; azocararse; fruncirse; jabonarse
scarf mascada
scatterbrained azurumbado; azurumbrado; loca; tilingo; volado
scheme caula
school boy escuelero
school boy or girl escuelante
school girl escuelera
school subject that is easy to pass costura
school system, level of the ciclo
school topic, boring jarta
scold barbear; plaguear; retar
scolding that lasts and lasts barbero; sonsonete
score escor
Scotch Tape™ escotch
scoundrel lana
scratch chuchear; escarchar
screen escrin
screwdriver desarmador
script escrip
scrotum (vulgar) bolsa; güevas; huevas; huevos; mochilas; turmas
scrub tallar
sea wall molo; tajamar
search for something jurungar
seasoning ahogado; recao; recaudo
seaweed, special type of cochayuyo; huiro; luche
second floor tabanco
seconds revirar

secret coroto
secret place caleta
secret, unable to keep a resfriado
secure firme como un peral; macizar
sediment gazpacho
see through calar
seek favors through gifts manzanear
seesaw buinsuan; cachumbambé;
mataculín; sube y baja; suinsuan
segment of a fruit casco
segregate negrear
self-confident despercudido
self-control self control
self-interested calculador
selfish azadón; esmayao; lambío;
ojete; repuñoso(a)
self-service selfservice
self-serving vivanco
sell pitar
sell cheap machetear
semen (vulgar) leche; naturaleza
send to prison emplumar
sequence, without al cuete
serenade albazo; esquinazo; gallo
serious seco
serious, little paquete
servant cachifa(o); chajal; chino(a);
guachiman; mayordomo; mucama;
servicial
service colocho
servile person alzacola
set setear
set bones componer; sobada; sobijo
setback mecha
severe trancado
several things spread on a surface
tendal
sewer, main hole in a meinjole
sex appeal, with sexapiloso
sex, have (vulgar) abrocharse;
acostar; acostarse; afilar; cachar;
chapetear; chichar; chingar; coger;
culear; echar un polvo; encamarse;
jalar; montar; pichar

sexual attraction berraquera;
verraquera
sexual desire naturaleza
sexual excitement arrechera; arrecho;
calentura
sexually attractive person
buenote(a); levantador(a)
sexually excited, be arrechado(a);
estar caliente
shabby butuco; potoco; rungo
shack cobacha
shackles brete
shake chequear
shake, violent cimbronazo;
hurgandilla; jamaqueo
shame cisca
shame, cause achumar
shameless cachafaz; cariduro;
caripelao; conchudo; desharrapado;
fregado; fregón; raspado; zafado
shanty town callampas; cantegril;
población callampa; ranchería; villa
miseria
shapeless masatudo
shapeless object mamotreto
sharp person agarroso; amarroso;
puntudo
sharpen afilar
shave barbear
shave the head tusar
shavings virusa
shawl estola; mantilla; mantón; paño;
pañoleta; serape
shed, large open galpón
shelf chelv
shell corroncha
shellfish, a kind of concha; guacuco;
macha; piure
sherbet cepillado; cherbet; copo de
nieve; granizado; helado de agua;
nieve; pabellón; piragua; raspado;
rasco-rasco; raspadilla; raspado;
sorbeto
sherbet in a cone canuto

sheriff cherife
sherry sherry
shift key tecla shift
shinbone canilla
shirt, woman's camisón
shirt worn in the Caribbean
  guayabera
shish kebob anticuchos
shiver chucho
shock choc
shock absorber shoquer
shoe chalán
shoe, big banasta; calamorro;
  camambuses; chambón
shoe, Indian caite
shoe, old chaguala; chalupa;
  chancharreta; chancleta; guaraches;
  sueco; zueco
shoe store peletería
shoelaces agujetas; cabete; cintas;
  correa; pasaderas; talego; trenza
shoeshine boleadores; grasa
shoeshine box lustrín
shoeshine, give a embolar
shoeshine person lustrabotas;
  lustrador
shoe's sole, change a remontar
shoot chutar; chute
shooting plomera
shop chop; chopa; chope shop, to
  chopear
shop, small baratero; chinchorro;
  ratonera; ventorrillo
short cut atrecho; chaquiñán;
  deshecho
short, fat person cuico; paturro, taco
short person apachurrado; chaparro;
  chicoco(a); chingo; cuto(a); lepe;
  petiso; petizo; potoco; retacón;
  rungo; taco
short socks zoquete
shorten achicar
shorts entrepiernas; mameluco;
  pantaloneta

short-sighted person chicato
short-tailed choco(a)
shoulders, with wide espaldón
shout loudly acogotar; berrear
shovel, wooden gualmo
show a fake intention to do
  something cachaña
show boldness with gestures
  encocorarse
show off bacilón; brejetero; cajetilla;
  mico show off, to creerse; hacer
  fiero; pantallear
shower chagüer; lluvia; pluma;
  regadera
shreds chirajos; chiras; chiros
shrimp chacalines; chacolín
shrimp, big gamba
shrink back achucutarse; fruncirse
shrivel achucutar
shrubs, clear of socola
Shut up! icho!
shy apartado; buchipluma;
  chuchipluma; penoso; ser aguasado
sick person acabado; calandraca;
  malanco(a)
sickly morroño
sickly-looking person cignato
sickness, high-altitude puna
sideboard seibo
sidewalk andén; banqueta; sardinel;
  vereda
sift harnear
sigh angelar
sign anuncio; aviso; rótulo; sain; valla
  comercial sign, to sainear
signature, short pategallina
silly, act babosear; destorrentarse;
  lesear; ser pavo; tilinguear
silly, feel tupirse
silly person (vulgar) asopao;
  azurumbrado; baboso; berracá; bola;
  bolsa; bolsiflay; bolsón; bolsudo;
  boludo; caído del catre; camote;
  casimiro; chauchón; chayote; chirote;

233

chitrulo; chotón; cipote; comebola;
crestón; dundo; fallo; firulístico; gil;
gracejo; guanaco; güevón; huevón;
jetón; jil; junípero(a); leso(a);
mamerto; menso; morolo; nabo;
pánfilo(a); papayudo; pavuncio(a);
pendejo(a); pistolo(a); salame;
suncán; tilango(a); tilico; tilingo;
tórtolo; vejiga
silly thing (vulgar) güevonada;
huevonada; patilla; pistolada
similar guareto; pintado
simpleton alumbrado; cachencho;
tilango(a)
sinecure mamada
sing monotonously canturria
singer of popular songs gardelito
sink fregador; lavadero; lavamanos;
lavatorio; pileta; sinc
sink, kitchen lavaplatos; sinc
sirloin chorizo
sit with the legs crossed arrodajarse
skating rink skeitinrom
skeleton carcancha
sketch esquech **sketch, to**
esquechar
skillful caperuzo; habiloso;
rebuscador; tinoso
skills, acquire jubilarse
skin irritation sisote; tacotillo
skin on a fat person, hanging
charcheta
skin, person with fair lavado
skin, person with stains on the
pañoso
skin that is eroded by the cold
pasparse
skinny arenque; flacuchento;
flamenco; fliche
skip someone or something comer
skirt enaguas; follón; funda; naguas;
pollera; saya
skunk hediondo
slacks eslacks

slander alacraneo; calumnia;
conventilleo; recorte
slang caló; coa; lunfardo
slap aletazo; cachetada; chalchazo;
chirlo; galleta; galletazo; gaznatón;
moquete
slash latiguear; somatar
slashes on the buttocks from a belt
cuartada; cuartazo; cuartiza; reatazo
slaughter faenar
sleep apolillar; guindar; hacer tuto
sleep off a hangover dormir la mona
slice torreja; troncha
slide slaid
slide, playground canal; chorrera;
deslizadero; resbaladera; resbaladero;
resbaladilla; zurra-zurra
slingshot biombo; guaraca; haraca;
ratonera; tirador
slip fondo; refajo; saya interior;
sayuela **slip, to** resfalar
slip (underwear for a male) eslip; slip
slip away pelar
slippers babuchas; chanclas;
chancletas; chinelas; chopos; gutara;
zapatillas de levantarse
slippery liso
slogan eslogan
sloppily dressed escrachao
sloppy (vulgar) pelotudo; tirao
sloven desgualetado
slow learner burro; chuzo
slow reactions, person with
albóndiga; corroncho; durazno;
lenteja; pajarón; salame
sluggishness pachorrada
slum ratonera
sly cuatrero; guillado; lángara
small amount pite; pucho
small cup of any alcoholic drink palo
small person chingo; guatoco;
mirringo; pirringa
small talk bembeteo
small, very pichiruche

smart jaiba; pierna
smart move caribería; gallada; parada; ranada
smarten up desparpajar
smash apachurrar
smear embijar
smell of dirty feet cicote; sicote
smog smog
smoke chupar; pitar
smoking esmoquin
smooth suave
smuggle chancuquear; trapichar
smuggling of alcoholic drinks and/or tobacco chancuco
snack botana; causeo; lonche; onces; pasabocas; picada; picadito; puntal
snail churo; turo
snake machala
snake, poisonous guata
sneakers championes; champions; esnikers; tenis; zapatillas
sneaky person cachorro; tapado
snob (vulgar) come mierda; concheto; esnob; sifrino
snoop mosquear; pispar; pispiar
snout (derogatory) bemba; matatudo
snub someone bochar
soak enchumbar; ensopar
soaked entripado
so-and-so galla(o); perencejo; perico
soap, last piece of calilla
soccer field gramilla
soccer game fútbol
soccer match, informal pichanga
social class, person of low (derogatory) arrotado; jincho
social climber metido
social misbehavior derraparse
social status status
social status, person of low alpargatón; alpargatudo; carajo; chancletero; lana; pinganilla; ruanetas
social value, person without carajo; sardina(o)

socks calcetas; escarpines; medias
soda bebida; refresco
soft aguada(o); biche; suave
software softwere
soil, wet bañado; estero; vega
solemn prosudo
someone who avoids a commitment liso
someone who is always exploiting others arrimado(a); bolsero; goterero
someone who is not serious pinganilla
something bad feo; gacho; malinche
something with little or no value basura; lesera; lesura
son chino
son of a bitch ahijuma
son of one's grandson chorlo
son, youngest cuneco; cunene; maraco; pucho
soon ahora; ahorita
soon, very automático; en un improviso
sore cáncer; chaquira; chira; cizote
soup, a special kind of ajiaco; caldillo; cuchuco; mondongo; sancocho; valdiviano
sour choco(a); joco; juco
sour, turn acidarse
souvenir suvenir
space between two objects luz
Spaniard, nickname for a chapetón; coño; gachupín; gallego; ladino(a)
spank sonajear; spankear; zarandear
spanking batida; cueriza; fuetera; garrotera; muenda; trilla
spasm puntada
speak a lot without any substance cantinflear; cantinfleo; carreto; rollo
speak ill of someone zumbar
speak nonsense tilinguear
speak vehemently with passion regarse

speak with a peasant's accent
cacaquear

speaker corneta; parlante; spiker

speaks too much, person who
bembón(a); caña hueca; carreto;
chachalaquero; cotorra; palangana

speaks too quickly, person who
carretilla

speech espiche; spich

speed, at full embalado

spell (witchcraft) daño

**spell, person who harms by means of
a** dañero

spell, to espelear; espeliar

spendthrift botarata

sperm (vulgar) canela; leche;
naturaleza

spices recado

spike tapilla

spirited zafado

spiritualism, someone who uses
espiritero

splash zarpear

splinter cuña

spoil tongonear

spongy biche

sponsor esponcear; esponsor

sponsorship esponsorizar

sport esport

sports, promising in prospecto

sportsman sportman

sporty sportivo

spot espatear

spray lepe

spread embarrar

spreadsheet on a computer
spreadsheet

spree rumbo; sandunga

spring esprín; vertiente

sprint sprintar

spur picana

spy sapo **spy, to** orejear; pavear;
vichar

squander money cancanear

squash zapallo **squash, to**
apachurrar; despichar; machetiar

squat aparragarse

squeamish resabiado

squeeze achurrascar; amuñuñar;
apurruñar; despichar

squinty-eyed biscornio; bizcorneado;
bizcorneo

squirt lepe

stab charquear; charrasquear

stack estacar

staff estaf

stain empichar

stained curtido

stamp cuño; estampa; sello; timbre

stand estand

standardization estandarización

standardize estandardizar;
estandarizar

staple grampa **staple, to** engrampar

stapler grampadora

stare at someone with desire velar

**stares at someone else with desire,
person who** velón

start an activity with enthusiasm
fajarse

start an engine estariar

start doing something hincarle el
diente

starting money in a business plante

starving galgo; garifo; gorozo;
hambrío(a)

station wagon guagua

stay arranchar

stay up very late malanocharse

steak bife; churrasco

steal afanar; alzar; amolar; batanear;
bolsear; chorear; encaletar;
guachapear; guachapiar; hueviar;
jabear; jalar; jolopear; pitar; refalar;
tocar el piano

steering wheel cabrilla; guía;
manejera; stering; timón

stencil estencil

stencil machine polígrafo
step stepiar
stepladder burro
sterile capón; horro; jorro
stew cocido; guiso; patasca; pipián;
  salcocho; sancocho
stewardess aeromoza; auxiliar de
  vuelo; cabinera; camarera; erjostes
stick chaparro; garrote; leño; rolo
sticky alaste; masatudo; mazacotudo;
  pegotudo; plegoste
stiff trinco; tringo
stilts sango
stimulate incentivar
stimulating ají
sting chute
stinginess pichirrear
stingy, be amellarse; lecherear
stingy person agalludo; chucho;
  conservativo; garrotero; hambriento;
  judío; lechero; maceta; machete;
  pichirre; pinche
stink baranda
stinks fo
stinky gacho
stir hurgüetear; meneada
stock estoc; stock **stock, to** stocar
stomach guata; lipa; pipa
stomach ache embuchado; estar
  rebotado; insulto; jaleo
stomach, upset (child's) empacho
stone, big bolón; camote; peñazco
stone, paving solera
stool catre; pata de gallina
stop apozarse; chantar
stop it now parála
stoplight estop
storage place bodega
store chop; chopa; estor; negocio
store, articles for sewing and knitting
  paquetería
store, food and liquor taguara
store, meats and sausages
  salsamentaria

store, medicinal herbs botánica
store, small baratillo; boliche;
  chinchorro; linterna; quincalla;
  ratonera; taguara; tarantín; tendajo;
  ventorrillo
stove estufa; fogón; reverbero
stowaway colero; pato; pavo
straight al cuete
straitjacket canana
stranger afuerino
straw, drinking calimete; cañita;
  carrizo; pitillo; popote; sorbete;
  sorbeto
strawberry estraberry; frutillas
street light foco
street urchin gamín; palomilla; títere
street vendor maritata
strength garnacha; garra; polenta
strength, with all possible al carajo
strength, without mamado
stress estrés
stressful situation estresante
stretcher chacana
strict fregado
strike machetiar; straique
strike (in bowling) boche
strikebreaker carnero; escab; krumiro
string cabulla; cabuya; cañamo;
  curricán; guato; lazo; lienza; pita;
  ropo
string bean ejote
strip naked (vulgar) empelotarse;
  encuerar
strip paint from a wall descascaranar
striptease striptease
stroke estroc
strong firme como un peral; machín;
  machina; morocho; morrocotudo;
  polenta
strong person firme como un peral;
  guayacán; machete; ternejo
structure carcancha; encatrado
struggle bregar
strum charrasquear; surrunguear

stubborn arranchado; cabeciduro; cachorro; conchú; enhuevado; fregado; macho; sesudo; taimado

stubborn, be amacharse; enmular; machetear

stuck-up facistor(a); pije

stud padrón

student, college colegiante

studies a lot, person who estofón; mateo

study hard estofarse; matearse

stuff berenjena; bicha(o); broma; charada; chereques; chunches; chivas; coroto; coso; deso; estaf; féferes; gabela; ichu; pallasá; perol; tiliches; vaina; verga

stuff (very vulgar) güevada; huevada

stuff with taquear

stump chonco; ñoco; soco; zoco

stunned turulato; zurumbático

stunned, be atotumarse; azurumbarse

stunted in physical growth, be apachurrado

stupefied acarajado; apendejado

stupid (vulgar) arao; baboso(a); bola; bolsa; bolsiflay; bolsón; bolsudo; boludo; buey; chitrulo; chorizo; cipote; collera; comebola; crestón; enfermo(a); guanaco; güevón; huevón; jetón; ñangue; pelotudo; pendejo(a); redondo; sángano; sorete; surumbo; tapado; tórtolo

stupid, extremely (very vulgar) bolas de cuero; pelota; ser calzón; ultraboludo

stupidity (vulgar) charada; chirotada; güevonada; huevá; huevonada; pendejada

stutter canacanear; cancanear; gagear; gagüear; gaguear; mudenco

stutterer gago; lenco; lenguachuta; tartancho(a)

submissive chupamedia

subordinate suche

substitute in a job fungir

subway metro

successful, be embocar

succession of rapid events virivira

sucker (vulgar) asopao; caído del catre; gil; hueva; jil; marrano; papayudo; pavuncio; pelotudo; salame; zanahorio

sucker, be taken for a embarcar

suffer a hard blow (vulgar) sacarse la cresta

suffer the consequences llevar el bulto

sugar, solid block of unrefined chancaca; empanizado; panela; panocha; panuela

sugar, unrefined azúcar negra; panuela

sugar-cane liquor aguamiel; caña

suit jacket leva; paletó; saco; vestón

suit jacket, boy's saquito

suit, men's flux

suit, two-piece man's ambo

suit, woman's vestido de sastre

suitcase papelera; saco de viaje; suitqueis; valija; velís

sunglasses espejuelos de sol; gafas; lentes ahumados; lentes oscuros

sunstroke, get atarrillarse

superior maldito(a)

supernatural powers, person with alumbrado

superstitious person agüerista

supplementary suple

support baqueo; vaqueo

sure thing ir a fiesta; posta

surf surfear

surfer surfista

surfing surf

surly person cachorro

surpass bañar; comer; machetiar

surprise clavo **surprise, to** abismar; trincar

surrender cuartear

surveillance, under cachado
suspicious cabreado; cachudo; emponchado
swaggering bocatero(a)
swallow the wrong way trapicar
swamp agualotal; curiche; manigua; suamp; suampo
sweat transpiración
sweater chaleca; chomba; chompa; pulover; suera; suéter; yersey
sweet, extremely ampalagoso; hostigoso; relajante
sweet potato boniato; camote; chaco
sweetheart camote; chaval, chavala
sweets, fond of galgo
swell bufar
swelling chorcha; gualuche
swig of liquor cañonazo; guamazo; jalón; lamparazo; matracaso; palo; tacazo
swimming pool alberca; pileta; pool
swindle cabra; forro **swindle, to** conejear
swindler conejero; lana
swing colombina; mataculín; suing **swing, to** hamaquearse
switch, electric apagador; chucho; llave de la luz; suich; suiche
sycophant alcahuete; cepillo; chupa; chupahueso; jalabola; jalador; jalamecate; labioso(a); lambón; patero(a); sacamicas
symposium symposium
syrup sirop
syrup cake chancaca; empanizado; panela; panocha; panuela
tableland of the Andes puna
tack taquilla
tail, having no choco(a)
taillight calavera
tailor tailor
take agarrar; chapar; nancear
take a chance agarrar chansa
take a short cut deshechar

take a spell off someone by praying rezar
take advantage pechar; sacar la leche
take an exam rendir examen
take an exam a second time reparar
take and keep agachaparse; embolsicar
take away refalar
take courses in school agarrar clases
take it easy cógelo suave
take off refalar
take somebody else's things cuminar
take something without complaint mamar; pujar para adentro
tale macana
talk a lot without substance cantinflear; chamullar; pajudear; rollar
talk about one's misfortune plaguear
talk too much bembetear; latear; palanganear
talk, too much bembeteo
tall person bimba
talkative person bembón; bocatero(a); boquique; caña hueca; carreto; chachalaquero; cotorra; ladino(a); palangana; pispireta
tantrum cachicha; chivo
tape güincha; huincha; teip **tape, to** taipear
tape recorder pasacintas
tapping of a rubber tree pica; pique
tar neme
taste of fruit when it is not ripe tetelque
taste, without pariguayo; periguallo
tatting frivolité
tattletale acusete; alzafuelles; lambon(a); tapudo
taunt pitanza
tax tax; taxa
taxi driver tachero
taxi girl taxi girl
tea, medicinal cocolmeca; guarapillo; guarapo

tea, typical Argentinean mate; yerba

teacher ticher

teacher or professor, female cucha

teapot pava

tear hacer garra; hacer tira

tear apart desplomar

teenager chamo; chango; colino; lolo(a); pavito(a); sardina(o)

teeth (incisors) chocleros

teeth, without cholco; mueco

teetotum guazapa; pirinola; tirubaqué

tell desembuchar

ten-dollar bill chiva; chivo

tent carpa

termites comején; sepe

terror escame

test testiar

testicles (vulgar) blanquillo; bolones; gobelinos; hueva; huevos

text mode in the computer text mode

theft cacho

thick substance chorota; mazacotudo

thief choro; chorro; galafardo; gato; lanza; manilarga; manilargo; monrero; pato; punga; ratero; robón(a)

thief, look-out campana; loro

thin and long tasajudo

thin person acartonado; alambrito; angarillo; angarrio; arenque; charcón; cuico; fifiriche; flamenco; huesudo; langaruto; lumbriz; pacho; palillo; palitroqui; silgado

things bicha(o); broma; chereques; chivas; chunches; coroto; coso; deso; estaf; féferes; perol; tereque; verga; vaina

think cabecearse

thinker, slow conchudo; quedado(a)

thorns or spines, with ganchudo

those who steal from drug dealers torcidos

thoughtless young woman marocha

throw aventar; largar

throw stones peñasquear

ticket tiquete

ticket, cut a tiquetear

ticket, punch a tiquetear

tie chalina; tai

tie up tightly atracar; atrincar; empatar

tiger, Central American manigordo

tiger in the Chaco region bicho

tight-fisted conservativo

tight-fitting arrequintado

tile, floor solera

timing taimin

tin can tarro

tinware container latería; perol; perola

tip camarón; feria; vendaje

tipsy achispado; apintonearse; tomado

tipsy, get acatarrar

tire caucho; llanta; neumático; tair

tire of an activity encandilado(a)

tire repair shop llantería

tired desguañangado

toast toast

tobacco plantation vega

toddler barrigón; cagón; carricito; chamaquito(a); chavalo; chirringo; chirriquitín; cipote; lepe; patojito; pelaíto

toes, an irritation in the mazamorra

toilet excusado; inodoro; poceta; pompón; taza del baño; tóilet; water; waterclo

toilet paper papel de toile

tolerate bancar; calar

tomboy machona

tongs gato

tongue, smooth labia

tonsils glándulas; mompes

tool used to make holes coa; macana

tooth, without a cholco

toothache, have a destemplar

top hat bolero; bomba; cúbilo

top, spinning china; guasapa; guazapa; güila; zaranda

topic tópico

topless toples

tortilla, special kind of Mexican arepa; casabe; casave; chalupa; chilaquila; enchilada; envuelto; memela; pelliscada; pupusa; repocheta

toucan pico

touch in a sexual manner (vulgar) agarrón; amasar; jamonear

touchy necio

tough atrincado

toupee cabellera

tow truck reca

town taun

toy, cup-and-ball bolero

toy that buzzes runrún; zumbador

trade fajar

trademark trademark

traffic circle rondpoint

traffic jam taco; tapón; tranca; trancón

traffic stop stop

trailer dobletroque; tractomula

train conductor el chancho

traitor malinche; matamama

transvestite encamisonado; transformista

travel allowance, give beatificar

travel gear tapeque

traveler's check travelchek

tray bateya; charola; fuente

treasure, buried tapado

treat, sweet mecato

trench trencha

trichinosis zaratán

trick cabra; cachirulo; chiva; coba; descrestada; embarque; jarana trick, to chapuzar; enchilar; engrupir; pichulear

trick, dirty carajada; chanchada; perrería

trick used to avoid work roña

tricked, be comer pavo

tricks, full of enjaranado

trickster cuentero; cuentista; lana

trifle chingadera; insoria

trinkets achimes; baratillo; baratos; cacharpas; cacharros; cachivaches; chalchiuite; chécheres; chunches

trip raid trip, to dar un boniato

tripe soup guata; menudo; mondongo

trips, make tripear

triviality gurrumina

trouble malhora; pedo; revolú

troublemaker buscamoscas; chavón; cuchillero

trough bateya

trousers, baggy mameluco

truck troc; troca; troces

truck, heavy-duty jaula

truck, pickup pick up

truck, small delivery panel

trumpet butute

trunk cajuela; castaña; petaca; tronk

trust trastear; trostear

trustee trustí

trustful person alférez; ficha; ficho

truth, hide the amapuchar

T-shirt franela; polera; ticher

tumor tacotillo

tuna fish tuna

tune in agarrar la onda

turbid and/or secret activity quiquirigüiqui

turkey chompipe; chumpipe; guajalote; jolote; pisco

turn a vehicle voltear

turn on an electric device prender

turn on the TV or the radio ponchar

turncoat camarón

turtle huistora

tuxedo sacoleva; sacolevita

TV tiví

twins chachos(as); cuache; jimaguas; morochos; tuines

twins, identical chachos(as); cuache; cuapes; gemelos; mellos; morochos
twist enchuecar
twisted cheuto; chueco; virado; viroteao; visorioco
type taipear; tipear
typical típical
ugh! (interjection) ichis!
ugliness feúra; maluquera
ugly person bagre; botago; bufeo; feto; gacho; moscarrofio
ugly woman bagre; garabato
umbrella paragüe; sombrilla; umbrela
unable to understand chicato
unattractive majunche
unbaptized person moro
uncommon choro
uncouth cabestro; cerrero
under the influence of something empatucado
undercover agent camarón
underpants, long godos
undershirt camisilla; franela
underskirt hormadoras; naguas; peticote; saya interior; sayuela
understand cachar; caer el veinte; mangar
underwear, men's pantaloncillo
underwear, women's calzones; cuadros; cucos; pantaleta
undesirable zaragate
uneasy, be sanjuanear
uneducated person chongo; guasamaco; guaso
unemployed, be estar en banda
unfortunate torcido
unfriendly person higadoso; sangriento
unimportant issue (vulgar) güevonada; huevonada
uninterrupted action al hilo
uninvited guest chicle; paracaidista
union unión

unique machún; maco
unirrigated land de rulo
unit, one machún; maco
unit used for measurement cartabón
unlucky salado
unnecessary inoficioso
unpleasant bagre; balurdo; chocante; feo; higadoso; parche
unproductive or useless person cacatúa
unrefined sugar cake chancaca; empanizado; panela; panocha; panuela
unscrupulous turco; vivaceta; vivanco; vivaracho
untied thing aguada(o)
untrustworthy person buchipluma; chuchipluma; fayuto
upper floor los altos
uproar brollo; escándalo; fajazón; furrusca; garata; guato; margayate; molotera; tilingo
upset calentar; entripar; hinchar
upset, be arrechado(a); bravito; estar caliente
upset, get chivarse; encachorrarse; enchivarse; entromparse
upstart metido
up-to-date, the most la última chupá
urge aleonar; carbonear; chucear; enchinchar; incentivar; jochear; puyar
urinate (vulgar) desaguar; hacer chi; pillar
urine chi; pichí
Uruguay, native of charrúa
U.S., Anglo-Saxon in (derogatory) gabacho; gabardina
used object chiva
used too much se choteó
useless objects alaco; changle; chueco; coroto; féferes
useless person alaco; maraca
U.S., those who live in gabardinos

U.S., white person from the
gringo
utensils of poor quality, household
trique
vagina (vulgar) agujero; bizcocho;
bollo; cachimba; cachucha; chicha;
chimba; chocha; choro; chucha;
chuspira; concha; conejo; crica;
cucaracha; cueva; linda; pancho;
panocha; papaya; raja; tatú
vagrant bichicome
vagueness desbole; despelote;
despiole
vain, be atufarse
vain person estilozo(a); ñoño; pepe
valiant agallado
value, without torreja
vanish alcanforarse
varnish tapón
vegetable vainica
vegetable peel cachaza
vegetable stew calalú
vegetable that is not completely
cooked jojoto
vegetables served with meats
vianda
vehicle, battered batata; burra;
cacharra(o); cafetera; charchina;
cucaracha; fodongo; garnacha;
matraca; tartana
vehicle for transporting people, large
guagua
vehicle, four-wheel drive campero
vehicle license padrón
vehicle that doesn't work
accidentado; varado
vehicle that stops continuously
lechero
vehicle with wheels rodado
venereal disease chinche
Venezuelan Christmas carol
gaita
Venezuelan folk dance joropo
Venezuelan folk music chipola

Venezuelan folkloric musical
instrument furruco
very re
very little of something nadita
very much a la lata
vessel made from a squash
nambira
vessel, tall earthenware tinaco
vest centro
village elder amanta; amauta
village, small vereda
villain (vulgar) guache; muérgano;
sorullo; vergajo
violence garnacha
violent discussion garrotera
violent person machetero(a)
violent temperament rebotado
voices, noisy algaraza
voices, sound of runrún
voluminous balumoso
voluntary work cayapa
vomit basca; guacara; traboco **vomit,**
to debocar; deponer; trasbocar
vulgar and rude person cochino;
guache; pedrero
vulgarity guachada
waffle guafles
waffle machine guaflera
wait aguántele
wait, long embarque
waiter coime
waitress copera
wake up desparpajar
walk, take a chotear
walk without direction brujulear
walkie-talkie waquitoki
walks a lot and/or fast andón
wall zanja
wander matrear
wardrobe chiforobe; escaparate
wart on the finger mezquino
wash basin lavabo; lavacara; lavado;
lavatorio
wash clothes tallar

washer candeleja; golilla
washer, water-valve guasa
waste a rolete; desparringarse; desperrindingarse; retobo
waste time mangonear; tangalear
watch guacha **watch, to** chapar; guachar; guillar
watch, pocket molleja
watchman guachiman
water cannon truck guanaco; huáscar
water carrier aguatero
water container chirigua; cumbo; huacal
watered down chirre
watermelon melón de agua; patilla
wax waxear
waxed hulado
weak aguada(o); biche; cacarico; fifiriche; morroño; ñecla; neneque; patuleco; sute; tilico
wealthy fondeado
wealthy person caletudo(a); jaibón; sólido
weaning despecho
wedding casorio
weekend wiken
weld gueldear
welfare welfare
well-considered estar cotizada(o)
well-dressed person aliñado; cachaco; chiche; empaquetado; manga; pintoso
well-preserved morocho
western western
wheat, boiled mote
wheat flour dough boiled in soup pancutras; pantrucas
wheelbarrow carreta; carretilla
whimsical, become ponerse tere
whip acial; atajona; chilillo; chucho; coyunda; cuero; foete; fuete; fute; guasca; penca; rejo; verga **whip, to** chicotear

whip a liquid meneada
whisky (Scotch) escotch
whistle at pifiar
white beans coscorrones
white blond alien who speaks Spanish with a foreign accent gringo
white person canche; catire; chele; choco(a)
white person from the U.S. gringo
white person with curly hair grifo
whither achucutar
whore alegrona; anafre; bofa; cabaretera; campechana; capulina; chiva; chuquiasa; cuero; fletera; guaricha; güila; maraca; nochera; pajuela; patín; pellejo; perra; salquipanqui; turra; vagamunda; wuiza
whorehouse quilombo
wicked chorizo; zoquete
wide and flat pando
wife costilla; doña; guaife; vieja
will to do something tener polenta
willingness to enjoy fondling manilarga
win blanquear
win big dar una pela; pampear
win the heart of curucutear
wind norte
windmill ringlete
window, shop vitrina
windshield güinchil; vidriera
windshield wiper guaiper
wind up enchipar
wine, mild sweet chacolí
wire used to penetrate pipes laucha
wise-guy cheche; chenche; despercudido; parejero
witchcraft fufú
with low intelligence quedado(a)
with one limb shorter than the other tunco

without class (derogatory) majunche; mengalo; picante

without manners arrotado; guasamaco; jicate

without strength, be left desgonzarse

wizard alumbrado

woman cabra; chata; chavona; galla; imilla; jeva; llokalla; vieja

woman, attractive bien hecha; budín; célebre; churro; lechuguita; macanuda; machota; macita; mamazota; mazota; piba; potra; trozo; yegua

woman, coquettish bacana; betibú; chiva; mica

woman, easy (vulgar) banda; corbejo; pistolita

woman, lively chata; tusa

woman, peasant china

woman, responsible and courageous macha

woman, sterile (vulgar) machorra

woman, ugly bagre; garabato; gurgucia; prójima

woman who is not married cotorra

woman who likes younger men pollera

woman with a bad reputation bacana; banda; cabra; chingona; cojín; corbejo; cuero; manoseada; pistolita; rabúa; refistolera

womanizer (vulgar) bregador; cabro; chimbero; faldero; lacho; vagamundo

wood used as a blunt weapon macana

woodshaving colocho

word, erudite palabrota

word processor wordprosesor

words that do not make any sense coroto

work bregar; chambiar; jalar; laburar

work laburo; voleo

work a little magancear; mangancear

work, avoid ahorrar; baracutey; capear

work day by day rebusque

work extra hard (vulgar) camellar; cuidar la cuchara; descrestarse; fajarse; monear; ponerle mucha tiza; remar

work in a small job pichulear

work in odd jobs brujulear

work patiently rustir

work reluctantly hacer la roña

worker at the lowest level pinche

worker who defends the interests of the boss apatronado(a)

worms that live in the human intestine piduye

worry comején

worst seat in the theater gallinero

worthless person pendejo(a); tusa

worthless thing mecha

wound estacar

wound from a shot guamazo

wound, infected cáncer; cizote; lacra

wound made with a sharp object hincada; tajeadura

wrap embojotar

wreck quiñazo; reca

wrestling match in which the blows are faked cachacascán

wrist canilla

X-ray or picture taken by scanning device escanograma

yams boniato

yard yarda

yes claro

yogurt jocoque

you are welcome a la orden; con mucho gusto

you lose sonastes

young, feel pintonear

young man carajito; chamo; chango; cipote; imilla; llokalla; pelao; pibe

young man, oversized macuco; tarajallo

young man who behaves as a child guagualón; malgansón

young person lolo(a)

young person who consistently follows others coliche

younger member of the family coyote; cuneco; cunene; maraco; tierno(a)

you (pronoun) che; vos

yucca mandioca

zero grade huevo

zipper cierre; cierre relámpago; síper

zipper in trousers or pants marrueco

Spanish Index

¿**A dónde vas?** ¿A dónde la llevas?; ¿Para dónde tú vas?

a golpes a rolo

a la fuerza a juro; a la brava; a la machimberra

a la temperatura ambiental al clima

a medio cocinar saltón

a mí no me importa me vale un cacao; me vale un pepino

abandonar largar; rajarse

abandonar el juego como ganador amellarse

abandonar la escuela dropearse

abandonar un establecimiento, sin pagar conejear; fanfultear; fullería; hacer perro muerto

abarrotes grocer; groceri; grocería

abeja colmena

abogado licenciado

abombado acarajado; apendejado

abrasadera clam

abrazar apuchungar

abrelatas abridor

abridero abridura

abrigo femenino sobretodo; tapado

abstraerse embolatar; envolatar

abucheo pifia; silbatina

abuela la vieja; mama grande; viejita

abuelo papa grande; tata; tatá

abundancia jaracotal; tendal

aburrido cansón

aburrimiento aburrición; jarto

abusa del permiso reposero

abusón barsa

acabado, estar estar sonado

acalorado sancochao

acampar campin

acampesinado cachaco; guasca

acariciar ajonjear; chinchinear; tolonguear

acariciar eróticamente (vulgar) atracar; jamonear

acarrea riesgo sobado

¡acaso no lo ves! ¡muchacho!

acechar pavear

acelerador de un vehículo chancleta

acelerar puyar; sprintar

acento mote

acepta abusos, el que aguantón

aceptarlo sin reclamo mamar; ponerse

acera andén; banqueta; sardinel; vereda

acercarse asomar

achacoso traqueado

achisparse, con la bebida apintonearse

acicalado empaquetado

acné barro

acobardarse acholarse; achucutarse; arrugarse; culipendearse; enculillarse; fruncirse

acolchado quilto

acometer fajar

acomodar embonar; setear

acompañamiento a las carnes vianda

acoplado trailer

acortar achicar

acosar atiquizar

acostarse con alguien (vulgar) encamarse

acostumbrarse amañarse; aquerenciar

acto sexual, realizar el (vulgar) abrocharse; acostar; acostarse; cachar; chapetear; chichar; chingar; coger; culear; echar un polvo; encamarse; jalar; montar; pichar

acuario acuarium

acueducto pipeline

acuerdo entre caballeros gentleman
agreement
acusado sindicado
acusar chotear; sindicar
adefesio mondongo
¡adelante! ¡éntrale!; ¡siga!
adelanto a cuenta del jornal suple
aderezado con chile enchilado
adhesivo glu; pega; pegante; resistol
adicto a las drogas pichicatero
adinerado(a) caletudo(a); catrin(a);
fondeado; jaibón; morrocotudo;
palote; sólido
adiós bai; chao
adiosito chaito; chau
adivinar la intención calar
administra un garito chinguero
administrador manayer; manejador(a)
administradora de un prostíbulo
cabrona
admirador(a) fan
adolescente chamo; chango; colino;
lolo(a); pavito(a); sardina(o)
adoptar las costumbres del campo
aguajirarse
adoptar las costumbres y usos del
nativo acriollarse
adornarse con objetos de poco valor
emperendengarse
adornarse de las mejores galas
cacharpearse
adorno de plata virola
adulación jaladera; madera; mecate
adulador(a) (vulgar) alcahuete;
alzafuelles; cepillo; chupa;
chupahueso; jalabola; jalador;
jalamecate; labioso(a); lambón(a);
patero(a); sacamicas
adular hacer la pata; mecatear;
peinar; sobar
adulterar chimbear
adúltero(a) cojín; juguetón(a)
adulto que se comporta como joven
lolei

afeitar barbear
afeminado (vulgar) amariconado;
aviador; cueco; de agua; manflora;
pájaro; pato; torolo; trolo; volteado
afición goma; hobby
afición por jalar para
aficionado fan; inquieto
aficionado a las fiestas arrocero;
garufa; patalegre; rumbero
afinidad raport
afortunado fortunoso; suertero
afortunado con las mujeres
bacán
afrecho jachi
afuerano fuereño
agarrar chapar; trincar
agazaparse aparragarse
agente de aduanas despachante
agente de inmigración correa;
empleado(a)
agente encubierto camarón
agentes de Inmigración de los
Estados Unidos migra; la migra
agradable chévere; chiche; cuquera;
fullero; paponia
agradar cuadrar
agraviado torcido
agredir atracar; fajarse
agregado a de forro; de llapa; de
ñapa; de yapa; ganancia; ipegue;
pesuña
agriarse acidarse
agrietarse la piel por efectos del frío
pasparse
agringarse abolillar
agrio agarroso; choco(a); joco; juco;
suche
agrupación para obtener beneficios
económicos trenza
aguacate palta
aguacero invierno
aguachento aguachoso
aguado chirre
aguador aguatero

aguantar calar
aguantar sin quejarse pujar para adentro
aguardiente de mala calidad cachaza; guandolo; guaripola; jobo
aguardiente de uvas, un tipo de pisco
aguardiente mezclado miche
agudo amarroso
aguijón chute; lanceta
aguijonear chucear
agujero hureque
agujero en las medias papa
ahínco berraquera; verraquera
ahogador en el carburador choc
ahorita horita; horitita
ahorrando, estar siempre amarrete; apretado(a)
ahorrar forrar; salvar
aislado, lugar chifurnia
ajarse achucutar
ají, un tipo de locoto; rocoto
ají verde muy picante gárnica
ajustar embonar
al acecho tantear
al contado cach
al que se le respeta por su antigüedad amanta; amauta
alambre de acero para penetrar cañerías laucha
alameda camellón
alardear hacer fiero
albahaca basilico
albaricoque apricot; damasco
albaricoque, una variedad de chabacano
albino talamoco
alboroto alacamunería; argüende; baluma; balumba; bayú; bembé; berrinche; batiboleo; boche; borlote; bronca; bululú; chirinola; escándalo; fajazón; furrusca; garata; guachafita; guato molotera; montante; rebolotú;

reborujo; revulú; tangána; tángana; titingó
alborozarse estrepitarse
alcanzar nancear
alcohol que se agrega malicia
aldea pequeña vereda
alegre inquirriado
alegría, interjección de ijipa!
alejarse picárselas
alelado acarajado; apendejado
alemán, apodo para un boche
alentar aleonar
alerta, estar abusado(a); brincar a la cuerda; estar pilas
alerta, esté avíspese; póngase las pilas
aleta gualeta
alfajores de pinol gofio
alfarero locero
alfombra carpet; carpeta; choapino; jerga
alfombra de pita costal
alguacil cherife
alicaído engerirse
alimentador fider
alimento en vías de descomposición cignato
alimento pesado llenador
alimento quemado rechinado
alimentos para hacer un viaje bastimento; provista
almacén bodega
almacenar stocar
almeja clam; taca
almidón de patatas chuño; tunta
almorzar lonchar; lonchear; lunchiar
almuerzo lonch; lonche; lunche
alojado arrimado(a)
alojar arranchar
alquilar rentar
alta sociedad, creerse de la concheto
altanero alabao
alteración producida por la droga traba; tronada

alterar a alguien calentar
altivez, abatir la achantar
alto stop
alucinarse friquear
alud volcán
alusión sarcástica chinita
amancebarse (vulgar) amachinar;
  encuerarse
amante china; jebo
amargo agarroso
amaricado cueco; pájaro
amarrar atrincar
amazacotado masatudo; mazacotudo
ambicioso agalludo
ambiente elegante y fino pituco
ambiente previo bakgraun
amígdalas glándulas; mompes
amigo(a) cercano(a) alicate; broder;
  cabro; cuatezón(a); iloco!; loro;
  manito(a); pana
amigos, hacerse amistarse
amilanarse amusgarse; azararse
amonestar taquear
amontonados apilonados
amontonar abalserar
amorío secreto quiquirigüiqui
amortiguador de un vehículo
  shoquer
ampollarse envejigarse
amputado broco; cholco; chuto(a);
  cuto(a)
amuleto cábula
anaquel chelv
ancho y aplastado pando
anciano(a) angarrio(a); rodillón
anda de casa en casa, el que
  mosquero
anda mucho andón
andar de arriba a abajo matrear;
  tumbear; voltear
andar en aventuras amorosas
  gatear
andar siempre juntos amorochados
andarivel tarabita

andrajos chanchira(o); güilas; huilas
andrajoso culirroto; hilachento(a);
  pililo; rotoso
anécdota cacho; pasaje
**anglo que simpatiza con la causa
  chicana** chicanglo
**anglosajón de los Estados Unidos
  (peyorativo)** gabacho
anguila congrio
anillo matrimonial aro
animal sin cuernos muco
animar aleonar
animarse arrebolarse
ano (vulgar) ojal; ojete; poto
anonadar calar
anotar en un libro buquear
ansioso cachero
antecedentes bakgraun
anteojos espejuelos; foco; gafas
anticiparse sobrar
anticonceptivos birdcontrol
anticongelante antifris
antídoto contra
antipatía aburrición
antipático(a) bagre; higadoso(a)
antiséptico para la boca listerina;
  listerine
anular nulificar
anunciador mural espaciador; boletín;
  tablero de anuncios; tablilla de
  anuncios
anuncio aviso
añadidura de forro; ipegue; ganancia;
  llapa; pesuña; yapa
añorar faltar
apabullar calar; machetiar
apagado of
apalear bejuquear
aparatoso buchipluma
aparecer adinerado catrin
**aparenta fidelidad y está
  traicionando, el que** vendido
aparenta ser blanco y rubio
  catirruano

aparentar intención de hacer algo
cachaña
apariencia falsa pantalla
aparqueadero parkin; parking
apartado de correos casilla
apartarse abrirse
apedrear peñasquear
apellido nombre de familia
apenas a gatas
apesadumbrado apensionado
apesta fo
apetito sexual naturaleza
apilados apilonados
apilar estacar
aplanado pacho
aplaudir clapiar
apocado tilico
apoderarse de algo chapar
apodo mote
aprehensión flato
aprende lento, el que burro; chuzo
aprendiz cadete
apresurar apurar; de raspa; sacar
chocoliya
apretado apurruñado; arrequintado
apretujar achurrascar; amuñuñar;
apurruñar; despichar
aprieto brete
apropiarse de una cosa cuminar
aprovechador argollero; bolsero;
mamador; parche; pechuga; vivaceta;
vivanco; vivaracho
aprovecharse de otros bolsear;
pechar; sacar la leche
aprovisionarse de comida forrar
aproximarse asomar
apto caperuzo
apuntador (teatro) soplador
apunte esquech
apurado ajorado
apurarse rachar
¡apúrate! ¡ándale!; ¡métele!; ¡órale!
aquél que no se desea nombrar
elote

¡aquí! ¡órale!
arandela candeleja; golilla; guasa
araña viuda negra capulina
árbitro réferi
árbol en el desierto chaparro
archivo file
arcilla greda; masilla
ardid caula
argentinos, apodo para los che
argumento sanata
argumentos falsos, usar engrupir
armadillo cusuco; quirquincho
armado estructural de un objeto
carcasa
armario biblioteca; bufete; cabinete;
chiforobe; estante
armazón carapacho; farmaleta
armazón que sostiene la cama catre
armónica organillo
aro (rueda del automóvil) llanta
arrancar un motor estariar
arrancarse fletar
arreglar bichar; setear
arrendar rentar
arrepentirse fruncirse; rajar
arrestar apañar
arribista social metido
arriesgado endiablado
arrogante recargado
arrojar aventar; largar
arrollar enchipar
arroyo estero
arruinado bruja; quemado
arruinado, está está jodido
arruinado, estoy estoy hecho pistola;
estoy jodido; estoy cachimbeado
artesa bateya
asado rosbif; rost
asaltar por la calle cogotear
asalto match
asalto en un combate de boxeo
raund
ascender política y/o
económicamente encarapichar

ascensor elevador
aserruchar serruchar
asestar un golpe canchar
asfalto alquitrán; brea; chapapote; chicle
asiento contable rubro
asignatura fácil costura
asistencia médica medicaid
asistir a fiestas caculear
asociación pool
asombrar abismar
asombro, interjección de ¡chucha!; ¡pucha!
asombroso, es le ronca el clarinete; le zumba el mango
aspaviento aguaje
aspecto el look; pinta
áspero(a) morroño; roñoso(a)
astillar escarapelar; estillar
astucia jaibería
astucia para evitar el trabajo roña
astuta, acción caribería; gallada; parada; ranada
astuto(a) abusado(a); avispado(a); bagre; bala; banana; bicho; bocho(a); caperuzo; chucho; culebrero; jaiba; ladino(a); lángara; lanza; lobo; macuco; malva; recurso; tinozo; zamarro; zorrongo
asunto bicha(o); broma; charada; chimbo; coroto; coso; deso; estaf; gabela; ichu; pallasá; perol; vaina
asunto inmoral o escabroso cahuin; chanchullo; fritera
asunto peligroso papa caliente
asunto secreto cuita
asustado(a) cabreado(a); paniqueado(a)
asustarse azocararse; fruncirse; jabonarse
atado joto; lulo
atajo atrecho; chaquiñán; deshecho
atareado(a) festinado(a)
atareado, muy abacorao

atasco impase
atemorizarse abatatarse
atención, ponga ojo
atiborrar atucuñar; atapuzar
atizar atiquizar
atolladero impase
atolondrado azurumbado; tilingo; volado
atolondrarse atotumarse; atufar; azurumbarse; tilinguear; trabucarse
atontado acarajado; apendejado; zurumbático
atorarse trapicar
atracción hacia otra persona traga
atracción sexual berraquera; verraquera
atractiva, persona bizcocho; churro; cuero; levantador(a); machote; mango; tipazo(a)
atractivo glamur
atractivo sexual sexy
atractivo sexual, tiene sexapiloso
atrasarse colgarse; embromar
atrevido cachafaz; conchudo; raspado; zafado
atrofiado apachurrado
atún tuna
aturdido grogui; surumbo
aturdirse atotumarse; atrojar; atufar; azurumbarse; pasmarse
audacia pechuga
auge boom
aula de enseñanza salón
ausentarse de la escuela sin permiso capear escuela; hacer la chancha; hacer la cimarra; hacer la pinta; jubilarse; juqui
ausente de la escuela o el trabajo jubilado(a)
auténticamente mexicano tapatío
autobús bas; camión; chiva; colectivo; guagua; micro; microbus; omnibus
autobús pequeño chivita; busito

autocontrol self control
automatización automación
automóvil carro; coche; máquina
automóvil grande cadilaque; nave
automóvil viejo o en mal estado
batata; burra; cacharra; cacharro;
cafetera; charchina; cucaracha;
fodongo; garnacha; matraca; tartana
autopista jaiguey
autoservicio selfservice
autovía autocarril
avanzar forwardear
avaricia agalla
avaricia, actuar con alagartarse
avaro amarrete; apretado(a);
hambriento; maceta
ave pequeña piririta
avena cúaquer
avenida jirón
aventura amorosa movida; volada;
volantín
avergonzado(a) acholado;
embarazado(a)
avergonzar acholar; achumar;
amostazar; empavar
avergonzarse achuncharse;
amusgarse; azarearse; pasme;
picharse; tupirse
avería de una maquinaria pana;
vararse
aversión hacia una persona o asunto
bronca
avinagrarse acidarse
avión a chorro jet
avión pequeño pipilacha
avíos de viaje tapeque
aviso bil; pasacalle
axila arca; chucha; encuentro
ayudar a que una pareja se conozca
hacer gancho
azada lampa
azafata aeromosa; auxiliar de vuelo;
cabinera; camarera; erjostes
azafate charola; fuente

azotaina fuetera; garrotera; muenda;
trilla
azote cuartada; cuartiza; cuartazo;
cuerazo; reatazo
azotes, dar de latiguear;
zarandear
azuzar jochear
azuzar una pelea, interjección para
¡cúchale!; ¡cúchele!
bailar guarachar; rumbear
bailar; al que le gusta mucho pata
alegre; rumbero
bailarina balerina
baile familiar charanga; charranga;
charonga
baile, un tipo de cueca; danza;
jarana; joropo; marinera; pachanga;
porro
baja estatura, de chaparro(a);
chicoco; cuto(a); lepe; petiso; petizo;
potoco; taco
bajo la influencia de algo o alguien
empatucado
bajo los efectos de la droga
arrebatao; embalao; empepado;
engrifado; pepo
balanceo suing
balancín buinsuan; cachumbambé;
mataculín; sube y baja; suinsuan
balazo plomazo
balcón volado
balde bote; cubeta; cubo
baldosa de piso solera
balón bola
balón-mano handboll
balsa panga
banana butuco; cambur; guarán;
guineo; maduro; plátano
bancarrota jorobado; saltar
matojo
banco de una corriente de agua
vereda
bandeja bateya; charola; fuente
bandido matrero

bandita de goma banda de caucho; elástico; goma elástica; gomita; liga; resorte

bañera baño; batea; tina; tina de baño

baño batrom; water; waterclo

baqueano chane

baratija cacharro; pichiflina

baratijas achimes; baratillo; baratos; cacharpas; cacharros; cachivaches; chachivaches; chalchiuite; chécheres; chunches; muérgano

baratillo barata

barato y de baja calidad baratieri; chafa; macano(a)

barba chiva

barbacoa barbekiu; parrilla; parrillada

barniz tapón

barquillo para el helado barquilla; cucurucho; sorbete

barranco cajón

barriga guata; lipa; pipa

barrigudo(a) lipón(a); pipón(a); pipudo(a); tripón(a)

bártulos féferes

barullo baluma; boche; bembé; revolica

bastón del tambor mayor guaripola

bastón policíaco luma; macana; rolo

basura bachata; charbasca

basurero bote de basura; latón de basura; safacón; tacho de la basura; tarro de la basura; zafacón

bata de levantarse levantadera

batahola balumba; bayú; bembé

batata boniato; camote; chaco

batir chequear

baúl cajuela; castaña; petaca

beato cucufato

bebé bebito; beibi; beiby; chichí; cipe; guagua; nenito

bebé cagón poposeador

bebé que llora mucho cipe

bebé que mama mucho mamón

bebe y come a costas de otro bolsero; goterero

bebedor tomador

beber bebidas alcohólicas chupar; jalar; mamar

bebida alcohólica para un velatorio gloriado

bebida alcohólica, un tipo de aloja; campechana; caña; chicha; curda; gas; mezcal; mingui; pisco; pulque

bebida espesa mazamorra

bebida sin azúcar amargo

bebida sin gusto aguachada

bebida, un tipo de aguapanela; api; atole; champús; mate; pinole; piñol; pinolillo; pozol; resbaladera; ulpo

bellaco zoquete

beneficio propio, el que usa su autoridad para chapacaca

benjamín coyote; cuneco; cunene; maraco; tierno(a)

berrinche cachicha; chivo

berruga mezquino

besar apretar; dar un pico

beso pico

beso apasionado chupón

betún para el calzado grasa

biberón bibi; botella; chupo(a); chupón; mamadera; mamila; pacha; pomo de leche; tetera; tetero

bicho pajarito

bicicleta baicicle; burra; cicla; juila

bicoca bica

bidón caneca

bien macanudo; nítido; okei

bien conservado morocho

bien parecido bien hecho; bizcocho; chinazo; chiva; churro; cuero; fuerte; gallo; macanudo; machote; papasote; papazote; pintón; por el libro; potro; roscón; tipazo; yeguo

bien vestido aliñado; cachaco; chévere; churro; chute; macanudo; mamito; perchudo; pintoso; titino

bienes robados por funcionarios chunchullos; chunchurria

bienestar social welfare

bigotes boso

bilis, ataque de rebote

billete fasulo; tíquet; tiquete

billete de cien pesos cupón; gamba

billete de cinco mil pesos gabriela

billete de diez dólares chiva; chivo

billete de mil pesos luca

billete de un peso papel

billetes de dólares lechugas

binoculares anteojos largavista; gemelos

biólogo biologista

biombo cancel

bísceps conejo; gato; lagartija; lagarto; mollera; molleros; ratón

bisexual bugarón

bistec bife

bizco bizconeto; biscorneo; bizcornio; choco(a)

bizcocho panatela

blanda y sin consistencia, cosa aguada(o)

blando suave

blanqueador blich

blusa cota

bobalicón cachencho

bobo camote; chorizo; cipote; guanaco; suncán; tilingo

boca (vulgar) buchaca; jeta

boca grande tarasca

bocadillo pichanga; snack

boceto esquech

bochinche bolate; bonche; volate

bocina (electrónica) corneta; espiquer; parlante

bocina del automóvil corneta

bocio cantimplora; chorcha; coto

bocota guayaba

bofetada aletazo; chirlo; galleta; galletazo; moquete

bofetadas, dar de dar galleta

boleto tíquet

boleto de la lotería suerte

boliche; juego de las bolas bolero

boliche, juguete bolero; emboque

bolígrafo biromé; esferográfico; lapicera; lapicero; lápiz de pasta; pluma

bollos bolillos; bollitos; mascadura; pancitos; panecillos; panecitos; rolos; rols

bolos bouling

bolsa funda; huacal; jaba; morral

bolsa de papel cambucho; cartucho

bolsa fuerte y resistente costal

bolsillo bolsa

bolsillo lateral del pantalón grillero

bomba pompa

bombero lumbrero

bombillo(a) ampolleta; bolb; bombita; foco; lamparita

bonito(a) chévere; chirote; chiva(o); chulo(a); encachado(a); nítido(a); pepeado(a); pirulo

bonito(a), es muy bacán; bien hecho(a); budín; cuquísima; está papa; polenta; por el libro; por la maceta; repiocha

boquete de manguera pitón

borrachera (vulgar) curda; juma; jumado; montera; papalina; rasca; tomatera; tranca; vacilón

borracho, completamente está hasta el birote; pluto

borracho; ebrio ajumado; almareado; birote; bolo; caneco; cañoneado; chumado; cocido; como cuba; como huasca; como huevo; como pickle; como piojo; como poto'e guagua; cuete; curado; curdeao; curdo; embolado; en fuego; engorilado; entre pisco y nazca; estar en fuego; guarape; guarapeado; guarapero; guaro; guayao; jalado; jumado; jumeta; jumo; mamado; pernicioso;

petardo; picao; prendido; rajao; tacuache; tomado; trinco; trompeta; zumbado

borracho, estar andar con el gorila; andar pedo; andar pisto; estar bomba; estar con el gorila; estar con la caña; estar con la mona; está hasta el birote

borrar deletear

bosquejo esquech

botadero dumping

¡bótalo! ¡órale!

botar dompear

botar como desperdicio yonquear

bote ancón; chalupa; panga

bote salvavidas life boat

bragas calzones; cuadros; cucos; pantaletas; pantis

bragueta marrueco

bramadera runrún; zumbador

bravata entablonada

bravucón bragado

brazalete esclava; pulsera

brazo del delta de un río caño

brea neme

bribón cuatrero

brizna grisma

brocha de afeitar hisopo

brocha para pintar cabra

broche desabrochador; pin

broche, un tipo de chulo

broma ancheta; changuería; chapa; chercha; jarana; mecha; pandorga; talla; vellón

broma grotesca joda

broma que causa daño cacho; joda; vacilada; vacilón

bromas, decir echar tallas

bromear bachatear; brincar; changuear; chingar; chucanear; gufear; hechar tallas; tandear; vacilar

bromista célebre; chango; mozón; vacilón

brujería fufú

bruto tapado

budín pudin

buen jinete chalán

buen negocio ancheta; movida

buena presencia, de simpático

buena relación raport

buena suerte chepa; liga

buenmozo chivo

bueno(a) chévere; chingón; chuchin; groso; gufeao; macanudo; machín; machina; nítido; pleno; tuanis

bueno(a), es muy por la maceta

bueno para nada (vulgar) huevón; güevón

bufanda mascada

bufón chucán; gracejo

buhardilla desván; tapanco

búho chuncho; mochuelo; múcaro; tecolote

buhonería achimería

buhonero achimero; achín; achún; cacharrero; cangallero; maritata; sencillero; varillero; ventero

buitre carancho; chulo; gallinazo; jote; samuro; tincute; tiñoza; zamuro; zopilote

bujía eléctrica ampolleta; bolb; bombita; foco; lamparita

bulevar búlava

bulla bochinche; laberinto; rochela

bullicio de voces algaraza

bullicioso guanguero; guatoso

bulto bojote

buñuelo dona; donat; picarón

buque insignia flagship

burla chercha; chinga; costeo; jarana; pitanza; relajo; tiradera; trisca

burlarse bacilar; chotear; costear; relajo; soguear; tandear; tomar para el fideo; triscar; vacilar

bus; autobús bas; camión; chiva; colectivo; guagua; micro; microbus; omnibus

bus pequeño buzeta

busca relaciones amorosas, el que bregador
buscapleitos buscamoscas
buscar busconear
buscar favores con regalos manzanear
buscar tesoros escondidos guaquear
butaca pata de gallina
butacazo suelazo
caballa jurel
caballero gentleman
caballete para serrar burro
caballitos calesita; carnaval; carrusel; machina; volantín
caballo blanco palomo
caballo de sillín pingo
caballo que luce muy mal chongo; mocho
cabaret night club
cabeza (vulgar) azotea; cachola; chola; chirimoya; chompa; coco; jupa; la sabiola; mate; pepa; piojosa; terraza; testa; tusta; zabeca
cabeza dura conchú
cabezón cacholón
cachazuda conchudo
cachete cachetada; chalchazo; galletazo; gaznatón; moquete
cachivaches féferes; tareco
cacique chacón; curaca
cacique político gamonal
cacto quisco
cadena network
caderas juanetes
caerse escocotarse
café cofiro
café, color braun; carmelita; castaño; chocolate; marrón
café con poca leche marrón
café descompuesto cache
café pequeño perico
café solo negro; tinto
caída matada
caimán sudamericano yacaré

caja congeladora frisa
caja de material sólido cajón
calabaza bulto; cutuco; zapallo
calabaza, un tipo de chayote; jícara; poronguito
calaña, de baja mugre; mugroso
calavera abandonado
calcetín corto zoquete
calcetines calcetas; escarpines; medias
caldera boila
calentador jira; jiter
calidad inferior, de bodrio; chimbo; medio pelo; pacotilla; penca
callarse la boca comer machica
¡cállate! icho!
callos (estómago de la vaca) guata; menudo; mondongo
calvo(a) cocopelao; coquipela; pelón; tuso(a)
calzada andén
calzado del indio caite
calzado deportivo championes; champions; esnikers; tenis; zapatillas
calzón mameluco
calzoncillos pantaloncillo
calzones pantis
cama de campaña catre
camaleón camarón
camarera copera; gata; mucama
camarero barman; coime
camarógrafo cameraman
camarón grande gamba
camarones chacalines; chacolín
cambiar de ideología voltear
cambiar las cosas de su sitio curucutear
cambio (dinero) chirola; chirona; feria; menudo; sencillo; vuelto
cambio de suela remontar
camilla chacana
caminar sin hacer nada pavear
caminata futin; jaic
camino rural vereda

camión troc; troca; troces
camión con remolque dobletroque
camión grúa reca
camión para carga pesada jaula; tractomula
camión pequeño de reparto panel
camisa de dormir camisón; camizón
camisa de fuerza canana
camisa de mujer camisón
camisa típica del Caribe guayabera
camiseta camisilla; franela
camisón bata de dormir; dormilona
campamento campin
campeón(a) champion
campesino canario; chagra; inquilino; jíbaro; montañero; motoso
campo cultivado chacra; fil
campo de juego pleigraun; fil
campo, del campirano; guaina
campo, el cauntri
campo sembrado de maíz milpa
canal diche; zanjón
canasta de comestibles ancheta
canasto, un tipo de mochilón
cancelar nulificar
cancha de fútbol gramilla
candelabro candil
cangrejo buruquena; cacarico; crab; jaiba; juey
cangrejo de río bruquena; seboro
cangrejo pequeño cocolía
canicas ágatas; agües; agüitas; balitas; bolas; bolitas; garbinche; garvinche; metras; papangos; tiros
canicas, un juego de pepa y palmo
canijo sute
canoa banasta; bató; chalupa; panga; piragua
cansado choreado; desguañangado
cansado(a) de una actividad, estar encandilado(a); estar podrido; estar quemado(a)
canta muy bien, el que gardelito

cantidad, en gran choretó
cantina pobre boliche; botiquín
cantinero bartender
canto del payador payada
canto folclórico navideño venezolano gaita
canto monótono canturria
cantor que crea versos improvisados payador
caña de pescar carrizo
caña para picar al buey picana
cañería paipa
cañonera ganbout
capacidad intelectual mate
capacidad y voluntad de hacer algo bien tener polenta
capar arreglar; componer
capataz forman
capaz capo; machete
capirotazo pastorejo; tincazo
capital con que se inicia un negocio plante
capota del automóvil bonete
capricho birria
caprichoso, ponerse ponerse tere
captar con palabras lisonjeras aguachar
cara de enfado caracho; malacaroso
caracol cambute; churo; turo
¡caramba! ¡Ay bendito!
caramelo candi
¡caray! ¡carajo!
carbonilla carboncillo
cárcel bartolina; bote; buchaca; cana; capacha; chirola; chirona; jeruza; joyolina; tambo
carente de entusiasmo aplastado
carga en exceso soborno
cargado de deudas embrollao
cargador terciador
cargar terciar
cargar a la cuenta charchiar
cargo público, lograr un encamburarse

cargos políticos, desempeño de varios a la vez policamburismo
caricaturas cómicas; comiquillas
cariñoso querendón
carne asada churrasco
carne de carnero hecha cecina chalona
carne de cordero seca chalona
carne del lomo del vacuno chorizo
carne en salmuera carne bif
carne enrollada y aderezada arrollado
carne seca charqui
carnes que empiezan a pudrirse aventado
carnicería pesa; tercena
carnicero bachajé; pesador
carpeta folder; cartapacio
carpeta sobre el escritorio vade
carrete de hilo carretón
carretera de circunvalación by pass
carretilla de mano carreta
carrillera carretilla
carrillo abultado, con un cachipuco
carrillos, de grandes cachetón
carro policial que lanza agua guanaco; huáscar
carrusel volantín
cartapacio bulto
cartel anuncio; aviso; rótulo; sain; valla comercial
cartera bolsa; bolso
carterear bolsear
carterista gato
casa de empeño tía rica
casa de huéspedes asistencia
casa de prostitutas quilombo
casa, la chante
casa muy pequeña y arruinada sucucho
casamiento casorio
casarse amarrarse

casas de material ligero cantegril; población callampa; ranchería; villa miseria
cascabel maruga; ronrón
cáscara de un vegetal cachaza
casino ilegal timba
¡cáspita! ¡ijito!
casquivana loca
castigar físicamente fajar; hacer sonar
castigo corporal pela
castigo máximo en el juego penal
castrar arreglar; componer
casualidad, por chiripa; de chiripa; por chiripa
cataplasma cayanco
categoría ranquin
categorizar ranquear
católico(a) fanático(a) pechoño(a)
católico, muy mocho; pechoño
catre de madera marquesa
caucásico bolillo
causa daño con brujerías, el que dañero
causa molestia lavativoso
causar daño embarrar
causar embriaguez rascar
cazar con las boleadoras bolear
ceder aflojar
cédula de identificación, otorgar una carnetizar; cedular
celebración feria
celo, estar en alzado
celos gararey
cementerio chacarita
ceniciento nixte
censura pipo
centavo chele; kilo; peni
centavo, un chavo
centro del blanco blanco; fama; mosca
cepillo para botellas churrusco
cepo brete
cerca reja; talanquera; zanja

cerdo chancho; cochino; cuchí; lechón; macho; marrano; tunco
cerebro coco
cereza capulín; cherry; guinda
cerillo fósforo; mach
cerner o cernir harnear
cerradura candado; chapa
cerrar a medias entrecerrar
cerril cerrero; jicaque
cerveza biela; bironga; birria; chela; pola
cerveza con gaseosa refajo
cerveza del barril shop; sifón
cerveza helada fría
cerveza oscura malta
cerviz tungo
césped grama; gras; lon; manga; prado; yerba; zácate
cesta(o) canasta(o); huacal; mochilón
chabacano pilinqui
chabolas callampas; cantegril; población; ranchería; villa miseria
chacota chercha
chacotear brincar
chal estola; mantilla; mantón; paño; pañoleta
chalado craqueao
chaleco de un traje centro
chancaca azúcar negra; empanizado; panela; panocha; panuela
chancear changuear
chancleta gutara
chancletas guaraches
chaqueta americana; campera; casca; chamarra; manuela
chaqueta de un traje leva; paletó; saco; vestón; yaket
chaqueta o blusa tejida suera; yersey
charco cocha
charcutería rosticería
charlatán charlón
chasco magna

chasco, llevarse un enchilar; magnarse
chato chingo
cheque viajero travelchek
chequear chulear; inspectar
chicha aloja
chichón cocotazo; cototo; marranazo; tutuma
chicle chuingom
chiflado chiflis; desvirolado
chile verde ají
chileno, apodo para un roto
chinche alepate
chisme alacamunería; argüenda; bochinche; borrego; chimentos; conventilleo; pelambre; recorte; zumbido
chismear acarrear; cacarear; chimentar; copuchar; desparramar; jacalear; pelar
chismorreo andar de jacalera; bembeteo; conventilleo; sopa de cuerda
chismoso(a) bochinchero; camarón; chirinola; chivato(a); conventillero(a); enredista; lenguón(a); lleva y trae; llevacuentos; oreja; pajudo; pajuo; pendenciero; tapudo
chiste talla
chocolate con atole champurreado
chofer chofero
choque cantaso; cantazo; chancacazo; choc; estrellón
chorritos, en lepe
choza bajareque; bohio; callampa; caney; jacal; quilombo; rancho; ruca
chucherías chalchiuite
chuleta de cerdo chapa
chuleta para copiar en un examen bate; chivo; comprimido; droga; torpedo
chupete (del bebé) biberón; bobo; caldera; chupo(a) de entretención; chupón; mamón; pacifair; tete

chupetín   caramelo; chambelona; chupaleta; chupeta; chupete; colombina; paleta; pilón; pirulí

cicatería   agalla

cicatero   garrotero

cicatriz pequeña   ñañara

ciego(a)   choca(o); tuerto(a)

ciénaga   suamp; tocotal

cierre de cremallera   cierre; cierre relámpago; síper; slíper

cigarrillo   faso; frajo; pitillo; tusa

cigarrillo de mala calidad rompepecho; chicote

cigarrillo de marihuana   bacha; bazuco(a); cachaflín; cacho; coso; moto; pepa; pito; vareto; varillo

cigarrillo de marihuana, lo que queda del   chicho

cigarro puro   tabaco

cinco arrobas   tercio

cinco centavos   vellón de cinco

cine, el   el mono

cinta   güincha; huincha; teip

cinta adhesiva   escotch

cinta metálica   güincha; huincha; suncho

cintarazo   cinchazo

cinturón   chicote

cinturón de salvavidas   life belt

círculo para jugar al trompo mancha

cirio de gran tamaño   velón

cita   apoinmen; deit

citar al juzgado   infraccionar

ciudad   taun

clase media   medio pelo

clavar   enterrar

clavarse   estacar

clavícula   eslilla

cliente regular   casero

cloro   clorex; clorina

club nocturno   night club

cobarde   cagacatre; chabelón(a); chayote; cochino(a); cucamba; culilludo(a); mantilla; maula; pendango(a); pendejo(a); ratón

cobardía   canilla; pendejada; tilico

cobertizo   galpón

cobija   frisa

cobrar o dar soborno   matraquear; matraqueo

cobrar un precio excesivo   garrotear

cocaína   perico

cocaína que se aspira   pase

coche cama del tren   eslipincar; polín

cochinada   chanchada

cociente   ratio

cocina   estov; estufa; fogón

cocinar   cuquiar

cocinilla   cocineta; reverbero

coco verde   pipa

codicia   angurria

coger   agarrar; nancear

coger un camino   cortar

cohete   rastrero; roquet; volatero

cohibido, sentirse   ajibararse

coito (vulgar)   polvo

cojear   chuequear

cojo   patojo; patuletas

colar   meneada

colchón de muelles   somier; tambor

colchón de paja   pallasa

colgar   abrirse; berretín; guindar

colibrí   burrión; chupa-mirto; chuparosa; chupaflor; esmeralda; quinde; tentenelaire; visita flor; zumbador; zunzun

colilla de cigarrillo   bacha; chinga; cusca; pucho

colilla de puro   breva; cabo; chacuaco; mocho; pucho

colinas   cerros

colisión   cantaso; cantazo; choc; estrellón

colombianos, cualquiera que viva en los llanos   llanero

colorante para las comidas   achiote; color

colorear las mejillas chapetear

columpiarse hamaquearse

columpio colombina; mataculín; suing

combate match

combatir los hechizos, lo que se usa para contra

combinar machear

combustible fiul

comedor lonchrum

comenzar a hacer algo hincarle el diente

comer filear; manyar

comer bien forrar

comer chile picante enchilar

comer en la casa de otro lamber; velar

comer excesivamente atracar; batear; darse un panzazo; darse una jartera; empacar; empanzar; empanzurrar; jambar; jamonear

comer íntegramente jartar

comercia en la yerba mate yerbatero

comestible edible

cometa barrilete; bomba; caite; chichigua; chilito; chiringa; huila; pandorga; papalote; piscucha; volantín

cometa pequeño chonchón; falucho; güila; ñecla; papagallo; papagayo

cómico costiante

cómico, aquel a quien todo se le hace célebre

comida mastique

comida de bajo costo puchero

comida de maíz morocho

comida de tarro enlatado(a)

comida indígena nicaragüense indio viejo

comida mal preparada frangollo; sambumbia; tumba

comida preparada con los restos de otra ropa vieja

comida, puesto de comeivete; friquitín

comida sin valor nutritivo embeleco

comidas de cerdo, especializado en lechonera

comilón garoso; gorozo

comisión, el que trabaja por una coyote

comisión ganancia

¿cómo se llama Ud.? ¿cual es su gracia?

¿cómo te llamas? ¿cómo tú te llamas?

compadre broder; cuate; llave; mano; parna

compañero broder; cuate; mano; parna; parner

competente capo

compinche caballo; gallo

complacer sólo por interés cotonear

completo full

complicadas, hacer las cosas emborujar; encarajinar

cómplice bastonero; campana

componer bichar

comporta como un niño, el que se guagualón

comportarse, el que no sabe como carajo; carretonero; guasamaco; pariguallo; periguallo

comprender agarrar la onda

comprometer en una situación difícil clavar

comprometerse amarrarse

computador compiuter

computadora personal PC

con la resaca después de una borrachera con el cuerpo cortado; con el ropero a cuestas; con el hachazo; con la caña mala; con la mona viva; enguayabado

con manchas en la piel pañoso

con pretensiones y sin mérito carcamán

con toda la fuerza posible al carajo; a todo dar

con una extremidad más corta que la otra tunco
concertar casar
concha corroncha
conchabar amangaluar
conciliador peismeker
concubina china
condescendiente mantequilla
condición status
condición social, de baja (peyorativo) arrotado; jincho; roto
condición socioeconómica, de baja alpargatón; alpargatudo; carajo; chancletero; lana; pinganilla; ruanetas
condimento achiote; color; recao
condón (vulgar) forro; goma
conducir un vehículo draivear; manejar
conducta descuidada al tuntún
conducta necia ñeñeñe
conducta no convencional relajo
conducta típica del chicano chicaneo
conductor de ómnibus colectivero; guaguero
conectado on
conectar prender
conejillo de indias apereá; conejo de las indias; curiel; curí; cuy; güimo
conexión link
confabulación manguala
confabular amangaluar
confesar desembuchar; espepitar
confianza trust
confianza o desconfianza, persona de ficha; ficho
confianzudo parejero
confiar trastear; trostear
confidencialmente of de record
confirmar conformar
confitado helado
confundido, estar empelotado; pelar
confundir boruquear; calar; emborucar; engalletar
confundirse abatatarse

confusión barata; brollo; galleta; desbole; despelote; despiole; mazamorra; revolica
congelado frisado
congelar frisar
conjunto de objetos monos
conjunto musical combo
conmoción shock
conocedor del camino rumbeador
conquistador de mujeres bacilón; cabro; gaucho; vagamundo
consecuencias, afrontar las chupar
conseguir lo que se desea apañar; cachar; levantar; mecha; pechar
conseguir un empleo enchafainarse
conserje, el el super
conservador (política) godo; mocho
conservarse bien pintonear
consorcio pool
constipación aguda entablazón
constreñido trancado
contacto político, comercial o profesional brazo; cuña; gancho; pala; palanca
contaminación polución
contaminar polucionar
contenedor container
contenerse atajarse
contonear chiquear; dengue; tongonear
contrabandear chancuquear; trapichar
contrabandista butléger
contrabando de alcohol o tabaco chancuco
contradictorio contrecho
contrariedad mecha; vaina
contratiempo guamazo; mamonazo
contrato de renta lease
contribución para comprar en grupo serrucho; vaca
controla votantes, el que cacique
contubernio político conchupancia
convaleciente cacreca
convenir casar

conversación interviú
conversación bulliciosa chercha; corrincho; mololoa
conversacion larga y tediosa cotorra
conversación sin importancia cháchara; jarabe de lengua
conversador ladino(a)
convertir en dinero efectivo cachar
convivir sin haberse casado arrimarse
copado full
copiar en un examen chivear; copietas; pastelear
copiar en un examen, papel para bate; chivo; comprimido; droga; torpedo
coqueta pispireta
coquetear caculear; fletar; flirtear; floretear
coraje caliente; pechuga
coraje, tener tener pana
corajudo atrincado
corbata chalina; tai
corbata de lazo corbata de gato; corbata de humita
cordel cabulla; cabuya; cañamo; curricán; guato; lazo; lienza; pita; string
corpulento cipote; maceta; morrocotudo
corral grande pampón
correazos, dar de chicotear; fajar
correcto chévere; legal
corredor (edificio) hol; jol
correo certificado recomendado
correr un riesgo agarrar chansa
cortafrío cortahierro
cortar mochar
cortar con cuchillo filerear
cortar con machete chapear
cortar el boleto tiquetear
cortar la taquilla cortar pantrucas
cortar las malezas despagar
cortar más de lo necesario ponchar

cortar y peinar el cabello peluquear
corte de carne de vacuno lagarto; lomo; malaya; muchacho; palomilla; picana; sobrebarriga
corte de pelo motilado; pelado; peluqueada; peluqueado; recorte de pelo
corte muy corto al pelo, tener quedarse mocho
cortejar atacar
corto chingo
cosa (vulgar) bicha(o); broma; chereques; chivas; chivo; chunches; coroto; coso; deso; estaf; perol; tereque; vaina; verga
cosa buena machera
cosas de baja calidad, persona que sólo compra pichinchero(a)
coscorrón caibo; cocotazo; coscacho; marranazo
cosecha pizca
cosecha entre varios tarea
costal guangoche; saco
costarricences, apodo para los ticos
costra en las heridas lacra
crespo(a) culisada; enrizado(a); pasa; pelo enrulado; pelo rizo
cresta de ave cenca; chorcha
criado guachiman; mayordomo; servicial
crines del caballo tusa
crisis impase
crítica pipo
criticar tusar
criticón triscón
cruce de círculo rondpoint
crucero crus
cruzar el Río Grande brincar el charco
cuadrilátero para los encuentros pugilísticos ring
cuadro de calificación listing
cualquiera, una bacana; banda; cabra; cojín; corbejo; cuero; pistolita; rabúa; refistolera

cuarto pieza
cuarto de dólar, un cuora
cuarto de galón, un litro
cuarto para descansar den
cuarto pequeño cobacha
"cuatro ojos" (peyorativo) gafufa
cubanos, de los campos guajiro
cubo bote; cubeta
cubre los errores, el que palero
cubrecama bedspred; cobo; colcha;
  edredón; sobrecama
cucaracha barata; chiripa; roche
cuchilla de afeitar hoja de gilet;
  hojillas; navajas de rasurar
cuchilladas, dar muchas charquear
cuchillo chafirro; faca; filera
cuclillas, ponerse en aplatarse
cuco macuco
cucurucho de papel cambucho
cuello cocote
cuenca de un río hoya
cuenta bil
cuentagotas gotario; gotero
cuento macana
cuerda cabestro; mecate; ropo; soga
cuerda para saltar cuica
cuernos cachos; chifles; cuaco; tarro
cuesco pepa; pepita
cuestión (vulgar) berenjena; bicha(o);
  bichar; charada; chereques; chivas;
  chunches; coroto; deso; estaf; feferes;
  gabela; ichu; pallasá; perol; tiliches;
  vaina; verga
cuestión enredada berraquera;
  verraquera
cuestiones chereques; chunches;
  coso; deso; tiliches
¡cuidado! ¡chivísima!
cuidador(a) de niños sentador(a)
cuidador del cementerio
  camposantero
culebra machala
culo (vulgar) ancas; aparato; cola;
  cueva; el queque; fundifá; fundillo;

popi; popín; popó; poto; rabo; siete;
tambembe; traste
cultura africana, relativo a la
  garífuna
cultura chicana chicanismo
cuna camita
cuneta cordón; encintado de la acera;
  orilla; sardinel; solera
curandero(a) callahuaya; machi;
  piacha; tegua; yatiri; yerbatero
curiosear mosquear
cursi bagre; cuico; pije; siútico
cursilería huachafería
dádiva erogación
dado chincharro
daga facón
da las cartas, el que gurupie
dale un beso dale un pico
¡dale! ¡imétele!
dame un respiro dame quebrada
dañar bichar; choretear;
  desperfeccionar; envainar; fregar;
  joder
dar largar
dar examen tomar examen
dar gratificación al cliente encimar
dar muerte descocotar
dar un regalo pitar
darse cuenta de realizar
darse de golpes monear
dársena dock
de acuerdo, estar kupia-kume
de carácter fuerte guayacán
de improviso paratatú
de inmediato ahora; ahoritica;
  ahoritita; altiro; en un tilín
de nada a la orden; con mucho gusto
de poco valor lesera; lesura; torreja
débil aguada(o); cacarico; morroño;
  neneque; patuleco; tilico
débil de carácter, persona biche
decadencia, en tirá; tirao
decaimiento aplanche
decano (académico) dean

decir algo indirecto sanguaraña
decir o hacer una lesera lesear
declarar falsamente jesusear
dedicarse con ahínco fajarse
defecar (vulgar) hacer el dos; hacer la
  caca; hacer pupu; votar
defecto cuija; dinga
deformar eschoretar
degradar algo o a alguien (vulgar)
  putear
deja de hacerlo ahora parála
idéjalo! iórale!
dejar dropear
dejarse estar achanchado; despatarro
déjate de decir tonterías acábala
  farolito
idéjese! órale!
idéjese de molestar! iábrase!
delatar aventar; batir; chivatear;
  chivar; chotear; pajear; sapear
delator chota; pinche
deletrear espelear; espeliar
delgado acartonado; alambrito;
  angarillo; angarrio; arenque; charcón;
  cuico; flamenco; fliche; huesudo;
  langaruto; lumbriz; palillo; palitroque;
  silgado; tasajudo
delicado chiche; cuquera
delincuente malevo; palomo; pato
  malo; punga
delirium tremens diablo
delito crimen; felony
demonio chucuto
idemonios! icoño!
denostar retar
dentadura postiza caja de dientes
denunciar batir; chivatear; chivar;
  pajear; sapear
dependiente en la tienda de
  abarrotes bodeguero
deportes, prometedor en los
  prospecto
deportista sportman
deportivo esport; sportivo

depositar o retirar dinero del banco
  banquear
depósito estoc
depósito de chatarra yonker
deprimido, estar tener un bajón
derecho de paso en las vías públicas
  prelación
derechos de autor copirrait
derribar con violencia voltear
derrochador botarata
derroche a rolete; cancanear
derrota garrotiza; pela
derrotar chingar; garrotear
desabrido aguachoso; terco
desafiar chorear
desafinado desorejado
desafortunado torcido
desagradable bagre; balurdo;
  chocante; feo; higadoso; parche
desagrado, interjección de imorite!
desairar bochar
desaliñado desgualetado
desanimado aguacate
desaparecer alcanforarse;
  empuntarlas
desarmado descachalandrado
desarmar desconchinflar
desarraigadora ruter
desastre quilombo; tendalada
desatento, estar pavear
desatino chayotada
desbrozar socola
descabalar descompletar
descalabrarse descocorotarse
descalificar descualificar
descanso breca; breik; breique;
  breque
descarado desharrapado; fregón
descaro concha; empaque; impavidez
descascarar descarachar;
  descascaranar
descomportarse descompasar
descompuesto, está está chingado
descomunal sendo

desconectado of
descongelar desfrozar
descontrolarse friquear
descortés migueleño
descuento rebaje
descuidada y pobre, cosa albóndiga; falopa; rasca
descuidado(a) (vulgar) batata; pelotudo(a); quilombero(a); tirá; tirao
descuidado(a) en el vestir descachalandrado(a)
descuidado(a), ser pelar
desea obtener cosas gratuitamente, el que golillero
desembolso erogación
desempate, partido de playoff
desempeño performans
desempeño de un papel rol
desempolvar dostiar
desengaño chasco
desentenderse de un problema abrirse de piernas
desentona balurdo
deseos de comer o beber provocación
desfachatez cachaza
desgañitar acogotar
desgarrar desplomar
desglosar itemizar
desgracia guamazo; mamonazo; salado
desgracia, poner en hacer sonar
desgraciado(a) torcido(a)
desgreñado(a) cacurúo(a)
deshonesta, actividad quiquirigüiqui; rebusque
desilusionado, estar amachinarse
desinflar un neumático fletear
desistir correrse
desleal fayuto
desmantelado(a) desconchiflado(a)
desmigamiento desmoronamiento
desnalgado culipando; culiseco

desnudar encuerar
desnudarse (vulgar) empelotarse; encuerar
desnudo(a) (vulgar) avirote; calato(a); en cueros; en pelotas; pilucho; viringo
desnudo(a), estar andar en pelotas
desodorante antipespirante; deodoran
desorden barajuste; chamuchina; desbole; despelote; despiole; merequetén; pango; reguerete; relajo; revolú; revulú; tripulina; tendalada; voleo
desorden, quedó un quedó la escoba
desordenado(a) desconchiflado(a); empelotado(a); escrachao
desordenar regueretear
desorganización guachafita
desorientado azurumbrado
despabilar desparpajar
despachurrar apachurrar; despichar; machetiar
despecho pica; pique
despedida cariñosa adiosito
despedido(a), ser mochar
despedir de un trabajo botar; descolar; desocupar
despegue de un avión decolaje
despejado cliar
desperdicio retobo
despierto recuerdo
despilfarrar desperrindingarse; desparringarse
despistarse embolatar; envolatar
despreciable tusa; zaragate
después lueguito
desquiciado(a), está muy más loco(a) que una cabra; zafado
desquitarse sacarse el clavo
desquite retaliación
desteñido curtido
desternillarse de risa destornillarse de risa
destete despecho
destilería ilegal sacotín

destituye a otro de su empleo el que descamburador

destornillador desarmador

destruir blanquear

destruir la reputación de otro(s) empatucar

desván ático; detur; entretecho

desvanecimiento taranta

desventaja handicap

desvergonzado(a) cachafaz; cariduro(a); caripelao; conchudo(a); desharrapado(a); fregado(a); fregón; raspado(a); zafado(a)

desviarse embolatar; envolatar

detallar itemizar

detallista detalle

detective (vulgar) gofia; petejota; raya; tira

detener stop

detenerse apozarse; arrejarse

deteriorado, muy hecho torta

deteriorarse descachalandrarse; jubilarse

deuda acreencia; cacalota; calillas; dita; jarana

deuda que no se paga clavo

deudas, llenarse de enditarse; enjaranarse

devolver los golpes ripostar

devorar jartar

devoto fan

devuélvela dala para atrás

devuélvelo llévalo para atrás

devuélvemela dámela para atrás

día de paga raya

diablo, el chucuto; cozco; cuco; el uñudo; mandinga; pingo

diagrama de flujo flowshart

diapositiva slaid

diarrea (vulgar) abradera; cagadera; cagalera; cagarreta; cagueta; charretada; charreteada; churra; churretada; churria; chorro; corredera; currutaca; cursera; obradera; soltura

diarrea, con (vulgar) churrete

diarrea, tener (vulgar) estar churrete

dibujo al carbón carboncillo

dibujos animados curiositas; cómicas; comiquillas; monos; muñequitos

diccionario mataburros

dientes (incisivos) chocleros

diestro tinoso

diez centavos vellón de diez

difamación alacraneo

difamar alacranar

difícil duro; fregado; salado; teso

difícil, está está cabezón; está del carajo

difícil, persona arrecho; fregada; jodido; sobado; tostón

dificultad handicap; pacaya

digno alturado

dinero (vulgar) biyuya; biyuyo; chavos; chicharrones; chirola; chirona; guano; guita; jando; la mosca; lana; machacante; mangos; moni; morlacos; mosca; pachocha; pisto; sencillo

dinero en efectivo cash-flow

dinero, pedir machetear; pechazo

dinero recolectado en grupo formar; vaca

dinero, sin andar ficha; andar pato; andar quebrado; arrancado; arrancao; estar ahorcado; estar pato; helado; jorobado; lámparo; pato; pelado; seco

dinero, tener encaletado; rayado; tener guano; torteado

Dios el colochón; papachú

¡Dios santo! ¡coño!

dique tajamar

directo al cuete

director manayer; manejador(a)

director del espectáculo showman

dirigir empuntar; jefaturear

dirigir el juego por llevar la mano ganadora mandar

dirigirse a un sitio coger; jalar

discar el teléfono dailear; dalear; dialear

disco compacto cidi

discurso espiche; spich

discurso poco sustancioso rollo

discutir atracar

diseminadas, profusión de cosas tendal

disgustar entripar

disgusto cocora

disgusto, hacer a mamarse

disimulada(o) lángara

disimular quillarse

disiparse alcanforarse

dislocación recalcadura; troncha

dislocar desconchabar

disparatada, una enflautada

disparate caballada; coroto; despapucho; macana

dispositivo anticonceptivo churrusco

dispositivo controlador de disquetes drive

distancia entre dos lugares jalón

distancia entre dos objetos luz

distinguir espatear

distraído(a) englobado(a); envolatado(a)

diversión chacota

doblado chueco

dócil chupamedia

dogo buldog

dólares, un millón de palo verde

dolor agudo punzada

dolor de dientes, tener destemplar

dolor de estómago, tener embuchado; estar rebotado; insulto; jaleo

domesticar una bestia aguachar

don nadie, un pinche

dormir apolillar; guindar; hacer tuto

dormir la borrachera dormir la mona

dormitorio cuarto; habitación; pieza; recámara

droga ilegal falopa; pichicata

drogadicto colino; grifo; moto; pichicatero; tecato

drogado doping

drogado(a), estoy estoy embalado(a)

drogas, abastecimiento de cachucha

ducha chagüer; lluvia; pluma; regadera

dudosa, cosa macana

dulce candi

dulce, extremadamente relajante

dulce, un tipo de bienmesabe; cajeta; cazuela; gofio; huevochimbo; matagusano; quesillo; tapado

dulzura sabrosura

durmiente en la vía del tren polín

ebrio; borracho ajumado; almareado; birote; bolo; caneco; cañoneado; chumado; cocido; como cuba; como huasca; como huevo; como pickle; como piojo; como poto'e guagua; cuete; curado; curdeao; curdo; embolado; en fuego; engorilado; entre pisco y nazca; estar en fuego; guarape; guarapeado; guarapero; guaro; guayao; jalado; jumado; jumeta; jumo; mamado; pernicioso; petardo; picao; prendido; rajao; tacuache; tomado; trinco; trompeta; zumbado

ebrio, casi a medio filo; ajumao; copetón; encopetonarse; está chapetón

ebrio, estar (vulgar) andar con el gorila; andar pedo; andar pisto; estar bomba; estar con el gorila; estar con la caña; estar con la mona; está hasta el birote

echar fletar

echar bravatas guapear

edad madura, de jecho

edad madura, la vejentud

edificio bilding; finca

editorial mancheta

edredón quilto

269

efectos de un narcótico turra
eficaz machete
eficiente capo
egoísta azadón; esmayao; lambío; ojete; repuñoso(a)
ejecutar algo a medias chancar
ejemplar de algún impreso copia
ejemplo machote
ejerce el comercio sexual, el que salquipanqui
ejército, el ormy
el domingo pasado el último domingo
el escondite, juego infantil tuero
el especial . . . mero
el gran . . . mero
el mejor paquete
el poco que queda pucho
el super . . . mero
el único . . . mero
elección escogencia
electrochoque electroshock
elegante cachaco; chévere; chiche; chute; mamito; manga; perchudo; pintoso; titino
elegir chusear
elegir un candidato electar
elevada estatura, persona de bimba
elevarse de rango social encampanar
élite social, la jai; jetset
elogiarse mutuamente cumbearse
eludir el pago amallarse; lambizque
eludir un compromiso culebrear; pijotear
embarazo encargo
embaucar cabulear; embachichar
embestir barajustar
embolsar agacharparse; embolsicar
emborracharse, embriagarse abombar; agarrar la tetera; amarrarse; chumar; curar; empedar; guarapear; jalar; jumarse; ponerse pedo; rajarse; traguearse
embotado embarado

embreagar un vehículo enclochar
embriagado rascado
embriagarse con vino enguainar
embriaguez bomba
embriaguez colectiva rascazón
embrollo brollo; latifundio
embrujar enyerbar
embustero brollero; cachero; cuentamusa
emigrar ilegalmente a los Estados Unidos brincar el charco
empacar enterciar
empalmar embonar; empatar
empanadilla pastelillo; salteña
empapado entripado
empapar enchumbar; ensopar
emparedado bocadillo; bocadito; sanduche; torta
emparedado de chorizo choripán
empatar tangalear
emplasto vigo
empleada(o) doméstico(a) chajal
empleado(a) de comercio dependiente
empleado(a) de última categoría suche
empleado(a) público(a) (peyorativo) mamón(a)
empleado de la estancia estanciero
emplear para un trabajo específico conchavar
empleo brete; cuchara; jale
empleo conseguido por medio de influencias chanfaina; corbata
empresario(a) manayer; manejador(a)
empujar contra algo atracar
empuje berraquera; punch; verraquera
empuje, tener apechugar
en este instante ahorita
en este momento ahoritica
en exceso de vicio
en partes iguales miti miti
en un momento ahora; en un improviso

en venta for sale

enaguas fondo; hormadoras; naguas; peticote; refajo; saya interior; sayuela

enamoradas, dos personas pestillo

enamoradizo chivo; gallinazo; paquete

enamorado, completamente tragado

enamorado(a), estar empelotado(a); estar gas; templado(a)

enamorar afilar; atacar; curucutear

enamorarse amelcocharse; encularse; enfuscarse; templar

enano apachurrado; corrotoco

encaja huesos quebrados, el que sobador; sobandero

encajar huesos sobada; sobijo

encajarle a alguien un asunto canchar

encaje tejido a mano frivolité; ñandutí

encarcelar enguandocar; entambar

encariñar aguachar

encasquetar endilgar; endosar; enflautar

encendedor laira

encender ponchar; prender

encendido on

encerado hulado

encerar waxear

encerrar laquear

enchufe brazo; palanca

enclenque fifiriche; muchitanga; ñecla

encolerizarse encohetarse

enconado cizote

encontrón caballazo; quiñazo

encopetado pije

encuadernación en rústica peiperbac

encubrimiento forro

encuentro match

encurtido pickle

endeudado enjaranado

endrogarse darse un paseo

enérgico zafado

energizar retamblar

enfadado soplado

enfadar calentarse; condenar; encachorrarse; enchismar

enferma, persona malanco(a)

enfermedad dengue; maluquera; norsa

enfermedad producida por la altura sorochi

enfermedad venérea chinche

enfermizo acabado; calandraca; cignato; traqueado

enfermo, estar jorobado; tener dengue

enfermo mental (vulgar) tocado

enfiestado bonchón

enfriar culear

enfurecerse arrecharse; enchivarse; enfogonarse

engaña al astuto, el que carbonero

engañado, ser comer pavo

engañar cabulear; carbonear; chapuzar; dar capote; embachichar; embolatar; envolatar; epichulear; fulear; fumar; marranear; meter el choclo; tantear

engaño caula; embarque; forro; jarana

engrasar embijar

enlace link

enlucido de un muro empañetado

enmarañado, cabello chasca

enmarañado (persona) chascón(a)

enmohecerse azumagarse

ennegrecer entilar

enojado(a) amargo(a); andar bravo(a); arrechado(a); bravito(a); bravo(a); calentura; enchinchado(a); está de maleta; estar caliente; guapo(a); tener coraje

enojarse berrear; empacarse; empavar; enchicarse; enchismarse; entromparse; entunarse; prenderse

enojarse, fácil de malaley

enojo arrechera; arrecho; coraje

enorgullecerse atufarse

enredado(a) cahuinero(a); galletoso(a); maneado(a)

enredar embarbascar

enredo atao; brete; cahuin; candinga; emborujo; frangollo; julepe; mazamorra; pango; quilombo; reblujo; rebujo; revolica

enredos, provocar empatucar

enrizado enchinado

enrollar encartuchar; enchipar

ensalada, un tipo de guacamole; salpicón

ensimismado alepantado

ensortijado (cabello) colocho; rizado

ensortijado, persona de pelo chino(a)

ensuciar batir; empatucar; empichar

enteco sute

entender cachar; caer el veinte; mangar

entendimiento, de escaso alumbrado

enterarse acatar; acatarrar

¿entiendes? ¿cachay?

entorpecer chalequear

¡entre! ¡siga!

entrenador coch

entrepiso mesanín

entretenerse echarle al pelo

entrevista interviú

entristecerse amurrarse

entrometerse comedirse

entrometido(a) aprontao; arbolario; brejetero; brujo(a); cuico; entrador(a); huelefrito; metete; metiche; metido; nariz; refistolero(a); refitolero; zaragate; zaramullo

entumecido emparamado

entumecimiento monguera

entusiasmar entotorotar

entusiasmo berraquera; verraquera

entusiasta con el sexo opuesto picado(a) de la araña

envalentonarse agallarse; embraguetarse

envejecer emplumar

envejecido traqueado

envidioso engurrioso

envoltorio de dinero para estafar balurdo

envolver bolear; embojotar

envolver en deudas entortar

envolverse en una pelea trenzarse

equipo de empleados estaf

equivocación gajo; pelada

equivocarse pelarse

¿eres estúpido? ¿estás enfermo?

erosión de la piel paspadura

error embarrada

error, cometer un caballada; embarrar; gajo; meter las extremidades; meter la pata; pelada; pelarse; tirarse la plana

error, cometiendo un embarrándola

error gramatical mote

eructo chancho

esbozo esquech

escala de tijeras burro

escalofrío chucho

escándalo ajiaco; bullaranga; chambrana; laberinto; toletole

escaparate vitrina

escaparse abrirse; arrancar; destaparse; embalar; emplumárselas; enfletar; fletar

escarabajo ron-ron

escarbar chuchear

escarcha lancha

escatimar lecherear

escoba pichanga

escoba gastada soco; zoco

escolar escuelante; escuelero(a)

esconder encaletar; enguacar; enhuacar; fondear

esconder la verdad amapuchar

esconderse por razones políticas o judiciales enconchar

escondite abrigada; caleta
escribir en un teclado tipear
escritorio carpeta
escroto (vulgar) bolsa; huevas;
  huevos; mochilas; turmas
escrúpulos, sin podrido; turco
escuela secundaria escuela superior;
  high school
esforzarse puyar; remar
esfuerzo final en una carrera sprint
eslabón cheje
esnob come mierda
eso es mentira salta pa'l lado
espacio gap
espacio publicitario spot
espaldas anchas, de espaldón
español, apodo para un chapetón;
  coño; gachupín; gallego; ladino(a)
esparcir embarrar
especias recado; recaudo
espere aguántele
espermio (vulgar) canela
espeso mazacotudo
espía sapo
espiar orejear; pavear; vichar
espinilla canilla
espiritista espiritero
esponjoso pana; panita
esposa costilla; doña; guaife
esposas canana
esposo jebo
esqueje patilla; sarmiento
esqueleto carcancha
esquirol escab; krumiro
está al día up to date
está bien fain; okei; íorale!; ta; vaya
  pues
¡está buenísimo! ¡de a cachimba!;
  ¡deacá!
está en el ataúd está en la piyama de
  madera
está en la política por ganancias
  personales colmilludo
está enamorado está hecho un cabro

está viejo pasao
estación de gasolina gasolinera; grifo;
  bomba de bencina
estación fría del año, la escarcha
estacionar parkear
estadounidense gringo(a)
estadounidense de origen africano
  (peyorativo) llantón
estafa aletazo
estafador conejero; cuentero;
  cuentista; embrollón
estafar chapuzar; conejear; fumar;
  morder; pulpear
estampa religiosa registro
estampilla cuño; estampa; sello;
  timbre
estancamiento impase
estante cabinete; librera
estaquilla tapilla
estar a cargo bate
estar de novios pololear
estar en estado de jolgorio
  enfiestarse
estar en un lugar sin hacer nada
  brujulear; pajarear
estar fuera de sí andar lurias
estar sin deseos de continuar
  achantarse
estás mintiendo donde la viste
¿estás trastornado? ¿estás
  enfermo?
estéril, animal horro; jorro
estéril, persona capón
estimación al tuntún
estimulante ají
estimular incentivar
estirar la pata estirar la jeta; estiró
  los caites; peló el ajo
estofado cocido; guiso; patasca;
  pipían; salcocho; sancocho
estómago de la vaca, guiso con el
  guata; menudo; mondongo
estopa guaipe
estoy de acuerdo fain

¡**estoy maldito! (vulgar)** ¡me lleva la chingada!

estrafalario circunstanfláutico

estrella star

estrellitas yacks; yaquis

estreñido estítico; tapado; trancado

estreñimiento, tener entablazón; estar prendido; trancarse

estribillo cantaleta

estricto fregado

estructura débil encatrado

estrujón exprimión

estudia mucho, el que estofón; mateo

estudiante universitario colegiante

estudiante universitario del primer año fresco; mechón

estudiar con ahinco estofarse; matearse

estudio mal preparado crudo

estúpidamente, comportarse patanear; ser calzón; ser pavo

estupidez (vulgar) güevonada; huevá; huevonada; pendejada

estúpido(a) (vulgar) arao; baboso(a); calabaza; enfermo(a); güevón(a); huevón(a); ñangue; pelota; redondo(a); sángano

estúpido(a), ser tratado como un(a) embarcar

evadir definiciones guabinear

evaporarse alcanforarse

evita comprometerse, el que liso

evitar sacatear

evitar el trabajo ahorrar

exagerado alaraco; arbolario; farolero; irse al chancho; pasarse la nota

excede las capacidades, el que cuellón

excelente legal; pepeado; piocha; soda

excepcional, persona jamón; terciazo

excitación sexual arrechera; arrecho; calentura

excitado(a) sexualmente, estar arrechado(a); estar caliente

excremento cacana, meca

excremento animal bosta; guano

excremento en los pañales maleta

excremento sólido mojón; sorete

excusado pompón; taza del baño

exención de aduana liberación de aduanas

exhalar cuando se fuma chicotear

exhibición show

exigente y poco complaciente trabajoso(a)

existencias stock

éxito, tener embocar

expendio de embutidos salsamentaria

experiencia, con canchero; curtido

experto cuatriborleado; sabido; taco

exposición show

expreso expres

expulsado de la escuela dropeado

extranjero (vulgar) yoni

extranjero rubio gringo; mister

extraordinariamente bueno bien padre; polenta

extravagante discante

extraviarse destorrentarse

fábrica factoría

fabricado en meidin

fabuloso como coco; padre; padrísimo

facha, de mala picante

fácil abanico; asopao; bilí; bizcocho; botana; chancaca; chiche; es papaya; golilla; guame; jauja; mogollo; papa; paseo

facilidad de palabra labia

facsímil o facsímile fax

falda enaguas; follón; funda; nagual; naguas; pollera; saya

fallar chingar; irse al tacho; ponchar; se fue al pihuelo

fallar un examen colgarse en la escuela; colgarse en un examen; jalar el examen; ponchar
fallido(a) chinzado(a)
falsa(o) chimbo; fulera(o); julera(o)
falsedad feca; macana
falsificar chimbear
falta en un juego de pelota faul
faltar mistear
faltar a una cita chantar
fanático de la salsa salsómano
fanático del rock roquero
fanfarrón aguajero; bocatero(a); cañero; carrilero; chanta; chantún; clueco; fafarachero; fafaracho; falfullero; farfullero; guapo(a); pantallero; plantilla
fanfarronada bluf; caña
fanfarronear balaquear; blufear; entablar; pantallear
fantástico bárbaro; maldito(a); suave; vacano
farmacia dragstor
farol foco
farsa papelada
farsante cachiporra; fayuto; papelero
fastidiar albardear; amolar; echar jareta; engorrar; jericoplear; manganear; remoler
fastidio sobadera
fastidioso ácido; ají; carlanca; chicle
favor colocho
favor, hacer un gauchada
favores políticos, dar o recibir clientelismo
favores, siempre anda pidiendo arrimado(a)
fea, persona bagre; feto; moscarrofio
fealdad feúra; maluquera
fechoría, envolver en una encochinar; entortar
femenino feminil
feo bufeo
feo, es es óxido

feo, muy botago
féretro cajón
feria turno
fermentar enchichar
ferretería mercería
ferroviario ferrocarrilero
feses ñoña
festival folclórico jarana
fiambrería rosticería
fibroso hebrudo
fideicomisario trustí
fiebre, con mucha calenturiento
fiesta arroz; atolada; bayú; borlo; calducho; chancleo; charranga; chingana; chorcha; jarana; lonche; malón; movida; pachanga; pary; pereque
fiestas, andar de bonchar; cumbanchear
fila cola
filloa panqueque
filmina slaid
filtrar liquear
filtro de aire de un motor calabaza
filudo agarroso
fin de semana wiken
fina y delicada, persona aliñada
finca pequeña hijuela
fino chiche
firma de identificación personal pategallina
firmar sainear
fisgonear pispar; pispiar
flaco(a) acartonado(a); alambrito; angarillo; angarrio; arenque; charcón; cuico; flamenco; fliche; huesudo(a); langaruto; lumbiz; palillo; palitroque; silgado; tasajudo
flacucho flacuchento
flatulencia (vulgar) bomba; peo; ventoso
flauta hecha con bambúes quena
flema (vulgar) pollo
flequillo capul; chasquilla; pollina

flojera fiaca; locha; monguera
floreado florecido
florecer florear
flotar flout
fofo biche
fontanero gásfiter
forastero afuerino; arribeño
formal, persona (peyorativo) almidonado
formulario esqueleto; forma
fornido morrocotudo
fortuna, amasar una taparse
fortuna, una cachipil
fracasado, ser un no estar en nada
fracasar corchar; feilear; sonar
fracasé en el examen me colgué en el examen
frambuesa mora
franco franque
francote claridoso
fraude aletazo; descrestada; forro; manguala
fraudulento chimbo
frazada chamarra; cobija; colcha; cuilca; friza; manta; serape
fregadero fregador; lavabo; lavadero; lavaplatos; pileta; sinc
fregar el suelo mapear; mopear; suapear
fregasuelos bayeta; coleto; mapo; trapeador; trapero
freír friar
frenar un vehículo manear
freno(s) breca; breik; breique; breque; retranca
fresa estraberry; frutilla
fresco fregado; liso
fricción fletación
frío intenso helaje; pacheco; tornillo
frío, tener empalarse
fritos en general cuchifrito; cuchufrito
fritura, un tipo de alcapurria; bacalaito; tacón
frívola, persona pinganilla

frotamiento fletación
fruta ácida amarroso
fruta seca pasado
fruta, un tipo de catuche; chirimoya; guayaba; lúcuma; mamonsillo
fruto a medio madurar camuliano; celeque; sarazo; tetelque; zarazo
fruto maduro jecho
fruto podrido jojoto; malanco(a)
fruto sin sabor aguanoso
frutos víveres
fuego de artificio, un tipo de cuete; guatapique; tote; volatero; yacks; yaquis
fuera aut; autsai; of
fuera de sitio visorioco
fuera del juego ofside
fuera, me estás dando lata fochi
fuerte firme como un peral; macha; machín; machina; morocho; morrocotudo; polenta
fuerza garnacha; garra; polenta
fulano gallo; perico; perencejo
fumar chupar; pitar
función show
función vespertina intermediaria; vermuth
funcionar funcar
furioso(a), estoy estoy puto(a)
furtivamente, comportarse hacerse el cucho
furúnculo nacido
gabinete cabinete
gafas espejuelos de sol; lentes ahumados; lentes oscuros
gajo casco
galán cabrón
galanteador afilador; chivo; gallinazo; lacho; mariposón; tenche
gallera palenque
galleta choca; cuki; galletica; galletita
gallina gumarra
gallo amarillo giro
gamberro pavito

ganancia ilícita tragada
ganar blanquear; pampear; ponchar
ganar experiencia jubilarse
ganarse la vida busconear; changar
gancho sex appeal
ganga jamón; pichincha
gangoso fañoso
ganó la lotería le pegó el gordo
gargajo (vulgar) pollo
garganta gaznate
gargarizar corcorear; gargarear
garrafa pomo
garrotazo leñazo
garrote macana
gaseoducto pipeline
gaseosa bebida; refresco; soda
gasolina bencina; gas; gasolin; nafta
gasolinera bomba de bencina;
　estación de servicio; expendio de
　gasolina; grifo
gato bibicho; cucho; mico
gato del automóvil gata; yaque
gaznate guargüero
gemelo de la camisa collera;
　mancorna
gemelos(as) chachos(as); cuache;
　cuapes; mellos; morochos
generoso(a) abiertazo(a);
　espléndido(a); manirroto(a);
　manoabierta; rasgado(a)
genital (vulgar) bicha(o); coroto; cosa
gente importante gente copetuda
gentes aglomeradas apilonados
gerente manayer; manejador(a)
gestionar con mucha política
　muñequear
gesto con la mano para un conjuro o
　maleficio bicho
gesto de total desinterés (vulgar)
　hacer tapa
gesto insultante pistola
gesto irónico miñoco
gigolo crestón
girar un vehículo voltear

gitano húngaro
globo balún; bomba; chiras; vejiga
glotón(a) bosgo(a); comején; lambío
gol en el fútbol pepino
golfillo camín; palomilla; pelusa; títere
golosina mecato
golosina, un tipo de alfeñique; beso;
　panucha
golpe al ojo bergantín; fundoso;
　piñazo
golpe con los dedos chirla; chirlito
golpe de pie en el fútbol chute
golpe de puño camotazo; castañazo;
　chingazo; chingadazo; guascazo;
　moquetazo; punch; tabaco
golpe de suerte batatazo
golpe en el juego del trompo canco
golpe imprevisto y repentino
　guaracazo
golpe oblicuo chanfle; suing
golpe violento batacazo; batatazo;
　bichazo; cachuchazo; cantaso;
　cantazo; cascarazo; chafirrazo;
　chingazo; coñazo; guamazo;
　lamparazo; mamonazo; matracaso;
　palotazo; punch; tanganazo; toletazo;
　totazo; turcaso
golpeado, ser coger pela
golpear chantar; dar candela; fajar;
　garrotear; machetiar; quiñar;
　tamboreatear; trincar
golpiza chanca; garrotiza; paleada;
　pela; tanda; tunda; turqueada; zurra
golpiza como broma camotera
golpiza, dar una dar una tanda; fletar;
　sacarle la ñoña
goma de borrar borrador; desborrador
goma de pegar glu; pegadura;
　platicola
gomero hule
gordo(a), persona albóndiga;
　amasadito(a); bachicha; bombo(a);
　batata; botija; fodongo; pamplón(a);
　tripón(a)

277

gorduras del cuerpo chichos; mangoso
gorra biscera; cachucha; montera
gorro militar prepucio
gotear liquear
gotera chorrera
grabar electrónicamente teipear
gracejo garabato
gracioso charro; fullero
graduarse egresar
gran cantidad cachá; poconón; pocotón; una barbaridad
gran jefe indio toqui
gran número de personas parranda
gran personalidad vacano
grande, persona bárbaro; bimba; botija; caballón(a); chirote; cuajado(a); maceteado; morrudo; ropero
grandullón macuco; malgansón; mamón; pailón
granero colca
granjero farmero
grapa grampa
grapadora grampadora
grapar engrampar
grasiento y de mal olor cochambriento
gratificación que el vendedor da al comprador ancheta; de forro; de yapa; ganancia; llapa; ñapa; pesuña; yapa
gratis de golilla
grave seco
gresca follisca
grifo canilla; caño; chorro; focet; llave; pila; pluma
grillo caballete; caballito del diablo; siripita
gripe flu; gripa; monga
gris, color plomo
gritar acogotar; berrear
grocería guachada

grosero caballo
grúa pequeña donkey; señorita
grueso butuco
grupo pool
grupo de mala conducta chillería
grupo que realiza una actividad fajina
grupo sin ningún orden choclón
guante de béisbol mascota
guapetón cajetón; garrotero
guapo machote
guarapo aguamiel
guardaespaldas espaldero
guardafangos botafango; botalodo; faldón; fenda; fender; tapabarros; tapalodo
guardametas arquero; golkiper
guardapolvo broga
guardarse el dinero que se va ganando apuñalearse
guardián ronda
guarida abrigadero; cucho; guarimba
guatemaltecos, apodo para los chipines
guerra química gas warfare
guía baqueano, baquiano; buscones; chaneque
guión escrip
guisado guiso
guisado, un tipo de ajiaco; calalú; carapulca; chupe; patasca; pepián; pipián; pirco; revuelto(a); tomaticán
guisante alverja; alverjón; arveja; arverja; chícharo; pees; petipóas; petipúa; pitipuas
guitarra charranga; jarana
gusto, de mal penca; picante
ha conseguido un empleo desvarado
haber fracasado estar sonado
habichuelas caraotas; cocoles; frejoles; frijoles; frísoles; frisoles; porotos
habichuelas blancas coscorrones
habichuelas negras negritas

habichuelas tostadas cancha; canchitas; canguil
habichuelas verdes chauchas; ejotes
hábil caperuzo
hábil en la política, ser tener muñeca
habilidoso habiloso
habilitar implementar
habitación ambiente
habla muy de prisa carretilla
hablador(a) bembón; bocatero(a); boquique; caña hueca; carreto; chachalaquero; cotorra; ladino(a); palangana; pispireta
hablar acampesinado cacaquear
hablar con vehemencia regarse
hablar de los infortunios plaguear
hablar en voz baja runrún
hablar mal de alguien acabar; zumbar
hablar mucho chamullar; latear
hablar sin decir nada babosear; cantinflear; cantinfleo; comer bola; macanear; pajudear; tilinguear
hace de todo, el que todero
hace las cosas a su gusto, el que esplayao; realengo
hace muy poco reciencito
hacer algo imperfectamente dar mateo; echar mateo; machetear
hacer algo rápido esmandarse
hacer esfuerzos pechar; ponerle empeño; ponerle pino
hacer novillos capear; hacer la cimarra; hacer la chancha; hacer pinta; jirola; jubilarse; paviarse; ratearse de la escuela; volarse de la escuela
hacer pedazos hacer garra; hacer tira
hacer pucheros hacer cuchara
hacerlo confuso dar birote
hacerse cliente amarchantarse
hacienda estancia; finca; hato; rancho
haciendo un puño empuñar
¡hágalo! ¡éntrale!

halago servil jalada
halar jalar
halcón gavilán; guaraguao
hamaca, un tipo de campechana; chinchorro
hambre angurria; fatiga; fiaca; gurbia; ragú
hambriento(a) galgo; garifo; gorozo; hambrío(a)
haragán (vulgar) aguada(o); almágana; arreado(a); baracutey; bernia; croto; empelotado; fodongo; machetón; mamalón; maqueta; pernicioso; quisio
haraganear maquetear
harapos chanchira(o); chiringo; piltrafas; piltrajas
harina de maíz, un tipo de chuchoca; funche; polenta
harina tostada de maíz gofio
harto(a) cabriado; pimpo; pachigua; popocho(a)
harto de una comida, estar hostigar
¿has perdido el juicio? ¿estás enfermo?
hasta el final a concho
hasta la coronilla hasta la tusa
hasta luego chau
¡hay alguien aquí! ¡upe!
hay un problema se formó el tilingo
hay una gran cantidad hay a patadas
¡hazlo! ¡imétele!
heces gazpacho
hechizado alumbrado; chorizo
hecho artesanalmente hechizo
heladera cúler
helado aiscrim; gelati; leche nevada; mantecado; nieve; paico
helado de barquillo aiscon; cono; cucurucho
hélice propela
hemorragia cerebral estroc
hereje pirujo
herencia mortual

herida cáncer; cizote; hincada; tajeadura
herida de bala guamazo
herida mortal, provocar una desgraciarse
herir charrasquear; fastidiar; joder; straique
hermano broder; ñaño
hermoso pepeado
herradura casquillo
herramienta para hoyos coa; macana
hez del guarapo cachaza
hielo raspado copo de nieve; piragua
hierbas medicinales anamú; pamita
hierbas medicinales, tienda de botánica
hígado de animal pana
hija menor maraca
hijo(a) chino(a)
hijo de mala madre ahijuma
¡hijo de p...! (vulgar) ¡joepuchita!; ¡puchita!; ¡a la gran puchica!
hijo del tataranieto chorlo
hijo menor pucho
hilachas chirajos; chiras; chiros
hilos para controlar un cometa frenillo; gaceta
hincharse bufar
hinchazón chorcha; gualuche
hinchazones, con boludo
hipar jipar
hipocresía, proceder con camandulear
hipócrita chepe; fayuto; tapado
histeria matropa
historietas chistes; comiquitas; cuentos; fonis; monitos; muñequitos; paquines; tiras cómicas
hocico (peyorativo) bemba
hocicudo matatudo
hojalata, envase de perol; perola
hojalatería latería
hojas de cálculo spreadsheet

holgazán aplatanao; batata; echado; maganzón; manganzón; pata de rolo; paterrolo
holgazaneando hangueando
holgazanear bartolear; chotear; hangear; magancear; mangancear; manguarear; manguerear
holgazanería bausa; maganza; manganza; maquetería; paterrolismo
hombre chavón; jevo; man
hombre blanco huinca
hombre de mucha fuerza física fuerte; macanudo; machete; ropero; tenche; ternejo
hombre de negocios bisnesman
hombre pequeño chichimeco
hombre que coquetea gallinacea
hombre que se refugia detrás de las mujeres calzonudo; pollerudo
homosexual (vulgar) aviador; chupón; culero; gay; hueco; loca; mamalón(a); manflor; maraco; marico; pájaro; pato; rosca; rosquete
homosexual, demostrar que se es cucarronear
honda biombo; guaraca; haraca; ratonera; tirador
hondureños, apodo para los catrachos
honesto alférez; franque; redondo; seguro; zanahoria
hongos callampas; champiñones; machrum; paragüita de sapo; setas
horadado forado
horario completo fultaim
horno cocedor
horqueta garabato
horquilla ganchito; gancho; incaible; pasador; pin; pinche; presilla
hostigamiento fregadera
hostigar abacorar
hostil sangriento
hoyo cucho; hueco; pozo
hoyos de viruela tusa

huérfano(a) (peyorativo) huacho(a); guacho(a)

hueso de la fruta pepa

huesos de las piernas tabas

huéspedes, encargado(a) de una casa de bordera(o)

huevo blanquillo

huevo podrido güero

huevos revueltos huevos pericos

huidizo huilón

huir abrirse

humillar achicar; negrear

humor, de mal engreñao

huraño apartado; lobo

hurgar hurgüetear; jurungar

hurtar guachapear; guachapiar; hueviar; jabear; refalar; solfear

husmear mosquear

idéntico(a) entero(a); enterito(a); pintado(a)

idiota aguacate; ñangue; surumbo

ignorante baboso(a); buey; burro(a); jicate; machetero(a); menso(a); menzo(a); tapado(a)

ignorar hacer tapa

igual enterito; entero; guareto; pintado

igualar machear

iguana garrobo; jama

ilusiones, hacerse vanas soñar con pajaritos de oro

imbécil corneta

imitación barata trucho

imitar changuear

impaciente, está le pica

impedido tupido

imperdible alfiler; alfiler de criandera; alfiler de gancho; asegurador; broche; gancho; gancho de nodriza; segurito; seguro

impermeable abrigo de lluvia; capa de agua; capote; gabardina; piloto

impertinencia, cometer una descache

impertinente chocante; sobrado(a)

imponer el poder roncar

imponer reglas estrictas atracar; atrincar

imponer sobre los demás entablar

importante, persona cangrimán; cocoroco; papapúa

importunar jeringar

imprecisión desbole; despelote; despiole

impresora printer

impresora de agujas pín printer

imprudencia, cometer una meter las extremidades; tirarse la plana

impudicia empaque

impuesto gabela; tax; taxa

impuesto municipal, un tipo de detalle

impuestos sobre la renta income tax; incomtax

incapaz cabestro

incita a la pelea, el que carbonero

incitar aleonar; carbonear; enchinchar; incentivar; jochear; puyar

incoherente revirado

incompleto, dejar algo dar mateo; echar mateo

incorrectamente, actuar derraparse

incredibilidad ¡apucha!

incredulidad, interjección de ¡adiós!

incumbencia atingencia

indecente bascoso

independentista en Puerto Rico pipiolo

indeseable zaragate

indiferencia paterrolismo; terquedad

indiferente pata de rolo; paterrolo

indigencia carraplana

indignación calentera

indio, comportarse como (peyorativo) aindiado

indio de Chile mapuche

indio ecuatoriano joven longo

indirecta, se dice de una manera sangaraña

indiscreto resfriado
indisposición de vientre, con
embuchado
indocumentado alambrista; aliento
ineficacia guachafita
ineficiente cacatúa
inescrupuloso vivaceta; vivaracho
infernáculo golosa; peregrina; pata
sola
inflamado cizote; sisote
influencia, camarilla de rosca; rosco
influencia política, persona de cuña;
palanca
influencias, usar palanquear
influyente, persona fuerte
informado leído
informar a la policía tirar el dedo
infusión medicinal guarapillo;
guarapo
ingenioso ideoso; ideático
ingenuo (vulgar) asopao; caído del
catre; gil; hueva; jil; marrano;
papayudo; pavuncio(a); pelotudo;
salame; zanahorio
inhalación de marihuana toque
iniciar con entusiasmo fajarse
ininterrumpídamente al hilo
injuriar rezondrar
inmaduro biche; ñoño
inmediatamente después despuesito
inmoral (persona) gusano
innecesario inoficioso
inodoro excusado; taza del baño;
tóilet; water; waterclo
inquietar latir
inquieto chiririco; tilingo
inquieto, estar sanjuanear
inservible chueco
insignia charola
insignificante chingadera; pichiruche
insincero paquete
insistente, muy cargoso
insistir machetear
insolación, sufrir una atarrillarse

inspeccionar inspectar
inspector controler; el chancho
instruido leído
instruir instructar
instruirse jubilarse
instrumento musical discordante
chicharra
instrumento musical, un tipo de
bandola; charango; furruco; guiro(a);
juque; maraca; tango; taramba;
trutruca
insultar amontonar; faltar; intratar;
rajar; rezondrar
insulto (vulgar) bollo; quemón; reto;
sángano; sorete
insulto indirecto pipo
insulto que menciona a la madre
madrazo
inteligencia bombillo; chipote; coco
inteligencia, de poca gafo; mate
inteligente banana; bocho(a); pierna;
porra
interesado calculador
interesante choro
interiores del cerdo fritos cuchifrito;
cuchufrito
interiorizar internalizar
interrumpir chalequear
interrupción de una actividad risés
interruptor eléctrico apagador;
chucho; llave de luz; suich; suiche
intersección bocacalle; cruce; crucero
intervalo gap
intervenir en conversación ajena
meter la cuchara
interventor controler
intimidar padrotear
intriga laberinto
intrigar camandulear
intruso(a) metiche
intuición tincada
inundarse aguachinarse
inútil alaco; cacho; changle;
macuache; maraca; zoquete

invendible, mercancía cacho; hueso
inyectar una droga abujazo
ir de tiendas chopear
ira, con mucha envenenao
irascible sulfúrico
irresponsable buena pieza;
  desobligado(a); tilango(a); tilingo(a);
  tocado(a)
irritable arrecho; chinchudo; volado
irritación en los dedos de los pies
  mazamorra
irritarse arrufar
irrumpir en una fiesta descolgar
irse echarse el pollo; embocar;
  empuntar; mandarse mudar; pelar;
  picar
irse del lugar sin pagar conejear;
  fanfultear; fullería; hacer perro
  muerto
italiano, apodo para un bachicha;
  tano
jabón usado, lo que queda del calilla
jalea yely
jamba banderola
jarabe acaramelado sirop
jarana rumbo; sandunga
jardín infantil cero; escuelita;
  guardería; jardín de infancia; jardín de
  niños; kindergarten; la creche
jarrón de arcilla cacharro de greda
jerez sherry
jerga del hampa caló; coa; lunfardo
jersey pulover
jilipollas gil; pelotudo
jornalero bracero; lunguero
joroba maleta; totuma
jorobado cucho; curco; curcuncho;
  gocho
joven carajito(a); lolo(a)
**joven presumido que no le gusta
  trabajar** patiquín
joven que sigue a los otros coliche
jovial chaneque
joyas prenda

juego match
juego de canicas, un tipo de
  chocolón; uñita
juego de dados cacho; canilla
juego del boliche enchute
juego del corro ronda
juego erótico jamón
juego infantil, un el luche; gallito;
  listones; luche; macalililia; tugar-tugar
juego informal de fútbol pichanga
juego limpio fairplay
juego sin dinero jugar vicio
juerga bachata; remolienda
juerguero rumbero; vagamundo
jugador de caballos burrero
jugo de caña guarapo
jugo de la carne greive
juguete infantil china; ringlete
junta mecánica empaque
juntar gente para actos políticos
  acarrear
juntarse mitiar
justo justiniano
la muerte la fulera; la pelada
la pata coja avión; bebe-leche; el
  luche; el tejo; golosa; llorosa; luche;
  pata sola; pelegrina; peregrina
la rayuela el tejo
la tele tiví
labio deformado, persona con
  boquinche; boquineto(a); cheuto;
  janano(a); janiche; morocho
labios (vulgar) bemba; bembé; jeta
labios grandes, persona con los
  jetón(a); bembudo(a)
labios gruesos, boca de bimba;
  chambe
laboratorio de cocaína cocina
ladrón(a) choro; chorro; galafardo(a);
  gato(a); lanza; manilarga; manilargo;
  monrero(a); pato; punga; ratero(a);
  robón(a)
ladrón de poca monta galafardo
lagartija pichete

laguna cocha
laguna pequeña tajamar
lameculos (vulgar) cepillo; chupa;
chupahueso; chupamedias;
lambeache; lambeculo; lambehuevos;
lambeojo; lambiache; lambiscón(a)
lamentar repelar
lamento sonoro leco
lamer liquear; lambucear
lámpara globo
lámpara de parafina chonchón
lancha de velocidad voladora
lanchón bacha
lanudo pachón
lanzar largar
lanzar al aire flipear
lapicera pluma
lápiz labial lipestic
largarse rápido emplumárselas;
enfletar
larva comestible de insecto
mojojó
larva de la mariposa churrusco
lastimar afectar
lata bote; conserva; pote; tarro
latigazo chuchazo; cuerazo
látigo acial; atajona; chilillo; chucho;
coyunda; cuero; foete; fuete; fute;
guasca; penca; rejo; verga
**latinos que siguen costumbres
anglosajonas** agringados
lavabo excusado; inodoro; lavamanos;
lavatorio; lavatory
lavadero loundri
lavamanos lavatorio; lavatory
lavativa visitadora
lazos de zapatos agujetas; cabete;
cintas; correa; pasaderas; talego;
trenza
le falta un diente, al que cholco
le fue mal, al que le fue de la patada
le gusta andar de fiestas, al que
gozón
le gusta pelear, al que faitoso(a)

le gustan los anglosajones, al que
gabachero(a)
le mataron, al que le dieron el paseo
**lealtad y ahínco, el que trabaja para
otro con** goma
leche choca; milque
leche agria angola
lechuguino futre; pituco
lechuza búho; mochuelo; múcaro;
tecolote
legítimo rajado
lejos, en un lugar donde el diablo
perdió el poncho
lengüetazo lambetazo
lengüetear lamber
lentes gafas
lento, muy lenteja
lerdo albóndiga; bolsa; corroncho;
durazno; marmolín; pajarón;
quedado(a); tronca
lesbiana (vulgar) arepera; cachapera;
pata; tortillera
letrero aviso
letrina pompón
libélula matapiojo; pipilacha
libertino pavito
librado de compromiso ensabanado
libre cliar
libro voluminoso mamotreto
licor barato guarapo; guaro
licor de alto grado alcohólico fuerte
licor de caña de azúcar caña;
guarapo
licor de yuca güero; huero
licorería estanco; estanquillo
licores, tienda de botillería; taquilla
liendre liendra
limpiabotas lustrabotas; lustrador
limpiado al seco draicliner
limpiado al seco, tienda de cliner
limpiaparabrisas guaiper
limpiapiés felpudo
limpiar blanquear
limpio clin; fresquesito

línea de omnibuses boslain
linterna eléctrica flash
lío malhora; ¡qué brete!
liquidación baratillo; especial; oferta; realización; rebaja; sail; sale; venta
liquidación, en en especial
líquido que forma un charco aposar
lisiado tunco
lista de los candidatos tíquet
lista para envíos mailing list
listo avispa; bala; bicho; canchero; culebrero; jaiba; lobo; malva; pierna; piola
llaga chaquira; chira
llamada a los pollos ¡cutí!; ¡cutú!
llamar a través del beeper bipear
llanta en la rueda de un vehículo rin
llanura sin árboles pampa
lleno full; pachiqua
lleno(a) de comida empancinao; estar satisfecho(a); pipocho(a); piponcho(a); popocho(a); taqueado(a)
lleno de trucos enjaranado
llorar berrear
llorón bicho chillón
llovizna chinchín; cilampa; garúa; garuga; serenar
lloviznar harinear; serenar
lluvia con sol chirapa
lluvia fuera de estación norte
lo entendió se le encendió el bombillo
lo malo dentro de un conjunto mona
lo mejor la última chupá
lo mismo para ti escoba
lo que está o es seguro ir a fiesta; posta
lo que hace el mujeriego lachar
lo que se come después de un licor pasador; pasante
lo que se ve bien potro(a); yeguo(a)
local doméstico

localidad más barata del teatro gallinero
loco guano; tostao; turuleta
locura piantadura
locutor spiker
lodo de un alud mazamorra
logra familiaridad rápidamente, el que entrador(a); pechuga; puntudo(a)
lograr lo máximo ponerle la tapa al pomo
loly chupetín; pirulí
lombrices del intestino piduye
loro chocoyo; cotorra; perico
los militares ormy
los que arremeten contra algo cayapa
los que roban a los traficantes de drogas torcidos
lotería, boleto de cacho
luces traseras calavera
lucha brega; match
luchar bregar
lucifer el uñudo
lucirse bacilón
lugar donde se lava guachatería
lugar especial para comer o comprar picada
lugar o región valle
lugar para meriendas ligeras lonchería
lugar seguro, poner en un macizar
lugar solitario o vacío íngrimo
lugar sucio y desordenado chinchería; chinchero; cucarachero
lujurioso (vulgar) chimbero
lustrabotas boleador; bolero
lustrar bolear; embolar; lujar
luz de freno estop
maceta macetero
machete chinga; cutacha; paila
madre la vieja; taita; viejita
madre tierra pachamama
madriguera abrigadero; cucho

maestra de párvulos jardinera prescolar; kindergarterina
maestro(a) ticher
magnífico bacán; piocha
maíz abatí; avatí; choclo; elote; olote
maíz cocido, grano del mote
maíz cocinado en chile esquite
maíz machacado chancao
maíz para aves de corral malamé; pozole
maíz purpúreo pujagua
maíz tierno chilote
majadero chavón
mal colocado viroteao
mal corte de pelo tusada
mal de ojo mabita
mal educado jicate
mal estado, está en malanco(a)
mal hablado boquisucio
mal hecho, está birriñaque
mal humor argel
mal olor baranda
mal olor de la boca tufo
mal olor de pies cicoto; sicoto
mala figura, de chichimeco
mala jugada carajada
mala memoria memoria de gallina
mala suerte mala leche; mufa; salado; salazón
mala suerte, el que tiene quemado
mala suerte, persona que trae mabita
mala suerte, ser de estar salado
mala suerte, tener ser la sal
malas condiciones, en escrachao; jodido
maldito(a) maldingo(a)
malecón molo
maleficio daño
maleta valija
maletero del automóvil baúl; cajuela; castaña; tronk
malévolo malevo
malhechor malevo

malhumorado argelado
malicia visage
maliciosa, acción chingadera
maligno jodido
malo como la mona; feo; gacho; malinche; pichirre; turro
maloliente, quedar emberrenchinarse
malvado malinche; maluco
malversación peculado
mamá, en sentido cariñoso cucha
mamporro tiestazo; totazo
manantial vertiente
manantial de petróleo mene
manchado curtido
manchar con pintura embijar
manco soco; zoco
mandadero cadete
mandar a la prisión emplumar
mandíbula carretilla
mandioca yuca
mango mangó
mango de un bolígrafo canuto
manguito de unión niple
maní cacahuate; madubí; pínut
manía follón; grillo
manifestación rally
manioca yuca
manosear dar carpeta
manosear sexualmente (vulgar) chapar
manta poncho; serape
mantequilla manteca
mantillo capote
mantis religiosa palote
manubrio manejera
manzanilla albarillo
mañoso(a) jaiba
maquillador(a) beutichian
máquina de discos vellonera
máquina lavadora de platos fregadera
máquina para guafles guaflera
marca de revisión chulo
marca deportiva record

marca en la piel chorcha
marca registrada trademark
marcado(a) con una cicatriz jachado(a)
marcador plumígrafo
marcar tarjeta en el trabajo ponchar
marcha futin
marcha atrás reversa
marcharse embocar; empuntar; mandarse mudar; picar; rispar
marchitarse achucutar
mareado cucufato; tomado; turulato
margen de ganancias brutas gross margin
marginar negrear
mariconear mariquear
marido engañado cabrón; cachero; cachón; le pegaron el tarro
marihuana maría; mariela; marimba; mota; varilla; yerba
marihuana de baja calidad pasto; ripio; zácate
marihuana de máxima calidad punto rojo
marihuanero fumón
marimacho amachada; machera; machona; marota
marimacho, comportarse como una machonear
mariposa paloma
marisco concha
marrón braun
más tarde luegito
masa de harina de maíz bola
masaje fletación
masturbación (vulgar) casqueta; cocolía; manuela; paja; puñeta
masturbarse (vulgar) chaquetear; hacerse la paja; jalársela; pajearse
matar achicar; fregar; mamar; pelar; quebrar; quiñar; soplar; victimar
matar el tiempo jangiar
matón(a) bule

matrícula de un vehículo licencia; patente; placa; pleit; tablilla
mazo de hierro almádana
mazorca abatí; avatí; choclo; chocolo; choglo; coronta; elote; jojoto; olote
me encontré, junté, reuní mitié
me juntaré contigo te miteo
mecedora buinsuan; suinsuan
mechón de pelo gajo
medallones de plátano frito chifles; mariquitas; patacón; platanutre
medianamente malo(a) maloso(a)
medicina para provocar sudor sudor
medicinas, llenarse de emboticarse
medio ebrio ajumao; cucufato
medio hermano cachirulo
medio tiempo en el juego jalf
mediocre majunche
mejillas abultadas, con las chalchudo
mejillón choro
mejillón grande cholga
mejillón pequeño chorito
mejorar impruviar; remodelar
melancolía flato
melancólico amacolao
melaza sólida panetela; raspadura
melindre disfuerzo
melindroso cismático; resabiado
mellizos cuache; chachos(as); gemelos(as); jimaguas; morochos(as); tuines
melocotón durazno; pich
melocotón blanco blanquillo
melocotón deshidratado huesillo
memoria, de botella
memoria de la computadora memory
mendigar bombear
mendigo limosnero
mensajero chasqui
menstruación asunto; doña Rosa; luna
menstruando estar caer mala
menta pepermin

mentir (vulgar) cañar; guayabear; mojonear

mentira aguaje; argüende; barreta; calumnia; carretilla; carril; chile; chiva; coba; cuentazo; feca; globo; grupo; guaragua; guayaba; lana; levante; mula; paquete; pura paja

mentiras, el que dice macumba

mentiras, sarta de bochinche; carreta

mentirilla jarana

mentiroso(a) (vulgar) argüendero(a); brollero; cachero; cisnero(a); cuentamusa; mojonero; mulero; pajudo; pajuo; paquetero

mentón cumbamba

menudo sencillo

mercado marqueta

mercado de contrabando sanandresito

mercado muy grande parián

mercancía regalada alipego

mercancías en existencia stock

merecer ameritar

merienda picnic

mesa para planchar burro

mescolanza mazamorra

meseta de los Andes puna

mestizo (despectivo) acepillado; cabecita negra; cholo(a); coyote; grifo; ñapango; roto

meteprisa azarozo

meter en un asunto ilegal enzanjonar

meter en una zanja enchambrar

meterse indebidamente en la fila colear

metiche aprontao; arbolario; brejetero; cuico; entrador; huelefrito; metete; nariz; refistolero(a); refitolero(a); zaramullo

metido cuico

mezcla champurriado; ensalada; pupurrí

mezcla de frutas tutifruti

mezcla de licores carabina; ponche

mezcla de magia y religión santería

mezcla de materiales de construcción mezclote

mezcla racial, provenir de encartado

mezclado y desorganizado masacota; masacote

mezcladora de jugos molenillo

mezclar camburrear; misturar; mixtiar

mezcolanza frangollo

mezquino lechero; seco

miau ñau

microfilme microfilm

miedo chucho; escame

miedo, apodo para el mieditis

miedo, sentir abrirse

miedoso(a) culiche; culilludo(a)

miel joni

migaja buruza; chinguito

militar (despectivo) cachaco; milico

militar golpista gorila

millón, un palo; un palo

mimado, hacerse el mingonear

mimar añoñar; chocholear

mimos ñoñerias

miope chicato

mira lorea

mirar chapar; echar pupila; guachar; luquear

mirar a un desnudo (vulgar) cuarteo

mirar con deseo velar

miserable arrastrado

mitones guantes; manillas; manopla

mochila chiba; guipe; maleta; morral; motete

moda, a la up to date

modales finos, persona de aliñada; don de gentes; fifí; místico

modelo machote

moderno la última chupá

modificar remodelar

modo gráfico en la computadora graficmode

mohoso amohosado

mojón lindero

moldura rodón
moler chancar
molestar acatarrar; chavar; chingar;
  chinguear; chipiar; chucear; cuquear;
  dar candela; dar carpeta; empatar;
  emporrar; entripar; esgunfiar; fregar;
  fuñir; güevear; hinchar; huevear;
  jeringar; jeringuear; joder; latir;
  mamar gallo; mosquear; poner sebo;
  ratón; romper
molestarse chivarse
molestia camote; chingadera;
  jodienda; mecha; roncha; vaina
molesto(a) amargo(a);
  enchinchado(a); está jodido(a); le
  pica
molestoso bomba; cargoso; catete;
  chavón; fregado; fregón; gadejo;
  jeringón; jerigonzo; jodón; jorobón;
  ladilla; llenador; perecoso; perecudo;
  secante
molido ñuto
molleja contre; molleja de pollo
molusco, tipo de guacuco; loco;
  macha; pinuca
monada micada
moneda vellón
moneda de cinco centavos
  caló
moneda de diez centavos de dólar
  daim
monedas de poco valor chochas
monedero chacára
mono bata; broga; machín;
  mameluco; mico; overol
monopolizar la conversación
  sentarse en la palabra
montón de granos banco
montón, un burujón
moño cachirulo; chongo; molote;
  moña
morcilla moronga; prieta; sangre
mordiscón tarascón
moretón machucón; morete

morir estirar la jeta; guindó los tenis;
  pelar; quedarse tieso; templarse;
  totearse
morirse quedarse tieso; templarse
morral mochila
mortero pilón
mosquerío mosquero
mosquitero toldillo
mosquito mbarigüí; rocoroco; zancudo
mostrar envalentonamiento
  encocorarse
mostrar que no se quiere hacer algo
  amurrarse
mostrar respeto y admiración
  sacarse el sombrero
motel a la orilla del camino estadero
motoniveladora buldoser
motor de arranque starter
mover rápido y con energía
  jamaquear
movimiento mágico mariguanza
mucha pico
mucha conversación bembeteo
mucha gente viviendo junta en pocos
  cuartos conventillo
muchacha china; vieja
muchacha alocada marocha
muchacha bonita máquina
muchacha de gran tamaño pioscota
muchacha pobre (vulgar) griseta
muchachito chigüín; purrete
muchacho chamo; chino; cipote;
  patojo; perinola
muchacho muy crecido y corpulento
  para su edad macuco; tarajallo
muchacho que prefiere jugar sólo
  con niñas calzonudo; pollerudo
muchacho vagabundo palomilla
muchedumbre soez y grosera
  muchitanga
mucho a la lata; chorro; harto; hereje
mucho dinero guita loca
mudanza trasteo
mueble(s) fornitura; furnitura

mueble para la ropa escaparate
mueble para la vajilla seibo
muelle suave
muerte pateteada; peteteada
muertos y heridos casualidades
mugre pegostre
mugre en el cuello o las orejas cota
mujer cabra; chata; chavona; galla;
  imilla; jeva; llokalla; vieja
mujer alegre y vivaracha tusa
mujer atractiva bien hecha; budín;
  célebre; churro; lechuguita;
  macanuda; machota; macita;
  mamazota; mazota; piba; potra;
  trozo; yegua
mujer de mala reputación (vulgar)
  bacana; banda; cabra; chingona;
  cojín; corbejo; cuero; pistolita; rabúa;
  refistolera
mujer del campo china
mujer elegante china
mujer estéril (vulgar) machorra
mujer fea bagre; garabato; gurgucia;
  prójima
mujer joven imilla; lechuguita;
  llokalla; piba
mujer pobre gurgucia; prójima
mujer provocativa bacana; betibú;
  chiva; mica
mujer que dirige el tráfico vehicular
  chupa
mujer sexy machota
mujer valiente macha
mujeriego (vulgar) bregador; cabro;
  chimbero; faldero; lacho; vagamundo
multitud (peyorativo) bola; bolón;
  catajana; jaracotal; la gallá; tracalá
muñeca canilla
muñeca fea monicongo
muñeco para brujería monicongo
muñón chonco; ñoco; soco; zoco
murciélago lechuza
murmuración runrún
música de cabaret bachata

**música folclórica venezolana, un tipo
  de** chipola
músico que toca la bandola
  bandolero
muslo de ave trutro; tutro; tuto
muy re
muy apegado(a) a otra persona
  arriquín; chipe
muy bueno (vulgar) arrecho; ¡ay
  chihuahua!; bacano; bárbaro; buena
  esa; chévere; ¡chihuahua!; como tuna;
  de la madona; descueve; está cabrón;
  legal; macanudo; padre; padrísimo;
  pulento; soda
muy cerca a pata; de mingo
muy dulce ampalagoso; hostigoso
muy enojado(a) encandilado(a)
muy extraordinario acabose
muy grande la yegua; macho;
  manso(a); media
muy lejos en los quintos infiernos
muy malo (vulgar) ¡ay chihuahua!;
  ¡chihuahua!; como el forro; como las
  huevas; está cabrón
muy nublado nublazón
muy poco nadita
muy rápido como cuete; soplado
nacional doméstico
nada ni cacho
nalgadas cueriza
nalgas (vulgar) ancas; aparato;
  cachetes; cola; fundifá; fundillo; rabo;
  traste
nalgudo(a) nalgón(a)
naranja china; oranch
narigón(a) chamborote
nariz chopo; ñatas
nativo(a) de Bogotá cachaco(a)
nativo(a) de Ciudad de México
  chilango(a)
nativo(a) de Guadalajara tapatío(a)
nativo(a) de Paraguay guaraní
nativo(a) del Callao chalaco(a)
nativo(a) del Uruguay charrúa

náusea ansia
Navidad crismas
necedad chirotada; lesera; lesura
necio(a) chayote; jicate; junípero(a);
  pavuncio(a)
negocio bisnes
negocio de poca monta ancheta;
  chimbo
negocio fácil y ventajoso mantequilla
negocio ilícito palangre; rebusque
negro(a) (peyorativo) angolo(a);
  chombo(a); jamaiquino(a);
  molleto(a); prieto(a)
negro(a) de la piel clara mulato(a)
negro de los Estados Unidos moyo
negroides, con rasgos (despectivo)
  niche
neumático caucho; llanta; tire
neumático desinflado flat
neumático, parte interna de un
  carcasa
ni esto ni lo otro ni fu ni fa
nicaragüenses, apodo para los nicos
nido tasin
niebla camanchaca; cerrazón; lancha;
  sabora
niebla tóxica smog
niña buca; cabra; carajita; chamaca;
  changa; chapul; china; molacha;
  nena; ñaña
niña recién nacida chancleta
niñera(o) beibisiter; cargadora; casero;
  china
niño botija; cabro; cachifo; chamaco;
  chapul; chaval; chavo; chico; chiquilín;
  fiñe; ñaño; nene; pelado; pelao; pibe
niño(a) con retraso mental inocente
niño de corta edad barrigón; cagón;
  carricito; chamaquito; chavalo;
  chirringo; chirriquitico; chirriquitín;
  cipote; lepe; patojito; pelaíto
niño del campo gurí
niño enfermo por un mal de ojo
  empacho

niño(a) entrometido(a) siripita
niño(a) inteligente aribe
niño lactante enfermizo cipe
niño(a) malcriado(a) chinche;
  chipón(a)
niño(a) pobre chino(a)
niño precoz amayorado
niño que vende el periódico canilla
niño travieso chirote
niño vagabundo chino; gamín;
  palomilla
nitrato natural salitre
nivel de escolaridad ciclo
no cumplir con un compromiso
  mamar; mamarse
no decir ni una palabra no chillar
no entiende lo que pasa, el que
  chicato; pánfilo(a)
no entiendes colgado(a); no estay ni
  ahí
no es atractivo, el que majunche
no está o no es dulce, el que cerrero
no está relacionado, el que na' que
  ver; nada que ver
no funciona está chingado
no interfieras salta pa'l lado
¡no lo estropees! ¡nojuña!; ¡no fuña!
¡no lo puedo creer! ¡chale!
no me importa me importa tres pitos
no sabe guardar un secreto, el que
  resfriado
no se relaciona con otros, el que
  jojoto
no se vende abollado
no soy bobo yo no me chupo el dedo
no tener empleo estar en banda
no tiene solución está chingado
nodriza chichi
nombrar mentar
norteamericanos gabardinos
nostálgico cabanga; cavanga
nota cero huevo
noticias chiba
noticias falsas bola; bomba; caña

novio(a) camote; chavala; chaval; costilla; jeva; pestillo; pololo(a)
nudo mal hecho amarradijo
objeto cilíndrico lulo
objeto sin forma mamotreto
objeto usado chiva
objetos en desorden arrume
objetos sin importancia burundanga
observado cachado
observar carpetear
observación tonta (vulgar) güevada; huevada
obsesión coco; follón; grillo
obsesionarse empuntar
obstáculo entablazón; handicap
obstinación birria
obstinado arranchado; cabeciduro; cariduro
obstinado, ponerse amacharse
obstruido tupido
obstruir taquear; tupir
obtaculizar hacer bulto
obtener por las malas a la diabla
obtener previlegios apitutarse
obvio de cajón
obvio e inevitable cajonero
obvio, es está de cajón
ocelote manigordo
ocioso realengo
ocupado ajorado
odio birria; riña
ofenderse chillarse
ofensa bollo
ofensor(a) ofendor(a)
oficina de aduana garita
ofrece mucho y no cumple el que farfullero
oír pispar; pispiar
ojeriza cocora
ojo amoratado pistero
olla de gran tamaño biche
olor a podrido olor fuerte
olor ácido olor fuerte
olor de la carne chiquije

olor de las axilas chucha; grajo; monate
olor de los pies cicote; pacueca; pecueca; pesuña; sicote
olor humano o animal catinga
ombligo cachube
ombliguero candonga
omitir comer
ómnibus bas; camión; chiva; colectivo; guagua; micro; microbus
ómnibus pequeño buseta
operacional operático
operador de grúa donquero
operaria laburanta
operístico operático
oportunidad chanse
oportunista político pancista; panzú
oración gramatical sentencia
ordenar en rangos ranquear
ordinario chongo; picante
oreja, con una sola gacho
organillo cilindro
orgía partuza
orgulloso tufoso
originario de Ciudad de Guatemala chapín
orina pichí; chichí
orinal mica
orinar (vulgar) desaguar; pillar
oruga cuncuna
oscuro prieto
ostentación chamberinada; echonería
ostentoso(a) chamberí; echón; fachoso(a); farolero(a)
oveja negra mancha negra
oxidado amohosado
pachotada pachorrada
paciente, extremadamente aguantador(a)
pacto, hacer un kupia-kume
padrastro padastro
padre taita; tata; tatá

padres parientes
paga por todos, el que siempre
paganini
pagar chipiar; enterar
pagar en cuotas exhibir
pagar una cuota enterar
pago contra entrega ciodi
pago inicial enganche; pie
país cauntri
paja para beber calimete; cañita;
carrizo; pitillo; popote; sorbete;
sorbeto
pala de madera gualmo
palabra grandielocuente palabrota
palabra obscena bachata
palabrería insulsa ancheta
palangana apaste; bacín; lavacara;
lavado; lavatorio; platón
palanqueta diablito
palidez jipato
pálido(a) cherche; nixte; pánfilo(a)
paliza capa; canquiza; entrada;
garrotiza; paleada; reatiza; sopletón;
trompicón; zurra
palmadas, dar de sonajear;
spankear
palmera guano
palo garrote; leño; rolo
palo, un mamón
paloma doméstica zuro
palomilla palomita
palomitas de maíz alboroto;
alborotos; cancha; canchitas; canguil;
cotufa; crispetas; crispeto; esquite;
maíz piro; pacón; popcón; poporopos;
rosetas de maíz; rositas de maíz
paludismo chucho
pan, un tipo de arepa; guafles;
hallulla; marraqueta; pandebono;
pupusa; roscón; sopaipilla; tortilla;
tortilla de rescoldo; trama
panadería donde se amasa a mano
amasandería
páncreas del animal pafarilla

pandilla barra; chorcha; corillo;
cuerda; ganga; gavilla; palomilla;
patota
pandillero ganguero; patotero
panecillo bisquete; mogolla
panorama divisa
pantalla escrin
pantalón corto entrepiernas; short
pantalones, un tipo de blue jeans;
bombachas; jeans; eslacks; overol;
vaquero
pantano agualotal; curiche; manigua;
suamp; suampo
pantorrilla batata; camote; canilla;
cañuelas; chamorro; choclos; ternera
pantuflas babuchas; chanclas;
chancletas; chinelas; chopos;
zapatillas de levantarse
pañales chapeta; culero; diaper;
mantillas; taparrabos; zapeta
paño jerga
paño de cocina repasador
pañuelo paliacate; paño
papá cucho
papada chalcha
papanatas (vulgar) pelotudo
paparruchada guata
papaya fruta bomba; lechoza
papel higiénico papel de toile
paperas cantimplora; falfallota
papilla dulce mazamorra
papudo chalchudo
paquete postal encomienda
parabrisas güinchil; vidriera
paracaidista parachutista
parachoques bamper; bompa;
bomper; paragolpes
paraguas paragüe; sombrilla; umbrela
paraguayos, apodo para los curepa;
curepí
parar chantar; stop
parcha chinola
parche cachirulo
parche medicinal parcho

293

pardo carmelita
parear machear
pareja parna; parner
pareja amancebada marinovios; vivir
  arrimado
pariente relativo
parir liberación
parlanchín boquique
parlanchín(a) bembón; caña hueca;
  carreto; chachalaquero; cotorra;
  palangana; pispireta
párpados hinchados apajuatao
parranda bachata; rumbo
parrandear pachanguear
parrilla gril; grilla
partes iguales, en apartido
participa en una minga, el que
  minguero
participar sin poner nada de cachete;
  ir de cachete
partido match
pasajero en la motocicleta parrillero
pasar la frontera, el que cobra por
  ayudar a coyote
pasar la noche, lugar para dormida
pasarlo bien cacheteo; fonazo; vacilar
pasatiempo hobby
¡pase! ¡éntrale!
pasear chotear
paso, dar un stepiar
pastel, un tipo de capirotada;
  mamón; mollete; panocha
pasto gras
patata de mala calidad toya
patata dulce boniato; chaco
patinaje skating
patio yarda
patituerto patuleco
patizambo cazcorvo; chapín; garetas;
  maneto; patasagrias
patrocinador esponsor
patrocinar esponcear; esponsorizar
patrón bos; trompa
patrón de referencia cartabón

patrón para reproducir estencil
patrullero policial dama gris
pavo chompipe; chumpipe; guajolote;
  jolote; pisco
payaso clawn
pechos femeninos (vulgar) chiche;
  chichi; goma; marías; marujas;
  pampalinas; pechugas; puchecas
pedacito chilingo; chinguito; cuecho;
  chinchín
pedante facistor(a); facistol(a);
  firulístico
pedigüeño güiña
pedir peticionar
pedir mimos mimosear
pedir trámites ruleteo
pedo (vulgar) peo; ventoso
pedrada peñascazo
pegajoso alaste; pegotudo
pegamento glu; pega; pegadura;
  pegante; plasticola; resistol
pegar atracar
pegarle dar una pela
peinado en dos trenzas clineja;
  crineja
peinar combiar
peine desembarañador; peineta;
  peinilla
pelado(a) tuso(a)
pelar frutas desconchar
pelea bronca; fajina; garrotera; mocha;
  rosca; tángana
pelea de puños agarrón; canco
pelear agarrarse a cancos; darse zoca;
  guindar
pelear cuerpo a cuerpo mancornar
pelele esquimal
peliagudo peludo
pelicano tocotoco
película de vaqueros western
películas el mono
peligroso endiablado; jodido
pelirrojo(a) mechicolorado(a)
pellizcar piñiscar

pelo mecha
pelo ensortijado churrusco; musuco; pasudo; pelo malo
pelo liso chuzo
pelo rojizo ensortijado, persona de bachaca
pelón(a) tuso(a)
pelos de punta, con los cereta
pelota bol; bola
pelotera furrusca
peludo(a) pachón(a)
pena cabanga; grima
pendencia boche; bronca; chirinola; patasca
pendenciero abusado(a); cuchillero; guapo(a)
pendientes aretes; aritos; aros; candongas; chapeta
pene (vulgar) balone; baloni; bicho; binbín; chale; chile; chimbo; guasca; güevo; huevo; pájaro; paloma; penca; perico; picha; pichula; pico; pija; pinga; pipi; tembó; verga
pene de los niños chichí; pichulín; pirulo; tula
pensar cabecearse
penurias gajo
peonza guasapa; güila; zaranda
pepino chucumber
pequeña cantidad chinchín
pequeñez gurrumina; insoria
pequeño guatoco
perchero junto a la cama capotera; solterón
percudido curtido
perder algo ponchar
perder de vista despintar
perder el juicio alunarse; friquear
perder el tiempo mangonear
perder los estribos cabrearse
pérdida de esperanza desespero
perdido(a), muy más perdido(a) que el hijo de Limber; más perdido(a) que el teniente Bello

perdiste sonastes
perdonar excusar
perengano perencejo; perico
pereza cholla; choya
perezoso(a) arranao; bausón(a)
perfume de baja calidad pachulí
perilla candado; chiva; chivera
perinola guazapa; pirinola; tirubaqué
periódico papel
perjudicar afectar; echar jareta; fuñir
permanecer arranchar
permiso para conducir cartera dactilar; pase
permiso sin restricciones largona
perro chico pichicho
perro vago quiltro
persona aburrida (vulgar) calilla; camote; ladilla
persona agradable campechana; chusco; gumarra
persona ambiciosa calango(a)
persona bien vestida manga
persona blanca y rubia canche; catire; chele; choco(a); grifo
persona bonita bien hecho(a); por el libro; potro(a); yeguo(a)
persona de mundo recorrido(a)
persona hosca cachorro
persona mala amarrete; basca; cachorro; jodido; jodón; lechero; muérgano; perro; pichirre; pinche; pingo; podrido; sorullo
persona no confiable buchipluma; chuchipluma
persona no invitada chicle; paracaidista
persona pequeña mirringo; pirringa
persona sin bautizar moro
persona sin compañía íngrimo
persona sin experiencia carajito
persona sin gracia aguado(a)
persona sin miedo agalla
persona sin valor social (peyorativo) carajo(a); sardina(o); torreja

persona sin viveza aguada(o)

personaje típico chileno guaso; huaso

personal, el estaf

personalidad, con chorizo; choro

personas asociadas combo

peruano(a), apodo peyorativo cholo(a); perulero

pescuezo cocote; gaznate

pestañar espabilar

petardo cuete; guatapique; tote

petimetre cajetilla; catrin; pepe

petróleo canfín

pez pequeño mote

picado de viruelas sipo

picante ají; ají picante; chiltoma

picante verde chile verde; ají verde

picapleitos huisache

picardía ranada

pícaro banana; camote; confiscado; lepe; maleta; piola; zaragate

picazón rasquera

pico picada

picotada picada

picotazo picotón

pie grande gamba; patricia

pie hinchado ñame

piedra grande bolón; camote

piedrecillas grabol

piel clara, de la lavado

piel del cerdo cuero; garra

piel irritada, con la safornado; sollamado

piel morena, persona de trigueño(a)

piel oscura, persona de (peyorativo) arrosquetado; cholo(a); cuarterón; curiche; cururo; morocho; pardo; urraca; zambo

¡piérdase! ¡ábrase!

piernas largas trancas

pieza blanca del dominó caja blanca; chucha

pieza dramática tanda

pijamas payamas; piyamas

pila balsa; ruma

píldora cacahuate; pepa

pillo cachafaz

pilluelo títere

pinchar chuzar; puyar

pinta de ron caneca

piña ananá

piña, variedad de esmeralda

piojo caranga

pipa paipa

piragua pelota

pirulí chambelona; chupaleta; chupeta; chupete; colombina; paleta; pilón

piscina alberca; pileta; pool

piso de arriba, el altos; los altos

pisotón pisón

pistola escuadra

pistolero ganman

pizarrón tablero

pizca fisca; grisma; pite

planeamiento planin

planta de la marihuana cañamo

planta marina, un tipo de cochayuyo; luche

plantación de tabaco vega

plantar chantar

plantón embarque

plátano dulce guineo; maduro

plátano originario de Costa Rica butuco

plátano verde frito chatino; chicharritas; mariquitas

plato típico ajiaco; asopao; bacán; caballo; cebiche; ceviche; chanfaina; charquicán; chirmol; chupe; fufú; gandinga; jaconta; locro; machito; mangú; matrimonio; mofongo; mojito; mole; mondíngalo; moros y cristianos; ñachi; pastel; plantón; pozole; salcocho; sancocho; seco

pleno, en el boliche boche

plomería ploming

plusmarquista recordman

pobre arrastrado; pelado
pocilga cochera
poco inteligente (vulgar) bolsa; bolsón; bolsudo; pigmeo
poco o nada un carajo
poco serio paquete; tocado
podar camochar; desahijar
policía (vulgar) aguacate; botón; cachaco; cana; chapa; cilón; cuico; jura; paco; palomita; placa; tombo; verde; yuta; zopilote
policía, agente de carabinero; gendarme; oficial de policía; polisman
policía, la (peyorativo) cachucha; jara; la cana; la chota
polilla palomita
político sin escrúpulos coyote
polizón colero; pato; pavo
pollo de cualquier ave pichón
polo franela; polera; ticher
polvo para hornear bakin; beiquinparer; salarete
pomelo greifú; greifrut; toronja
pompa bomba; bombo
pomposo llambaroso; mamón; pintor; prosudo
poncho, un tipo de chamanto; chamarreta; chamerrata; hunco; jorongo; poncho de sesenta listas; ruana; sarape
poner chantar
poner el pie encima stepiar
poner la comida al fuego montar
populacho chamuchina
poquito chinchí; chischín; chispito; piñisco
por el puro gusto de vicio
¡por favor! ¡ay bendito!
por la fuerza a la brava
porfiado fregado; macho
porfiar enmular
porra de la policía bolillo
porrazo tiestazo; totazo
porro cacho

portadocumentos papelera
portalámparas socate; socket
portamonedas chauchera
portátil portable
posibilidades avenidas
posición status
postre, un tipo de capirotada; maíz caqueado; majarete; marifinga; matagusano; natilla; requesón; tembleque
postular aplicar
poza fangosa curiche
práctica, adquirir jubilarse
practica la santería, el que santero
practicar la santería brujear
precipitarse a algo esmachetarse
preferente preferencial
pregunta cuestión
preguntar mucho, el acto de preguntadera
premiar premiación
premio mayor, sacarse el bingo
premios aguares
prenda de baja categoría chamarro
prenda que se presta chiva
preocupación comején; pensión; tarugo
preparación apronte
prepararse afilar
presentar introducir
presionar presin
preso embarcado
prestamista garrotero
préstamo manga
prestar largar
prestigio status
presume de elegante y rico el que cheto; refistolero(a); refitolero(a)
presumido(a) brejetero(a); cachetón(a); chanta; chantún; fachoso(a); fullero(a); monifato(a); parejero(a); recargado(a); sobrado(a); vaselino

presumir quillarse
presupuesto badget
primavera esprín
primer ministro premier
primer premio paquete
primeras lluvias del verano
  cabañuelas
probar testiar
problema beguiansa; brete; brollo;
  cangrejo; forro; pedo
problema, crear un embarrar
procedimientos ilegales malpractis
procesadora de textos wordprosesor
producto de la herrumbre cascarria
profesor(a) cucho(a); ticher
prologar prefaciar
promedio averach; average
pronto ahora; ahorita
propina camarón; feria; ganancia;
  vendaje
proponer la candidatura nominar
proporción ratio
proporcionarse placeres
  castigarse
prostitución chivería
prostituta (vulgar) alegrona; anafre;
  bofa; cabareta; campechana;
  capulina; chiva; chuquiasa; cuero;
  fletera; guaricha; güila; maraca;
  nochera; pajuela; patín; pellejo; turra;
  vagamunda; wuiza
proteger apañar
protestante, de religión canuto
protestar chichar
provisional provisorio
provoca risas, persona que
  mojiganga
provocación puya
provocar chucear; cuquear;
  embochinchar; enchinchar; puyar
provocar sexualmente dar picón
publicista relacionista
pudrirse abombarse; empicharse
pueblo taun

puerco chancho; cochino; cuchi;
  macho; marrano; tunco
puerta vidriada mampara
Puerto Rico, lo que es de borincano;
  borinqueño
Puertorriqueño boricua
puesto estand; stand
puesto de venta callejero ventorrillo
puesto público cambur; coroto
¡puf! ¡chis!
pulir chainar
pulla chifleta
pulpa del coco vaca
pulsera brazalete; pulso
pum-pum tun-tun
puntaje escor
puntapié en el trasero chuleta
punto en las transmisiones
  inalámbricas stop
punzada puntada
punzar chuzar; estacar; puyar
puñado manotada; pucho
puñetazo aletazo; bimbazo; bollo;
  bombazo; burrunazo; cachimbo;
  combo; mangazo; ñeco; pajuelazo;
  piña; piñazo; puño; reatazo;
  trompada; trompón; zoquete
puño de hierro manopla
pupitre carpeta
puré de patatas molo
pus materia; postema
que así sea vaya pues
¡qué chistoso(a)! ¡que plato!
que cobra por rezar en el funeral,
  el/la rezandero(a)
que defiende los intereses de la
  compañía, el/la apatronado(a)
¡qué desagradable! ¡qué clase de
  bomba!
¿qué diablos quieres? (vulgar) ¿qué
  chingados quieres?
¡qué mala suerte! ¡qué vaina!
que no tiene gusto, el/la pariguayo;
  periguallo

que no vale nada, el/la pendejo(a)
¡qué persona más avara! ¡huy que avión!
¡qué problema más complicado! ¡qué vaina!
¡qué ridículo! ¡que plato!
¡qué terrible! ¡muchacho!
quebradura crack; craqueado; resquicio
quebrar descorotar; escrachar
quebrarse abrirse; totearse
queda mal, el que calceto
quedarse con las ganas cuello
quedarse sin fuerzas desgonzarse
queja complain; pipo
quejar chillar
quemado achicharrado
quemadura quemada
quemadura grande quemón
querella complain
querendar aguachar
querido(a) joni; mi cielo
querido papito o mamita cochote
queroseno cocinol; kerosene
quijada carretilla
quisquilloso brejetero; necio
quitar refalar
quitasol sombrilla
rabón cuncuno; choco(a); chucuto
racimo de bananas cacho
radio portátil chicharra
radiodifusión, radioemisora brodcastin
raíces comestibles víveres
rama para azotar chaparro
rana nativa de Puerto Rico coquí
rango más bajo del ejército congrio
rapar tusar
rápido bolón; embalao; esmandao; puntudo
rápidos de un río cabezón; chorro
rapiña agalla
rasgos asiáticos, apodo para cualquiera con chino(a)

rasguear charrasquear; surrunguear
raspar escarchar
rata guarén; pericote; petota
ratón laucha; maus
rayuela peregrina; pelegrina; golosa
raza negra, de la (peyorativo) angolo(a); arrosquetado; changa(o); chocolate; cholito; cholo; chombo; chuga; cuervo; cururo; garífuna; mollete; moreno; prieto
realizar algo brillante fajar
reanimación revival
rebelde alzado
rebotar picar
rebozar apanar
receloso cabreado; orejero
receptáculo candungo
receta médica fórmula
recetar medicinas formular
rechazo boche
rechiflar pifiar
rechoncho(a) barrilito; cambuto; catimbao; cuico; parraneto; paturro; petacón(a); potoco; retacón; rungo; taco
recibo tíquet
recipiente cumbo; pipote
recipiente hecho del jícaro huacal; jícara
reclamar cleimiar; patalear; pitear
recoger colectar; pañar
reconocimiento reconociencia
¡recórcholis! ¡puchica!
recordar recolectar
recuerdo suvenir
recuperarse alentar
red neta; netawork
reducir achicar
reemplazar socapar a uno
reemplazar en un empleo fungir
reformar remodelar
refresco fresco
refresco, un tipo de agua de piringa; aguachacha; aguada(o); aguadulce;

aguapiringa; champola; chingue; chorote; orchata; pinolillo

refrigerador frigider; heladera; hielera; la refrigeradora; nevera

regalo al que hace una fiesta jocha

regalón, el querendón; ñaño

regalonear tongonear

regañar barbear; plaguear; retar

regañina desplomo; sonsonete

regaño boche

regañón barbero

regar irrigar

regenta de un prostíbulo madama; patona

registro padrón

regla rula

regordete pachango

relación amorosa brega; brete; chillo; rebusque

relajo vacilón

relegar emplumar

religioso, extremadamente mocho; pechoño

reloj guacha

reloj de bolsillo molleja

remedar reparar

remiendo billete

remolacha betabel

rencor cocora

rencoroso cachorro

rendimiento irregular falencia

rendirse cuartear

reparadora de neumáticos llantería

reparar provisionalmente un vehículo desvaradar

reparte a domicilio, el que casero

repartidor del periódico rutero

repartir chismes desparramar

repetir sin entender paparrotear

repetirse una comida revirar

repostería tanela

reprender taquear; trancar

represa resaca

representación performans

representación, con habilidades en el arte de la lírico

reprimenda (vulgar) aplanchar; enjabonada; luma; palo; penca; puteada; rajatablas; raspa; taqueada; trancada; vaciar

reprobar un examen colgarse; corchar; feilear; partir; ponchar; quemarse; rajar; raspar

reprobar una materia colgarse; flonkear; quemarse; raspar

repugnancia, interjección de ifo!

reputación, persona de mala cuero; ficha; rabúa; refistolero(a); refitolero(a)

resaca cruda; estar engomado; guayabo; largar; mona; ratón

resbaladizo liso

resbalar resfalar

resentimiento pica; pique

reserva estoc

resfregar tallar

resfriado constipado

resfriar acatarrar

residencia estudiantil dormitorio

resina cipe

respaldar baquear; vaquear

respaldo baqueo; vaqueo

respirador respirator

responder ripostar

respondón boquiduro

responsable, hacerse apechugar

restaurante de mala calidad asistencia

restaurante de pollos pollera

restos de un puro chicote

resucitación revival

reteniendo joldin

retirarse a algún lugar lejano encampanar

retractarse llamar

retraerse entumirse

retrasado en el crecimiento apolizmado

retraso en los pagos colgada

retrete excusado; inodoro; poceta; pompón; taza del baño; tóilet; water; waterclo

reunión calpul

reunión bulliciosa bola

reunión de las tribus indias malón

reunión desorganizada machitún

reunión para confabular choclón

revancha retaliación

revelar un secreto soltar prenda

reventón bloaut; totazo

reverencia caravana

revisar chequear; chulear; inspectar

revision chequeo

revoltijo frangollo; reblujo; rebujo

revolver arrebrujar; bichar; rebrujar; rebujar; rebullir

rezongar plaguear

riachuelo estero

ridículo, hacer el papelón; plancha

ridículo, quedar en violín

rígido por risa, llanto o ira secarse

riguroso(a) guapo(a)

rimel pestañina

rincón cucho

rinconera esquinera

riña tángana

ritmo suing

rizado, de pelo muy murruco

rizo chongo; churo; colocho; marrón

robar (vulgar) afanar; alzar; amolar; batanear; bolsear; chorear; encaletar; jalar; jolopear; pitar; tocar el piano

roble chapote; moray

robo aletazo; alzo; cacho

roca peñazco

rodaja torreja

rodilla chocozuela

rodillo de pastelero palote; uslero

rojo oscuro, color guindo

roldana rondana

rollo de gordura charcheta

rollo de monedas chorizo

romo pompo

rompehuelgas carnero; escab; krumiro

ron cañita; guaro; tafia

roncha chorcha

roña carca

roñoso pichirre

ropa barata (peyorativo) garra; pilchas

ropa, con mucha empalmado

ropa sucia loundri

ropa vieja chirapa; garra; mecha

rosca dona; donat

rosetas de maíz alborotos; cancha; canchitas; canguil; cotufas; crispetas; esquites; maíz piro; pacón; odoropos; popcón; pororó; rositas de maíz

rubio(a) cano; chancaco; chele; fula(o); güero(a); locho(a); macho; mono(a); rucio(a)

ruborizarse tupirse

ruedo de gallos gallera

ruido bochinche; laberinto; rochela

ruido, hacer rochelar

ruin basca; cachorro; chichimeco; jodón; muérgano; perro(a); pinche; pingo; podrido; sorullo

ruleta pica

rumiar remascar

rumores bomba; borrego

rústico cabestro; campirano; guaso; guajiro

sabana cocha; pampa

sabihondo cheche; chenche; despercudido; parejero

sabio despercudido

sacafaltas triscón

sacar refalar

sacar el aire espichar

saco gabán; paletó; vestón

sacrificarse (vulgar) fajarse; sacarse la cresta

sacudida cimbronazo; jamaqueo
sagaz macuco; zamarro
sagrado, lugar huaca
sala cuna norseri
sala de estar living
salario diario jornal
salchicha corta y gruesa gorda
salida éxito
salir cachiflín
salir apresuradamente pitar;
  raspar
salón de baile balrum; dancing hall
salón de belleza biutichap
salón de patinaje skeitinrom
salpicar zarpear
salsa chorota
saltamontes chapulín; chicharra;
  esperanza; langosta; saltagatos
saltar jumpear
saltar a la cuerda bailar la suiza;
  brincar a la reata; brincar la cuerda;
  saltar el lazo; saltar la cuica; saltar la
  soga
saludo rechazado oso
salvadoreños, apodo para los
  guanacos
sanar curar
sancochar salcochar
sandalias chalas; chanclas; guarache;
  huarachas; ojotas
sandía melón de agua; patilla
sandwish torta
sangría, dejar indentar
sanguijuela choncaco
santurrón(a) santulario(a)
sarna cancha; caracha; zarate
sarnoso carachoso
sartén acero
sastre tailor
satírico bomba
satisfecho(a) ensabanado(a)
sazón ahogado; ahogo; hogo
se acabó pompón; tilingo-tilango
se deja manipular, el que dejón

se destaca por su intelecto, el que
  célebre
se murió cantó el manicero; guindó
  los tenis; guardó el carro
se produjo un lío se formó el tilingo
secreto coroto
secreto, lo que se tiene en
  enmochilado
secuestrar plagiar
secuestro plagio
sedal guaral
seducir, fácil de pariguayo; periguallo
segundo piso tabanco
¡seguro! ¡órale!
seguro seguranza
seguros, compañía de seguranza
selectivo disticoso
sembrado tala
semejante guareto
semen (vulgar) canela; leche;
  naturaleza
semental padrón
sencillo (dinero) feria; single; vuelto
sendero huella; pica; picada; pique;
  trillo; vereda
sensual, ambiente sexy
sentarse arrodajarse
señal de muerte calaca
señal donde alguien murió en el
  camino animita
señora laidi; misia; mádam
ser bueno ser arrecho
ser cruel tener muñeca
ser osado tener agallas
ser tímido ser aguasado
serenata albazo; esquinazo; gallo
serie set
serio seco
serpiente venenosa guata
servicio colocho
Servicio de Inmigración de los
  Estados Unidos migra; la migra
servilleta limpiamanos; mantelito;
  secador

servilón alzacola; chupamedias; lambeache; lambebotas; lambeculos; lambehuevos; lambeojos; lambiache; lambiscón

servir el mate cebar

severo trancado

sexo con varios, la que tiene (vulgar) chingona; manoseada

sexo con varios, tiene (vulgar) chingón(a)

sexo, tener (vulgar) abrocharse; acostartse; afilar; chapetear; chichar; chingar; coger; culear; echar un polvo; encamarse; jalar; montar; pichar

sexualmente atractiva(o) buenote(a)

shorts pantaloneta

sí claro

siempre se opone el que contreras

siempre se queja el que argüendero(a)

silenciador del automóvil mofler

silencio chillo; dejen de relinchar

silla de descanso perezosa

sillón couch

simpático célebre; sabrosón

simple, persona tilango(a)

simposio symposium

sin ambición achantao

sin clase (despectivo) bodrio; majunche; mengalo; pacotilla; picante

sin comentario nocomen

sin dientes mueco

sin fuerzas mamado

sin gracia fome; terco

sin modales arrotado; guasamaco; jicate

sin orden al cuete

sin pagar, el que se va del restaurante conejea; fanfullero; fullero; hace perro muerto

sin restricciones chipe libre

sin valor mecha; pichiflina; tepalcates; torreja

sindicato unión

sinvergüenza conchudo(a); lana

sirviente(a) cachifa(o); chino(a); gata; guachiman; mayordomo; mucama; servicial

sistema social establichment

situacion difícil forro; fregada; tostón

situación difícil, estar en una embromado; estar montado en la vaca

situación engorrosa arroz con mango; lava; macán

situación molesta chinchín

situación problemática forro; jaleo; verga

sobornar aliñar; engrasar; untar la mano

soborno coima; matraca; mordida

sobras de comida retallón; salcocho; sancocho; sarapa

sobras en la botella aunche; hunche

sobre de marihuana pelpa

sobrenaturales, con poderes alumbrado

socio(a) parna; parner

sol, el care gallo

sola unidad machún; maco

solapado guillado

soldar gueldear

solicitar peticionar

solicitud aplicación

soltar relís

soltero single

solterona beata; cotorra

sombrero, un tipo de bolero; bomba; charra; chupalla; cúbilo; jipa

sombrero viejo guaracho

sonajero margua; ronrón

sonar un timbre ringuear

sonido previo pleibac

sonrojarse flochar

sopa, un tipo de caldillo; cuchuco; menudo; mondongo; valdiviano

soplón(a) acusete; alzafuelles; lambón(a); tapudo

soportar rustir
soporte cuña
soporte físico del sistema informativo hardwear
sorbete cepillado; cherbet; granizado; helado de agua; nieve; pabellón; rasco-rasco; raspadilla; raspado; sorbeto
sordo juicio
soroche puna
sorprender cachar; rochar; trincar
sorpresa clavo
sorpresa, interjección de (vulgar) iapucha!; ichucha!; ihíjole!; ipucha!; ireflauta!
sortija alianza; anillo; argolla; aro
sospechoso cabreado; cachudo; emponchado
sostén senos ajustador; brasier
sótano beisman; subterráneo
subalterno suche
subasta remate
subastador martillero; rematador
subastar rematar
substancia espesa chorota
substancia pegajosa plegoste
sucesión muy rápida virivira
suceso en la música jit
suchil suche
suciedad de las rodillas cabra
sucio(a) chanco; chorreoso(a); cochino(a); curtío; manteco(a); zoquete
sudado sancochao
sudor transpiración
suelto (dinero) aguada(o); feria; vuelto
sueño tuto
suerte (vulgar) cueva; leche; tarro
suerte, con buena chepudo; tener leche
suerte, dar o tener mala empavar; torcido; yetatore

suéter chaleca; chomba; chompa; pulover
sufrir daño chavarse
sufrir una gran pérdida sonar
sujetar atracar; atrincar
sumamente bueno del carajo
sumamente viejo del año del caldo
sumergir consumir
superar a otros bañar; comer; machetiar
superior maldito(a)
superticioso agüerista
suplemento suple
suprimir deletear
surtido stock
suspirar angelar
susto batata; cisca; jabón; terronera
taberna grifo; pub; taquilla
tabla pastelera patineta
tablero de anuncios boletín; espaciador; tablilla de anuncios
tacañería amellarse; pichirrear
tacaño(a) (despectivo) agalludo(a); chucho; conservativo(a); garrotero(a); hambriento(a); judío(a); lechero(a); maceta; machete; pichirre; pinche
tachar tarjar
tachuela taquilla
tafetán adhesivo vendita
tajada troncha
taladro mecha
taller del fotógrafo retratería
tallo del cochayuyo hulte
talón jarrete
tamales humista; humita
tambor bomba
tapa de botella chapa; corcholata; ficha
tapa del alcantarillado meinjole
tapioca yuca
tardo corroncho
tarifa inicial en un taxi banderazo
tarjeta de embarque pasabordo

tarro de conservas bote; conserva; lata

tartaleta pai

tartamudear canacanear; cancanear; gagear; gagüear; gaguear

tartamudo(a) gago; lenco; lenguachuta; mudenco; tartancho(a)

tasa ratio

taxista tachero

tazón bandeja; cazo

ite lo digo! imuchacho!

té que se sirve en la tarde onces

teatro de variedades music hall

techo rufo

tecla de bloqueo de mayúsculas tecla shift

teclado kibord

teclear taipear; tipear

técnico en el laboratorio de cocaína cocinero

tejido de punto flexible punto jersey

tela barata, un tipo de brin; choleta; gangoche; lona; tocuyo; zaraza

tela o traje muy sucio percocho

tema tópico

tema aburrido jarta

temerario(a) guapo(a)

temeroso(a) buchipluma; chuchipluma

temperamento violento, el que tiene rebotado

temporada de las lluvias invierno

tenaz taimado

tenazas alicate; alicates; gato; pinzas; pláier

tenazas pequeñas playo

tener antecedentes calificar

tener bajo control planchar

tener un orgasmo (vulgar) acabar

tengo hambre me está arañando el tigre

tengo sueño tengo el hojo empillamado

tengo una corazonada me tinca

tentempié, un tipo de botana; causeo; pasabocas; picada; picadito; puntal; snack

terco cachorro; sesudo

terminar un noviazgo le dió la quiebra

termitas comején; sepe

ternera vaquilla

terreno abandonado potrero; rastrojo

terreno anegado bañado; estero; vega

terror escame

tesoro escondido botija; tapado

testaferro calanchún

testículos (vulgar) blanquillo; bolones; gobelinos; güevas; huevas; huevos

tetera (bebé) bobo; caldera; chupo(a) de entretención; chupón; mamón; pacifier; pava; pepe; tete

tetilla del biberón chupete; chupo(a); chupón

tez blanca y pelo negro, de menudo

tiempo empleado taimin

tienda (campamento) carpa

tienda (comercio) chop; chopa; chope; estor; negocio

tienda de abarrotes abarrotería; abasto; almacén; bodega; changarro; colmado; el chino; grocer; groceri; grocería

tienda de fiambres fiambrería

tienda que vende barato baratero; baratillo; quincalla

tienducha baratillo; boliche; chinchorro; linterna; quincalla; ratonera; taguara; tarantín; tendajo; ventorrillo

tiene alcohol está cabezón

tiene alguna deformidad, el que choreto

tiene espinas, el que ganchudo

tiene éxito con las mujeres, el que tiburón

tiene malanco, el que malancón
tiene que hacerse rápido automático
tiene recursos recursivo(a)
tierno suave
tierra de secano de rulo
tieso tilinte; trinco; tringo
tiesto callana
tiesto pequeño mate
tigre del Chaco bicho
tijeras clipa
tímido(a) aguasado(a); penoso(a)
tina bañadera
tinaja pondo
tintorería cliner
tiovivo calesita; carnaval; carrusel;
  machina; volantín
tipeja (despectivo) galla; tipa
típico típical
típico de la cultura chicana
  pachuquismo
tipo de lagarto teyú
itíralo! iórale!
tirar aventar
tiras cómicas chistes; comiquitas;
  cuentos; fonis; monitos; muñequitos;
  paquines
tiro de la chimenea tiraje
tiroteo plomera
tiza choc; gis; tizate
toallas higiénicas femeninas cotaco
tobogán canal; chorrera; deslizadero;
  resbaladera; resbaladero; resbaladilla;
  zurra-zurra
toca por oído lírico
tocacintas pasacintas
tocar en un sentido sexual (vulgar)
  agarrón; amasar; atracar; jamonear
toldo tolda
tolerar aguantar; bancar
tolondrón turupe
toma de agua boca de agua; boca de
  incendio; bomba de agua
tomador de ollas bajaollas
tómalo con calma cógelo suave; funá

tomar agarrar; chapar; nancear
tomar el pelo cachar; mamar gallo;
  pitar; tomar para el fideo
tomar en el aire barajar
tomar examen dar examen; rendir
  examen
tomar un atajo deshechar
tomar una postura firme amarrarse
  los huevos
tomar una siesta sestear
tomarse la autoridad que no le
  corresponde facultoso(a)
tomarse unas copas canchar
tontear destorrentarse; lesear; ser
  pavo; tilinguear
tontería al pedo; ancheta; chantada;
  charada; chayotada; despapucho;
  lesera; lesura; pallasá; patilla; pavada;
  pistolada; zoncura
tonterías, hacer (vulgar) huevonear
tonto(a) (vulgar) aguacate; agüevado;
  ahuevado; apendejao; azurumbrado;
  baboso(a); berracá; bola; bolsa;
  bolsón; bolsiflay; bolsudo; boludo;
  buey; caído(a) del catre; camote;
  cipote; casimiro; chauchón; chitrulo;
  chotón; collera; comebola; crestón;
  dundo; fallo; firulístico; forro; gil;
  gracejo; guajolote; guanaco;
  guarango; güevón; huevón; jetón(a);
  jil; leso(a); mamerto; menso(a);
  menzo; morolo; nabo; pánfilo(a);
  papayudo; pendejo(a); pigmeo;
  pistola; pistolo; salame; suncán;
  surumbo; tarado(a); tilango(a); tilico;
  tilingo; tórtolo; vejiga; zaramullo
tonto, absolutamente (vulgar) bolas
  de cuero; ultraboludo
torcer enchuecar
torcido cheuto; chueco; virado;
  viroteao; visorioco
torpe (vulgar) caballo; chalungo;
  chirote; ganso; gocho; güevón;
  huevón; gurundango; machetón(a);

mamao; mamerto; matungo; menso;
muchitanga; navo; pajarón; pariguayo;
pavo; pendango; periguallo; tapado;
turupe

torpemente, actuar (vulgar) güevear;
huevear

torpeza gafo

torta bizcocho; bizcochuelo; pastel;
queik; queque

torta de maíz perrerreque

tortilla omelet; torta

tortilla mexicana, un tipo de arepa;
casabe; casave; chalupa; chilaquila;
enchilada; envuelto; memela;
pelliscada; pupusa; repocheta

tortuga huistora

tosco lanudo; pedrero

trabaja en la marqueta, el que
marquetero

tostada toast

trabajar bregar; chambiar; jalar;
laburar

trabajar con ahínco camellar; cuidar
la cuchara; descrestarse; fajarse;
monear; ponerle mucha tiza; remar

trabajar con desgana hacer la roña

trabajar con paciencia rustir

trabajo brete; camello; chamba;
cuchara; jale; laburo; pega; voleo

trabajo a destajo chamba; trabajo a
trato

trabajo, contratar para un conchabar

**trabajo de poca monta, realización
de un** pichulear

trabajo esporádico brujulear; faena;
pituto; pololo(a); rebusque

trabajo fácil batata; botella; mamada

trabajo ilegal pichulear; rebusque

trabajo pequeño chiripa

trabajo voluntario cayapa

trabarse manearse

trabas, poner entrabar

traer mala suerte salar

traficante de marihuana marimbero

tráfico, atasco del engalletar; taco;
tapón, tranca; trancón

trago de licor cañonazo; guamazo;
jalón; lamparazo; matracaso; palo;
tacazo

traicionar chaquetear; chivatear;
chivar; poner el gorro; sapear

traicionero malinche

traje de baño bikini; calzoncillo de
baño; calzoneta; malla; pantaloneta;
ropa de baño; trajebaño; trusa;
vestido de baño

traje de etiqueta sacoleva; sacolevita

traje de hombre ambo; flux; terno

traje de niño mono

traje sastre vestido de sastre

trajín corredera

tramar brujulear

trampa cabra; chiva

trampear chingar; fonchar; mogallar

tramposo(a) chapucero(a); chira;
chueco(a); lana; mulero

tranquilízate aguántate

transbordador ferry

transgresor(a) ofendor(a)

transmisor-receptor portátil
waquitoki

transparente cliar

transporte gratuito, dar bolear; cola;
dar botella; dar paloma; dar un
aventón; dar un jalón; dar un pon;
jaiyakin

transporte gratuito, pedir bolear;
cola; hacer dedo; jaiyakin; pedir
botella; pedir paloma; pedir un
aventón; pedir un jalón; pedir un
pon; pon; tirar el dedo

transporte lento lechero

trapear mapear; mopear; suapear

trapero bayeta; coleto; malaya

trapero gastado soco; zoco

trapos güila; peleros; tiras

trasero (vulgar) ancas; aparato; cola;
cueva; el queque; fundifá; popi;

popín; popó; poto; rabo; siete;
tambembe; traste

trasnochar malanocharse

trasto coroto; féferes; traste

trasto viejo muérgano; tereque

trastornado por el alcohol
engasado

trasvasar trasvasijar

tratamiento de respeto doctor;
maestro; mister; missy; tata; tatá;
taita

tratar mal pesetear

travesear miquear

travestido(a) encamisonado;
transformista

travesura avería; perrería

trazar esquechar

trecho jalón

tremendo(a) maldito(a); padre;
padrísimo

tren subterráneo metro

trenza chimba; simpa

tributo gabela

trifulca bronca

trigo hervido mote

tripas para comer chunchules;
chunchullos; chunchurria

triquinosis zaratán

triste amongado(a); amurrugado(a);
enguayabado(a)

triste, encontrarse amachinarse

tristeza grima; macacoa; mucepo

trompadas, dar cachimbear; sacarle
ñachi

trompeta butute

tronera buchaca

tropezar dar un boniato

trozar toletear

trozo cachito; cacho; rolo

trozo de piel frita (cerdo o pollo)
chicharra; chicharrón

truco cachirulo

tú (pronombre) che; vos

tucán pico

tuerto chueco

tumor tacotillo

tumulto acabose; bola; escándalo;
fajazón; garata; guato; margayate;
molotera; reborujo

tunda chanca

tupé cabellera

turbado turuleta

turnio bizcorneado

úlcera chira

ulceración en el talón jarretera

único machún; maco

urina chi

usarlo demasiado chotear

uso de cualquier droga ilegal pase

utensilios de mala calidad trique

uva gajo

vaciadero dumping

vaciar un líquido flochar

vacío biche; gap; güero; huero

vado chimba

vagabundo candil; linyera

vagancia manguareo

vagar brujulear

vagina (vulgar) agujero; bollo;
cachimba; cachucha; chicha; chimba;
chocha; choro; chucha; chuspira;
concha; crica; cucaracha; cueva; linda;
pancho; panocha; papaya; raja; tatú

vago bichicome

valentía arrecho; pana

valentón(a) añiñado(a); añiñao; bule

valiente agallado; caliente; castao;
guapo(a); panudo(a); ternejo

valija lágach; maleta; suitqueis; velís

valla verja

valor guaramo

valores, mercado de stock

valores sociales, persona sin
tilango(a)

vanidoso(a) estilozo(a)

vano ñoño

vaquero cowboy

vaquero argentino gaucho

vaquero chileno huaso
vaquero colombiano llanero
vaquero mexicano charro
vaquero uruguayo gaucho
vaquero venezolano llanero
variación del joropo gabán
varicela lechina
vasija chirimbolo; tiesto
vasija, un tipo de chirigua; jícaro;
  mate; nambira; porongo; tinaco
vaso con asa moca
vaso grande caña; potrillo
iváyase! iábrase!
iváyase de aquí! imándese mudar!
vegetal vainica
vegetal a medio cocinar jojoto
vehículo averiado accidentado; reca;
  varado
vehículo con ruedas rodado
vehículo en mal estado batata; burra;
  cacharro(a); cafetera; charchina;
  cucaracha; fodongo; garnacha;
  matraca; tartana
vehículo para pasajeros guagua;
  microbus
vehículo para todo terreno
  campero
vehículo policial bola; chota; jaula;
  julia
veinticinco centavos de dólar
  cuartilla
veinticinco libras de hojas de coca
  cesto
velatorio velorio
velocidad, a toda a todo jender;
  embalado
vencer dar una pela; soplar
venda de parche banda
vende helados, el que nievero
vende objetos usados, el que
  chivero; garrero
vendedor ambulante achín; achimero;
  achún; cangallero; maritata;
  sencillero; varillero; ventero

vendedor de periódicos canillita;
  papelero; suplementero(a); voceador
vendedor(a) en el mercado de
  comestibles vivandero(a)
vendepatrias matamama
vender pitar
vender barato machetear
vender carne pesar
veneno muy potente canjura
venganza retaliación
vengarse chingar
ventaja gabela
ventaja, dar encimar
ventajista argollero; parche; vivanco
ventana gráfica window
ventilador abanico; fan
verde grin
verdura vegetable
vergüenza chasco; cisca; muela; pena;
  quemón
vergüenza, pasar una planchar
¿ves? ¿cachay?
vestíbulo hall; lobi
vestido chachae; dres; traje
vestido de verano solera
vestido formalmente palta
vestido liviano de mujer camisón
vestido pobremente apuercado
vestimentas de mala calidad
  piltrafas; piltrajas
vestirse canchar
vestirse con esmero arriscarse
vestirse elegante apitiguarse;
  arrejarse; empilcharse
viajar tripear
viaje raid
viático, dar el beatificar
vida llena de padecimientos vidurria
viejo(a) (despectivo) angarrio;
  bejuco(a); cacarico; vejuco(a);
  vejucón(a); veterano(a)
viejos vicarios
vigía durante una fechoría
  campanero; loro; sapo

vigilante guachiman; rondín
vigilar guillar
villano (vulgar) guache; muérgano;
  sorullo; vergajo
vínculo liga
vino suave y dulce chacolí
violación (vulgar) capote; redoblón
violador rapista
violento(a) machetero(a)
viril, muy chingón
viruelas, con cicatrices de borrado
virutas colocho; virusa
vivaz avispa; minga; pierna
vive a costas de otros, el que
  bolsero; garrotero; mamador(a);
  vividor(a)
víveres cocaví
vivienda pobre ratonera
viviendas pobres callampas; cantegril;
  población callampa; ranchería; villa
  miseria
vivir sin casarse conchabar
volado, estar estar jai
volador volatero
volante del automóvil cabrilla; guía;
  manejera; stering; timón
volarse con drogas caballón(a);
  gira
volquete dumper
voluminoso balumoso
volver a revisar doblechequear
vomitar debocar; deponer; trasbocar

vómito basca; guacara; traboco
voz para llamar al gato cuchito
vuelta lup
vulgar cochino; guache; pedrero
vulgaridad guachada
vulva (vulgar) bizcocho; conejo
whisky escotch
yerba gras
yerbazal pajonal
yeso tizate
yugurt jocoque
zancos sango
zanja chamba; herido; trencha
zapatería peletería
zapato chalán
zapato fuerte y resistente banasta;
  bototo; calamorro; chambón
zapato viejo chaguala; chalupa;
  chancharreta; chancleta; sueco; zueco
zapatos de lluvia zapatones
zapatos deportivos de goma
  championes; snikers; zapatillas
zapatos grandes banasta; calamorro;
  camambuses; chambón
zarcillos aros; caravanas; pantalla;
  topos
zarigüeya chucha
zorrino hediondo
zurdo izquierdista; lluqui; macueco
zuro olote; tusa
zurra batida; felpa; fuetiza
zurrar atracar; latiguear; somatar

Country Indexes

a esta altura del
partido
a gatas
a rolete
abatatarse
abatí
abrirse
abrirse de piernas
acábala farolito
acabar
acatarrar
achanchado
achinado
achispado
acusete
afanar
afilador
afilar
aflojar
agallado
aguasado
aguatero
ahora
ají
ají verde
al pedo
al tuntún
alacranar
alacraneo
albóndiga
almacén
almidonado
altos
alverja
alzado
alzar
amargo
amarrete
ambo

amolar
ananá
ancas
andar con el
gorila
andar pato
angurria
anillo
anteojos
largavista
apañar
apensionado
aplastado
apretado
apretar
apronte
aquerenciar
araucano
aros
arquero
arrimarse
arrollado
arrugarse
arveja
arverja
asunto
avatí
azotea
bacán
bacana
bachicha
bagre
balaquear
balurdo
banana
baqueano
baquiano
barajar
baranda

baratieri
baratos
bárbaro
batata
batir
baúl
bebida
biblioteca
bicho
biromé
biyuya
biyuyo
bizcochuelo
bocacalle
boche
bodrio
bola
boleadoras
boliche
bolichero
bolitas
bolón
boludo
bombachas
bombita
bosta
botón
brete
bronca
budín
burrero
burro
cabecita negra
cabrearse
cachar
cachetada
cachete
cacheteo
cachivaches

cadete
cafetera
cafiche
cafiolo
cagadera
cajetilla
cajón
calar
calesita
camisón
camote
campana
campera
cana
canasta
canchero
canilla
canillera
canillita
caña
cañonazo
carancho
caravanas
carcamán
carpa
carpetear
carretilla
casorio
castañazo
castigarse
catinga
cebar
cerrazón
chacarita
Chaco
chacota
chalchazo
chamuchina
chamullar

chancaca
chancao
chanchada
chancho
chanchullo
chancletas
chanfaina
chanfle
changador
changar
chango
chanta
chantada
chantar
chantún
chapar
charango
charcón
charqui
charquicán
chauchas
chauchón
chavona
chavón
che
cheto
chicato
chicha
chicote
chicotear
chillar
chimentar
chimentos
china
chinche
chinchudo
chinchulines
chingana
chingar
chirola
chirona
chitrulo
chivarse
chocante

choclo
cholo
choncaco
chongo
choripán
chorro
chotón
chucear
chuchoca
chueco
chulo
chumar
chuño
chupamedia
chupar
chupe
chupete
chupetín
churrasco
churrete
churro
ciclo
cierre relámpago
coche
coger
coima
cola
colectivero
colectivo
como la mona
concha
conchavar
concheto
contre
contreras
conventillo
cortahierro
croto
cuico
culo
cuña
curado
curar
curda

cuy
damasco
de chiripa
de vicio
denso
desbole
desembuchar
despatarro
despelote
despiole
donde el diablo
    perdió el
    poncho
durazno
El Chaco
embancarse
embocar
empacarse
empanada
empelotado
empelotarse
empilcharse
encarajinar
enchinchado
encintado de la
    acera
encocorarse
encomienda
endiablado
enfermo
engorilado
engrupir
ensopar
entretecho
es un clavo
escándalo
esgunfiar
eslilla
esquinazo
está papa
estación de
    servicio
estancia
estanciero

estante
estantería
estar ahorcado
estar churrete
estar con la mona
estar en banda
estar pato
estar podrido
estar sonado
estirar la jeta
faca
facón
faenar
fajar
falopa
fama
farolero
faso
fasulo
fayuto
feto
fiaca
fiambrería
fiambres
fifí
formar
fruncirse
fuerte
fumar
funá
funcar
gabardina
gallego
gallo
galpón
gamba
gancho
gardelito
garúa
garufa
gato
gauchada
gaucho
gay

gelati
gendarme
gente copetuda
gil
globo
gobelinos
goma
gomita
gorila
gotero
grandulón
grillero
gringo
griseta
grupo
guacho
guaraní
guaripola
guasca
guaso
guata
güevada
güevas
güevón
güevonada
guinda
guita
guita loca
gusano
hacer gancho
hacer la cama
hacer pucheros
hay a patadas
hay ropa tendida
hecho torta
hediondo
heladera
helado de agua
hinchar
huella
huevada
huevas
huevo
huevón

huevonada
huinca
impavidez
irse al tacho
jabón
jabonarse
jaiba
jeme
joder
jodido
jodienda
jornal
jorobado
jugar
justiniano
kimono
la fulera
la mosca
la pelada
la sabiola
la yegua
laburanta
laburar
laburo
lacra
lamparita
lanza
largar
latear
latería
lavatorio
lechuguita
leso
licenciado
liga
linyera
llave de luz
loca
¡loco!
locro
lona
luca
lunfardo
lustrabotas

lustrador
macana
macanudo
machetiar
machi
machona
machonear
madama
maíz
mala leche
malevo
malla
mamadera
mamado
mandarse mudar
manga
mangos
manopla
manyar
máquina
mariquitas
marmolín
marrón
martillero
mascada
matambre
mate
matrero
maula
mazamorra
mecha
medio pelo
mentar
meter el choclo
milico
mimosear
misturar
mona
¡morite!
morrocotudo
mosca
mote
movida
mufa

mulero
muñequear
nada que ver
nafta
naftazo
navo
nena
nene
nenito
neumático
ni fu ni fa
ni muy muy ni
   tan tan
nieve
nochera
obradera
ojo
olor fuerte
oreja
orejear
oso
paja
pajarón
pajearse
pajero
pajonal
palanca
palangana
palanquear
palo
palo verde
palote
palta
pampa
pancho
pango
papa
paponia
paquete
paquetería
paquetero
paracaidista
parála
parar la olla

pardo
parrilla
parrillada
patente
pato
patota
patotero
patuleco
pava
pavada
pavo
payada
payador
pechar
pechazo
peinar
peineta
pelo enrulado
pelota
pelotudo
pepino
perezosa
petiso
petizo
piantadura
piba
pibe
picana
picárselas
pichicata
pichicatero
pichiflina
pichincha
pichón
pichulear
pierna
pieza
pifia
pifiar
pija
pijotear
pilchas
pileta
pillar

piloto
pinche
pingo
pintón
pintor
pinzas
piña
piojosa
piola
pispar
pispiar
pitillo
pituco
piyamas
planchar
plasticola
playa
playa de
    estacionamiento
podrido
polenta
pollera
pollerudo
polvo
poncho
ponerse
por chiripa
poronguito
posta
potrero
potro
ipucha!
pucherear
puchero
pucho
pulover
punga
puntudo
pupurrí
purrete
ique plato!
quedarse piola
querencia
quilombo

ragú
ranada
ratearse de la
    escuela
re
refalar
remar
rematar
remate
rendir examen
resfalar
resfriado
retar
revirado
rodado
romper
roncar
ronda
ropa vieja
ropero
roto
rotoso
rubro
rumbeador
runrún
salado
salame
sanata
secante
seguro
shop
siete
silbatina
sobar
sobrar
solfear
soltar prenda
sonar
sonastes
sorete
sorullo
sube y baja
suertudo
tabas

tachero
tacho de la
    basura
taita
tajamar
tajeadura
tapado
tarascón
tarro
tata
tatá
tener polenta
tentenelaire
ternera
tiburón
tilango
tilinguear
timba
tipa
tira
tocado
tocuyo
toletole
tomador
tomar para el
    fideo
tornillo
tortilla
tortillera
trabucarse
tragada
tranca
trancarse
trenza
trigueño
trincar
tripulina
trolo
trompa
trompada
tronco
trucho
trutruca
tufo

tumba
tun-tun
turra
turulato
tusa
ulpo
ultraboludo
una barbaridad
un palo

untar la mano
valija
vaquero
vaquilla
vejentud
vendido
vereda
verga
vermuth

veterano
vichar
villa miseria
virado
virola
vivanco
vivir arrimado
vos
yeguo

yerba
yerbatero
yoni
yuta
zabeca
zafado
zapallo
zapatillas
zurra

BOLIVIA

aburrición
acholarse
achuncharse
acusete
ahora
ají
alianza
aloja
alpaca
alverja
amauta
amayorado
ancheta
anticuchos
api
aro
arveja
arverja
auquénido
bagre
baqueano
baquiano
bebida
boche
bochinche
bravo
cabañuelas
cabra
cachivaches
cachos
callahuaya
camote
canasta
caneco
cañonazo
capacha
carabinero
catinga
catre
cesto
Chaco
chacra

chala
chalona
chancaca
chancho
changar
chapa
charango
charqui
che
chicha
chicotear
chirapa
chocante
choclo
choco
cholo
chueco
chuño
chuto
cochayuyo
coima
conejo de las
  indias
conventillo
cueca
culo
curcuncho
curiche
cuy
damasco
de yapa
debocar
empanada
empanizado
encohetarse
estancia
estanciero
fama
foco
galpón
gamonal
gárnica

garúa
gatear
grifo
gringo
guacho
guagua
guanaco
guano
guaraní
guarapo
guasca
guato
guatoco
hacer perro
  muerto
hoja de
  gilet
huella
humista
hunco
imilla
jachi
jaconta
jacú
jalón
jara
jeme
jipijapa
jochear
jornal
jugar
juma
jumado
kantuta
la yapa
leche
legal
lenguachuta
leso
liso
lisura
llama

llapa
llokalla
locoto
macana
madama
madubí
malevo
mandioca
manta
marinera
matatudo
mate
matrear
mazamorra
milico
mogallar
montera
mordida
moro
mote
mucama
neumático
ojotas
pachamama
pampa
papa grande
papango
parcela
patasca
patuleco
pechoño
pechuga
pelota
pepe
petaca
petiso
petizo
pingo
pisco
pollera
poncho
porotos

CHILE

a capela
a concho
a medio filo
acabar
acachao
acatarrar
acholado
acholar
achurrascar
acusete
afilar
aflojar
afuerino
agallado
agarrar
agarrar la onda
agarrón
aguachar
aguantador
aguántele
aguasado
aguatero
ahora
aindiado
ají
ají verde
ajiaco
al cuete
al tuntún
alaraco
aleonar
aletazo
alfiler de gancho
alicate
almacén
altiro
altos
alverja
alzado
amallarse
amariconado
amarrete

amasandería
ambiente
ambo
amellarse
amohosado
ampalagoso
ampolleta
amurrarse
anchoveta
andar pato
anillo
animita
anotarse un
  poroto
anteojos
  largavista
anticuchos
añiñado
apanar
apañar
apatronado
apechugar
apitiguarse
apitutarse
aposar
apretado
apronte
apurar
araucano
argolla
¡aro!
aros
arquero
arranao
arrancar
arreglar
arrollado
arrotado
arveja
arverja
asomar
asopao

atao
atracar
atrincar
autocarril
auxiliar de vuelo
azumagarse
bachicha
bacilarlo
baqueano
baquiano
barajar
barata
baratero
baratieri
baratillo
barreta
barsa
bartolear
bata
batatazo
bebida
bencina
berrear
blanco
blanquillo
bocacalle
boche
bochinche
bodrio
bolas de cuero
boliche
bolichero
bolitas
bolón
bolsear
bolsero
bolsiflay
bomba de
  bencina
bosta
botarata
botillería

bototo
bravo
brin
bronca
burra
burro
caballazo
cabecearse
cabra
cabriado
cabro
cabrón
cabrona
cachá
cachaña
cachar
cacharpearse
cacharro
cacharro de greda
¿cachay?
cachencho
cachero
cachetada
cachete
cacheteo
cachetón
cachiporra
cachirulo
cachito
cachivaches
cacho
cachos
cachuchazo
cachudo
cacique
cafiche
cafiolo
cahuin
cahuinero
caído del catre
cajón
calamorro

318

calar
calcetas
caldillo
caldo de cabeza
calducho
calentarse
calenturiento
calillas
callampas
calumnia
calzones
calzonudo
camanchaca
cambucho
camisón
camote
camotera
campechana
cana
canasta
canchero
canilla
canillera
canillita
cantinflear
cantinfleo
canuto
caña
caña hueca
cañamo
cañonazo
cañoneado
cañuelas
capacha
capear
caperuzo
capo
capote
carabinero
caracho
carajada
carajo
carboncillo
carbonero

care gallo
carretilla
carretonero
carril
carrilero
carro
carrusel
casaca
cascarria
casero
casilla
casimiro
castañazo
catete
catre
causeo
cebiche
cerros
ceviche
cháchara
chacolí
chacota
chacra
chaito
chalas
chalcha
chalchudo
chaleca
chalupa
chamanto
champiñones
champurriado
chamuchina
chamullar
chanca
chancaca
chancacazo
chancao
chancar
chanchada
chancho
chanchullo
chancleta
chanfaina

chanfle
chantar
chao
chapa
charango
charcheta
charquear
charqui
charquicán
charretada
charreteada
chasca
chasco
chascón
chauchera
che
cheuto
chicha
chicharra
chiche
chicoco
chicotear
chilote
china
chingar
chipe libre
chipiar
chirimoya
chiripa
chirlito
chiva
choapino
choca
chocante
chocleros
choclo
choclón
choclos
choco
choleta
cholga
cholito
cholo
chomba

chonchón
choreado
chorear
chorito
chorizo
choro
chorro
chucha
ichucha!
chuchoca
chueco
chuleta
chulo
chuncho
chunchules
chuño
chupalla
chupamedias
chupar
chupe
chupete
churrasco
churretada
churrete
churro
chute
chuzo
cilón
cimarra
claro
clavo
coa
cocaví
cochayuyo
cochino
cocido
cocinería
cogotear
coima
cola
colcha
colgado
color
combo

como cuba
como cuete
como el forro
como huasca
como huevo
como la mona
como las huevas
como pickle
como piojo
como poto'e
 guagua
como tuna
componer
con el cuerpo
 cortado
con el hachazo
con el ropero a
 cuestas
con la caña mala
con la mona viva
concha
congrio
constipado
contre
conventilleo
conventillera
conventillo
coño
copuchar
coronta
cortar
cortar pantrucas
cortarla a cincel
coscacho
coscorrones
coto
cotorra
cototo
crestón
cruce
cuadros
cuarteo
cuchito
cucho

cuco
cucufato
cueca
cuello
cuentero
cuero
cuete
cueva
cufifo
cuico
cuita
culear
culo
cuncuna
cuña
curado
curanto
curar
curcuncho
curda
curiche
curtido
cururo
cuy
damasco
dar examen
dar una tanda
de cajón
de llapa
de ñapa
de rulo
de vicio
de yapa
descrestarse
descueve
despercudido
despintar
despunte
diablito
donde el diablo
 perdió el
 poncho
donde la viste
durazno

echar tallas
echar una
 pestaña
echar un polvo
echarle al pelo
echarse el pollo
el luche
el queque
elástico
embalado
embalao
embancarse
embarrada
embarrándola
embarrar
embeleco
emboque
emboticarse
empacho
empalarse
empanada
empelotarse
emplumárselas
empuñar
en cueros
en pelotas
encachado
encamarse
encargo
encatrado
enchuecar
encielar
encomienda
endiablado
engorilado
engrasar
engrupir
ensopar
enterrar
entrador
entrecerrar
entrepiernas
entretecho
erogación

es papaya
es pintado
es un clavo
escándalo
escoba
esquinazo
esquinera
está cabezón
está de cajón
está de maleta
estante
estantería
estar churrete
estar con el gorila
estar con la caña
estar con la mona
estar pato
estar prendido
estar satisfecho
¿estás enfermo?
estero
estítico
estrellón
fachoso
faenar
fama
felpudo
fiambrería
fiambres
firme como un
 peral
flacuchento
fletar
flor
fome
fonda
fondear
forado
forro
fósforos
fregado
fregar
frivolité
frutillas

fulera
futre
gabela
gabriela
gajo
galla
gallo
galpón
gamba
ganso
gargarear
garra
garrotear
garrotero
garuga
gásfiter
gasfitería
gata
gauchada
gaznate
gil
gloriado
golilla
goma
gorda
gotario
gotero
greda
gringo
groso
grupo
guachapear
guachapiar
guacho
guagua
guagualón
guaina
guaipe
gualeta
guanaco
guano
guapear
guaraní
guarén

guaripola
guasamaco
guasca
guaso
guata
guatapique
güero
güevada
güevas
güevear
güevón
güevonada
güila
güilas
güincha
guinda
güiña
gusano
habiloso
hacer cuchara
hacer dedo
hacer gancho
hacer la chancha
hacer la cimarra
hacer la pata
hacer perro
  muerto
hacer sonar
hacer tapa
hacer tira
hacer tuto
hacerse el cucho
hacerse el/la
  pituco
hacerse la paja
hallulla
harto
hasta la tusa
hay ropa tendida
hechizo
helado
herido
hierbatero
hijuela

hincarle el diente
hinchar
hisopo
hoja de gilet
hostigar
hostigoso
huacho
huáscar
huaso
huella
huero
huesillo
huevá
huevada
huevas
huevear
huevón
huevonada
huilas
huincha
huiro
hulte
humita
hurgüetear
impavidez
inquilino
irse al chancho
jaiba
jaibón
jalar
jalón
jauja
jeme
jeta
jetón
jil
joder
jodido
jodienda
jornal
jote
jugar
jurel
krumiro

la gallá
la última chupá
la yegua
lachar
lacho
lacra
ladilla
ladino
lagarto
laja
lanceta
langosta
lanza
lápiz de pasta
largar
largona
lata
latear
laucha
lavamanos
lavaplatos
lavatorio
le pica
lechugas
lenteja
lesear
lesera
leso
lesura
liberación de
  aduanas
lienza
limosnero
llama
llanta
llapa
llave
llenador
lobo
loca
loco
lolei
lolo
lomo

peo
pepa
pepino de fruta
perico
pericote
petiso
petizo
pica
picada
picado
picante
picarón
picarones pasados
pichanga
pichí
pichicata
pichicatero
pichicho
pichiruche
pichón
pichula
pichulear
pichulín
pico
picotón
piduye
pié
pieza
pifia
pifiar
pije
pilchas
pililo
piltrafas
piltrajas
pilucho
pinche
pinganilla
pingo
pinta
pintado
pinuca
piñiscar
piñisco

pirco
pirinola
pirquinero
pirulo
pisco
pispireta
pita
pitanza
pitar
pitear
pitillo
pito
pituco
pituto
piure
piyamas
plancha
playa
playa de
   estacionamiento
plomo
po
población
   callampa
polenta
polera
pollera
pollerudo
pollo
pololear
pololo
polvo
poncho
poner el gorro
ponerle empeño
ponerle pino
popi
popín
popó
porotos
poto
potoco
potrero
potrillo

prender
prosa
prosudo
provisorio
¡pucha!
puchero
pulento
pulpear
puna
punga
puntada
punto jersey
puntudo
pupurrí
puyar
¡que plato!
quedado
quedó la escoba
quemado
quena
quiltro
quiñazo
quirquincho
quisco
rajar
rasca
rastrojo
ratero
ratón
ratonera
re
realización
reciencito
¡reflauta!
reja
relajante
rematar
remate
rendir examen
repelar
resfalar
resquicio
retar
reversa

rochar
rodado
rodón
roncear
ronda
rondín
rosca
roto
rotoso
rubro
ruca
rucio
runrún
sacarle la ñoña
sacarle ñachi
sacarse el
   sombrero
sacarse la cresta
saco
salado
salitre
salpicón
salta pa'l lado
saltón
sandunga
sapo
sarmiento
se fue al pihuelo
seco
sencillo
ser pavo
shop
silbatina
sindicado
sindicar
siútico
sobrado
sobretodo
solera
somier
sonar
sonastes
sopaipilla
sota

COLOMBIA

candongas	chécheres	choglo	colgarse
caneca	chepa	cholla	colino
canilla	chepudo	chorizo	colombina
cantaleta	chévere	chorlo	color
caña	chiba	chorro	comején
cañar	chicha	chota	componer
cañero	chichar	chucha	comprimido
capear escuela	chicharra	chueco	concha
capote	chichí	chulear	conejear
capul	chicho	chulo	conejero
¡carajo!	chicote	chunches	conejo
carreta	chicotear	chunchullos	confiscado
carretilla	chiflis	chunchurria	conserva
carreto	chilingo	chupa	consumir
carro	chimba	chupaflor	copera
carrusel	chimbear	chupahueso	copetón
casar	chimbero	chupeta	copietas
casco	chimbo	chupo	corbata
castaño	china	chupón	corchar
catire	chinazo	churro	corredera
cazcorvo	chincharro	churrusco	correrse
célebre	chinche	chusco	coso
cerilla	chino	chuspira	costura
cerrero	chirajos	chuzar	crestón
chacára	chiras	cicla	crispetas
chacra	chirimoya	cimbronazo	crudo
chaguala	chirinola	circunstanfláutico	cuajado
chalán	chirlo	cismático	cúbilo
chalupa	chiros	clavar	cucaracha
chamba	chirringo	clavo	cucarrón
chambiar	chirriquitico	clientelismo	cucarronear
champús	chirriquitín	cobija	cucha
chanchira	chiva	cochera	cuchara
chanclas	chivar	cochino	cucho
chancuco	chivatear	cocina	cuchuco
chancuquear	chivato	cocinero	cucos
chanfaina	chivera	cocineta	cuellón
changuear	chivo	cocinol	cuete
chantar	chocante	coima	cuetear
chapetón	chocha	coime	cuidar la cuchara
chapín	chocholear	cola	culear
charanga	choclo	colada	culipando
charranga	chocolo	colcha	culipendearse
charro	chocozuela	colgada	culirroto

culiseco
cumbamba
cuncuno
cuquera
cuquísima
curaca
curco
curdeao
curdo
curí
cursera
curtido
curtir
curucutear
cusca
¡cutí!
¡cutú!
dama gris
daño
dar un pico
darse un paseo
de cachete
de la madona
de llapa
de ñapa
de yapa
decolaje
del carajo
del coño de su
  madre
dengue
desaguar
descache
descarachar
descocorotarse
descompletar
descorche
descrestada
desespero
desgonzarse
desgualetado
deshechar
deshecho
deslizadero

desmoronamiento
desperrindingarse
despichar
destape
desvaradar
desvarado
desvirolado
determinar
divisa
dobletroque
doctor
don de gentes
dulceabrigo
durazno
echar pupila
edredón
el que con niños
  se acuesta,
  cagado amanese
embarcado
embarrándola
embarrar
embocar
embolar
embolatar
embromado
empanada
empañetado
empaque
empaquetado
emparamado
empatar
empelotarse
empepado
emplumárselas
empuntar
empuntarlas
en un improviso
en un tilín
encabar
encachorrarse
encaletado
encaletar
enchafainarse

enchambrar
enchipar
enchivarse
encimar
enclochar
encochinar
encomienda
encopetonarse
encularse
endilgar
endosar
enflautar
enfletar
engerirse
englobado
engrampar
engrifado
enguandocar
enguayabado
engurrioso
enjabonada
enlagunado
enredista
ensalada
entrabar
entrador
entromparse
entumirse
entunarse
envejigarse
envolatado
envolatar
envuelto
erogación
escándalo
escaparate
escogencia
escuadra
escuelante
escuelita
esferográfico
esmeralda
espaldón
esqueleto

esquimal
está chapetón
estadero
estar caliente
estar cotizada
estar en la
  pitadora
estar montado en
  la vaca
estar pilas
estar quemado
estar rebotado
estítico
estop
estoy embalado
estoy puto
estrellón
estufa
etiqueta
excusado
fafarachero
fafaracho
fajar
falencia
farmaleta
feo
feúra
ficha
ficho
foco
fogón
fórmula
formular
franela
fregado
fregar
fresco
frijoles
frisoles
frísoles
fritera
fuetera
fufú
fullero

funda
furrusca
fute
gabardina
gabela
gadejo
gafufa
gaguear
galafardo
galgo
gallada
gallera
galletica
gallinacea
gallinazo
gallo
galpón
gambetear
gamín
gamonal
gancho
gancho de
  nodriza
ganchudo
garabato
garbinche
garetas
garoso
garra
garrotera
garvinche
gas
gavilán
gavilla
gaznatón
gemelos
gil
gis
glándulas
godo
godos
gofia
golosa
goma

goterero
gotero
gozón
gramilla
grampa
grampadora
grifo
grima
guacal
guachada
guache
guacho
gualmo
guandolo
guanguero
guantes
guapo
guaquear
guaquero
guaracazo
guaracha
guarapo
guargüero
guaricha
guaro
guasa
guasca
guascazo
guata
guayaba
guayabo
güevón
güevonada
gumarra
gurbia
hacer fiero
hacer la caca
hacer la roña
hamaquearse
hambriento
harnear
harto
helaje
hijoemadre

hijoepucha
hilachento
hogo
hormadoras
horro
hoya
huacal
hueco
hueso
huesudo
hueva
huevón
huevonada
huevonear
huevos pericos
hule
hunche
hureque
¡huy que avión!
infiernillo
inoficioso
invierno
ir a fiesta
ir de cachete
jai
jaiba
jarana
jardinera
  prescolar
jarrete
jarretera
jarta
jarto
jaula
jecho
jeme
jeringuear
jetón
jipa
joder
jodón
jorro
joto
jubilarse

jugar vicio
juma
jumado
jumarse
junípero
lagartija
lagarto
lambeculo
lambiscón
lambón
lamparazo
lámparo
lana
langaruto
largar
lavaplatos
lazo
le dieron el
  paseo
le falta la
  persiana
leche
lechero
legal
levantadera
levantar
liberación
liga
liso
llanero
llanta
llantería
llapa
llave
llenador
llevar el bulto
locero
locha
locho
lonche
lonchería
luca
lueguito
lunguero

luz de la calle,
oscuridad de la
casa
macanudo
machera
machetear
machín
macho
machona
macumba
madrazo
maduro
magancear
maganza
maganzón
maíz piro
malacaroso
malaley
maldingo
maleta
maluquera
mamá
mamado
mamar
mamar gallo
mamarse
mamazota
mamón
mamonsillo
mancorna
manearse
manga
mangancear
manganza
manganzón
mangazo
manguala
manirroto
manotada
manteco
mantilla
maqueta
maquetear
maquetería

maraca
marías
marico
mariela
marimba
marimbero
mariquear
mariquitas
marranear
marrano
marrón
marujas
más cansón
más loco
más perdido
masatudo
mascada
mataculín
mate
materia
mazacotudo
mazamorra
mazota
mecate
mecato
mecha
mechicolorado
memoria de
gallina
mesanín
mica
microbus
minga
minguero
miñoco
miquear
mirringo
misia
mister
místico
miti miti
mochar
mochila
mochilas

mochilón
mochuelo
mogolla
mogollo
mojojó
molleto
monicongo
monitos
mono
monos
montañero
moña
morir soñando
moro
morocho
morral
morrocotudo
motilado
muchacho
mueco
muenda
muérgano
mugre
mugroso
naguas
natilla
naturaleza
necio
negrear
neme
nena
nene
nevera
no estar el palo
para cuchara
no estar en nada
no raja ni presta
el hacha
número
ñaño
ñapango
ñoco
ojal
pachanga

pacueca
padrón
pafarilla
paganini
paja
pájaro
pajearse
pajero
pajudear
palanca
palanquear
palillo
paloma
palomilla
palomo
pampa
pampalinas
pandebono
pando
pandorga
panel
panela
pánfilo
panocha
pantallero
pantaloneta
panucha
pañar
pañoso
Papa Noel
papayudo
papazote
papel
papelada
papelera
papelero
paquete
paracaidista
parada
parece un silbido
de culebra
parranda
partir
pasabocas

pasabordo
pasacalle
pasacintas
pasador
pasaje
pasante
pase
pasmarse
pastelear
pastelero
pasto
pastorejo
pasudo
pata sola
patacón
patalegre
patanear
patasagrias
pategallina
patilla
pato
patojo
patuletas
paturro
pavear
pechuga
peculado
pedir limosna con
  escopeta
pedir una
  paloma
pedo
pedrero
pegante
pegostre
pegotudo
peinilla
pelada
pelado
pelaíto
pelao
pelar
pelarse
pelotudo

pelpa
peludo
peluqueada
peluqueado
peluquear
peluquearse
pena
pendejada
pendejo
penoso
pensión
pepa
pepo
perchudo
perecoso
perecudo
peregrina
perencejo
perezosa
perico
pernicioso
perrería
pestañina
pica
picadito
pichanga
pichar
pico
pigmeo
pintoso
pinzas
piñazo
pipa
pipo
pipocho
pipón
piponcho
pipudo
pique
piqueteadero
piragua
pirringa
pisco
pistero

pistola
pita
pitar
pite
pitillo
piyamas
placa
plante
platón
plomazo
plomera
pluma
plumígrafo
poconón
pocotón
pola
polín
pollera
pompo
ponche
poncho
poner sebo
ponerle mucha
  tiza
ponerse tere
póngase las pilas
popocho
poposeador
porra
porro
postema
postrera
prado
prelación
prepucio
prospecto
provocación
puchecas
pucho
pulso
puntal
punto rojo
pupurrí
puscafé

puyar
que la felicidad te
  atropelle
quebrar
iquedetallaso!
quiñar
rabo
rajar
rajarse en el
  examen
rajatablas
rancho
rascado
rasgado
raspa
raspado
rastrero
raya
realización
rebaja
rebanar
reblujo
rebolotú
rebotado
rebote
rebrujar
rebujar
rebujo
rebullir
rebuscador
rebusque
rechinarse
recocho
recomendado
recorderis
recorrido
recursivo
redoblón
refajo
regadera
regarse
registro
rejazo
rejo

relacionista
remascar
remontar
repasador
resabiado
resbaladera
resorte
retobo
retranca
reverbero
reversa
rezar
ringlete
ripio
ripostar
rochela
rochelar
rodillón
rompepecho
rondpoint
roña
rosca
rosco
roscón
ruana
ruanetas
rumbero
sabido
sacar la leche
sacarse el
  clavo
saco
saco de viaje
sacoleva
sacolevita
sacotín
salado
salar
salchicha
salcocho
salón
salpicón
salsa
salsamentaria

salsómano
saltagatos
saltar el lazo
saltar matojo
saltón
samuro
sanandresito
sancochar
sancocho
sanduche
sanjuanear
sanjuanito
sapear
saquito
sarapa
sarazo
sardina
sardinel
secarse
seco
sentarse en la
  palabra
ser la sal
serenar
sexapiloso
sifón
isiga!
simpático
sindicado
sindicar
sobada
sobadera
sobado
sobador
sobandero
sobijo
sobrebarriga
sobrecama
soco
socola
soda
soguear
solterón
soltura

sombrilla
sonsonete
soñar con
  pajaritos de oro
soplado
sudor
suiche
surrunguear
sute
tabaco
tablero
tablero de
  anuncios
tajamar
talanquera
talego
tanda
tapado
taparse
tapón
taqueada
taqueado
taquear
taquiara
tarabita
tarasca
tarro
tarugo
tegua
tener dengue
tengo el hojo
  empillamado
tenis
tercena
terciador
terciar
tercio
terraza
terronera
teso
testa
tetera
tetero
tiestazo

timón
tinto
tiquete
tiquetear
tirarse la
  fiesta
tirarse la
  plana
titino
todero
tolda
toldillo
toletear
tomado
tombo
topo
toque
torcidos
tórtolo
totazo
tote
totearse
toya
traba
trabado
trabajoso
traboco
tractomula
traga
tragado
traguearse
trancada
trancado
trancar
trancón
trapichar
traqueado
trasbocar
traste
trasteo
trilla
trisca
triscar
triscón

COSTA RICA

aguada
aguadulce
alepate
alipego
amarrarse
arrodajarse
atrincar
barbear
barbero
bolero
bolo
bolsear
butuco
cabanga
cachero
cacho
camarón
cambute
campirano
cancanear
canfín
cantaleta

cañamo
chafirrazo
chafirro
chilaquila
chinga
chinguear
chinguero
chirote
chocolón
cholo
chonco
cicote
cilampa
cinchazo
cipe
cobo
colocho
con mucho
  gusto
copo de nieve
detalle
dormida

echado
emporrar
enchilar
encohetarse
encomienda
enjaranado
entortar
entotorotar
feria
fifiriche
fogón
gangoche
garifo
guamazo
güila
hacer cuchara
higadoso
invierno
macana
macho
maganzón
manganzón

maraca
pantalla
polígrafo
ratón
salado
sicote
sólido
tanela
tapilla
tarasca
ticos
tiradera
tolonguear
trillo
turno
tusa
iupe!
vaina
vainica
vereda
yautía
zapoyol

CUBA

abanico
achiote
aeromosa
aguacate
aguajirarse
aguantar
aguantón
ahora
ají
ají picante
ajiaco
ajustador
al tilín
al tuntún
aletazo
alfiler de
  criandera
alverja
amarrarse
amelcocharse
ameritar
anillo
aretes
arroz con mango
arveja
arverja
atrincar
automático
avenidas
aventar
aviador
aviso
bacán
bailar la suiza
bañadera
baracutey
baratillo
bárbaro
basura
bata
bata de dormir
bate

batear
batiboleo
bayeta
bebito
bembón
berracá
betibú
biberón
bicho
bingo
blanquear
boca de agua
bocacalle
bocadillo
bocadito
bocatero
bochinche
bodega
bodeguero
bohio
bola
bolas.
bolitas
bollo
bolso
bolsón
bolsudo
bomba de agua
bombillo
boniato
borrador
botafango
botella
brincar a la
  cuerda
bronca
burro
burujón
cabra
cachorro
cachucha
cachumbambé

cagadera
cagalera
camisón
campechana
canal
cantó el manicero
capa de agua
carajo
carmelita
carro
carrusel
cartera dactilar
cartucho
caucho
chambelona
champiñones
chancho
chancletas
chapapote
charranga
chatino
chicharra
chicharritas
chicharrón
chiche
chinelas
chivato
chotear
chucho
chupón
cicote
coco
colcha
colgarse en la
  escuela
colombina
comer bola
cono
cotorra
cuarto
cubo
cucurucho

culero
cuño
curiel
dar botella
dar un boniato
dormir la mona
echar una bomba
el tejo
embancarse
empelotarse
empelotarse con
escarpines
esmeralda
espantar el lomo
espejuelos
espejuelos de sol
esperanza
espléndido
estar con la
  mona
estar salado
estola
estufa
fajazón
fallo
fama
finca
fiñe
flato
fletar
fletera
florecido
foco
fogón
fondo
forro
fósforos
franela
frigider
fruta bomba
fuente
gafas

334

galletazo
galletica
ganchito
gancho
garrotero
gasolinera
gato
gavilán
gemelos
goma elástica
gotero
grama
granizado
guacamole
guagua
guajiro
guano
guantes
guapo
guardó el carro
guaso
guayaba
guayabera
habitación
huevos
inodoro
jaba
jarana
jardín de infancia
jardín de niños
jimaguas
jubilarse
juma
jumado
kilo
la creche
lata
latón de basura
lavado
lavatorio
le pegaron el
  tarro
le ronca el
  clarinete

le zumba el
  mango
legal
lentes ahumados
lentes oscuros
leño
licencia
liga
llave
macho
mandarse mudar
manoabierta
mantecado
mantón
maraca
mariquitas
maruga
mascada
masilla
mazorca de maíz
me hace tilín
me importa tres
  pitos
medias
melón de agua
menudo
meter La Habana
  en Guanabacoa
mocho
molleja de pollo
molleros
mondongo
moros y cristianos
mulato
muñequitos
nevera
obradera
pájaro
paleada
palomilla
palote
panecillos
panecitos
panetela

papagallo
papagayo
papalote
papaya
parejero
pasa
pastel
pato
payamas
pedir bola
pega
peletería
pena
pendenciero
penoso
perico
perro caliente
petipúa
picada
pichón
pila
pinga
pinzas
piragua
pita
pitar
piyamas
placa
pluma
pomo de leche
ponchar el
  examen
ponerle la tapa al
  pomo
presilla
prieto
pulso
pupurrí
¡qué brete!
¡qué clase de
  bomba!
quedarse mocho
quemado
rajar

rancho
rasco-rasco
raspado
raspadura
ratero
refajo
refresco
regadera
rizado
ropa vieja
rosetas de maíz
rositas de maíz
saco
salar
salcocho
saltar la soga
sancocho
saya
saya interior
sayuela
se formó el tilingo
se le encendió el
  bombillo
sello
sicote
sobrecama
soda
sombrilla
sorbete
tabaco
tablilla de
  anuncios
tan rápido como
  entierro de
  pobre
tanda
tángana
tareco
tarro
te la comiste
tener guano
tener pasas
tener una
  botella

335

DOMINICAN REPUBLIC

a la brava
a la diabla
abanico
abridor
abrirse
acabose
achiote
acriollarse
iadiós!
adiosito
agacharse
aguaje
al carajo
alabao
amachada
amasadito
amongado
añoñar
apachurrado
aplatarse
apozarse
apuñalearse
arenque
arrancado
arrancao
atrincar
azotea
bacán
bachata
bacilón
balsa
batata
bemba
bembé
bembudo
bergantín
bienmesabe
billete
binbín
bizcocho
bizcorneado
boche

bodega
bohio
bolear
bollo
bolsa
bomba
boso
botánica
bragado
bravito
bregar
brollo
brujear
brujulear
buscones
caballada
caballo
cabeciduro
cabo
cachaza
cachetada
cagadera
cagueta
calalú
calentar
calimete
camarón
camisilla
cancanear
cantaso
cantazo
carne bif
carro
casabe
casave
chambe
champola
chancleta
chancletas
chancletero
chanfle
changuería

chele
chichar
chícharo
chichí
chichigua
chinchín
chinchorro
chinguito
chino
chirimbolo
chiririco
chiva
chivear
chivo
chocha
chorota
chorreoso
chupar
churria
cicote
cicotudo
clueco
cocotazo
cocote
colgarse
comebola
conchudo
congri
coquero
coraje
coroto
corredera
cota
crica
cubo
cuero
culebrear
culebrero
cumbanchear
cuquear
curtío
dar candela

dar carpeta
descascaranar
descocotar
descolgar
desconchabar
desconchinflar
destaparse
destornillarse de
   risa
duro
egresar
embochinchar
embolsicar
embuchado
enchinchar
encuerar
enfogonarse
engreñao
enmarañado
enterito
especial
estillar
estrepitarse
exprimión
fajar
fajarse
faldero
fanfullero
fanfultear
féferes
feúra
firulístico
fletación
fletar
floretear
ifo!
franela
frenillo
fuete
fuetiza
fullería
fullero

ECUADOR

abarrotería	barata	chauchera	duro
abrigo de lluvia	baratillo	che	elástico
acabado	bascoso	chicha	embancarse
acabar	bembeteo	chichos	embonar
achumar	berrear	chicotear	empanada
acial	biela	chifles	empaque
acusete	biscera	chilito	empavar
agalla	blanquillo	chimba	emplumar
agalludo	boche	china	empuntarlas
aguada	bomba de agua	chingar	encartuchar
ahijuma	bravo	chinola	enchivarse
ahorrar	buchaca	chirimoya	encomienda
aindiado	cachaco	chirla	entripar
ají	cacho	chirotada	esclava
alegrona	cachos	chistes	espaciador
alentar	calumnia	choclo	estanco
alepantado	camin	cholo	estanquillo
alfiler de gancho	camote	chompa	estar salado
alianza	canguil	choro	fama
almacén	cañita	chucha	farfullero
alverja	cañonazo	chueco	féferes
amañarse	cargoso	chumado	felpa
amontonar	carpeta	chupete	ferrocarrilero
amostazar	carrusel	chupón	flacuchento
ancheta	cartucho	churo	fo
anillo	casaca	cocha	fochi
anteojos	casco	coima	foco
largavista	cebiche	comedirse	follón
apachurrar	ceviche	comején	fósforos
apartido	chacana	comer machica	fregado
arveja	chacra	concha	fuereño
arverja	chagra	costal	fundifá
asomar	chajal	crimen	fundillo
atrincar	chancaco	cucho	gallinazo
atufar	chancho	cuerazo	galpón
aviso	chapa	cuico	garrotero
avispado	chapacaca	curco	garúa
bacán	chapar	curcuncho	gaznate
bajaca	chaquiñán	cuy	gil
baluma	charango	damasco	grajo
baqueano	charlón	desperfeccionar	grifo
baquiano	charrasquear	durazno	gringo

guacho
guagua
guaipe
guanaco
guano
guapo
guaraca
guarape
guarapeado
guarapero
guarapo
guasca
guata
guiso
hacer el dos
harto
huella
huilón
jaiba
jarana
jebo
jocha
joder
juma
jumado
lana
lancha
latear
lavacara
lavadero
lavatorio
leche
legal
liso
lisura
llambaroso
llanta
llapa
llevacuentos
lluqui
longo
machona
malanocharse
mamadera

mamerto
manganear
mangoso
manta
marinera
marinovios
mate
menso
menzo
molacha
molo
moro
morocho
mote
mucama
neumático
nieve
ñaño
ñeco
ñuto
oferta
ojotas
omnibus
pacheco
palta
pampa
pana
pancho
panela
papa grande
papasote
partir
pasaderas
pato
patuleco
pechuga
pecueca
pega
peinilla
pepa
pepita
perico
pesuña
pica

pico
pingo
pique
pisco
plantilla
playo
pleno
pluto
pollera
pomo
poncho
pondo
porotos
prosa
prosudo
pucho
puna
puntada
puntudo
quena
quinde
rajar
redondo
rizado
roñoso
ropa de baño
rosca
roto
ruma
salchicha
salpicón
saltar la soga
sangaraña
seguro
sencillero
silgado
sindicado
sindicar
sipo
soborno
socapar a uno
soplador
suche
suelazo

suertero
sulfúrico
taco
talamoco
taparrabos
tapilla
taquilla
tarascón
tareco
tarro
tarro de la basura
tasin
templado
templar
templarse
tercena
terco
ternejo
terquedad
tina
tinaco
tincazo
tirar el dedo
tiros
tracalá
trenzarse
trigueño
trompeta
trompón
tumbado
tun-tun
turro
vaca
vega
vendaje
vetazo
volatero
wuiza
zambo
zancudo
zanja
zapallo
zapatillas
zoquete

GUATEMALA

hueco
huisache
ideoso
jabear
jalapeño
jalón
janano
jaracotal
jarana
jericoplear
jeruza
jesusear
jicaque
jícara
jobo
joco
jolote
joyolina
ladino
lana
lapicero
le fue de la
　patada
le pegó el
　gordo
leche
librera

licenciado
liso
lisura
llanta
machina
maleta
malhora
mamar
mamón
mancha
maneto
manigordo
maraca
matagusano
metete
mica
micada
mico
milpa
molotera
mondongo
moronga
motete
nenito
ni cacho
no chillar
norte

olote
otate
pacaya
panela
paquínes
pateteada
patojito
patojo
pena
penoso
pepe
pica
pirujo
pisto
poporopos
pozole
prieto
prosa
prosudo
provisorio
quedarse tieso
remoler
rentar
retratería
rosticería
rumbo
salazón

sarape
se choteó
soplador
sorbete
surumbo
tapado
tapanco
taquilla
tarro
templarse
tenis
tierno
tina de baño
tincute
tiras cómicas
tuanis
tuero
tuerto
tufoso
tusar
vejiga
vereda
yautía
zopilote
zoquete
zumbado
zumbar

HONDURAS

abalserar
abarrotería
abiertazo
abismar
abridura
abrigada
acatar
achimería
achimero
achimes
achín
achiote
achucutar
achún
agarroso
aguacate
aguachacha
aguachada
aguachinarse
agualotal
aguanoso
alaco
albardear
albarillo
alborotos
alcanforarse
alentar
aletazo
alférez
algaraza
almádana
almágana
alverja
alzo
amarradijo
amostazar
amurrarse
amusgarse
andén
angelar
angola
apachurrar

aparragarse
apartado
apaste
arepa
aribe
aritos
arreado
arrimado
arriquín
arveja
arverja
atajona
atiquizar
atolada
atole
atracar
atributo
atucuñar
azadón
azarearse
azocararse
azurumbarse
azurumbrado
bagre
bajareque
balumoso
bató
beatificar
bernia
bibicho
bimba
birriñaque
blanquillo
bocatero
bolero
bollo
bolsear
bomba
borrego
bote
botija
bravo

bulto
burrión
butuco
butute
cacalota
cacarico
cachar
cachicha
cachiflín
cachipuco
calentarse
calilla
calzoneta
camión
camochar
camuliano
candinga
candonga
canilla
canjura
cantaleta
cañamo
capa
capotera
caranga
caravana
carlanca
carretón
cartabón
catrachos
catre
caula
cayanco
centro
cepa
chachos
chacolín
chamaca
chamaco
chamaquito
chamarro
chane

chapa
chapulín
chaquira
charra
chayote
cheje
chele
chercha
cherche
chicha
chicharra
chicharrón
chiche
chifleta
chigüin
chile
chile verde
chinchinear
chinga
chingar
chiquear
chiras
chiringo
choco
chocolate
chorcha
chotear
chucho
chumpipe
chupar
cipe
cipote
colocho
confiscado
corretaje
corroncha
cotonear
cucamba
cucho
cuerazo
cumbearse
cumbo

cuminar
cutacha
deponer
desharrapado
desparpajar
destorrentarse
diablo
embolado
emperendengarse
empichar
enchicarse
enchilada
enchute
enfiestarse
enflautada
enjaranarse
ensopar
enterar
enterrar
entilar
estacar
estar bomba
estrellón
faltar
flamenco
forrar
fregado
fresco
fungir
gajo
gallera
gancho
garífuna
garnacha
garúa
gazpacho
gendarme
grisma
guanaco
guangoche
guaracho
guaragua
guarapo
guaro

guazapa
hacer bulto
hacer cuchara
hacer garra
huacal
hueviar
huistora
hulado
hurgandilla
ideático
inquieto
inquirriado
intratar
irse de levante
jachado
jalapeño
jalón
jama
jambar
jarana
jeruza
jicate
jolote
joyolina
juanetes
juco
juicio
jupa
lana
lapicero
latiguear
lazo
leche
lenco
levante
licenciado
liga
limpiamanos
lindero
liso
lujar
machina
machote
maleta

malhora
mamar
mameluco
mamón
mantadril
mantilla
maraca
marocha
mascadura
matada
matropa
me colgué en el
  examen
mecha
memela
micada
mico
migueleño
milpa
mingui
mololoa
molotera
mona
mondongo
monear
montante
montera
mora
moray
morete
morocho
morolo
moronga
morroño
mortual
moscarrofio
motete
mucepo
muco
mudenco
muela
musuco
nagual
nalgón

nambira
nancear
neneque
nixte
no chillar
norte
olote
otate
pachigua
pachón
palomilla
panela
panuela
paquínes
pataste
patojito
patojo
pena
penoso
percocho
pichete
pinole
pinolillo
piñol
pioscota
pitón
provisorio
¡qué vaina!
rentar
revolica
rispar
ronrón
ropo
rungo
sesudo
somatar
sorbete
suampo
suncán
surumbo
tangalear
tango
tantear
tapado

tapiscar	tiras cómicas	tuanis	zamarro
taquilla	tizate	tunco	zaratán
taramba	tocotal	vigo	zarate
taranta	torcido	vivandero	zarpear
tenis	totazo	yautía	zopilote

MEXICO

¿a dónde la
  llevas?
¿a dónde la tiras?
a la brava
a secas
a todo dar
abanico
abarrotería
abolillar
abujazo
abusado
acarrear
acartonado
acatar
acatarrar
acero
agarrar clases
agarrar de puro
  pedo
agarrar la onda
agarrar la tetera
agarrarse a cancos
ágatas
agringado
aguacate
aguada
agües
agüitas
agujero
agujetas
ahora
ahorita
ahoritita
al hilo
alambrista
albazo
alberca
aliento
aliñado
alverjón
alzado
amacharse

amarrarse
amarrarse los
  huevos
americana
ameritar
ancheta
¡ándale!
andar bravo
andar de jacalera
andar en pelotas
andar ficha
andar juntos
andar lurias
andar pedo
andar pisto
andar quebrado
apachurrar
apagador
apañar
aparato
apartado
apaste
¡apucha!
apuercado
arca
aretes
argüenda
argüende
argüendero
arrancar
asegurador
atole
atracar
atrojar
aventar
avería
avión
avirote
¡ay chihuahua!
baboso
bacha
bala

balone
baloni
banco
bandeja
banqueta
baño
barata
baratero
barro
basca
bata de dormir
batiboleo
batir
bebe-leche
betabel
bica
biche
bien padre
bironga
birria
blanquillo
bobo
boche
bofa
bola
boleadores
bolero
bolillo
bolillos
bolitas
bolón
bolsa
boludo
bomba
bombo
borlo
borrador
borrego
boruquear
bosgo
botana
bote

bote de basura
botella
botija
bracero
bravo
brete
brincar a la reata
brincar el charco
brincar la cuerda
broche
bronca
bruja
buca
buchaca
buenote
buey
bufar
burro
buscamoscas
caballazo
caballete
caballito del
  diablo
caballón
cabellera
cabestro
cabrón
cacahuate
cacarear
cachar
cachirulo
cacho
cachucha
caer el veinte
cagadera
cajón
cajuela
calabaza
calaca
calango
calavera
caldillo

calentarse	cero	chi	chulo
calilla	cerros	chicaneo	chupa-mirto
caló	chabacano	chicanglo	chupa-rosa
calzoncillo de	chachalaquero	chicanismo	chupaleta
baño	chafa	chicano	chupón
cambiado	chalán	chícharo	cilindro
camello	chale	chicharra	cintas
camión	ichale!	chicharrón	cisca
camita	chalupa	chichi	cisnero
camizón	chamaca	chichimeco	cizote
camotazos	chamaco	chicle	claridoso
camote	chamarra	ichihuahua!	cobija
campechana	chamba	chilango	cocedor
camposantero	chamorro	chile	cochino
canacanear	champiñones	chile verde	cochote
canco	champurreado	chillarse	cocido
candil	chanclas	chinchería	coco
canilla	chancleo	chinchero	cocoles
canquiza	chancletas	chingadazo	cocolmeca
cantinflear	changa	chingadera	cofiro
cantinfleo	changarro	chingar	coger
canuto	changle	chingazo	cojín
capa de agua	changuear	chingón	cola
capirotada	chante	chino	colcha
capón	chapa	chinzado	coliche
capulín	chapapote	chipón	colmena
capulina	chaparro	chira	conchabar
caquis	chapeta	chiringa	conejo
icarajo!	chapetear	chirinola	cono
caravana	chapote	chirola	conservativo
carbonear	chapucero	chirona	contrecho
carbonero	chapul	chiva	coraje
carnaval	chapulín	chivas	corbata de gato
carrizo	chapuzar	chivo	corcholata
carro	chaquetear	chofero	cordón
cartapacio	charchina	chompa	correa
casco	charola	chongo	corredera
casero	charrasquear	chopo	costilla
casqueta	charro	chopos	coyote
castaña	chaval	chorcha	cozco
catre	chavala	chorizo	crucero
catrin	chavo	chorro	cruda
cazo	chela	chotear	cuaco
célebre	chepe	chucho	cuartada

húngaro
incaible
inocente
insulto
izquierdista
jacal
jacalear
jalapeño
jalar
jalársela
jale
jalón
jando
jarana
jeme
jerga
jiriola
ijito!
jocoque
joder
jodido
jodón
jorongo
jubilarse
juguetón
juila
julia
juma
jumado
jura
la raza
laberinto
labioso
ladino
lambeache
lambehuevos
lambiache
lambizque
lamprear
lampriar
lana
lángara
lapicero
largar

lata
latinos
lavado
lavaplatos
leche
leche nevada
lechuza
leído
lejecito
lenguón
lentes ahumados
lentes oscuros
lepe
leva
licencia
licenciado
liga
linda
linterna
lírico
listones
llamar
llanta
llantón
llave
lobo
loro
luis
lumbrero
lumbriz
luna
macalililia
macano
machetón
machín
machina
machito
macita
macizar
macuache
macueco
madera
magüey
malamé

malanco
malancón
maldito
maleta
malinche
malva
mama grande
mamada
mamador
mamalón
mamila
mamón
mancha negra
manear
manejera
manflor
manga
manillas
manito
mano
manopla
manoseada
mantelito
mantillas
manuela
manzanear
mañanitas
máquina
margayate
maritata
marota
marrana
marrano
masacota
masacote
mascada
ime lleva la
    chingada!
mecate
medias
meneada
menso
menudo
mero

imétele!
mezcal
mezquino
mi cielo
milpa
moca
mocho
mojado
mole
molleja
mollete
molote
moquetazo
mordida
mosca
mota
movida
naguas
nariz
navajas de
    rasurar
nieve
nievero
norte
obradera
ojete
olote
iórale!
otate
pabellón
pachanga
pachocha
pachuco
pachuquismo
padre
padrísimo
pajuela
pajuelazo
palabrota
palenque
palero
paliacate
paloma
palomilla

palomita
palotazo
palote
pamita
pana
panita
panocha
paño
papa grande
papalote
paquete
paquínes
para acabarla de
  chingar
paragüe
parche
parián
pasado
pasador
pastel
patojito
patojo
pedir un aventón
pegadura
pelado
pelliscada
pena
penoso
perico
perinola
perro caliente
petaca
picada
picha
pieza
pinche
pingo
pintado
pinzas
piocha
piragua

pisto
pita
pitar
piyamas
pizca
placa
plomo
pluma
pochos
ponerse pedo
popote
pozole
provisorio
pulque
i¿qué chingados
  quieres?!
quemado
quemón
queque
rajar
rancho
raspado
rasquera
raya
rayado
reatazo
reatiza
rebaje
reborujo
recámara
recargado
recaudo
recorte
redondo
regadera
relajo
rentar
repiocha
repuñoso
resaca
resbaladera

resbaladero
resbaladilla
resistol
resquicio
robón
rosca
rosetas
  de maíz
rótulo
rutero
sacatear
saco
salar
salarete
sandunga
sardina
se le pegaron las
  cobijas
secador
segurito
seguro
serape
sesudo
sisote
sobrecama
socapar a
  uno
soda
solera
soltura
sonajear
sopletón
sorbete
suave
sube y baja
tablero
taco
tacotillo
tacuache
tallar
tambo

tambor
tamboreatear
tanda
tángana
tantear
tapado
tapatío
tecolote
tendajo
tenis
tepalcates
tetera
tiliches
timbre
tomado
toronja
torta
tortilla
trama
trapeador
trinco
tripón
trique
trusa
urraca
vacilar
vacilón
varillero
vejiga
vendita
ventoso
vereda
vidriera
vieja
volada
volantín
zácate
zancudo
zapeta
zopilote
zumbido

NICARAGUA

ia la gran puchica!
achicharrado
achún
aguada
ahora
ahorita
al bote y al miado
al mejor mico se
le cae el zapote
alagartarse
alaste
almareado
alzo
amarrarse
apartado
arrecho
atracar
autocarril
babosear
bajo
bichero
bienmesabe
birote
bufete
caballo
cachimbear
cachimbo
cachipil
cacreca
cada lora a su
guanascate
caite
cajeta
calandraca
camión
cancanear
cavanga
celeque
cepillo
chacalines
charbasca
chavalo

chécheres
chereques
chicha
chigüin
chilillo
chilote
chiltoma
china
chingo
chingue
chipote
chiquije
chiripa
chirre
ichivísima!
icho!
choco
chocoyo
chorcha
chueco
chunches
chuzo
cipe
cipote
coco
colocho
comal
cotonear
coyunda
cuajada
¿cual es su
gracia?
cuapes
cuechos
currutaca
cusuco
ide a cachimba!
ideacá!
dejen de relinchar
dundo
échele chicha al
cumbo

el colochón
el uñudo
embolado
enchichar
es óxido
está en la piyama
de madera
está hasta el
birote
está jodido
estiró los caites
estoy
cachimbeado
estoy hecho
pistola
estoy jodido
fregado
gancho
garnacha
garrobo
gofio
guachiman
guanaco
guayaba
guineo cuadrado
hacer garra
huevochimbo
huila
huipil
¿ideay?
indio comido
puesto al
camino
indio viejo
ipegue
jeta
jícara
jícaro
jincho
jocote
ijoepuchita!
jupa

kupia-kume
la chota
le dió la quiebra
lluvia
lo peor es un
indio
repartiendo
chicha
machala
mamar
mamón
matamama
me esta arañando
el tigre
me vale un cacao
me vale un
pepino
mengalo
meter las
extremidades
molenillo
morral
motete
murruco
nacatamal
nambira
nicos
orchata
pacha
pachango
pacho
paila
panga
papachú
papalina
pata de gallina
peleros
peló el ajo
pereque
perrerreque
peteteada
pinche

PANAMA

abatí
aguada
ajumado
amachinarse
amarrarse
avatí
baúl
bemba
biche
biombo
bohio
bola
bolas
borrador
búho
buinsuan
busito
cabanga
cachos
camisón
capote
capul
caramelo
carrizo
carro
cartucho
chachae
chancletas
charrasquear
chichí
chiva
chivita
chocolate
chombo

coa
cobija
cocido
coco
cómicas
comiquillas
cueco
cuí
culisada
durazno
en fuego
enguacar
enhuacar
enrizado
estar en fuego
estar engomado
excusado
finca
fogón
fósforos
fregador
frijoles
frisoles
frísoles
fula
gallera
ganchito
gancho
gasolinera
gavilán
guardería
guineo
hacer pupu
huevos

jamaiquino
jumado
la refrigeradora
lata
lavamanos
librera
liga
llanta
lleva y trae
macana
medias
mellos
mollera
nevera
obradera
pájaro
palitroqui
palomilla
pancitos
panela
pañoleta
paquínes
paragüita de
  sapo
patacón
patacones
pato
paviarse
pechuga
pedir un aventón
pelaíto
pelao
perro caliente
pesuña

peticote
petipóas
picha
pilinqui
pipi
piyamas
placa
playa de
  estacionamiento
presilla
prieto
pulsera
recámara
revulú
saco
sobrecama
soda
sorbeto
subterráneo
suinsuan
tablero
tina de baño
tinto
torta
traje
trapeador
tunda
vestido de
  baño
visita flor
yerba
zapallo
zapatillas
zurra-zurra

PARAGUAY

abatí
acabar
achinado
acogotar
afilador
afilar
amistarse
anotarse un
  poroto
apereá
apintonearse
apronte
argel
argelado
atajarse
avatí
bagre
balita
banda
banderola
bañadera
bañado
bárbaro
barbear
biblioteca
bocho
boliche
bolichero
cábula
cachafaz
cacho
cachucha
cadete
cajón
calentón
calentura
calesita
camandulear
camburrear
camisilla
camisola
cana

canilla
canillera
canillita
cañonazo
caracha
catinga
cebar
cerrazón
Chaco
changar
chucho
churrasco
ciclo
cierre
concha
cortahierro
cuentero
cuentista
curepa
curepí
darse un panzazo
de vicio
dependiente
desgraciarse
despachante
en los quintos
  infiernos
encomienda
escuelero
estancia
estanciero
estero
fiambrería
fiambres
frisa
ganadero
gaucho
greifú
gringo
guaraní
guaripola
guasca

guasupyta
guayaquí
güevón
hacerse la paja
heladera
hinchar
huevón
impavidez
joder
jodido
jugar
kimono
la cana
la vieja
largar
latería
lavatorio
liga
loca
locote
lona
los altos
lustrabotas
lustrador
luz
macana
macanear
macanudo
machona
machonear
madama
malevo
manflora
manteca
matambre
mate
mbarigüí
milico
mimosear
nacido
ñandutí
olor fuerte

organillo
paja
pajearse
pajero
pajonal
pancearse
pandorga
panzazo
paquetería
paragolpes
paspadura
pasparse
pavada
peineta
pelotudo
peluqueada
peluqueado
peluquear
peluquearse
petiso
petizo
pibe
picharse
pichincha
pichinchero
pichulín
piririta
pispar
pispiar
pituco
plaguear
playa
polenta
pollera
poncho
poncho de
  sesenta listas
pororó
porotal
porotos
pozo
prójima

PERU

cruce
cúaquer
cuatrero
cuchí
cucho
cucufato
cueca
curado
curcuncho
cuy
damasco
de llapa
de ñapa
de yapa
debocar
desorejado
despapucho
discante
disfuerzo
disticoso
donde el diablo
  perdió el
  poncho
durazno
duro
edredón
el chino
elástico
embarrada
embarrar
empanada
empaque
empavar
emponchado
encomienda
enflautada
enlatado
entablar
entablonada
entre pisco y
  nazca
erogación
escándalo
esclava

espaciador
estar salado
excusado
fama
flacuchento
fletar
florecido
foco
forado
fósforos
frangollo
fregado
fuereño
gago
gaguear
gallinazo
galpón
gancho
gargarear
garrotero
garúa
gásfiter
gasfitería
gaznate
gotero
grifo
gringo
guacho
guagua
guanaco
guano
guapo
guaraca
guarapo
guasca
guata
güevón
guiso
hacer el dos
hacer garra
hacer perro
  muerto
haraca
harto

hoja de gilet
huaca
huachafería
huella
huevón
jalar el examen
jarana
jeme
jirón
jornal
lacra
lambebotas
lampa
lapicero
lata
latear
latifundio
lavadero
lavaplatos
lavatorio
leche
legal
liga
liso
lisura
llama
llanta
llapa
llevacuentos
locoto
maceteado
macuco
mamadera
mampara
manoabierta
manopla
manta
marinera
martillero
mate
mayordomo
mazamorra
me tinca
mecha

menudo
meter la pata
molleros
monrero
montera
moro
morroño
mote
motoso
mozón
mucama
muchitanga
nieve
ñaña
ñaño
oferta
ojotas
omnibus
palangana
palomilla
palta
pampa
pampón
Papa Noel
paparrotear
parrilla
parrillada
patasca
patuleco
pechuga
peineta
pepián
perezosa
pericote
perra
perulero
petacón
pica
pichón
pifia
pifiar
pingo
pintado
pique

pisco
pitar
piyamas
playa de
  estacionamiento
pollera
poncho
porongo
porotos
poto
prosa
prosudo
puna
puntada
puntudo
pupurrí
quena
quipe
rajar
raspadilla
ratero
ratonera
redondo
remolienda

retamblar
rezondrar
ricoto
rizado
rocoto
ropa de baño
rosca
rosquete
roto
rotos
ruma
salchicha
saltar la
  soga
sandunga
sango
sanguaraña
seguro
sello
sencillero
ser aguasado
simpa
sobrecama
soda

sombrilla
sorbete
sube y baja
suche
suerte
suertero
taco
tanda
tapado
taparrabos
taquilla
tarasca
tarro
tarro de la
  basura
taza del
  baño
templado
templar
tentenelaire
ternejo
tilingo
tina
tirar el dedo

tiros
tortilla
trapeador
trenzarse
trigueño
trompada
trompeta
trompón
troncha
tun-tun
tupido
ulpo
velón
vereda
vicuña
virado
vuelto
zambo
zapallo
zapatillas
zaragate
zaramullo
zoncura
zoquete

PUERTO RICO

a la brava	aprontao	biscornio	burundanga
a todo jender	arao	bizcocho	buruquena
abacorao	aro	bizcorneo	busconear
abanico	arrebatao	bobo	cabete
abombarse	arrebolarse	boca de incendio	cabra
abrigadero	asalto	boche	cabrear
aburrición	asopao	bochinche	cabro
acepillado	atracar	bochinchero	cabrón
achantao	atrecho	bodega	cabulla
achantarse	aventado	bohio	cabuya
achiote	aviso	bola	cacahuate
ácido	iay bendito!	bolitas	cacatúa
afectar	bacalaito	bollitos	cachapera
agallado	bachata	bolones	cachaza
agallarse	bachatear	bomba	cachola
agua de piringa	balumba	bombazo	cacholón
aguacate	banasta	bombear	cachorro
aguachoso	baratillo	bonete	caculear
aguajero	barquilla	boquiduro	caer mala
aguantador	barrilito	boquisucio	cagacatre
aguántate	bartolina	boricua	cagarreta
aguapiringa	batacazo	borincano	caja blanca
ajibararse	batata	borinqueño	cajetón
ajorado	batatazo	botago	calculador
ajumao	bate	botalodo	camarera
alcapurria	batida	botánica	camarón
alicate	baúl	botar	canasta
alzacola	bayú	botella	candungo
alzado	beguiansa	brea	caneca
amacolao	bemba	bregar	canela
amapuchar	bembé	brete	cangrimán
amarillo	bembeteo	breva	canilla
amarrarse	bembón	broco	cano
amasar	besito de coco	bronca	cansón
anafre	bibi	bruquena	cantaso
anamú	bicho	buchipluma	cantazo
ancón	bien hecho	buena pieza	cañita
angolo	bienmesabe	bufeo	icarajo!
ansia	bife	bugarón	cariduro
apajuatao	bilí	bulto	caripelao
apendejao	billete	bululú	carne bif
aplatanao	bimbazo	burrunazo	carro

falfallota	gasolinera	jevo	más enamorado
falfullero	gata	jíbaro	que un cabro
falucho	gavilán	jodón	matrimonio
farfullero	gira	jonrón	matungo
fastidiar	golosa	jorobón	medias
feca	goma	juey	menudo
fiambrera	gomita	jueyero	minga
finca	gotero	julepe	missy
firulístico	grama	juma	mister
flamenco	grifo	jumado	mofongo
fliche	guagua	jumeta	mollero
flipiadora	gualuche	jumo	mondongo
florecido	guame	labia	monga
foete	guantes	lacra	monguera
fogón	guarachar	lambeojo	moto
follón	guaraguao	lambío	moyo
fósforos	guarán	lata	múcaro
franela	guarapillo	latear	¡muchacho!
fregado	guarapo	lavabo	muchitanga
fregón	guareto	lease	muñequitos
fresco	guayaba	lechón	naranja
fresquesito	guayabear	lechonera	navajas
friquear	guayabera	litro	nevera
friquitín	guayacán	macana	nítido
friza	guayao	maceta	no vuelvo ni a
fuente	gufeao	machacante	buscar billetes
fufú	gufear	machina	ñangue
fuñir	guía	machorra	ñeñeñe
gabán	guillado	machota	ñoña
gaceta	güimo	machote	ñoño
gacho	guineo	maduro	orejero
gafas	guineo niño	majarete	pachó
gagüear	gurundango	malgansón	paico
gallera	hacer cuchara	mamao	pajarito
galleta	hol	mamito	pala
galletita	jaiba	mamotreto	paleta
gallito	jaibería	mangar	palo
gallo	jaleo	mangó	palomilla
gandinga	jalón	mangonear	pamplona
gandul	jara	mangú	pana
garabato	jarana	mantecado	pancista
garata	jeringar	maraca	pantalla
garrote	jeringón	marifinga	pantaloncillo
gas	jeva	marranazo	panzú

papa caliente
papel de toile
papi
paquete
paquetero
paquínes
parejero
parraneto
pasao
pase
paseo
pasme
pastel
pastelillo
pata
patilla
pato
patona
payamas
pedir un pon
pegado
peinilla
pela
pelegrina
pelón
pendango
pendejo
pepa
pepita
peregrina
pestillo
petardo
petipúa
pica
picao
pichón
pilón
pimpo
pinche
pintado
pipa

pipiolo
piragua
pirulí
pistolita
pitiyanqui
pito
planchar
platanutre
plegoste
pluma
pollina
pon
por el libro
por la
  maceta
pote
prender
prenderse
prieto
pujar para
  adentro
puñeta
puño
puyar
quemarse
quenepa
quenepe
querendón
quillarse
rabúa
rajao
rajarse
ratonera
recao
recorte de
  pelo
refajo
refistolera
refistolero
reguerete
regueretear

relajo
rentar
revolú
riña
rótulo
rumbear
rumbero
saco
safacón
salado
salar
salcocho
salón
saltar la cuica
sambumbia
sancochao
sancocho
sandunga
sángano
santería
santero
se le pegó el
  vellón
seibó
sello
setas
sicote
sombrilla
sorbete
sorbeto
sube y baja
tablilla
tala
tangána
tapalodo
tapón
tartana
tecato
tembleque
tenche
tener leche

tenis
tereque
tetera
tirá
tirao
títere
titingó
tongonear
tortillera
tostao
tostón
traje
trillo
trinco
tringo
trompicón
tumbe
tun-tun
tupido
turuleta
tusa
vaca lechera
vacilón
vaina
vellón
vellón de cinco
vellón de diez
vellonera
verja
vianda
virado
virivira
viroteao
visorioco
votar
yautía
yerba
yompear
yuca
zafacón
zumbador

EL SALVADOR

abarrotería	chamaco	culero	liso
acatar	chamaquito	culiche	machina
achimería	chaneque	cusuco	maleta
achimero	chapa	cuto	malhora
achimes	chapear	cutuco	maraca
achiote	chapulín	dar birote	mico
agarroso	cheje	dar un	milpa
aguacate	chele	jalón	motete
aguachacha	chicha	darse zoca	norte
alaco	chicharra	embolado	otate
alborotos	chicharrón	enchilada	pacha
amarrarse	chiche	faltar	panela
amarroso	chichí	feria	paquínes
andén	chifurnia	fresco	patojito
apachurrar	chile	gallera	patojo
arepa	chile verde	garúa	pelo rizo
aritos	chingar	gendarme	pena
arrecho	chira	grama	penoso
baboso	chiras	guanacos	piscucha
bagre	chochas	guaro	pitar
bicho	choco	güisquil	pitipuas
chillón	chocolate	huacal	¡puchica!
blanquillo	chocolón	jalón	pupusa
bobo	cholco	janano	rentar
bolo	chompipe	janiche	sacar chocoliya
borrego	chorcha	jeruza	ser arrecho
bote	chorro	joder	sorbete
bravo	chotear	jodido	tapado
cachar	chueco	jodión	taquilla
cachero	chunches	joyolina	te voy a
calentarse	chute	juque	chillar
calzoneta	cilampa	lambeculo	vaya pues
canilla	cipe	lambiscón	vejiga
chachivaches	cipote	lapicero	vereda
chacuaco	colcha	leche	yautía
chalchiuite	colocho	licenciado	zopilote

URUGUAY

abatí	campera	empacarse	mamado
abombar	cana	empanada	mamar
afilar	canario	empelotarse	mandarse
agarrar	canilla	encomienda	mudar
ají	canillita	endiablado	manteca
alcahuete	cantegril	es un clavo	marrón
almacén	caña	estar pato	mate
amargo	cañonazo	facón	matrero
ambiente	carancho	fiaca	milico
ambo	caravanas	fiambrería	montar
ananá	carretilla	fiambres	moquete
andar pato	cebar	forrar	moreno
anillo	chalupa	forro	morocho
apolillar	championes	fósforos	morrudo
arquero	chancho	gallego	mosca
avatí	chanfle	galpón	mosquear
bachicha	chanta	gancho	mula
bancar	chantún	garra	mulero
bárbaro	charqui	garúa	nabo
batir	charrúa	gaucho	nafta
berretín	chasqui	gendarme	nena
bichicome	chicharrones	gringo	nene
blanquillo	chiche	guacho	nenito
bocacalle	china	guano	nieve
bochinche	chingar	guarango	ojotas
bodega	chiquilín	guaraní	omnibus
boleadoras	chirola	güevón	palo
bolear	chirona	guita	palta
boliche	choclo	gurí	paquete
boludo	cholo	heladera	paquetero
bombita	chorizo	huevas	pardo
boniato	chueco	huevón	parrilla
botija	chupar	impavidez	parrillada
cachar	churrasco	jornal	patota
cachetada	coche	judío	peinar
cachete	coger	laburar	peineta
cacheteo	coima	laburo	pelota
cacho	concha	lapicera	pelotudo
cajón	cuentamusa	llanta	pesetear
caldera	cuña	macana	petiso
calentar	curado	macanudo	petizo
camambuses	embancarse	machete	picada

pija

pilchas

pillar

pingo

pinzas

piña

piñazo

pitar

pitillo

pituco

polenta

pollera

polvo

poncho

porotos

pupurrí

quilombo

rancho

resfriado

retratería

seguro

sorete

ta

tano

tarado

tener un

  bajón

valija

vaquilla

vejiga

vereda

verga

vermuth

yapa

yerba

yerbatero

VENEZUELA

a juro
a la machimberra
a pata
a rolo
abacorar
abasto
abollado
abombarse
abradera
abrirse
acatar
acatarrar
accidentado
achucutarse
agalludo
agarrón
aguacate
aguada
aguajero
aguamiel
aguapanela
aguarapado
ahoritica
ajumado
alacamunería
alcanforarse
alfeñique
alfiler
alumbrado
alverja
amachinar
amarchantarse
amarrarse
ameritar
amolar
amorochados
amuñuñar
amurrugado
ancheta
andón
ansia
apilonados

apuchungar
apurruñado
apurruñar
arbolario
arepa
aro
arrechado
arrecharse
arrecho
arrejarse
arrequintado
arrocero
arrosquetado
arroz
arrufar
arrume
arveja
arverja
atacar
atapuzar
atarrillarse
atole
atrincado
atrincar
avispa
azotea
bachaca
balurdo
bambalina
banderazo
bandola
bandolero
bañar
barajustar
barajuste
barrilete
bastimento
bastonero
bejuco
bemba
berenjena
berrinche

beso
bicha
bichar
bicharango
bichazo
bicho
bienmesabe
bocatero
bochar
boche
bojote
bola
bollo
bolsa
bonchar
bonche
bonchón
boquinche
boquineto
botiquín
botiquinero
brega
bregador
brejetero
brincar
broga
brollero
brollo
broma
brujulear
buchipluma
bullaranga
bulto
buruza
buseta
caballo
cabestro
cabra
cabulla
cabuya
cachaco
cachado

cachapera
cachar
cacharra
cache
cachero
cachifa
cachilapo
cachimba
cachimbero
cacho
cachorro
cachube
cachucha
cacurúo
cajón
cajonero
calar
calentarse
calentera
cambur
camisón
campechana
canchar
caney
cangrejo
canuto
caña
caño
cañonero
carabina
carajito
carajo
caraota
carapacho
cargadora
caribería
carraplana
carricito
cartnetizar
cartón
casabe
casave

casero
casquillo
catajana
catire
catirruano
catre
catuche
cayapa
cazcorvo
cedular
cepillado
cerrero
chaco
chalequear
chamarra
chamarreta
chamba
chambrana
chamerrata
chamo
chancleta
chapa
chaparro
chapín
charrasquear
chercha
chévere
chicha
chicle
chimbo
chinchín
chinchorro
chingo
chinita
chipola
chirigua
chirimoya
chiripa
chiva
chivero
chocante
choretear
choreto
chorro

chuchazo
chuchear
chucho
chucuto
chuequear
chupón
chuzo
cignato
cipote
clineja
coba
cochino
coco
coger
cola
colear
colero
coleto
comején
comer
comiquitas
conchabar
conchudo
conchupancia
condenar
confiscado
conformar
contra
coñazo
corneta
coroto
corredera
corrincho
corroncho
cosa
cota
coto
cotorra
cotufa
crineja
crispeto
cuadrar
cuatriborleado
cuerazo

cuerda
cuero
culilludo
cuneco
cunene
cupón
curda
curdeao
curdo
curucutear
dañero
daño
dar capote
dar mateo
dar picón
de golilla
de mingo
de raspa
derraparse
descachalandrado
descamburador
desconchar
descorotar
desparringarse
desplomar
desplomo
doctor
dormilona
echar jareta
echar mateo
echón
echonería
embarbascar
embarque
emberrenchinarse
embojotar
embraguetarse
empatar
empatucado
empatucar
empavar
empicharse
emplumar
empuntar

encaletar
encamburarse
encamisonado
encampanar
encarapichar
enchumbar
encomienda
enconchar
encuerarse
encullillarse
engalletar
engorrar
engrasar
enguayabado
enjabonada
enmochilado
enquesarse
ensabanado
ensopar
envainar
enzanjonar
erogación
es papaya
escaparate
eschoretar
esmachetarse
espabilar
espaldero
espichar
facistor
fajar
fajarse
fajina
faldellín
fañoso
fatiga
festinado
ficha
fisca
fiscal
flacuchento
flato
florear
flux

follisca
fondeado
franela
fregada
fregado
fregar
fría
fullero
fumón
funche
fuñir
furruco
gabán
gafo
gago
gaita
gajo
galleta
galletoso
gallinero
garetas
gocho
gofio
golilla
golillero
gorozo
grillo
guabinear
guacal
guachafita
guacuco
guamazo
guaral
guaramo
guarapo
guarimba
guata
guayaba
güero
güevón
güevonada
guillar
guindar
gutara

hacer garra
harinear
hato
helado
hereje
hincada
hojillas
huelefrito
huero
huevón
huevonada
implementar
íngrimo
insoria
intermediaria
invierno
jacal
jalabola
jalada
jaladera
jalado
jalador
jalamecate
jalar
jalar para
jalón
jamaquear
jamaqueo
jamón
jamonear
jara
jarabe de lengua
jartar
jaula
jefaturear
jerigonzo
ijipa!
jipato
joda
joder
jojoto
joropo
jubilado
jubilarse

jumo
jurungar
kindergarterina
ladilla
ladino
lagarto
lamber
lambucear
lanudo
lanza
latir
lava
lavado
lavativoso
lecherear
lechero
lechina
leco
levantador
liendra
limosnero
lipa
lipón
liso
lisura
lonchería
lonchero
mabita
macacoa
macán
macha
machete
machetero
machún
maco
maestro
magna
magnarse
majunche
maloso
maluco
mamarse
mamonazo
mancheta

mandar un golpe
mandinga
manejar
maneto
mango
manguarear
manguareo
manguerear
manigua
manteca
mantequilla
maraca
maraco
maría
marico
mariquear
marrón
mascota
mastique
matada
matraca
matracaso
matraquear
matraqueo
mazacotudo
mazamorra
mecate
mecatear
mecha
mene
menudo chichero
merequetén
metra
mezclote
miche
mingonear
mocho
mojiganga
mojito
mojonear
mojonero
monifato
mono
montar

Index of Words
Borrowed from English

(**RAE** = recognized by the Real Academia de la Lengua Española)

acuarium
agarrar chansa
aguares
aiscon
aiscrim
antifris
aplicación
aplicar
apoinmen
apricot
ático
aut
autoestop
automación
autsai
averach
average
bacín
badget
bafle (RAE)
bai
baicicle
bakgraun
bakin
balasto (RAE)
balerina
balrum
balún
bamper
banda
bángalo (RAE)
banquear
baquear
baqueo
barbekiu
barman
bartender

bas
basilico
básquetbol (RAE)
bate (RAE)
batrom
bazuca (RAE)
bedspred
beeper
behaviorismo
 (RAE)
beibi
beibisiter
beiby
beich (RAE)
beicon (RAE)
beiquinparer
béisbol (RAE)
beisman
best-séller (RAE)
beutichian
bikini
bil
bilding
biologista
bipear
birdcontrol
bisnes
bisnesman
bisquete
bisté (RAE)
bistec (RAE)
bit (RAE)
bíter (RAE)
biutichap
blackpawer
blich
bloaut

bloque (RAE)
blue jeans
blues (RAE)
bluf
blufear
boicot (RAE)
boila
bol (RAE)
bolb
boletín
bompa
bomper
boom
bordera
borlote
bos
boslain
bouling
box (RAE)
boxear (RAE)
boxeo (RAE)
boxer
brandy (RAE)
brasier
braun
breca
breik
breique
breque
brodcastin
broder
búlava
bulchitero
buldog
buldoser
bule
buquear

butléger
by pass
byte
cabinete
cach
cachacascán
cachar (RAE)
Cadi
Cadilaque
caite
calificar
camamila (RAE)
cameraman
cámper
campin
candi
carcasa
carne bif
carpet
carpeta
cash-flow
casualidades
cauntri
chagüer
chainar
champion
champions
chanse
charchiar
chárter (RAE)
chelv
chequear (RAE)
chequeo (RAE)
cherbet
cherife
cherry
chip (RAE)

371

felony
feminil
fenda
fender
ferry
fider
fil
file
film (RAE)
filme (RAE)
fiul
flagship
flash
flat
fletear
flipear
flirtear
flochar
flonkear
flout
flowshart
flu
focet
folder (RAE)
fonazo
fonis
for sale
forma
forman
formatear
formateo de disco
fornitura
forwardear
franque
friar
frisa
frisado
frisar
fulear
full
fultaim
fútbol (RAE)
futin
ganbout

ganga
gangster (RAE)
ganguero
ganman
gap
garden party
gas warfare
gasolin
gentleman
gentleman
   agreement
gigabyte
glamur
glu
gogo-girl
golkiper
grabol
graficmode
gras
greifrut
greive
gril
grilla
grin
gripa
grocer
groceri
grocería
grogui
gross margin
guacha
guachar
guachatería
guachiman
guaflera
guafles
guaife
guaiper
gueldear
güinchil
hall
handboll
handicap
hangear

hangueando
hardwear
high school
hobby
hot dog
ichu
iglú (RAE)
impase
impruviar
incentivar
income tax
incomtax
indentar
infraccionar
input
inspectar
instructar
internalizar
interviú
introducir
irrigar
itemizar
jaic
jaiguey
jaiyakin
jalf
jamburguer (RAE)
jazz
jeans
jeep
jersey (RAE)
jet
jetset
jipar
jira
jit
jiter
jol
joldin
joni
jumpear
juqui
kerosene
kibord

kilobite
la migra
labor
lágach
laidi
laira
landromat
laquear
lavatory
legalismo
líder (RAE)
liderato (RAE)
liderazgo (RAE)
life belt
life boat
link
lipestic
liquea
liquear
lis
listerina
listerine
listing
living
llévalo para atrás
lobi
lock out
lon
lonch
lonchar
lonche
lonchear
lonchera
lonchrum
loundri
lunche
lunchiar
lup
mach
machear
machrum
mádam
mailing list
malpractis

man	nulificar	pepermin	queik
manayer	of	performans	quilto
manejador	of de record	peticionar	rachar
mapear	ofendor	pich	raglan (RAE)
mapo	oficial de policía	pick up	raid
marketing (RAE)	ofside	pickle	rally
marqueta	okei	picnic	RAM
marquetero	omelet	pin	ranquear
match	on	pin printer	ranquin
maus	operático	pínut	rapista
medicaid	oranch	pipeline	raport
megabytes	ormy	pláier	ratio
meidin	output	planin	raund
meinfreim	over booking	playoff	realizar
meinjole	overol	pleibac	reca
memory	pacifair	pleigraun	recolectar
microfilm	pacón	pleit	reconociencia
migra	padoc	ploming	record (RAE)
milque	pai	poliéster (RAE)	recordman
mimeógrafo (RAE)	paipa	polisman	réferi
mistear	palchó	polución	relativo
mitiar	paniqueado	polucionar	relís
mitié	pantis	pompa	remodelar
mitin (RAE)	panty	ponchar	respirator
mixtiar	papel	póney (RAE)	retaliación
mofler	papelero	poni (RAE)	revival
mohair	¿Para donde tú	pool	rin
mompes	vas?	popcón	ring
moni	parachutista	portable	ringuear
monquiar	parientes	poster (RAE)	risés
mopear	parkear	prefaciar	roche
motocross	parkin	preferencial	rock
music hall	parking	premiación	rol
neta	parna	premier	rolos
network	parner	preseki	rols
night club	pary	presin	roquero
niple	PC	printer	roquet
nocomen	pedigrí (RAE)	propela	rosbif
nombre de familia	pees	pub	rost
nominar	pega	pudin	rufo
noqueado	peiperbac	pullman	rula
noquear	peismeker	pulover	ruter
norsa	penal	punch	sail
norseri	peni	puzzle (RAE)	sain